AMERICA: REPENT OR PERISH

Psalm 911

He that dwelleth in the
secret place of the Most High
shall abide under the shadow
of the Almighty.

Printed in the United States of America

Library of Congress
Cataloging-in-publication
ISBN 1-57558-120-5

AMERICA: REPENT OR PERISH

Dr. Bree M. Keyton, Th.D., D.C.E.
and Stephen T. Keyton

Special Guests Publishing
2002

Table of Contents

President Abraham Lincoln's Proclamation,
April 30, 1863, for a National Day of
Fasting, Humiliation and Prayer

We have been the recipients of the choicest bounties of
heaven. We have been preserved, these many years,
in peace and prosperity.
We have grown in numbers, wealth and power,
as no other nation has ever grown.
But WE HAVE FORGOTTEN GOD.
We have forgotten the gracious hand which preserved us
in peace, and multiplied and enriched and strengthened
us;
and WE HAVE VAINLY IMAGINED,
in the deceitfulness of our hearts,
THAT ALL THESE BLESSINGS WERE
PRODUCED BY SOME SUPERIOR WISDOM AND

VIRTUE OF OUR OWN.
Intoxicated with unbroken success, we have become too
self-sufficient to feel the necessity of redeeming
and preserving grace,
TOO PROUD TO PRAY
to the God that made us!
It behooves us, then to HUMBLE OURSELVES
before the offended Power,
to CONFESS OUR NATIONAL SINS,
and to PRAY FOR CLEMENCY AND FORGIVENESS.

George Washington's Vision of Three Wars

The following, an edited version of **George Washington's vision,** describes the events an angel showed him at Valley Forge. Three wars were revealed to be fought on American soil: the Revolutionary War, the Civil War, and the third, **the most terrible, is yet to come.**

An Uninvited Guest

"I do not know whether it is owing to the anxiety of my mind, or what, but this afternoon, as I was sitting at this table engaged in preparing a dispatch, something in the apartment seemed to disturb me. Looking up, I beheld standing opposite me a singularly beautiful being. So astonished was I, for I had given strict orders not to be disturbed, that it was some moments before I found language to inquire the cause of the visit. A second, a third, and even a fourth time did I repeat my question, but received no answer from my mysterious visitor except a slight raising of the eyes."

First Great Peril

"Presently I heard a voice saying, 'Son of the Republic, look and learn,' while at the same time my visitor extended an arm eastward. I now beheld a heavy white vapor at some distance rising fold upon fold. This gradually dissipated, and I looked upon a strange scene. Before me lay, spread out in one vast plain, all the countries of the world. Europe, Asia, Africa and America. I saw rolling and tossing between Europe and America the billows of the Atlantic, and between Asia and America lay the Pacific. 'Son of the Republic,' said the same mysterious voice as before, 'look and learn.'

"At that moment I beheld a dark, shadowy being, like an angel, standing, or rather floating in mid-air, between Europe and America. Dipping water out of the ocean in the hollow of each hand, he sprinkled some upon America with his right hand, while with his left he cast some over Europe. Immediately a cloud arose from these countries and joined in mid-ocean. For awhile it remained stationary, and then it moved slowly westward, until it enveloped America in its murky folds. Sharp flashes of lighting gleamed through it at intervals, and I heard the smothered groans and cries of the American people. (This may be interpreted to have been the Revolutionary War then in progress)."

Second Great Peril

"'Son of the Republic, look and learn.' I cast my eyes upon America and beheld villages and towns and cities springing up one after another until the whole land from the Atlantic to the Pacific was dotted with them. Again, I heard the mysterious voice say, 'Son of the Republic, the end of the century cometh, look and learn.'

"And this time the dark shadowy angel turned his face southward. From Africa I saw an ill-omened specter approach our land. It flitted slowly and heavily over every town and city of the latter. The inhabitants presently set themselves in battle array against each other. As I continued looking, I saw a bright angel on whose brow rested a crown of light, on which was traced the word 'UNION.' He was bearing the American flag. He placed the flag between the divided nation and said, 'Remember, ye are brethren.'"

"Instantly the inhabitants, casting down their weapons, became friends once more and united around the National Standard."

Third and Most Fearful Peril

"Then my eyes beheld a fearful scene. From each of these continents arose thick black clouds that were soon joined into one. And throughout this mass there gleamed a dark red light by which I saw hordes of armed men. These men, moving with the cloud, marched by land and sailed by sea to America, which country was enveloped in the volume of cloud. And I dimly saw these vast armies devastate the whole country and burn the villages, towns and cities which I had seen springing up.

"As my ears listened to the thundering of the cannon, clashing of the swords, and the shouts and cries of millions in mortal combat, I again heard the mysterious voice saying, 'Son of the Republic, look and learn.' Where the voice had ceased, the dark shadowy angel placed his trumpet once more to his mouth, and blew a long and fearful blast."

Heaven Intervenes

"Instantly, a light as of a thousand suns shone down from above me and pierced and broke into fragments the dark cloud which enveloped America. At the same moment, the angel upon whose head still shown the word UNION, and who bore our national flag in one hand, and a sword in the other, descended from the heavens attended by legions of white spirits. These immediately joined the inhabitants of America, who I perceived were well-nigh overcome, but who, immediately taking courage again, closed up their broken ranks and renewed the battle.

"Again, amid the fearful noise of the conflict I heard the mysterious voice saying, 'Son of the Republic, look and learn.' As the voice ceased, the shadowy angel for the last time dipped water from the ocean and sprinkled it upon America. Instantly the dark cloud rolled back, together with the armies it had brought leaving the inhabitants of the land victorious.

"Then once more, I beheld the villages, towns and cities springing up where I had seen them before, while the bright angel, planting the azure standard he had brought in the midst of them, cried with a loud voice: 'While the stars remain, and the heavens send down dew upon the earth, so long shall the UNION last.' And taking from his brow the crown on which blazoned the word 'UNION,' he placed it upon the Standard while the people, kneeling down said, 'Amen.'"

The Interpretation

"The scene instantly began to fade and dissolve, and I, at last saw nothing but the rising, curling vapor I at first beheld. This also disappeared, and I found myself once more gazing upon the mysterious visitor, who, in the same voice I had heard before, said, 'Son of the Republic, what you have seen is thus interpreted: Three great perils will come upon the Republic. The most fearful for her is the third. But the whole world united shall not prevail against her. Let every child of the Republic learn to live for his God, his land and UNION.' With these words the vision vanished, and I started from my seat and felt that I had seen a vision wherein had been shown me the birth, the progress, and destiny of the United States."

"Such, my friends," the venerable narrator concluded, "were the words I heard from Washington's own lips, and America will do well to profit by them."

This vision was related by George Washington to Anthony Sherman. He presented it in July 1859, when he was ninety-nine years old, to a reporter named Wesley Bradshaw. It was reprinted in the *National Tribune,* December 1880.

Chapter 1

America—This Is Your Wake-Up Call! Repent!

On Tuesday, September 11, **[911]** 2001, America received an emergency call. The wake up call was from God, and it was heard around the world. God has our attention, and it is time we listen as if our lives depend on it. The hedge of protection around the United States has been lifted because of unrepented sin, pride, and the innocent blood on our hands. We have refused to heed the warnings of God's prophets. God is asking us to choose this day whom we will serve: God or mammon. America was granted a period of sovereign mercy, but that mercy is close to an end.

This is a message to the president and the body of believers in Christ. We can fall on our knees and **repent** for our nation and the actions of its leaders, or we can ignore the warning and be judged with our nation. Through fervent prayer, we can still witness the greatest revival America has ever known. How? As always, God watches for repentance.

> *If My people, which are called by My Name, shall HUMBLE THEMSELVES AND PRAY, and seek My face, and TURN FROM THEIR WICKED WAYS; then will I hear from heaven, and will FORGIVE THEIR SIN, and will HEAL THEIR LAND.*
>
> —2 Chronicles 7:14

We, the people of America are like the buildings of the World Trade Center, hanging in the balance in a moment of time before the collapse. But unlike the twin towers, we have a choice. This was, symbolically, a graphic picture of America. **We simply cannot save ourselves! Only God can save us.** We must humble ourselves and pray like never before. Open our eyes, oh God, for we've been slumbering. We do not know that we, the people of the Laodicean church in Revelation 3, are like the twin towers, vulnerable because of our sin. We need to see that spiritually we are poor, blind, naked and wretched. Give us eye salve that we may see!

Chapter 2
The Key to Victory

There is one more element that is the key to victory. Our leaders must humble themselves and repent if our nation is to continue into the future as we know it today. Individual salvation and national salvation are different. An individual can call upon God at any time during his life and God will forgive all his sins and welcome him into His kingdom. However, the salvation of a nation is predicated on how much collective sin has accumulated according to God's weights and measures. When the cup of iniquity is full, judgment comes against that nation *(Revelation 19:2)*. God does not execute this judgment, but rather He pulls back His hedge of protection, and Satan and his hordes, always built up into a frenzy, invade and destroy. Because of his hatred for mankind, Satan's judgments are not fair or merciful, and he destroys at random, the innocent with the guilty.

If the people of America will pray that God will change the hearts of our leaders into an attitude of humility, and lead us into repentance for the sins of our nation, God will heal our nation and continue to protect and bless our nation as He has always done.

Chapter 3
Calling on President Bush and Our Leaders

If we trust in the arm of the flesh or the pride of our nation, we will lose this battle. Prayer and repentance are the only weapons we have in this spiritual battle. The only effective way to victory now, is to repent and cry out for God to save us. Pride, armies and smart bombs will only destroy both us and them. Don't misunderstand, in the natural we have every right, even the responsibility to go after the terrorists and the nations that protect them, to bring them to justice, and stop their ability to strike again.

However, according to more than one of God's prophets, "terror upon terror" will come upon this nation and its people. This indicates that there are several terrorist events yet to come in the USA, as

well as natural disasters such as earthquakes, vol-
canos, hurricanes, tornados, drought, floods, even
meteor strikes. Through it all, God will protect His
own. Make certain you are born again and close
enough to Him that He recognizes you as one of
His own. God has promised revival will spring up
at the same time judgment falls. Many prophets have
declared the coming revival will strengthen God's
people "through" the judgment, and that prayer warriors will rise up, in the spirit, pulling down strongholds, resulting in whole families and neighborhoods
coming to Jesus Christ (Yahshua Messiah). Those
same prophets also proclaim that our "banks will
be in turmoil" and our economy will "fail and fall to
dust" if our leaders do not turn, seek God now and
lead our nation into sincere repentance. God is also
warning us to cover our president with prayer, for
murderers will attempt to destroy him and many
will perish.

I call on the leaders of this nation to lead us in
repentance. Individuals who call on the LORD and
repent will be saved, but the **leaders of a nation
must repent for a nation to be saved**. I call on
President Bush to declare a **National Day of Re-**

pentance, just like Abraham Lincoln did (see his statement on the back of this book), that would include repentance, fasting, humbling ourselves and fervent prayer. Please read the following scriptures with holy fear and trembling before a holy God.

> *If that nation, against whom I have pronounced, turn from their evil, I will repent of the evil that I thought to do unto them. . . . IF A KINGDOM DO EVIL IN MY SIGHT, THAT IT OBEY NOT MY VOICE, THEN I WILL REPENT OF THE GOOD, WHERE WITH I SAID I WOULD BENEFIT THEM. . . . Because MY PEOPLE HATH FORGOTTEN ME, they have burned incense to VANITY, and they have CAUSED THEM TO STUMBLE IN THEIR WAYS FROM THE ANCIENT PATHS. . . . I WILL SCATTER THEM AS WITH AN EAST WIND BEFORE THE ENEMY. . . .*
>
> —Jeremiah 18:7–17

America Addicted—Impaled on Icon of Wickedness

In the spring of 2002, an item in the news stood

out: A woman struck a homeless man, impaling him on the icon on the front of her car. Rather than stop and help him, she drove home, parked in her garage, and shut the door. She allowed him to hang there three days until he died. Then she called friends to help her hide the body. When she was caught and sentenced, the testifying physician stated that the man would have lived if she had taken him to a hospital.

This story reflects the spiritual condition of America. We are being driven by wickedness and we are flailing and hanging on helplessly. Yet, no one seems able to stand up for the truth, effectively. We are bleeding and in the death throws as a nation, yet we seem oblivious. We are so caught up in our own selfishness and greed, that we do not hear the cries of the helpless, the homeless, the unborn child, the spiritually lost. But the Ancient of Days is watching and judgment is coming, ultimately. It is sure—and unavoidable.

Chapter 4

A Tale of Two Towers

A tale of two towers unfolded in the 1970s, builtproudly to reach the heavens, the tallest buildings in the Big Apple. The people said in their hearts: ***Let us build us a city and a tower, whose top may reach unto heaven; and let us make us a name*** *(Genesis 11:4),* as did Babylon of ancient times. The people raised up icons of steel and glass to their own glory. Thus, the towers stood, almost defiantly. God waited many years, for He is slow to anger and full to overflowing with mercy.

Early on the morning of September 11, the twin towers stood glistening in the early morning sunlight of what promised to be a perfect summer day. People hustled purposefully toward the city for trading and profit, ambivalent toward God. Many of those who believed in Him either saw Him as a distant, uncaring entity, or someone irrelevant they had summarily dismissed. They were lukewarm on that day, as they had been for many years. The people said in their hearts, "We are rich and have need of nothing. We can live like kings. We are invincible!"

Twin gods of Greed and Pride

A plot was hatched to tear down the twin temples of the World Trade Center. Many who worked there marched in step, even worshiped at the feet of **greed** and **pride**, the two spirits that resided there. According to Howard Pittman, who saw the spirit of greed, it is a demon with human looks, wearing a business suit. I see greed personified just like the pirates of Wall Street and the financial district. He traffics in human souls, but can only be distinguished from humans by his cat-like eyes, that glitter with delight as he makes conquest after conquest. His followers worship at his feet in this age, without pity or remorse, as he foments insatiable avarice by promising wealth and power. The chief place of commerce for corporate America, in the principle city to do worldly business, was the World Trade Center, and Greed had his headquarters there.

Chapter 5
It Was the Worst of Times

The twin towers shimmered in the sunlight, beautiful in their symmetry.

> *For when they shall say peace and safety;*
> *then SUDDEN DESTRUCTION cometh*
> *upon them, as travail upon a woman with*
> *child; and they shall not escape.*
>
> —1 Thessalonians 5:3

On September 11, 2001, hijackers turned jumbo jets into terrorist bombs. While the world watched on television, one plane, then another hit the towers. A gaping black hole appeared and fire burst out the side. Still the towers stood, for a long moment, winking in the relentless sun, viewed from sea to shining sea, in a last moment of pride and strength, as if completely unaware that the support columns were weakening around the burning, black hole of its wounds, until buckling under its own weight, each floor collapsed on itself. Oblivious to its own eminent demise, it appeared to be waiting for the financial kings of Wall Street to give it the nod. They simply did not know that **pride goes before a fall**.

People who had begun to evacuate the buildings were told by their leaders to return to their desks. The ones that returned and failed to recognize the warning signs to get out of the towers, were crushed.

Finally, breath seemed to leave the tower's bodies. The buildings, built by the arm of the flesh, fell by the arm of the flesh. In despair of support, they imploded like an accordion, falling forever in seeming slow-motion, leaving only what looked like a rib cage on the New York skyline. These steel bars have been graphically and prophetically described as "The Gates of Hell," by the rescue workers. Pride, wealth, accomplishments, plans, dreams, all gone, as the buildings gave a last gasp, exhaling fire and smoke from the very jaws of death. The stench of destruction and density of thick, black smoke now choked the city in the natural, that had been choking them in the spiritual for a long time.

The reeking odor billowed toward heaven. Still photographs taken by CNN and the Associated Press caught the attention of many who said they could see eyes, a nose, a mouth and horns in the cloud formations arising from the destruction.

I stared in horror at the TV, numbed by the shocking image of a Boeing 757 hitting the World Trade Center. I felt as if a gong was striking in my head as they replayed the scene again and again. I thought of the dead that would never have a chance to ask God's forgiveness, or say goodbye to their loved ones, and of the families that had suffered irreparable loss. I, like many Americans, wept for hours, until I could weep no more.

Pride—Downfall of Man

In **pride**, America imagines herself to be strong and invincible, able to overcome any threat. One target of the terrorists, the **White House**, remained unharmed, to give our country and our President **space to repent**.

The country that thinks it can be victorious without God in control is a country that is too proud. **The handwriting is on the wall for America. She**

has been WEIGHED in the balance, and found wanting *(Daniel 5:18–27)*. Whitaker Chambers, in his book *Witness*, states, "History is cluttered with the wreckage of nations that have become indifferent to God, and died."

As In the Days of Noah

Our God sent His prophets to warn the people of America, to call them to repentance, but the people laughed them to scorn. The church and the people continued as they had since the times of Noah, in wickedness, and violence, in the vain imaginations of their own hearts, doing evil continually. ***For as in the days that were before the flood they were eating and drinking, marrying and giving in marriage, until the day that Noah entered into the ark, and KNEW NOT UNTIL THE FLOOD CAME, and took them all away . . .*** *(Matthew 24:38)*. The people **"KNEW NOT,"** yet Noah preached to them for one hundred and twenty years. Their hearts were hardened and filled with such wickedness that they could not hear.

Chapter 6
Hedge of Protection Lifted

The **hedge of protection** was lifted from America over the course of the summer of 2001, allowing demons of great destruction, hatred, pestilence and murder to begin moving their forces inland. Without the protective hand of God, America was naked and vulnerable.

At the end of June, the LORD sent our family to Florida for two weeks. While in New Smyrna, after doing a radio show, the Father sent us to the beach, where He allowed us to be witnesses; to literally see fiendish principalities, powers, and demon forces without number roiling in from over the sea. I saw a great dragon in the vanguard. The hordes of demons released from **the deep** on America was beyond belief, unstoppable, and furious. Their assignment was to kill and destroy Americans.

A few months later, I spoke with a former diplomat to the Mideast who witnessed the same dragon, with hordes of demons, "leave the middle east" in the spring of 2001, a short time before I saw them enter America.

This great armada of demons was able to invade the shores of America because those standing in "The Gap" (a real place), though valiant and true prayer warriors, were not enough to stop the attack. In the days before the terrorist's attack, Steve and I waited with great concern, not knowing how what we had witnessed would manifest. All was calm, but we knew that this was "the calm before the storm." America was naked without the covering from the true and living God, for the first time since its inception 225 years ago. There *was* an advance warning of the World Trade Center attacks. It was subtle but the news carried it daily before the terrorists hit.

Chapter 7
The Year of the Shark

CNN labeled 2001 "The Year of the Shark," an extraordinarily prophetic statement. From the deep comes our attacker. Fear had come and what can match the fear generated by the silent, ruthless killing machines we call sharks. Beginning in the summer of 2001, an unprecedented number of vicious and fatal shark attacks occurred. Early July brought attacks in Pensacola on the gulf coast. Bob Clark, sheriff of Escambia County (Pensacola), stated, **"Sharks all over, up and down the whole entire gulf coast."** Sharks were loosed from **the deep**.

The relentless character of the shark is symbolic of the demons swarming our country, and the Arab terrorists that were preparing to assault us. Sharks appear out of nowhere, attack and disappear. They do not stop or discriminate. They might bite off a leg and then, inexplicably, leave. Terrorists attack, seemingly without reason, and then hide. Sharks are like the Terminator: without pity, and they will not stop, ever. Terrorists are much the same. I must point out that it is the demonic forces *behind* the terrorists that fully influence and empower them to commit atrocities.

There were an astonishing number of further shark attacks. The bulk of them occurred at New Smyrna Beach, twenty the last I heard. This was possible because the hedge that once covered our great nation was being lifted, and the wicked spirits of the deep were being released. The demons were moving toward the coastlines for the kill, just as the sharks did. (As in the spiritual, so in the natural.) Sharks continued to attack on the gulf coast, the east and west coasts of Florida, and the eastern seaboard.

The sharks were a **warning** that went unheeded: **Our coasts can be breached!**

Chapter 8
Does America Deserve Judgment?

We, the people, stood by silently, as the fruit of wickedness abounded. The gaping, black, billowing stench of our wickedness has come up before the nostrils of a holy God. Danger lurked, as **our support base** was collapsing around our ears, but we blissfully ignored it. It is God alone Who raises up, or pulls down nations.

Wickedness is big business in America. Just ask the people in the abortion and porn industries. Greed pushed the propaganda that **abortion** is right because it is very profitable. Once he got the healers to become killers, he pushed the idea: "Why not profit from selling fetus body parts? After all, they're already dead. Right? You profited on the abortion, so why not exploit it all the way, and profit on the remains of the fetus." Abortionists discovered that infant tissue is worth enormous sums, more when it is fresh, so they set up businesses harvesting body parts right in the abortion clinics, and designing the type of abortion to fit the individual daily demands. Greed nodded and smiled. This was easier than he thought. He just had to nudge them in the right direction, and they took off creatively on their own.

Selfishness and **pride** jumped in the circus ring, and promoted the idea day and night, that women have the right to kill their own offspring if it does not conveniently fit their schedules. Women bought it, packaged seductively as freedom. After all, everyone wants to be free, right? This so-called liberation brought an even greater bondage: the sin of murder.

Blood On Our Hands

When Cain murdered Abel, he was told that Abel's **blood cried out from the ground**. The blood of the senseless slaughter of millions of unborn babies cries out from the ground in America, today. God, forgive us. We elected a president, not once but twice, who refused to stop the wickedness. He promoted abortion worldwide, and the UN began funding abortions throughout the globe. Remember, as the leaders *we* elect lead, so shall the people be judged. When the Chief executive is a liar, an adulterer, a sexual predator, and flaunts his immorality as a badge of dishonor, he takes the country down several notches with him. ***For they have sown the wind, and they shall reap the whirlwind . . .*** *(Hosea 8:7).*

Once President Clinton refused to sign a bill to stop partial birth abortion, a bill the American people wanted and Congress voted for, judgment was imminent. Innocent blood is crying out from the ground. The blood of our most helpless is running in the streets. Between 1973 and 1996, 38,103,780 million preborn children were slaughtered. Since then, 1,365,730 abortions have occurred each year, according to Allen Guttmacher, President of Planned Parenthood. This **WEIGHS IN** at about forty-five million by the end of 2001. These are just the reported abortions. The figures are probably much higher. Other sources say the truth is, the number of abortions in America is closer to seventy-five million. What should be the **WEIGHT** of this judgment? God said:

> *And when ye spread forth your hands, I will hide My eyes from you: yea, when ye make many prayers, I WILL NOT HEAR: Your HANDS ARE FULL OF BLOOD.*
>
> —Isaiah 1:15

The publicized kidnappings, rapes and murders have become daily news. America is number one in teen pregnancy, violent crime, drug use, divorce, illiteracy, and abortion. 150,000 youth carry guns to public school. In the 50s, when we still had prayer in schools and the Ten Commandments were posted in courthouses, the worst problems we had in schools were chewing gum and talking. Now, in the new millennium, the schools have metal detectors, police who stand guard in the hallways, along with the constant threat of rape and murder. Pat Buchanan stated on page 1-2, in *The Death of the West*:

> In half a lifetime, many Americans have seen their God dethroned, their heroes defiled, their

culture polluted, their values assaulted, their country invaded, and themselves demonized as extremists and bigots for holding on to beliefs Americans have held for generations.

Chapter 9
Seared Consciences

With **seared consciences** and **hardened hearts**, the people accepted **pornography** with the evening news during the Clinton years. Jezebel took over the White House, to bring in a spirit of whoredoms and perversion. Our Commander in Chief demonstrated to all hopefuls, that being a liar, adulterer and sexual predator is the way to succeed. Lies and deception have become tools to manage the public.

As their politics and behavior became public, it trickled down to the people. Scandals began to rock the churches and the news. Leaders of major denominations were exposed in embezzlement schemes. Some Catholic priests are still being exposed as pedophiles. In the permissive atmosphere and tone set by the White House, teen promiscuity and abortion escalated.

Ultimately **slumber** and indifference gripped the general public. Young women, selling soft drinks, while writhing in near nakedness, became commonplace. If these same commercials and pornography, passing as entertainment, had aired in the 50s, the entertainers and producers would have been arrested.

We, the people, slept as Samson once did on Delilah's knees, while our power was being cut off from us. We became numb to wickedness and blatant sin as our leaders wantonly degraded and defiled America with their **immorality**, dishonesty, **perjury**, deceits, encouraged rampant **homosexuality** in the military and elsewhere, traded precious military secrets to the Chinese, and attempted to dismantle the military. Armed forces were reduced by 50%, while weapons research was curtailed, and new weapons were restricted. The public does not know that the USA's military is ranked 7th or 8th in the world. Yet we beat the war drum to send our military overseas, leaving our own country short on protection. Illegal aliens flood our country at the rate of a million a year, and there have been recent shootings on the border, but we seem powerless to stop it.

General **rage**, exemplified by road rage, hit our country, and the hatred against Christians and Jews has been building, both in this country and worldwide. The rise of **Humanism**, **sorcery**, **Satanism**, **witchcraft**, **cults**, **new age religions**, the worship of self, and a propensity toward general wickedness has given Satan deep level access to our country. The rise of pagan worship and occultism permeates the movies, television, books, video and computer games, until there is nothing in our culture that is not profoundly tainted. Psychics, which are really false prophets, are on every channel. Though some have been involved in scandals and shut down, it seems that ten more spring up to take their places. People are so desperate to know what to do that they will do anything. There is even a psychic who, instead of reading palms, reads rear ends. What will it take for people to wake up. Meanwhile, lawsuits to remove God's name from our money and public meetings are at epic proportions. We are thumbing our noses at a holy God, and there is a price to pay.

Chapter 10
The God of Mammon

Is our economy more important than righteousness? The voters of this nation thought so, overwhelmingly. Because the people elected Clinton, not once but twice, we signaled our holy God that His laws meant nothing to us; that the god of **mammon** (money and greed) was more important than living righteous lives with godly leaders that would steer the ship of state toward morality.

God was watching! If mammon was our god, then He would allow our economy to be seriously hit. The World Trade Center was destroyed and Wall Street was shut down. Airlines were grounded, and with them commerce screeched to a halt. The airlines claimed loses near 250 million dollars per day. Wall Street plunged continually, reporting the largest drop since the Great Depression. The tenuous support beams of our civilization were buckling.

Scandals hit the financial community and rocked Wall Street. As they scrambled like rats to cover their lies, thievery, embezzlement, and artificially inflated stocks, they betrayed one another with regularity. Companies consumed with deception and greed such as Enron, WorldCom, Global Crossing, Xerox and many others yet to be exposed, have turned their backs on God's Ten Commandments. Their consciences are so seared that some top executives express no feelings of guilt for their actions, even though many investors lost everything.

> ***I have written to him the great things of My law, but they were counted as a strange thing.***
>
> —Hosea 8:12

This country is six trillion dollars in debt. Millions have lost their jobs in this deep recession. We are in a free fall, with no way out except turning back to God and repenting.

> ***The earth also is DEFILED under the inhabitants thereof; because they have***

transgressed the laws . . . broken the EV-
ERLASTING COVENANT.

—Isaiah 24:5

Chapter 11
Generation Without Prayer

In this country we behave as if we are ashamed of our God. **Forty years** have passed since we **took prayer out of the schools**. Our God has shown mercy for a whole generation, as we simply put Him out of our plans. We **removed God's laws from our courthouses, public places and schools**. Christians stood by, while our civil liberties were taken away, one by one. Our right to the freedom "of" religion has become twisted by satanically motivated politicians and judges into the freedom "from" religion.

In the **educational** arena, the public schools and their teachers taught meditation, witchcraft, and concepts of new age religions on a daily basis in the classroom. In the name of tolerance, our country allows gross wickedness to claim the schools and children, while being amazingly intolerant toward Christianity. Our educational system was originally founded in this country for the purpose of learning to read the Bible. What has happened? This generation has never known true right from wrong, nor heard the Ten Commandments.

The Supreme Court judges are as much to blame as the President for passing wicked laws. Our **courts** and **congress** declare right is wrong and wrong is right. They've said in their hearts, "Poor old God. His system of justice is hopelessly outdated. We have to fix things by legislating immorality into becoming the new morality." The people do not want God telling them right from wrong.

> *WOE TO THEM THAT CALL EVIL GOOD, AND GOOD EVIL . . . that are wise in their own eyes . . . WHICH JUSTIFY THE WICKED FOR REWARD, and take away the righteousness of the righteous from him!*

—Isaiah 5:20–21, 23

Evolution and **progress** have become the new theology. There is no moral compass, save their own wavering judgments, based on nothing. Our schools replaced God with **humanism, psychology and evolution**. They taught that we can save ourselves; that **we are our own gods**, on the throne of our own selfish hearts. The state of Kansas was ridiculed and humiliated before the whole world when the people wanted to teach creationism, the Holy Bible treated like a foolish, antiquated myth. Those that fought against creationism, and forced the THEORY of evolution back on the children, have forgotten that theirs is a religion that has not one shred of evidence to support its beliefs. Whereas, the Bible has mountains of historical documentation to back it up. Proudly the twin towers of greed and pride glittered the gold of the sun back at us. Fool's gold.

In our charge toward greed and mammon, we chose to ignore the danger of training Arab nationals and pilots from other countries that are our enemies. Embry-Riddle and the many other flight schools located in Florida are loaded with foreign nationals, some of whom could pose a threat. Why are tens of thousands of foreign and even unfriendly United Nations military troops allowed to train and occupy numerous bases on American soil, including Fort Hood, Texas? This is an unbelievably dangerous policy. In our **arrogance**, we have literally trained our enemies how to attack us, and opened our treasure houses for them to tour and inspect. God's Word clearly instructs us not to make covenants with His enemies.

Any person or nation that is against Israel, and fails to stand by her, is the enemy of YHWH, our God. We are to pray for the peace of Jerusalem. America's destiny is inextricably tied to Israel. Those who bless Israel will be blessed; those who curse her will be cursed.

> *Pray for the peace of Jerusalem: they shall prosper that love thee.*
>
> —Psalm 122:6

> *Take heed to thyself, lest thou make a COVENANT with the inhabitants of the land whither thou goest, lest it be for a snare in the midst of thee . . . and . . . go a whoring after their gods, and do sacrifice unto their gods. . . .*
>
> —Exodus 34:12–15

When King Hezekiah of Judah, in his pride, opened up all his treasures for the wicked ambassadors of Babylon (where modern day Iraq is) to tour, God was very displeased and told him that because of this, all his treasure would be carried off to Babylon, along with his sons.

Chapter 12
Islam Vs. Christianity

Islam is one of the fastest growing religions in the world. Is Islam the peaceful religion that the news media has portrayed? **Here are a few quotes from their holy book, the Quran (Koran).**

> Fight and **slay the pagans** wherever ye find them, and seize them, beleaguer them, and lie in wait for them in every stratagem of war.
>
> —Quran, Sura 9:5

> Prophet, **make war on unbelievers** . . . hypocrites . . . deal rigorously with them.
> —Al Tawbah (The Repentance) Sura 9:73

> Let not the unbelievers think they will ever

get away. They have not the power to do so. Muster against them all the men and cavalry at your command, so that you may **strike terror into the enemy of God** (Allah) and your enemy. . . . Prophet, rouse the faithful to arms! If they incline to peace (accept Islam) make peace with them.

—Al Anfal (The Spoils) Sura 8:59

Believers, **take neither Jews nor Christians to be your friends**: they are friends with one another. Whoever of you seeks their friendship shall become one of their number, and God does not guide wrongdoers.

—Al Maidah (The Table) Sura 5:51-74

Article by Douglas Davis, *Jerusalem Post*, August 6, 2001

LONDON—Scores of Palestinian women have responded to a fatwa issued by the High Islamic Council in Saudi Arabia last Wednesday to become suicide bombers, according to yesterday's London Sunday Times.

It said, "The terrifying zeal of those willing to undertake suicide missions leaves the security services with an almost impossible task as they try to prevent atrocities." The paper also quoted Israeli-Arab spiritual leader Sheikh Abdullah Nimr Darwish as saying that, "The women, too, will fight," he said. . . .

He spoke of seeing Palestinian women wearing white shrouds at funerals—a sign of their readiness to become a shuhada, or martyr—and the paper quoted Palestinian security sources describing how the women shouted in exultation: **"MAKE A BOMB OF ME, PLEASE!"**

"Israel has the Dimona nuclear plant, but **we Palestinians have** a stronger Dimona—**the suiciders**," added Darwish. **"We can use them on a daily basis."**

In another development, the London-based *Sunday Telegraph* reported that leading Arab intellectuals are calling on Palestinian women to join the war against Israel as **"BIOLOGICAL WEAPONS."**

YHWH is the true name of our God, which, despite what you have been told, is a different God from Allah, the one the Muslims worship. Every time you see the word LORD all in caps in the Old Testament, this is actually the word YHWH. According to extremists of Islam, their god, Allah, frequently calls for jihad (so-called holy war is really the slaughter of anyone who opposes their fanatical beliefs).

It is faithfully reported in *The Voice of the Martyrs* magazine, that time and again Christians are specifically targeted by advancing Islamic soldiers. All over the Moslem world atrocities against Christians are commonplace. In Turkey, believers are threatened and imprisoned, Cyprus—no Christian witness is tolerated, Iran—witnessing is banned and several pastors were murdered, Iraq—tens of thousands were gassed, shot or forced to leave their homes, Kuwait—only Moslems may become citizens and Bibles are burned, Maldives—all Christians were arrested, Morocco—Christians are imprisoned, Egypt—Christian girls are raped and forced to marry Muslim men. Islamic persecution of Christians continues in India, Laos, Tunisia, United Arab Emirates, Comoro Islands, Libya, Syria, Bhutan, Brunei, Equatorial Guinea, Yemen, Oman, Somalia, Malaysia and Qatar.

In Pakistan, our supposed new ally, false accusations against Christians abound resulting in mob murders. Loudspeakers call loyal Muslims to burn Christian buildings, beat the men and rape the women. One pastor was imprisoned in a tiny cell with no toilet, his feet beaten 100 times, his hands tied to a stick from which he was hung for four hours. In Saudi Arabia, another of our allies, converts to Christianity face execution, imprisonment or beheading. Indonesia—Moslems on jihad attack Christians and kill and force them from their homes, Myanmar—Christians are singled out for repression, Mauritania—Christians are charged with treachery and imprisoned, Nigeria—Christians are killed and their buildings burned, Azerbaijan—Moslem mobs burn Christian homes, churches and businesses, Uzbekistan—churches are forcibly closed, Algeria—100,000 people have been brutally murdered by the Islamic Salvation Front since 1992, Tajikistan—Muslims planted bombs at a church murdering many.

Throughout the world Christians are tortured by Islamic fundamentalists, captured and turned into slaves. The Muslim's horrific torture of Christian men, women and children in the Sudan is reprehensible:

mother's breasts are cut off and they are forced to watch in agony as their infants starve to death, some are skinned alive, babies are torn from their mother's arms and drowned before their eyes, they are denied access to water wells, pastors and children are shot in the head for refusing to renounce Christianity, the women are raped, whole congregations are locked in their churches and burned alive, people are imprisoned, tortured, forcibly deprived of sleep until they die, given severe electric shocks, and some are even crucified.

Despite the horrors all around them, here is what one Sudanese pastor said: "Suffering is a beautiful gift from God." He states that because of the suffering, tribal barriers and hatred have ceased, denominational walls have fallen, the Body of Christ is unified and the purified church is growing. In Bangladesh a Christian converted from Islam shared, ". . . my wife and I have lost our house. They have burned our clothes. They have burned our furniture, but they cannot burn Jesus from our hearts."

(Our appreciation to Voice of the Martyrs *for the above information.)*

Chapter 13

Fake Palestinian Funeral—A Shocking Tale of Visiting Hell

On Friday, May 3, 2002, there appeared an ar ticle entitled, "IDF films fake Palestinian funeral in Jenin." Film was actually made of the "funeral." The men carrying a shrouded figure accidentally dropped the man "they themselves" had beaten into unconsciousness. Thinking him dead, they called the press and paraded him through the streets to illicit world sympathy, blaming the Israelis for the death. When he hit the ground the "dead" man took off running and a reporter, named Ariel O'Sullivan, pursued him for five blocks, where the frightened man related the following story.

The man, clearly terrorized, related that when he was in an unconscious state he opened his eyes and was engulfed in flames. He saw his dead relatives tormented in the fires of hell, screaming in pain. They told him that their lies about seventy virgins to wait on them in paradise were untrue, and that they had met their god in hell, who ruled them in "vengeance, hate, and pride," and this was their lot for all eternity.

Even as they faded away they shouted over the "din of anguish and fiery torment," the "People of the Book" were right, and begged him not to continue on his present course, or he would surely end up as they were.

(Reported by Michael Rood on his website: www.2000.com.)

Chapter 14

Islam—
A Religion of Love or Hate?

Under Osama bin Laden and the Taliban, the people were ruled with an iron fist. *Globe Magazine* quotes several expert sources on the subject in the October 9 issue. According to Alison Kelly, a British humanitarian aid worker, women are prisoners who must completely cover themselves. Recently, a woman was beaten to death by an angry mob when she accidentally exposed her arm. Even the windows of their homes are painted so no one may look in. Woman have little or no health care because male doctors are forbidden to touch them. They cannot laugh or talk loudly in public. Beating, rape and kidnapping of women is commonplace. They are not permitted to work, be educated or travel alone. Husbands can kill their wives if they are offended in any way. Their fingernails and toe-nails are torn out if they are painted.

A recent news story detailed the unfortunate death of an Arabian princess. While she was asleep in her bed, a man broke in and raped her, yet "she" was put to death for supposedly tempting "him." The man was dismissed without even a reprimand. This clearly demonstrates the inequity of the Islamic system.

Osama bin Laden, a total hypocrite according to experts, is an opium addict who has made millions selling heroin from the rich poppy fields of Afghanistan. According to Larry Johnson, ex-CIA agent and former deputy director of Counter-Terrorism at the State Department, Osama and his military captains live a very hedonistic lifestyle. He condones gang rape, drinking and carousing. Daniel Pipes, director of the Middle East Forum and expert on bin Laden, says, "They're drawn to porn like moths to a flame. They have even used porn websites to pass on secret messages." Steven Zunes, assistant professor of politics at the University of San Francisco stated, "Pretending to be devout is just a ruse he uses to attract the religious zealots he needs to carry out his barbaric acts." Osama preaches death to Christians and Jews.

Our military actually had a part in training Osama bin Laden and equipping his army for a war fought in Afghanistan. We trained and equipped Sadam Hussein, and that dog has come back to bite us, too.

What Did the Terrorists Really Hope To Gain?

Do the terrorists know something we do not know? Will their Muslim brothers rally round them in the end, causing catastrophic world war? ***And the nations were angry, and Thy wrath is come . . . (Revelation 11:18).*** The hatred against Christians and Jews is monumental, worldwide. Only demonically inspired people, whipped into a frenzy by fanatical religious extremism, are capable of such acts. They were willing to die for what they believe. Are we? Are we willing to lay down our lives for the **LORD's cause**? Are we willing to preach the truth, even though it is not a popular message?

Chapter 15

America—
Turn to a Higher Way

A merica is experiencing **THE BIRTH PANGS**, the beginning of sorrows, yet it is not too late to repent and still see one last revival in America. People want to hear about peace, love and safety, yet they want to dwell in the land of **pride** and **revenge**. God allowed these things to happen because of our own nation's wickedness, yet I say again, we can still turn from wickedness and be overcomers. In the book of Revelation we are told, ***And they OVERCAME him (the devil) by the blood of the Lamb, and by the word of their testimony; and THEY LOVED NOT THEIR LIVES UNTO THE DEATH*** *(Revelation 12:11)*.

Jericho

Fear gripped the people of Jericho, who in their

pride had called themselves self-sufficient. They had a strong city, and were proud of the fortress that surrounded them. They trusted in their thick walls to protect them, but within was the stench of wickedness that the great I Am had to judge. Fear opened the door to their downfall. The manmade fortress they built was not enough in their day of trouble, for the trumpet of God was blown. The Hebrews, at YHWH's direction shouted, and the wicked walls of Jericho fell.

Terrorism—Rooted in Fear

Fear was one of the keys to the downfall of Jericho. Fear was a major key loosed against America. Many of those coming into the hospitals in the first hours after the attack were suffering from panic attacks and heart trouble. ***Men's HEARTS FAILING THEM FOR FEAR, and for looking after those things which are coming on the earth: for the powers of heaven shall be shaken*** *(Luke 21:26)*. The Bible states that in the end times, men's hearts will fail them because of fear. Fear is the opposite of faith. Fear will kill you. Fear causes a multitude of diseases. Take authority over fear and choose to place your life in the Father's hands.

Our president stated that our new war is between "freedom and fear." Freedom in God's eyes, however, does not mean freedom to do wickedly. It means freedom to experience God's fullness by loving Him and trusting Him. Our forefathers sought freedom on these shores to worship the one true God. Fear is not so much the enemy of freedom, as it is the enemy of faith; faith in our God's ability to save and protect us.

Anger

I believe action should be taken against the perpetrators of the atrocities against America, but the anger, hatred, revenge and retaliation on everyone's minds is eclipsing what must be our true focus. If we export revenge and anger to the nations, we will surely lose in the war against terrorism. Regardless of the necessary actions taken to stop terrorism, forgiveness must be in the hearts of all true believers, or it will destroy us, affecting our judgment and actions. It must be turned into national repentance for the things that caused God's hedge of protection to fall in the first place. Pray that President Bush will listen to his heavenly Father, rather than his earthly father and advisors, who are all rattling their sabers.

Nineveh

Nineveh, one of the wickedest cities of old, modeled the *right* reaction. When the prophet Jonah warned them of impending judgment, the king and all the people, even the animals fasted and repented. Their lives were spared by a merciful God.

Hezekiah and the Assyrians

In ancient Judah, when the Assyrians (Syria today) railed against the God of the Israelites, threatening and frightening the people of Judah, **King Hezekiah and the prophet Isaiah prayed and cried out to heaven** *(2 Chronicles 32:17–20)*. That night the LORD of Hosts sent an angel who killed 185,000 Assyrians in one night *(2 Kings 19:35)*. Hezekiah spoke great words that we should heed, right before this victory. *. . . **There be more with us than with him: With him (Assyria) is an ARM OF THE FLESH; but with us is the LORD our God (YHWH our Elohim) to help us, and to fight our battles** . . . (2 Chronicles 32:7–8)*.

Chapter 16

A Holy God Must Have a Holy Bride

There was an **even greater danger after the battle**. After this great victory Hezekiah's heart became lifted up because of the power and wealth that was given him. Because he was **proud**, he was struck with a sickness unto death. When he humbled himself and prayed the LORD healed him. Once again God's wrath was averted. So must it be for America and our president.

God has desired to wed a holy bride, His church, but instead our country has embraced the wicked spirit of Jezebel (see my new book *Jezebel vs. Elijah* for more detail) and gone whoring after other gods. The bride has become a harlot. Therefore, we are being allowed a taste of what it is like without God's protection. **Worse things will fol-**

low unless we choose to repent. There are numerous examples of Israel and Judah, in the Old Testament, coming under attack and being carried off into captivity because of God's judgments. The time of grace is past for America. It ended in August, 2001. The time of a holy God winking at our manifest wickedness has come to an end.

We have preached a milquetoast, weak gospel and a wimpy God of love, love, love. Yes! Our God is love, but we have forgotten that He is a jealous God, zealous for a pure bride. We truly have forgotten the holiness factor. I want to throw myself, my family, and my nation on the mercy of God. His judgments and . . . ***counsels of old are faithfulness and truth,*** and He is still a righteous and holy God. Wickedness has reached the fullness of time. The cup of iniquity is full. Now, everything that can be shaken, will be shaken *(Haggai 2:6; Hebrews 12:27).* **The LORD of Hosts is like a hammer that shatters the rock of darkness**, and exposes the wickedness in our own hearts *(Jeremiah 23:29).* He will bring purity, though it be a painful process, to the earth. Because He loves us, He will purge us. Even Christians will be angry at God for the shaking, not only for the World Trade Center and Pentagon attacks, but other dreadful events to follow.

Chapter 17
God's Side or Our Side?

We, as individuals and as a nation, must repent and **get on God's side**. We cannot simply expect Him to be on our side, just because we are Americans. We must not resist Him.

In the book of Ruth, Naomi and her sons and husband tried to escape the judgments of God by running to Moab to hide. The result was that they all died except Naomi, herself.

Joshua was confronted by a stranger with a drawn sword in his hand before the battle of Jericho. He asked: *Art thou for us, or for our adversaries? And he said, NAY; BUT AS CAPTAIN OF THE HOST OF THE LORD AM I NOW COME* (Joshua 5:13–15). The LORD has asked us a question, **"Are we with God, or are we asking God to be with us?"**

A trap has been laid for us by our adversary.

Our enemy is not any human being, it is the devil, the dragon, that old serpent, which deceives the whole world *(Revelation 12:9)*. ***For we wrestle not against flesh and blood, but against principalities, against powers, against the rulers of the darkness of this world, against spiritual wickedness in high places*** *(Ephesians 6:12)*. He is very clever and should not be underestimated. He is wily and elusive. We can only win if we rise up as Elijah's who are willing to stand alone if necessary and throw down Jezebel from her ivory tower. We must stand against the false prophets that preach peace and safety. The time has come to get off the fence. Wake up, America!

The End-Time Laodicean Church

We are the Laodiceans mentioned in Revelation, the last of the seven churches. And the LORD of Hosts responds to the Laodicean's in the following manner:

So then because thou art LUKEWARM, and neither cold nor hot, I will spew thee out of my mouth. Because thou sayest, I

AM RICH, and increased with goods, AND HAVE NEED OF NOTHING; and KNOWEST NOT that THOU ART WRETCHED, and MISERABLE, and POOR, and BLIND, and NAKED: I counsel thee to buy of Me gold tried in the fire, that thou mayest be rich; and white raiment, that thou mayest be clothed, and that the shame of thy nakedness do not appear; and anoint thine eyes with eyesalve, that thou mayest see.

—Revelation 3:17–18

The people of Noah's day *"KNEW NOT"* that their hour was upon them, and the wretched, poor, blind Laodicean church *"KNOWEST NOT"* that their hour has come. They are being **WEIGHED in the balances and found wanting**. The true prophets have warned America for years to repent, to turn from their wickedness, yet they laughed and went about their merry way. Those who have not willfully sinned against God's law have stood back and allowed wickedness to abound all around them. They have stubbornly voted for immoral leaders and stood apathetically by, while iniquitous legislation and deeds were done. If America insists on sowing to the wind, then she must reap the whirlwind.

Chapter 18
America: Repent or Perish!

We may conclude that if America will repent, she can be saved. If she rises in self-righteous **pride**, and fails to heed the warning of the true prophets, if her arrogance abounds rather than her once strong faith, she will fall. Rather than saying we are proud to be Americans, we should say that we are humbly thankful to be Americans. So far, the response of our leaders has been, "America is strong. Watch out enemies of America! We will find and destroy you! We are the biggest bully on the block and you don't mess with us!" Rather than, "We repent and turn from our wicked ways. We have sinned against You alone, oh God!"

If we confess our sins, He is faithful and just to forgive us our sins, and to cleanse us from all unrighteousness.

—1 John 1:9

Terrorists we cannot find are symbolic of demons we cannot see. Even if we find a few terrorists, more will spring up. If we cast out demons, they will return unless we get rid of the garbage that they feed on; sin. America is full of garbage, and rats (demons) feed on it. When will we learn that the key is to eliminate the sin, in order to get rid of the demons. If we think we can pull ourselves up by our own bootstraps without repentance, we are deeply deceived.

Conversely, if we carry bitterness against our enemies, as they have so graphically carried against us, we will destroy ourselves. Bitterness destroys from within, causing cancer and other diseases. Anger and bitterness destroy nations from within. Rage ultimately brings destruction. This anger must be given to the Father Who loves us.

> **Dearly beloved, avenge not yourselves, but rather give place unto wrath: for it is written, Vengeance is mine; I will repay, saith the LORD.**
>
> —Romans 12:19–20

We are given a powerful mandate, straight from the

heart of God. Among Yahshua Messiah's (Jesus Christ's) last words, were these nuggets of pure gold.

> *Whosesoever sins ye REMIT, they are remitted unto them: and whosesoever sins ye retain, they are retained.*
>
> —John 20:23

REMIT means to restore to the original state, forgive a sin, abate, refrain from exacting a penalty.

Am I saying the USA should do nothing to defend itself? Definitely not! I am simply calling our leaders and country up to a higher way. I am exhorting them to trust in YHWH, our God. Not in their own strength. To ask for His guidance, before charging in for revenge: **To humble ourselves, and cast out pride**, which will be our downfall.

So America: Repent or Perish!

Chapter 19

We, the People

This could be our finest hour, or our worst. If we run in **fear**, we are dead as we live. If we fight the good fight of **faith**, we are victorious no matter the circumstances that surround us. It is a matter of history that when the Christians were thrown to the lions, in their darkest hour they displayed such courage and faith, even forgiving the Romans as they were torn to pieces, that for every Christian killed, ten Romans converted to the faith. We must remember that Shadrach, Meshach and Abednego refused to bow their knee to worship false gods, and so must we. They were saved because they trusted in the God of Abraham, Isaac and Jacob. They walked through the burning, fiery furnace because the Fourth Man (Jesus) was there with them, and He is here with us *(Daniel 3)*. We need not **fear**. There are greater terrors yet to face.

How we face them will bring honor or shame to our God, YHWH. We must live for what is written in heaven and **humble ourselves** under the hand of Almighty God. Instead of **retaliation** in our hearts, we need **repentance**.

> *If My people, which are called by My Name, shall HUMBLE THEMSELVES AND PRAY, and SEEK MY FACE, and TURN FROM THEIR WICKED WAYS; then will I hear from heaven, and will forgive their sin, and will HEAL THEIR LAND.*
>
> —2 Chronicles 7:14

I exhort you this day to strengthen your hearts, and place your trust in the LORD. The attack on America is only the beginning of sorrows. It is the beginning of birth pangs.

> *But when ye shall hear of WARS and commotions, BE NOT TERRIFIED . . . NATION SHALL RISE AGAINST NATION, and kingdom against kingdom: And GREAT EARTHQUAKES shall be in divers*

places and fearful sights and great signs shall there be from heaven. But before all these, they shall lay their hands on you, and persecute you, delivering you up to the . . . prisons. . . . And ye shall be betrayed . . . For in these days of vengeance, that all things which are written may be fulfilled . . . there shall be great DISTRESS in the land, and WRATH upon this people. . . . And there shall be signs in the sun, and in the moon, and in the stars; and upon the earth distress of nations, with perplexity; the sea and the waves roaring; MEN'S HEARTS FAILING THEM FOR FEAR, and for looking after those things which are coming on the earth; for the powers of heaven shall be shaken.

—Luke 21:9–26

Chapter 20

Savior or Judge

There is a story of a young man in India who became so despondent that he threw himself into a river to drown. Another man jumped in and saved him. The young man began to lead a life of wickedness and crime, killing and stealing, until he was finally caught several years later. When he was brought before the judge he was all smiles, because he recognized the same man who had saved him years before from drowning. He imagined in his heart that the man would let him off for his crimes. However, the judge sentenced him to death. Now in great fear he asked him why he didn't receive mercy, and the judge replied, "The first time I came as your savior. This time I come as your judge."

I have heard the president and others calling out for justice, over and over. This is a mistake. If our country gets the justice they are clamoring for, it will be utterly destroyed. Instead of justice, we need mercy. Take heed, America!

Chapter 21

Prayer for the Individual and the Nation

Glory and honor and praise to YHWH, our glorious LORD, Who inhabits the praises of His people. Almighty God, All Consuming Fire, we declare that we, as individuals and as a nation have done wickedly in Your sight.

Heavenly Father, we fervently repent for our sins; for our failure to place You and You alone on the throne of our hearts. We make You LORD of our lives right now! We repent for trusting in the arm of the flesh, and in our own ability to help ourselves, for building towers of greed and pride, instead of building a relationship with You. We repent of the rampant greed of ourselves and our nation. We repent of the pride of life that has been our downfall, both for ourselves and our nation, instead of humbly trusting in Your ability to save us. We have been so busy that we programmed you right out of our lives, and our hearts were so hardened that we didn't even realize we had left You. But You are blowing the shofar one last time, calling a repentant, humbled people back to You. Help us! Have mercy on us, heavenly Father. Save us in our day of trouble.

The Bible declares in John 20:23 that the sins we remit will be remitted. Therefore, we, the people, remit the sin of those people responsible for bombing and threatening our nation. We ask You to deal with them and with those who are planning further attacks on our country. We repent for our nation that has willfully turned its back on You and raised themselves up to the heavens, placing themselves on the throne of their own hearts. We weep in sorrow for taking prayer out of the schools, and ask Your forgiveness, merciful Father. We remit this sin for our nation. We ask Your forgiveness for the slaughter of unborn babies. They were our godly heritage, and we destroyed them. Forgive us for standing back and allowing these things to happen. We remit this sin for our nation and ask You to deal

9

with those individuals who brought this sin on us, even as we forgive them. We ask you to forgive us for teaching evolution, instead of honoring You, our creator.

We remit the sin of a people deeply in error, worshiping false gods of greed, pride, Satan, and other false religions. Forgive us for allowing pornography and perversion to be a constant way of life, ever before our eye gates, polluting our very souls. Forgive us for willfully electing wicked leaders that brought us swiftly toward the lifting of our hedge of protection, and onto a slippery precipice, the very brink of judgment. Though we have sent missionaries around the world to preach the gospel, and have stood (sometimes halfheartedly) by Israel, we ourselves are in danger and in desperate need of the truth. As we somberly face the ripened fruit of our own iniquity, we remind ourselves of your Word.

> *O ye sons of men, how long will ye turn my glory into shame? How long will ye love vanity, and seek after sin?*
>
> —Psalm 4:2

Yet, hear us oh God, we beseech You with Your Word: If we humble ourselves and pray, and seek Your face, and turn from wickedness, You will hear and forgive us our sins, and heal our land *(2 Chronicles 7:14)*. Before You, oh God, Who hold the worlds in the palm of Your hand, we humble ourselves now, to fast, pray and repent.

We throw down pride, and a false sense of self-sufficiency. In these last times, as we are cleansed by the blood of Jesus, the Messiah, we can only safely hide ourselves under the shadow of Your wings *(Psalm 91:1)*. You, alone, are our hiding place *(Psalm 32:7)*. Your angels will encamp round about us because we fear You with a holy fear *(Psalm 34:7)*. Save us, oh YHWH, our God, as we place our trust in You alone.

> *Give us help from trouble: for vain is the help of man. Through God we shall do valiantly: for He it is that shall tread down our enemies.*
>
> —Psalm 108:12–13

Yes, we ask you to tread down our enemies.

Oh God, King of the Universe, purge us with hyssop, and we shall be clean. Create in us a clean heart, and renew a right spirit within us *(Psalm 51)*. Let us rise up once more, mighty warriors dressed for battle, and run once more, as Elijah did, before the King's chariot. Let us do great exploits in Your Name, bring only glory and honor to Your Name, the Captain of our salvation. We cry out once more for repentance, holy worship and revival to sweep our nation. The fields are white unto harvest in this day. Give us the heathen for our inheritance and the uttermost parts of the earth for Thy possession. Turn our nation into a land that calls on the Name of YHWH, our LORD, that we may be saved. Amen.

Prayer for the Victim's Families

Father, we are heartbroken over the loss of life in all these tragedies. We ask You to send Your Holy Spirit, the Comforter, to those who are grieving. We mourn with those who mourn, today. Fill them with the peace that passes all understanding, that they may rest in You, even in times of great trial and tragedy. Father, when King David came home and found his wives and children gone, he only turned to you, and encouraged himself in the LORD. Oh, that they would come to know You, Father, to lean on you. We ask You to impart comfort, peace, strength and provision to the victim's families.

I pray that You would strengthen them moment by moment, and that they would forgive their enemies that have murdered their loved ones, as Your Son Jesus Christ did when He hung on the cross, forgiving those who killed Him. I pray for the salvation of every person involved in this tragedy, that they would not wait another day to give their hearts to you.

I pray for all the rescue workers, the police, firemen, and medical personnel that gave of themselves selflessly and tirelessly to comfort, rescue and give assistance to the wounded, the trapped, the desperate, the hurting, the despondent. Thank you, heavenly Father, for imparting boldness and strength to them in their continuing efforts. Thank you for those who bravely laid down their lives to help their friends and others trapped in the buildings. They are an inspiration to us all. They are more than conquerors, even in death. Amen.

An Open Letter to
the President

**Dear President Bush and all the leaders of the
United States of America,**

We come as citizens today who love our country, to
request an action by our leaders that could make
the difference between our nation being destroyed
as we know it, or surviving with honor. America
has been blessed above all nations, but we have
forgotten by whose hand we have been preserved
and prospered these many years. God alone can
take credit for our success!

We: ". . . have vainly imagined all these blessings were produced by some superior wisdom and
virtue of our own" **(President Lincoln's Proclamation for a National Day of Fasting, Humiliation [Repentance] and Prayer, April 30, 1863)**.

The terrorist attack of 9-11-01 was an emergency call to wake us up, and drive us to our knees to repent. God's hedge of protection around the United States has been lifted because of unrepented sin, pride, the innocent blood on our hands and because we have refused to heed the warnings of God's prophets. Judgment has begun, but it can be stopped. How? As always, God watches for repentance.

> *If My people, which are called by My Name, shall humble themselves, and pray, and seek My face, and turn from their wicked ways; then will I hear from heaven, and will forgive their sin, and will heal their land.*
>
> —2 Chronicles 7:14

We call upon you today, to lead us in repentance by confessing our national sins, humbling ourselves before God and asking God for forgiveness, a return of His hedge of protection, and His grace and blessing on our nation.

Individual salvation and national salvation are

different. The salvation of a nation is determined by the actions of its king (President). The collective sins of our nation, its leaders, judges and citizens, weigh heavily on God's scales of justice. According to examples in the Bible, the king or leaders of a nation must humble themselves and repent if a nation is to survive, once the judgment cycle has begun. An individual, on the other hand, can call upon God at anytime during his life and God will forgive all his sin, welcoming him into His kingdom. (We commend you on your war against terrorism, and we are **not** saying to do nothing to defend ourselves. Rather, we are calling you to a higher way; to trust in God, not in ourselves.)

President Bush, it is our job to remind you, but it is your job to take the responsibility to lead our nation through repentance. **We call upon you today to declare a NATIONAL DAY OF REPENTANCE**, just as **President Lincoln did in the midst of a national crisis**, to include fasting, repentance and fervent prayer. We the people of America are like the buildings of the World Trade Center, hanging in the balance in a moment of time before our ultimate collapse. Our steel may have been dented, but we still have a nation to fight for, on our knees. Our most effective response will be to call on our God with a penitent heart.

We simply cannot save ourselves! Only God can save us. Failure to turn this nation to repentance will result in a near total destruction of this country. **George Washington's Valley Forge vision** prophesied of only a remnant of America surviving this calamity, and Mr. President, you can change the course of this tragedy.

Without your action on this, more terrorism, earthquakes, volcanoes and nuclear war is coming to the land that we love.

We are only one sincere repentance and forgiveness away from being saved. Mr. President, please hear us and act accordingly. This could be America's finest hour! Oh God, please hear our President's plea and save our nation!

Dr. Bree M. Keyton
Stephen T. Keyton

About the Author

Dr. Bree M. Keyton is the author of several books. She holds two teaching certificates in English and in Speech and Theater. She holds doctorates in Theology and in Administration and Education. Bree is director of research for Faith Bible College in Kansas City.

Bree ministers in power evangelism, brandishing a sword of steel while exercising the sword of the Spirit. Thousands have been saved, delivered and received physical and emotional healing by the awesome power of God.

Bree ministers in music, has a CD that received nationwide airplay for three years, and travels preaching the gospel. She has a zeal for soul winning, healing the sick and setting the captives free. She has hosted a national TV talk show and served as a worship leader.

Before being born again, Bree traveled as a warm-up act for rock stars and had her own nightclub act. She was shot in the head, and through the miraculous intervention of the living God, she lived to tell the story and share God's great healing power with others.

Bree has appeared on *"The 700 Club," "It's Supernatural"* with Sid Roth, the National Right to Life Convention, the International Counter-Cult Conference, and the National Full Gospel Business Men's Convention. Bree has ministered in arenas, churches, music halls, prisons, malls, parks, high schools, colleges, retreats, crusades, seminars, coffee houses, and outdoor festivals.

Additional Materials Available Through:

Bree & Steve Keyton Ministries

PO Box 17802

Kansas City, MO 64134

1. ***Jezebel vs. Elijah* $12.95 (book).** Anointed revelationary teaching on the great struggle going on right now in our country, our churches, and our homes. Put on your seat belts. This one packs a wallop!

2. ***Heart & Soul Surrender* (music) $15.95—CD $12.95— cassette (comes with study guide).** Receiving nationwide airplay for three years. Anointed music to lead the listener into the presence of God, bringing salvation, healing, deliverance and worship. Includes four electrifying dramatic works, "Stripes," through which thousands have been healed, "Nails," "Thorns," and "The Blood."

3. ***Stripes, Nails, Thorns and The Blood* $24.00 (book).** An essential study guide for in-depth spiritual warfare, healing and deliverance, and a dynamic manual of healing scriptures; tackles tough questions: how to receive and maintain your healing and deliverance; vivid and intense teaching on demonic spirits and strongholds; testimonials; prayers and much more.

4. ***Healing Scriptures* $10.00 (cassette).** 100 minutes of healing scriptures, exhortation, and music; the most riveting and complete healing tape of its kind.

5. ***Bitter-Root Judgments, Inner Vows & Soul Ties* $10.00 (cassette).** We have all made them—they are destroying

our lives—get set free with this insightful teaching that has already helped so many.

6. ***Victorious Scriptures* $12.00 (two 90 minute cassettes).** For the overcomer; powerful, uplifting scriptures, exhortation and music throughout; indispensable.

7. ***Victorious Scriptures* $10.00 (book).** A strategic and forceful work that includes complete victorious scriptures, names of God and their significance, exhortation and prayers.

8. ***Advanced Spiritual Warfare* $40.00 (12 part cassette series).** Anointed training for the serious prayer warrior, and preparation for ministry. Potent and compelling. An accredited college course.

9. ***Song of Solomon, Esther and Ruth* $12.00 (two 90 minute cassettes).** For the bride: A vibrant and profound, eye-opening message; truly a blessing.

THE GREAT END TIME CLASH

JEZEBEL VS. ELIJAH

The spirits of Jezebel and Elijah live in America today.
God's whirlwind of judgment is at the door,
for it has reached the fullness of time

by Dr. Bree M. Keyton, TH.D., D.C.E.

BERLITZ®

KENYA

By the staff of Berlitz Guides

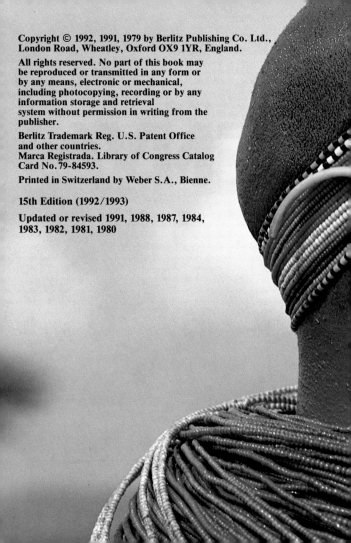

15th Edition (1992/1993)

Updated or revised 1991, 1988, 1987, 1984,
1983, 1982, 1981, 1980

How to use our guide

- All the practical information, hints and tips that you will need before and during the trip start on page 103.

- For general background, see the sections Kenya and the Kenyans, p. 6, and A Brief History, p. 13.

- All the sights to see are listed between pages 28 and 87. Our own choice of sights most highly recommended is pinpointed by the Berlitz traveller symbol.

- A Who's Who in the Animal World section on pages 39 to 49 fills in on the background to the habits and particularities of the major species you're likely to meet.

- Entertainment, nightlife and all other leisure activities are described between pages 89 and 99, while information on restaurants and cuisine is to be found on pages 100 to 102.

- The Index on page 127 will help you to find what you are looking for.

- Finally, at the back of the book, there's a checklist of animals you might sight.

Text: Jack Altman
Photography: Jürg Donatsch
Layout: Doris Haldemann
Illustrations: Aude Aquoise
We wish to thank Ray Morrell and Odhiambo Okite for their contribution to the preparation of this guide. We are also grateful to African Safari Club, the Kenya Tourist Office and T.K. Ngaamba for their valuable assistance.
Cartography: 🌀 Falk-Verlag, Hamburg.

Contents

Found an error or an omission in this Berlitz Guide? Or a change or new feature we should know about? Our editor would be happy to hear from you, and a postcard would do. Be sure to include your name and address, since in appreciation for a useful suggestion, we'd like to send you a free travel guide. Write to: Berlitz Publishing Co. Ltd., London Road, Wheatley, Oxford OX9 1YR, England.

Although we make every effort to ensure the accuracy of all the information in this book, changes occur incessantly. We cannot therefore take responsibility for facts, prices, addresses and circumstances in general that are constantly subject to alteration.

Kenya and the Kenyans

The first phenomenon you'll notice in Kenya is the sky, something you might take for granted amidst urban horizons. Here it is quite simply endless and constantly changing in depth and colour. In the heat of the day you'll discover blues, pinks, reds and golds in the light that you never saw before, for Kenya is a feast of colour, light and movement. And in between the stimuli are the most restful beach resorts a tired body could want.

Even on a cloudy day there never seem to be enough clouds to cover the whole sky. You'll watch buffaloes in huge herds making their way across the plateau of the Masai Mara, a few thousand at a time, and the sky will swallow them up. Sitting in a land-rover or minibus, you may suddenly feel very

small, yet somehow at ease to find your proper niche in the scheme of things.

Equally fascinating is the play of colour on every side: the deep red of the soil of Amboseli and Tsavo, the icy white of snow-topped Mount Kenya and the dazzling white of the sandy beaches, the tranquil blue of the ocean and a blue in the lakes that suddenly turns pink when blanketed with a million flamingos, the hot dry green of the savannah and the lusher green of the Aberdare forests.

Movement is similarly diverse. In Nairobi, the pace of the people is an easy-going amble, a swinging gait that reflects the rhythm of the capital's

The vastness of the African skies is a source of perpetual wonder.

business—lively but not frenetic. In the sultry port town of Mombasa the pace is languid; only mad dogs would want it otherwise. Inland to the west, human movement slows to the infinitely patient wanderings of Masai herdsmen, the pace of nomadism itself.

But in the wilds the human being no longer dictates the speed of life. Your eye is taken by the gallop of a herd of zebras, the scamper of an excited troop of baboons or an anxious family of warthogs, the golden flash of a cheetah, the slither of a crocodile in the mud or the slow, purposeful progress of a herd of elephants. This country may be ruled by men and women, but animals are the most honoured tenants.

Kenya is equatorial and thus can offer you the searing heat of Samburu's semi-desert, or the soothing, lukewarm waters of the Indian Ocean; the saturating torpor of Mombasa, but also the heady, bracing air of the cool highlands around Nairobi. Although the capital is less than 150 kilometres from the Equator, you will need a jacket in the

Cabbages, coconuts and mangoes —Nairobi market's exotic mix.

evenings at 1,660 metres above sea level. After a day spent in the parched bush of the Masai Mara, you will greet the regular afternoon rains of the Kericho tea plantations as a refreshing respite.

Kenya has emerged as an oasis of calm and stability on a continent that has known little but turmoil in the decades since decolonization. While this has been a great advantage in attracting the tourist trade, it is paradoxically a source of occasional embarrassment. Nairobi is the preferred East African headquarters for news correspondents and is consequently the routine date-line used for reporting wars and political unrest in neighbouring countries. Many inattentive newspaper readers imagine all these disturbances are happening in Nairobi and need to be reassured that Kenya is a safe place for a holiday. The peaceful transition of power after the death of President Kenyatta was a source of surprised admiration to some, but Kenyans themselves found it perfectly natural. They attributed the apprehension of outside observers to the contagious effect of reporting power struggles in other African countries.

The Kenyan people have a **9**

pronounced taste for the quiet life and a relatively carefree nature that the government is sometimes at pains to stir up into more energetic productivity. But their easy-going character has had the beneficial effect of overcoming the old tensions of tribalism, a major source of conflict elsewhere in Africa. The tribes are formations that rarely go back more than a couple of hundred years and were sustained as elements of colonial administration at a time when they were progressively dissolving and merging into the national unity they are achieving today.

The divisions that Kenyan Africans themselves make in defining their origins are linguistic rather than racial: Bantu-, Nilotic-, Nilo-Hamitic- and Hamitic-speaking peoples. The Kikuyu of the central highlands, part of the Bantu-speaking majority, achieved a dominant position by their direct association with colonial authority after Nairobi was sited on the border of Kikuyu lands. The tribe continues to enjoy considerable prestige and influence despite efforts made by Jomo Kenyatta, the late president and former tribal leader, to dispel ideas that the Kikuyu were in any way superior to other Kenyans.

Daniel arap Moi, member of the minority Nilo-Hamitic Kalenjin tribe, was chosen to succeed Kenyatta in order to combat tribal rivalry between the Kikuyu and the Nilotic-speaking Luo. The Luo, from the shores of Lake Victoria, have developed a reputation as the country's leading intellectuals because of their long connection with European missionary schools, and they fill many of the top university posts.

The most independent of Kenya's tribes is the Masai, a group of tall pastoral nomads who resist the encroachments of modern technological civilization. The Masai guard their herds with spears and still favour the traditional long cloak, though occasionally you may see a young boy wearing a tie-dyed T-shirt.

Kenya's national language is Swahili—Bantu with Arabic influences. This term also refers to the Mohammedan Bantu inhabitants of the coast, distinctive for their mixture of African and Arab features and their pride as merchants with historic ties across the Indian Ocean and Persian Gulf.

Of Kenya's estimated 20,000,000 population, only about 25,000 are of European (mostly British) origin, 80,000

Chadors emphasize beautiful eyes on the predominantly Muslim coast.

are Indian and approximately 30,000 Arab. The European and Indo-Pakistani contingents are what remain of some 60 years of British colonial administration, but the Arab residents go back much further to the settlements founded along the coast from Mombasa up to the island of Lamu in the Middle Ages. The Europeans range from long-established businessmen, hotel managers and farmers to palaeoanthropologists investigating the origins of man and zoologists for whom Kenya is a researcher's paradise. The Indians, Pakistanis and Arabs form distinct commercial classes living in self-contained communities.

The colonial legacy is **11**

marked by the prevalence of the English language, customs and, for want of a better word, cuisine. Vehicles drive on the left. The design of traffic signs, army uniforms and newspapers, the structure of government and public services all show the abiding influence of British models. Even the style of English spoken by African Kenyans reveals colloquialisms from the British colonial and civil services of the 1920s.

But the echoes of the colonial past have been invested with the Kenyans' own casual humour and self-assurance. Conversations about national events of the day are not at all defensive or cautious, as may sometimes be the case in less confident African countries. People have a free-and-easy readiness to criticize shortcomings in authority without at the same time sacrificing an assertive national pride.

When you go to Kenya, be prepared for an exciting sensory experience. You will have a holiday there as you never had before. And come back keener, more alive, more demanding of your usual surroundings.

Don't go out in Malindi's noon sun unless you're born and bred in it.

A Brief History

The first human being to appear in Kenya was perhaps the first human being to appear anywhere. Give or take a few hundred thousand years, he seems to have set up house some 2,500,000 years ago in northern Kenya near the eastern shore of Lake Turkana, or Lake Rudolf as it was known in British colonial times. A fossil of his skull was dug up there in 1972 by a team of palaeo-anthropologists led by Dr. Richard Leakey, the director of the National Museum in Nairobi.

Identified at the National Museum simply as No. 1470, the remains of Kenya's first man predate those found in Java, China and elsewhere in East Africa. Scientists speculate that mankind appeared first in this part of East Africa, rather than anywhere else in the world, because the climate and topographical conditions were appropriate for evolution.

Kenya had changed from a cover of dense rain forest to ever-widening expanses of open savannah. A creature best described as a man-like ape, agile at using trees for his habitat and moving about the ground on all fours, emerged **13** from the forest. In order to look out over the tall savannah grass, to loom larger as a greater apparent threat to predators and to carry food from where it had been gathered or hunted to a safe place for eating, the creature stood up on his hind legs and developed feet for walking and hands for gripping. He became an ape-like man.

The rest, as they say, is history. But it is a history with only the sketchiest of records until the European colonial era. For the rest we must rely on the diggings of palaeoanthropologists and archaeologists.

Stone Age Society

The Stone Age in Kenya seems to have progressed in the classic manner, with fire coming into systematic use around 50,000 B.C. Tools and weapons were progressively refined, particularly with the migration of Caucasoids from south-west Asia and northern Africa. They brought stone arrowheads, knifeblades and ornamental beads made from seeds and discs of ostrich eggshell, dating from around 15,000 B.C.

At this time significant cultural advances took place in the Rift Valley, the great volcanically caused geological fault running through Kenya from Mount Elgon to Mount Kilimanjaro. In the region between Eldoret and Nairobi, ceremonial burial sites have been found, suggesting the first systematic religious practices. Natural volcanic glass or obsidian was used to make knives that were much longer and more effective than had previously been possible.

By dating rock paintings of long-horned cows found on Mount Elgon and grindstones, pestles, bowls and pots used for grain, it has been estimated that cattle-herding and agriculture emerged only around 1,000 B.C. In fact society in Kenya seems to have remained largely at a Stone Age level until about A.D. 1000, when signs of iron-smelting appeared. Throughout this period there was a constant migration and merging of peoples now identified as Bantu-, Nilotic-, Nilo-Hamitic- or Hamitic-speaking. The gradual change from a hunting-and-gathering society to one of agriculture or pastoralism led to rapid increases in population in the more fertile areas of the highlands and the grazing plateaus of the south-west.

This fellow was perhaps the first human being, found on the banks of Lake Turkana. He's called 1470.

Settlement of the Coast

While the Kenya interior has a written record that goes back only 100 years and sparse information from an oral tradition at most 500 years old, the history of the coastal area begins in Roman times. A Greek merchant living in Roman Egypt made a trip down Africa's east coast to explore trade prospects sometime in the 2nd century A.D. His anonymous account, *The Periplus of the Erythraean Sea* (the Roman name for the Indian Ocean) describes places we know as Lamu, Mombasa and Zanzibar, where the local inhabitants—very tall pirates and seafarers—were ready to trade in ivory, tortoiseshell, rhinoceros horn, coconut oil, gums and spices.

In the next few centuries Arab, Persian, Indian and Chinese merchants arrived on the coast with the help of the Trade Winds. From November to March the north-east monsoon carried them across the ocean to barter for African goods with ceramics, metal hatchets, daggers, lances, glass, wine and wheat. They made the return journey in April, when the south-west monsoon blew their dhows back to the Persian Gulf or India. By the 8th and 9th centuries Arabs began to settle on the north Kenya coast in

what they called the land of the Zenj (the black people). The 10th-century Arab geographer Al-Masudi described the Zenj as a people ruled by elected kings with standing armies and priest-advisors. They used oxen harnessed like horses for transport and for war. They cultivated bananas, millet and coconuts and ate meat and honey.

Trading settlements were established on islands in the Lamu archipelago and spurs of land surrounded by creeks and swamps where their wealth could be easily defended without protective ramparts. The excavated town of Manda in the Lamu archipelago shows an affluent community living in impressive coral-rock houses set with mortar, of a massive construction not found elsewhere in Africa south of the Sahara. In addition to the export of ivory, ambergris, leopard skins, tortoiseshell and gold brought up from what is now Zimbabwe, there are the first records of trade in African slaves, sent to Iraq.

The Shirazi, immigrants from the Persian Gulf, progressively colonized the coast in the 12th century, intermarrying with Africans and developing within two or three generations the mixed Bantu-Arabic language of Swahili, or more pro-

perly, Kiswahili. In trading centres established at Malindi and Mombasa, this Islamic Swahili ruling class kept Africans in a state of slavery, performing menial tasks and tilling the fields. The coastal dwellers thus dealt exclusively with the outside world and had few links to the Kenya interior.

Portuguese Domination

The Portuguese explorer Vasco da Gama arrived on the coast in 1498. The Portuguese, with

16

Mombasa was always a place worth fighting for, and Fort Jesus was for the Portuguese an almost impregnable stronghold for a hundred years.

commercial centres already established in India, were more interested in setting up new bases for trade across the Indian Ocean than in opening up and colonizing East Africa itself. They were able to make a trading alliance with the Shirazi Sheikh of Malindi, but other city-states, especially Mombasa, resisted Portuguese encroachment.

Mombasa was attacked and plundered by the Portuguese three times in the 16th century—1505, 1528 and 1589—before surrendering its independence. Functioning both as an island-state and a mainland power, with access to military **17** aid from non-Swahili Africans in the hinterland, Mombasa impressed the Portuguese with its great resilience and the material resources it derived from trade with the Middle East and India. In fact it was Mombasa's pre-eminent position that had provoked Malindi's jealousy and pushed it into alliance with the Portuguese.

In the 1580s the Turks, long-time trading partners of Mombasa, sent two expeditions to break the Portuguese blockade of the port. Portuguese retaliation was massive and Mombasa's resistance was overcome by a simultaneous attack in the rear by Zimba warriors who had migrated from the Zambezi valley. Mombasa recovered enough to stage a counter-attack on Malindi, but Malindi's Bantu allies, the Segeja, won a bloody battle, and the town of Mombasa was handed over to the Sheikh of Malindi and the Portuguese in 1592.

Mombasa became the mainstay of Portuguese authority on the coast, placed under the rule of Sheikh Ahmad of Malindi and backed by a Portuguese military garrison in the newly built Fort Jesus. During the next century the whole Swahili coast acknowledged Portuguese supremacy paying customs and tribute to the King of Portugal through his representative, the Captain of Mombasa. But tribute was never paid placidly. The Swahili rulers were encouraged to stage revolts as the Portuguese hold on the coast was gradually weakened by mounting threats to their position elsewhere in the Indian Ocean from the Dutch and British, and from the Persians and Arabs in the Gulf.

After a ferocious assault on Fort Jesus in 1631, the Portuguese were obliged to rule without a sheikh as intermediary. The Imam of Oman supported a major revolt on Pate Island, just north of Lamu, and Fort Jesus was again besieged and plundered in 1660. The Portuguese were finally driven out of Mombasa in 1698. They returned briefly in 1728 but lost their control of the coast for ever the following year.

Having supported Swahili opposition to the Portuguese, Omani Arabs wanted in turn to supplant the Portuguese as the effective rulers of the coastal region. But the Swahilis decided they had had enough of foreign overlords and successfully withstood Omani pressure for over 100 years. Finally Oman's Sayyid Said bin Sultan was able, with political support and second-hand but nonetheless superior naval technology from the British, to establish a foothold on the northern coast with a base at Lamu. In 1837 he was able to conquer Mombasa, but it was felt to be too precarious a place for his seat of power, and he preferred to rule the Eastern African coast from headquarters further to the south in Zanzibar. This Arab supremacy would never have been possible without aid from the region's future rulers, the British.

The Interior in Pre-Colonial Times

During the period prior to British colonization, Kenya's interior was populated—as far as can be ascertained from oral tradition and scanty archaeological findings—by groups that took a long time to achieve the political cohesion of tribal unity. The Nilotic-speaking Luo migrated along the foothills of Mount Elgon from Uganda and Sudan in small family groups, rather than as a tribe—a large group sharing beliefs in a common ethnic identity based on a single mythical founder. They arrived on the shores of Lake Victoria in what is now Nyanza province in the 16th century, but it was not until the late 18th century that they developed a tribal identity, after the change from pastoral to agricultural life and the subsequent fight for land-ownership. Luo tribal unity solidified through the 19th century in wars against neighbouring Nilo-Hamitic tribes of Masai and Nandi. The Masai controlled the grazing lands of south-central Kenya's open plains, while the Nandi held the hill country.

Political organization varied greatly, inevitably clashing later with the uniform system of chieftainships imposed by the British colonial administration. The Bantus of north-western Kenya, for instance, did have a certain centralized organization, with a council of elders advising a clan leader paid for his services in meat, grain or beer. But the eastern Bantu people—most prominently the Kikuyu—occupying the region between Mount Kilimanjaro and Mount Kenya, were organized in peer-groups known as age-sets, each serving a military, police or judicial function in ruling the tribal lands. Solidarity came through kinship and territorial allegiance, rather than loyalty to a central council or chief.

The first Arab contacts with the Kenya interior were cau-

tiously confined to caravans organized from Mombasa, trading cloth, wire, beads and firearms in exchange for ivory, mainly from the Kamba tribe. (Unfortunately for Kenya's elephants, the quality of the ivory from their tusks was considered superior to that of Indian elephants and sold better in the Orient.) In the early part of the 19th century attempts at slave-raiding for the thriving Zanzibar trade were quickly abandoned because the Arabs were afraid of risking Masai, Nandi and Kikuyu attacks, which would have jeopardized food and water supplies on the long-distance ivory safaris. The Kikuyu accepted to trade with the Kamba but never allowed the Arab traders into Kikuyu territory.

The caravans opened up routes from Mombasa to Kilimanjaro, and across the Rift Valley, via what is now Nairobi, to Lake Victoria and as far north as Lake Turkana. The Arabs spread the Swahili language along these routes but were never able to gain a hold on the interior itself.

For a Samburu tribesman the fierce wars against European colonizers are just a faint ancestral memory.

Under the Union Jack

In the European partition of Africa in the 1880s, the British colonized Kenya almost as an afterthought. They were mainly interested in strengthening the economic and strategic positions they held in Zanzibar and Uganda. They wanted a means of transport between the coast and the sources of the River Nile. In the first instance this meant building a railway from Mombasa to Lake Victoria. It was only incidentally that they discovered the central highlands through which the railway passed to be good farmland well worth settling. What began as a protected transport corridor was expanded into the full-fledged colony of Kenya.

The first European explorations of the interior were carried out in the 1840s by two Germans, Johann Ludwig Krapf and Johann Rebmann, who worked for the British Church Missionary Society. They located Mounts Kenya and Kilimanjaro, John Hanning Speke discovered Lake Victoria in 1858 and Joseph Thomson explored Masai territory in 1883. (Africans try not to smile patronizingly at European "discovery" of places that they have known about since the beginning of time.) **21**

These men mapped out the territory to be exploited by the Imperial British East Africa Company, set up in 1888. Inept management forced the British government to take over operation of what it called the East African Protectorate seven years later in preparation for the building of the Uganda Railway.

The construction was a legendary struggle against malaria, dysentery, man-eating lions and guerrilla warfare waged by Kamba, Kikuyu and Nandi tribesmen. Some 13,000 Indian coolies formed the backbone of the railway's work force. Hundreds were killed by disease and heat and 28 of them were eaten by lions at Tsavo.

In 1899 the railway reached a well-watered place that had been established during reconnaissance as a staging depot for oxen and mules. It was also the last flat land before the railway would have to make the difficult descent of the Escarpment towards Lake Naivasha. It was decided to make this the new administrative headquarters for the railway and so the town of Nairobi was founded.

When the railway reached Lake Victoria by 1901, Indian traders and European missionaries and settlers had established themselves all along the route—Tsavo, Nairobi, Naivasha, Nakuru and the terminus, Kisumu (Port Florence in those days). The first settlers had come to Kenya in 1896, but official encouragement to people in South Africa, Australia, New Zealand, Canada and Britain began under Commissioner Sir Charles Eliot (1900–04). In 1903 Lord Delamere, a pioneer agriculturalist, was given a grant of 40,000 hectares of rich farmland on the plateau that came to be known as the White Highlands.

When British settlers persuaded the Colonial Office to reserve the White Highlands for them, it was a move not only to exclude the Africans but also the growing number of Indian settlers. Having participated in the construction of the railway and contributed soldiers to the armed force used to crush African resistance, the Indians felt they had a stake in Kenya's future. They had even been encouraged by British commissioners in Uganda and Zanzibar to think of this newly opened territory as a potential "Indian America".

It was in large part to counteract this Indian campaign that the decision was made to shift the capital away from Mombasa, where Oriental traditions were felt to be too strong. Nairobi was made the capital of the Protectorate in 1907, but it was not until 1920 that the region became known as the Crown Colony of Kenya, a name derived from the country's highest peak.

African Ascendency

The British colonial administration interrupted a series of changes taking place among Kenya's tribes by imposing control through a system of tribal chiefs, whom they chose from among men who had led caravans, recruited labour for the railway and new farms or could act as go-between by speaking the growing lingua franca of Swahili. New rivalries developed among ambitious young Africans competing for the wealth and privileges conferred by these chieftainships.

At the same time the British were providing the Africans with weapons for their independence. Christian missionaries gave Africans a European-style education. The revolutionary movements of the 1920s found leaders among graduates of the schools at the Kikuyu Mission Station and the East Africa Scottish Mission at Kibwezi. They were mostly Masai refugees from famine and epidemic, or children of dispossessed landowners from the Highlands. At the Luo Nomia Mission, John Owalo developed a vision of a heaven where he and his African followers, together with Jews and Arabs, would be admitted, while Whites and Indians, he prophesied, would be excluded.

During World War I Kenyan Africans provided several thousand soldiers and over 150,000 military labourers for the campaign in German East Africa. Living and fighting side by side with Europeans, they gained their first direct experience of the white man's real strengths and weaknesses. Veterans of the war returned to lead such militant groups as the Kavirondo Taxpayers and Welfare Association (KTWA) and the Kikuyu Central Association (KCA).

Grievances grew out of the labour recruitment laws. Forced migration moved Africans off their own lands to work in the White Highlands. Herdsmen became farm labourers and fishermen became domestic servants. A policy of "separate development" placed Africans not working European-owned land on "native" reserves, clearly delineated to protect them against illegal encroachment and amended **23**

Indians were among the first foreigners to settle down in Kenya. This frieze in a Swami temple testifies to their pious traditions.

when, in 1931 for instance, gold was found on one of them. Apart from the Swahili towns on the coast, Kenya's urban areas were all European in origin. Africans could work but not live there, except as "sojourners" in shanty towns on the outskirts.

Cutting across tribal lines, the rural KTWA allied Luo with Luyia and the Nairobi-based KCA included both Kikuyu and the Kamba Muslims. Leaders of the movements used their newly acquired education and experience of European ways to combat both colonial practices and the traditional tribal conserv-

atism that kept Africans in submission. An editorial of the KCA newspaper in the 1920s said: "An educated tribe or nation defeats an uneducated tribe or nation. You better swallow that". The writer was a man named Jomo Kenyatta. The British defused the militancy by forcing all grievances to pass through local native councils where the young radical leaders were counterbalanced by moderate elders and British-appointed chiefs under the presidency of the District Commissioner.

The British continued to try to control the drive for independence by courting the moderates among the African leaders. In 1944 Eliud Mathu, educated at Fort Hare University in South Africa and Balliol College, Oxford, was made the first African member of Kenya's Legislative Council. In the same year the colonial administration permitted the formation of a group of African advisors for Mathu, but insisted it be called the "Kenya African Study Union" rather than the too nationalistic-sounding "Kenya African Union". Two years later, Jomo Kenyatta returned to Nairobi after 16 years of study, teaching and political activism in England. He took over Mathu's advisory group, dropped the word "Study" from its title and, as its president from 1947 until it was proscribed in 1952, turned the Kenya African Union from a small educated élite into a mass political movement open to workers, the uneducated and veterans of World War II.

Differences grew between Kenyatta's radicals, who sought independence through revolutionary methods, and the moderates surrounding Mathu, who wanted a gradual, reformist approach. The moderates especially resented Kikuyu domination of the KAU and Kenyatta was agreed that multi-tribal leadership was essential to national independence—a problem that continued to plague him after independence was achieved.

The Mau Mau

The radicals gained the upper hand and events moved relentlessly towards the Mau Mau uprising (the name is believed to have been derived from a Kikuyu warning that the enemy was coming) in 1952, when the Kikuyu led Meru and Embu tribesmen in guerrilla warfare against settlers in the White Highlands. The fighting was fierce. Kenyatta was imprisoned and then exiled to the desert lands of the northern frontier district. Thousands of Kikuyus, Embus and Merus were resettled in guarded areas. Finally in 1956 British troops drove the Mau Mau bands into the Mount Kenya and Aberdare forests, where they were either killed or captured. The casualties of the Emergency, which officially ended in 1960, numbered over 11,000 Mau Mau and close to 2,000 African civilians. Some 50 British troops and 30 European civilians also died.

Armed resistance was broken, but colonial authority was at an end. In 1960 the White Highlands, which cover 800,000 hectares, were opened **25** up to black ownership. British Prime Minister Harold Macmillan spoke of Africa's "winds of change". But Kenya's tribal conflicts were still unresolved as the Kikuyu-dominated Kenya African National Union (KANU) competed for power with the Kenya African Democratic Union (KADU) of the minority tribes. Kenyatta returned from exile to lead the KANU in 1961. Independence was finally achieved on December 12, 1963, and when a republic was proclaimed the next year, Kenyatta was named president.

Independence

The national flag of Kenya is black, red and green—black for the Africans who rule the country, red for the blood shed in the fight for independence and green for the land.

The post-colonial period has been marked by steady Africanization. The land of the old White Highlands has been progressively transferred to African families. An African commercial class has evolved to participate increasingly in previously entirely European- or Asian-owned manufacturing, construction, transportation, tourism and trading businesses. Kenya has developed a mixed economy of private enterprise and state ownership—particularly in banking, petroleum and electricity—as an alternative to the African socialism of neighbouring Tanzania.

Efforts to create an East African Common Market among Kenya, Uganda and Tanzania, particularly through the 1969 Treaty for East African Cooperation, have constantly foundered on the same obstacles that beset the beginnings of the European version: reluctance to relinquish economic sovereignty, imbalances in trade (Tanzania has a chronic trade deficit with Kenya) and recurring political conflicts. Kenya has tried to steer an impartial course, resisting, for example, Tanzanian pressures to close off Uganda's trade access to the Indian Ocean through Mombasa.

Mzee (Honourable Old Man), as Kenyatta was known, exerted a unifying and charismatic leadership through the 15 years of his presidency. His international prestige, even among his old British enemies, greatly boosted Kenyan self-confidence. His successors have a solid foundation to build on.

Modern times have not yet brought industrial air pollution. Clothes hung out to dry won't come in dirty.

What to See

Nairobi

It's a good idea to spend at least a couple of days in Nairobi before heading for the coast or the game reserves. You'll understand why Kenya has been so successful in making the transition from colony to stable republic. It's important to remember that Nairobi was never conceived as an African town; it was artificially created as a convenient place for railway builders and then colonial administrators. For most of the colonial era Africans weren't even allowed to live there. Now you'll see a city whose European beginnings are gradually being Africanized while drawing on modern European and American technology.

Nairobi is the largest of the East African cities, with a population currently estimated at one million. In a country where hurry is nowhere considered a virtue, the central streets of Nairobi almost bustle. What makes this even conceivable so close to the Equator is the mile-high town's delightfully temperate climate, which greatly influenced the British in their choice of a capital for their colony.

But in 1899 when construction first began, Nairobi was described as "a bleak, swampy stretch of soggy landscape, devoid of human habitation of any sort". The Masai were more complimentary, calling the area *Nakusontelon* (The Beginning of All Beauty). Certainly the climate has since borne out the Masai rather than the railway builders, making it possible for Nairobi to boast the name "City of Flowers" with abundant hibiscus, jacaranda, bougainvillea, frangipani and acacia along highways and roundabouts and in lush parks and gardens.

In 1902 the place was nearly abandoned when plague swept the town, which was burned to the ground on the recommendation of a doctor. "Town" was a big word for it—a few rows of tents, barracks slapped together out of corrugated iron, some Indian shops, a soda-water factory, railway yards and one ramshackle hotel called Wood's. It was a frontier town, in fact.

Despite another plague in 1904, Nairobi was rebuilt and by the time the Protectorate had officially established its headquarters there in 1907 the great white hunters were

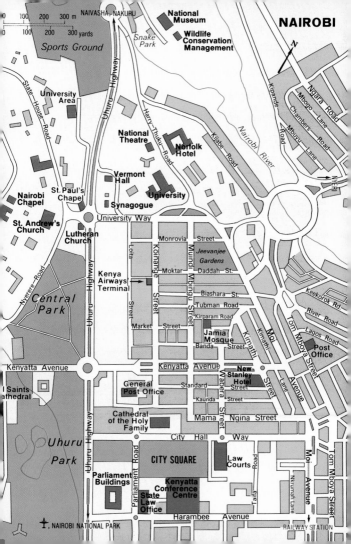

streaming in to start off on safari from the Norfolk Hotel. The most prominent of them was Theodore Roosevelt, the United States president, who headed a safari with 500 porters, all dressed in blue and each carrying 25 kilos of supplies. In ten months—while out of office—Roosevelt bagged 296 animals.

But it was not till the 1930s that Nairobi began to emerge from its primitive frontier beginnings to look something like the city of today, which covers 650 square kilometres, including the airport and the Nairobi National Park. Because it is hemmed into a triangle by the Nairobi River on the north, the railway on the south and the six-lane Uhuru Highway on the west, the central area is developing skyward with high-rise buildings rather than expanding outwards.

The building that dominates the skyline, the huge **Kenyatta Conference Centre,** neatly symbolizes the interaction of Nairobi's European origins and

African destiny by combining a cylindrical skyscraper that would not be out of place in London, Brussels or Frankfurt with a cone-shaped congress hall reminiscent of tribal African thatched structures. It's worth a trip to the top of the Conference Centre (completed in 1973) for the view of the city and the surrounding hills. It is found in City Square along with the old—to the extent that anything in Nairobi is old—neo-Classical Law Courts, the very model of an English county court building, and other administrative offices.

White-columned arcades, the dominant feature of architecture in the business district, are perfectly adapted to the climate, protecting you from the sudden rains or midday sun as you make your way around town. These typical arcades shelter the shops and restaurants along Mama Ngina Street—formerly Queensway and now named after Kenyatta's wife—and Kimathi Street, named after Dedan Kimathi, a Mau Mau leader executed by the British in 1957. Kenyatta Avenue is the broadest of the central streets; it was constructed in pioneer days to enable 12-span oxcarts to wheel around without difficulty.

Jomo Kenyatta's Conference Centre towers over Nairobi's skyline just as he dominates Kenya's history.

31

Two of the great traditional meeting-places of Nairobi are the Norfolk and New Stanley Hotels, which you can enjoy even if you are staying elsewhere. The **Norfolk,** in Harry Thuku Road—damaged in a fire in early 1981—is only eight years younger than Nairobi itself. Have tea on the Delamere terrace or a gin and tonic in the bar with its caricatures of old colonial types on the walls and you'll catch a whiff of the decades when the lion, the symbol of Kenya, had a Union Jack on its tail.

The **New Stanley's** claim to fame is its Thorn Tree, a café in Kimathi Street. Hunters and other travellers would leave messages pinned to the trunk of a huge acacia with yellow bark rising from the middle of the café and the tradition remains, although the hunters have been replaced by tourists and the old acacia has been replaced by a new one: Franz tells Heidi (and the rest of us) that he'll meet her in Cairo, and Debbie tells Billy Joe she won't be able to join him in Marrakesh.

Nairobi is quite ecumenical in its religious buildings. The Jamia Mosque was built in 1933 by the Sunni sect of Islam on the Kirparam Road, north of Kenyatta Avenue. Mass is said in Swahili and hymns are sung in traditional African rhythms at the modern Cathedral of the Holy Family on City Hall Way. The Anglican All Saints Cathedral, west of Uhuru Park, is the epitome of English ecclesiastical architecture. There is also a synagogue, west of the University of Nairobi.

The **National Museum,** on Museum Hill at the northern end of Uhuru Highway, deserves a visit above all for its prehistoric collection, depicting the origins of man and various animals. On exhibit here is No. 1470, the skull of our two-and-a-half million-year-old ancestor discovered at Lake Turkana (see p. 13). There are also the findings from Olduvai Gorge in Tanzania: fossilized remains, perhaps 1,650,000 years old, of *homo habilis,* the first tool-making man, with his stone hand-axes and cleavers; and *homo erectus,* a 1,150,000-year-old man coming closer to the brain capacity of *homo sapiens.*

The remains of prehistoric animals include a giant ostrich, a rhinoceros that makes his present-day descendant look like a rabbit, and a two-million-year-old fossilized elephant, which could be brought into the museum only by knocking down one of the walls. In the museum courtyard is the stuffed version of a modern-day monster: Ahmed, the legendary elephant from Marsabit, with huge tusks, who was declared a national monument by President Kenyatta after two American hunters threatened to shoot the beast. Ahmed died a natural death in 1974, aged about 60. On a smaller scale are the magnificent bird, insect and butterfly collections—the latter protected from moths by camphor balls.

Opposite the National Museum is the **Snake Park,** where you can see snakes, crocodiles, lizards and other examples of Kenya's reptile life. For those who like that kind of thing, you can watch the snakes being "milked" for their venom, usually on Wednesday afternoons.

If you are visiting Nairobi before you set off for the national parks and game reserves, you may want to tour the **Nairobi National Park.** Established in 1945, this was the first national park to be created in Kenya. It has a beautifully varied landscape of forest, hills and savannah; but if you've already visited other parks, Nairobi's well-marked, smooth-surfaced roads may seem a little too tame and civilized in comparison to, say, Samburu or Masai Mara.

Otherwise Nairobi makes a good introduction.

There are lots of lions, and the gate keepers at the park entrance may tell you where they are to be found each day. Also look out for the ostriches (who do *not* bury their heads in the sand), baboons, zebras, giraffes, warthogs, and elands—antelopes whose tasty meat and milk have attracted the interest of animal breeders hoping to develop herds on special farms. Although the animals are fenced off on one side of the park from the Nairobi–Mombasa highway, they have free access for migration to and from Amboseli and Tsavo across the Athi and Kaputei Plains. If you have missed some of the animals at the other parks and reserves because they were too shy, you will find them so blasé about vehicles here they'll practically pose full-face, profile or rear view as requested. One of the great advantages of Nairobi National Park is for the photographer.

At the western end of the park is the **Animal Orphanage,** founded in 1963, mostly with donations collected by Dutch schoolchildren to provide a home for young animals deserted in the wild by their parents and unable to survive alone. Zoologists who care for

The neo-Classical architecture of Nairobi's Law Courts is a strong reminder of the country's British colonial past, set against a solid background of modern progress. All of which can be said with flowers.

them until they are able to be returned to the reserves have a chance to study these animals up close and children can take their first easy look at Kenya's animal riches. But for the rest of us, with the abundance of wide-open parks and reserves so easily available, the orphanage is little more than a glorified zoo and has a limited appeal.

If your appetite for prehistoric remains has been whetted by the National Museum, you might be tempted to make an excursion to **Olorgesailie,** 40 miles west of Nairobi. A national park has been declared to protect the Stone Age camp-

site excavated in the 1940s by Louis and Mary Leakey, the famous palaeoanthropologists whose son is now director of the Nairobi Museum. In thatched-roof shelters is an excellent collection of the tools and weapons that were found lying about the ground, exposed to the elements but miraculously preserved. Among the implements discovered are what seem to be early versions of Argentinian *bolas*, stones grouped in threes, strung to-

gether and thrown at the legs of running animals to trip them up.

The ride down to Olorgesailie is also an expedition to the bed of the **Rift Valley,** and you will see a lot of that awe-inspiring phenomenon as you make your way to the game reserves. To obtain an overall view of the immensity of the valley, try to make at least one journey between the national parks and the capital by small aircraft. **35**

National Parks and Game Reserves

Every nation has its monuments and Kenya's are not cathedrals, palaces or museums, but rather the wildlife that roams the length and breadth of the country. Animals and birds are accorded a privileged position in the life of Kenya and are protected against the wanton hunting and poaching that have nearly decimated many species. For instance, the elephant population dropped from 165,000 in 1970 to at most 60,000 by 1978. Leopards, between 2,000 and 5,000 in 1971, are now seldom seen.

As the human population has grown, urban areas and farmland have expanded and a system of national parks and game reserves (operated by local authorities) has been developed to protect humans from the wild animals and vice versa.

This system has enabled the wildlife to survive in its natural habitat—though the old migration patterns have necessarily been somewhat modified and ecologists are studying what long-range effect this might have. It has also provided tourists with the perfect opportunity to view the animals going about their normal business of hunting, eating, drinking and mating.

Safaris (a Swahili word meaning simply "journey") are organized into the bush in jeeps and minibuses with adjustable roofs to see the wildlife at close quarters. It is quite exhilarating to wake at dawn and have a quick cup of coffee or tea with the sunrise and then go on a game-run at the best time for viewing animals on the move, before they settle down to rest in the heat of the day. And you return to your lodge or campsite for a proper English-style breakfast.

You will have many opportunities for photographing, filming and simple viewing with binoculars. But it's important to remember as you read or hear about what animals you can expect to see at this or that park, that they're not always to be found in the same place; they migrate, weather conditions change and availability of food and water varies from day to day. With so much arranged for you, don't be too upset if some animals don't choose to conform to the tour organizers' plans. A guide to some of the "monuments" of Kenya with their Swahili names begins on p. 39.

Dos and Don'ts in the National Parks and Game Reserves

You soon learn to accept the rules and restrictions operating in the parks and reserves as more than reasonable in the interest of preserving both the wildlife and the natural beauty around you.

National parks exclude all human residence except hotels, lodges and specially designated campsites, while game reserves permit only a limited number of herdsmen with their cattle. No other creatures, including your pet dog, are allowed to enter these areas.

Touring the parks and reserves is permitted only during daylight hours—roughly from 6 a.m. to an elastic 6 p.m. You very quickly get into a rhythm of early rising and early nights to take maximum advantage of the chances to see wildlife up close. There is plenty to be seen throughout the day, but it is a good idea to take a siesta in preparation for one last run before dusk. This is when the carnivores begin their hunt for dinner, and it's the only time of day when the more elusive animals come out of hiding.

For their own safety and to avoid disturbing the animals, tourists are confined to their vehicles during a safari, except at special signposted sites where it is permitted to walk about. This may at times be frustrating but it has a certain humbling effect on human beings, who for once are caged in while the animals roam free in their natural habitat.

Driving speeds are usually limited to 48 kilometres per hour inside the parks, but it is best to drive even slower than that. You will see more, disturb the animals less and stir up less dust. It is a deliberate government policy not to tarmac the park roads, which are uneven and often potholed so as to force traffic to slow down and to keep the parks in their natural state.

The Ministry of Tourism and Wildlife will assign rangers to accompany you on game-runs and it is highly recommended that you make use of this service. The rangers are usually local residents who know the game country inside out and can guide you to the places most likely to shelter the more elusive animals, as well as provide information and folklore about the animals' habits.

In some parks you are allowed to leave the roads and go across open country—make sure you have a sturdy four-wheel-drive vehicle—but it is advisable not to do this without a ranger. Be sure to take a little food and drink in case your car breaks down.

Who's Who in the Animal World

Elephant *(Tembo or Ndovu).* Although the lion has long been regarded as the king of beasts, when you see animals working out their own hierarchy in nature, you are likely to conclude that the real supreme monarch is the elephant. Certainly the lion himself makes way. You cannot fail to be impressed, even awed, by the prodigious nobility of elephants as they wander around in search of fresh grass, leaves or juicy bark, a cool water-hole or some mud to wallow in. You may also see them blowing dust over themselves with their trunks, then rubbing themselves against trees to remove ticks.

An adult male, three metres tall, often weighs around 5,400 kilos and each tusk may weigh up to 90 kilos. The female, just under three metres, weighs a mere 2,700 kilos. But the females do all the work and are the leaders of herds that group their own baby and

There's something about an elephant that inspires respect. It's a matter of unquestionable dignity.

adolescent offspring and that of their daughters. Male elephants are chased away from the herd as soon as they are old enough to fend for themselves, at around 12 to 14 years, and join up with other males.

Enormously affectionate mothers, the females also do all the fighting to protect their young from lions and hyenas. The males turn up only when one of the females goes into heat. Pregnancy lasts up to 22 months, the longest of any mammal. Living till about 50–60 years, elephants are known to bury their own dead and indeed other dead animals, even dead humans they have killed; but, contrary to legend, they do not have mass burial grounds. (When elephant skeletons have been found en masse, it has invariably been due to mass killings carried out by humans encircling an elephant herd with fires.)

Lion *(Simba).* It may be arguable whether the lion is the king of the jungle, but nobody would dispute that this is the most feared of African predators. Lions are ferocious hunters, but in the daylight hours when you will see them, they are more likely to seem docile, lazy and imperturbable and downright friendly. Unless, of course, they were unable to find a meal during the night, in which case their hunger might rouse them to action.

Lion prides, comprising several small families spread over a wide area, are more loosely knit groups than elephant herds. Lions roam over a territory that covers perhaps 50 square kilometres in threes and fours, usually lionesses with their cubs, while male lions roam together, keeping separate from the females until mealtime.

With an arrogance that would enrage the mildest feminist, the male leaves almost all the hunting to the female and just waits for the kill, at which point, weighing up to 180 kilos compared with the 110-kilo female, he moves in, fights off the lioness and her cubs and takes—the lion's share. But it should be said in the male's defence that his presence as a sentinel does keep the pride area safe for the lioness and her cubs.

The lion's favourite prey is zebra and buffalo. Both are big enough for a hearty meal for the whole family but also strong enough, especially the buffalo, to require group effort to make the kill. Most antelopes can be knocked off single-handed.

Lions are very sensuous beasts and like to lick, groom and rub up against each other, often as an act of group solidarity before the hunt or just out of good fellowship during the after-dinner siesta. Males are especially vain about grooming their opulent mane, their chief sexual selling-point. The roar, heard most often before dawn or early evening, is a crescendo of deep rolling grunts quite unlike that fabricated MGM groan.

Baboon *(Nyani).* Behaviourists have used the *baboon* as an analogy for theorizing about natural aggressiveness and male dominance among human beings. Quite apart from the dubious value of making such parallels, recent observations of baboons have shown them to be motivated not by fear and brutal tyranny, as had been claimed, but by strong family relationships and social co-operation.

While the males play an important role in guaranteeing the safety of the baboon troop, it is the females who provide the troop's stability. Females stay in the troop all their lives, while males are constantly on the move. Social cohesion is built around the family, with perhaps as many as 20 related units of mother and offspring.

The males form a separate band moving on the outskirts of the troop as it hunts for food.

You will frequently see male, female and baby baboons grooming each other. Their communal search for ticks, knots and dirt is an activity which reinforces group solidarity and what zoologists do not hesitate to call friendship. Male and female baboons form companionships independent of sexual mating. There is a hierarchy of prestige among female baboons, and the males seek a reflected glory by associating with prominent females, who are the troop's effective leaders and decide when it is time to move and which direction to take.

Baboons will eat young shoots of savanna grass, shrubs and herbs, but their favourite food is fruit, especially figs. They also occasionally turn carnivore and hunt down birds, hare and young gazelles. Nothing would be safe on an unguarded picnic. Baboons, ever playful, are frequently naughty, even vicious when provoked, but a long way from being obnoxious criminals.

Giraffe (*Twiga*). In 1414 the Chinese Emperor was sent a unicorn as a gift through Arab traders in Malindi; but when it turned out to be a giraffe he was reportedly not disappointed. Giraffes are the best argument for seeing animals in Kenya in their natural habitat, rather than in a zoo. You may think you already know what this weird beast looks like, but a delightful surprise awaits you when you finally spot one towering over the plain or decorously moving out between the trees on a hillside.

The giraffe seems to have achieved a state of grace, an ineffable dignity, just from being quite literally above it all—as much as 5 metres for males. He relies on acute eyesight and his privileged vantage point to see potential dangers long before they arrive, fleeing instead of coping with them in a fight. He gets his liquid from juicy or dew-covered foliage, so as not to have to bend down too often to drink ground water in an ungainly split vulnerable to attack from lions.

Females give birth standing up and the calf, already almost two metres tall and weighing 65 kilos, is dropped over a metre to the ground, head first and with a considerable thud. The fall

Next page: *You might catch the attention of a hyena, giraffe or lion. Baboons prefer nit-picking.* **41**

Picturepoint Ltd, London

breaks the umbilical cord. Freud would not be surprised to learn that this rude arrival on earth prepares the calf for a not very affectionate upbringing from the aloof female giraffe.

Hyena *(Fisi)*. You're not supposed to like hyenas. With their oversized heads, sloped backs, scruffy fur and clumsy gait, they're ugly. They have a dozen ways to make a horrible din, including a whoop, a groan, a low giggle, yell, growl, whine and the famous blood-curdling laugh. And they have a miserable reputation as cowardly scavengers, waiting for other predators to do their hunting for them and feeding off the remains.

But field studies have revealed hyenas to resort much more to hunting than scavenging for their food. They hunt with considerable intelligence and courage, even attacking rhinoceros and young elephants. In fact, precisely because lions are stronger than hyenas, they can always steal the latter's kill and actually rely more on scavenging than the much maligned hyenas. So much for reputations.

Grouped in closely knit clans of up to 20 members, they live in a den with entrance holes connected by a network of tunnels. They mark out the clan territory with their dung and go on regular border patrols to keep out rival clans. Unusual among the mammals, the females are stronger and heavier than the males (58 as against 54 kilos). This evolution is thought to result from the mother's need to protect her young against the male hyena's frequent cannibalistic tendencies.

Clan solidarity is constantly reinforced, particularly before a hunt, with elaborate meeting-ceremonies: hyenas sniff each other's mouths, necks and heads, raise a hind leg and lick each other before going off, reassured, on the group activity. Hunting is carefully co-ordinated. Typically, hyenas will start to chase a herd of wildebeests (gnus) and suddenly stop again to take stock of the herd in motion. One of them spots a weakling and the chase resumes. They bring down the chosen victim with a series of well-aimed bites and the end is swift.

Rhinoceros *(Kifaru)*. There is a certain sad poetry in the thought that the huge, lumbering, ill-tempered rhinoceros has a horn which in powdered form is believed in the Orient to be an aphrodisiac. The historic and highly profitable quest for his horn has aggravated the poor rhino's temper. Other animals on the game reserves have grown used to human beings, but every time a rhino sees us —and his tiny eyes don't see very well—he assumes we're after his blessed horn again.

Rhinos in Kenya have dwindled from 8,000 in the 1960s to about a thousand now. Although they may move around in twos and threes, they are more often seen alone. There is nothing more desolate than the screaming groan of a solitary rhino disturbed by another at his water-hole.

The one creature that can approach the rhino with impunity is the oxpecker (or tick bird) which perches on the rhino's back. In exchange for the rhino's ticks and flies, the oxpecker provides a loudly chattering alarm system to warn the sleeping rhino of any approaching danger.

Mother rhinos are ferocious defenders of their young. A concerted attack by three male lions on a rhino calf resulted in one of the lions being killed and the other two slinking away. The rhino can move his 1,350-kilo bulk up to 55 kilometres per hour, at least as fast as a lion, with amazing ability to wheel suddenly to face an attack from the rear.

There's nothing delicate about rhinos, not even their love making, which is accompanied by a lot of ferocious snorting and jousting resistance from the female before she finally submits. Unlike the few seconds expended by most animals, copulation between rhinos lasts more than 30 minutes and this is thought to account for the mythic properties attributed to that horn.

Zebra (*Punda Milia*). The big question is not how the zebra got his stripes, but why he bothered in the first place. The stripes don't act as effective camouflage nor are they a means of sexual attraction, since males and females have essentially the same coats— with sub-species ranging in colour from black and white to brown and beige. The best guess so far is that the subtle individual variations of zebras' stripes enable them to recognize each other at a distance. Whatever the explanation, the optical effect of a couple of hundred zebras at full gallop can make your head spin.

The herd consists of strong family units, in which a stallion

On following page: *A cheetah can be distinguished from a leopard by his smaller head. Zebras, rhino.* **45**

Fritz Bucher, Zürich

stays together with up to six mares and their foals, and groups of male bachelors. The bachelor groups are quite frivolous, like American college fraternities, spending most of their time racing, wrestling and generally fooling around. Relations between the stallion and his "harem" are cordial, enhanced by mutual grooming. If you have a nice striped coat, you keep it in good shape. Unlike many animals, the zebra stallion does not seem to fear being cuckolded and is friendly and courteous to other stallions.

When lions or hyenas threaten, the stallion stands his ground, biting and kicking them to give his family time to escape. This ploy is often successful because lions prefer to rely on surprise attack, rather than a pitched battle, for making their kill and hyenas much prefer to tackle a weakling, rather than a stallion.

Cheetah *(Duma).* How do you tell a cheetah from a leopard? First, his body markings are round spots with pronounced black "tear-marks" on the face, whereas the leopard's spots are like groups of five fingerprints and the face is spotted rather than "tear-marked". More importantly, if you get the chance to watch

them, you will see the cheetah is much more lithe and elegant, and taller and slimmer than the leopard. If you want to compare the leopard to a handsome woman, then the cheetah is a superb mannequin with the same cool aloofness.

Cheetahs are not very gregarious, often hunting alone and so unable to protect their kill when attacked by scavenging lions, hyenas or even vultures. A mother will dutifully rear her cubs and then part abruptly from them. They never acknowledge each other again. Male cheetahs fend for themselves, occasionally hunting with a couple of other males, and meeting up with females only for mating and then only after a fierce fight.

The mother's training of her cubs for hunting is a careful affair, as befits the fastest mammal on earth, 112 kilometres per hour compared with the fastest racehorse's 77 k.p.h. At first the mother cheetah makes the kill herself, usually by biting through the prey's windpipe. The cub picks up the dead prey by the throat and "strangles" it again. Gradually the mother lets the growing cub have first go at catching the prey and only if he botches it will she intervene so as not to risk losing the meal altogether.

Closed Season

The Kenyan government declared a total ban on hunting in May 1977, in an attempt to restore ecological balances after years of wholesale killing threatened many species with extinction. The sale of trophies is also outlawed.

Government officials do not want to commit themselves on when hunting might be restored, but it would be only on the strictest quota system for a few animals reaching ecologically excessive numbers.

Or else the mother makes the first thrust and then leaves the weakened prey for the cub to finish off. By about the age of 14 months the cub is ready to do the job alone. Mother can go. You have a fair chance of witnessing some of this, as the cheetah is the only big cat to hunt by day, mostly in the early morning.

Leopard *(Chui)*. Leopards are always described as elusive and you will indeed be lucky to see one unless you are in one of those game lodges that lures leopards to floodlit platforms with bait. They keep to the cover of trees and dense undergrowth and their solitary, stealthy habits are enabling them to survive poachers much better than lions and cheetahs.

While females seem to roam at will, male leopards are definitely territorial, staking out their home ranges by spraying urine along the boundaries and fighting off other males who might trespass. A leopard's usual roar sounds like wood sawing, but during mating there's a snarling and caterwauling reminiscent of alley cats, only ten times louder. The females make affectionate mothers and, unlike cheetahs, continue to meet with their offspring after they've grown up and left home.

Leopards are nocturnal beasts, spending the day resting in the shade, either under an overhanging hillside rock or up a tree, anywhere where they can survey the surrounding countryside. Weighing between 35 and 55 kilos on an average, they are very powerful and versatile hunters, prepared to kill anything from small birds to animals three times their size. Leopards can carry 45 kilos of uneaten meat up into the higher branches of a tree out of the reach of scavengers. They particularly like eating other carnivores such as foxes, jackals and serval cats, which accounts for their notorious partiality for domestic dogs on occasions when they have wandered into town.

49

Aberdare and Mount Kenya

Aberdare* National Park, north of Nairobi and west of Mount Kenya, is a good place to begin sightseeing. Animals here don't have to run fast to get away from predators—or human beings—because they have the protection of concealment in dense rain forest and bamboo jungle. Consequently, since it is not easy to catch sight of them when you are driving around the park, several hotels have been built as viewing-posts (to be sure of getting a reservation, book well ahead). They are perched high on stilts in the middle of the forest, usually near a water-hole.

The pioneer of these is **Treetops,** on the eastern edge of the park. It was originally built in 1932, a single cabin for a few guests who would go there on moonlit nights to see the wild animals wander over to the water-hole and natural salt-lick (soil covered with natural deposits of sodium chloride). By

---

*Aberdare is the old colonial name, after the Victorian President of the Royal Geographical Society. The Kikuyu name, Nyandarua, is replacing it but hasn't wholly caught on yet.

With Mount Kenya in the background, waterbucks drink before the elephants and buffaloes arrive.

50

Bruce Coleman Ltd, Uxbridge

1952 its popularity had grown and it was expanded and spruced up to receive an illustrious young couple, Princess Elizabeth and the Duke of Edinburgh. (The night of their stay, news came of the death of King George VI and Princess Elizabeth's accession to the English throne.)

An "artificial moon" was installed—floodlighting—and a little extra salt was added to the lick to keep the animals happy. However disturbing they might be to the sensibilities of nature-loving purists, the artifices of floodlighting and extra salt don't seem to upset the animals themselves. Why shouldn't the moon shine every night? Wild dogs have not been observed to go wilder; they apparently know the real thing.

The Aberdare forest provided natural cover for the Mau Mau when British armed forces mounted their counter-attack in the 1950s. In 1954 the Mau Mau burned down Treetops—not a difficult operation as it was, and is again, made entirely of wood. It was rebuilt three years later.

Because of the proximity of the wild animals, you and the other guests will be asked to meet in the nearby town of NYERI (at the Outspan Hotel, whose grounds contain the old home of Robert Baden-Powell, founder of the Boy Scouts) to be driven in mini-buses to the edge of the forest. There a guide armed with a rifle will usher you cautiously on foot to the hotel. You'll be warned to keep together and be quiet so as not to disturb the odd—and lethal—buffalo that might be in the neighbourhood. The path to the hotel is dotted with little timbered enclosures in which you can take cover if surprised by a wild visitor.

At the hotel you will be served tea and cakes, which you may have to share with the baboons and hornbills who find this hotel-on-stilts formula an excellent supplement to their diet. For the rest of the evening and after dinner as late into the night as you care to stay awake, you can settle down to a parade of elephants, rhinos, antelopes and buffaloes. Watching them congregate around the waterhole, you can observe how they accept their hierarchy. The antelope makes way for the buffalo, who steps aside for the rhino, and they all move out of the way for the elephant. However late you may have stayed up, it is worth getting up at dawn to see the sun rise over the snowy peaks of Mount Kenya.

The Ark, closer to the Aberdare mountain range and accessible via the Aberdare Country Club, has the same formula as Treetops, but on a more luxurious scale. As its name suggests, it is built—again on stilts— in the form of Noah's ark, with a gangplank leading you over the trees to the entrance. There is a "dungeon" in the basement to give you an elephant's eye-view of the animals. If you are lucky, you may catch a glimpse of the rare *black* leopard or smaller *black* serval cat. This rarity is due to the high altitude—over 2,500 metres—which is thought to cause melanism, a blackening of the animals' coats.

In **Mount Kenya's** forest-covered foothills, which also constitute a national park, is another hotel-on-stilts: **Mountain Lodge,** at the south-west edge of the mountain, is accessible by car. Mountain Lodge brings you right to the heart of the rain forest, compared with Treetops, where the elephants' destruction of the trees has greatly expanded the clearing around the water-hole. There is even a "game-watchman" who will wake you up without fail if one of the animals you have "asked for" appears at the water-hole. Here you are plunged into a clamour of sounds and the heady smells of primeval forest, the Africa you dreamed of.

But the chief attraction of the region is Mount Kenya. The snow-covered peaks of Africa's second highest mountain are right on the Equator. When the German missionary-explorer Johann Ludwig Krapf reported this fact to Europe in 1849, he was laughed at. It was not until Joseph Thomson, a Scotsman, confirmed his observation 34 years later that the equatorial snow was accepted as fact.

There are three peaks—Batian (5,199 metres), Nelion (5,188 metres) and Lenana (4,985 metres)—all lava "plugs" that thrust through volcanic eruptions when the mountain was 1,800 metres higher ten million years ago. The two highest peaks are regularly scaled by experienced climbers, while the Lenana is a relatively easy climb and has become known as "Tourist Peak".

The origin of the mountain's name is disputed and has developed into a matter of tribal pride, since it became the name of the country. The Masai call it *Erukenya* (Misty Mountain), which is romantically true for nine months of the year. The Kikuyu call it *Kirinyaga* (White and Glorious Mountain) and **53**

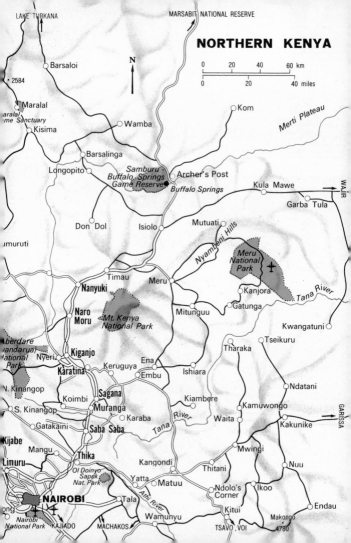

THE MOUNTAIN LODGE

ALTITUDE
7200 FEET
2195 METRES

the Kamba call it *Kya Nyaa* (Hill of the Cock Ostrich).

If you have the time and a good pair of lungs, it's well worth attempting the Lenana climb at least. After being cooped up in a vehicle during most of your day-time safaris, you'll enjoy the chance to walk through dense forest changing to bamboo jungle at 2,500 metres and then, at 3,000 metres, to clearings surrounded by charming Abyssinian Hagenia trees (the fruit of which is a fine antidote to stomach-worms) hung with orchids, old-man's beard and other creepers. The walk is a botanist's delight and experiences like this change steel-and-concrete city dwellers, who never thought of "nature" as being anything but cats, dogs, pigeons and dandelions, into amateur zoologists, ornithologists or botanists overnight (see p. 92).

The climb is not likely to be dangerous. The animal you will see most frequently is the little hyrax, sometimes called a rock-rabbit. However, it has hoofs rather than paws and this, plus its digestive system,

Hotels on stilts, a speciality of Kenya's animal-watching, are made from the wood of the rain forests.

relates it, believe it or not, to the elephant.

Three jet-setters got together in 1958 to convert the Mawingo Hotel in NANYUKI to a deluxe complex, the **Mount Kenya Safari Club.** In a superb 100-acre landscaped garden, there's everything from airstrips to bird observation towers, from swimming pools to restaurants to entertain you—lavishly.

Samburu

The Samburu-Buffalo Springs Game Reserve, on the River Uaso Nyiro north of Aberdare, is small by Kenyan standards. You'll have excellent opportunities to see a wide variety of game in a compact area of 330 square kilometres.

At the **Samburu Game Lodge,** a well-equipped hotel beside the river, you can go down to the Crocodile Bar at the water's edge and sip an evening aperitif with a ringside view of crocodiles having their supper (thoughtfully served on the river bank by the hotel kitchens). The lodge lures leopards out of the dense forest with meat on a floodlit platform. It's a very rare treat indeed when this Greta Garbo of the animal kingdom deigns to make an appearance. Most often the bait is gobbled up by little genet cats or white-tailed **57**

A photo safari on the game reserve caters to every need and comfort. Camps have tented dining rooms.

mongooses—a less spectacular act, perhaps, than the star performance the public is waiting for, but endearing nonetheless.

On the early morning game-run you will be able to criss-cross the reserve in search of lions or rhinoceros—this is one of the reserves where the country is flat enough for your vehicle to leave the regular roads. In your search for the hunters' famous Big Five—lions, leopards, elephants, buffaloes and **58** rhinos—your best bet is to stay close to the river, especially in the dry season. But be sure you don't miss Samburu's special attractions: the reticulated giraffe, treasured for his bronze, web-patterned coat as the most handsome of the species and found only here and, less visibly, at Meru and Marsabit reserves; and the equally scarce Grevy's zebra, with trumpet-shaped ears and a coat more intricately striped than that of the common variety.

If you want to avoid hotel life, there is a campsite where tents can be rented in BUFFALO SPRINGS, south of the river. There are also several other tented campsites, both

on the bank of the Uaso Nyiro and to the south-east along Champagne Ridge, where you'll have a good view across the reserve. Camping is particularly recommended for bird-watchers, for whom Samburu provides a bewildering variety. One expert has spotted 363 species, including the African hawk eagle, the buff-crested bustard, the Egyptian goose and the lilac-breasted roller; but even a complete amateur will grow to know and love the schoolmasterly hornbill, the idiotic guinea fowl and, everybody's favourite, the vulture, nature's most efficient garbage collector. One of the good things about vultures is that if you see them clustered in the trees somewhere, they act as a good signpost to one of the big cats sitting by the remains of his prey—while the vultures wait their turn.

Lakes Nakuru and Naivasha

After the restrictions, however necessary, of the big game parks it makes a pleasant change to visit the tranquil lakes of Nakuru and Naivasha, south-west of Samburu, and walk in broad daylight without worrying about being eaten alive. A variety of birds are **59** attracted to the area, with several hundred species counted at each lake.

Lake Nakuru is considered by leading ornithologists to be quite simply the finest in the world for sighting birds. But even if that doesn't impress you, the sight of hundreds—in exceptional years thousands —of pink flamingos in a wide band along its shoreline should. And then there are hundreds of other species to be seen, if you care to persevere. The lake is surrounded by a national park, where you'll be in the company of docile waterbuck, impala and baboons galore. The park extends to the foothills of the Mau Range, in which rhinos roam around as well as a few lions and leopards.

But the real attraction is the lake itself, a haven of peace. There's a lodge away from the lake, but the lake area is worth camping in and the camps are well equipped. Make your way through the forest to the lakeside and watch the cormorants, herons, pelicans, storks and sandpipers. Enjoy the morning sun with the hippos at Hippo Point.

Drive around to the west side of the lake where you can visit the President's Pavilion on the lakeshore. You'll have a close-

All About Nakuru Ecology

Why do the flamingos favour Nakuru rather than other lakes? The explanation is a perfect ecological cycle. The water comes into the lake through three inlets but has no outlets and so the minerals build up to give the water a high alkaline content.

There are some blue-green algae that thrive on it and the flamingos in turn thrive on the algae. They eat an average of 135 metric tons of algae a day and deposit 45 metric tons of droppings, which in turn decompose and interact with sunlight to enable the algae to double their numbers in a few hours. So the flamingos dine on more algae and it begins again…

There's even a carotene pigment in the algae which adds a pink hue to the flamingo's white feathers. (It's only fair to point out that some years this ecological cycle is upset by excessive rains, which flood the normal lakeshore and make it impossible for the flamingos to wade out to their beloved algae. In which case they fly off to some other lake, so make sure where they are before you plan an excursion.)

Lake Nakuru's best-known attraction is its numbers of pink flamingos.

The tranquillity at Lake Nakuru is a lure for both birds and humans, and if you're tired of travelling, you can enjoy it over a cup of tea.

up view of the flamingos in one of their favourite congregating points. (Why else would a president have his pavilion here?) But for a better sense of the sheer immensity of the flamingo phenomenon, go up to the look-out point on Baboon Cliff, also on the western side, for a panoramic view of the whole lake.

The size of **Lake Naivasha** varies according to the rains and it once formed a single lake with Elmenteita and Nakuru. You can go by punt, for hire at the Marina Club, to Crescent Island, a wildlife sanctuary at the eastern end of the lake, and this is by far the most pleasant way to enjoy it. Walk up to the highest point of the island and

you'll have a fine view of the Rift Valley, the Aberdares and the Mau Range.

The lake used to have no fish in it at all, but the Government's wildlife and fisheries department has stocked it with tilapia and black bass, if you want to try your luck from the punt. You'll probably find the shores of Crescent Island too swampy to fish from there. Choose an early week-day morning and you and a few gazelle and tiny dik-dik ante-lopes will be alone with the malachite Kingfisher, pelican, spoonbill and Hottentot teal.

Without the more spectacular beasts of prey as competition, the antelopes are well worth a closer look—they're more delicate and graceful than Walt Disney ever imagined. You may spot a couple of sleepy hippos out in the water. As fascinated as you might be to see them, they, luckily, will be totally bored by you. If you should by the remotest chance **63** come upon a hippo on dry land, be sure not to stand between him and the water. It's the one thing that upsets him. It's his element, not yours. Let him through.

If you are interested in Kenya's prehistoric beginnings, you might like to stop on your way up to Nakuru at the Stone Age sites of Kariandusi and Hyrax Hill. You can see examples of obsidian handaxes and cleavers and some fossilized bones at **Kariandusi,** a palaeolithic campsite perhaps as much as 400,000 years old. **Hyrax Hill** is probably the more interesting of the two sites. A neolithic village of pit dwellings that may be 10,000 years old and a later cemetery in which skeletons were found are visited on the guided tour.

The skeletons were uncovered in a curled-up position, about half of them female. In each case the females were accompanied by utensils, flat stone dishes, platters, mortars and pestles. The males had nothing. Some people have concluded that the burials paid ritual tribute to the fact that the women did all the work. Defenders of the male sex suggest it might merely be that grave robbers carried off the men's belongings. The utensils and other artefacts, including some beautiful beads, are on view at the small museum.

You can also see a version of the famous *bao* game still played throughout Africa on the hillside site, cut right out of the rock. It consists of two parallel rows of small cavities in which counters, in this case pebbles, are transferred from one to another until captured by one of the two players.

Masai Mara

If your trip to Kenya allows you time for only one game safari, then Masai Mara Game Reserve is almost certainly the place to go. Geographically an extension of Tanzania's world-famous Serengeti National Park, Masai Mara gives you the best chance of seeing all, really all, the major wild animals in a superb rolling landscape of gentle hills, acacia woodland and the sinuous River Mara.

In the heart of Masai land, that is to say land ruled for centuries by pastoralists rather than hunters, the wildlife population has managed to maintain a constant level and now enjoys the protection of an enlightened local authority. Although Masai Mara has the official status of a game reserve and herdsmen are permitted to reside with their cattle, an inner 500 square kilometres, where

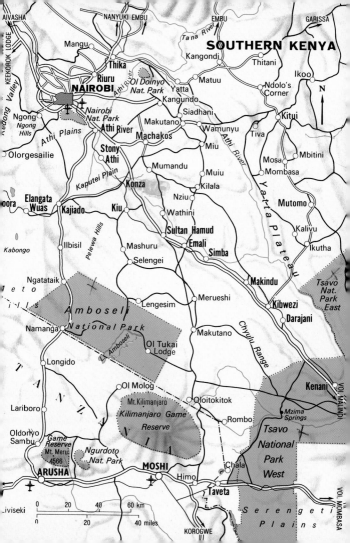

The Masai

While most of Kenyan society has been rushing pell-mell into the 20th century and getting ready for the 21st, the Masai tribe has remained steadfastly conservative, clinging to centuries-old traditions that resist modern institutions. The proud, faintly mocking young warriors *(moran)* with their plaited hair, red cloaks and spears, challenging your curiosity and your camera, recall the fierce reputation the Masai enjoyed in their 19th-century heyday. They fought off Arab slave-traders and rival tribes and intimidated European explorers, before succumbing to the destruction of their cattle by rinderpest and the decimation of their tribe through cholera and smallpox.

The Masai remain committed to cattle-herding as a way of life, living on a diet of milk, tea, maize and blood extracted from their cattle, which they rarely use for meat. During a major drought in the early 1970s they were obliged to leave their traditional grazing lands in search of pasture. They finally found it at Nairobi Airport and the government had a hard time persuading the Masai and their cattle to leave the runways.

The Masai still practise the circumcision and initiation rites that take a male from boyhood to warrior status and then to marriage as an elder. As a warrior he is expected to protect the cattle and the tribe against wild animals—and human beings.

the wildlife is at its densest, is treated as a national park area, excluding all human habitation except for two lodges.

In the north-west, **Mara Serena Lodge** is up on a bluff near the River Mara and looks down over the plain towards the Tanzanian border. From the terrace you can watch the movement of huge herds of migrating buffaloes, zebras, wildebeests and elephants. The lodge is an imaginative modern adaptation of traditional Masai architecture in a "village" of individual huts with external walls of reddish-brown mud.

Down in the plain at the eastern end of the reserve is **Keekorok,** one of Kenya's oldest game lodges, also laid out with individual accommodation, this time bungalows, and a swimming pool as well as an artificial water-hole, far enough away for there to be no danger from the elephants and buffaloes it frequently attracts. It also boasts hot-air balloon safaris—book in advance through a travel agent.

If you want to camp among the animals, **Governor's Camp,** by the river in the north-west corner of the reserve, is well-guarded and luxurious enough for the most pampered city-dweller. You'll be plunged into all the sounds and smells of the animal world, and you'll feel very much one of *their* guests. Driving off the marked tracks across open country is permitted in Masai Mara, but it's advisable to take a Ranger, the Masai being particularly good-humoured companions for the drive. You'll see lots of lions, sometimes in prides up to 20 and 30 strong, and have the best opportunity of sighting a leopard without the aid of a flood-lit baited platform. The open plain is the perfect arena for the cheetah to show his speed. You are likely to find yourself driving through a thicket of acacias out of which a herd of 50 elephants will suddenly materialize. They'll surround your car, but you need not panic—they're more accustomed to you than you are to them. Whatever Mohammed Ali may claim, *they* are the greatest.

Masai are among the handsomest and proudest of Kenya's nomads.

Kericho

Before or after your trip to Masai Mara, particularly if you've spent a long time on the hot, dry and dusty road, you may find yourself for the first time in your life crying out for rain. There's one place that guarantees satisfaction—Kericho with its famous tea plantations about 250 kilometres north-west of Nairobi. There is hardly a day in the year when it doesn't rain. People set their watches by it.

You'll have a morning of brilliant sunshine, not a cloud in the sky at lunchtime, and you'll wonder what local people mean when they say that at 3 p.m. it will rain. Then suddenly the rain comes and you may well be tempted to dance around in the clean, re-freshing showers. But first look at your watch: it will almost certainly be 3 p.m.

You can enjoy this spectacle at the Tea Hotel, one of the more elegant vestiges of co-

Tea is by no means a casual local industry. Picked in Kericho's green fields, it's a major export product.

tea-pickers plucking the buds and topmost young leaves and tossing them into wicker baskets on their backs. You can also visit the local tea factories on estates near the town for a fascinating explanation of the cutting, fermenting and drying stages that go into tea processing.

Kenya's tea industry prospered in the 1920s when experts decided Kericho's soil was perfect for producing the best quality tea from Ceylonese and Indian plants. You suddenly realize how the British Empire functioned as a gigantic holding company, enabling the transfer of whole industries from one continent to another. These old imperial origins are neatly underlined by the inscription on a vintage tea-processing machine at one of the factories: "The Britannia Balanced Pucca Tea Sorter (Calcutta, India)".

Kericho is also an excellent centre for fishing expeditions up the Kiptiget River and to the lovely Lower and Upper Saosa Dams, where chances for rainbow trout are good.

lonial times. The unmistakable Englishness of the immaculate green lawns—a welcome change from the arid savannah—is perhaps due to the way the warm sun and sudden rain conjure up nothing so much as the perfect English summer's day. It's altogether fitting that the region produces tea.

The plantations are well worth a visit. There are miles of lush green bushes tightly packed in a shoulder-high carpet dotted with the heads of

Amboseli, Kilimanjaro and Tsavo

Although the wildlife is abundant and easily accessible, the most important reason for recommending **Amboseli National Park** is the simple fact that the elephants, cheetahs and giraffes that you are likely to see there become an unforgettable spectacle against the background of MOUNT KILIMANJARO. Except for the very beginnings of its northern foothills, Kilimanjaro is entirely inside Tanzania, but the awe-inspiring view of it from anywhere in Amboseli makes it an undeniable part of Kenya's landscape, too.

One of the joys of Amboseli is viewing the herds of elephants caked with whitish-grey mud from wallowing in Amboseli's swamps and spraying clouds of dust over their backs. A herd of 40 or more elephants in the mellow evening sun setting over Kilimanjaro is an impressive sight. Naturally, all the wallowing animals in Amboseli turn whitish-grey, except the hippos who wash off their muddy coat.

Elephants take off for Mount Kilimanjaro across the Tanzanian border, leaving us to sit and dream.

Fritz Bucher, Zürich

71

The most comical of them are the warthogs. These funny little beasts, rarely more than 75 centimetres tall, are dismissed by most people. They remember warthogs from picture books as ugly, even repulsive, because they are usually photographed in close-ups showing those nasty protuberant warts beside each eye and their clumsy little tusks. But when you see them grubbing around as a family, tentatively trying to claim territory at the water-hole while the big brutes are not watching and then, when frightened, scampering away with their tails in the air like tiny flagpoles, warthogs *seem* as endearing as any household pet. They are, however, dangerous and bad-tempered and will not hesitate to charge.

Tsavo National Park, the largest in East Africa, covers about 20,000 square kilometres and is divided into eastern and western sections by the Nairobi–Mombasa highway. After years of drought and forest fires, Tsavo's vegetation has gradually grown back with the aid of newly bored water-

Beauty, they say, is in the eye of the beholder. Behold this warthog.

Kilimanjaro

"As wide as all the world", wrote Hemingway in his famous short story, "great, high and unbelievably white in the sun". The legendary Kilimanjaro is Africa's highest mountain, 5,895 metres. This massive extinct volcano stretches across an 80 by 50 kilometre area and has three marvellous peaks. The highest is the great snow-covered table known as Kibo, but called Uhuru (Freedom) since Tanzania gained independence. The western peak, Shira, is only 4,005 metres and the jagged eastern peak is Mawenzi, 5,150 metres high but much tougher to climb than Kibo. In fact in 1973 a New Zealander went up Kibo on a motorcycle.

Legend has it that the son of King Solomon and the Queen of Sheba, King Menelik of Abyssinia, also made it to the top. In heroic battles he conquered all of East Africa and then, as death approached, he climbed Kibo. He disappeared into the crater with his slaves, who carried all his jewels and treasures, including King Solomon's ring. Find that ring and you'll inherit Solomon's wisdom and Menelik's courage. Failing that, take a good look at one of the great wonders of the world, all the more splendid for standing there alone and unchallenged.

holes. You will see a mixture of dense bush, palm thickets and thorn-tree groves and a less parched savannah than in the bad years of the early 1960s.

The hill country is especially rich in elephants, claiming the largest herds in Kenya. It is not unusual to see a mass of over 100 elephants—still red from their last bath—ambling across a hill in search of water. Solitary giraffes take on a new majesty as they haughtily watch your car curve down the hillside. Once again, you're made to feel an intruder.

The Shaitani lava flow from a volcano extinct only 200 years, at the northern end of Tsavo West, offers an otherworldly landscape. The volcano is said to have buried a Kamba village and as you clamber over the black lava a stretch of your imagination lets you hear beneath the lava, as the legend insists, the Kamba still going about their business with their cattle, goats and dogs.

A cooler, more relaxing experience is yours at MZIMA SPRINGS, where you can see the

Marabou storks, vultures, baboons and ostrich wait around for lunch.

pure, underground water from the Kyulu Hills gush out into limpid pools. The spring provides Mombasa and Malindi with millions of litres of drinking water daily. A crocodile or two can be seen on the banks of the pools—the *far* banks—and the hippos appreciate the purity of the water.

You can watch them at their own level, in a concrete-and-glass underwater observation tank built into one of the pools at the suggestion of a couple of Walt Disney cameramen. You'll also come eye-to-eye with mudsucker fish and bream. Black-faced vervet monkeys scamper through the umbrella thorn-trees and "toothbrush" bushes, the twigs of which can be used for cleaning teeth after a picnic by the Lower Pool.

Tsavo boasts over 500 species of birds, and a lot of them will save you the trouble of searching for them by visiting you on the long terrace at the **Kilaguni Lodge;** the hornbills will particularly welcome a share of your sandwich from the bar. On the road you'll see ostriches running like prim schoolmistresses trying to catch a bus, and the exotic fluffy-headed secretary birds, standing dreamily around unable to take dictation from anyone.

Mombasa and the Coast

The fact that Mombasa is not the capital of Kenya has done nothing to diminish its pride. It has an independent spirit that sets it apart from the rest of the country, and an exoticism derived from its long history and constant contact with the Orient that leaves Nairobi a little jealous. Its climate may be less congenial than the highlands of the interior, but the slower pace adds a languorous fantasy to its streets.

Mombasa has been in existence longer than anyone can remember. Some versions of its history claim that as early as 500 B.C. Phoenician sailors travelling around Africa for the Pharaoh of Egypt put in at a coastal port that would correspond to Mombasa Island. The Greeks noted its trading potential in the first and second centuries A.D., and the Arabs arrived to exploit that potential in the 9th century.

Dhows, carried by the northeast monsoon from the Persian Gulf across the Indian Ocean, made their way along the East African coast looking for an opening in the treacherous coastal reef. The most navigable was at Mombasa, making the city a natural magnet for Arabs, Persians, Turks, Indians, Portuguese and the British, all of whom left their mark on the town.

The island city, linked to the Nairobi road by a causeway, the north mainland by a bridge and the south mainland by a ferry service, is inevitably more Asian than African in its architecture. But the people, the Swahili mixture of fine Arab and lithe African, are a handsome expression of the historic marriage of the two races. You'll find them the blithest of spirits, not easily upset. But this is a demeanour acquired after centuries of fighting off a foreign foe, then absorbing him and fighting off the next one.

When the Portuguese explorer Vasco de Gama arrived at Mombasa in 1498, the people gave him a cold reception and he had to move up the coast to Malindi. It took the Portuguese 100 years of repeated assaults on the island stronghold before they could set up shop for their Indian Ocean trade behind the coral-rock walls of Fort Jesus. That century of Portuguese attack, siege and plunder destroyed medieval Mombasa, and the town we see today is essentially 19th century, except for the remains of Fort Jesus.

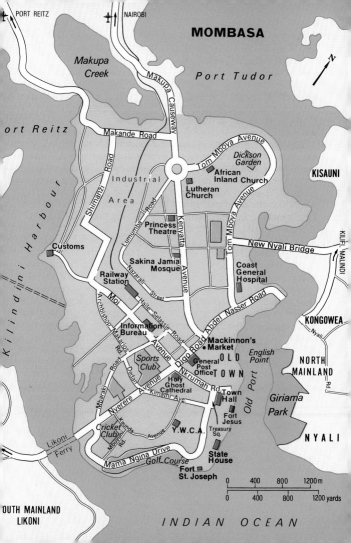

Before you start your tour—and Fort Jesus is the place to start—be warned that the most comfortable way to see the town is to stay outside it and see the sights only in the early mornings and late afternoons. Don't venture out in the midday sun.

The one monument you won't miss, coming in or out of town, is the **double arch** across Moi Avenue formed by four huge sheet-metal tusks, which symbolize the source of Mombasa's fortune and misfortunes.

Fort Jesus, strategically placed at the southern entrance to Mombasa Harbour, stands on a coral ridge and has ramparts several metres thick. Inside you can make your way along the parapet walk, step up on the firing positions and imagine what it must have been like to defend this redoubt against marauding infidels—Muslims or Christians or "pagans" according to who held it, since both Portuguese and Arabs made it their stronghold (right up to 1895 when the British took over and turned it into a prison).

With its foundations of solid coral rock, it could not be undermined and any attackers attempting to scale the walls would have been hurled to the dry moat below—now a car park. It was more often taken by guile and bribery than by force.

The ground plan that you see today is much the same as that designed in 1593 by Italian architect Giovanni Battista Cairato for the first Portuguese captain of Mombasa, Mateus Mendes de Vasconcelos, which included a barracks, chapel, water cistern and well, guard rooms, houses for a priest and governor and a storeroom for gunpowder.

During the Arab conquest of the Fort in 1698, the powder magazine was the scene of one of history's recurring acts of mad heroism: a Portuguese officer told the Arabs the storeroom held the garrison's gold treasure, led some Arab soldiers to collect it and blew them and himself to smithereens. The cannons in the courtyard are English 18th- and early 19th-century naval guns brought there in 1837. The Fort also has a museum worth a brief visit. Look at the collection of artefacts from up and down the coast, including Persian, Portuguese and medieval Chinese ceramics, the latter imported from India.

At Mombasa's Old Port, dhows still carry goods to the Persian Gulf.

Behind the Fort, on Treasury Square, is the Government Game Department's **Ivory Room,** where you can see elephant tusks, rhinoceros horns, hippopotamus teeth and other animal trophies confiscated from poachers or taken from dead animals on the reserves. Auctions are held twice a year and you can buy these hot items with legal government permits.

To conserve your energy, limit your walking tour to the **old town.** You'll see the most fascinating part of Mombasa. This area just north of Fort Jesus comprises the mosques, the shops and stalls of silk, spice

This Jain Temple is a fine symbol of the prosperous Indian community.

and perfume merchants, goldsmiths, ivory- and horn-carvers—hustlers all, but with the most amiable of manners. The atmosphere is especially lively at Mackinnon's Market, whose colonial name seems to be resisting the new official title of Municipal Market.

Quickly work your way past the fish market to the **old port** where a sign telling you to "Keep Out" can safely be ignored if you're not part of a big tour group. At the quayside you can watch the loading or unloading of the last of the dhows that still ply between Mombasa and the Gulf. These craft with their large lateen sails, now supplemented by a motor, were once a familiar sight here, coming in with the wind by January and leaving again in June. Now there are just a few dozen.

With a winning smile you may be able to wangle your way aboard and join the haggling for brass chests, Arab silverware, ornate tiles, Persian carpets, furniture, spices and dates. The merchants will be happy to take your money, but their business is usually by barter for ivory, horn, animal skins, sugar, coffee, coconut oil and timber.

The **South Coast,** going down to the Tanzanian border at Tanga, is reached from Mombasa by the Likoni Ferry. This is the only means of transport connecting Mombasa and the beaches of the south. The leisurely ferry takes about ten minutes to travel from the island to LIKONI.

The beauty of the South Coast is in its beaches. The white coral sand is smooth and usually free of seaweed, except in the rainy season, and the beaches are quieter than most of the North Coast's resort areas. The best of the beaches is

the **Diani,** whose major landmark, near the Trade Winds Hotel, is a 500-year-old baobab tree measuring over 20 metres in circumference and protected from felling by presidential decree. Elephants and trees, much more than man-made monuments, are Kenya's protected heritage.

Once you've seen the baobab there is blissfully little to do but watch the sun rise and set, not that sunrises and sunsets here are anything to sneeze at. If you want to give your sun-tan a rest, you can go inland to the little game reserve at **Shimba Hills,** a pleasant wooded plateau rising to 450 metres. Go early in the morning —do everything around here early in the morning or late afternoon—and you should see the splendid sable antelopes with scimitar-shaped horns, rare in Kenya. The males have magnificent coats of reddish-black, while the females are a chestnut-brown colour. There are no lions, so it is safe for the antelopes and you to walk on the higher slopes. But look out for the odd python!

The **North Coast** is where Mombasa's Asian, European and new African élite have their homes, often palatial residences shrouded in hibiscus and bougainvillea and watched over by guard dogs. The area abounds in luxury hotels, for the most part well-run, which will satisfy your every hedonistic need, though some are guilty of exploiting the package-tour trade. The beaches are for the most part clean but some of the hotels are less than efficient about clearing away the seaweed, more prevalent than on the South Coast.

Across the six-lane New Nyali Bridge from Mombasa, the road south leads to ENGLISH POINT, with a monument to the man who explored the Kenya interior on behalf of the British Church Missionary Society, Johann Ludwig Krapf, and the graves of his wife and child.

There are two sets of Arab ruins as you go up to Malindi. The first is at JUMBA LA MTWANA (Home of the Slave-Master), just a couple of miles north of Mombasa. As the town was abandoned in the 15th century, there are only traces of mosques, a characteristic pillared tomb and some houses, one of which was a bakery judging from the large ovens for the baking of millet bread.

The carpenter shapes his dhow with traditional tools following the time-honoured methods of his craft.

The coconuts are ripe and ready to drop. Malindi's smiles are irresistible.

More substantial is the 15th-century town of **Gedi,** close to Malindi. Sunset there is both eery and romantic as you pick your way among the walls of the palace, mosques, houses, pillared tombs and market place. It's likely that the only dramatic event in Gedi's otherwise unremarkable history was its destruction and desertion in the early 1500s, probably dur-

ing one of Mombasa's wars against Malindi.

Somali tribesmen resettled it briefly at the end of the 16th century but left in a hurry with the news that fierce Galla warriors were on their way south. The palace includes a strong-room where cowrie shells were stored as money. For one gold dinar you had to shell out 40,000 cowries. Another room

in the palace is protected by a *fingo* pot, buried in the floor of the threshold, containing a genie to deal with anyone after the cowries.

Just before you reach Gedi, you'll see the enchanting **Watamu Marine National Park.** Like the nearby Malindi Marine National Park, it is a protected area of white coral sand beaches and clear, deep-blue lagoons, where it is forbidden to fish or collect coral and seashells. Instead you can view

these marvels of nature by skin-diving or snorkelling. If you are staying at a hotel in Malindi, you should definitely visit these marine national parks, as the water is as pure as proverbial crystal, whereas the sea at Malindi is for the most part brown with the mud of the Sabaki River.

If you've had a hard year and you just want to sleep for a week or two in the sun, with no demands on your energies, then **Malindi** may be the place for you. You'll have clean beds, wholesome food, swimming-pools and sun-tan lotion. There is some excellent fishing, but it's usually too hot to move around, so you don't have to feel guilty about relaxing until you fly home.

There was a time when Malindi was more lively. With an eye to the main chance, the Sheikh of Malindi decided not to follow Mombasa's hostile example; he received Vasco da Gama hospitably on that 1498 trip and gave him food and water for his voyage to India. It paid off with some golden years of trade with the Portuguese during the 16th century, until Mombasa's resistance was broken and the Portuguese transferred the sheikh there. Malindi then sank back into the torpor that you'll see today.

If you feel up to a short walk, there's a monument to that brief moment of glory out along the cliffs on the promontory at the southern end of the Malindi harbour—the Padrão or Cross of Vasco da Gama, engraved with Portugal's coat of arms and presented to the sheikh by the explorer in gratitude for his warm reception. It has survived the ravages of the Turks, Arabs and British and is one of the few authentic Portuguese relics left on the coast.

For an idea of what Malindi—or Mombasa for that matter—really looked like when the Arabs ruled the coast, you must go up to the island of **Lamu.** "Must" makes it sound like a duty, when in fact it is pure pleasure. Lamu is a delightful backwater of Swahili culture, basking peacefully in splendid isolation at the northern end of the coast. No motor vehicles are allowed other than that of the District Commissioner. People walk about smiling, as if they know something the rest of us don't. And they probably do.

They fish a little and sell some cattle for shipment to Mombasa. Wood-carvers work at their trade and women make their way through the narrow back streets swathed in black *baibuis*. But nobody works too hard. People have a sense of life's priorities on Lamu. They always have time to talk to each other and to strangers. The friendliness is not pushy, not obtrusive, not meant to please a tourist for a tip; it is in the best sense disinterested.

The local inhabitants take pride of place on Lamu; the visitors are always a tiny minority and by no means over-privileged. They have to make their way to the island in small ferry boats, after travelling to nearby MANDA by small aircraft, as the overland route from Mombasa is very rough and often flooded. Once there, visitors are happy to make do with adequate, but never luxurious, lodgings.

The centre of activities, regardless of where you're staying, is the bar at **Petley's Inn.** It's right on the port. This institution is where local people and visitors gather together to talk of cabbages and kings. Nowhere in Kenya do Africans and Europeans mix more easily. Noon and 6 p.m. at Petley's are moments not lightly to be missed. The inn is named after its first owner, Percy Petley, who is said to have thrown unruly women guests down the stairs and to have killed a leopard with his bare hands. Since one version you will hear says he did it by strangling and another with one blow of his fist, probably neither is true.

The most beautiful feature of Lamu's houses is their carved wooden doors and moulded plasterwork. Some of them date back to the 18th century, but even the most modern retain the style, forms and craftsmanship of centuries-old traditions. Some excellent examples are on display in the nicely organized **Lamu Museum.** There are reconstructions of typical Lamu interiors, including a traditional bridal chamber. But the pride of the museum is the two magnificent *sivas* (ceremonial horns), one of carved ivory, two metres long, from Pate Island, and the other of brass, slightly shorter, from Lamu.

There's the fine **Riadha Mosque,** where infidels dressed with due decorum—and without shoes—are admitted. The massive fort built in the early 19th century is now the town prison, which you may look at but not photograph. As the market outside the prison has a lively auction on Saturdays, you could say you were photographing the auction, but it's risky—the prison isn't very appealing inside.

If you want to swim, there's a beach three pleasant kilometres down the road at SHELA, whose Friday Mosque has a distinctive minaret.

Lamu is one island in an archipelago in which Manda and Pate were politically and economically much more important, competing for coastal supremacy and playing foreigners off against each other. They declined while Lamu, quiet and unambitious, survived quite nicely, thank you. There's a moral there somewhere.

What to Do

Sports

Kenya offers the supreme outdoors holiday and opportunities for the sportsman seem endless, despite the current embargo on hunting. **Fishing** is encouraged and there is no closed season. Deep-sea or big-game fishing has taken over from hunting as Kenya's lure for the outdoor man. It's ranked among the best in the world.

At all the breaches in the coral reef up the coast—from the Pemba Channel near the Tanzanian border, to Mombasa, Kilifi, Mtwapa and up to Malindi—you'll find fishing clubs and boat-charter services, many of which have desks at the major hotels. You can rent anything from a little speedboat with an outboard motor to a luxury yacht complete with cabins, showers and fully equipped kitchen. The price, of course, varies greatly. The hotels and fishing clubs will provide you with the indispensable fishing licences. All boats come with an expert crew, rods, reels, bait and all the harness equipment necessary to haul in the big ones.

Do your fishing in the morning and you can expect to grapple with barracudas, kingfish, tunas, marlins, sailfish, dolphins and sharks. Kenya's rivals to *Jaws* include the vicious mako, tiger and hammerhead sharks. Sailfish have been known to come in at over 60 kilos and marlins at over 225. The champion in Kenya waters is a 336-kilo tiger shark, landed in 1973 by a West German after a two-and-a-half-hour struggle.

The best time of year for the biggest fish is November and December, but there isn't really a bad time. Practically all the fishing clubs let you keep everything you catch—if you can eat that much—or you can sell your haul to defray the costs of boat hire.

The peace-loving fishermen on the coast are happy to stand or sit on a rocky promontory and angle their day away half-asleep. You can go surf-casting inside the reef in waters rarely more than thigh deep. There is also good underwater spear-fishing for rock-cod.

Inland you can enjoy fine

The intricately carved wooden doors of Lamu Island are coveted by visitors. You can buy replicas.

fishing for rainbow or brown trout in the streams around Mount Kenya, the Aberdares and up at Mount Elgon. Among the best areas near Mount Kenya are the Naro Moru River to the west and the Rupengazi to the east. The trout are delicious at a kilo and may weigh as much as $3\frac{1}{2}$ or $4\frac{1}{2}$. Again, equipment may be hired and you need a licence. The maximum daily bag is six rainbow and four brown trout.

One of the great challenges is fishing for the big Nile perch—weighing up to 90 kilos—in the north at Lake Turkana. You can get equipment at Lake Rudolf Angling Club and Eliye Springs. The perch are also a prime target at Lake Victoria. Lake Naivasha is famous for its black bass and tilapia.

If you prefer to leave the fish where they are, there are other **water sports** to consider. You'll find the coastal waters delightfully warm for swimming, with none of the health risks or crocodiles of the inland rivers and lakes. The sharks stay outside the reef. To explore the coral beds you can hire a wet suit for **skin-diving** or equipment for **snorkelling.** You can also observe sea life from glass-bottomed boats for hire at hotels.

Even if you are a non-swimmer, you can safely go out to the reef in one of the punts steered by local youths and observe marine life, but note that removing shells is now forbidden. Wear rubber-soled shoes to protect your feet from the razor-sharp coral. There are also several possibilities for **water-skiing** and even a little **surfing** off Malindi.

While you can hire miniature sailboats on the coast, the real **sailing** is done on the tranquil waters of the inland lakes, the best being Naivasha, Nairobi Dam and Lake Victoria (at Kisumu). For the truly adventurous there is **canoeing** on the Tana River.

Riding, an imperial legacy, is most popular in the Highlands. You'll find superb trails in the Ngong Hills, where Danish Baroness Karen Blixen, author of *Out of Africa,* had her farm in the 1920s. It is possible to hire horses, and the best place to enquire is at the Karen *dukas* (shopping centre).

Kenya's thriving bloodstock industry makes for exciting **horse racing.** During the season, which runs from September to July, weekly meets are held most Sunday after-

If tennis strikes you as a bit too strenuous in the coastal heat, you can do nothing at all by the pool.

There are few more peaceful moments on earth than sailing in a dhow around the island of Lamu. You may never want to go back home again.

noons at the Jockey Club of Kenya in Nairobi. Facilities at the track are excellent, and racing enthusiasts claim that the course is one of the most attractive in the world.

Sitting and dreaming at the foot of Mount Kilimanjaro, tantalizingly across the Tan-

zanian border, you may feel the urge to go **mountain climbing.** In which case you have to head for Mount Kenya—at least a thousand others do each year. Thoughtfully providing for the varying abilities of Kenya's tourists, Mount Kenya offers three peaks, each with a dif-

Climbing is organized by the Nairobi-based Mountain Club of Kenya and two Austrian-trained rescue teams are on hand all year round. Climbs begin at the Naro Moru River Lodge, which hires out porters and equipment. Take two days for Lenana and three for Batian or Nelion. There's a longer tour that takes you round all three peaks.

Which brings you to the more conventional sports of **tennis** and **golf,** both well provided for in this former British stronghold, especially in the Highlands. Although there are tennis courts on the coast, have a heart check-up before you play in that heat. The Royal Nairobi, Limuru and Karen golf clubs all accept tourists as guests. The Royal Nairobi's course is of championship calibre and there is a museum commemorating past players in the old-fashioned club-house. The Karen offers parkland greens with a par of 72 and vistas of Nairobi, the Athi Plains and sometimes even Mount Kilimanjaro that may put you off your stroke. Some of them have quaint rules of penalty and compensation if your ball is given a helpful kick or is eaten by a passing animal. In elephant footprints, bunker rules usually apply.

ferent degree of climbing difficulty. The lowest peak, Lenana, rises gently and is within the reach of any reasonably fit person with a head for heights and lungs strong enough to handle the rarefied air at 5,000 metres. If your doctor assures you that you run no risk of pulmonary edema you might even consider the higher peaks. But Batian and Nelion demand expertise rated by professionals as Grades VI and V—Lenana being a mere II.

93

Photography

Kenya's abundant animals and birds, picturesque peoples, magnificent scenery, colourful flowers and regular sunshine make it a photographer's heaven. Photo safaris are organized in the same way as the old hunting safaris, some of them almost on the scale of Teddy Roosevelt's extravaganzas. You will tour the game reserves and national parks in plush jeeps, bedding down in luxury tented camps complete with iced champagne and the finest cuisine, served by a staff of six or more. Your armed guide will protect you while you wriggle up close to photograph lions and elephants in intimate poses not always possible on the average tour. Certainly by getting away from other tourists, you'll be seeing an Africa closer to the Hemingway dreamland.

But you'll still take some great photographs on the group game-runs led by government rangers in a jeep or minibus. The roof of the minibus will open to give you unimpeded standing shots.

Wild flowers are just as exotic as wild animals—and don't move.

You'll often find the animals so close that your telephoto lens will be a hindrance.

One of the problems of the group runs is that when one vehicle has found a pride of lions basking in the sun after a good meal, other vehicles will rush to the spot and encircle the poor beasts, limiting photographic alternatives. It is a good idea, if the terrain allows it, to pull back from the lions once you've found them and shoot telephoto at a distance in such a way that other groups won't notice your find.

You will occasionally see signs at game reserves forbidding you to take photos of Masai or other tribesmen. This is partly because many of them quite simply object to undignified invasions of their privacy. (Leopards feel that way, too.) But the ban also seeks to avoid the unseemly haggling over payment which many of them not unreasonably ask for posing. You will, however, with proper and discreet preparation find opportunities to photograph the tribesmen in areas where it is not forbidden. You may even find them flagging down your vehicle, to do a dance for you on the road—not exactly *cinéma-vérité* but colourful all the same—for appropriate payment.

Camping

If you can't afford the high-style camping of the luxury photo safaris, there is still a lot of fun to be had camping out in the special sites set aside for those wanting to rough it in the game parks. You can choose from the more than 200 officially recognized campsites throughout Kenya, charging variable (but small) amounts per night. A few are elaborately fitted out with rentable caravans and permanent huts, and have central facilities for cooking, showers, safe drinking water, etc.

There is a scout on hand at most campsites. He is usually armed, but is under strict orders not to shoot an animal except in extreme emergencies. Animals are generally wary of people and should keep their distance unless provoked; but an occasional baboon or vervet monkey might invite himself to dinner if you leave food untended.

Shopping

The big problem in shopping for souvenirs of your stay in Kenya is sorting out the genuine artwork from mass-produced junk. The first rule of thumb is to avoid any shop with a sign that offers "curios". These may well be hand-carved as advertised, but on an assembly line without the careful craftsmanship of the real thing. Authentic, traditional African artwork may be well-nigh impossible to find any more, and your best bets are the wood-carvings at Lamu and replicas of old moulded plasterwork. If these are too pricey, you can also buy the beautifully fashioned brass locks and padlocks made by Lamu locksmiths.

If you do want some of the more modern sculpture, you can find quite good likenesses of elephants, lions or giraffes in wood or soapstone. The best selection will be in Nairobi, rather than out in the countryside. Your best buy on the road is a Masai or Samburu spear or shield. You will also find various versions of the African *mbao* board game (see p. 64) in Nairobi.

In Mombasa shop for antiques—Arab brasswork, trays and "Zanzibar" chests. You'll find good buys, but nothing will be inexpensive. Animal skins purchased without government

Kenya's best craftwork is as good as any in Africa, but you must be careful to avoid mass production.

permits—and you won't get one—are strictly illegal.

Crafts cooperatives representing rural artisans have retail shops in the towns. Other important sources of souvenirs are prison industries shops, which are found in most of the major urban centres. You can also recall your stay in Kenya with the safari suits and light cotton or Indian silk *kanga* wraps and dresses that will be tailor-made overnight. However, you may find they lose some of their appropriateness in a European or American context.

Entertainment

The big show is Kenya itself, but if you occasionally have a homesick urge for discotheques or night clubs, Nairobi and Mombasa can satisfy your needs. For the most part you'll be entertained by professional bands, performing European and American pop music with incredible fidelity to the originals, rather than by records.

On the coast the hotels stage disco shows as well as programmes of **native dancing.** But the latter most often bears the same relationship to the real thing as the "curios" in souvenir shops do to authentic African art. The women wear bras. This is less a sign of prudishness in a European sense than an implicit expression of the incongruity of performing dances with religious or ritually erotic symbolism at a hotel.

A more genuine display of African dancing is available at the Bomas of Kenya near the Nairobi National Park where you can see Samburu war dances, Kamba acrobatics, a Giriama wedding dance and a slightly expurgated version of the Kikuyu circumcision ceremony—still carried on by men though suppressed by women, feminism being a growing movement in Kenya championed by Kenyatta himself and enthusiastically carried forward by the new leadership.

You can gamble at roulette, baccarat and chemin-de-fer at Nairobi's International Casino and watch a Bluebell Girls floorshow to console you for your losses. More decorous entertainment is available in the capital and occasionally elsewhere from various theatre clubs and groups, but Kenya doesn't provide much in the way of European-style nighttime entertainment.

Authentic tribal dancing is often hard to find but worth looking for.

99

Wining and Dining

Wining can be very easily dealt with—drink the beer. Kenya's local brew is excellent, served "cool" or "warm"—that's what they say—according to your preference, as the barman or waiter defers to old colonial tastes. Imported red wines are inevitably over-heated, given the usual room-temperatures, and white wines are refrigerated out of all recognition. Champagne, away from those luxury safaris, is likely to be flat. In hotels and restaurants, all imported wines and spirits are expensive. In shops, wines are expensive, spirits less so. On the coast you might like to try the very potent palm wine. But not at midday.

Dining in Kenya owes much, probably too much, to the colonial past. Most hotels and restaurants offer a faithful and

Without a doubt, the most delicious food in Kenya is the fish at the coast. And nobody ever complained that the portions were too small.

usually unimaginative reproduction of English cuisine, with blandly cooked beef and pork and overdone vegetables.

The great, truly great exception to this is the seafood served on the coast: large succulent spiny lobsters, superb shrimp and prawns—all astoundingly cheap compared with European or American prices—and excellent kingfish and swordfish. If you order them grilled simply, with at most a butter sauce, you will have Kenya's best meals.

Cheeses and desserts, it should be added, are an honourable supplement to the meal, especially with the delicious pineapples and mangoes, though the bananas may seem strange to the European palate. Also, on the game reserves, you will be glad of the English breakfasts served after a dawn game-run.

Nairobi and Mombasa have several fine Indian and Chinese restaurants, and the hotels and lodges do much better with the Indian cuisine than with the English.

African food is a taste perhaps difficult for Europeans and Americans to acquire on a first visit. But the more adventurous might like to try *sukuma wiki na nyama*, sauté of spinach with meat; *kuku wakupaka*, spiced chicken from Lamu; or the ubiquitous *irio*, a Kikuyu mixture of mashed chick peas, maize, pumpkin and potatoes, eaten with meat or fish.

You'll find the service friendly and willing, but sometimes rather over-trained. The waiters have been told to keep your table uncluttered with unused cutlery, plates and glasses and some of these may disappear before you've finished with them. The buffet service favoured by most hotels for at least one of the meals gives you as generous portions as you could wish. In Kenya, to eat well and cheaply, go for the buffet spreads and seafood.

101

To Help You Order...

Good evening. I'd like
a table for three.

**Habari za jioni. Napenda
kupata meza ya watu watatu.**

I'd like a/an/some...

Nitapenda...

aperitif	**kinywaji kabla ya chakula**	milk	**maziwa**
beer	**bia [pombe]**	potatoes	**mbatata**
bread	**mkate**	rice	**wali**
butter	**siagi**	rolls	**mkate wa kusukuma**
cheese	**jibini**	salad	**saladi**
coffee	**kahawa**	salt	**chumvi**
dessert	**chakula mwisho**	seafood	**vyakula vya bahari**
fish	**samaki**		
fruit	**matunda**	soup	**supu**
ice-cream	**aiskrimu**	sugar	**sukari**
lemon	**ndimu**	tea	**chai**
meat	**nyama**	vegetables	**mboga**
mineral water	**maji safi ya kunywa**	(iced) water	**maji (baridi)**
		wine	**divai [mvinyo]**

...and Read the Menu

avokado	avocado	**mbaazi mbichi**	green peas
biringani	aubergine (eggplant)	**mbuzi**	goat
		mchuzi wa nazi	cream of coco-nut soup
choroko	lentils		
embe	mango	**mtama**	millet
kaa	crab	**ndizi**	bananas
kababu	meat balls	**nyama ya kuponda**	minced meat
karoti	carrots		
kipande cha kondoo	lamb chops	**peschi**	perch
		saladi ya figili	lettuce salad
korosho	cashew nuts		
liiki	leeks	**soseji**	sausages
maji ya matunda	fruit juice	**steki**	steak (in general)
mabalungi/ machungwa	grapefruit/ orange		
		tikitiki maji	melon
nanasi/nyanga	pineapple/ tomato	**tilapia**	a local salt-water fish

102

BLUEPRINT for a Perfect Trip

How to Get There

Although the fares and conditions described on pp. 104–105 have all been carefully checked, it is advisable to consult a travel agent for the latest information on fares and other arrangements.

From Great Britain

BY AIR: Flights leave daily from London (Heathrow) to Nairobi (some flights are direct to Mombasa), stopping at different places en route according to the day of travel. Passengers from Eire and the provinces must connect at London. There are flights linking Nairobi to Mombasa and other airports in Kenya.

The fares available are first class, economy class, an excursion fare and an APEX (Advance Purchase Excursion) fare. The price of APEX tickets (low compared with other fares) varies according to season—June to September and December to January are considered "high" seasons. You can make stopovers en route with all fares except APEX. Reductions are available for children.

Package Tours: Although there are no charter flights from London to Kenya, package tour operators charter seats on scheduled flights for their clients. A comprehensive range of tours is available, from full board in a top class hotel including safaris, to camping on beaches. Safaris are often organized for groups with special interests like historians, anthropologists and geologists. You may find that package tours which start from other European cities are even cheaper.

Hire cars are available for independent travel in Kenya.

BY SEA: The Canberra World Cruise stops in Mombasa for 47 hours, otherwise there are no cruises or passenger berths on cargo boats available to East Africa from Europe.

BY ROAD: There is a route from Europe to Kenya and you can join overland package holiday groups driving from London to Nairobi.

From North America

BY AIR: Nairobi is serviced by direct flights from New York City on Tuesdays, Thursdays, and Fridays. Connections can be made daily from many American and Canadian cities. Those travelling between New York, Houston or Toronto and Nairobi have the most flights and departure times from which to choose.

Three fares at present available to Kenya are economy, first class, and the 14- to 45-day excursion. The excursion fare is least expensive and can be booked at any time. It permits two stopovers in each direction if the trip is made via Europe. If travel takes place on a weekend, a surcharge must be paid. Children 2 to 11 years of age fly for 50% of the adult excursion rate.

Charter Flights and Package Tours: A variety of Group Inclusive Tours (GIT), usually of three weeks' duration, combines visits to cities like Capetown, Cairo and Casablanca with wildlife tours of Kenya. Several programmes include Brazil as the first stopover point. From there, travel is due east to South Africa and then north to Victoria Falls, Kenya, and the Sudan. Included in the cost of the tour are roundtrip air transport transfers, accommodation at de luxe hotels and lodges, all or most meals, tips, and the services of a guide. A 15-day OTC (One-Stop Inclusive Tour Charter) has been designed for the traveller who wants to visit only Kenya and to spend nine days on safari.

Previous restrictions on travellers arriving from the Republic of South Africa no longer apply.

When to Go

Since Kenya is on the Equator, climate remains pretty stable throughout the year. Temperatures in Nairobi, the Highlands and other mountainous areas are modified by the altitude; days are generally sunny and hot but nights can be cool. The recommended time to visit is the period between mid-September and mid-October, as flowering trees are at their best, weather and roads are good (prior to the rains from late October) and accommodation in hotels and lodges is reasonably priced.

Note, also, that temperature can vary significantly between day and night. The following charts give you an idea of the average monthly temperatures and rainfall in two different areas of Kenya. Water temperature remains fairly constant all year—from 23 °C (73 °F) to 26 °C (79 °F).

Nairobi	J	F	M	A	M	J	J	A	S	O	N	D
°C max.	26	27	27	26	24	23	23	23	26	26	25	25
min.	13	13	14	15	15	13	12	12	13	14	14	14
°F max.	79	81	81	79	75	73	73	73	79	79	77	77
min.	55	55	57	59	59	55	54	54	55	57	57	57
Rainfall (in inches)	2	3	5	8	6	2	1	1	1	2	4	3

Mombasa	J	F	M	A	M	J	J	A	S	O	N	D
°C max.	32	32	32	31	29	29	28	28	29	30	31	31
min.	23	24	24	24	22	22	21	21	21	22	23	23
°F max.	90	90	90	88	84	84	82	82	84	86	88	88
min.	73	75	75	75	72	72	70	70	70	72	73	73
Rainfall (in inches)	1	1	3	8	13	5	4	3	3	3	4	2

Planning Your Budget

To give you an idea of what to expect, here are some average prices in Kenya Shillings. They should be considered only as guidelines, however; inflation is as rampant in Kenya as elsewhere.

Airport departure tax. U.S.$20 (to be paid in freely convertible currency).

Baby-sitters. $4–8 per day plus transport.

Camping. In national parks and reserves $2–3 per person per night to camp in own tent (Masai Mara the same), plus $22 booking fee per site; "tented camps" $30–50 per person.

Car hire (Nairobi). *Daihatsu Charade* (4 seats) $50 per day, $0.20 per km., $360 per week with unlimited mileage. *Isuzu Trooper* (large 4-wheel drive) $153 per day, $0.50 per km., $1,500–1,800 per week with unlimited mileage. All prices include compulsory insurance.

Charter flights. 5 passengers $2 per mile, 7 passengers (or 8 without luggage) $2.70 per mile.

Cigarettes (per packet of 20). Local brands $0.60–1.00, locally manufactured foreign brands $1.30–1.50, imported brands $2.10–2.40.

Hairdressers. *Woman's* haircut $10–17, shampoo and set $8–14, blow-dry $3–5, permanent wave $54–65. *Man's* barber cut $8–10, stylist cut $10–13.

Hotels. Luxury, double room $110–122, single room $89–96. First class, double room $60. Second class, double room $29–40, single room $18–26. Rates are higher in August.

Meals (medium-priced restaurant). Breakfast $1.50–3.50, lunch $2.50–5, dinner $5–10. Service tax to be introduced in 1992.

Scheduled local flights. From Nairobi to Mara $85, return $150, to Amboseli $68, return $120, to Samburu $100, return $184, to Lamu $131, return $250, to Turkana $141, return $274.

Trains. Nairobi to Mombasa, private first class compartment for two, $21 (single occupancy $21), second class $11. Nairobi to Kisumu, first class $26 for two (single occupancy $26), second class $6.50. Return ticket double.

An A–Z Summary of Practical Information and Facts

> A star (*) following an entry indicates that relevant prices are to be found on page 107.

A

AIR CHARTERS. Chartering an aircraft has not been till now a millionaire's prerogative in Kenya—mercifully, since distances are vast and roads forbidding. A few hours' flight to Lake Turkana, instead of several days' ride on an endurance-testing, backbreaking bus, may mean saving more than time alone. This pleasant situation is, however, fast degenerating, owing to the oil crisis in the Middle East.

Kenya Airways have regular flights to Mombasa and Malindi. In addition there are several charter airlines, which have turned Nairobi's Wilson Airport into Africa's busiest. Cessnas, Pipers and Beechcrafts buzz in and out of the airport at two-minute intervals during peak hours and serve the more than 200 airstrips that dot the Kenyan countryside. Most hotels and lodges outside the main urban centres have landing strips nearby.

Air Kenya (see below) operate regular flights from Nairobi's Wilson Airport to Lamu, Masai Mara, Turkana and Amboseli.

Other large charter airlines based at the Wilson Airport are Boskovic Air Charters and Safari Air Services.

Addresses:

Boskovic Air Charters: P.O. Box 45646, Nairobi; tel. 501210/9.
Safari Air Services Ltd.: P.O. Box 41951, Nairobi; tel. 501211.
Air Kenya: P.O. Box 30357, Nairobi; tel. 501601/2/3/4, 501421/23
P.O. Box 84 700, Mombasa; tel. 43 39 82

AIRPORTS★. Kenya is served by two of the largest, most modern and efficient international airports in Africa. The Jomo Kenyatta International Airport is half-an-hour's drive from Nairobi's city centre, where most of the better hotels are located. Mombasa's Moi International Airport on the Kenya coast is closer to the town centre, but most of the tourist hotels are at various distances from the town.

At both airports, electronic conveyor belts ferry baggage close to customs officials, and there are teams of porters ready to carry heavy bags to the customs zone without charge. Another team of porters will carry luggage beyond customs to bus stops and taxi stands for modest tips.

Most tourist hotels have their own minibuses at the airports to transport guests, while airlines provide transport to terminals in the city centres. Kenya Airways buses leave on the hour to a central terminal, stopping at main hotels on the way and every hotel within Nairobi. A public bus serves both the Jomo Kenyatta and Moi airports. Numerous taxis are on hand.

Kenya Airways buses leave the city-centre terminals (at Sadler House, Koinange Street, Nairobi; and Jubilee Building, Moi Avenue, Mombasa) on the hour.

There is an airport tax for departing passengers.

BABY-SITTERS (*msaidizi wa kutazama mtoto*). Most hotels will arrange baby-sitting services for their guests. Rates vary widely depending on the location of the hotel or lodge, and on the number of children, but are never excessive.

CAMPING. Camping is a way of life in the warm Kenyan sun, and some people would say it is the only way to experience the real Kenya. Wherever you want to camp, you are certain to be surrounded by magnificent scenery, and in some places, by a wide range of wildlife. You can book sites on the spot or at the town hall.

Camping has become a thriving "extra" for Kenya's tour operators, and the better-off visitor can experience the thrill of Kenya's vast skies and the *bundu*—the endless bush—at a comfortably fitted campsite that serves champagne for breakfast! But for the adventurous and the enterprising visitor (and resident alike), camping in Kenya's wild bushlands can be an inexpensive and delightful do-it-yourself holiday, and an unforgettable experience.

Find a site well before sunset, for in tropical Africa it can be pitch dark half-an-hour after the sun starts to go down. Choose level ground with short grass and plenty of shade, but beware of the type of tree you camp under: thorn trees are good for shade and have no climbing leopards and snakes, but underneath them there is usually a thick carpet of thorns; some trees exude sap, and trees with lots of bird nests mean there will be unwelcome bird droppings.

In hot, low-altitude areas, temperatures inside a tent can be unbearably high, so make sure the rear windows face the prevailing wind.

Do not set camp on, or too near, a sandy expanse of a dry riverbed—a tropical rainstorm miles away can send unbridled water gushing down towards you.

C Avoid camping right across or too near a game trail. Not only might your tent attract some unnecessary curiosity, but you could find an animal stumbling into your guy ropes.

There is always the danger of a fire going wild. Learn to build "safe" fires, with stones around the campfire, and keep the flames under control at all times.

Camping equipment: if you intend spending the whole holiday under canvas, bring as much equipment as your light-weight allowance will permit, although you can actually, in case of need, buy or rent supplies in Nairobi at very attractive prices.

The main items include: tent (with a sewn-in groundsheet and mosquito-netted windows); camp beds (airbeds are vulnerable to thorns), sleeping bags; folding chairs and table; local pots and pans (Kenyan lightweight ones are excellent for direct fire use); plastic airtight containers for bread, sugar, salt, etc.; axe and machete; *karai* —a wide metal bowl useful for heating water, for washing, or covering the fire when it rains; a two-burner gas stove with spare gas; torch (flashlight); plates, mugs, spoons, knives, kitchen knives; folding spade; wooden board for cutting bread and vegetables; gas lamps; insulated boxes; personal equipment; binoculars; plenty of drinking water; food (which you need to plan with care depending on which part of the country you are heading towards); appropriate safari clothes.

CAR HIRE*. Nairobi boasts more than 200 car hire firms. This says more about Kenya's spirit of free enterprise than about the state of the car hire business in the country. At the airports and hotels you'll see the familiar names. But look through the phone book first and see what other companies there are before you make arrangements. Prices are generally higher than in Europe and North America. A tour agent or hotel concierge can help you select the firm that best suits your needs and pocket.

Before you hire a car, be aware of the many deterrents to self-drive (see DRIVING).

CIGARETTES, CIGARS, TOBACCO* *(sigara, sigaa, tumbaku).* Imported European and American cigarettes are available in the large towns and cities, but are generally dearer than at home. Cheaper local brands are made to surprisingly high quality. Bring your own cigars.

A packet of…/A box of matches, please.	**Pakiti ya…/Kibiriti, tafadhali.**
filter-tipped/without filter	**zenye filta/isioyo na filta**

CLIMATE and CLOTHING. See also page 106. Temperatures in Nairobi and throughout the highlands are never excessive, thanks to high altitudes, but bear in mind, nevertheless, that Nairobi is only 60 miles south of the Equator and that the sun can be strong. Those not acclimatized should wear hats. Evenings are cool and can be chilly. Warm clothing is therefore necessary after sunset, especially on safari.

On the coast, beachwear is sufficient for day-time in hotels, with a loose cotton dress or shirt worn to meals or when walking or shopping. Nylons and other synthetic materials prove very hot for the coast; cotton is much more suitable. Incidentally, nudity on the beaches or in any public place is against the law in Kenya.

COMMUNICATIONS. Post offices are indicated by the letters PTT (Post, Telephone, Telegraph). Mail boxes are painted red. You can also buy stamps at stationers, souvenir shops and small grocers' shops.

Post office hours: From 8 a.m. to noon and from 2 to 4.30 p.m., Monday to Friday, from 8 a.m. to noon only on Saturdays.

Poste Restante (General Delivery): Letters can reach you, but the system in Nairobi is a little haphazard. At the post office on Kenyatta Avenue you ask for the letters beginning with your initial and look through the bunch for your mail. Since the clerk is not very strict about checking your identity, you may find letters "going astray". It's best to have mail sent to a listed address, but allow plenty of time. An airmail letter from Europe can take between three and ten days, from the U.S.A. sometimes as long as two to three weeks.

Telegrams: These can be sent by telephone through the operator. Ask at the information office or hotel reception desk for the nearest telex facilities. When possible, it is recommended to send messages by telex.

Telephone: From Kenya you can dial direct to many countries both in Africa and overseas. For details on international subscriber dialling, contact your hotel manager or a branch of the post office.

City telephone kiosks are painted red. If you cannot locate one, or if you find one out of order, approach the nearest hotel, restaurant or shop; they will allow you to use their telephone at double the normal rate. Long distance calls are cheaper between 6 p.m. and 6 a.m.

CONVERTER CHARTS. For fluid and distance measures, see page 113. Kenya uses the metric system.

C Temperature

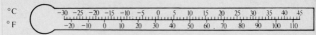

Length

Weight

CRIME and THEFTS. There are some areas in Nairobi and Mombasa where it is inadvisable to wander after dark. Avoid going into poorly lit areas or buildings in the towns, or strolling alone on empty highways, lanes or on the beaches at night.

Remember that Kenya is still a country of great contrasts in wealth, with most of the African population living on very modest means. Do not carry large sums of cash or traveller's cheques on you. Deposit what you do not require immediately with the manager of your hotel for safe-keeping. Lock all articles in the boot of your car, and lock the car too. Similarly, do not leave valuable personal belongings unattended on beaches and in public places.

If you feel in the slightest worried, you should discuss the current local situation with your hotel manager or your tour leader.

D DRIVING IN KENYA. To drive a hired car in Kenya all you need is a valid international driving licence. But bear in mind that this is the home of the famous Safari Rally, designed to test to the limit the endurance and toughness of both the driver and the car. Roads are being improved all the time and at a faster rate than in many other African countries, but if you are on holiday, you may want to leave much of the driving, especially on the off-beat sandy and muddy roads, to experienced and well-trained tour drivers. On the main road from Mombasa to Uganda there is a small toll for private vehicles.

Although it's rather unlikely that you'll ship your car to Kenya, if you do, you would be wise to check beforehand how long you are allowed to use it without having to pay import duty. Have it cleared by customs as soon as it arrives, or you'll have heavy storage charges to pay. To take your car into Kenya you will need:

- an international driving licence
- car registration papers
- an international insurance certificate
- a nationality plate or sticker

Driving conditions: As an inheritance of the British past, Kenyan motorists drive on the left and overtake (pass) on the right. Most vehicles have the steering wheel on the right. Roads are generally narrow, so make sure you have full view of the stretch ahead before you attempt to overtake.

Driving in the national parks: Speeds are strictly limited to 30 or even 20 m.p.h. (50 or 30 k.p.h.), so as not to frighten the wild animals. For the same reason all loud noises and brusque movements should be avoided, both when driving and while taking photographs. Don't try to nudge animals out of the way; just enjoy the occasion and wait for them to move on.

Fluid measures

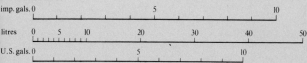

Distances: Here are some approximate road distances in kilometres between major centres:

Nairobi–Eldoret	310	Mombasa–Eldoret	800
Nairobi–Kisumu	350	Mombasa–Kisumu	845
Nairobi–Malindi	615	Mombasa–Malindi	120
Nairobi–Marsabit	560	Mombasa–Marsabit	1,110
Nairobi–Mombasa	490	Mombasa–Moyale	1,380
Nairobi–Nanyuki	200	Mombasa–Nakuru	650
Nairobi–Nyeri	160	Mombasa–Namanga	605

To convert kilometres to miles:

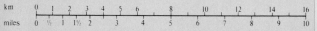

D **Traffic violations:** For minor traffic offenses the police usually impose fines on the spot against your signature on a sheet admitting the charge. Send your cheque by registered post to the address of the traffic court given on your charge sheet. Following this procedure can save you a great deal of time, for local traffic courts are quite busy.

Breakdowns: Before setting out for long-distance driving, get in touch with the Automobile Association of Kenya, with headquarters in Nairobi. The A.A. will advise on the road conditions ahead, and on how you can obtain help in case of emergency.

Telephones:	Nairobi:	720382/3
	Mombasa:	26778
	Eldoret:	27000
	Kisumu:	41361
	Nakuru:	44811

Are we on the road to…?	**Tuko katika njia sawasawa ya kwenda…?**
Fill the tank, please.	**Tafadhali jaza tangi.**
normal/super	**standardi/premium**
I've had a breakdown.	**Imeniharibikia nilipokuwa.**
There's been an accident.	**Kumetokea ajali.**

E **ELECTRIC CURRENT.** Major towns and cities are supplied with 240 volts, 50 cycles A.C. Some lodges have independent power generators which vary in voltage.

Tourist hotels and lodges generally provide an adaptor for 220 and 110 volts. The plug in use throughout Kenya is of the three-pin 13-ampere type.

EMBASSIES, CONSULATES, HIGH COMMISSIONS. Kenya maintains diplomatic relations with more than 80 countries.

Australia:	High Commission: Riverside Drive, P.O. Box 30360, Nairobi, Tel. 749955/6/7.
Canada:	High Commission: Comcraft House, Haile Selassie Avenue, P.O. Box 30481, Nairobi. Tel. 334033.
Eire:	Embassy: Monrovia Street, P.O. Box 30659, Nairobi. Tel. 226771.

United Kingdom:	High Commission: Bruce House, Standard Street, P.O. Box 30465, Nairobi. Tel. 335944/60.
U.S.A.:	Embassy: Moi Avenue, P.O. Box 30137, Nairobi. Tel. 334141.

Denmark:	Embassy: H.F.C.K. Building, Koinange Street, P.O. Box 40412, Nairobi. Tel. 331088.
	Consulate: Mr. J.H. Nielsen, Liwatoni Bay, P.O. Box 99543, Mombasa, Tel. 316051/3.
Finland:	Embassy: International House, City Hall Way, P.O. Box 30379, Nairobi. Tel. 334777/8.
Netherlands:	Embassy: Uchumi House, Nkrumah Road, P.O. Box 41537, Nairobi. Tel. 332420.
	Consulate: ABN Bank, Hassanali Bldg., Nkrumah Road, P.O. Box 90230, Mombasa. Tel. 25241.
Norway:	Embassy: H.F.C.K. Building, Koinange Street, P.O. Box 46363, Nairobi. Tel. 337121.
	Consulate: Mrs. Sondhi, Reef Hotel, P.O. Box 82234, Mombasa. Tel. 471771.
Sweden:	Embassy: International House, Mama Ngina Street, P.O. Box 30600, Nairobi. Tel. 229042/3/4/5.
	Consulate: Southern House, Moi Avenue, P.O. Box 86108, Mombasa. Tel. 20501.

EMERGENCY and SERVICES TELEPHONE NUMBERS

Police, Fire, Ambulance anywhere in Kenya	999
Police Headquarters, Nairobi area	222251
St. John's Ambulance, Nairobi	222396/224066
Time	993
Long-Distance Calls	0196
Dialling Assistance	900
Nairobi Airport Information	822111

ENTRY FORMALITIES and CUSTOMS CONTROLS. Citizens of Great Britain (except passport holders of Indian and Pakistani origin), **115**

E Eire and Canada are entitled to a three-month visitor's pass—issued on arrival—and no visas are required. The same applies to citizens of a limited number of other countries. All other nationals should obtain visas from one of the embassies, consulates or consular representatives in their countries. A deposit (refundable on departure) of the equivalent of £250 sterling per person may be required upon arrival, but visitors holding a ticket for the return or onward journey are normally exempt from this. Visitors are also required to carry a minimum sum of £200 sterling or the equivalent in a convertible foreign currency.

The following chart shows what main duty-free items you may take into Kenya and, when returning home, into your own country.

Into:	Cigarettes	Cigars	Tobacco	Spirits	Wine
Kenya	200 or	50 or	250 g.	1 l. or	1 l.
Australia	200 or	250 g. or	250 g.	1 l. or	1 l.
Canada	200 and	50 and	900 g.	1.1 l. or	1.1 l.
Eire	200 or	50 or	250 g.	1 l. and	2 l.
N. Zealand	200 or	50 or	½ lb.	1 qt. and	1 qt.
U.K.	200 or	50 or	250 g.	1 l. and	2 l.
U.S.A.	200 and	100 and	*	1 l. or	1 l.

*a reasonable quantity

Currency restrictions: Import and export of Kenya Shillings is not permitted. You can bring any amount of foreign currency into Kenya, but it must be declared upon arrival. Great care must be taken of the declaration form which will be required on departure. Leaving the country, you can take with you up to the equivalent of 4,000 Kenya Shillings, provided the amount is entered in your passport.

G **GUIDES and INTERPRETERS.** Trained tour guides and interpreters have been graduating from the Kenya Utalii (Tourism) College (the only such centre in Black Africa) since 1974; but there is still a serious shortage of guides. All available are employed by the tour companies and hotels and their charges are included in hotel or tour bills.

HITCH-HIKING. This is not yet a very practical way of travelling in Kenya, except on the Nairobi–Mombasa Highway. Also, hitch-hiking is viewed with suspicion in Kenya and you may be expected to pay for the ride. However, it's an effective way of meeting some residents.

Can you give me a lift to…?	**Unaweza kunichukua garini kwenda…?**
Where to?	**Wapi?**

HOTELS and ACCOMMODATION*. Kenya's hotels and lodges are classified in four categories. The luxury hotels offer extremely high standards of service and are comparable to the best hotels anywhere in the world with rates on an international scale. First-class hotels offer comfortable accommodation, efficient services, a variety of international dishes or specialized dishes of various nations, and all rooms have private bath and toilet, telephone, radio and television. Second class hotels and lodges offer reasonable comfort and a range of European-type food, and they generally have showers in rooms. Third-class hotels and lodges are not recommended for tourists; services are limited.

Kenya also has a few motels that offer good accommodation, food and reasonable services for the motorist. In many urban centres, there are guest or boarding houses for those who want to stay for extended periods. Some of these boarding houses are extensions of large hotels.

On the coast a large number of comfortably furnished bungalows can be found, usually near beaches, for families and groups who desire a homely atmosphere and who want to do their own cooking.

Most hotels offer a reduction of 50% for children under 12. At the height of the tourist season, hotel accommodation in Kenya can be scarce, so an early reservation—and confirmation—is always advisable. But if stuck without a room, ask for the tourist information office, which you will find in most major towns throughout the country.

Where is the tourist information office?	**Wapi ofisi ya habari kwa watalii?**

LANGUAGE. Swahili, the lingua franca of East Africa, was originally written in Arabic characters. When British missionaries introduced the Latin alphabet, they adopted as phonetic a transliteration as possible, so that Swahili is rather easy to pronounce. More than 40 tribal languages are spoken in Kenya. Most educated people, however, speak English remarkably well, and so English, whatever accent you have, will be understood, except well off the beaten track, where you'll need

L　Swahili. The Berlitz phrase book SWAHILI FOR TRAVELLERS will help you get by in just about any situation you're likely to meet.

Hello	**Jambo**
Good morning	**Habari za asubuhi**
Good afternoon	**Habari za alasiri**
Good evening	**Habari za jioni**
Good night	**Lala salama**
Please/Thank you	**Tafadhali/Asante**
You're welcome	**Karibu**
Goodbye/See you soon	**Kwa heri/Tutaonana**

LAUNDRY and DRY-CLEANING (*dobi mfua nguo; dobi wa nguo za sufu*). Hotel laundry is generally done well and, if you insist, overnight. If you are in central Nairobi, you may want to try one of the many fast-service dry-cleaners. Ask at the reception desk for the one nearest your hotel, as the in-house charges may be rather high.

I want these clothes...	**Nataka nguo hizi...**
cleaned	**zisafishwe**
ironed	**zipigwe pasi**
pressed	**zipigwe pasi**
washed	**zioshwe**
I need them...	**Nazitaka...**
today/tonight/tomorrow	**leo/usiku/kesho**

M　**MAPS.** Most of the hotel stationery shops are well stocked with brightly illustrated maps of city centres, game parks, campsites, roads, etc. Maps are distributed by tourist information offices in the major towns. In Nairobi and Mombasa, precise but complicated maps can be obtained from the Land's Offices.

MEDICAL CARE

Vaccinations: Yellow fever and cholera inoculations are advisable, but obligatory only if you enter from an infected area.

　　You can safely swim in the sea, but avoid swimming, bathing in or drinking from lakes (especially Lake Victoria), rivers or open natural reservoirs because of the risk of bilharzia, parasites, typhoid or dysentery bacilli (a vaccination against typhoid and paratyphoid fevers is recommended). All swimming pools are safe and usually well cared for.

Malaria is still a problem all over the country. Nairobi is officially malaria-free, but don't run unnecessary risks; take one of the many reliable prophylactics for two weeks before you arrive in Kenya, all the time you are in the country, and for four to six weeks after you return home. Consult your doctor and bring your favourite insect repellent.

Insurance: If your medical insurance cannot be extended to foreign countries, you may want to take out special travel insurance to cover yourself in case of accident, illness or hospitalization during your trip.

Doctors: There are highly qualified doctors, surgeons and dentists in both Nairobi and Mombasa.

Doctors' surgeries are open from 8 a.m. to 5 p.m., some till 6 p.m. or later. Lodges in remote game reserves have resident medical staff. The lodges have radio or telephone contact with the Flying Doctor Service in Nairobi. If travelling under your own steam, camping, etc., you should think of joining the Flying Doctor Service as a temporary member for a small fee. The postal address in Nairobi is P.O. Box 30125; tel. 501301 or 500508; fax 506112.

Pharmacies: Pharmacists in the major urban centres take turns to stay open late—till about 9 p.m.; rosters are published daily in the newspapers. Pharmacies at the major hospitals remain open 24 hours a day.

Hospitals: The major hospitals in the **Nairobi** area are all well-equipped:

The Kenyatta National Hospital is the nerve centre of Kenya's hospital system and a university teaching hospital. Large and modern. Tel. 334800.

Nairobi Hospital, private and expensively fitted out, offers the most modern equipment and comfort, as well as an impressive number of highly qualified consultants. Tel. 722160.

Gertrude's Garden specializes in children's illnesses. Tel. 65305.

The Aga Khan Hospital boasts a large team of resident doctors. Tel. 742531.

Mater Misericordiae Hospital specializes in maternity and related cases. The hospital is run by an order of Catholic sisters and is noted for excellence in nursing care. Tel 556666.

The major hospitals in the **Mombasa** area are fully equipped:

The Coast General Hopital is the largest. Tel. 314201.

The Katherine Bibby Hospital is comfortable and expensively fitted out. Tel. 312191.

M **Health precautions:** Visitors heading for the coast are advised to take all things in moderation at the start. There is a clinical condition known as "heat exhaustion" which is generally brought about by an excess of eating or drinking, sun-bathing or exercising, not just by temperature. Although sunstroke is rare on the coast, sunburn is very common. Bring your favourite suntan cream with you.

MEETING PEOPLE. By and large, Kenyans are friendly and easy-going, perhaps more so in Mombasa than elsewhere. In Nairobi, people are courteous but a little more businesslike in their manner. In the countryside there is a certain shyness, but this derives more from the unfamiliarity of English or other European languages—or even Swahili as opposed to local dialects—than from any unwillingness to communicate. In Nairobi, the most likely place for you to meet with African or European residents is at the New Stanley's "Thorn Tree" (see p. 32). In Mombasa the discos and other nightclubs are frequented by Europeans and Africans alike. Probably the best place in all of Kenya for meeting people is the island of Lamu, especially down by the harbour at Petley's Inn.

MONEY MATTERS

Currency: Kenya's unit of currency is the Shilling (abbreviated Sh(s), written 1/–, 2/50, etc.), divided into 100 cents (c). There are copper coins of 5 and 10c and silver coins of 50c and Sh 1/– and 5/–. Banknotes come in denominations of Shs 10/–, 20/–, 50/–, 100/–, 200/– and 500/–. It is an offence to deface or damage Kenya currency in any way. For currency restrictions, see ENTRY FORMALITIES AND CUSTOMS CONTROLS.

Exchange control regulations: Visitors are particularly warned against those "unofficial" money changers who will offer incredible deals in the street—you will be breaking the law and will usually end up with a handful of paper or forged notes. Foreign currency, including traveller's cheques, may be exchanged for cash only at a commercial bank or an authorized hotel. It may also be used for purchases of goods from persons licensed to accept foreign currency.

Banking hours: Banks in Nairobi and the major towns west of Nairobi open from 9 a.m. to 2 p.m., Monday to Friday, from 9 a.m. to 11 a.m. on Saturday. In addition, some banks open from 4 to 7 p.m. on Friday and Saturday. Banks in Mombasa and along the hot coastal belt open and close half an hour earlier. Some of the banks at the international airports open round the clock every day, while others begin at 6 a.m. and go on till midnight every day.

Foreign exchange departments of major banks in Nairobi stay open till 4.30 p.m. from Monday to Friday. You can also change money in most of the major hotels and resorts throughout the country, but at a slightly disadvantageous rate.

Credit Cards and Traveller's Cheques: Only a small number of international credit cards are accepted in Kenya. Traveller's cheques are readily recognized and accepted at most international hotels and tourist agencies.

Prices: Visitors are often surprised by the high prices, particularly of imported items, of goods in the shops, but there are very heavy import duties and sales tax. If you consider that you are being exploited, consult your tour leader or travel agent.

NEWSPAPERS and MAGAZINES. Kenya has three well established English-language daily papers, the *Nairobi Times,* the *Nation* and the *Standard,* and their Sunday counterparts. There is also a weekly English-language magazine and a wide range of monthlies. Many international newspapers and magazines are sold on newspaper stands and in stationer's shops in the large hotels several days later—unless you come across private entrepreneurs who pick up second-hand copies left by travellers at airports and re-sell them for the full cover price.

PHOTOGRAPHY. Well-known brands of film are on sale, but prices are higher than in Europe and the United States. You will need high-speed film for animal shots. Zooms are useful and telephoto lenses essential for good wildlife photography in Kenya. A 135-mm. lens is sufficient for animals, perhaps a 200-mm. for birds. Some Nairobi and Mombasa photo shops have good selections of still or cine cameras for sale or hire.

Your camera will require more than usual protection. While in the bush on dusty roads, keep camera and lenses in polythene bags, preferably shopping bags, where they can be reached easily. The dust goes everywhere, even into tightly closed car boots. Do not leave your camera in the sun or locked in your car in the heat; the colours will be washed out of the film. Keep it away from sand and salt water. And when you go through security checks don't allow your camera and film to be submitted to detection devices; Kenyan authorities will readily examine these separately.

It is forbidden to photograph the national flag, the president, state lodges, soldiers, prison officers, prisoners, prison establishments and (for the time being) the late President Kenyatta's mausoleum. Failure

P to observe this regulation will invariably cost you your film or even camera, and may lead to a court fine.

Some of Kenya's more colourful tribespeople have become wise to tourist ways and may demand a small fee to pose for a photograph.

Can I take a picture? **Naweza kupiga picha?**

POLICE. All policemen and policewomen are friendly and helpful to tourists and are the most reliable source of any kind of information you require. There are various branches of the Kenya Police, but the two types you are likely to meet are the traffic and the criminal police. If they cannot help you, they will tell you where to obtain the information you need. They are also the most efficient source of help in case of emergency of any kind. In an emergency, dial 999.

PUBLIC HOLIDAYS

January 1	New Year's Day
May 1	Labour Day
June 1	Madaraka (self-rule) Day
October 10	Moi Day
October 20	Kenyatta Day
December 12	Uhuru/Jamhuri (Independence/Republic) Day
December 25	Christmas Day
December 26	Boxing Day

Movable Dates:
Good Friday, Easter Monday, Idd-ul-Fitr

R **RADIO and TV.** Kenya has one English-language radio station that can be picked up throughout the country. The station broadcasts from 6 a.m. to 11.10 p.m. You can tune in to international news at 7 a.m., 9 a.m., 1 p.m., 5 p.m., 7 p.m. and 9 p.m. International news summaries are broadcast every hour, on the hour. The Swahili station is strong on good local and international popular music.

On the coast, the Mombasa station adds some occasional local programming to the Nairobi broadcasts.

On Kenya's single TV channel, Swahili and English programmes come on the air at 5.30 p.m. and go off at about 11 p.m. Popular English-language features include international favourites and film **122** series from Britain, Germany, the United States and Australia.

RELIGIOUS SERVICES. Christianity is the dominant religion of Kenya with adherents divided roughly equally among Roman Catholic, Protestant and Independent African faiths. There are also large communities of Moslems on the Coast and smaller communities in the north-eastern region, where people of Somali origin live. About one-third of the rural population still adheres to a variety of traditional religions. In the urban centres mosques and temples of various eastern faiths are much in evidence.

Nairobi is a major centre of the Independent African Church Movement. Every Sunday hundreds of groups gather on street corners, at bus stops, in parks and public halls for worship. Others march up and down the streets to the rhythm of drums in colourful clothes, carrying flags, singing and preaching. Some of the groups welcome guests, but most are suspicious of newcomers.

English services of the major Nairobi Catholic and Protestant congregations are announced in the daily newspapers on Saturdays.

church	**kanisa**
synagogue	**hekalu la kiyahudi**
mosque	**msikiti**
mass/the service	**sala ya misa/ibada**

SIGHTSEEING. Numerous tour operators offer excursions to points of interest in the major towns and cities, as well as to game parks and other sights. Hotel chains organize their own sightseeing tours en route from one hotel to another. Ask at a tourist office for a list of possible tours and firms.

You can with advance planning embark on a private photo safari, guided and protected by a professional armed hunter whose equipment and staff may include four-wheel-drive cars, five-ton lorries, trackers, gun-bearers, camp cooks and aides. The expedition can hardly be rushed, so plan on up to a week in the Kenyan bush. There is no doubt that this is the most exciting way of seeing the country, but the cost is prohibitive. Even a privately organized group safari is expensive and conditions are more cramped. Unfortunately, if you have to ask the price, the chances are you can't afford it.

TIME DIFFERENCES. The East African countries of Kenya, Uganda and Tanzania are on standard time, three hours ahead of GMT. It remains constant throughout the year (see chart on p. 124).

Sunrise and sunset times for major urban centres are published in the daily newspapers.

T **Winter Time chart:**

New York	London	**Kenya**	Sydney	Auckland
4 a.m.	9 a.m.	**noon**	8 p.m.	10 p.m.

TIPPING. Tipping is often discouraged, but not forbidden in Kenya as it is in some of the African countries. So if you appreciate a service, tip at your discretion, but keep it moderate. Most good hotels and restaurants include a ten-percent service charge in the bill.

Is service included?   **Eti pamoja na utumishi?**

TOILETS (*choo,* pronounced "cho"). Ladies and Gentlemen are almost always indicated in English, accompanied by male and female symbols.
  Wanawake (Ladies) and *Wanaume* (Gentlemen) appear in bold letters in public lavatories, and are generally warnings that the places ought to be avoided—unless in cases of extreme emergency. A 10-cent coin will open toilet doors in the public areas of hotels, but surprisingly, in the generally tourist-only areas, no charge is made.

TOURIST INFORMATION OFFICES. Bring your queries to the local tourist office, which will recommend the best shops, car hire firms and hotels and advise on tours, recreation and any other subject. A wide range of guide-books, maps and pamphlets are also available.
  The Nairobi Bureau, operated by the Kenya Tourist Development Corporation, is centrally located near the Hilton Hotel, in City Hall Way.

P.O. Box 30471, tel. 21855 (open from 8.30 a.m. to 12.30 p.m. and 2–5 p.m., Monday to Saturday).

Similar information is available on the coast at the Mombasa Information Bureau near the tusks on Moi Avenue (formerly Kilindini Road), tel. 23509/20627 (open from 8 a.m. to noon and 2–4.30 p.m.).

Kenya Tourist Offices abroad:

United Kingdom: 25 Brooks Mews, London W1Y 1LJ; tel. 071-355 3144.

U.S.A.: 424 Madison Avenue, New York, N.Y. 10022; tel. (212) 486 1300.
Doheny Plaza, Suite 111–112, 9100 Wilshire Boulevard, Beverly Hills, California 90212; tel. (213) 274 6634.

TRANSPORT

Buses: City buses operate in Nairobi and Mombasa and provide an excellent opportunity for seeing the city centres and suburbs at low rates. Visitors are advised to avoid peak hours, when the buses will be very crowded. The best times to use the city buses are from 9.30 a.m. to 12 noon and 2.30 to 4 p.m. Fares are paid on the bus to the conductor.

There are no route maps on the streets or at bus stops, as these change frequently. Maps of current routes are available at the tourist office and most hotels.

There are inter-city buses of a reasonable standard connecting Nairobi with all main centres and crowded country buses connecting villages to the latter. These local buses are not reliable nor recommended except in an emergency.

Taxis: There are four types of taxi in the major urban centres of Kenya: Kenatco-owned, Yellow band, private and long distance. None have meters. Whatever you do, establish the fare *before* getting into the taxi.

Kenatco taxis use Mercedes Benz 200 vehicles. They charge per kilometre and you can consult lists of approximate distances to prominent landmarks and places of interest posted in most good hotels. Check the authorized fare with their office at the airport or at hotel reception desks.

Yellow band taxis come under the control of the municipal councils. Visitors should always check with the information bureau about the approximate charge for a journey before boarding the vehicle.

Private taxis come under no particular control and the vehicles may not be properly insured. Charges for waiting time and extra passengers are negotiable.

In addition to these, there are long-distance Peugeot taxi services which are shared by passengers who book their destination in advance. Prices are quite reasonable, and the ride relatively comfortable. These operate only between the major urban centres and do not go off the paved roads.

Matatus: These local private taxis compete directly with the bus services. They are often built from the wrecks of old cars and are filled to overflowing. Their—usually—unlicenced drivers will have no insurance and are particularly accident-prone. To be avoided at all costs.

Trains*: Passenger service on Kenya's single railway line from Mombasa to Kisumu is a railway enthusiast's dream. Trains are clean, cheap

T and supplied with good restaurant cars and well-stocked bars. Going at the leisurely pace of 35 miles per hour, the overnight trains are timed to leave the major stations of Mombasa, Nairobi and Kisumu about sunset and to arrive at these stations just after sunrise, providing good opportunities for day-long visits to either Mombasa or Kisumu from Nairobi, or day-long stopovers or visits to Nairobi from either place. Two consecutive nights on the train can prove tiring, however, so allow for at least one night's stopover.

W **WATER.** Other than in Mombasa's hotels, Nairobi is practically the only town where the tap-water is 100 per cent safe for drinking. However, if you are in doubt, bottled water is always available in bars. Nearly all lodges keep filtered water in jars or thermos jugs beside the bed. That is a direct warning that water from the tap is not safe, even for brushing teeth.

WILDLIFE ORGANIZATIONS. Conservationists and wildlife enthusiasts visiting Kenya may want to get in touch with the following societies:

Mountain Club of Kenya, P.O. Box 45741, Nairobi.

Members meet on Tuesday evenings at the Mountain Club of Kenya Clubhouse, Wilson Airport, from 7.30 p.m. Clubhouse telephone: 501747.

Cave Exploration Group of East Africa, P.O. Box 47583, Nairobi.

Other societies of interest are:

Geological Club of Kenya, P.O. Box 44749 Nairobi (no telephone).

East African National History Society, P.O. Box 44486, Nairobi; tel. 20141.

East Africa Wildlife Society, Nairobi Hilton Hotel, P.O. Box 20110; tel. 27047.

Wildlife Clubs of Kenya, National Museum, P.O. Box 40658, Nairobi; tel. 742161.

Geographical Society of Kenya, P.O. Box 41887, Nairobi.

Museum Society of Kenya, P.O. Box 40658, Nairobi; tel. 742131/2/3/4.

Index

An asterisk (*) next to a page number indicates a map reference. For index to Practical Information, see inside front cover.

127

SAFARI ROUNDUP

☐ Oryx ☐ Impala ☐ Eland ☐ Gerenuk

☐ Thomson's Gazelle ☐ Wildebeest ☐ Bongo ☐ Buffalo

☐ Greater Kudu ☐ Sable Antelope ☐ Dik-Dik ☐ Coke's Hartebeest

☐ Lizard ☐ Gecko ☐ Boomslang ☐ Leopard Tortoise

☐ Butterfly ☐ Termite ☐ Safari Ant ☐ Centipede

 ☐ Nile Crocodile   ☐ Bush Pig   ☐ Giant Forest Hog   ☐ Hippopotamus

"Udaipur ... must lie, I think, within a magic circle, for it is a place of utter enchantment ... it seemed as if with every step we were being drawn into another world, a world imagined in an oriental fairy tale."

Roderick Cameron

A bagpipe procession at Bikaner, with the old fort in the background.

The Rajput and the British shared a common interest: the *shikar,* or hunt. Tiger shooting became an obsession from the early 19th century.

EVERYMAN GUIDES
PUBLISHED BY DAVID CAMPBELL PUBLISHERS LTD, LONDON

RAJASTHAN – ISBN 1-85715-887-3

© *1996 David Campbell Publishers Ltd, London*
© *1996 Editions Nouveaux-Loisirs, a subsidiary of Gallimard, Paris*

NUMEROUS SPECIALISTS AND ACADEMICS
HAVE CONTRIBUTED TO THIS GUIDE:
WE WOULD LIKE TO GIVE SPECIAL THANKS TO:
ASOK KUMAR DAS, KAILASH SANKHALA, AMAN
NATH AND DIVYABHANUSINH CHAVDA FOR
REVIEWING THE VARIOUS SECTIONS OF THE
GUIDE AND TO NADIA CORNELIS FOR
EDITORIAL ASSISTANCE.

RAJASTHAN:
EDITORS: Vivien Crump, Irene Toh
PICTURE RESEARCH: Umaima Mulla-
Feroze, John Falconer
NATURE: Kuldeep Bhan, M.K. Ranjitsinh,
Kailash Sankhala
HISTORY: Anjula Bedi, Asok Kumar Das
ARTS AND TRADITIONS: Anjula Bedi,
Asok Kumar Das, Sharada Dwivedi,
Tripti Pandey
ARCHITECTURE: Rahul Mehrotra
RAJASTHAN AS SEEN BY PAINTERS:
Asok Kumar Das
RAJASTHAN AS SEEN BY WRITERS:
Sharada Swivedi
ITINERARIES: Anvar Alikhan
TEXTILE MOTIFS: Asok Kumar Das
THE TIGER – TOWARD CONSERVATION:
Sherree Desai, Kailash Shankhala
WALL PAINTINGS OF SHEKHAVATI:
Aman Nath

WEAPONRY: Anvar Alikhan
CAMEL CORPS: Anjula Bedi
SCULPTURES OF OSIYAN, RANAKPUR AND
DILWARA: Saryu Doshi
FOLK ART: Anjula Bedi
THE RAJ: Sharada Dwivedi
BIRDS OF BHARATPUR: Kailash Sankhala,
Sherree Desai
DEEG PALACE: Anvar Alikhan
PRACTICAL INFORMATION:
Tripti Pandey, Anar Alikhan, Amita Sarwal
GLOSSARY: Anvar Alikhan

ILLUSTRATIONS:
NATURE: Anuar bin Abdul Rahim, Lim Yew
Cheong, David Rankin
ARCHITECTURE: Kathryn Blomfield
PRACTICAL INFORMATION:
Heather Thompson

PHOTOGRAPHY:
Jagdish Agawal, Joh Burbank, Suresh Cordo,
Chelna Desai, Sally Holkar, Farooq Issa,
Nitin Jhaveri, Samar Singh Jodha,
K.B. Jothady, Benoit Juge, Roy Lewis,
Jimmy Ollia, Avinash Pasricha, Nitin Rai,
Raghu Rai, M.D. Sharma, A.L. Syed,
Daulat Singh Shekhavat, Mahipal Singh,
Kailash Sankhala

EDITED AND TYPESET BY EDITIONS DIDIER MILLET PTE LTD.
PRINTED IN ITALY BY EDITORIALE LIBRARIA.

EVERYMAN GUIDES
79 Berwick Street
London W1V 3PF

Rajasthan

Everyman Guides

CONTENTS

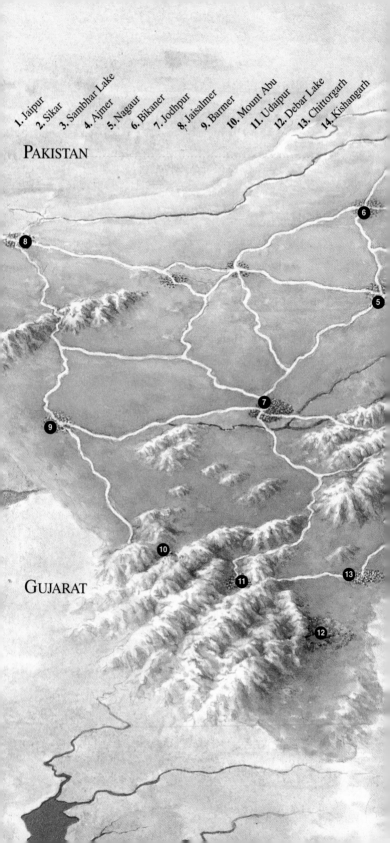

1. Jaipur   2. Sikar   3. Sambhar Lake   4. Ajmer   5. Nagaur   6. Bikaner   7. Jodhpur   8. Jaisalmer   9. Barmer   10. Mount Abu   11. Udaipur   12. Debar Lake   13. Chittorgarh   14. Kishangarh

PAKISTAN

GUJARAT

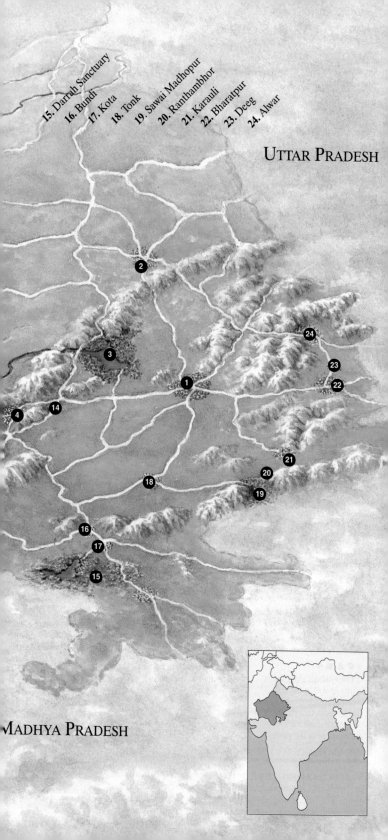

UTTAR PRADESH

15. Darrah Sanctuary
16. Bundi
17. Kota
18. Tonk
19. Sawai Madhopur
20. Ranthambhor
21. Karauli
22. Bharatpur
23. Deeg
24. Alwar

MADHYA PRADESH

How to Use this Guide

The symbols at the top of each page refer to the different parts of the guide.

■ NATURAL ENVIRONMENT
● UNDERSTANDING VENICE
▲ ITINERARIES
◆ PRACTICAL INFORMATION

The itinerary map shows the main points of interest along the way and is intended to help you find your bearings.

The mini-map locates the particu[...] itinerary within the wider area covered by the guide.

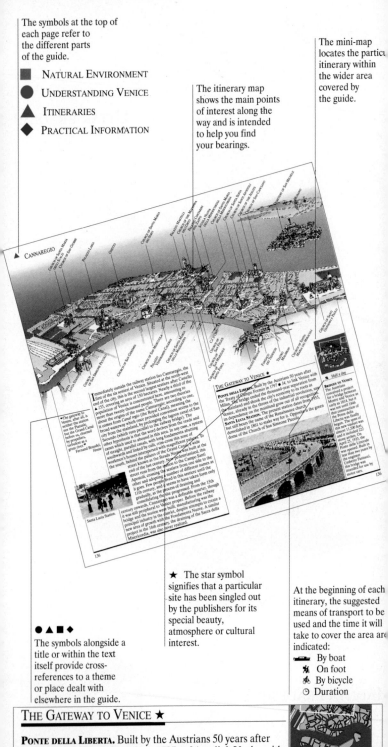

◀ CANNAREGIO

Immediately outside the railway station lies Cannaregio, the first of the six sestieri of Venice. Situated at the north-west end of the city, this is the second largest sestiere after Castello ▲ 155, covering an area of 130 hectares. Nearly a third of the population of Venice is concentrated here, amounting to more than twenty thousand people. There are two theories about the origins of the name Cannaregio, according to one, it comes from Canal regio (the Royal Canal), meaning the broad waterway which once provided convenient access to the city from the mainland, by prolonging the lagoon canal of San Secondo (which runs parallel to the railway bridge). The other hypothesis is that the word derives from the reeds and canes which used to abound in this area. In any case, a system of straight, parallel canals, with long cross-cross rows of workmen's houses interspersed with the magnificent palaces abutting the south, behind the palaces of the Grand Canal, is a wide street known as the Strada Nova. Near the sestiere of the end of the last century. Now decorated at the Campo Santi Apostoli, crossing the sestiere from one side to the other and adopting a number of different names as it goes. Few people lived in this sestiere until the 11th century, and it seems to have taken form only gradually, as the process of draining and consolidating the mainland was gradual. From the 15th century onwards, Cannaregio was a definable quarter, though it was still peripheral to Venice proper. Before the railway bridge and the station were built, manufacturing was the principal industry in this district, despite attempts to create a new area of growth with the Fondamenta Nuove. A similar project in the 16th century, the draining of the Sacca della Misericordia, was also never realized.

The gateway to Venice, after all, is neither the station nor the Piazzale Roma, but the Grand Canal before us, churned so often as a great river.
Fernand Braudel

Santa Lucia Station.

136

THE GATEWAY TO VENICE ★

PONTE DELLA LIBERTA. Built by the Austrians 50 years after the Treaty of Campo Formio in 1797 ● 34, to link Venice with Milan. The bridge ended the thousand-year separation from the mainland and shook the city's economy to its roots as Venice, already in the throes of the industrial revolution, saw its dependence on the mainland grow out of all recognition. **SANTA LUCIA STATION.** The present station dates from 1955, but still bears the name of the Renaissance church demolished in 1861 to make way for it. Opposite is the green dome of the Church of San Simeone Piccolo.

★ Half a day

BRIDGES TO VENICE
The Austrians conceived a project for a viaduct between Mestre and Venice early as 1814, but it was not until 1846 that connection of Ponte della Liberta was finally begun. The span of the new 11,500 feet long structure, with its 222 stone arches, was opened [...] April 25, 1933, the Ponte della Liberta was then two years [...] the engineers' [...] this bridge was [...] intended for use [...] motor cars.

136

★ The star symbol signifies that a particular site has been singled out by the publishers for its special beauty, atmosphere or cultural interest.

● ▲ ■ ◆
The symbols alongside a title or within the text itself provide cross-references to a theme or place dealt with elsewhere in the guide.

At the beginning of each itinerary, the suggested means of transport to be used and the time it will take to cover the area are indicated:
🚣 By boat
🚶 On foot
🚲 By bicycle
🕐 Duration

THE GATEWAY TO VENICE ★

PONTE DELLA LIBERTA. Built by the Austrians 50 years after the Treaty of Campo Formio in 1797 ● 34, to link Venice with Milan. The bridge ended the thousand-year separation from the mainland and shook the city's economy to its roots as Venice, already in the throes of the industrial revolution, saw

🚶 Half a day

BRIDGES TO VENICE

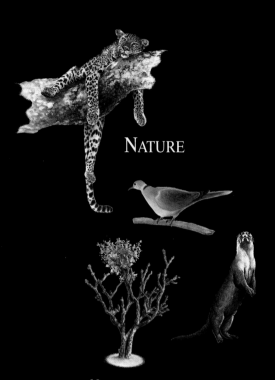

NATURE

Human activity, including an ever-increasing population and excessive grazing by livestock, has had a severe impact on the natural ecosystems in Rajasthan. The lack of rainfall, poor vegetation, low soil fertility, susceptibility to erosion, and a

series of droughts have also left their mark on this region. Yet fascinating vestiges remain of the original topography and natural ecosystems. While the claim that Rajasthan's desert is entirely man-made is an exaggeration, the role of the human population in accentuating aridity cannot be denied.

LUNI RIVER

1. SANDY ARID PLAINS (MARUSTHALI) This region, also known as 'Thar Desert', comprises sand dunes interspersed with silt-covered valleys. It extends to about 40,000 square miles.

2. SEMI-ARID PLAINS These stretch from Shekhavati in the north to the Godawar plain, north of Mount Abu in the south, with the Aravallis to the east. Seasonal water courses, such as the Sukri-Jawai, originating in the Aravallis, flow through it. The plains, sparsely covered with trees and bushes, are studded with rocky outcrops and sand hills called *bhits*.

3. ARAVALLI RANGE The most distinctive and ancient mountain chain of peninsular India, the Aravallis mark the site of one of the oldest geological formations in the world. Heavily eroded and with exposed outcrops of slate rock and granite, it has summits reaching 4950 feet above sea level. It bisects the State of Rajasthan.

4. EASTERN PLAINS Sloping gradually eastward from the Aravallis, the plateau consists of undulating, once forested hills, especially in southern Mewar around the Bagad region of Udaipur, where there is more rainfall.

5. CHAMBAL VALLEY The middle portions of the Chambal, the largest river and most reliable water source of Rajasthan, are marked by heavily eroded valleys and ravines. The region is a low plateau, cut by the Vindhya range, and covered with shallow soil, exposed rock, and coarse grasses in the upper reaches.

SECTION OF DESERT

STABILIZED SAND DUNES
Some sand dunes have been stabilized by *Calligonum polygonoides* shrubs and clumps of *Panicum turgidum*.

LONGITUDINAL SAND DUNES
The dunes, often parallel, usually run in a northeast to southwest direction, corresponding to the prevailing monsoon and winter wind directions.

WOOD FOSSILS
During the Jurassic age some 180 million years ago, the western region of Rajasthan was covered by forest. Now much of the region is desert. The forest was fossilized in geological times and buried by soil and sand in recent times. Wind and water erosion has exposed colorful wood fossils of large conifer trees. These fossils are scattered over a large area 11 miles south of Jaisalmer.

SHELL FOSSILS
Shell fossils are the remnants of the marine life which existed in the desert region of Jaisalmer some 2000 million years ago.

ARAVALLI RANGE

MOUNT ABU
The Abu massif in the southwestern corner of Rajasthan rises from the plains, a rocky outcrop separated from the Aravalli range, forming a distinctive microcosm of its own. Its highest point, Gurushikhar peak, reaches 5693 feet above sea level.

GEOLOGY

Rajasthan is rich in mineral deposits, both metallic ones, such as copper, zinc, lead, and tungsten, and non-metallic ones, such as limestone, super lime, marble, dolomite, soapstone, sandstone, gypsum, granite, and mica, as well as carbonaceous fuel minerals such as lignite. Explorations are in progress for fossil oil since natural gas has already been found in the desert region. Precious stones such as diamonds and emeralds are also being prospected in Ajmer district. Mining of copper, zinc, and lead, and quarrying of sandstone, limestone, marble, mica, silica, and gypsum are some of the principal economic activities of the state.

DISTRIBUTION OF MINERALS

▲ Asbestos
▲ Barytes
▲ Beryllium
▲ Clay
▲ Copper
▲ Emerald
▲ Feldspar
▲ Garnet
▲ Gypsum
▲ Iron
▲ Kyanite
▲ Lead and zinc
▲ Lignite
▲ Limestone
  Manganese
  Sandstone

▲ Rock phosphate
▲ Marble
▲ Mica
▲ Salt
▲ Silica sand and quartz
▲ Steatite
▲ Tungsten
▲ Vermiculite
▲ Granite

4. COPPER
Copper pyrite is found in hydrothermal veins in the Delhi series of rocks in Khetri (Jhunjhunu district) and Khoh Dariba in Alwar. A large smelting plant has been established at Khetri.

ROCK STRATIFICATIONS

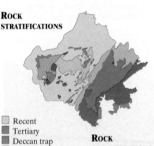

Recent
Tertiary
Deccan trap
Triassic-cretaceous
Permo-carboniferous
Marwar supergroup
Malani igneous suite
Delhi supergroup
Aravalli supergroup
Bhilwara supergroup
Vindhyan supergroup

SANDSTONE
Sandstone, shown in situ above, is largely found in the Vindhyan supergroup in Dholpur and Karauli and in the Marwar supergroup of rocks in Jodhpur and Nagaur districts. It is used exclusively for building construction.

ROCK STRATIFICATIONS
The geology of Rajasthan represents all major rock stratifications, from some of the oldest fragments of the earth's crust of the

Bhilwara supergroup formed some 2500 million years ago to the sedimentary Delhi series, Vindhyan, Marwar super and Deccan trap to the recent sand-dune formations.

7.

7. ROCK PHOSPHATE
Rock phosphate deposits have been discovered in the Aravalli supergroup of rocks and in Jaisalmer, Jaipur, and Banswara. It is a direct fertilizer, ideal for tea gardens where the climate is damp.

Left to right: Granite rock field; marble ready for cutting; mini cement plant.

1. LIMESTONE
Limestone is found extensively in the Vindhyan supergroup deposits in Alwar, Sawai Madhopur, Chittorgarh, and Jaisalmer. It is used for cement manufacture. A high-quality limestone discovered at Jaisalmer is used in the steel industry.

2. IRON
Iron ore was known to early Iron Age civilization. It is found in Jaipur and in small deposits in Udaipur.

3. PINK QUARTZ
Quartz varies in color according to the iron compound present in the rock. It is used for the manufacture of ceramic wares and optical instruments. Quartz is found in Alwar, Ajmer, and Sirohi.

5. MICA
Mica is a group of minerals (silicates of aluminium) which is capable of splitting in thin laminas. The commonest form, called muscovite, is used as insulating material in electric appliances and fillers in rubber tyres. Mica is found in Bhilwara, Rajsamand, and Jaipur.

6. PINK GRANITE
Granite is predominantly a crystalized homogenous rock of quartz and feldspar with subordinate quantities of other minerals such as mica and hornblende. Granitic rock occurs in the Delhi series in Alwar and Aravalli formations in Pali, Sirohi, Ajmer, Jalore, Barmer, Bhilwara, and Banswara.

9. MARBLE
Marble is a metamorphosed form of limestone rock. The marble of Makrana made the famous Taj Mahal. Marble is also quarried in Bundi, Ajmer, Nagaur, Rajgarh and Sirohi. Presence of iron salts creates different colors in the marble.

10. LEAD ORE
Lead is found in Jawar, Dariba, and the Rajpura-Agucha mines in the Aravalli series of rocks in Udaipur.

8. GARNET
Garnet, a semi-precious stone, is found in high-grade pellet-like sediments of pre-Aravalli age in Udaipur and Tonk. It is transparent and colored red, lilac, or pink.

19

■ TRADITIONAL AGRICULTURE

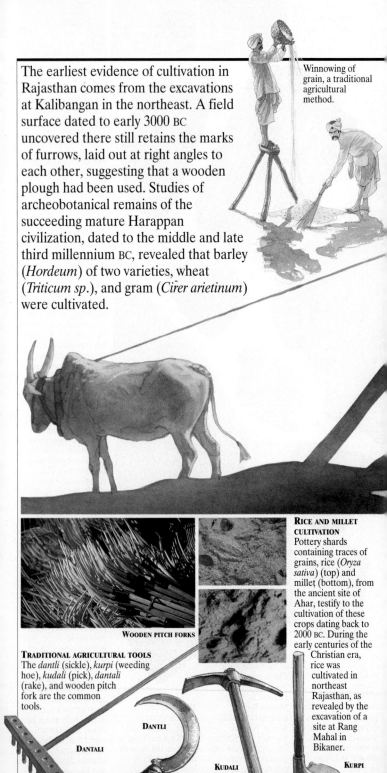

The earliest evidence of cultivation in Rajasthan comes from the excavations at Kalibangan in the northeast. A field surface dated to early 3000 BC uncovered there still retains the marks of furrows, laid out at right angles to each other, suggesting that a wooden plough had been used. Studies of archeobotanical remains of the succeeding mature Harappan civilization, dated to the middle and late third millennium BC, revealed that barley (*Hordeum*) of two varieties, wheat (*Triticum sp.*), and gram (*Cirer arietinum*) were cultivated.

Winnowing of grain, a traditional agricultural method.

WOODEN PITCH FORKS

TRADITIONAL AGRICULTURAL TOOLS
The *dantli* (sickle), *kurpi* (weeding hoe), *kudali* (pick), *dantali* (rake), and wooden pitch fork are the common tools.

DANTALI

DANTLI

KUDALI

KURPI

RICE AND MILLET CULTIVATION
Pottery shards containing traces of grains, rice (*Oryza sativa*) (top) and millet (bottom), from the ancient site of Ahar, testify to the cultivation of these crops dating back to 2000 BC. During the early centuries of the Christian era, rice was cultivated in northeast Rajasthan, as revealed by the excavation of a site at Rang Mahal in Bikaner.

Ploughing with camels (left); monsoon ploughing (right).

Irrigation using a mote (the sewn-up skin of a large domestic animal) was once a common method in the arid western region.

CROSSED FURROWS
The pattern of the crossed furrows (right), closely spaced in one direction and more widely spaced in the other, is still used for planting two crops simultaneously.

TRADITIONAL IRRIGATION METHODS
The Pratapgarh inscription of AD 946 records the various methods of irrigation prevalent at that time. The main devices include a leather bucket, called a *koshavahaka*, pitchers, and the Persian wheel ■ *23*. In the 15th century, Babur also wrote about the use of a leather bucket tied with a length of rope which passed over a roller, with the other end of the rope being tied to a bullock. This simple irrigation method is still practiced today.

■ AGRICULTURE AND IRRIGATION

Rajasthan's economy is mainly agriculture-based. About 80 percent of the population lives in rural areas and is dependent on farming. Cereal crops such as *bajra*, *juar*, wheat, and barley cover the largest cultivated area. About 30 percent of the total cultivated area is irrigated. The Indira Gandhi (or Rajasthan) canal provides irrigation to the arid western districts of Bikaner and Jaisalmer. Ganganagar district is irrigated with water from the Ganga canal in the Punjab ▲ *194*. Irrigation projects have also developed on the Chambal and Luni rivers. The western region grows predominantly *kharif* (monsoon) crops, while the eastern belt, which has better rains and soil, grows both *kharif* and *rabi* (winter) crops. The latter is grown under rain-fed farming conditions or in irrigated areas.

KEY	
1. Juar	
2. Maize	
3. Bajra	
4. Cotton	
5. Wheat	
6. Gram	
7. Sesame	
8. Groundnut	

BAJRA
Bajra
(*Pennisetum typhoideum*) is consumed by the rural poor, particularly the nomads. Rajasthan is the largest producer of *bajra* in India.

JUAR
Juar (*Sorghum vulgare*) is an important pulse crop during the monsoon.

BARLEY
Barley (*Hordeum vulgare*) is the second largest crop in Rajasthan.

SESAME
Rajasthan provides the second highest quantum of sesame (*Sesamum indicum*) in India. One of its common uses is as an ingredient in sweetmeats.

GRAM
Gram (*Cicer arietinum*) (right) is another major pulse crop grown in *rabi*.

MAIZE
Maize (*Zea mays*) is a staple crop for the Bhil tribes in the Aravallis. In northern Rajasthan, maize is a delicacy eaten with butter and the green leaf of the mustard plant.

WHEAT
Wheat (*Triticum sp.*) is cultivated on irrigated land.

GROUNDNUT
Groundnut is a major *kharif* oilseed crop.

COTTON
Cotton (*Gossypium sp.*), used to make the famous Rajasthani textiles, is a major cash crop.

Sugarcane, sold in the market (right), is grown in irrigated areas, mostly in the eastern region.

SIDE VIEW

Drive arm

The cogs in the main drive wheel interlock with the cogs of the small shaft wheel to set the latter in motion.

Main lifting wheel

Small shaft wheel

Main drive wheel

Drive arm

Bullocks yoked to the long arm turn the main wheel.

Drive shaft

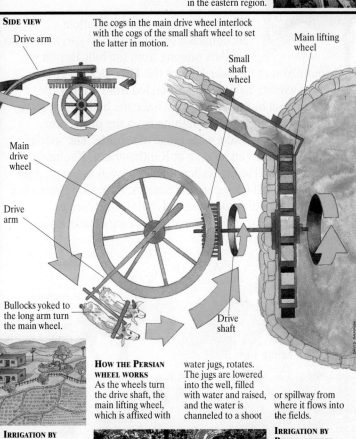

HOW THE PERSIAN WHEEL WORKS
As the wheels turn the drive shaft, the main lifting wheel, which is affixed with water jugs, rotates. The jugs are lowered into the well, filled with water and raised, and the water is channeled to a shoot or spillway from where it flows into the fields.

IRRIGATION BY ELECTRIC PUMP
Electricity is supplied to about 80 percent of the villages, energizing pumps and tube wells.

WOODEN PLOUGH
Traditionally, the plough is the most vital agricultural implement.

IRRIGATION BY PERSIAN WHEEL
The Persian wheel method is popular in the central and eastern region where the ground water table is comparatively high. One Persian wheel can irrigate up to one hectare of land ▲ 258.

The plough consists of a *hal,* or wooden boot, attached to an upright shaft, a draught pole projecting in the front, a *jori* or neck-yoke for the bullocks, and the *jot,* or collar strap.

23

■ FAUNA

COMMON LANGUR
The common langur, with its shiny, white-gray coat, jet black face, and lanky limbs with long fingers, is a leaf-eating monkey.

The nature reserves of Rajasthan encompass a broad biological spectrum, with habitats ranging from the hilly terrain of Mount Abu to the heartland of the Thar Desert. These special wildlife habitats are protected from human depredation by law. Some were once the hunting preserves of the maharajas and, benefiting from the protection afforded, now hold a wide range of wildlife. The species featured here can be seen at Ranthambhor, Keoladeo Ghana, and Desert National Park, as well as sanctuaries such as Gajner, Tal Chappar, and Sariska. Keoladeo Ghana is a World Heritage site recognized by UNESCO. Reserves such as Kumbhalgarh and Sitamata are being developed as national parks.

SAMBAR
The *sambar,* with its magnificent antlers, is the largest deer of India. When danger is sensed, it gives a high-pitched, metallic, trumpet-like call. If repeated, the call confirms the presence of a predator.

CHINKARA
The *chinkara* lives in small family herds in dry, deciduous, bracken, rocky, open country, as well as in sandy deserts.

Punjab

Pakistan

RAJASTHAN

Gujarat

Madhya
Pradesh

SLOTH BEAR

The sloth bear is a clumsy-looking, shaggy animal which lives in deciduous forests. It feeds on fruit and honey, but its favorite food is termites which it obtains by breaking into termite mounds using its strong claws. Sloth bears are nocturnal and do not hibernate, although they may shelter and sleep in secluded dens.

PROTECTED AREAS

1. Desert
2. Wood Fossil Park
3. Kanodiawala Rann
4. Gajner
5. Tal Chappar
6. Sariska
7. Keoladeo Ghana
8. Baretha
9. Vanvihar
10. Ranthambhor
11. Chambal
12. Ramgarh
13. Darrah
14. Jawahar Sagar
15. Sitamata
16. Jaisamand
17. Mount Abu
18. Kumbhalgarh
19. Doli-Dhawa

ROCK PYTHON

The rock python is a large, sluggish reptile which preys on small mammals by strangling them. It swallows its prey in one piece.

MARSH CROCODILE

The Indian marsh crocodile, or mugger, is the largest aquatic predator of rivers and lakes in India. It feeds on insects, frogs, and fish, while adults prey on small mammals, birds, snakes and even deer and buffalo. The female lays forty to fifty eggs, which are buried in the sandbank to be hatched by the sun's heat.

FOUR-HORNED ANTELOPE

The four-horned antelope is a solitary animal which lives in hilly regions with tall grass. It walks with graceful yet jerky movements.

CHITAL

In color, design and shape, the *chital* is the most handsome deer of India. It lives in forests interspersed with patchy, open meadows, in herds which swell to a few hundred.

BLACKBUCK

The blackbuck, with its long, pointed, spiraling horn, is an impressive creature. Males live in open, grassy wastelands in the company of ten to fifteen hornless female bucks. The bucks fight fierce territorial battles and are often seen chasing their errant females to bring them back to their harem.

JACKAL

The jackal, with its conspicuous evening howling chorus, was once a common scavenger of the forests and villages. It has been heavily hunted for its skin.

NILGAI

The *nilgai* is a robust antelope which lives in open country. The bull is ashy black with spiky, forward-turned horns. The female is fawn-colored. The *nilgai* moves in an ungainly fashion.

SMOOTH INDIAN OTTER

The smooth Indian otter, which is exclusively a fish predator, is the most common otter in India although its habitat has become increasingly threatened in recent years.

25

For decades, over a hundred tigers were shot in the annual hunts of the maharajas of Rajasthan. Other hunts, such as the unleashing of cheetahs on blackbucks, and caracals on game birds, were also a princely pastime ▲ *176*. Even Akbar hunted antelopes with his favored cheetah in the open wastelands of Sanganer near Jaipur. But such scenes are now a thing of the past. Overhunting for trade and the loss and destruction of natural habitats constitute the main threats to wildlife. A total ban on hunting and the emergence of national parks and sanctuaries are helping to protect some of the threatened species.

LEOPARD
The leopard has a great talent for survival, feeding on deer, antelopes, and other small mammals, as well as birds. It lives in thick forests and open arid country, including rocky outcrops. Overhunting for its spotted, light golden colored coat has made it an endangered species.

STRIPED HYENA
The striped hyena feeds on carrion since its body structure is not adapted for the speed and agility needed for killing fast-running animals except when two or more corner a helpless antelope or deer.

WOLF
The wolf preys on antelopes, deer, rabbits, and livestock. It lives in pairs or small family packs in open wastelands and mountains.

DESERT FOX
The desert fox preys on gerbils, lizards, birds, and insects and, when in season, on desert fruits. It breeds in spring, commonly raising two to four pups.

SIBERIAN CRANE
The Siberian crane breeds in south Siberia and arrives at the marshes of Bharatpur for feeding during the winter months ▲ *307*. It has become endangered probably as a result of hunting and the disappearance of wetlands. No birds arrived at Keoladeo Ghana in 1994.

GREAT INDIAN BUSTARD
The Great Indian Bustard is the state bird of Rajasthan. It feeds on lizards, locusts, beetles, and small birds. These birds make a nest in which a single egg is laid. The eggs are often destroyed by cattle.

CARACAL
The caracal is an agile cat of the open jungle. It feeds on small mammals and birds.

TIGER
The tiger, one of the most magnificent animals of India, has long fascinated people with its awesome power and beautifully patterned coat. Adult tigers are solitary animals. Male and female tigers remain together only for a short period when the latter is in heat. Two to three cubs are born, but on average just one survives. Cubs remain with their mother for two years, by which time they have learned to fend for themselves.

GHARIAL
The long, thin snout of the gharial (right) is designed for catching fish such as catfish and tilapia. The females bury their eggs in a deep nest dug in a sandy bank above the flood level; as many as sixty eggs may be laid. The female guards the nest against predators.

27

■ BIRDS

The metallic blue neck and open crest add grace to the peacock, India's national bird.

SARUS CRANE
In summer, they gather in their hundreds at drying lakes ▲ *307*.

The sub-tropical forests of Mount Abu, the dry, deciduous, hilly forests of the Aravallis, and the arid, open grasslands of the Thar Desert, with its dry land farming, create ideal habitats for birds and support a wide range of the birdlife of Rajasthan. But the feature which makes the State unique is its location on the bird-migration flyways: not only for water birds flying from Siberia to the tropical and sub-tropical wetlands, but also for the terrestrial houbaras, sandgrouse, larks and cranes, and their predators, the eagles, falcons, and hawks in the desert lands. Rajasthan is also on the flight path of birds flying from the south to the Himalayas.

PEACOCK
The peacock's elaborate train, with its colorful moons and crescents, allures peahens to mate during the monsoon when many mating calls can be heard.

RING DOVE
The ring dove, a common bird, is a symbol of peace and charity. It feeds on small grains and constructs a simple nest in which two eggs are laid. These are incubated alternately by both parents.

COMMON SANDGROUSE
The common sandgrouse flies for miles every morning to congregate noisily in the hundreds at waterholes to drink.

GRAY PARTRIDGE
The gray partridge is a prized bird of open scrub jungles. Its elegant walk and high-pitched challenging calls make it conspicuous. It nests on the ground and raises a covey of eight to ten chicks.

BLOSSOM-HEADED PARAKEET
It lives in small flocks feeding on shoots, flowers, and fruits.

PHEASANT-TAILED JACANA
The pheasant-tailed jacana is a wetland species. The male develops a beautiful tail as a breeding plumage. The female constructs a well-anchored floating nest and lays four eggs which are hatched by the male.

KING VULTURE
King vultures survive on carrion. They nest on the ledges of steep escarpments or the upper branches of tall trees. Their red heads and wattles give them a regal appearance. They live in pairs.

CRESTED SERPENT EAGLE
The crested serpent eagle is a bird of open forests with well-distributed waterholes. Perched on a tree, the eagle keeps a watchful eye open for game birds coming to drink, as well as snakes that emerge from ponds in search of rodents and lizards.

SMALL GREEN BEE-EATER
The small green bee-eater feeds on bees and insects.

FLAMINGO
The flamingo is a mysterious bird; its nesting places are located in inaccessible, brackish marshlands. One such site is the Rann of Kachchh, where they breed. The birds live in large flocks and feed by sifting tiny plankton from the brackish waters. Their walk, flight, and landings are delightfully graceful.

STONE CURLEW
The stone curlew is a curious-looking bird, with its round, large eyes and its body perched on long legs. Living on open ground, it relies on the subtle colors of its plumage for camouflage against predators. It spends much time surveying the ground before returning to its nest.

DEMOISELLE CRANE
The demoiselle crane, or *kurja*, migrates to Rajasthan in large flocks in late September, where it breeds. The flocks scatter in search of drying lakes, and ripening gram and groundnut fields for feeding.

◼ FLORA

ANWAL
The bark of *anwal* (*Cassia auriculata*), a perennial shrub, is a source of tanning material.

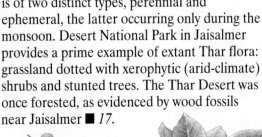

The natural vegetation of Rajasthan is of two distinct types, perennial and ephemeral, the latter occurring only during the monsoon. Desert National Park in Jaisalmer provides a prime example of extant Thar flora: grassland dotted with xerophytic (arid-climate) shrubs and stunted trees. The Thar Desert was once forested, as evidenced by wood fossils near Jaisalmer ◼ *17*.

KHEJRI
Khejri (*Prosopis cineraria*) is an all-purpose tree held sacred by the Vishnoi community ▲ *202*. Its pods are eaten as vegetables, while its leaves provide valuable fodder. During famines, even its bark is consumed.

AKARO
Akaro (*Calotropis procera*), a commonly found plant, is widely used: its fibres for making rope; its latex and root-bark for medicine; and the soft floss from its seeds for stuffing pillows.

BABUL
Babul (*Acacia nilotica*), which flourishes in valleys and places where the soil is deep, is found particularly in the Chambal Valley.

ROOT SYSTEM
Perennial xerophytic plants have deep tap roots. The roots of a 20-foot high *khejri* tree may penetrate 100 feet beneath the top sandy soil to find water.

TUMBO
Tumbo (*Citrullus colocynthis*) (above) is a perennial creeping plant. Its fruit is used in indigenous medicines and as a purgative.

BORDI
Bordi (*Zizypus nummularia*) has delicious, red berries and leaves that are relished by camels and goats. Its dried twigs are used with the aromatic roots of the *khas* grass (*Vetiveria zizanioides*) for making screens.

KER
Ker (*Capparis decidua*) is commonly found on rock, gravel and sandy plains. Its unripe fruit is eaten as pickles and vegetables. The plant flowers twice a year.

DESERT GRASS
Perennial grasses such as *Eragrostis plumosa* not only help bind soil and dunes together, but are also a good source of fodder for livestock.

HISTORY

Sculpture from Kalibangan (left) and Harappan seal (right).

2500 BC TO EARLY RAJPUTS

On the northwestern limits of India lies Rajasthan. The name literally means the "Land of Kings (rajas)". Since a large part of the State is covered by the arid and desolate Thar Desert, its very inhospitality had bred a race of tough and brave warriors, the Rajputs. The land fostered independent kingdoms and also attracted enterprising merchants.

2500 BC – HARAPPAN CIVILIZATION. In 1965 archeologists discovered the site of Kalibangan in the Ganganagar district of Rajasthan, just 100 miles from the famous site of Harappa. Kalibangan is located on the left bank of the now dry river, Ghaggar. The excavations at Kalibangan established a link with the Harappan era which flourished between 2500 and 1500 BC and was part of the Indus Valley Civilization, which had been traced back to 6000 BC. Harappa represented the zenith of the Bronze Age and was the high watermark of the Indus Civilization. Its emphasis on town planning was a mark of a well-established society.

THE ARYANS. When the Indus Valley Civilization was dying out, a new group of migrants, the Aryans, moved from an area in Central Asia through Iran into the Indian subcontinent. With them, they brought a new religion, the Vedic religion, based on their holy books, the *Vedas* (derived from the word *vid*, which means "to know") ● *44*. The first of these was the *Rig Veda,* believed to have been composed in 3000 BC. The *Vedas* were written in an older form of Sanskrit, the Aryan mother tongue in India. Thus this period, from the coming of the Aryans to around 500 BC, is known as the Vedic Age.

ORIGIN OF THE RAJPUTS. According to orthodox Hindu views, the Rajputs of Rajasthan were the direct descendants of the Kshatriyas or warriors of Vedic India. They were first mentioned in the oldest Hindu stories, the *Puranas,* between the 3rd and 7th centuries BC, as the "solar" or *suryavanshi* – those descended from Rama, the hero of the epic *Ramayana* – and the "lunar" or *chandravanshi,* who claimed descent from Krishna, the hero of the *Mahabharata*. A third clan was the *agnikula* or fire-born, said to have emerged from the ritual fire or *yajna* on the top of the sacred mountain, Mount Abu, in Rajasthan ▲ *269*.

HISTORICAL RECORDS. The conquests by many races have perhaps been responsible for the lack of historical records in India. For the history of

2700 BC
Date of the Indus Valley seals found at Kish.

2500–1500 BC
Indus civilization in India.

1435 BC
Aryan kings in Western Asia.

550–477 BC
Mahavira, the founder of the Jain sect.

Harivamsha Purana manuscript (right). (Below) Colonel Tod at the Mewar court.

Rajasthan we are dependent on the accounts of
foreigners such as Alberuni, an Arab scholar, in the 11th
century, or Ferishta, a Deccanese Muslim scholar, in the 16th
century. Information can be also gleaned from inscriptions,
old coins, sculptures and deeds commemorating the gift of
land, wells, temples, and the like by the ruler to his subjects.
But perhaps the best record of events and descriptions of
kingdoms and battles fought between them is contained in
the *khyats* or historical prose and verses written by the royal
bards, the Charans and the Bhatts ● *54*, who were
patronized by the rulers. The best known of these are
Nainsi, from the court of Jodhpur, and Chand Bardai, who
immortalized the last Hindu ruler of Delhi, Prithviraj
Chauhan. With the advent of the British came Colonel James
Tod, who wrote *Annals and Antiquities of Rajasthan*, which
became one of the sources of Rajasthani history.

THE FIRST RULERS. There is evidence of the Kushanas ruling
western India in AD 40. The Kushanas came from Central
Asia and straddled the Hindu Kush mountains in the north,
establishing their capital at Peshawar on the Great North-
West Road between the Indus and the Khyber Pass. Their
supremacy lasted between the 1st and 3rd centuries AD. The
Aryans settled down to different occupations, which later led
to the creation of the caste system.

RAJPUT STRONGHOLDS. It has been accepted that the Rajputs
were divided into thirty-six races and twenty-one kingdoms.
The leaders were the Sisodias of Mewar (Udaipur), the
Kachwahas of Amber (Jaipur), the Rathors of Marwar
(Jodhpur) and Bikaner, the Haras of Kota and Bundi, the
Bhattis of Jaisalmer and the Chauhans of Ajmer. From
earliest times, the Rajput kings were called upon to play a
difficult role: to defend their faith, to preserve their traditions
and to protect Hindustan from the marauding attacks of the
Muslim invaders. They had to pay a heavy price, for their
lands were frequently ravaged, and their strongholds captured
by the superior Muslim forces. But such was their remarkable
valor and tenacity that they refused to be beaten despite the
odds. The history of Rajasthan is the stuff of legends. The
rajas fought for their honor, while the ranis who sent the men
off to the field urged them to return victorious, or to die
fighting on the battlefield. Suryamal, the
royal bard of Bundi state in the 18th
century, epitomized the valor of
the Rajputs when he
wrote, "The
mother, while
rocking the
cradle, sings
of bravery
and
sacrifice,
preparing
her son for
death on the
battlefield,
rather than
the
dishonour of
retreat."

327 BC
*Alexander enters
India.*

322 BC
*Accession of
Chandragupta
Maurya.*

269 BC
*Coronation of
Ashoka.*

AD 320
*Beginning of Gupta
era.*

AD 500–42
*Hunas rule in
Malwa and
Rajputana.*

Rajput noblemen.

Sun symbol of
the Sisodias.

MEWAR. Of the Rajput states which kept alive the tradition of independence, pride of place undoubtedly belongs to Mewar and the Sisodias, who to this day are acknowledged as the first family in the Rajput hierarchy ▲ 240. The founder of this dynasty was Bappa Rawal, who established the capital city of Chittor in the 8th century AD. Because of the indomitable spirit of the rajas, the conquest of Chittor became a point of prestige for all invaders. It was attacked over the centuries by Alauddin Khilji, Sultan of Delhi, Bahadur Shah, Sultan of Malwa, and even the great Mughal, Akbar. Consequently in AD 1567, Udai Singh had to establish a new capital, Udaipur. The Sisodias produced a line of kings who became legendary heroes – Rana Kumbha, a man of letters who patronized the arts and built the Kirtistambha, or Tower of Fame, and the great fort, Kumbhalgarh ▲ 260; Rana Sanga, who carried the scars of battle, having no less than eighty-four wounds on his body; and Maharana Pratap, who introduced guerilla warfare and refused to bow before the Mughals; he died an uncrowned king ▲ 242.

MARWAR. The Rathors were a proud race that ruled over the states of Bikaner and Jodhpur. The founder, Rao Siyaji, took shelter in the desert of Rajasthan after the destruction of the north Indian kingdom of Kannauj. His descendant, Rao Jodha, established the kingdom of Jodhpur, and Rao Jodha's son Bika ruled the state of Bikaner. In the 16th century, Raja Maldev annexed Bikaner state, exalting Marwar to the first place among Rajput states. When the Mughal emperor Humayun was defeated by the Afghan Sher Shah in 1540, Maldev offered him refuge in Marwar. Sher Shah took revenge and defeated Maldev. Maldev's son, Chandra Sen, succeeded him in 1562, but in 1572 Rai Singh of Bikaner attacked and occupied Marwar, severely wounding Chandra Sen. With the accession of Chandra Sen's brother, Udai Singh, Marwar's struggle against the Muslims and Mughals came to an end, and peace was established. In 1639, Jaswant Singh was the first ruler to be recognized as maharaja by the Mughal emperor, Shah Jahan.

JAISALMER. An oasis in the desert, Jaisalmer was important because it lay on the trade route from Jodhpur to Sind. The Bhattis, who founded the state in the 10th century AD, had been driven there by the pressure of the Arabs, and in 1156 Rao Jaisal founded the fort and city of Jaisalmer. For centuries it was an independent state, until Alauddin Khilji of Delhi captured the fort in 1294 and left it desolate for years. In 1570, the ruler Har Rai submitted to the Mughal

emperor Akbar by giving his daughter in marriage. Consequently, from 1626 to 1702, Jaisalmer became one of the leading Rajput states.

BIKANER. In 1485, Bika, the son of Rao Jodha of Jodhpur, built the fort of Bikaner and three years later founded the

city. When Bika died in 1504, his influence extended to the
borders of Ajmer, Delhi, and southeastern Punjab. There
were frequent forays between the kingdoms of Jodhpur and
Bikaner, which were suspended only with the supremacy of
the Mughals. One of the most influential princes at the
Mughal court was Rai Singh. Under his reign, Bikaner grew
into a prosperous town, and the gigantic fort erected in
1588–92 was one of the most impressive in Rajasthan. Later
Raja Anup Singh (reigned 1674–98) ▲ 199 encouraged art,
science, and literature. Bikaner rose in prominence, along
with Jaipur and Jodhpur.

AMBER. The erstwhile rulers of Amber (Jaipur) belonged to
the Kachwaha clan, which migrated to Rajasthan around
AD 1093. The founder, Duleh Rai, defeated the Mina
tribesmen who had lived in and ruled Amber for centuries.
His son, Kakil Dev, established his kingdom at Amber in
1135. Amber rose to prominence in the 16th century under
Raja Prithviraj, a great statesman and visionary. His son, Raja
Bharmal, thought it wise to ally himself with the Mughals of
Delhi, since Amber lay closer to Delhi than any of the other
Rajput kingdoms. In 1727, Sawai Jai Singh II decided to
establish the new city of Jaipur, which even today is
considered a unique example of town planning ▲ 92. Amber
produced a number of rulers of exceptional abilities,
including, among others, Bhagwan Das, Man Singh ▲ 131,
Sawai Jai Singh II (regarded as one of the most remarkable
men of his age, being an astronomer, mathematician, and
patron of the arts ▲ 131), who raised the house of Amber
from obscurity to prominence.

AJMER. The Chauhans of Ajmer were once a great power in
northern India. Their rule extended to Delhi till AD 1192,
when with the death of their ally, Prithviraj Chauhan, the last
Hindu king of Delhi, they were eventually crushed by
Shihabuddin Ghori in the Battle of Tarain.

BUNDI-KOTA. These two states were known as Haravati, or
the Garden of the Haras, the most important branch of the
Chauhan line. The founder was Rao Dewa, who captured the
area from the Mina tribesmen. The name Kota came from
Koteya, the chief of the Ujala Bhil tribe, who ruled this
kingdom.

BHARATPUR. It is significant that this is the only Jat kingdom
in a part of the country which has known only Rajput
supremacy. Under Raja Ram the Jats were organized
into a predatory power, looting caravans that passed
the road from Delhi to Agra. The Jats were of
peasant stock, and though they did claim descent
from the moon, they were never accepted as
Rajputs and could not intermarry with other
Rajput clans. Historians have observed that
up to the middle of the 18th century there was
no Jat state, only a robber leader whose success
had netted many as partners in plunder. Around
1722 Badan Singh organized these scattered
units and established his supremacy ▲ 300. His
son, Surajmal, raised Jat power to the pinnacle
of its glory. With the murder of Surajmal's son in
1768, Jat power declined. In 1826 the fort was
captured by the British ▲ 301, but the Jats
continued to rule till 1947.

Prithviraj Chauhan
(top) and Sawai Jai
Singh II (bottom).

1497–98
*First voyage of Vasco
da Gama.*

1526
*First battle of Panipat.
Founding of the
Mughal Empire.*

1556
*Death of Humayun.
Enthronement of
Akbar.*

Jat noblemen.

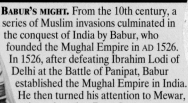

Emperor Akbar.

Rana Sanga.

1562
*Akbar marries a
princess of Amber.*

1567
*Fall of Chittor.
Foundation of
Fathepur Sikri, Agra.*

1600
*English East India
Company founded.*

1602
*Dutch East India
Company founded.*

1615
*Submission of Mewar
to the Mughals.*

1632–53
*Building of the Taj
Mahal.*

Shah Jahan as a
prince.

BABUR'S MIGHT. From the 10th century, a series of Muslim invasions culminated in the conquest of India by Babur, who founded the Mughal Empire in AD 1526. In 1526, after defeating Ibrahim Lodi of Delhi at the Battle of Panipat, Babur established the Mughal Empire in India. He then turned his attention to Mewar, where the ruler, Rana Sanga, presented a threat to his position. With better arms and military tactics, Babur won the Battle of Khanwa in 1527. The conquest of Rajasthan became one that earned prestige for subsequent Mughal rulers.

AKBAR. Babur's son, Humayun, was beset with enemies and had to take refuge at the Marwar court. But his son, Akbar, the greatest emperor of the Mughal dynasty, ascended the throne of Agra in 1556 and extended his hand of friendship to convert his inveterate foes into steadfast friends. His liberal policies and far-sightedness attracted many of the Rajput princes as vassals.

MATRIMONIAL ALLIANCES. The Rajput princes realized the futility of fighting against a superior force, so they cemented their bonds through matrimonial alliances. The first alliance was that of the daughter of Bharmal of Amber with Akbar. His son, Bhagwan Das, gave his daughter Man Bai in marriage to Prince Salim, later to become Emperor Jahangir. Salim also took the Jodhpur princess, Jodha Bai, as his wife. Man Singh, Bhagwan Das' son, became one of Akbar's most trusted generals. Thus, by the time Akbar's grandson, Shah Jahan, was born, the Mughal emperor had three parts of Rajput blood.

PERIOD OF PEACE. It can be said that the golden age of Rajput civilization was closely linked with the destiny of the Mughal Empire. Rajasthan's political and cultural contacts with the rest of India were considerably widened. This encouraged an assimilation of several cultures into the arts and traditions of the Rajput kingdoms, which were already renowned as centers of art and learning. *Karkhanas,* or craft workshops, were started, based on the Mughal model; Mughal miniature paintings aroused interest and Muslim artists came under royal patronage; Mughal buildings influenced Rajput architecture, and even the red sandstone color of the monuments of Agra inspired the "Pink City" of Jaipur. The musician, Behram Khan, from the Mughal court, was invited and established the tradition of *dhrupad* music in the Jaipur *gharana* style. Rajasthan still retains its position as a leader in the fields of arts and crafts, and dance and music, in India.

THE RESISTANCE. The proud ranas of Mewar had singularly refused to bow before the Mughals. In 1572, by the time Maharana Pratap came to the throne, the princes of Amber, Bikaner, Jaisalmer, Sirohi, and Bundi had come into the Mughal orbit. But Maharana Pratap chose to take on Akbar's forces at the Battle of Haldighati in 1576 ▲ *242*. Though he was defeated, he continued guerilla warfare tactics for several years, eventually recovering a large part of his territory.

JAHANGIR. Akbar's son, Jahangir, sent a force under his son, Khurram, to subjugate the indomitable Maharana Pratap's son, Amar Singh. Amar Singh was forced to sign a treaty with the Mughals and for the first time a Mewar rana paid

Haldighati battle scene.

obeisance at the Mughal court.

SHAH JAHAN. When Prince Khurram, later to become Shah Jahan, rebelled against his father, Jahangir, he sought refuge with Amar Singh's son, Karan Singh, at the beautiful palace on Lake Pichola, Jag Mandir ▲ *251*. But when Karan Singh decided to restore Chittorgarh, Shah Jahan, as Emperor, invaded the fort and subverted Karan Singh's plans. Jaswant Singh of Jodhpur served Shah Jahan loyally for twenty years, but the civil war after Shah Jahan's dethronement forced him to join forces with the heir-apparent, Dara, who was finally defeated by another son, Aurangzeb.

AURANGZEB. In 1658, Aurangzeb deposed his father, Shah Jahan, and usurped the throne of Delhi. Initially, the Rajput vassals of the Mughals were loyal to him. But Aurangzeb's anti-Hindu policy and religious fanaticism provoked a violent reaction and once again the Rajputs renewed their conflict with the Emperor of Delhi. Aurangzeb's proposal of marriage to the Princess of Roopnagar was taken as an insult to Rajput womanhood. She appealed to Raj Singh of Mewar, who, displaying true Rajput chivalry, married her to save her honor. From then on, he assumed the leadership of the Rajputs. In 1679, when Aurangzeb escheated the property of Jaswant Singh of Jodhpur and declared Marwar a centrally established territory, Raj Singh gave refuge to Jaswant Singh's wife and restored their son, Ajit Singh, to his rightful position as heir-apparent, bringing the wrath of the Mughals upon himself. The formidable alliance he built was an example to the other Rajput states, who decided to avenge their pride after years of subjugation.

LATER MUGHALS. After Aurangzeb's death in 1707, the Mughal Empire showed signs of disintegration. The time was favorable for the princes of Rajasthan to regain their independence. Ajit Singh of Marwar, Sawai Jai Singh II of Amber, and Amar Singh II of Mewar made a pact in 1708 to protect their territories from the Mughals. And even though peace with the Mughals was made in 1710, in the words of the historian, Satish Chandra, "the gulf with the Rajputs was narrowed but not bridged".

Firman, or order, dated 1605, soliciting Raja Rai Singh of Bikaner's presence at Akbar's sick bed.

1678
Marwar occupied by the Mughals.

1826
Fall of Bharatpur.

Shah Jahan's palace on the island of Jag Mandir.

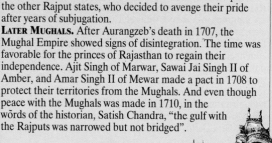

RAJPUTS AND THE BRITISH

The Imperial Assemblage held at the *durbar* in New Delhi in 1877.

1829
Prohibition of sati *by Lord William Bentick, Governor-General of India.*

1853
First railway from Bombay to Thana.

1854
Lord Dalhousie introduces postal and telegraph system.

1857
The Sepoy Mutiny.

1858
British India placed under the direct government of the Crown.

1877
Queen Victoria's Proclamation as Empress of India.

1876
The Royal Titles Act.

1885
Foundation of the Indian National Congress.

A tiger hunt in Rajasthan.

THE TAKEOVER. The East India Company, which started as a trading company, eventually took over as rulers. In 1807 the Company signed a treaty of protection and paramountcy with the Rajput states. Rajputana at that time consisted of eighteen native states and the British district of Ajmer. The five important courts of Udaipur, Jaipur, Jodhpur, Bharatpur, and Kota had British Political Agents representing the Governor-General ▲ *253*, while all the other states were directly under him. In time the influence of the Company over the internal administration of the states increased considerably.

BRITISH PROTECTION. British protection restored peace in Rajasthan. Although the princes were convinced that under no government would their rights be so well-protected, they considered the British a necessary evil. The British introduced education and banned social practices such as *sati* (the burning of a widow on her husband's funeral pyre). Several reforms were made and state debts paid off. It is significant that in the great Uprising in 1857, when armies elsewhere revolted, there was no trouble in the Rajput states.

THE CROWN. The Rajput support of the British was rewarded when, after 1857, India came directly under the Crown, and the princely states were allowed to remain separate entities. The rule of the princes was thus perpetuated. The new policy was to punish the princes for misdeeds by deposing them, but their states could not be annexed to the Empire. One of the main points of resentment, however, was the British right to recognize a ruler's successor. All successions had to be accepted by the Paramount Power and confirmation given through a letter of authority handed over at a special *durbar*.

RAJPUT-ANGLO RELATIONS. The Rajputs believed that they had several traits in common with the British. Their traditions of chivalry and gallantry, their courtesy and large-heartedness toward their adversaries, their love of sports and horses, all combined to build a good social rapport. Despite political differences, the Political Agents enjoyed being guests of the princes, especially during the Christmas sandgrouse shooting season. Several of the rulers were sent to England to study administration and brought back Western influences to their lifestyles and government. After the first Imperial Durbar of 1877 at New Delhi, when Queen Victoria was declared

The Maharaja of Jaipur's first interview with the British Political Agent.

Maharaja Ganga Singh of Bikaner.

Empress of India, several Rajput princes, following the British royal tradition, fashioned coats-of-arms for their states.

WORLD WAR ONE. Until 1916 the states were treated as isolated foreign units and no formal relations, either political or social, between the states, were tolerated. The permission of the Political Agent was necessary even for courtesy calls among the princely states. World War One loosened the shackles of this isolationist policy, since the princes had cooperated wholeheartedly with the British government during the war. A conference of princes was summoned by the Viceroy, Lord Hardinge, in New Delhi in 1916. The rulers of Jaipur and Jodhpur were among those who attended. In 1917, at the Imperial Conference in London to boost the war effort, the Maharaja of Bikaner, Ganga Singh, figured most prominently among the princes. He was elected the first Chancellor of the Chamber of Princes in 1921. The Indian National Congress had appealed to the princes in 1920 to permit a fully responsible government in the states. In 1927 the All India States Peoples' Conference was formed to support popular movements in the Princely States. But ordinary citizens did not respond to this attempt at politicization and the idea of power-sharing or a democratic self-government did not meet with success.

POST-WORLD WAR TWO. With the end of World War Two, the British days in India were numbered. The Indian Independence movement gained momentum under Mahatma Gandhi, and, with it, the idea of democracy. It was clear that the Princely States could not last long. In 1946 the rulers met with the Cabinet Mission which came to India. They were advised to organize themselves into viable units and to deal directly with the new Indian rulers. When, in April 1948, a number of states, led by Bhopal Singh, Maharana of Udaipur, merged to join the Rajasthan Union, Nathudan wrote, "Oh Eklingji [the family deity of Udaipur], why was he crippled in his legs [Maharana Bhopal Singh was paralysed from the waist down ▲ 248]? It should have been in his hands so that he would have been unable to sign."

1914–18
World War I.

1920
Khilafat (Non-Cooperation) Movement.

1930
Civil Disobedience Movement. First Round Table Conference.

1934
Civil Disobedience Movement called off.

1939
World War II begins.

1943
Lord Mountbatten, Supreme Commander of southeast Asia.

INDEPENDENCE

Lord Mountbatten of Burma was appointed Viceroy to facilitate the transfer of power and the partition of the subcontinent into India and Pakistan. At first the princes were assured that they would be part of a federation and retain their states. But a month before the takeover a new State Department was formed under Sardar Vallabh bhai Patel, who urged Mountbatten to persuade the princes to sign an individual Instrument of Accession to either of the new states of India or Pakistan, according to their geographical contiguity. India became independent on August 15, 1947, and the rule of the British and the princes came to an end.

Lord Mountbatten, the last Viceroy of India.

39

DISBANDING OF PRINCELY STATES

1947
India gains independence on 15th August. Pandit Jawahar Lal Nehru, India's first Prime Minister. Dr. Rajendra Prasad, India's first President.

Gayatri Devi of Jaipur (above) was a candidate of the opposition Swatantra Party in 1962. She won a spectacular victory, beating the ruling Congress Party candidate by a margin of 175,000 votes.

1948
Mahatma Gandhi assassinated. Sri C. Rajagopalachari appointed Governor-General.

1949
State of Rajasthan formed.

Bhopal Singh of Udaipur (left) with Ganga Singh of Bikaner. This picture was taken in the 1920's.

ACCESSION. The first to sign the Instrument of Accession was Maharaja Sadul Singh of Bikaner. For many of the princes, a free India was the prime consideration. Others such as the Maharaja of Jodhpur (who is said to have pulled out a pistol in anger) signed because they had no choice. But by March 30, 1949, all the princes of Rajasthan had acceded.

PRIVILEGES. In return for signing over their lands, the princes were allowed certain privileges in the Indian Union. They were given privy purses annually, the percentage being worked out according to revenue collected. The Maharana of Udaipur received the highest, with 2 million rupees. The princes retained the State number plates for cars, were exempted from paying wealth tax and were allowed to import goods without paying customs duty. The Maharaja of Jaipur was named Rajpramukh, equal in status to the governor of a state. Many of the maharajas and maharanis joined politics, prominent among them being Gayatri Devi of Jaipur, who was one of the founders of the Swatantra Party.

DEMOCRACY. In 1951, India had its first general elections to the Lok Sabha, or the Central Parliament, as well as to the State Legislatures. The Congress Party, which had emerged as the symbol of the protest against the British, naturally won the elections in most states, including Rajasthan. It took about eight years for the state of Rajputana to come into its present shape, and it was only on November 1, 1956, that it acquired its new name, Rajasthan. Now India was well and truly on the road to its avowed goal of a socialist society.

WITHDRAWN PRIVILEGES. In 1970, the Prime Minister, Indira Gandhi, dealt a severe blow to the princes by withdrawing the privy purses and canceling their privileges, an act which alienated many of the princes who had joined the Indian Union with great hopes. There is no doubt that their contribution to Indian history was considerable. They had been a symbol of unity between the ruler and the ruled and were, by and large, looked upon by their subjects as their *mai-baap* (mother-father). Once the custodians of Indian tradition and culture, they were now effectively consigned to history. Several of the princes tried to adapt to the changed times and carved out careers for themselves in the armed forces or the foreign service. Sawai Man Singh of Jaipur was given an ambassadorial assignment in Spain. Karni Singh of Bikaner represented India at three Olympic Games.

TOURISM. One of the major contributions of the princes, especially after the withdrawal of their privileges, has been to the tourist industry. Many palaces and hunting lodges have been converted into luxurious hotels, and tourists from all over the world visit Rajasthan to experience for themselves the lost lifestyles of the princes of Rajputana. Some of the world's best hotels are Rambagh Palace, Jaipur, Lake Palace, Udaipur and Umaid Bhavan Palace, Jodhpur. Another great success was the Palace on Wheels, a train which ran between Delhi, Jaipur, Jodhpur and Jaisalmer, with saloons of the former rajas providing the visitor with a taste of mobile luxury. Many of the rulers took great interest in the development of the fabled handicrafts of Rajasthan. They started their own workshops for the production and export of the famous block prints, blue pottery, camel-hide items and other crafts.

Samode Palace near Jaipur, like many Rajput palaces, has been turned into a splendid hotel.

1949
New Constitution of India adopted and signed.

CONTEMPORARY RAJASTHAN

Rajasthan supports a population of 43,880,640 in an area of 342,239 square miles. Once one of the most backward states industrially, it is fast making up for lost time. Jaipur, the capital, is one of the fastest growing cities in India. Though traditionally arts and crafts form the mainstay of the economy, natural resources such as zinc, mica, feldspar and precious stones such as emeralds and garnets are also the State's assets ■ *18*. The glorious history, myriad handicrafts, and fairs and festivals of Rajasthan ensure that its tourism industry flourishes.

AGRICULTURE. With the building of the Rajasthan Canal, also known as the Indira Gandhi Canal, in northwest Rajasthan, the greening of the desert has been extremely successful, especially in Ganganagar and the northeastern part of Bikaner district, which boasts several lucrative farms, orchards and vineyards. Even the Kota-Jhalawar area in the southeastern region, which was mostly stony uplands, has now been successfully irrigated with water from the Chambal River and its tributaries. A state suffering a deficit in food grains in the pre-Independence years, Rajasthan has adopted a pro-agriculture economic policy and produced 110,000 tons of food grains in 1990–1. Several public-sector enterprises provide employment to thousands of people.

INDUSTRY. Cement, fertilizer, fabric and chemical plants and big public-sector companies, Hindustan Salts, Hindustan Zinc, Instrumentation Limited, and Hindustan Copper, are just a few of the many important industrial units. Light industries, including television and precision instruments assembly, are rapidly expanding. The main industrial complexes are located at Jaipur, Kota, Udaipur and Bhilwara. Given Rajasthan's location, constant surveillance against illegal immigrants and smuggling is a high priority in the extensive, sparsely populated border area in the northeast.

1950
India celebrates first Republic Day on 26th January.

1950
Sardar Vallabhbhai Patel, India's "Iron Man", dies.

1964
Death of Pandit Nehru.

1966
Lal Bahadur Shastri, the country's second Prime Minister, dies.

1984
Indira Gandhi assassinated.

1991
Rajiv Gandhi assassinated. Narsimha Rao sworn in as Prime Minister.

● LANGUAGES

HINDI AND RAJASTHANI

While Hindi is the official language of the State, there are important local dialects with regional variations. In fact the word "Rajasthani", often used to identify the local language, has emerged only after the union of the Princely States and represents the dialects spoken in those states. It is only in recent years that the issue of getting Rajasthani constitutionally recognized as the original language has been taken up by a few, but the matter remains unresolved. Since Rajasthani dialects have the same roots as Hindi, it is not difficult for locals to understand Hindi, which is widely used in the big cities of the State. Unlike some states of India, English has not really become the second language of Rajasthan, despite it being taught in the schools.

DIALECTS. The earliest reference to a dialect spoken in Rajasthan is to that of Maru Bhasha.

Today the recognized dialects are Marwari, spoken in Jodhpur, Bikaner, Jaisalmer, and Barmer; Dhundhari, spoken in the entire former Jaipur state, except the Shekhavati region; Mewati, spoken in the Alwar-Bharatpur belt; Mewari, spoken in Mewar, and in particular, the Udaipur-Chittorgarh region; Hadoti, spoken in the former states of Bundi, Kota, and Jhalawar; Vagadi, spoken in the area known as Vagad, covering Dungarpur and Banswara; and Malwi, spoken in the Malwa region, which includes certain areas of Mewar, Kota, and Jhalawar. Interestingly, these dialects also vary every few miles within their particular territory. Marwari is considered the most polite and sweet-sounding dialect.

SCRIPT. The different dialects have no characteristic script and today follow the pattern of the official script of India, known as Devnagari. In earlier times, the impure version of Devnagari was used by the Mahajans or Baniyas. Because of the twisting letters, the script was also known as Muria (meaning "twisting").

It is said that the script was developed by Raja Todarmal, one of the key administrators of the emperor, Akbar.

DINGAL AND PINGAL. Whenever references are made to the classical language of Rajasthan, many tend to name Dingal, as it has an extremely rich poetic heritage. Linguists have identified Dingal and another dialect, Pingal, as having two distinctively poetic styles. While the traditional bards, the Bhatts ● *54* and Charans, used Dingal to compose boastful sagas of heroic deeds, Pingal was used by the saints in their devotional writings. A salient feature of Dingal is its abundant use of adjectives. Pingal is conspicuously influenced by Brij Bhasha, the language of Krishna's land, or Brij Bhumi, which includes some parts of today's eastern Rajasthan.

LITERACY
Literacy rates are low in Rajasthan, with only about 40 percent of the State's population being literate. Female literacy is particularly low. However, in recent years, the State government has made great efforts to improve the situation, and many adult literacy programs have been implemented.

"Talwar ko ghav bhar jat, bat ko ghav kone bhare." (The wound of a sword can heal but one caused by words cannot.)
Rajasthani saying

Mewari script.

42

ARTS AND TRADITIONS

Most Indians are Hindus. Hinduism goes back to a hoary antiquity. Its earliest manifestation is seen in the *Rig Veda*, the oldest religious text in the world, whose principal divinities were, among others, Indra, the king of gods; Varuna, the omnipresent god of wind; Surya, the sun god; Agni, the fire god; and Yama, the lord of the dead. In the course of time, when the Vedic people settled down in northern India and spread out to all parts of the sub-continent, their religious beliefs, philosophy, and pantheon underwent gradual transformation. Besides the five principal cult divinities, Surya, Shiva, Vishnu, Ganesha, and Devi, numerous popular cults, local hero-spirits, and minor deities formed integral parts of the Hindu pantheon. In Rajasthan, the temples are all dedicated to these cult divinities with the sole exception of the Brahma temple on the bank of the Pushkar lake.

INCARNATIONS OF VISHNU
Vishnu, the Preserver, appeared in ten different forms known as *avataras* or incarnations in different *yugas* or ages, to save the world from the imminent danger of total destruction.

CHILD KRISHNA
Krishna is often worshiped as Bala Gopala, the Divine Child, full of childlike innocence, pranks, and playful acts despite his mighty power. Many of these stories are illustrated in the *Bhagavata Purana*, a popular and revered religious text of the Vaishnavas, the followers of Vishnu. In this detail the child Krishna is shown stealing butter from the churning pot of milkmaid Yashoda, his foster mother.

> ## "HE [KRISHNA] IS THE FATHER, MOTHER, FRIEND AND BROTHER TO ME – THERE IS NONE BESIDES."
> MEERA, 16TH-CENTURY SAINT-POETESS OF RAJASTHAN

Bhagavad Gita ("Song Celestial") forms part of the *Mahabharata*, the great Hindu epic. The other well-known epic is the *Ramayana*.

THE TRINITY

The three most important divinities of Hinduism are Brahma the Creator, Vishnu the Preserver, and Mahesvara or Shiva, the Destroyer. With the growing popularity of Shakti, the Mother Goddess, Brahma has been gradually relegated to near-oblivion.

KRISHNA

Krishna, the eighth incarnation of Vishnu, is the most popular god in Rajasthan. Easily identified with youthful exuberance, Krishna is the eternal hero, the symbol of life and joy, and man's communion with god. Apart from the standard daily rituals, the Krishna temples observe Dola-lila, or Holi, in the spring, Janamashtami, or Krishna's birth, in early autumn, Ras-lila ● 64, or the circular dance with the *gopis* (left), at the advent of winter, and Annakut on the day following Diwali.

BRAHMA

The God of Creation, Brahma, is four-headed, facing all four directions, symbolizing his presence everywhere. He is old, the prime godly spirit, and the creator of all gods and living beings. At Pushkar, in the only temple in India dedicated to Brahma ▲ 164, he is worshiped as any other cult god (right).

SHAKTI

Mother goddesses were worshiped in India from the dawn of civilization. They became Shakti, the strength of her male counterpart. The consort of Shiva is Parvati. In her powerful martial form she is Durga, and in her most grim aspect she is conceived as Kali (left). She protects everybody and destroys evil.

SHIVA

Shiva is a great ascetic. He wears his long matted hair in a top knot with the crescent moon, his forehead besmeared with lines of ashes round his all-seeing third eye and his neck garlanded with a black cobra.

MALE AND FEMALE DEITIES

Gods are mostly worshiped with their consorts. Often the male and female traits are combined into one syncretic form known as Ardhanarisvara, half male and half female, a combination of Shiva and his consort Parvati, or Vishnu and his consort Lakshmi. Even Vishnu and Shiva combine as Hari Hara and give birth to an offspring.

45

● HINDUISM IN DAILY LIFE

Gita-Govinda is a 12th-century poetical work in Sanskrit by Jayadeva on the love of Krishna for Radha and the milkmaids

Hindus generally visit a temple to worship a deity. On festive occasions large numbers of devotees throng a temple for a *darshan* (view) of the deity clad in suitable festive attire. Many Hindu homes have their own miniature shrine or *puja* (prayer) room. Besides the family's patron deity, small bronze or wooden images or paintings of other divinities also find a place there. The housewife performs all rituals, such as "waking up" the god or goddess in the morning, bathing and dressing it with appropriate clothing, and decorating it with sandal paste, vermilion, flowers, and perfumes, as well as performing the *arati* (worship) with a lighted lamp, camphor, and a yak-tail fly-whisk or *chauri*.

KARNI MATA
Karni Mata is the local Rajasthani incarnation of the Mother Goddess, worshiped by Hindus and tribal people alike. It is said that Karni Mata blessed Rao Bikaji, the founder of Bikaner, thus becoming the family deity of the State. Karni Mata Temple was built in the 16th century, and rats have always found refuge there ● *55* ▲ *207*. The rats are considered holy and their killing is prohibited.

PUJA
A priest offers prayers to the *Shivalinga*, or the phallic emblem of Shiva, the most popular form in which he is worshiped all over India.

DECORATED IDOLS
Hindu temples are generally dedicated to a principal cult deity whose image is installed in the sanctum chamber. Other cult deities are also present as subsidiary divinities. The image is decked in elaborate costumes and precious ornaments on special occasions. Temple idols are mostly carved from stone or metals such as copper, brass, or bronze, or even silver or gold. The use of wood and ivory is limited to miniature shrines.

NANDI
Nandi, the celestial bull, the mount of Lord Shiva, is an integral adjunct of all Shiva temples.

ELEPHANT GOD
Ganesha is the elephant-headed son of Parvati, the wife of Shiva. He is invoked first in every ritual and as god of prosperity, he is highly revered.

BATHING IN HOLY WATERS
The lake at Pushkar is called Tirtharaj, or the King of all Holy Places. Most Hindu temples have a "holy" tank where one must purify oneself before entering the temple.

PRAYER PARAPHERNALIA
For the daily *puja* or the elaborate temple ritual, a large variety of special vessels, lamps, and bells are used. Their shapes, forms, and sizes vary according to their use as containers of holy water from the River Ganga, or the various offerings of flowers, fruits, sweets, or perfumes. Every day the deity is offered *bhog*, or food, consisting of milk, honey, dry fruit, rice, yoghurt, and ghee.

SHIVA RATRI
The most important festival for the followers of Shiva is Shiva Ratri, observed on the day preceding the new moon in the spring. Devotees observe fasting and offer special *puja* throughout the night.

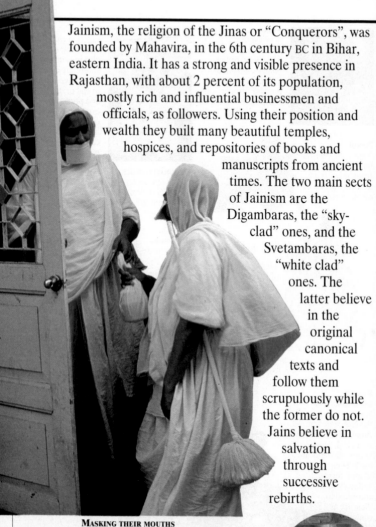

Jainism, the religion of the Jinas or "Conquerors", was founded by Mahavira, in the 6th century BC in Bihar, eastern India. It has a strong and visible presence in Rajasthan, with about 2 percent of its population, mostly rich and influential businessmen and officials, as followers. Using their position and wealth they built many beautiful temples, hospices, and repositories of books and manuscripts from ancient times. The two main sects of Jainism are the Digambaras, the "sky-clad" ones, and the Svetambaras, the "white clad" ones. The latter believe in the original canonical texts and follow them scrupulously while the former do not. Jains believe in salvation through successive rebirths.

MASKING THEIR MOUTHS
The mask worn by Svetambaras is to prevent them from inhaling living things accidentally. This stems from their belief that all life is sacred. *Ahimsa* ("non-violence") forms the cornerstone of Jainism.

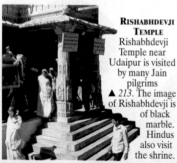

RISHABHDEVJI TEMPLE
Rishabhdevji Temple near Udaipur is visited by many Jain pilgrims ▲ 213. The image of Rishabhdevji is of black marble. Hindus also visit the shrine.

ASCETICISM
Jainism is a highly ascetic religion. Jains, who are strict vegetarians, do penance through fasting. During the holy week of Pajoshan, Jains abstain from leafy vegetables, roots, and unboiled water. They ask for forgiveness on the last day of

penance from any living creature they have wronged.

Jains revere their founder, Mahavira, who was the twenty-fourth and last *tirthankara* (saint), as well as the other *tirthankaras* who achieved salvation before him.

FIVE ESSENTIAL ITEMS

Pious Svetambaras carry all their earthly belongings with them: the *dhoti* (sarong), for a change of clothes which doubles as bedding, the *odhni* (mantle), as a covering and to sit on, the *rajo haran* (broom), to gently dust resting places without harming living creatures, the *patra* (vessel), to accept food given in alms (they do not accept money), and the eight-fold *muhpatti* (a mask) to cover the mouth.

DIGAMBARAS

Digambaras believe that man has to renounce all earthly possessions, including clothes, to achieve salvation. Thus their temples are more stark than the temples of the Svetambaras and their idols (above) unadorned.

PROCESSION

Smaller images from temples are brought home for special prayers with great ceremony and after ritual cleaning of the home. They may not be carried in any modern conveyance, only on foot or in bullock carts. After the prayers, they are returned to the temple. Jain processions are also held to felicitate those who have fasted for Pajoshan, or holy month (August to September). This rigorous fast is undertaken by adults and even children for as long as a month.

JAIN STATUE

The images of the Svetambaras have prominent enameled eyes, sometimes studded with precious gems, and an auspicious *tilak* or vertical mark on the forehead.

MONK

A Jain monk totally renounces all worldly possessions and attains ultimate discipline of mind and body by practicing twenty-two forms of endurance and penance.

JAIN BELIEFS

Jains believe that the practice of austerity will prevent a fresh inflow of *karma* (action) and destroy the undesirable existing *karmas*. The soul then realizes its inherent supreme knowledge, attains unlimited happiness and salvation (Moksha), and becomes the perfect being (Siddha).

Muslims paying obeisance at
the *dargah* at Ajmer.

Rajasthan was repeatedly ransacked
by Muslim invaders from the north
and northwest from the 11th
century. But Islam as a distinct
religious force became prominent
only from the 15th century. The
Mughals under Akbar and his
successors brought large parts of
the State under their direct control
to help the Muslims form integral
parts of its population and culture.
About 8 percent of its population are
Muslims. Muslims believe in one God, Allah, one prophet,
Muhammad, and one holy book, the Qur'an. Of the two
principal sects of Islam, the Shia and Sunni, the majority of
Indian Muslims belong to the latter.

**FLORAL
OFFERINGS**
Muslim
shrines use
only
fragrant
flowers
such as roses
and jasmine,
unlike the
Hindus who
offer all kinds
of flowers,
especially
marigolds.

COVERING THE GRAVE
It is customary to
offer flowers at the
grave of Muslim *pirs*
(saints). In return for
granted
wishes,
devotees
even offer
chaddars, or
sheets of
glittering
satins, to
cover the
grave.

**FASTING AND
PILGRIMAGE**
The month of
Ramazan is the
month when Muslims
observe a fast from
dawn till evening.
Many Muslims go to
Mecca for the Haj
pilgrimage on this
occasion and return
home with the title
"Haji", which they
add to their name, a
coveted distinction.

Arabic inscription at Arhai din ka Jhonpra ▲ 163.

DARGAH KHWAJA SAHIB

Ajmer is the principal center of the order of the Chistiyyas among the mystic Sufis, which has a large following throughout the Indian subcontinent. The most venerated saint Khwaja Mu'in-ud-din Chisti ▲ 162 settled and died here. The *urs*, the death anniversary of the Khwaja, is observed annually by Muslims in the month of Rajab. Thousands of devotees from all over India and neighboring Bangladesh, Pakistan, and Maldives attend.

MUHARRAM

For the Shia Muslims, Muharram is the month of mourning for their assassinated leader Husayn, grandson of the prophet Muhammad. The culmination of Muharram is a mourners' procession through the towns. Picturesque replicas of mausoleums, as tall as two-storied buildings, are carried during the procession.

SUNNI MUSLIMS

The majority of Muslims in Rajasthan are Sunnis, the sect to which the people of Arabia, North Africa, South and Southeast Asia, and Turkey belong. They follow all the basic tenets of Islam such as donating a certain portion of their income as *zakat* (charity), abstaining from liquor, eating only *halal* food, refraining from charging loan interest, and fasting during the month of Ramazan. The Islamic insistence on social homogeneity contrasts with the Indian tradition of rigid stratification according to caste. The tenet of equality, however, is limited to men, and women are not allowed to pray in mosques.

Rajasthan is the home of many tribes, such as the Bhil, Girasia or Garasia, Mangania, Kalbelia, Banjara, Rebari, Meena, and Gujar. Though many of them assimilated well with contemporary Hindu society, some still retain their traditional ways of life, social structure, religious beliefs, and occupations. Like all primitive people everywhere, the Rajasthani tribal people believe in evil spirits, and magical and supernatural phenomena. Local gods and goddesses, heroes and demi-gods, tree and snake spirits, and dead ancestors crowd their pantheon. Being poor, rootless nomads, it would have been impossible for them to survive in the harsh and hostile environment of this desert state without propitiating the evil spirits and malevolent forces that create natural calamities.

SNAKE CULT
The snake cult has an innumerable following among the tribes. The serpent represents the basic dormant energy and the source of all spiritual conquests. Gatodji or Gogaji (the snake god) is believed to have the power to relieve the sufferings of man and his cattle. Most villages have a temple dedicated to the snake god.

TRIBAL PRACTICES
The Bhils believe in witchcraft and resorted to many esoteric practices to get rid of the evil spirits. They – both men and women – tattooed their bodies (right). Now such practices are becoming rare.

SNAKE GOD IN PROCESSION
The Kalbelias, or snake-charmer tribe, carry the snake god in procession on the day of Nag-Panchami. People offer milk to snakes and alms to snake charmers on this day.

HINDU INFLUENCES
The Garasia, a tribe living in areas near Udaipur and Dungarpur, have converted to Hinduism. They worship Hindu gods and revere the cow. They were originally believers in ghosts, spirits, and black magic.

ANCESTOR WORSHIP
Most tribes believe in honoring their ancestors. The icon of a male ancestor (*chira*) is wrapped in white cloth, and that of a female (*mathori*) in red. Large numbers of tribes from southeast Rajasthan and the adjacent regions of Gujarat and Madhya Pradesh assemble at Baneshwar in Dungarpur district to immerse the

remains of their dead ancestors at the confluence of rivers Mahi and Som in February. The fair held there, known as Kumbh Mela, is the largest congregation of tribes in Rajasthan.

JATS
The Jats, an important agricultural community in northern and western Rajasthan, generally worship their own village deities (above) rather than the orthodox Hindu pantheon. Their temples include a number dedicated to deified heroes of the community.

SADHU
A sadhu is a man of peace, a mendicant who has renounced all earthly possessions.

LINGAM AND YONI
The temple of the Rebaris, who are cattle breeders, consists of small stones representing the *lingam*, the phallic symbol, and the *yoni*, the female symbol, placed under a tree, on which a few green petals are strewn occasionally. Water is too scarce to be poured over the shrine.

PABUJI
Pabuji is a warrior saint of the Rathors whose legendary battles are narrated in folk poetry and music by the Bhopas of southwest Rajasthan ● *55*. The painted *Pabuji-ka-phad* depicts the details of this long narrative that is part legend, part fact.

BABA RAM DEO
Baba Ram Deo (below), worshiped by Hindus and Muslims alike, helped the poor and the backward castes. The Meghwars and the Banjara tribes revere him as a saint. Ramdeo-ka-Karni, a fair held every year near Pokharan, between Jodhpur and Jaisalmer ▲ *218*, attracts a large number of devotees, both tribal and non-tribal.

Rajasthani folklore, which developed over the centuries, was closely linked with the nomadic existence of a large part of the population. Moving from court to court and village to village, the professional story-tellers, the Bhopas, Bhatts, Charans, and Bandis, developed their distinctive styles. Rajasthani folklore contains examples of some of the oldest handwritten tales. The common man was exposed to the oral, written, and pictorial versions of folk legends. In a land where heroism, valor, honor, and chivalry were given pride of place, it was but natural that many legends were created around heroic rajas, as well as ranis, whose beauty inspired superlative descriptions.

ITINERANT STORYTELLERS
Among the balladeers of Rajasthan are the Bhopas. The Bhopa, accompanied by his wife, the Bhopi, travels from village to village, narrating the stories of legendary heroes, usually tales of valor, through song and mime. They only use the twelve-stringed instrument, the *ravanhatta*.

> "ONE TALE FROM ANOTHER DIFFERS IN COURSE,
> YET ART IS ONE AND SINGLE ITS SOURCE."
>
> RAJASTHANI RITUAL VERSE

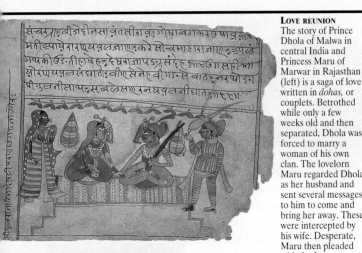

LOVE REUNION
The story of Prince Dhola of Malwa in central India and Princess Maru of Marwar in Rajasthan (left) is a saga of love, written in *dohas*, or couplets. Betrothed while only a few weeks old and then separated, Dhola was forced to marry a woman of his own clan. The lovelorn Maru regarded Dhola as her husband and sent several messages to him to come and bring her away. These were intercepted by his wife. Desperate, Maru then pleaded with the Langas, a community of wandering minstrels, to carry her message in song. Dhola heard their plaintive singing, and recognizing it as a call from Maru, he mounted his horse and, after overcoming several obstacles and defeating his rivals, was reunited with his betrothed.

KARNI MATA
Karni Mata was the daughter of a 16th-century Charan (bard). Married at twenty-seven, she became a *sanyasin* (ascetic) after her marriage was dissolved and decided to devote her life to the service of the poor. She is the Kuldevi (family deity) of the rulers of Bikaner who built the Karni Mata Temple ● 46 ▲ 206.

ROMANTIC WARRIOR
Prithviraj Chauhan (right) ● 35, son of the powerful Someshwar, the ruler of Ajmer, excelled in riding, war strategy, and the use of weapons. Fiercely independent, he refused to acknowledge the supremacy of Raja Jaichand of Kanauj. He is said to have received a message that Jaichand's daughter, Sanyogita, had chosen him as a husband, even though he was her father's enemy, and carried her off from her father's court, as she sat surrounded by suitors from among whom she had to choose a husband. Prithviraj rode through the gates into the court and vanished with Sanyogita on his horse before Jaichand's very eyes.

HONORABLE PABUJI
The story of Pabuji's sacrifice is sung by bards all over Rajasthan with the help of a pictorial scroll depicting his life (left) ● 53, 67. Legend has it that in return for a horse borrowed for his marriage procession, Pabuji gave his word of honor to a Charan woman that he would relinquish everything, even his new bride, if she ever needed his help. She later called upon Pabuji to save her cattle from a thieving neighboring clan, disrupting his nuptial ceremony in the process. True to his word, Pabuji left the ceremony halfway to ride forth to her defence. In the ensuing struggle, he unfortunately sacrificed his life.

BLOCK-PRINTED TEXTILES

Rajasthan is an important producer of textiles in India, especially the printed and tie-and-dye varieties. Textile printing is practiced in many areas of the State, with each having its special color scheme, design, and technique. The most important centers are Sanganer, Bagru, Jodhpur, Akola (in Chittorgarh district), Nagaur, Jaisalmer, and Barmer. In the last century, many printers of the Chhipa community, the traditional dyers and printers, came from Alwar, Sikar, Jhunjhunu, and other places to work in these cities. Handblock printing is perhaps the most popular kind of textile decoration as it allows the printer to produce a wide range of fabrics in bright colors and attractive designs to be made into saris, *odhnis*, bedcovers, and tablecloths.

AJRAKH PRINTS
Ajrakh prints are based on a special design in dark shades of blue and red geometrical patterns. These prints are used mostly for making turbans, coverlets, and *odhnis*, besides various other useful items. The designs of Jaisalmer and Barmer are similar to those seen in the *ajrakh* textiles of Sind in Pakistan.

PRINTING BLOCKS
The printing blocks used by the Chhipas are procured from the Khatis (carpenters) of Jaipur or brought from Delhi, Mathura, Farrukhabad, and Pethapur, where traditional woodcarvers create intricate traditional designs from blocks of *gurjun* or teak wood, as they have done for many generations.

BLOCK PRINTING
The process of printing is undertaken by the printer in his small workshop sitting before a low, wooden table.

DYEING
Reams of dyed cloth are hung on racks to dry. Black dyes are prepared by fermenting iron oxide with molasses and gum; red by extracting alizarin from madder roots and mixing with the locally available *dhawai* flower in lukewarm water in a large copper pot; blue from indigo extracted from the leaves of the *nil* plant (*Indigofera tinctoria*); yellow from pomegranate rind and raw turmeric. The millmade bleached cloth is prepared for handblock printing by washing and desizing for many hours.

SANGANER
With the foundation of Jaipur, the handblock printing industry in Sanganer flourished, enjoying phenomenal growth as a commercial center. Its origin as a textile producing center, however, remains shrouded in mystery. In the last few decades, the handblock printers who had been working in Sanganer for centuries received a renewed impetus. Now, sadly enough, most of the printers have resorted to screen painting instead of the time-consuming and costly block printing by hand.

DRYING BLOCK-PRINTED TEXTILES
The printed pieces of cloth are dried in the sun, and after the dyes are fixed, the cloth is given one or more washes and finally sized and dried before it is ready for the market.

● TIE-AND-DYE TEXTILES AND EMBROIDERY WORK

Tie-and-dye textiles, called *bandhej* or *bandhani*, are an important Rajasthani craft. From the 18th century, embroiderers from Delhi and Gujarat arrived in large numbers to work in the *toshakhanas* (royal wardrobe section) of the palaces at Amber-Jaipur, Jodhpur, Bikaner, and Udaipur. An array of court costumes and furnishings with elaborate and gorgeous golden embroidery works was produced for the Rajput courts. The main production centers today are Jaipur, Jodhpur, Udaipur, Alwar, Ajmer, Kota, Jaisalmer, Barmer, Sikar, and Jhunjhunu.

MIRROR WORK
In the areas adjoining Gujarat and Kutch, traces of the *mochi* technique, which uses small pieces of mirrors in cross-stitched designs, can be seen.

TURBAN CLOTH
Multi-colored turbans are often worn at festivals and weddings. Presents of bright, multi-colored turbans for respected elders are a must at a traditional Rajasthani wedding.

TIE-AND-DYE TECHNIQUE
The outline of the design is drawn or painted onto the cloth using a fugitive, or non-permanent, dye. The cloth is then tied with strings, usually by women who perform this task with remarkable ease. They pinch the cloth with their long fingernails and tie strings around the spots of the design. When the cloth is dipped in dye, the tied are; remain unaffected. The process repeated according to the intricacy of the design and the number of dyes used. The light and more fugitive dyes are used first, followed by red, chocolate brown, and black, or any other combination of colors.

ROYAL COSTUME
The costumes of royal ladies and their attendants show a profusion of *zari* and *gota* embroidery. In this replica of a court lady of Jaipur, an original 19th-century court costume made of tie-dyed cloth is shown. The borders and main field are in contrasting colors. The field is designed with dots and petals of stylized flowers.

EMBROIDERY
The Jat women of Sikar and Jhunjhunu embroider various geometric motifs as well as animal designs on long, flowing *ghagras* and on *odhnis*. Other handicrafts such as wall hangings, table cloths, purses, and coverings of palanquins are also richly embroidered.

LAHARIA
A special process of tie-and-dye creates the stylized wave pattern, or *laharia*, symbolizing water or the monsoon rain. Turbans and *odhnis* with *laharia* patterns are generally used on festive occasions, especially Teej.

Embroidered detail.

GOTA WORK

Gota work is a special kind of embroidery using the appliqué technique. Small pieces of *zari* ribbon are applied onto the fabric with the edges sewn down to create elaborate patterns. Lengths of wide, golden ribbons are similarly stitched on the edges of the fabric to create an effect of gold *zari* work. The *gota* method is commonly used for women's formal costumes. Khandela, in Shekhavati, is best known for its manufacture.

EMBROIDERY AND APPLIQUÉ WORK

Examples of embroidery work produced in Rajasthan (clockwise from bottom left): an animal-embroidered cloth from Jaisalmer, a quilt from Jaipur, and appliqué work with animal motifs.

ZARI EMBROIDERY

A form of raised *zari* metallic thread embroidery known as *karchobi* is created by sewing flat stitches on cotton paddings. *Zari* embroidery (above) in bridal and formal

costumes is still common. The wedding costume of a Rajasthani prince would invariably be of thick, brocaded silk with elaborate *zari* embroidery. The technique is also commonly used for velvet coverings, tent hangings, curtains, and the coverings of animal carts and temple chariots.

TIE-AND-DYE FABRICS

Rajasthani *bandhej* pieces are generally of fine *malmal* (delicate cotton cloth) for saris and *odhnis*, and medium or coarse cloth for the traditional *ghagra* (skirt), *lugri* (shirt), *choli* (bodice), and *odhni*. The designs are not as elaborate or delicately drawn as those in Gujarat.

59

To offset the barren, colorless landscape and the monotony of its cloudless sky, the people of Rajasthan show a distinct preference for bright costumes. From the simple village folk or tribal belle to the rajas and ranis, the preferred colors are bright red, dazzling yellow, lively green, or brilliant orange, highlighted by a lavish use of sparkling gold and silver *zari* or *gota*. The dyers of Rajasthan and neighboring Gujarat (many of whom migrated here) were masters of their craft from the dawn of history. Their unsurpassed skill is still evident in the costumes worn by the Rajasthani people, both rich and poor.

RAJPUT COSTUME

The Rajput kings, owing to their close proximity to the Mughal throne, adopted the Mughal court style in their formal dress. Richly brocaded materials from Benaras and Gujarat, embossed velvets, patterned silks, embroidered and woven Kashmiri shawls, and delicate cottons from Chanderi and Dhaka were procured at great cost. This formal dress made for Maharao Banai Singh of Alwar (1815–57) shows a strange admixture of Mughal and traditional styles.

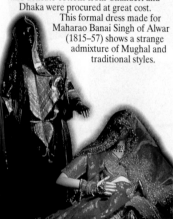

ODHNI

An *odhni* is 10 feet long and 5 feet wide. One corner is tucked in the skirt while the other end is taken over the head and right shoulder. Colors and motifs are particular to caste, type of costume, and occasion. Both Hindu and Muslim women wear *odhnis*.

ROYAL WARDROBE

The state records of Jaipur mention special departments in charge of royal costumes. While the *rangkhana* and the *chhapakhana* are departments that took care of dyeing and printing the fabrics respectively, the *siwankhana* ensured its immaculate tailoring. Two special sections, the *toshakhana* and the *kapaddwara*, took care of the daily wear and formal costumes of the king.

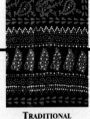

TRADITIONAL TEXTILES
Rajasthani daily wear such as saris, *odhnis*, and turbans are often made from textiles using either block-printed (above) or tie-and-dye techniques ● 56, 58.

WOMEN'S ATTIRE
The standard design is a four-piece dress which includes the *ghagra* (skirt), the *odhni* (head cloth), the *kurti* (like a bra), and the *kanchli* (a long, loose blouse).

MEN'S ATTIRE
The turban, variously called *pagari*, *pencha*, *sela*, or *safa*, depending on style, an *angrakhi* or *achakan* as the upper garment, and *dhoti* or pyjamas as the lower garment make up the male outfit.

TURBAN STYLES
Varying styles of turban denote region and caste ▲ 295. These variations are known by different names such as *pagari* and *safa*. A *pagari* is usually 82 feet long and 8 inches wide. A *safa* is shorter and broader. The common man wears turbans of one color, while the elite wear designs and colors according to the occasion.

PILA
An *odhni* with a yellow background and a central lotus motif in red, called a *pila*, is a traditional gift of parents to their daughter on the birth of a son.

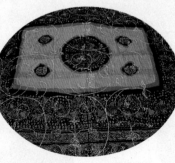

TYING THE TURBAN
Achieving different styles with just a length of material requires great skill. Specialists in this art, called *pagribands*, were employed by the royal courts, but Rajasthanis generally take pride in practicing and perfecting the art of turban-tying themselves.

● JEWELRY AND OBJETS D'ART

Enameled
liqueur sipper.

Rajasthan became famous for its jewelry industry from very early times, being an important source of precious and semi-precious stones ■ 18.
Sophisticated jewelry, set with precious stones using the *kundankari* technique, or decorated with bright enamel work, known as *minakari*, were made for the Rajput court and affluent people. Skillful artisans from Lahore, Delhi, Gujarat, and Bengal, attracted by the liberal patronage of the rajas, came to work in Jaipur, Bikaner, Udaipur, and Jodhpur.

THRONE
Silver was used extensively in the court to make cradles, carriages, *howdahs*, utensils, door panels, and thrones. The lion motif, as seen in this silver chair from Fateh Prakash Palace in Udaipur, could only be used for the throne or other formal furniture of the ruler.

ENAMELING
A lithograph of 1884 showing a typical workshop of a *minakar*. While three young assistants shape the ornament and engrave the design on it, the old master craftsman carefully fires it in the earthen *bhatti* (kiln) fired with charcoal. The process is not much different today.

MINAKARI
Enameling, or *minakari*, is not indigenous to Rajasthan. It was introduced at the turn of the 16th century by Raja Man Singh of Amber. He is said to have brought five skillful enamelers from Lahore where the craft had flourished under the Mughals. They settled in Jaipur and created fascinating types of jewelry and decorative pieces with exquisite enameling work in brilliant colors, such as this beautiful goblet and this necklace.

VILLAGE GOLDSMITH
In every small town or village, the resident *sunar* (goldsmith) produces traditionally designed ornaments to meet the needs of the tribes living in the surrounding areas and those of the ordinary village folk. He also works as the repair expert, money lender, and pawnbroker.

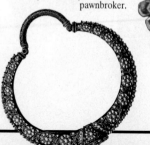

Enameled chess pieces.

KUNDANKARI TECHNIQUE

The Jaipur lapidary displays superior skill in carving from hard stones such as jade, rock crystal, agate, garnet, emerald, topaz, amethyst, and spinel. The *jadiyas* (stone-setters) create fabulous pieces of jewelry using the age-old *kundankari* technique. In this typically Indian technique, the gemstones are set within solid walls of gold.

TRIBAL JEWELRY

The ornaments of Barmer, Bhilwara, and of the Meos of Alwar follow age-old designs typical of a particular tribe. The designs often mimic the shapes of leaves, tendrils, and flower buds, finished with a classical simplicity.

TURBAN JEWELS

1. Following the Mughal emperors, the Rajput rulers wore costly turban ornaments, or *jigha*, made of dazzling, enameled gold and set with rare rose-cut diamonds, rubies, emeralds, sapphires, and pearls. Turban jewels like this one are still made by the jewelers of Jaipur.

2. The *sarpati*, made of enameled gold, is tied around the turban on formal occasions. The reverse of this piece is beautifully enameled in white, red, and green.

BODY JEWELRY

Women wear jewelry on many parts of their body. Personal ornaments include specific types worn on the feet, head, forehead, ear, nose, neck, chest, arm, wrist, fingers, and waist. Nose rings are attached to the earrings by fine gold chains, and globular pendants are worn on the forehead.

1.

2.

Rajasthani painting combines the exuberance of bright primary colors with the vigor of strong, bold lines. Early paintings illustrated religious and rhetorical texts such as the *Bhagavata Purana, Gita Govinda, Ramayana,* and *Ragamala*. From the mid-17th century, court portraiture and genre scenes gained in importance. The style of Rajasthani painting differs from state to state and from *thikana* to *thikana* (minor fiefdom). A variety of social, religious, and ethno-cultural differences gave rise to many distinct schools, the four major ones being Mewar, Marwar, Hara (Bundi-Kota), and Dhundhar (Amber-Jaipur). Several minor one include Kishangarh, Alwar, and Ajmer.

KISHANGARH
This small state produced perhaps the most distinctive religious paintings in Rajasthan. Nihal Chand, a highly innovative painter, transfigured his patron Maharaja Sawant Singh as Lord Krishna, his lady Bani Thani as Radha, and the lakes and gardens of Kishangarh as Vrindaban. Stylized linear distortions of the Mughal style were his hallmark, such as the curving elongation of the eyes and the sharp angular nose.

DHUNDHAR
Despite a close association with the Mughals, the early painting style of Amber reveals little of their influence. The foundation of Jaipur in 1727 resulted in a new wave of paintings comprising court, religious, and popular subjects, such as this splendid painting of Ras-lila (the circular dance of Krishna and the cowherd women).

MEWAR
By the end of the 16th century Mewari painting had developed its distinctive style as revealed by a fabulous group of *Ragamala* paintings. Between 1649 and 1653 a seven-volume *Ramayana*, profusely illustrated, was prepared for Maharaja Jagat Singh. From the 18th century the Mewari artists started to portray the patron maharajas in court scenes of a vast scale with innumerable courtiers.

This is a beautiful example of Mewar painting showing Maharana Fateh Singh of Udaipur crossing a swollen river in the rain during a hunting trip.

THE WEST

The most important centers in Marwar were Bikaner and Jodhpur, ruled by two collateral branches of the same family. The rulers employed Mughal-trained artists whose works display a distinct style – cool palette, delicate drawings, and restrained expression. This is particularly evident in Bikaner. Many paintings illustrating the seasons and manifold moods of lovelorn heroines as described in Hindi literature were produced, as were portraits of royal splendor. In Jodhpur paintings developed a robustly conservative Rajput style, full of verve and passion.

HARA

The rulers of Bundi were also close to the Mughal *durbar* and imbibed much court culture. The palette of the Bundi painters is often quite muted with patches of strong color for contrast (above). Court scenes, portraits, illustrations of religious and classical poetry, and the *Ragamala* were produced in large numbers in the 18th and 19th centuries. Much fauna, and flora such as banana trees and flower beds were often introduced as if to recreate the green verdure of this eastern Rajasthani state.

KOTA

The neighboring offshoot court of Kota, recognized as a separate kingdom from the early 17th century, continued the Bundi idiom. Later Kota works exhibit exceptional vitality and versatility. Hunting and wildlife scenes abound.

The small states of Uniara and Kaurali and the *thikanas* of Sarola, Indargarh, Antarda, and Karwar also reveal the strong impact of the distinct Hara style of Bundi and Kota.

● WALL AND CLOTH PAINTINGS

Kota mural.

Walls embellished with colorful paintings are a common sight in Rajasthan. The tradition of wall painting goes back to early times when the interiors of caves and temples were painted with religious scenes. Many towns contain numerous palaces, forts, temples, *chhatris,* and *havelis* with the walls covered in paintings. Some of the finest wall paintings are to be seen in the ancient towns of Bundi and Kota and the small fiefs of Shekhavati. In the temples, painted or printed cloths called *pichhvais,* which are hung behind a deity, serve as objects of devotion. As esthetic objects, they also provided a new genre in Rajasthani art.

GATHERING OF GODS
This interesting detail painted on a wall of a palace in Jhalawar depicts "Ram Durbar", an imaginary assembly of gods and goddesses – the five-headed Brahma, Shiva, Vishnu, elephant-headed Ganesha, Rama and Sita seated on a golden throne. The monkey god, Hanuman, is shown in the foreground seated with folded hands.

KOTA SCHOOL
This mid-18th century picture is a superb example of the Kota school ● 65. Two female dancers accompanied by musicians perform before the enthroned Brijnathji, the presiding deity of Kota State.

Pichhvais may be embroidered or woven with motifs derived from a vast repertoire of Vaishnava rituals. This design depicts the cowherd girls frolicking with Lord Krishna.

BUNDI STYLE
The paintings at the Chitrashala (painted pavilion) in Garh Palace are exquisite examples of the Bundi style ▲ *293*. Popular subjects include the Krishnalila (above) and *Ragamala* scenes.

SHEKHAVATI STYLE
Shekhavati has its own distinctive style ▲ *184–9*. Scenes of Krishnalila and *Ragamala*, erotic paintings, modern inventions, and genealogical portraits are common subjects. In this detail the painter has reproduced a familiar and popular subject, Lakshmi, the goddess of wealth, flanked and revered by four white elephants.

PICHHVAIS
Pichhvais are used in many Vaishnava temples of Rajasthan. In the temple of Shrinathji at Nathdwara, the *pichhvai* behind the principal deity provides a backdrop for worship on special occasions ▲ *257*. The *pichhvai* above shows Lord Krishna in full dancing attire before the image of Shrinathji. The principal devotee, Tilkayat, is shown on the left. Below, a painter works on a *pichhvai* at Nathdwara.

PHAD
The folk minstrels of the Bhopa caste use a kind of painted cloth known as the *phad* (above) ▲ *54*. Illustrated with the principal episodes of folk legends that the Bhopas narrate, these cloths are still being produced by a few surviving families of *phad* painters at Bhilwara. The style is simple, but the line work is extremely powerful and vigorous.

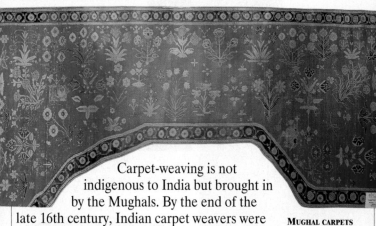

Carpet-weaving is not indigenous to India but brought in by the Mughals. By the end of the late 16th century, Indian carpet weavers were producing superior examples comparable with the finest products of Persia. The rulers of Amber-Jaipur took a great interest in carpets and built up a large collection of 16th- and 17th-century Persian and Mughal carpets. The carpet industry in Jaipur started only in the mid-l9th century when carpet-making was introduced as a jail craft. Ajmer and Bikaner were also selected as carpet-weaving centers.

MUGHAL CARPETS
This "shaped" Mughal carpet is from the Shah Jahani looms of Lahore. Mirza Raja Jai Singh bought a large number of such individually shaped carpets for spreading in his garden at Amber. The design shows rows of flowering plants of delicate hues similar to the design used in the palaces of the Red Fort and the Taj Mahal. Some representative Mughal carpets are on display at the Central Museum and the Maharaja Sawai Man Singh II Museum, Jaipur.

RAJASTHANI CARPETS
Modern Rajasthani carpets follow north Persian designs. Often dictated by the buyers' tastes, such designs frequently incorporate hunting scenes or romantic themes from Persian poetry.

DURRIES
A *durrie* is a cool, light rug. Rajasthani *durries* are smooth and closely woven. Pastel shades and a sparse use of geometrical and vegetal motifs are popular.

DURRIE-MAKING
Durries are woven all over the country where skilled labor is available cheaply ▲ 232. Durrie-making, which dates back to very ancient days in India, had been popular in eastern and northern Rajasthan, meeting a steady demand from the court and the general public.

WEAVING CARPETS
Carpet-weaving entails the combined efforts of the designer, dyer, weaver, and the knotter, whose skillful and deft fingers apply the delicate knots of different shades to bring out the design. The knots are then trimmed with a pair of carpet scissors, and the carpet is ready after a wash.

Leather saddles.

In every village of Rajasthan there are families of Chamars or Mochis, the lowly cobbler class, who collect dead animals for their hides. The hides are cleaned and processed by an indigenous method, and the processed leather is used to make shoes, sandals, bags, saddles, pouches, and other items. The quality of craftsmanship of the poor, neglected artisans in this trade is amazingly high.

SURAHI

Camel hide has many uses for the people of western Rajasthan. The tanned, soft inner hide is processed and polished till it is translucent and then molded to the desired shape to create various designs with gesso work. Tastefully painted flasks, jugs, *surahis* (long, narrow-necked water pots), like this example (right), and the lampshades of Bikaner, are made from camel hide.

KNUCKLE PAD

Knuckle pads, with padded inner lining for protecting the knuckles, are delicately turned out works of art. This example shows geometrical and floral patterns embroidered with delicate silk yarn.

SHIELD

A shield was not only essential armor; a specially made animal-hide shield, polished and decorated with painting and embellished with gold and silver bosses, or a shield of special steel with golden damascened decoration, was a symbol of high status for a Mughal and Rajput king or noble. Kota, Karauli, and Bikaner produced some of the finest animal-hide shields. Processing the toughest buffalo and crocodile hides and shaping them into shields was a difficult, time-consuming process. This shield (right) from the Maharaja Sawai Man Singh II Museum, Jaipur, with its lacquered painting, is a masterpiece.

JOOTIS

In Jodhpur, Jaisalmer, and Barmer, soft processed goat or sheepskin is decorated with colorful needle work. From these hides, *jootis* (leather sandals) (above), pouches, purses, belts, and saddle accessories are fashioned.

MUSICAL INSTRUMENTS

Leather is an essential raw material for making musical instruments, especially percussion instruments such as the *tabla, dhole,* and the *kamaycha* (left) and the stringed instruments used by Rajasthani folk singers.

● STONE CARVING

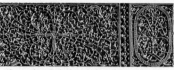

A panel of dancing figures decorate Jagdish Mandir in Udaipur (below left). Fine *jali* work from Jaisalmer (below right).

The geologically old land of Rajasthan is rich in different kinds of hard rocks, yielding granites, marbles, quartzites, slates, and other metamorphic rocks ■ *18*. With the ready availability of high-quality stone (the use of brick was almost unknown), it was easy for the Rajasthani builder to construct strong and beautiful forts, palaces, and temples. The full extent of the Rajasthani stone-cutters' skill can be seen in the richness and beauty of the large number of sculptures found in the temples built in ancient and medieval times in Bharatpur, Abaneri, Baroli, Ramgarh, Nagda, Ajmer, Chittor, Mandore, Osiyan, Jaisalmer, Bikaner, and Udaipur.

STONES FOR BUILDINGS
While Makrana produces white marble, Rupbas (near Agra) and Karauli produce red sandstone used by the Mughals to build their forts and palaces at Agra, Delhi, and Fatehpur Sikri; Kota in east Rajasthan produces gray stone for floor making; Barmer produces yellow marble for delicate carvings; and Ajmer produces granites.

STONE CARVING
The *silavat* (stone carver) carefully selects the stone, draws the design in charcoal and chips away the unwanted stone to create superbly reliefed *jali* works used to adorn temples, palaces, and forts.

FEMALE DANCER
This intricately carved sculpture is from Karni Mata Temple in Deshnoke, Bikaner ▲ *207*. Though it does not have the free-standing or high-relief sculptural decorations found in the earlier temples of Abaneri, Baroli,

Ramgarh, or Mandore, its delicate embellishments are no less striking. Stylized birds, flying, craning necks, or perching, form the border of this niche, with a female dancer hidden behind large leaves carved with immense care.

DEDICATED TO GODS

A row of figures (above) embellishes the Surya temple, Jhalarapatan, in southern Rajasthan. The stone carvers of this region, like their counterparts in north Gujarat and western Madhya Pradesh, produced some of the finest temples dedicated to Devi, Shiva, Vishnu, and the Sun God, adorning the buildings with many delicately carved figures of human and celestial beings.

THE GENIUS OF JALI

The genius of the Rajasthani *silavat* is seen in architectural pieces such as pillars, lintels, *jalis* (latticed grilles), and friezes. Some of the finest examples of *jali* work reign at Jaisalmer in unique mansions such as Patwon-ki-haveli, Nathmalji-ki-haveli, and Salim Singh-ki-haveli, where the stone carver has effectively transformed the hard surface of the yellow sandstone into soft, transparent traceries.

STONE MASONRY

Even as late as in the l9th and early 20th century the stone masons of Jaipur, Udaipur, Bikaner, Jodhpur, and Kota were capable of recreating the fine detail of earlier works, as can be seen in the delicate *jali* and relief works of the palaces and monuments. Mubarak Mahal in Jaipur's City Palace and the imposing gateway of City Palace, flanked by two monolithic white elephants (right), provide typical examples from this period.

ELEPHANTS IN HIGH RELIEF

This pair of elephants forms part of a sculptured panel from a Jain temple, Sat Bis Deorhi, in Chittorgarh. Hindu and Jain temples, Victory towers, and the palace coexist within the sprawling fort of Chittorgarh. Various panels within the temple display figures of men, women, and animals in high relief. The majestic figures of elephants abound everywhere.

● POTTERY

Pill containers made of blue pottery (right).

Clay – which could be obtained easily, shaped with little effort, and given some permanency after firing – is used extensively for making pots, dolls, and other objects in Rajasthan. Alwar, Pokharan, and Nohar near Bikaner are famous for pottery-making. Many beautiful terracotta plaques and figures come from the ancient sites of north and northwest Rajasthan. Some of them, discovered along the dried up Ghaggar basin at Rang Mahal near Bikaner, have excellent artistic merit and have been preserved in the Bikaner Museum.

BLUE POTTERY

Jaipur became a flourishing center of blue pottery from the middle of the 19th century. Vases, flower pots, plates, bowls, ewers, water pots, and other objects are produced in many workshops. Though traditional geometrical and floral motifs are used extensively, decorative water pots with hand-painted details of Rajasthani heroes and heroines are also common.

PREPARING BLUE POTTERY

The materials used are Multani clay or fuller's earth, quartz, raw glaze, and sodium sulfate. Once the piece is made, partly in molds and partly on the wheel, the artist draws the design with a soft brush on the surface using a copper sulfate pigment for turquoise blue and a cobalt oxide pigment for deep blue. The piece is then fired carefully in the kiln.

PAINTED EARTHENWARE

Images of folk divinities are sold in village fairs during festive times such as Teej, Gangaur, and Diwali. These icons are brush-painted.

THE POTTER

The potter uses clay to make *surahis* (water jugs) and *matkas* (water pitchers). Each area in Rajasthan creates its own special shape and design, as much depends on the quality of the clay and the expertise of the potter, or *kumbhar*.

MOLELA TERRACOTTAS

Like the large clay horses of Bankura in West Bengal or the different kinds of *gramadevata* figures found in Tamil Nadu, Karnataka, Maharashtra, and Andhra Pradesh, the clay plaques of Molela, a small town not far from Udaipur, are votive objects made in very high relief.

"...THEIR FACES, WITH LARGE ACCENTUATED EYES AND BOLD FEATURES, CONFORM TO THE GENRE OF THE FOLK PAINTINGS OF THE REGION."
UMA AMAND, *MANSIONS OF THE SUN*, 1972

Puppetry is an ancient, popular form of folk entertainment. The string puppets in Rajasthan are called *kathputlis*, or marionettes. The riveting histrionics of the puppeteers, like the full-throated songs of the Mirasis, Langas, and Manganiyars ● 79, belong to old pastimes, epitomizing a traditional, leisurely pace of life. No village fair, no religious festival, and no social gathering would be complete without them.

CONTROLLING THE PUPPET

The puppet is manipulated by strings which are looped into the puppeteer's hands and fingers. The puppets lie inert on the stage until they come to life when the strings are pulled. The puppeteers are usually from one family, such as a father-and-son team.

NARRATING FOLK LEGENDS

Heroic stories of folk divinities and Rajput heroes are popular with the Rajasthani puppeteer. This illustrated text (above) is of the love story of Dhola-Maru ● 55, a popularly narrated tale.

MAKING A PUPPET

The typical Rajasthani *kathputli* has a brightly painted face and a rough torso. Appropriate brightly colored male or female costumes are fashioned by the puppeteers themselves from patches of old cloth.

PUPPET THEATER

The traditional puppeteers are from the wandering community of the Bhatts. They move from village to village with their box of *kathputlis*, accessories, and *dholaks* during the festive seasons, returning to their villages to cultivate their small patch of land during the short rainy season.

The daily fare in Rajasthan typically comprises unleavened bread made of wheat, barley, millet, or maize, a soup of legumes flavored with red chili peppers, yogurt, or milk, and sometimes a vegetable such as *okra*, jackfruit, eggplant, mustard green, or fenugreek leaf. The wealthy can afford to eat meat regularly, but many abstain for religious reasons. The martial Rajputs are traditionally a meat-eating people. People who live in the deserts of Bikaner or Jodhpur may eat the bark of a bush, scraggly roots, berries, and the seeds of grasses. Spices and water are considered a luxury and are used sparingly.

MUGHAL-INSPIRED DISHES

The Mughals influenced the eating habits of the Rajput courts. From the simple grilled meats served on leaves, the royal kitchen introduced elaborate curries, *kebabs,* and *pulaos* (rice prepared with clarified butter, spices, meat, and vegetables) served on silver platters.

LASSI

Natural yogurt is churned to remove the butter content for the making of *lassi,* or buttermilk, a cooling summer beverage. The painting (left) shows Krishna's mother preparing a pot of *lassi*.

CHAPPATI-MAKING

The *chappati* is a flat, unleavened bread which serves almost as a spoon, for it is used as a scoop to transfer food to the mouth. It complements both the texture and flavor of the food it scoops up, absorbing runny sauces, balancing strong flavors, and pleasing the palate with its warmth and smoothness.

> "EAT FLESH AND YOU WILL GROW STOUT, EAT BUTTER AND YOU WILL GROW STRONG; EAT GREENS AND YOU WILL GROW POT-BELLIED AND HAVE NO STRENGTH AT ALL".
>
> OLD PROVERB OF THE RAJPUTS

FRYING PURIS
In this painting (left), a woman in the upper floor kitchen is frying *puris*. *Puris* are delicious, fried wheaten bubbles which have varied uses: as snacks, scoops for food, and as a complement to hot spices. Family members typically sit on the floor and are served piping hot food by the lady of the house.

KHUD KHARGOSH
Khud khargosh (hare or rabbit meat cooked in a pit) is a Rajput specialty during summer, when the hare is lean. The hare is skinned and stuffed with spices, wrapped in dough, and finally in layers of mud-soaked cloth. The ambrosial result is meat perfectly blended with the spices and dough.

THE INDIAN KITCHEN
The simple Indian kitchen has a brick-and-mud fireplace. Food is usually cooked over a wood or charcoal fire, in clay, brass, or copper utensils.

HOME-COOKED DESERT COOKING
Very little produce grows in the desert. Daily food mainly comprises *daal-bati* (cooked lentils and roasted balls of dough), accompanied by a variety of dried or pickled berries cooked in different ways.

● SULA

The painting below portrays a picnic, with *sula* being prepared in the foreground. Right, cooking *sula*, tender morsels of skewered meat.

In Rajput cuisine, *sulas* refer to tender morsels of meat, the most prized being wild boar spare ribs (*bhanslas*), marinated in a mixture of dry yogurt, browned onions, garlic, ginger, coriander, red chili, and *kachri*, a small pod which tenderizes meat and lends a particular sharp-sour flavor to many dishes. The marinated meat is smoked, spitted on skewers, and grilled over hot coals. Now that *shikar* (hunt) is a sport of the past, *sulas* are made of chicken, pheasant, mutton, or fish.

1. Pound *garam masala* ingredients and strain.

2. Pound *tandoori chaat masala* ingredients and strain.

3. To prepare mint sauce: grind cumin seeds and mango or pomegranate seeds. Add garlic paste, green chilis, and salt. Finally add mint and coriander leaves. Strain. Taste for saltiness and sourness. If needed, add lemon juice and lime cordial.

4. Fillet lamb leg and cut into thin one-inch strips (same as for *shashlik*). Sprinkle salt and marinate with half of malt vinegar. Put aside for two hours.

5. Mix ginger and garlic paste, red chili paste, salt, *garam masala*, mustard oil, pineapple juice, and the rest of malt vinegar with the curd (curd has to be hung in muslin cloth for two hours to obtain the solid coagulated substance, allowing the liquid to drain). Marinate

mutton pieces in mixture and keep in the refrigerator for at least eight hours.

INGREDIENTS FOR TANDOORI CHAAT MASALA
2¼ oz cumin seeds
2¼ oz black pepper corns
2 oz black salt
31½ oz dry mint leaves
a pinch of ajowain
a pinch of asafoetida
one drop of tartaric acid
½ oz mango, pounded
2 oz salt
¾ oz ginger, ground
¾ oz yellow chili, ground

INGREDIENTS FOR GARAM MASALA
2 lb cumin seeds
3½ oz cloves
3½ oz green cardamom
2 lb black cardamom
3½ oz cinnamon
3½ oz fennel seeds
150 g dry ginger
3½ oz bay leaf
5¼ oz black pepper corns
10 pieces nutmeg
3½ oz mace

INGREDIENTS FOR PUDINA (MINT) CHUTNEY
1¾ oz cumin seeds
2 lb raw mango
or or 7 oz pomegranate seeds

3½ oz garlic paste
5¼ oz green chili
salt to taste
2 lb mint leaves
6½ lb green coriander

INGREDIENTS FOR SULA

2 lb lamb leg (mutton, boneless)
salt to taste
1 oz malt vinegar
³/₄ oz ginger and garlic paste
17¹/₂ oz curd
³/₄ oz red chili paste
1³/₄ oz mustard oil
1³/₄ oz pineapple (raw) juice
1³/₄ oz butter
2 lemons
¹/₂ oz *garam masala*

7. Place skewered mutton in a moderately hot charcoal clay oven. After seven to eight minutes, turn over the skewer so as to ensure uniform cooking on both sides. Cook for another seven to eight minutes. Baste with butter using a brush. Place in oven for another two to three minutes' cooking.

6. Skewer mutton pieces. Allow eight to ten pieces per skewer.

8. Sprinkle with *tandoori chaat masala* and lemon juice. Serve with lemon wedges, onion rings, tomato quarters or slices, mint sauce, and Indian bread.

Music and dance are deeply ingrained in
Rajasthani life. The stillness of the desert
evening and the upsurge of life in the short-
lived rainy season or spring are filled with
soulful, full-throated music and rhythmic dance.
Instruments such as *sarangi, kamaycha, satara,
nad,* and *morchang* create a wide range of lilting
and melodious sound in accompaniment to the
music of the Bhopas ● *54,* Kalbeliyas, Langas,
and the Manganiyars ◆ *342* as well as the lively
and spontaneous dances, *ghoomar, gair,*
and *chari.*

MORCHANG
The *morchang*
(above) resembles a
jew's-harp. The
plaintive, melancholic
twang of the
morchang adds a
desolate dimension to
the songs of the
Manganiyars.

**OF BAMBOO, BRASS
AND BELLS**
The vast array of
Rajasthani folk
instruments is made
ingeniously from a
variety of materials.
Shells of dried
gourds of all shapes
and sizes are used
for stringed and wind
instruments, thick
gorse stems or
bamboo segments for
flutes, and baked clay
pots for drums.

Conch shells are
blown to produce full,
resonant sounds;
sticks create a rasping
rhythm; and
ghungroos (brass
bells) jingle on waists
and ankles.

KANJAR DANCE

It is only recently that the Kanjar women have come out of their villages to perform on the stage. Their dance, referred to as *chakri*, has the dancers moving in fast swirling movements.

SNAKE DANCE

The dance of the Kalbeliyas, the snake charmers' community, is a recent discovery ▲ 216. The dancers accentuate supple and snake-like movements.

FIRE DANCE

In the fire dance, the men dance on a platform of smoldering embers. Their movements grow more frenzied as the music reaches a crescendo. The dance is performed in Bikaner and Churu.

KAMAYCHA

The *kamaycha* has a big, circular resonator which produces a deep, booming sound. It is used exclusively by the Manganiyars in the Jaisalmer-Barmer region.

MANGANIYARS

The Manganiyars sing simple, full-throated folk songs, their skillful blending of voices weaving back and forth in an intricate tapestry of sound ◆ 342.

CHARI DANCE

Pots topped with lighted lamps are balanced on the head, and gentle steps and graceful hand movements come together in the *chari* dance of the Kishangarh area.

SATARA

This double flute, with its melodious and haunting sound, is evocative of the desert environs. It is played by both the Langas and Manganiyars.

FESTIVE DANCE

Rajasthani folk dances are performed during festivals and other ceremonial occasions. Each community and region has its own variations and the dances are accompanied by a particular type of music.

GAIR

The *gair* dance is performed during Holi, and the dancers are exclusively men. A series of half-swirls make up a simpler version. Based on the dancers' proficiency, the dance can build up to a series of intricate patterns. The striking of sticks gives the dance a vigorous character.

● FAIRS AND FESTIVALS

Camel polo (left) and folk dances (right) are featured during the Desert Festival.

There is a local saying that "Rajasthanis celebrate nine festivals in a week". In this State, seasons are heralded with a festive fervor; and cattle marts turn into delightful fairs. While some traditional *melas* (fairs) and festivals have a mythological origin, others commemorate a local hero or saint. Most of the traditional festivals fall in "the bright half of the month" (or when the moon is seen). To provide visitors with the opportunity to enjoy the romance of the full moon in the desert, new festivals such as the Desert Festival at Jaisalmer have been organized.

GANGAUR
Gangaur is based on the myth concerning the reunion of the goddess Gawa (another name for Shiva's consort, Parvati), and Lord Shiva after a long penance. Women revere the two deities to seek conjugal bliss. In Jaipur, following an age-old tradition, processions of stately elephants, camels, bullock carts, and caparisoned horses, all decorated in festive dress, emerge from the Tripolia Gate of the City Palace, accompanied by music.

ELEPHANT FESTIVAL
On the day of Holi, the entire elephant population of Jaipur assembles in the Chaugan stadium in a festive mood. The *mahouts* (elephant keepers) decorate their elephants with beautiful, colorful designs and dazzling attires.

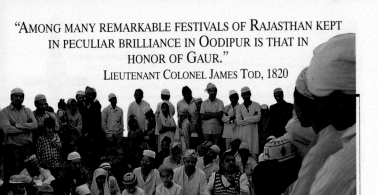

> "AMONG MANY REMARKABLE FESTIVALS OF RAJASTHAN KEPT
> IN PECULIAR BRILLIANCE IN OODIPUR IS THAT IN
> HONOR OF GAUR."
> LIEUTENANT COLONEL JAMES TOD, 1820

URS GHARIB NAVAZ

Devotees celebrate the death anniversary of the venerated Sufi saint, Khwaja Mu'in-ud-din Chisti, in the Muslim month of Rajab. Rich offerings of profusely embroidered tomb covers, fragrant flowers, and the lilting melody of Qawwali, devotional songs composed in honor of the saint, create a mystical atmosphere ● *51* ▲ *162*.

BOAT PROCESSION

In Udaipur, a boat procession on the serene waters of Pichola Lake is a magical sight during Gangaur. The glittering lights of the boats and their manifold reflections in the water create an unforgettable scenario.

TEEJ, THE MONSOON FESTIVAL

Teej (July–August) celebrates the onset of the monsoon. There is a spectacular procession in reverence to the goddess Parvati, known as Teej Mata. As in Gangaur, the procession emerges from the Tripolia Gate in Jaipur on both days of the Teej festival.

DESERT FESTIVAL

For three days in February, traditional performers gather in Jaisalmer to celebrate with folk music and dances. The sandstone city provides a golden backdrop to the popular festival, which was started in 1979.

HOLI

People throw colored powder all over each other in a riotous mêlée. Even myth describes Krishna and the *gopis* (milkmaids) playing with colors during Holi. It is a moment of joy for a lovelorn woman to be "colored" by her beloved. The mêlée is a celebration of the advent of spring and the harvest of the winter crop.

81

● FAIRS AND FESTIVALS

Traveling to Pushkar fair (left); Ravana effigy being prepared to be burnt on Dussehra festival, Kota (right).

From ancient times the fairs provided the best opportunity to buy and sell livestock and other essential items not available in nearby places. More than a dozen animal fairs, including large ones such as the Pushkar or Nagaur fairs, are held in the State. These are not only important trade events but also events of social and cultural interaction.

NAGAUR FAIR

Thousands of animals are gathered at the cattle fair of Nagaur, a small town in the Thar Desert ▲ 238. The cattle fair is reputed to be one of the best in the subcontinent. Nagaur itself is famous for a special breed of bull. There are two fairs annually, in February and August, named after local heroes.

PUSHKAR FAIR

Thousands of devotees take a dip in the sacred lake of Pushkar during the annual Pushkar fair (October–November) ● 47. Camels, horses, and bullocks are bought and sold in the hundreds. The bazaar sells camel decorations, saddlery, apparel for cattle, and handicrafts. Cattle races, plays, a fun fair, and a circus, with performers such as tightrope walkers, are other highlights.

SHEETLA FAIR

Devotees make offerings at the shrine of the Mother Goddess at the Sheetla fairs of Chaksu near Jaipur (below), and Kanana near Barmer. The Mother Goddess is believed to manifest her anger in diseases such as smallpox.

ARCHITECTURE

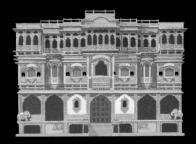

The architectural style of the rural house in Rajasthan is clearly a product of climatic conditions of intense, dry heat, desert storms, and a lack of building materials. The forms that emerge, mud or rubble masonry buildings, are firmly rooted in the landscape. Perhaps because of their remoteness from urban areas, they are expressive of the intuitive knowledge of materials held by local people and are ideally suited to the climate.

HOUSE
Every house in a typical Rajasthani village resembles a tiny fortress. Each is organized around an open courtyard, typically 400 to 600 square feet in area. This configuration is a response to sandstorms in the area, which blow drifts up against external walls, often to roof height.

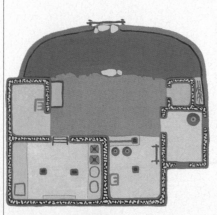

PLAN
The house is divided into a series of rooms, living, store, kitchen and so on, all oriented to face the internal, open-to-sky courtyard.

FAÇADE

The rural house usually has blank exterior walls, as most rooms are positioned facing the internal courtyard.

ROOF

The sloping roof is made with dried hay and supported by unplaned wooden rafters.

STORAGE UNITS

Rooms usually contain a variety of storage elements (below) which, besides their utilitarian function, serve as ornamental objects. Often these units comprise wooden chests, clay granaries of various sizes, clay storage units, and clay shelves with intricate decorative designs and inlaid colored glass and mirrors.

DECORATIVE MOTIFS

The homogeneity of building materials is broken by the motifs that decorate the openings of the houses. Doors and windows are outlined by colored bands, giving the houses a certain individuality.

The *haveli* is a prototype of the Rajasthani urban house – a superb response to the dense urban structure that characterizes towns throughout the State. Settlements usually comprise houses huddled together, collectively creating a micro-environment and shielding their inhabitants from the hot, dry climate. The *havelis* form a unit and have their entrances off the shady, narrow, winding streets which are lined with offices and temples. Within a city there is a consistency of building material, which ensures some unity despite variations in details. In Jaisalmer, for example, yellow sandstone unifies dwellings right across the fortified town ▲ *214*.

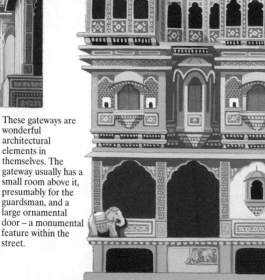

STREET GATEWAY
Galis (alleys) are often punctuated by *darwazas* (gateways) which act as security devices, shutting off entire streets and defining enclaves.

These gateways are wonderful architectural elements in themselves. The gateway usually has a small room above it, presumably for the guardsman, and a large ornamental door – a monumental feature within the street.

BALCONY
A common feature adorning *havelis*, with *chajjas* (sunshades) protecting against the desert glare.

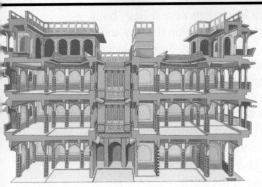

VIEWING WINDOW
Jarokhas (balcony windows) are diverse in form, but often include elaborately carved *jalis*, brackets and *chajjas,* the latter sometimes curved like a *bangla* roof.

SIDE SECTION
Although *havelis* can vary widely in plan, configuration, and scale, each is usually built around a courtyard, or several courtyards, at different levels. The *haveli* "breathes" through the courtyard, which provides adequate light and ventilation to the adjacent rooms, and it is topped by a roof terrace.

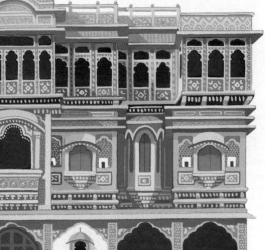

HAVELI FAÇADE
The façades of *havelis* vary in richness, texture, and detail from city to city and neighborhood to neighborhood. Usually, the buildings in the poorer quarters are simply white-washed, with some color to accentuate openings, cornice bands, brackets, and other decorative features. In affluent precincts, elaborately carved elements ornament the façade in the form of faceted *jarokhas*, while arches and recessed areas add to the variation in profile of the varied *haveli* façades.

STREET FAÇADE
The street façade of the *havelis* comprises elements such as balconies, *jalis* (screen windows), *jarokhas* (view windows), gargoyles, and decorated thresholds. The territory of each house is slightly extended toward the street by a raised platform or *otla*. In some areas, the richly carved wooden doors of individual *havelis* add yet another texture to the streetscape.

Palaces in Rajasthan were usually built as citadels located within the city and fortified by a high wall. Some palaces, such as those in Bundi and Udaipur, were built over several generations, and were therefore incremental, yet well integrated to create a whole. Public areas within the palaces consisted of the Diwan-i-Am (Hall of Public Audience), where the raja heard petitions from his subjects, the Diwan-i-Khas (Hall of Private Audience) for the council of ministers, the Sileh Khana for the display of armory, and the Daulat Khana, or treasury.

UMAID BHAWAN PALACE, JODHPUR
In colonial times, the need for fortified palaces disappeared, and many of the traditional-style retreats were abandoned in favor of stately mansions based on the Western model, such as the Umaid Bhawan Palace in Jodhpur. The Umaid Bhawan Palace ▲ *230* was built between 1929 and 1944. Its extended façade is clad in sandstone and is conceived in the grand, classical manner. The interiors are influenced by the Art Deco style in their use of materials and decorative motifs.

HAWA MAHAL, JAIPUR
Jaipur's Hawa Mahal, or Palace of the Winds ▲ *139*, makes use of elements such as *jalis* (intricately carved stone lattice screens). The *jali* has in a sense come to characterize Rajasthani architecture and with time has evolved an astounding variety of patterns.

"ONE OF THE MOST CURIOUS FEATURES OF THE PALACE
OF OUDEYPOOR IS, UNDOUBTEDLY,
ITS EXTENSIVE HANGING GARDEN."
LOUIS ROUSSELET, *INDIA AND ITS NATIVE PRINCES*, 1878

CITY PALACE, UDAIPUR
The City Palace in Udaipur ▲ *246* was built over some three hundred years, and consists of individual palaces connected by a labyrinth of corridors. This sprawling quality is what makes Rajput palaces different from those of the Mughals, who employed an architecture of perfect, preconceived symmetry. But later in the 18th century, the Rajput style changed under Mughal influence to become more formal in its planning and building concept, as exemplified by the City Palace in Jaipur.

DOOR
Doors are usually made of wood, with decorative studs in metal.

PARAPET
Stone filigree allows the breeze to penetrate the interior.

CUPOLA
Cupola-domed *chhatris* characterize the skyline of palaces and major public buildings in Rajasthan. *Chhatris* or pavilions were most often located at the highest corner points of the buildings.

BRACKET
Ornate carved stone brackets support balconies and *chajjas*.

PANEL
Made in stone relief, panels usually echo the patterns of openings, such as arches, in the rest of the building.

The fortresses of Rajasthan are strategically located on hilltops, rising abruptly out of the desert landscape. The defensive walls of the fort are often contiguous with the raja's palace (and sometimes other houses) contained within it, forming a single structure. The desert location of some of the forts influenced their architecture, which developed into interesting variations of the Rajput style. The fort symbolized power, and its function was to provide accommodation, a retreat for the Rajput warriors. The forts of Bikaner, Jodhpur, and Jaisalmer are some of the most dramatic and invincible in Rajasthan, having sheltered their inhabitants from several Muslim invasions.

JAISALMER FORT'S PLAN
Within the fort walls are the raja's palace, consisting of several buildings, *havelis*, a temple, and a bazaar. Like all forts, it is designed to be a self-sufficient entity, a city in the desert.

BASTIONS
Jaisalmer Fort has ninety-nine bastions built quite close together. During the 17th century, these semi-circular bastions (*burjs*) were furnished with platforms for wheeled guns.

WALL OF JAISALMER FORT
The snake-like fort wall ▲ *212*, which is several miles long, is made of local stone and built without any mortar.

The shifting sands of the desert cover the base of the bastions, creating the illusion of a fort rising out of the desert.

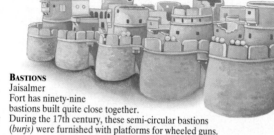

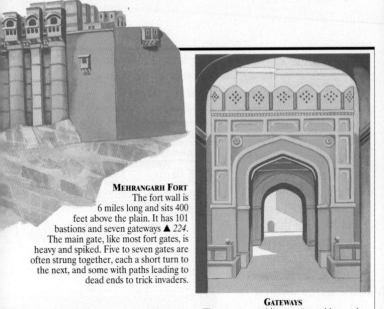

MEHRANGARH FORT
The fort wall is 6 miles long and sits 400 feet above the plain. It has 101 bastions and seven gateways ▲ *224*. The main gate, like most fort gates, is heavy and spiked. Five to seven gates are often strung together, each a short turn to the next, and some with paths leading to dead ends to trick invaders.

GATEWAYS
These gateways (*darwazas*) provide a series of protective locks along the main access route to Mehrangarh Fort.

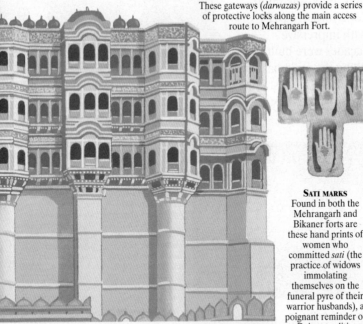

SATI MARKS
Found in both the Mehrangarh and Bikaner forts are these hand prints of women who committed *sati* (the practice of widows immolating themselves on the funeral pyre of their warrior husbands), a poignant reminder of a Rajput tradition.

GALLERIES
The western range of the Mehrangarh Fort-Palace is capped with tiered galleries. The soft sandstone of the region was ideal for fashioning the intricate lacework of the *jali* screens. The sandstone was easy to carve, and over time, hardened. Sandstone was also used to build the dramatic fort walls.

JAIPUR
A PLANNED CITY

Jaipur was one of the first examples in the world of city planning. In the 1720's architect Vidyadhar planned for Raja Sawai Jai Singh II a city of rectangular shape aligned on a grid pattern. The east–west axis of the new city was preordained by the existence of a ridge running from the Galta Hills in the east to Chandpole in the west. Following standard practice, Vidyadhar took the *haveli* or dwelling house as the smallest unit. Imposing multi-courtyarded *havelis* with impressive façades were built along the main bazaars and more modest ones along the smaller lanes.

CHANDRA MAHAL
The seven-storied Chandra Mahal, or Moon Palace, is the residential palace of the ruling family. Some of its floors, especially the upper ones, adhere to characteristically Rajput styles of decoration, while the lower floors also incorporate some Mughal and even European embellishments.

PLAN
Among the most far-sighted features of Vidyadhar's planning are the wide and straight axial roads dividing the nine *chokris* (city sectors), and the imposing gateways at the intersections of these roads. The two northern *chokris* were allotted mostly to high-caste officials, while the southern *chokris* were reserved for commercial activities and residences. Two *chokris* were added later, bringing their number to a magical nine.

SITE OF CITY PALACE
The palace complex ▲ *136* and all royal buildings, Jai Niwas garden, and the temple of Govinda Devji were constructed near the square-shaped Lake Talkatora, on the north of the east–west axis. Two city sectors lie on either side and four sectors of unequal size lie to its south.

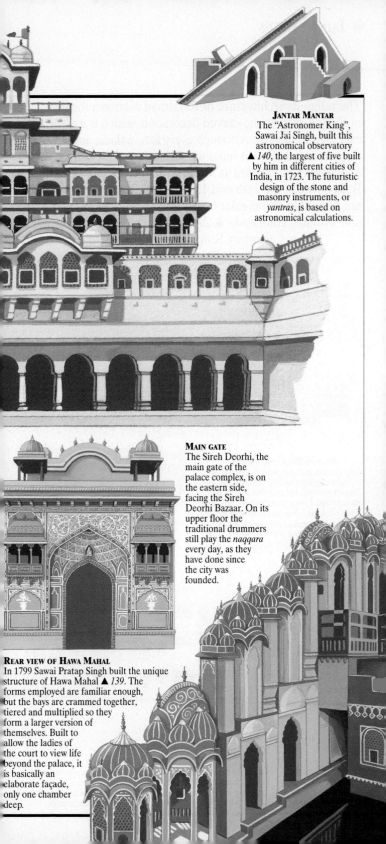

JANTAR MANTAR
The "Astronomer King", Sawai Jai Singh, built this astronomical observatory ▲ *140*, the largest of five built by him in different cities of India, in 1723. The futuristic design of the stone and masonry instruments, or *yantras*, is based on astronomical calculations.

MAIN GATE
The Sireh Deorhi, the main gate of the palace complex, is on the eastern side, facing the Sireh Deorhi Bazaar. On its upper floor the traditional drummers still play the *naqqara* every day, as they have done since the city was founded.

REAR VIEW OF HAWA MAHAL
In 1799 Sawai Pratap Singh built the unique structure of Hawa Mahal ▲ *139*. The forms employed are familiar enough, but the bays are crammed together, tiered and multiplied so they form a larger version of themselves. Built to allow the ladies of the court to view life beyond the palace, it is basically an elaborate façade, only one chamber deep.

The religious architecture of Rajasthan is known for the
profusion of its stone-carved decoration, which is usually
executed in marble. Although every fort, palace, and city in
Rajasthan has its own religious shrines, the Jain temples of
Ranakpur and Dilwara at Mount Abu are the most outstanding.
Built between the 11th and 13th centuries, the Dilwara temples
are set within rectangular courts lined with rows of small shrines
and a double colonnade ▲ 270–3. The chief glory of the 15th-
century Ranakpur Temple, set in the beautiful
Aravalli hills, is its profusion of marble
carvings ▲ 262–5.

CEILING
The ceilings of the Dilwara temples are
examples of the unsurpassed delicacy and
complexity of marble carvings.

PLAN OF RANAKPUR TEMPLE
The central chamber, which contains the
shrine, is approached through four
doorways from the cardinal directions.
Shrines with four entrances were popular
among the Jains because they were based
on the concept of *samavasarana*, an
audience-hall where the *tirthankaras* gave
their discourses.

RANAKPUR TEMPLE
The outer walls carry
depictions of Jain
saviors. A striking

feature of the interior
is the extraordinary
quality of the light,
with the sun's rays

streaming in through
the clerestories
created by the
multiple-level domes

supported on the
numerous columns
within the space of
the temple.

Sculptured panel from Ranakpur Temple.

PILLAR
The columns of the Dilwara temples are intricately decorated with figures of celebrating soldiers, dancers, and musicians.

DILWARA TEMPLES
The exuberant decoration of the interiors is in stark contrast to the unadorned outer walls. The wall niches of the sanctuaries house images of Jain saviors. The cool, white marble and the airy style of architecture symbolize an aloofness that defines the Jain aspirations of detachment and introspection.

DETAILED CARVING
The interiors contain incredibly complex and delicate decorations, such as this plaque of Parshva ▲ *265*.

DOORWAY
The doorways to the Dilwara temples are covered with finely carved friezes.

95

Jaswant Thada, Jodhpur.

ARCHITECTURAL PORTFOLIO
Architect Sir Swinton Jacob ▲ *134*, who lived in Jaipur, produced a celebrated portfolio of Indian architectural details (below) which virtually became the blueprint for British colonial designs all over India.

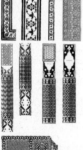

Albert Hall Museum, Jaipur.

Lallgarh Palace, Bikaner.

Gopal Bhawan Palace, Deeg.

Mehrangarh Fort, Jodhpur.

Bara Bagh cenotaph, Jaisalmer.

Balsamand Lake Palace, Jodhpur.

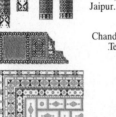

City Palace, Jaipur.

Chandravati Temple, Kota.

Amarsagar, Jaisalmer.

Umaid Bhawan Palace, Jodhpur.

Salim Singh ki Haveli, Jaisalmer.

RAJASTHAN AS SEEN BY PAINTERS

"THE FORT IS VERY LOFTY AND STRONG, SO THAT
THE LASSO OF THE IMAGINATION CANNOT REACH ITS
BATTLEMENTS, NOR THE CATAPULT."

ABU'L FAZL

The Mughal emperors often included painters in their entourage so as to have firsthand records of their campaigns and other activities. Some works are preserved in manuscripts and albums. One such is the *Akbarnama*, dating from the late 16th century, a chronicle of Akbar's life, written by his principal counselor, Abu'l Fazl. This is the first and most important artistic record of Rajasthan. Among the paintings of battles and sieges the most splendid is *Akbar directing the attack against Ranthambor Fort* (1), painted by Khem Karan, a master in Akbar's extensive studio. The painting comes from part of the *Akbarnama*, now at the Victoria and Albert Museum, London. At least fifty-seven painters were employed, with most of the miniatures being a joint work; the master drawing the composition, the junior artists applying pigments, and the portraitist often adding the important people. *Akbar visiting the shrine of Khwaja Mu'in-ud-din Chisti at Ajmer* (2), is also from the *Akbarnama*. The shrine is that of the patron saint of the Mughals. In *Akbar making a pilgrimage to Ajmer* (3), he is shown going on foot to give thanks for the birth of his son, Salim ▲ *162*.

| 1 | 2 |
| | 3 |

"THESE PICTURES ALSO REPRESENT THE CONTINUING
ACHIEVEMENT OF AN ANCIENT ARTISTIC TRADITION."

ANDREW TOPSFIELD

Some of the rulers of the different states of Rajasthan took a similar interest to that of the Mughal emperors in recording their activities. From the early 18th century the court painters of Udaipur prepared many large paintings showing the ruling maharaja holding court, visiting temples, and hunting and traveling in the countryside. Though their primary concern was to paint the ruler, they managed to portray monuments and landscape details with great vividness. The palaces of Udaipur, especially the two beautiful ones built on the islands in Pichola Lake ▲ *250*, received careful attention. *Maharana Ari Singh with his ladies at Jag Mandir*, c. 1767, by an unknown artist, shows the maharaja promenading with female attendants among the courtyards and gardens (1). Hunting trips in the hill country south of Udaipur were common, as shown in *Maharana Jawan Singh hunting tigers*, c. 1830, by an unknown artist (2). *Maharana Bhopal Singh inspecting the royal animals at Dassehra*, c. 1939, is attributed to Pannalal G. Sharma (1880–1950) and Chhaganal G. Sharma (1900–84) (3). It is one of the last pictorial records of the Dassehra festival at Udaipur.

1	
2	3

William Simpson (1823–99) was a Scottish painter and lithographer who first visited India between 1859 and 1862 to record the aftermath of the Indian Mutiny. His second visit was as a correspondent on *The Illustrated London News* with the party of the Prince of Wales in 1875. He was not much interested in formal court scenes and ceremonies. As a sensitive observer, he preferred the picturesque and subjects of human appeal. He was fascinated by the beauty of the deserted fort-palace of Amber, especially at the first light of dawn. The painting, *The Palace of Amber* (1863), shows the palace and its reflection in Maota Lake (1). He was attracted by the simple life of the villagers in their colorful dress and painted the striking *The Village Well* (1863) (2). To the water-starved Rajasthani the well has great significance. It is a common meeting point, with women coming to gossip and exchange information. *Dust storm coming on near Jeypore, Rajportana*, (1863), shows the startling beauty of a swirling dust storm or *andhi* enveloping the afternoon sky near Jaipur (3). Here at the edge of the vast Thar Desert dust storms are common at the height of summer.

1	
2	3

Oil paintings of Rajasthani scenes are comparatively rare as most of the visiting painters were amateurs or minor artists. Mortimer Menpes (1860–1938), was a professional artist who came to India from Britain to cover the grand Indian *durbar* of Lord Curzon in 1902–3 at Delhi for various London journals, such as *The Illustrated London News*, *The Pall Mall Gazette*, and *Punch*. He prepared a large number of paintings of the *durbar*. Following this work he traveled extensively in northern India and Rajasthan. Though he was more enthusiastic about the cities and monuments, many of his small-format oils show the love he developed for the rural scenes and landscapes of Rajasthan. Jaipur attracted him most and he prepared as many as eleven views of it, covering a wide range of subjects. In this street scene, *Jaipur*, c. 1900, Menpes shows a group of women clad in colorful, traditional clothing, covering their faces, emerging from a narrow lane. The pinkish *havelis* with small green windows belong unmistakably to Jaipur.

RAJASTHAN AS
SEEN BY WRITERS

RAJPUT TRAITS

The magnum opus of Lieutenant-Colonel James Tod (1782–1835) is considered to be the most authoritative account in English of the history and culture of the Rajputs and their traditions of valor, romance, and sacrifice. Tod joined the service of the East India Company as an army cadet. In 1818 he was appointed Political Agent to the western states.

❝The Rajpoot worships his horse, his sword and the sun, and attends more to the Martial Song of the Bard than to the Litany of the Brahmin.

A pledge once given by the Rajpoot, whether ratified by the 'eating opium together', 'an exchange of turbans', or the more simple act of 'giving the right hand', is maintained inviolable under all circumstances.

The Rajpoot is fond of his dog and his gun. The former aids him in pulling down the boar or hare, and with the stalking-horse he will toil for hours after the deer…. The practice of the bow is likewise a main source of pastime, and in the manner there adopted it requires both dexterity and strength. In these martial exercises, the youthful Rajpoot is early initiated, and that the sight of blood may be familiar, he is instructed, before he has strength to wield a sword, to practise with his boy's scimitar on the heads of lambs and kids. In this manner the spirit of chivalry is continually fed, for everything around him speaks of arms and strife. His very amusements are warlike; and the dance and the song, the burthen of which is the record of his successful gallantry, so far from enervating, serve as fresh incitements to his courage.❞

JAMES TOD, *ANNALS AND ANTIQUITIES OF RAJASTHAN*, LONDON, 1829–32

A PROFUSION OF TURBANS

Aldous Huxley (1894–1963) has published poetry, critical essays, short stories and works of an ethical and philosophical nature. His writings portray a witty satire on the moral anarchy of the times he lived in. "Jesting Pilate" was the diary he maintained while traveling through India, Burma, and America.

❝The long days of travelling through Rajputana seemed to me, as I sat entranced at the window, at once short and eternal. The journeys occupied only as much time as it took to fall into my trance, to eat lunch and relapse, to change trains and, once more settled, to relapse again. The remaining hours did not exist, and yet were longer than thousands of years. Much passed before my eyes and was seen; but I cannot pretend that I remember a great deal of what I saw. And when I do remember, it is not so much in terms of individual objects as of processes. Innumerable separate images, seen during hours of contemplation, have blended and run together in my mind, to form a single unit of memory, just as the different phases of the growth of plants or the development of caterpillars into butterflies are selected and brought together by the photographer so as to be seen as a single brief process in a five-minute cinema film. Shutting my eyes I can revisualise, for example, the progressive changes in colour, across the breadth of Rajputana, of the horns of the oxen; how they started by being painted both green, how the green gradually melted out of one and became red, how, later, they were both red, then both parti-coloured, then finally striped like barber's poles in concentric circles of red, white and green. More vividly still I remember a process connected with turbans, a gradual development, the individual phases of which must have been separately observed here and there through hundreds of miles of country. I remember that they started, near Jodhpur, by being small and mostly white, that they grew larger and larger and redder and redder, until, at a certain point where they came to a climax, touched an apogee of grandeur, they were like enormous balloons of dark crimson muslin with a little brown face peeping almost irrelevantly out of the middle of each. After that they began to recede again from the top of their curve. In my memory I see a process of gradual waning, culminating at Ajmere in a return to the merely normal. The train drew up in the midst of the most ordinary Indian headwear. I had seen the rise, I had been the entranced spectator of the decline and fall of the Rajput turban. **"**

ALDOUS HUXLEY, *JESTING PILATE: THE DIARY OF A JOURNEY*,
PUB. CHATTO & WINDUS, LONDON, 1927

UDAIPUR STREET SCENE

A member of the French aristocracy, Baron Jean Pellenc traveled extensively through Royal India in the years before the outbreak of World War Two. As a friend of many distinguished Indian maharajas, the Baron was afforded an intimate view of princely states, palaces, and royal family life.

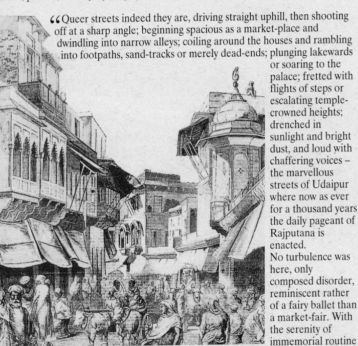

"Queer streets indeed they are, driving straight uphill, then shooting off at a sharp angle; beginning spacious as a market-place and dwindling into narrow alleys; coiling around the houses and rambling into footpaths, sand-tracks or merely dead-ends; plunging lakewards or soaring to the palace; fretted with flights of steps or escalating temple-crowned heights; drenched in sunlight and bright dust, and loud with chaffering voices – the marvellous streets of Udaipur where now as ever for a thousand years the daily pageant of Rajputana is enacted.

No turbulence was here, only composed disorder, reminiscent rather of a fairy ballet than a market-fair. With the serenity of immemorial routine a motley cortege streamed through the bazaar: cloven-bearded Rajput clansmen in rich brocades coming down from the palace, holding themselves haughtily erect, their swords enveloped in silken scarves; merchants in coloured turbans, their shirts dangling over their long white drawers; naked starveling "untouchables", members of the sweeper caste; Mohometan women, their faces veiled, in gaudy pantaloons looped in above their tinkling anklets; conventional Hindu matrons swathed in orange saris, or bold young Rajput beauties moving with a supple, dancing movement of the hips, dressed in the pleated Rajput skirt, their bellies bare to the navel, their firm breasts pointing under bodices of crimson silk. **"**

BARON JEAN PELLENC (TRANS. STUART GILBERT), *DIAMONDS AND DUST: INDIA THROUGH FRENCH EYES*,
PUB. JOHN MURRAY LTD., LONDON, 1936

107

THE ENCHANTED LAND

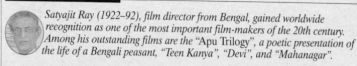

Satyajit Ray (1922–92), film director from Bengal, gained worldwide recognition as one of the most important film-makers of the 20th century. Among his outstanding films are the "Apu Trilogy", a poetic presentation of the life of a Bengali peasant, "Teen Kanya", "Devi", and "Mahanagar".

❝When we were very young, a Bengali book we were much taken with was called *Rajkahini*, or *Princely Tales*. The tales were about real kings and real princes; but so filled were they with the stuff of romance and chivalry that they didn't seem real. We read of a land of desert and forest and mountain fastnesses; of marble palaces rising out of lakes like gem-studded lotuses; of brave Hindu warriors on faithful, fearless steeds charging into battle against invaders; and of their womenfolk who threw themselves into the flames rather than be snatched away as prizes by alien conquerors.

I doubt if I'd have ever got to know Rajasthan well if I hadn't decided to become a film-maker. As a student of painting in Santiniketan, I had already discovered the exquisite world of Rajput miniatures, and realized that it wasn't just the martial arts that the Rajputs excelled in. And, of course, even as a child I knew some of the beautiful devotional songs of Mira, the Queen of Chittor who shed her finery to become a lifelong devotee of Krishna. Indeed, the lure of the enchanted land had grown over the years, and as soon as I found an opportunity, I decided to go filming in Rajasthan.

...The contrasts are enough to take one's breath away. In a country where for miles one sees nothing but sand and rock and brambles and camels, I have seen a seven mile stretch of marshland where thousands of birds from across the continents come and make their seasonal homes on treetops and tiny islets, filling the air with their calls and spattering the landscape with colour. I have seen fortresses perched on hill tops, fortresses rising out of barren plains, fortresses in forests, fortresses in the middle of cities, and fortresses nestling in the lap of mountains. I have seen palaces and *havelis* of marble and stone, airy ones and massive ones, all with exquisite carvings on them; and I have seen the ruins of a village of stone dwellings which go back a thousand years. In the museums I have seen swords and shields and lances the warrior kings fought with, some studded with jewels, all impeccably crafted; and I have seen paintings on the walls of present-day dwellings where the colour and the brushwork strike one dumb by their sweep and gaiety. And, of course, the women – and this goes for the whole of Rajasthan – women stepping straight out of the miniatures, decked out in brilliant reds and greens and yellows, disporting themselves with a grace that would rouse a queen's envy, and striking a joyous note in the drabbest of surroundings.❞

SATYAJIT RAY, FOREWORD TO RAGHUBIR SINGH'S
RAJASTHAN: INDIA'S ENCHANTED LAND,
PUB. PERENNIAL PRESS, BOMBAY, 1981

The Mirror Rooms at Amber

Aldous Huxley (1894–1963) has published poetry, critical essays, short stories and works of an ethical and philosophical nature. His writings portray a witty satire on the moral anarchy of the times he lived in. "Jesting Pilate" was the diary he maintained while traveling through India, Burma, and America in the 1920's.

❝There is a mirror room in the fort at Agra; there are others in almost all the palaces of Rajputana. But the prettiest of them all are the mirror rooms in the palace of Amber. Indeed, I never remember to have seen mirrors anywhere put to better decorative use than here, in this deserted Rajput palace of the seventeenth century. There are no large sheets of glass at Amber; there is no room for large sheets. A bold and elegant design in raised plaster work covers the walls and ceiling; the mirrors are small and shaped to fit into interstices of the plaster pattern. Like all old mirrors they are grey and rather dim. Looking into them you see 'in a glass darkly'. They do not portray the world with that glaring realism which characterizes the reverberations of modern mirrors. But their greatest charm is that they are slightly convex, so that every piece gives back its own small particular image of the world and each, when the shutters are opened, or a candle is lit, has a glint in its grey surface like the curved high-lighted in an eye.

They are wonderfully rich, these mirror rooms at Amber. Their elaborateness surpasses that even of the famous mirror room at Bagheria, near Palermo. But whereas the Sicilian room is nothing more than the old-fashioned glass-and-gilding merry-go-round made stationary, the Indian rooms are a marvel of cool and elegant refinement. True, this form of decoration does not lend itself to the adornment of large areas of wall or ceiling; it is too intricate for that. But fortunately the rooms in Indian palaces are seldom large. In a country where it rains with a punctual regularity and only at one season of the year, large rooms of assembly are unnecessary. Crowds are accommodated and ceremonials of state performed more conveniently out of doors than in. The Hall of Audience in an Indian palace is a small pillared pavilion placed at one end of an open courtyard. The king sat in the pavilion, his courtiers and petitioners thronged the open space. Every room in the palace was a private room, a place of intimacy. One must not come to India expecting to find grandiose specimens of interior architecture. There are no long colonnaded vistas, no galleries receding interminably according to all the laws of perspective, no colossal staircases, no vaults so high that at night the lamp-light can hardly reach them. Here in India, there are only small rooms adorned with the elaborate decoration that is meant to be looked at from close to and in detail. Such are the mirror rooms at Amber.❞

ALDOUS HUXLEY, *JESTING PILATE: THE DIARY OF A JOURNEY*,
PUB. CHATTO & WINDUS, LONDON, 1927

THE PALACE OF BUNDI

Born in Bombay, Rudyard Kipling (1865–1936) is renowned as a novelist, short-story writer, and poet. He is best remembered for his tales and poems portraying British imperialism in India and his stories for children. Kipling toured Rajasthan in search of "copy" for "The Civil & Military Gazette", for which he worked in Lahore as an assistant editor.

" It has been written 'the coup d'oeil of the castellated Palace of Boondi, from whichever side you approach it, is perhaps the most striking in India. Whoever has seen the Palace of Boondi can easily picture to himself the hanging gardens of Semiramis.' This is true – and more too. To give on paper any adequate idea of the Boondi-ki-Mahal is impossible. Jeypore Palace may be called the Versailles of India; Udaipur's House of State is dwarfed by the hills round it and the spread of the Pichola lake; Jodhpur's House of Strife, grey towers on red rock, is the work of giants; but the Palace of Boondi, even in broad day-light, is such a Palace as men build for themselves in uneasy dreams – the work of goblins more than the work of men. It is built into and out of hill side, in gigantic terrace on terrace, and dominates the whole of the city.

Like all the other Palaces of Rajputana, it is the work of many hands, and the present Raja has thrown out a bastion of no small size on one of the lower levels, which has been four or five years in the building. Only by scaling this annex, and, from the other side of the valley, seeing how insignificant is its great bulk in the entire scheme, is it possible to get some idea of the stupendous size of the Palace. No one knows where the hill begins and where the Palace ends. Men say that there are subterranean chambers leading into the heart of the hills, and passages communicating with the extreme limits of Taragarh, the giant fortress that crowns the hill and flanks the whole of the valley on the Palace side. They say that there is as much room under as above ground, and none know the whole extent of the Palace. Looking at it from below, the Englishman could readily believe that nothing was impossible for those who had built it. The dominant impression was of height – height that heaved itself out of the hillside and weighed upon the eye-lids of the beholder. The steep slope of the land had helped the builders in securing this effect. From the main road of the city a steep stone-paved ascent led to the first gate – name not communicated by the zealous following. Two gaudily painted fishes faced each other over the arch, and there was little except glaring colour ornamentation visible. This gate gave into what they called the chowk of the Palace, and one had need to look twice ere realizing that this open space, crammed with human life, was a spur of the hill on which the Palace stood, paved and built over. There had been little attempt at leveling the ground. The foot-worn stones followed the contours of the ground, and ran up to the walls of the palace smooth as glass. **"**

RUDYARD KIPLING, *LETTERS OF MARQUE*, PUB. H.M. CALDWELL CO., LONDON, 1899

THE LAKE PALACE AT UDAIPUR

Roderick Cameron, who traveled in India in the 1950's, has a remarkable eye for detail, as is evident from his description of the former summer palace of the rulers of Mewar, the Bari Mahal or Lake Palace at Udaipur, which he visited in the years before its conversion into a hotel.

  "I hesitate to describe the Bari Mahal, frightened that I shall be accused of exaggerating. Even now, when trying to recapture it, I wonder if I have not imagined the whole thing. Not that it is a particularly remarkable building, lots of it, in fact, being in rather questionable taste. Rather it is the poetry with which the whole thing has been conceived. Had Giraudoux's Ondine become a lady of fashion round about the eighteen-nineties, this is the kind of place one would have expected her to live in. Oscar Wilde might have stayed here, or Whistler. But even this does not give one quite the right idea, for they would have been figures met in one's dreams, where places and people are never quite real.

The drawing room is called 'The Light of the Moon'. The rooms are small and most of them have bay-windows that jut out over the lake, set on a skirting made of transparent alabaster. In 'The Light of the Moon' the doors are of mahogany but inlaid with panels of mirror, and all the table-tops are of glass. Fingers of sun crept in through the shutters, liquid sun that rippled over the crystal drops of the chandeliers.

We were shown His Highness's private sitting-room, reached by a lift connected with the landing-stage below. It is a pretty room, plastered in shining, ivory-colored *chunam* into which had been worked a pattern of green and amber roses made from flat pieces of glass. It is a happy, gay house and full of light. The Maharana's bedroom is minute, hardly more than an alcove, and frescoed all over with a landscape showing mountain scenery and rushing water-falls cascading down between tightly packed mango trees in which perch peacocks which leopards stalk, while tigers prowl around below. It is naively rendered, precise and detailed in the manner of Mogul painting, and has something about it of a miniature Douanier Rousseau.

We were fortunate in being shown the women's quarters, for visitors, I believe, are not often taken into this part of Bari Mahal. The rooms are more or less the same, except that they have shutters instead of doors. There appear to be a great many Bohemian chandeliers and all the windows are coloured.

There is a small section of the palace that is earlier than the rest and in it, in a rather dilapidated state, is the most enchanting courtyard planted with orange trees and jasmine. The walls are inlaid with seventeenth-century Persian glass mosaics made into panels of flowers, worked in a loose pattern with brown, green, blue, and silver mirrors. The surface of the walls has been made uneven purposely, so that no piece of mirror is quite flat, and in this way there is a play of light and the whole cloister shines.**"**

RODERICK CAMERON, *TIME OF THE MANGO FLOWERS*,
PUB. HEINEMANN, LONDON, 1958

JAIPUR SKETCHES

JAIPUR POMP

Sir Stanley Reed, editor of "The Times of India", lived in India for several years and was a popular and prominent citizen of Bombay. He accompanied the Prince and Princess of Wales during their tour of India in 1905–6 and recorded his colorful impressions in "The Royal Tour in India".

"From the station a broad straight road stretches for two or three furlongs before it turns sharply to the right towards the Residency, and this was lined with the retainers of the Maharaja and his feudatories in their most picturesque and characteristic garb. Here were the Maharaja's runners, lithe, active, bare-legged Nagas in green jerkins edged with gold, white turbans with feather aigrettes, and striped as to the lower extremities like a Muharram tiger. Their musician bore a noble war-horn on which he blew a weird conch-like blast. There were apparitions by the score, gorgeously dressed in scarlet and bearing silver staves; orange-robed messengers, spearmen by the hundred, and match-lock men in olive green, the guardians of the Maharaja's sleep. Now came camels with huge kettledrums, horses with kettledrums, and dancing horses gaily caparisoned in tinsel and green. A score of elephants themselves made a brave sight, with their gilded howdahs, trailing cloths of green and red and gold, and painted foreheads. And these served but as a further introduction to palanquins manned by red-coated bearers, bullock palanquins in red and in green, with the horns of the splendid Gujarati oxen brightly enameled. Then came a bullock battery with the tiniest of guns and camelmen with great swivel blunderbusses mounted on the pommels of their saddles and Sirdars on boisterous stallions.

Through this fascinating throng drove His Highness the Maharaja, in a carriage...to receive his royal guests, and he alighted at the station to the braying of war-horns and the strains of a most original anthem.**"**

STANLEY REED, *THE ROYAL TOUR IN INDIA*,
PUB. BENNETT, COLEMAN & CO., BOMBAY, 1906

THE BAZAAR

Ralph Oppenhejm's experiences as an inmate in a German concentration camp resulted in his first novel, "The Door of Death". The Danish author traveled extensively in India in the mid-1950's. "A Barbarian in India" was judged the best reviewed book of the year in Denmark.

"The bazaar, the town's great news-bureau, is the liveliest and gaudiest in all India, largely as a result of the Jaipur costume, which is a firework-display of colours. The men's turbans, overdoing all the rest of the peninsula in their volume – they take nine yards of material – are findant-pink and pistachio-green, cloud-white and sea-blue. The women's skirts, a blaze of yellow and puce, are set with little mirrors, coruscating in rivalry with such an abundance of silver ornaments that arms and legs, fingers and toes are stiff with them. Only women of the people move about the streets, but they move like queens, accompanied by the gay tinkling of their ankle-bells. They are among the handsomest in the country, the same golden-brown shade as the frescoed women in the thousand-year-old caves of Ajanta, with the same bewitching half-moon eyes. Though one is not often allowed to see their faces, which are usually screened by the big headcloths that make many Rajputana beauties look like walking ship's funnels.

Jodhpur has not the glamour of Jaipur. But perhaps it has more
character, and more shades of character. Dazzling beauties are apt to
come easily by everything, to excite immediate rapture – which often
gives place to a certain effect of emptiness, one day when we have
looked our fill; whereas the more modestly equipped, who have to
struggle for much the others take as a right, a matter of course, often
develop far more personality, and have always fresh surprises to offer.
While Jaipur is the only city in India, except New Delhi, to have been
built on a plan, Jodhpur – and this is not its least attraction – has grown out
of the varying taste and caprices of the generations. And if it yields to Jaipur
in purity of features and beauty of form, as a set-off it has a spontaneous,
natural charm, as it were a feminine inconsequence; it seems to have 'lived' – the
feeling which makes it so stimulating to meet certain women past their first
youth. **"**

RALPH OPPENHEJM, *A BARBARIAN IN INDIA*,
PUB. PHOENIX HOUSE, LONDON, 1957

JAIPUR LIFE

*R.N. Currey spent three years in India and was prize-winner of Lord Wavell's All India
Poetry Competition. Many of his poems have been broadcast and published in various
periodicals.*

JAIPUR (III)

The men had colour in their lives and movement.
Around the carpeted square durbar floor
That held the jewelled and enamelled hour
Flowered the rows on rows of intent turbans,
Ochre, and mauve, and scarlet; a disturbance
Of rumour like a breeze swept through the court;
And, in a gateway, swaying like their thought,
The howdah of an unknown elephant.

Outside was poverty. These roseate lives
Sucked blood from hungry men, but made a start
Between their gem-hilt wars upon the art
And building that are our inheritance:
Grant them aesthetic standards, positives
Yet to be made mankind's experience.

JAIPUR (IV)

Here in Jaipur the old and new worlds meet;
The forts, the temples, and the palaces
Look out on legislative offices
And schools and hospitals. This wide grave street
Worn by three centuries of slippered feet
And tripping pads of camels branches out
In roads that go impartially to meet
Old pleasure-gardens and new factories.

Here is a future growing from past beauty
Owning past inspiration – and a duty
To all men of all trades to build a city
Known for flourish of its industries;
Its roads made smooth for ordinary men
And knowledge climbing stairs to soar again.

R.N. CURREY, *INDIAN LANDSCAPE: A BOOK OF DESCRIPTIVE POEMS*,
PUB. ROUTLEDGE, LONDON, 1947

SIR PRATAP SINGH OF JODHPUR (1845–1922)

Maud Diver traveled through the Princely States in the years before World War Two. A prolific writer, her works include "The Englishwoman in India" as well as a series of novels about British life.

❝In almost every Indian State there is some special feature – building, personality, legend – that seizes one's interest and imagination. In Udaipur, it is the Palace and the tragic ruin of Chitor. In Jaipur, it is the deserted city of Amber. In Jodhpur, it is that work of demi-gods, the Fort; fit birthplace of the incomparable Sir Pratap Singh, whose name aptly signifies 'Lion of Glory'. Dead nearly twenty years, his influence still lives. Still they can say of him, 'He has no equal – he must have lived many times. Perhaps he will never need to live on earth again.' His record is unique among the Princes of India; and before his death he added lustre to a brilliant beginning. Far-famed and widely loved, intimate friend of three British sovereigns, he has been aptly named 'the first gentleman in the British Empire', using the demoded word in its higher meaning. A Rajput of bluest blood, he reckoned himself beyond all rules and codes except those dictated by his own sense of fitness, which was of the most exacting; a trait finely shown in the familiar story of an English subaltern who died at Jodhpur, and whose coffin could not be moved because one of the officers detailed to carry it was down with fever. No Hindu of caste could touch a coffin without defilement. An outcast scavenger seemed the only solution; but the officers reckoned without Sir Pratap. The young man had been his friend; and he promptly offered himself as pall-bearer with the characteristic remark, 'A soldier knows no caste with a brother soldier.' Perhaps only a Hindu could appreciate the spiritual significance of that simple courteous action. Rightly he belonged to the warrior desert tribe of Rajputs, the Rathores. 'Famous in battle,' and Sun-descended like the Seesodias of Udaipur, they trace back their pedigree for over fourteen hundred years. According to legend, the first Rathore sprang from the spine of Indra, god of storms and thunder-bolts; a legend in keeping with their history, that is mainly a red page written in their own blood. Always in the thick of danger or trouble, they welcomed any sacrifice that might save their land from the fanatic fury of Islam; and their unshaken courage has been embodied in the proverb, 'A wall may give way: a Rajput stands fast'.❞

MAUD DIVER, *ROYAL INDIA: A DESCRIPTIVE AND HISTORICAL STUDY OF INDIA'S FIFTEEN PRINCIPAL STATES AND THEIR RULERS*, PUB. D. APPLETON-CENTURY CO., LONDON, 1942

MAHARANA FATEH SINGH OF MEWAR (1853–1934)

Charles Allen, author of "Plain Tales from the Raj", and Sharada Dwivedi recorded the recollections of many of the former maharajas and nawabs and their family members and those of employees and officials.

❝A contemporary of Sir Pratap Singh who was as much concerned with Rajput honour – although displaying this in a very different way – was the ruler of Udaipur, Maharana Fateh Singh of Mewar. As Sir Pratap was the personification of the Rajput warrior, so Fateh Singh was the essence of Rajput kingship, a worthy occupant of the premier gadi in the land: 'The old man knew his power, he knew his position not only as the ruler of Udaipur but as the head of the Rajputs and virtually as the head of the Hindus. He could not accept his position

"TO CALL FATEH SINGH AN EXTRAORDINARY MAN IS ALMOST TO BELITTLE LANGUAGE. ONLY SUPERLATIVES APPROACH ADEQUACY IN DESCRIBING HIS QUALITIES, YET ONLY SIMPLICITY CAN PROPERLY CONVEY HIS VIRTUE."

BRIAN MASTERS, *MAHARANA – THE STORY OF THE RULERS OF UDAIPUR*

as head of the Indian fighting class and yet subservient to a foreign power, so at every opportunity he went against the British.'... Maharana Fateh Singh also had a low opinion of the honours and dignities handed out by the British for which so many Princes vied. During the First World War he was one of the few rulers who failed wholeheartedly to support the British war effort: 'He refused point-blank. He said, "When there is a fight in India, Europeans don't come here to die, so why should we send our Indians to die when Europeans fight?" But at the end of the war the British sent him the highest decoration for war services and when they brought this G.C.I.E. in a velvet case he looked at it and said to his interpreter, "It is the sort of thing that pattawalas (attendants) in offices wear. Put it on the horse. It looks better on a horse than a king." The interpreter on his own told the British officials that this was not an auspicious day, so His Highness would put it on some other time. Later when somebody asked him why he had got such a high honour for doing nothing, he said, "Because I rendered the British the highest service. While the British were away fighting the war in Europe, I didn't take over in Delhi. Isn't that a big enough service? " ' 〞

MAHARAJA GANGA SINGH OF BIKANER (1880–1943)

〝'What a towering man!' remarks M.M. Sapat, who came from Jaisalmer in 1924 to work in the Bikaner Secretariat. 'If you were to see him in just a vest and pyjamas among thousands of people you'd say, "Yes, there's a personality". What a man he was – with a voice like a tiger's.' But it was not character alone that distinguished him. 'My grandfather was the patriarch,' declares the present Maharaja of Bikaner. 'The people treated him like a father figure. Consequently he treated them like children. He always said to them, "I see no difference between my son and my grandchildren and you. You are all my children and your welfare is my first responsibility." He believed that, because he was a proud Rajput and the Rajput tradition means to protect. He could be a tyrant if he wanted to but at that time it was the only way to get work done. Anybody who stood in the way of progress he had to sweep to the side.'... Progress for Ganga Singh meant transforming Bikaner from a desert state into the granary of Rajasthan, a challenge that he first faced as a youngster in 1898: 'We had this terrible famine called the Chapna Kaal when my grandfather as a youth of eighteen went on camel-back from village to village and saw how hundreds were dying because of famine. He came to the conclusion that the only answer to this was canals – and railways so that you could bring in food quickly. So when he got his powers the first thing he worked on was the canals and the railway. Bikaner had no riparian rights but because he had that magnetism and personality he was able to influence the King and the Viceroy to gain access to the river Sutlej. That's how the Ganga Canal, which irrigated a thousand square miles, came about.' The Ganga Canal system was finally opened in 1927. 'The whole of that part of the country turned green,' remembers M.M. Sapat. 'As far as the eye could see there were green fields where the desert had been. And what a matter of pride it was, not only for him, but for all of us who went there and saw it.'〞

CHARLES ALLEN AND SHARADA DWIVEDI, *LIVES OF THE INDIAN PRINCES*, PUB. CENTURY, LONDON, 1984

PIG-STICKING AT BIKANER

One of the most brilliant diplomats of his time, Lord Hardinge of Penshurst was a close friend and trusted advisor of King Edward VII. He was Viceroy of India from 1910 to 1916. His memoir, "My Indian Years", was published in 1948.

❝It was a glorious winter's day with a bright sun, and as we stood on rising ground, watching a battalion of Bikaner Imperial Service Infantry beating a thick jungle, one felt, with the anticipation of exceptional sport, that life was really worth living. Presently an enormous herd of pig, estimated at over four hundred, emerged from the jungle, and immediately a dozen or more young Rajput horsemen belonging to the Maharaja's Staff galloped off and dashed into the herd, scattering them in every direction, and having spotted the old boar with the torn ear, gradually separated it from the rest of the herd. We followed slowly, and when it was clear that the old boar had become entirely detached from its associates, the Maharaja called out to me, 'There is your pig!' I started at once to gallop after the pig, but when I had approached it to within about a hundred and fifty yards the pig suddenly stopped, turned round and charged me at full gallop. I reined in my horse, and holding low the point of my spear, I pierced its tongue. The pig gave an angry shriek and dashed off in another direction. I followed at once in hot pursuit and on nearing the pig after a short distance, I dashed past, and my spear passed right through its body. I was disgusted to find that although, in spite of the heavy weight of the pig, I was able to retain hold of my spear, it broke in two, leaving half in the body of the pig. The impetus of my horse carried me on two or three hundred yards and I could see the pig on the ground with half my spear projecting on each side of its body. Happily my orderly galloped up to me and gave me the spare spear that he was carrying. Then, to my great surprise, I saw the pig suddenly get up and again charge me at full gallop. As I was unprepared I avoided the charge by quickly moving to one side, fearing that it might wound my horse, as often happens. The pig having missed me and my horse, turned and again charged, but this time I was prepared to receive the charge which was directed with such violence and speed that my spear entered the pig's chest and transfixed its body to such a depth that the pig, in its final struggle, was actually able to reach my boot and bite it. It was a fine pig of thirty inches, and most gallant. I felt profound sympathy for my brave victim. There is no doubt that the Indian wild boar is one of the bravest and most gallant of animals. It is absolutely fearless and will not hesitate to attack a tiger, and the latter is always afraid of a pig, while a panther stands no chance against a wild boar.❞

LORD HARDINGE OF PENSHURST,
K.G., *ON HILL AND PLAIN*,
PUB. JOHN MURRAY,
LONDON, 1933

THE SPLENDOR OF PEAFOWL

E. P. Gee has spent half a lifetime studying and photographing animals and birds in India. His book portrays a unique panorama of the wildlife resources of India – her sanctuaries, the animals that inhabit them, and the people who have helped to preserve them.

❝Peafowl are everywhere in this area, and cock birds do not let you forget their existence, with their loud screams of may-awe in the evenings and early mornings. These birds are protected in most parts of west, central and north India by legislation and, more significantly, by popular and religious sentiment. For the peacock is the vehicle of Saraswati (goddess of learning), Kartikeya (god of war) and Subrahmanya (god of yogic powers).

Consequently these spectacular, and to Westerners, exotic birds have become quite common in these parts, often proudly wandering and even nesting in villages totally unafraid of man.

It is recorded in history that Alexander the Great took back with him from India to Greece two hundred peafowl, and from Greece the birds spread to other countries of western Asia, north Africa, Europe and eventually to America. The Mogul emperors were greatly attracted by the beauty of this bird, and Shah Jehan's famous Peacock Throne was designed 'its pillars of emerald being surmounted by the two figures of two peacocks, ablaze with precious stones'.

Incidentally, the splendid ocellated 'train' of the peacock is not really its tail, but its upper tail-coverts enormously lengthened. For display these are erected and fanned out before admiring hens. Its crest feathers have fan-shaped tips, while those of the Burmese subspecies have pointed tips.

Peafowl, as well as langurs, are well-known as being among the first wild creatures to notice the approach of a tiger or leopard in the jungle and to sound their call of alarm, warning their fellow creatures that a predator is on the prowl.

Peacocks shed all their tail feathers each year and grow new ones. The old shed feathers are picked up and made into fans and widely sold in bazaars and elsewhere.

'The gorgeous peacock is the glory of God', said a Sanskrit verse, and in a country of pageantry and colour it is only fitting that the peacock has been officially proclaimed as the national bird of India.❞

E. P. GEE, *THE WILDLIFE OF INDIA*, PUB. COLLINS, LONDON, 1964

PADMINI OF CHITTORGARH

Margaret Noble came to India from Ireland and assumed the name of Sister Nivedita. She became an ardent disciple of Swami Vivekanand, the Hindu philosopher who attempted to combine the concepts of Indian spirituality with Western materialism.

❝It was almost midnight, as the moon grew near the full, when we looked for the first time on the fortress of Chitore. The lights in the village at its foot had been extinguished, and the hill with its great length stood dark and isolated against the sky. Silently we sat on a low stone a mile off and drank in the scene. Architecturally the splendour of the city justifies her pride. The rock on which she stands slopes inwards from all sides, with the result that there are innumerable tanks and a water supply practically unlimited. Within the walls are the remains of what has been virtually two cities, one to the north-east, the ancient capital of the time before Bappa Raoul, and one more modern which grew up between his accession in AD 728 and the evacuation under Akbar in 1568.

Long and narrow, like some lean grey lion crouching for the spring, lies the walled Chitore on its craggy hill. And the newly arrived traveller watching it may see it tonight, as the returning escort may have seen it when Padmini's marriage procession halted for the last time on the homeward way, more than seven centuries ago. Little can the "lotus fair" Padmini have slept that night, the last of the long journey from her father's distant stronghold. Rather must she have gazed on through hour after hour of waking dreamfulness, counting the tale of the turrets and bastions of the fortress that tomorrow she would enter as bride and queen. Within her was the confidence of the Indian wife, who thinks of herself as beginning what is only a new chapter in an old story, as recovering a thread that was held but a while ago, and dropped at death. Not for the first time were they to take up tomorrow the tale of life together – it was an ancient comradeship of the soul. Did no vision of the future cast its shadows across the path before her to make Padmini shrink and pause, in the glory of this her great homecoming? Had the bard whispered no word above her cradle of the tragedy of greatness that lay before her? Did she know that as long as winds should wail over Chitore they would sing her name, that with her would every stone and every building be associated in the world's memory till the end of time? To her, what would be was the following of the path of Rajput honour. Was it not always said that, in the hour of birth, the eyes of a boy were set upon a knife and those of a girl upon a lamp – for the man must leave life by way of the sword and woman by that of fire?❞

SISTER NIVEDITA, *STUDIES FROM AN EASTERN HOME*, PUB. LONGMANS, GREEN AND CO., LONDON, 1913

> "... SHE WAS THE FAIREST OF ALL FLESH ON EARTH. HER FAME WAS SUNG THROUGH THE LAND BY THE POETS, AND SHE BECAME, IN SOME SORT, THE HELEN OF CHITTOR."
>
> RUDYARD KIPLING ON RANI PADMINI

LAKE PUSHKAR

The Frenchman Louis Rousselet traveled extensively throughout India, and in particular, in the kingdoms of Rajputana in the middle of the 19th century. Profusely illustrated with fine drawings, his book acquaints the reader with the heroic traditions as well as the daily lives of the Rajputs.

❝One of the most sacred lakes in India is that of Poshkur, which is only rivalled by the lake of Mansourwar, in Tibet. It is situated in a narrow valley surrounded by immense mounds of shifting sand; and a few isolated peaks stand out on its borders with great effect. Its form is nearly a perfect oval, and at its southern extremity it empties itself by a narrow canal into an immense marsh. The origin of this lake is attributed to Lord Bramah. The story goes that the god, wishing to celebrate the sacrifice of Yug, stopped for that purpose in the valley, having first placed genii at the entrance of all the passes to keep off the evil spirits. Just as he was going to perform the ceremony, he perceived that his wife Sarasvati had not accompanied him; and, as the presence of a woman is necessary, he employed one of the Apsaras. Sarasvati was so grieved at this infidelity that she hid herself in the mountains to weep, and was transformed into a fountain. Several centuries after, one of the Purihara kings of Mundore lost his way while hunting, and, feeling thirsty, came to drink at the fountain of Sarasvati. He felt himself instantaneously healed of a disease previously incurable, and recognised the miraculous property of the spring. Shortly afterwards he returned, and had a basin dug out to receive the waters, which now form the lake of Poshkur.

This lake soon became a favourite resort of pilgrims, and during the Middle Ages the princely families of India vied with one another in covering its banks with temples and cenotaphs. Gradually quite a town of religious buildings sprang up, peopled by Brahmins. The wealthy pilgrims from all parts of India brought untold riches to Poshkur, and the princes spared no expense to enrich the holy inhabitants of the sacred town.❞

LOUIS ROUSSELET, *INDIA AND ITS NATIVE PRINCES*, PUB. BICKERS, LONDON, 1878

THE THAR DESERT – A DAILY PRESENCE

Born in Bombay in 1938, Dominic Frank Moraes was educated at Jesus College, Oxford. He is a prolific writer and has published several books of poems, essays, biographies, and travel books. He was awarded the Hawthornden Prize in 1958.

❝Time is very fixed. The courses of the sun are fixed. Night may be cold, as the heat evaporates from the sand, but from the second the blood-red rim of the sun appears on the horizon, and a pinkish light spreads swiftly over the sand, one is conscious once more of the heat filling and occupying the air. Within an hour everything is a single sterile blaze, intensifying until at noon, the sun at meridian, a bitter whitish glare blinds one. Dark spectacles are of little help against this, but squinting through them you may see the occasional penurious hamlet with its beehive haystacks; camels sitting with their legs folded under them, resting, or camels loping down the road, sometimes attached to carts of firewood and fodder; lean thrifty men with fierce moustaches and colourful turbans, women with their long skirts, longsleeved tunics and veils, the vivid clothes as stains of brilliance on the sand.

In the desert one meets people who have spent their whole lives here, and have lost the habit of speech. Memorable for their silence, they can find food, and even liquid from a species of cactus, or simply by knowing where to dig. But unlike Saint Exupery, most people find the desert unfriendly, and prefer not only not to live in it, but not to cross its borders into anarchy. For the desert is anarchic, in that it upsets the accepted convention of civilised man, that nature is friendly and a provider. For the people of Rajasthan, the desert is a daily presence for they live near it or around it or in it and it determines the patterns of their lives. The turbans of the men are not only ornamental but necessary, since they have to protect their heads from the hot wind and the sand it carries. The women wear the amount of clothing they do because it is sensible: it protects the body from the sun and wind, and it acts as insulation against heat.

There is a reason for everything one does in the desert. Nothing is or can be done except out of necessity. Desert economy is different. A cupful of water has an importance all its own. A plant means something quite different from what it does far from the dunes. Cattle and their fodder are to be protected by every means possible. Rain is a marvel sent directly from the deity. Most prayers are to do with rain. Most desert people who come to a place like Udaipur, seem awed, and amazed, childlike as they quench their eyes with the very sight of an element they hardly know. Many people have seen the immense luxury of the palaces, and this remains the image they hold of Rajasthan. Others find in the gaunt, grim, hill forts symbols of history – a history of passionate love, warfare, guns and swords and suicide charges, women rising in smoke from fiery pyres. But none of these is the truth. The truth is the desert, which made hard men cut their way to kingdoms, and turn from soldiers to sybarites in a generation.❞

DOMINIC MORAES, PHOTOGRAPHS BY GOPI GAJWANI, *RAJASTHAN*, *PUB.* HIMALAYA BOOKS, DELHI, 1989

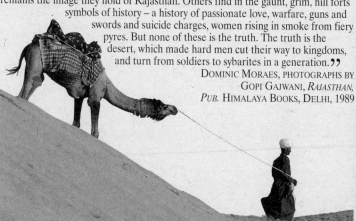

ITINERARIES

UDAIPUR STATE:
LAKE OF 1,000 ISLES.

▲ Jaisalmer city.

▲ Ajmer city.

Jodhpur Fort and city. ▼

City Palace, Udaipur. ▲

Amber Fort, Jaipur. ▲

▲ Ramdeora Fair near Pokharan.

▲ Pushkar Fair.

▼ Thar Desert.

▲ Udaipur.

▼ Barmer.

▲ Tilwara horse fair, near Luni River.

▲ Pushkar Fair.

Sariska Wildlife Sanctuary. ▼

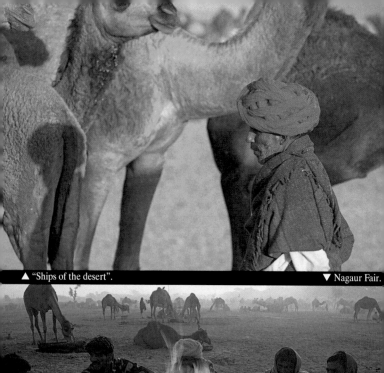

▲ "Ships of the desert".

▼ Nagaur Fair.

▼ The desert at Samm.

THE EAST

▲ THE EAST
JAIPUR

1. JAIPUR 2. JAL MAHAL 3. AMBER FORT 4. JAIGARH FORT 5. SISODIA RANI KA BAGH 6. GALTA 7. SANGANER 8. BAGRU 9. TONK 10. KISHANGARH

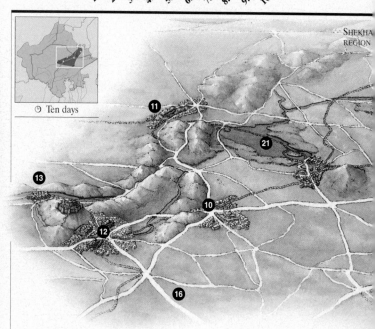

SHEKHA
REGION

🕐 Ten days

RAJPUTANA
The old name for Rajasthan was "Raputana" or "the land of the Raputs". Two years after India's independence in 1947, the Princely States of this region were merged, and the new political state that resulted was named "Rajasthan" or "the land of the rajas" ● 39.

Street scene, Jaipur, c. 1902.

The city of Jaipur is the logical starting point for anyone traveling in Rajasthan because of its central location and good air, road, and rail connections. To the West lies the desert region of Marwar (Bikaner, Jaisalmer, and Jodhpur), to the north and south run the craggy Aravalli hills. From Jaipur it is an easy drive to Alwar and the Sariska Tiger Reserve ▲ 174 in the northeast, or to Ajmer, Pushkar, and Kishangarh in the Southwest. Also within reach is the Shekhavati region in the northwest ▲ 180 and Ranthambhor National Park in the east ▲ 305.

HISTORY

The kingdom of Jaipur was originally known as Amber, which was also the name of its ancient capital, situated 7 miles away. Its history can be traced back to the 12th century, when Amber was the stronghold of the fierce Mina tribesmen. According to legend, the Minas once gave shelter to a young Rajput prince called Duleh Rai. But the prince later betrayed them by getting them drunk one night, slaying them, and taking over Amber. In the 16th century, Amber suddenly came to the fore when the Mughal emperor Akbar (reigned 1556-1605) married one of its princesses, the first of several shrewd matrimonial alliances between a Mughal ruler and a Rajput princess ● 36.

130

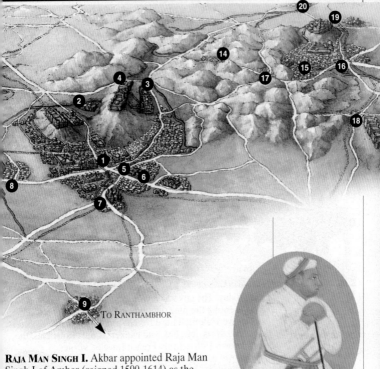

TO RANTHAMBHOR

RAJA MAN SINGH I. Akbar appointed Raja Man Singh I of Amber (reigned 1590-1614) as the Commander-in-Chief of the Mughal armies. Raja Man Singh I won a series of splendid victories for the Mughals all over India and helped them establish a vast empire, stretching from Kabul in the north to the Deccan plateau in the south. Apart from being an outstanding warrior, Raja Man Singh I was a great builder and a patron of the arts. It was he who built much of the impressive fort-palace complex at Amber. He was succeeded by Mirza Raja Jai Singh (reigned 1621-67), another great warrior and esthete cast in a similar mold.

RAJA SAWAI JAI SINGH II. The most brilliant of Amber's rulers was Raja Sawai Jai Singh II (reigned 1699-1743) ● *35.* The story goes that when, as a young boy, he was presented before Emperor Aurangzeb, the latter suddenly grabbed both his wrists and said, "Of what use is your sword now?" Jai Singh II calmly replied, "Your Majesty, when a bridegroom takes a bride's hand, he is duty-bound to protect her. Now that I have you to protect me, why do I need my sword?" Impressed by the repartee, Aurangzeb gave him the title "Sawai", which means "The One-and-a-Quarter", indicating that he was a notch above other men in intelligence. Sawai Jai Singh II was a man of many parts: soldier, mathematician, astronomer, statesman, and architect. It was he who reunited the Rajputs against the Mughals after Aurangzeb's death. With the turmoil of the last days of the Mughal Empire, Jaipur became a haven for the merchants, bankers, and jewelers of northern India and flourished, becoming, as a British visitor later wrote, "a sort of Lombard Street of Rajpootana".

THE GREAT CONQUEROR
Raja Man Singh I was a brilliant general who led Emperor Akbar's Mughal armies in campaigns from Afghanistan in the east and the Deccan in the south, contributing greatly to the rapid growth of the Mughal Empire. He amassed enormous wealth from his conquests which made Jaipur the powerful kingdom it was. According to legend, when Akbar once asked him what had happened to all the treasures of Deccan, Raja Man Singh I pointed to his battle wounds and said, "They're inside here."

131

Coin used during the
reign of Maharaja
Sawai Man Singh II.

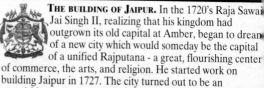

COAT-OF-ARMS
Jaipur's coat-of-arms
(right) incorporates
the ancient five-
colored flag of
Amber. The central
shield is flanked by a
lion (a symbol of
Rajput valor) and a
horse. It is topped by
a sun (representing
descent from the sun
god), or an image
of Lord Krishna
or Shiva, or a
helmet.

THE ONE-AND-A-QUARTER
Raja Jai Singh II was
given the title of
"Sawai", meaning
"The One-and-a-
Quarter", by
Emperor Aurangzeb
for his intelligence.
Ever since, the rulers
of Jaipur have flown
two flags, one full and
one quarter-sized, to
symbolize this title.

Jaipur, c. 1900.

THE BUILDING OF JAIPUR. In the 1720's Raja Sawai Jai Singh II, realizing that his kingdom had outgrown its old capital at Amber, began to dream of a new city which would someday be the capital of a unified Rajputana - a great, flourishing center of commerce, the arts, and religion. He started work on building Jaipur in 1727. The city turned out to be an astonishing well-planned one, based on the ancient Hindu treatise on architecture, the *Shilpa Shastra* ● *92*. The town planner was a talented, young scholar and engineer, Vidyadhar Bhattacharya (below), whose family had been invited to settle in Jaipur from the distant state of Bengal by Raja Man Singh I. Jaipur was built on a grid system. Its main streets, 119 feet wide were intersected at right angles by secondary streets, 60 feet wide, which were further criss-crossed by lanes and bylanes, 30 feet and 15 feet wide respectively. The streets were lined with fine buildings of uniform design and shaded by trees. In the middle of the main road run an aqueduct, and there were wells for drinking water at regular intervals, many of which are still used today. The city was divided into nine rectangular sectors (representing the nine divisions of the universe). Different streets were allotted for different professions such as potters, weavers, dyers, jewelers, and bankers. Louis Rousselet, the well-known 19th-century French traveler, wrote, "The town is built in a style of unusual magnificence... I doubt whether at the time it was built there were many cities in Europe which could compare with it." The 19th-century English bishop, Heber, wrote that it was comparable to the Kremlin in Moscow. Raja Sawai Jai Singh II named the new city after himself (fortuitously Jaipur also means "City of Victory").

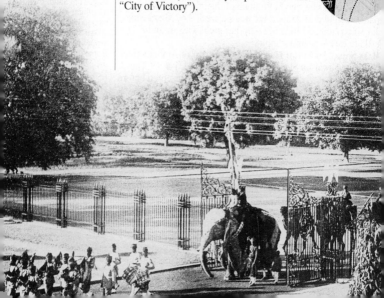

> "…THE GOOD PEOPLE OF AMERICA BUILDED THEIR TOWNS AFTER THIS PATTERN, BUT KNOWING NOTHING OF JEY SINGH, THEY TOOK ALL THE CREDIT THEMSELVES."
>
> RUDYARD KIPLING, *LETTERS OF MARQUE*, 1899

JAIPUR AND THE BRITISH.
During the early 19th century, plagued by the depredations of the Marathas from the south, the kingdom was thrown into confusion. In 1818 it signed a treaty of "defensive alliance, perpetual friendship, protection and subordinate cooperation" with the British. In the years that followed, the British handled Jaipur, and all the other Rajput kingdoms, with great shrewdness, drawing them into their fold. They elevated the major rulers from rajas to maharajas ("great rajas"), dished out gun salutes, and even had Robert Taylor, a heraldic novice in the Bengal Civil Service, design ornate, if slightly bogus, coats-of-arms for them, which Rudyard Kipling found "curious" and "interesting".

Maharaja Sawai Man Singh II, portrait (left) and in his carriage (right).

MAHARAJA SAWAI MAN SINGH II. The 1930's saw the beginning of a golden age in Jaipur, following the reign of Maharaja Sawai Man Singh II (reigned 1922-49), a glamorous young polo player and jet-setter. When he took his celebrated polo team to England in 1933 ▲ *144*, a newspaper breathlessly reported, "This Prince, who might have stepped straight from the pages of the Arabian Nights, is a slim, broad-shouldered Adonis. Champion polo-player of India, he can ride his horse like a Cossack, and has brought a team of princes, all of whom are related to him." Perhaps appropriately, he married in true fairy-tale. His third maharani was Gayatri Devi ● *40,* an exquisite princess of Cooch Behar, who was once listed, along with Vivien Leigh, as one of the ten most beautiful women in the world. The 1930's in Jaipur was an era of polo matches, tiger hunts, and fabulous royal parties. When a prince was born, for instance, he was promptly named "Bubbles", after the vast quantities of champagne that were downed in his honor. And when a princess was married, the wedding was so lavish that it was listed in the *Guinness Book of Records* as the most expensive wedding in the world. In 1949, after India's independence, all princely states of this region were merged ● *39.* Jaipur was made the capital of the newly formed state of Rajasthan.

FIRMAN
Raja Sawai Jai Singh II's *firman,* or order for the building of his dream city of Jaipur, was issued in 1726. In its planning 18th-century Jaipur recalled the legendary city of Ayodhya, described in the epic *Ramayana* as such: "A great and glorious city, divided into large fine streets, embellished with a royal avenue that cuts through it admirably ....The city has arched gates, well-placed markets and is occupied by all sorts of craftmen. Bards and heralds abound."

1. CITY PALACE **2.** HAWA MAHAL **3.** AMBER FORT **4.** JAIGARH FORT **5.** JAL MAHAL **6.** NAHARGARH FORT **7.** GAITOR **8.** ALBERT HALL MUSEUM **9.** RAMBAGH PALACE **10.** MOTI DOONGRI PALACE

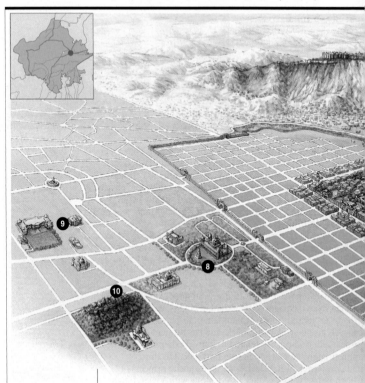

JAIPUR TODAY

Jaipur is the capital of Rajasthan, as was foreseen long ago by Raja Sawai Jai Singh II. It has a population of over 1½ million. Jaipur is called the "Pink City", for by law, all the buildings in the old city must be painted a deep saffron-pink. The practice follows a tradition that dates back to the visit of the Prince of Wales in 1876, when the entire city was freshly painted in his honor. (It might very well have been called the "blue" or "white" city, for these were some of the other colors that were apparently experimented with before pink was chosen.) Apart from being an important administrative, commercial , and educational center,

SIR SWINTON JACOB Several of Jaipur's buildings were designed by the architect Sir Swinton Jacob, who had produced a famous portfolio of Indian architectural details in the 19th century ● 96.

A miniature painting (top right) showing the pink gate and right, the pink gate as seen today.

"HIGHLY ORIENTED CURIOSITY...
ALL IN THE SOFT, RICH TINT OF STRAWBERRY ICE CREAM."

MARK TWAIN, *AROUND THE EQUATOR*, 1879

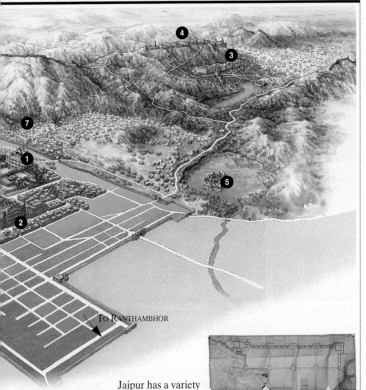

To Ranthambhor

Jaipur has a variety
of manufacturing industries.
It is especially known for its arts and crafts:
jewelry, enamel work, hand-printed fabrics,
and stone sculptures. Above everything, Jaipur
is an extraordinary colorful place. On its
streets you see women in their brilliant red and orange *odhnis*
(head coverings) and sweeping skirts, and men in their
equally vivid turbans and upturned mustaches. Both turbans
and mustaches have an entire non-verbal vocabulary of their
own: for instance, twirling one's mustache while looking at a
woman constitutes making a pass at her. And, as for a turban,
it can tell you the wearer's hometown, profession, and various
other personal details besides ▲ 295. If Jaipur is a city of
turbans and mustaches, it is also a city of polo, which has
curious variants: while usually played on horseback, it is also
played on elephants and, times being what they are, on
bicycles! The important sights to see in Jaipur are the City
Palace, the Jantar Mantar Observatory, and Amber Fort. But
do not miss the city's other fine public buildings such as the

Old map of Jaipur.

Albert Hall Museum.
While on the subject of
architecture, remember to
take a look at the grandiose
Raj Mandir cinema, whose
style could only be described
as "Cecil B. De Mille-Rajput
Rococo"!

Stone sculpture on a
wall in the city of
Jaipur.

135

SUN EMBLEM
This sun icon, composed of antique firearms and a Rajput shield, symbolizes the belief that the rulers of Jaipur trace their descent, through Lord Rama, hero of the great epic *Ramayana* back to the sun god himself.

Tripolia Gate.

The City Palace.

CITY PALACE ★

The sprawling City Palace was an integral part of Raja Sawai Jai Singh II's new city of Jaipur ▲ *132*. Of the nine blocks in the city plan, two were apportioned for the palace. It is almost a city within a city. The City Palace is a superb marriage of the Rajput and Mughal styles of architecture. The basic layout is in the Mughal style, with open, airy buildings designed for different functions, each one set in a geometrical garden of its own. But there is also a great deal, especially in the details of the palace, that results from centuries of Rajput (and Jain) architectural tradition. As you walk deeper into the palace complex, you come to buildings of an increasingly private function.

MUBARAK MAHAL. You enter through Atish Pol, or "Stable Gate" (the palace's great triple-arched Tripolia Gate is now reserved for the Maharaja's family, which still lives in a part of the palace). Passing through Chandni Chowk ("Square of Moonlight") and Gainda ki Deorhi ("Rhinoceros Gate"), you come to Mubarak Mahal (above). This was a royal guest house built in 1900 by Maharaja Madho Singh II. Designed by Sir Swinton Jacob ▲ 134, it now contains part of the palace museum. Here, in the *toshakhana* ("royal wardrobe" section), you can see some of the sumptuous brocade, silk, and fine muslin costumes of the royal family dating back to the 18th century.

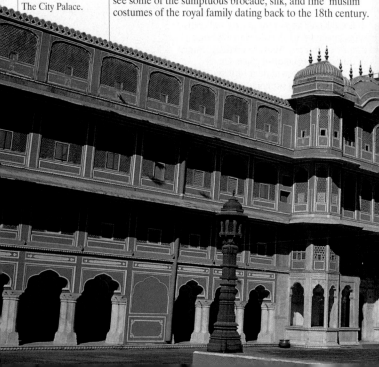

THE MAHARAJA'S SILK ROBE
An enormous silk robe worn by Raja Sawai Madho Singh I (reigned 1750-68) is on display in the museum at the City Palace. The Raja is said to have stood at over 6½ feet tall and weighed over 500 pounds.

SILEH KHANA. Nearby is Sileh Khana, the armory section, which contains one of India's finest collections of antique weapons, including Raja Man Singh I's massive cutlass (weighing 11 pounds) ▲ *200* and an interesting turban-shaped helmet that belonged to Mirza Raja Jai Singh I. Some of the weapons are real curiosities such as the dagger that has two miniature pistols built into its handle, hence leaving absolutely nothing to chance! There is also a bloodthirsty sword-like weapon - a predecessor of the dumdum bullet concept perhaps - that would spread open on being plunged into the unfortunate victim's body.

SINGH POL. Opposite Mubarak Mahal is Singh Pol ("Lion Gate"). This impressive gateway, with its ornate brackets, carved balconies, and brass-studded doors, is a fine example of the typically Hindu architectural elements that fill the City Palace. On either side of it are enormous white marble elephants (above) ● *71*. They were moved here from the *zenana* (private maharanis quarters) to mark the birth of Maharaja Bhawani Singh in 1931, the first direct male heir to the Jaipur throne in two generations.

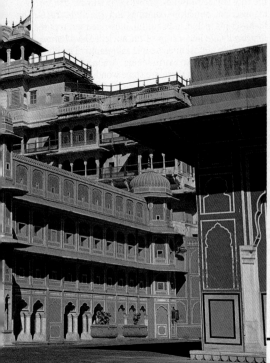

TAKING THE WATERS
When Maharaja Madho Singh II (reigned 1880-1927) (above) was going to England for King Edward VII's coronation in 1902, he had two enormous, solid silver urns made to carry sufficient sacred Ganges water for him to bathe with every day for four months! Measuring 5 feet high, they are listed in the *Guinness Book of Records* as the largest silver objects in the world. In addition, the devout Maharaja had the S.S. Olympia, a brand new ship that he had chartered, specially washed and purified, and had a temple to Lord Krishna made on board for the voyage across the "black waters".

▲ JAIPUR
THE CITY PALACE AND HAWA MAHAL

Chandra Mahal.

A portrait of Jesus Christ as an infant in the City Palace Museum.

Hall in Chandra Mahal.

Peacock gateway leading to Pritam Niwas Chowk.

DIWAN-I-KHAS. Beyond Singh Pol lies Diwan-Khas ("Hall of Private Audience"), a large, breezy, typically Mughal, pillared hall. Set within an impressive, deep pink courtyard, it has elegant rows of marble pillars and arches supporting its beautiful pavilion roof. Today, as a sign of the times, it is surmounted, incongruously, with a satellite dish antenna.

DIWAN-I-AM. To the right is Diwan-i-Am ("Hall of Public Audience"). Its ceiling, painted in the 1870's, is decorated with floral motifs in gilt, green, and red. Along one side are latticed galleries provided so that the maharanis of the household could watch the proceedings below without being seen themselves. Today Diwan-i-Am houses a major part of the City Palace Museum, known especially for its rare manuscripts, miniature paintings and splendid carpets. The manuscripts include a beautiful, illustrated scroll of the *Bhagavad Gita* and a copy of the ancient *Shiva Purana,* rendered in almost microscopic calligraphy. The illustrated *Geet Govinda* is also worth seeing. Among the miniature paintings, of which there are some wonderful examples here, two are particularly interesting. One is a painting of the Madonna and Child, in which Joseph is depicted in a European Renaissance style, but the Madonna, curiously, is wearing a typically Mughal headdress and earrings! Another outstanding painting is *Lovers at Night,* executed almost entirely in black and white, and brilliantly capturing the glimmer of moonlight on marble. The carpets dating back to the 17th century, came from Herat and Lahore. They are exquisitely woven, and measure up to 28 feet by 10 feet. The collection includes a carpet that is said to have been the throne carpet of the Mughal emperor, Jahangir.

PRITAM NIWAS CHOWK. Nearby is Pritam Niwas Chowk ("Square of the Beloved"). It is an enchanting enclosed courtyard with four 18th-century gateways, elaborately decorated in brilliant colors. This courtyard was originally used for royal dance performances. The balcony above one of the gates was used by performing singers.

CHANDRA MAHAL. Beyond Pritam Niwas Chowk lies the seven-storied Chandra Mahal ("Palace of the Moon"), with its Wedgewood-blue Chhabi Niwas hall, its beautiful, floral painted Sukh Niwas hall, and its even more beautiful Rang Mahal, an ornate Hall of Mirrors, based on the one at the Red Fort in Delhi. However, the Chandra Mahal complex is where the present Maharaja lives and is closed to the public.

GOVIND DEVJI TEMPLE. Walking back toward Sireh Deorhi Gate, you come to the large Jaleb Chowk. Here you will find Govind Devji Temple, the temple of Lord Krishna, in whose name the Kachhawaha kings used to rule Jaipur. The idol was brought back from Mathura, the birthplace of Lord Krishna, by Raja Sawai Jai Singh II and installed here in the 1730's.

HAWA MAHAL

Nearby is the ornate Hawa Mahal ("Palace of the Winds") ▲ *88, 93*. It is a delightfully idiosyncratic five-tier composition of arches and balconies with 953 casements set in a wide curve. However, it is little more than a façade, as most of the building is just one chamber deep. It was built in 1799 for the ladies of the royal household to enjoy the breeze and to look out to the outside world, without flouting the confines of *purdah*. The design of Hawa Mahal is said to have been inspired by Jain temple architecture, with its tradition of taking a single structural motif and repeating it, tier after tier, for the bold vertical thrust that it creates. The 11th-century Sas Bahu Jain temple near Gwalior is said to have been the model on which it was based.

RARE PHOTOGRAPHS
Maharaja Ram Singh (reigned 1835-80) was a passionate photographer in the 1860's who set up his own studio and darkroom within the City Palace. His photographs were praised by critics of his time. As a result, the City Palace Museum has a great collection of old photographic equipment, including Ram Singh's camera (above) and photographs. These include rare photographs of ladies of the royal family. (Normally, no aristocratic Indian lady of the time would allow herself to be photographed.)

Hawa Mahal.

▲ JAIPUR
JANTAR MANTAR ★

Narivalaya Yantra.

Jaiprakash Yantra.

SPREADING FAME
Raja Sawai Jai Singh II's observatory prompted the Portuguese Viceroy in Goa to send an emissary to Jaipur in 1729 to study it. Later, as its fame spread, French and German scholars, astronomers and priests also came here. Through his Portuguese friend, Padre Manuel de

The Jaipur astronomical observatory built by Raja Sawai Jai Singh II in 1827 is an amazing monument. Jantar Mantar (the name roughly translates as "The Formula of Instruments") was one of five observatories that he built in northern India.

Its instruments, which look like giant, abstract, futuristic sculptures, are actually highly sophisticated devices that could, among other things, mark time accurate to one second. The first observatory was built in Delhi. The second and more sophisticated one is at Jaipur. In addition, three smaller ones, in Varanasi, Ujjain, and Mathura, were built to supplement the observations made in Jaipur. (The Mathura one has since been destroyed.)

IN PURSUIT OF ASTRONOMY. Raja Sawai Jai Singh II eagerly devoured every known work on the subject written by Indian, Arab, and Greek astronomers and even went to the extent of having Ptolemy's *Almagest* and Newton's *Principia* specially translated into

Figueredo, Raja Sawai Jai Singh II procured the latest astronomical texts and instruments from Europe. Using his huge masonry instruments, he was able to detect errors in the well-known astronomical tables of Père de la Hire, who, like other European astronomers, used only standard-sized brass instruments.

Sanskrit for him. He greatly admired the work done by the Turkish royal astronomer, Ulugh Beg, who had built an observatory in Samarkand in the 15th century, which had produced the most accurate astronomical readings to date. In the introduction to his own comprehensive treatise, he wrote that since nobody had done any significant work in the field since Ulugh Beg, he would undertake the daunting task himself. He sent out his emissaries to collect all the most advanced astronomical instruments that were being used by 18th-century European and Islamic astronomers. During the course of his studies he discovered inaccuracies in the existing astronomical tables of the time. In the tables of the French astronomers, Père de la Hire, for example, he was able to detect a discrepancy of half a degree in the placement of the moon and planets. He was outspoken in his criticism and once wrote. "Ptolemy is a bat... the demonstrations of Euclid are an imperfect sketch of the forms of his contrivances." He concluded that the inaccuracies in the existing tables were all a result of mechanical limitations of the instruments used at the time - they were too small in size to be accurate, and their moving parts made them unreliable. His solution, therefore, was to build gigantic instruments from stone, masonry, and

Jantar Mantar.

Samrat Yantra.

marble instead of the conventional brass ones.

SAMRAT YANTRA. His great Samrat Yantra, for example, is basically a sundial, except that it is a massive 89 feet high and 148 feet wide. As a result, when the sun moves across the sky it casts a shadow on the finely calibrated quadrants on either side, which moves at a precise and measurable 0.08 inch every second. It was designed to measure local time as well as such things as zenith distances, meridian pass times and the declination of the stars with remarkable precision. Interestingly, the Samrat Yantra at each of his five observatories varies slightly in shape in order to ensure that the hypotenuse of its great triangle is aligned perfectly with the axis of the earth and the flanking quadrants are perfectly parallel to the Equator.

OTHER INSTRUMENTS. In all, Raja Sawai Jai Singh II invented fifteen different instruments, all of them based on his principle of accuracy through gigantic size. They ranged from Ram Yantra (below), which determines the azimuths and altitudes of various heavenly bodies, to Misra Yantra, which, among other things, tells the time at four different foreign observatories. The instruments are in such a good condition that, surprisingly, they are still used today. Samrat Yantra, for instance, is consulted every year on the full moon night of *Guru Purnima*, along with the ancient Sanskrit texts, to predict the onset of the monsoon. One of the instruments on display at Jantar Mantar and the City Palace Museum is a telescope, indicating just how aware the Raja was of the latest technology of his time. For all his brilliance, however, Raja Sawai Jai Singh II was touchingly ignorant of one little point: he thought, till the end, that the sun revolved around the earth.

Smaller Samrat Yantra (left).

MANUSCRIPT ON ASTRONOMY
Raja Sawai Jai Singh II's eclectic collection of astronomical instruments and manuscripts from all over the then known world are displayed at Jantar Mantar and the City Palace Museum.

KING OF ALL INSTRUMENTS
The astrolabe, a kind of celestial map engraved on a 7-foot wide metal disc, was one of the most sophisticated astronomical instruments of its time in the Western world. Raja Sawai Jai Singh II managed to get himself one, which he named Raj Yantra ("The King of All Instruments"). He wrote two volumes on the principles and utility of the device, which became one of his proudest possessions.

141

▲ JAIPUR BAZAARS

CHAND POL BAZAR
चांद पोल बाज़ार

Wandering through the bazaars of old Jaipur is an experience in itself, whether you buy anything (and there's lots to choose from) or not. They are colorful, noisy, and happily chaotic, and you can buy anything here, from Jaipur's famous *minakari* jewelry to bars of soap, marketed under the unique promise that they are made from holy Ganges water, to give you a holy Ganges water bath every time. The most interesting bazaars lie within the Pink City quarter. The best way to tackle them is perhaps by first taking a slow "recce" by cycle-rickshaw and then coming back to the parts you find most interesting.

SIREH DEORHI BAZAAR. A convenient place to start is Sireh Deorhi Bazaar, just outside Hawa Mahal. At street level is a jumble of colorful stalls, and above are the pink cupolas and ornate latticed windows of Raja Sawai Jai Singh II's old city. Here the shops selling brightly colored textiles begin. By the way, don't miss the little shop here that sells ready-made turbans, or the quiant, old Ramprakash cinema.

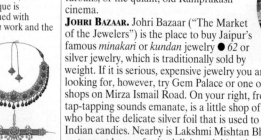

JOHRI BAZAAR. Johri Bazaar ("The Market of the Jewelers") is the place to buy Jaipur's famous *minakari* or *kundan* jewelry ● *62* or silver jewelry, which is traditionally sold by weight. If it is serious, expensive jewelry you are looking for, however, try Gem Palace or one of the other shops on Mirza Ismail Road. On your right, from where the tap-tapping sounds emanate, is a little shop of silver beaters who beat the delicate silver foil that is used to top traditional Indian candies. Nearby is Lakshmi Mishtan Bhandar, a restaurant known for its delicious *dahi wadas* and *kachoris*.

MINAKARI JEWELRY
Jaipur's *minakari* jewelry is gold jewelry that is lavishly enameled with glowing reds, greens, and turquoise blues ● *62*. Often, this technique is combined with *kundan* work and the

jewelry is further studded with gems. It is a painstaking craft (a single pendant can take months to make). Each piece passes through at least four master craftsmen. First, a goldsmith to craft the item, then a *minakar* to enamel it, then a gem-setter for the *kundan* work and, finally, another jeweler to add on the dangling pearls. It is said that Raja Man Singh I originally brought five master *minakar* jewelers here from Lahore in the 16th century. Some of today's well-known *minakaris* are directly descended from them.

142

Locally made handicrafts (left) and ready-made turbans (right) can be found in Jaipur's bazaars.

Inside, in the narrow maze of bylanes near Gopalji ka Rasta, are more tiny jewelry workshops and candy shops.

BAPU, NEHRU, AND INDIRA BAZAARS. Past Haldiyon ka Rasta, you turn at Sanganer Gate into the textile shops of Bapu Bazaar, Nehru Bazaar and Indira Bazaar. This is the place to buy Jaipur's well-known hand-block prints and vivid tie-and-dye fabrics ● 56. It is also the place for mirrored embroidery work and the embroidered camel-skin slippers called *mojris* , with their upturned toes. If you look up you can see the crenelated battlements of the medieval city wall running all the way along your left.

KISHANPOL BAZAAR. Turning up at Kishanpol Bazaar, you come to the shops selling decorative brassware and *ittar,* the heavily scented traditional Indian perfume. There are different seasonal fragrances that are supposed to cool you in summer and warm you in winter. Wander into Rang Walon ki Gali and you can see the textile dyers at work, tying and dyeing their flamboyantly colored fabrics. There is also an interesting old *haveli* here of the Commander-in-Chief of Jai Singh II: Natani ki Haveli (above), with its seven courtyards, now converted into a girls' school.

CHANDPOL BAZAAR. Past Khazane Walon ka Rasta, with its marble artefacts, you come to Chandpol Bazaar and its colorful little stalls selling everything from spices to delightfully kitschy lithographs of popular gods and goddesss. Stop by the little *haveli* here with its curious British-Rajput architecture. At the top of the tall classical columns, where you would expect to see Greek gods, are Indian deities instead! Inside, on your right, is Maniharon ki Gali, with its brightly colored bangle shops, where they specially twist lacquer bangles for you while you wait.

TRIPOLIA BAZAAR. Down Tripolia Bazaar are shops selling Jaipur's famous blue pottery and simple earthen water pots. There are two interesting, old *havelis* here - the *haveli* of Vidyadhar Bhattacharya, the architect of Jaipur (now converted into a museum) and the *haveli* of Nawab Faiz Ali Khan. Beyond Chaura Rasta, you come to Bari Chaupar, a good place to buy chunky rustic silver jewelry and traditional *mojri* slippers. Jaipur is also, by the way, an excellent place to buy carpets.

FAMOUS TEXTILE PRINTS

For more upmarket hand-block printed garments than the ones in the bazaars, try Anokhi at Tilak Marg. Featured in the pages of *Vogue* and *Elle* over the years, and with regular famous clients ranging from actress Felicity Kendall to author Doris Lessing, Anokhi has its own exclusive prints and designs. Most of what it makes is exported.

(Above) Models at an Anokhi fashion show.

Manak Chowk, Jaipur (center).

CANDY TREAT

Jaipur is known for its delicious traditional candies. A favorite is *ghevar,* a crunchy orange honeycomb-like disc made from cottage cheese. Probably the best-known candy shop in town is within the restaurant Lakshmi Mishtan Bhandar, said to have operated from the same premises since the 18th century.

A thoroughfare (left) with the gate, Chand Pol, at the far end.

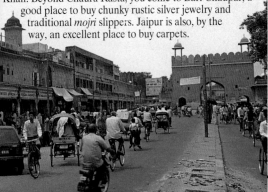

RAMBAGH PALACE

Rambagh Palace.

Rambagh Palace was the palace of Maharaja Sawai Man Singh II ▲ *133* in the closing decades of princely rule in India. A sprawling building with cupolas designed by Sir Swinton Jacob ▲ *134,* its gardens were once featured in Peter Coat's *The Most Beautiful Gardens of the World.* It has the unique distinction of being the only residence in the world with a polo field attached. Built originally as a garden house for a wet nurse of the prince, Ram Singh II, it later became a hunting lodge. (A princely guest once actually discovered a panther inside the palace and promptly speared it.) But by the 1930's, Rambagh had become the maharaja's official palace, with interiors furnished by Hammonds of London, including a magnificent red-and-gold Chinese room, Lalique crystal, Lalique chandeliers, Lalique fountains, and illuminated Lalique dining tables. It played host to a galaxy of international celebrities, from the famed Argentinian playboy (and polo player) Porfiro Rubirosa to Lord Mountbatten ● *39* and unexpectedly, the former U.S.S.R. premier, Nikita Khrushchev. Now it has been converted, like many Rajput palaces, into a splendid hotel. It is filled with the heirlooms of the last maharaja, including , in the Polo Bar, the mementoes of Jaipur's legendary 1930's polo team. Everywhere, you'll find details that speak volumes of the lifestyle of its former occupants.

Albert Hall Museum.

WINNING POLO
The Maharaja of Jaipur's polo team which visited England in 1933 was supposed to have been one of the finest the world has seen. It trounced the English teams so badly that this was how *The Tatler* depicted them.

ALBERT HALL MUSEUM

Set in Jaipur's spacious Ram Niwas Gardens, this stately building also designed by Sir Swinton Jacob, was modeled on London's Victoria and Albert Museum. It houses a collection of exhibits of Rajasthani folk arts. Take a look at the wonderful 30-foot long *phad* painting, for instance, depicting the ballad of the folk hero, Pabuji.

Drawing of
Rambagh Palace.

Various other exhibits include rare stone carvings dating back to the 2nd century and some fine miniatures. You will also discover, slightly unexpectedly, an Egyptian mummy. But the prize possession is a magnificent late 16th-century Persian garden carpet, considered one of the finest carpets ever woven.

RAJMAHAL PALACE

This charming 18th-century palace was built as a summer resort for the ladies of the royal household. Later it became the home of the British Resident in Jaipur, and ultimately the palace of the last ruling maharaja. Set in 52 acres of grounds, this was where the royal family lived till 1976.

HAVELIS

Jaipur probably had more nobles and wealthy landlords than any other Indian Princely State, except Hyderabad. And the *havelis* were the townhouses where they lived when they were in Jaipur ● 86. Between them, these *havelis* give you a peep into the lifestyle of the old feudal chieftains, with their chandeliers, hunting trophies, antique weaponry - and hybrid Rajput-British decor.

NARAIN NIWAS. Narain Niwas, one of the best examples, was the 19th-century *haveli* of the chieftains of Kanota. One of its occupants was Amar Singh of Kanota, a cavalry officer who fought with the Jodhpur Lancers in the Boxer Revolution in China in 1901 ▲ 220. His diaries, which consist of eighty-nine volumes covering the period 1898-1942, give a brilliant portrait of life in old Rajputana. Other interesting old *havelis* are Samode Haveli and Bissau Lodge. There are other well-known *havelis* in Tripoli Bazaar and Kishanpol Bazaar, but they are not in as good a condition.

MOTI DOONGRI PALACE

Moti Doongri Palace stands out eccentrically among the old Rajput palaces. Originally a small fort called Shankar Garh ("Shiva's Foot"), it was renovated by Maharaja Sawai Man Singh II - and idiosyncratically restyled to look like a Scottish castle! It was one of Maharaja Sawai Man Singh II's favorite palaces and was the location for glittering parties that he hosted for his intimate circle of friends. It had a rather grisly history, though, and is said to have been briefly used in the 1930's as a prison for a princeling who had cut off a boy's testicles in a fit of anger.

Moti Doongri Palace.

BLUE POTTERY REDISCOVERED
There are only a few rare pieces of Jaipur's beautiful 19th-century blue pottery ● 72 surviving today, and some of the finest specimens are in Rambagh Palace. The craft was practiced by just one family, who guarded its secrets so closely that the craft itself nearly died out. Then, in the 1950's, an artist named Kripal Singh, encouraged by Maharani Gayatri Devi ● 40, painstakingly pieced together its lost secrets, thus leading to a revival of the art form.

BLUE-TILED FOUNTAIN
This fountain at the Rambagh Palace was commissioned by Maharaja Sawai Man Singh II in the 1930's. The tiles were manufactured at the Jaipur School of Arts, which was founded in 1866 by Maharaja Sawai Ram Singh II (reigned 1835-80).

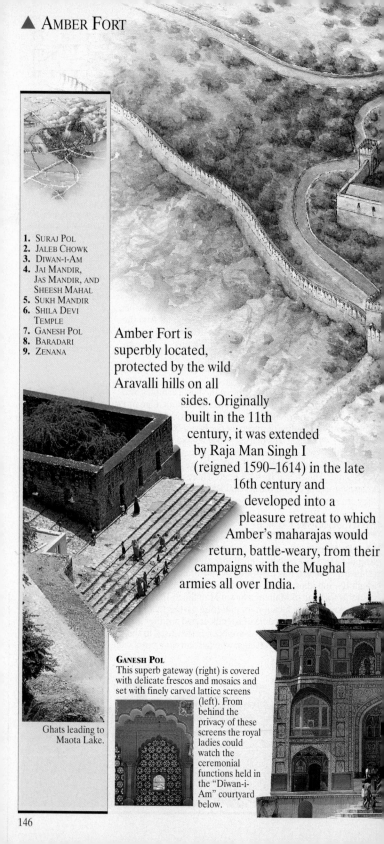

1. SURAJ POL
2. JALEB CHOWK
3. DIWAN-I-AM
4. JAI MANDIR,
   JAS MANDIR, AND
   SHEESH MAHAL
5. SUKH MANDIR
6. SHILA DEVI
   TEMPLE
7. GANESH POL
8. BARADARI
9. ZENANA

Amber Fort is
superbly located,
protected by the wild
Aravalli hills on all
sides. Originally
built in the 11th
century, it was extended
by Raja Man Singh I
(reigned 1590–1614) in the late
16th century and
developed into a
pleasure retreat to which
Amber's maharajas would
return, battle-weary, from their
campaigns with the Mughal
armies all over India.

Ghats leading to
Maota Lake.

GANESH POL
This superb gateway (right) is covered
with delicate frescos and mosaics and
set with finely carved lattice screens
(left). From
behind the
privacy of these
screens the royal
ladies could
watch the
ceremonial
functions held in
the "Diwan-i-
Am" courtyard
below.

Amber Fort.

AMBER FORT ★

Amber lies about 7 miles northeast of Jaipur. The name is derived from the goddess, Amba Mata, the Mother Earth, whom the Mina tribe used to worship at this site before the Kachhawaha Rajputs took it over and made it their capital. Amber remained the capital of the Kachhawahas till 1727, but even after that

SHEESH MAHAL
Virtually every major Rajput palace boasts a Sheesh Mahal ("Hall of Mirrors"), but the most lavish of all is the one at Amber ● *109*. Its walls and ceiling are entirely covered with an intricately patterned inlay of mirrors and colored glass. When a candle is lit in the darkness, the effect of an infinite starscape is created.

it was never completely abandoned. When the Mughal emperor Aurangzeb once asked Raja Sawai Jai Singh II what his capital looked like, it is said the latter cut open a pomegranate – to demonstrate how it lay in a protected valley. All around Amber, the hills are ringed with battlements and watchtowers, and within the valley lie the remains of the ancient capital. Much of it is now in ruins, including the 13th-century palace (only Bala Bai ki Sal is somewhat intact). There remains an ornate 17th-century water tank nearby, Panna Mian ka Kund, built by a eunuch, and Jagat Shiromani Temple, a fine marriage of north and south Indian architectural styles, with a superbly carved *torana* archway over its entrance. In addition, there is the 18th-century Chamwar Walon ki Haveli ("Mansion of the Fly Whisk Attendants"), which has now been painstakingly restored to its original condition. It is a private home, but worth seeing from the outside at least.

Jagat Shiromani Temple.

Jaleb Chowk.

GARDENS OF DILARAM BAGH AND MOHAN BARI. By the waters of Maota Lake lie the beautifully laid out old gardens of Dilaram Bagh and Mohan Bari. A formal garden was an idea largely unknown in traditional Indian palace architecture (although many palaces lay in beautiful natural surroundings) until this Persian concept was brought in by the Muslim invaders. The garden concept was one of many Mughal ideas that Raja Man Singh I imbibed from his close friend, Emperor Akbar, along with such details as cusped arches, domes and marble filigree-work grilles, all of

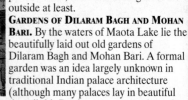

"…A LIVING PALACE WHERE THE SIGHTSEER KNOWS AND FEELS THAT…HE IS BEING FOLLOWED BY SCORES OF UNSEEN EYES."

RUDYARD KIPLING, *LETTERS OF MARQUE*, 1899

which he incorporated splendidly at Amber. Overlooking Maota Lake is the old Raj Mahal Palace, built from 1600 onward.

JALEB CHOWK. A steep cobbled path from Dilaram Bagh takes you up to Suraj Pol and Jaleb Chowk. Often mistakenly referred to as "Jalebi Chowk", or "The Candy Square", it actually means "The Square where Horses and Elephants are Tethered." Here lies Singh Pol ("Lion Gate"), an impressively fortified double gate, incorporating a blind turn and guard rooms on three sides. This was once richly painted with frescos, the fading remains of which you can still see.

Mohan Bari.

SHILA DEVI TEMPLE. Nearby is the beautiful temple to Kali, its pillars carved in the form of banana trees in delicate green marble. The image of the goddess was brought back from Bengal by Raja Man Singh I in 1580. The temple's priests had traditionally been Bengalis but now they are from Bihar.

DIWAN-I-AM. Opposite the Kali Temple lies the marvelous Diwan-i-Am ("Hall of Public Audience"), built by Mirza Raja Jai Singh I. On the southern side of Diwan-i-Am lies the splendid Ganesh Pol ("Elephant Gate"), described as one of the finest gateways in the world. It leads you into a lovely little Mughal garden, around which the royal apartment complex was designed.

JAI MANDIR AND JAS MANDIR. Jai Mandir, used as a hall of private audience, is created in white marble. Its floral ceiling is inlaid with intricate mirror-work. The walls are decorated with fine murals of leafy scrolls and flowers. The magnificent Sheesh Mahal ("Hall of Mirrors") has walls and ceilings entirely covered with intricate inlay-work of mirror and colored glass. The stained-glass windows here, by the way, were a later 18th-century addition, imported from Europe. Just above Jai Mandir is Jas Mandir, with a roof ablaze with spangled mirrors and lovely mosaics. Its entire eastern face is a filigreed marble screen, with a stunning view over Maota Lake and the rugged hills below, specially designed to catch the summer breezes and draw them in to cool the hall.

SUKH MANDIR. Opposite this complex, across the gardened courtyard, is Sukh Mandir ("Temple of Contentment"), an aptly named pleasure chamber, cooled by a marble water cascade. Do not miss the doors here, which are made of fragrant sandalwood, inlaid with ivory.

ZENANA. Beyond this lies the Zenana ("Palace of the Ranis"). Here, clustered around a large central courtyard, were what used to be the self-contained suites of twelve ranis, with chambers for concubines on the upper floor. There is a device for grinding millet in the floor of the favorite rani's suite: it apparently served as an exercising device to help keep her figure trim! In the courtyard is a fine *baradari* (pavilion) supported by stately carved pillars.

PLASTERED OVER Diwan-i-Am has a double row of red sandstone pillars with elephant capitals, and gray Mughal-style columns holding up its vaulted roof. The hall's magnificence is supposed to have provoked the jealousy of the Mughal emperor Shah Jahan, causing the Raja to prudently cover up the marble columns with plaster just before an imperial inspection. The plaster was finally removed only about fifty years ago, but if you look closely at the columns, you can still see traces of it. Nearby is a remarkable row of traditional *arayish* (lime stucco plaster) columns, so smoothly finished that you might mistake them for marble.

Jaigarh Fort.

JAIGARH FORT

High in the hills above Amber is the magnificent Jaigarh Fort. It was built in the 17th century to reinforce the defenses of the Kachhawaha capital. Its mighty ramparts stretch, seemingly for miles, across the hillsides, with embrasures cunningly designed to give the defenders a choice of three different angles for shooting down at their attackers. Also on the ramparts is an enormous watchtower, Diva Burj. Once it was seven stories high, but legend says that the lightning, jealous of the height of its flaming lamp, struck down the top two stories. The most interesting thing about Jaigarh Fort, however, is the legend of its buried treasure. Raja Man Singh I is said to have buried inside here the booty from his various campaigns, worth, according to one account, 1 080 million rupees (US$ 35 million) in the 1720's. The treasure was guarded by fierce Mina tribesmen. Over the centuries, each successive maharaja was led blindfold to the treasure by the Minas, once in his lifetime, and allowed to choose just one piece from it. In the 1970's the government of India launched one of the world's most ambitious treasure hunts ever to unearth his legendary treasure. It was, according to one theory, hidden inside the fort's huge water-tanks, but nothing was ever found. Some say the treasure is still in there, somewhere...

WORLD'S LARGEST WHEELED CANNON

The giant Jaivana cannon is the largest wheeled cannon in the world. Cast in 1720 in Jaigarh Fort's foundry, it is 9 feet high, over 20 feet long and weighs 50 tons. It took four elephants to swivel it around on its axis. Its sound was said to have been so terrifying loud that it caused the water in the nearby wells to dry up.

Wall painting in Nahargarh Palace.

JAIGARH PALACE. Inside the fort is a palace with a complex of royal apartments, build by various maharajas over a period of two centuries. In Lakshmi Vilas, there are some beautifully painted blue frescos, the remains of a lovely old Mughal garden and an interesting little theater where the maharajas used to watch dance, puppet shows, and music recitals (the ranis watched from a separate *purdah* section above). From here there is also an interesting view of a special fortified passage snaking down to a nearby lake which provided access to water in times of siege.

Decorative
arayish
plasterwork in
the palace of
Nahargarh Fort.

JAIGARH AND NAHARGARH FORTS ▲

CANNON FOUNDRY. The remains of Jaigarh's famous 16th-century cannon foundry, one of the few surviving medieval cannon foundries anywhere in the world, are here at Jaigarh Fort. You can see some of its products, including the mighty Jaivana cannon. Despite its awesome firepower, it is delicately decorated with scrollwork, birds, foliage and a roaring elephant at its mouth. There is also a point called Damdama ("continuous firing"), where a battery of ten great cannons was positioned to stop any approaching enemy with a furious fusillade. The curious thing is that this formidable battery was facing the approach from Delhi, leading one to believe that Raja Man Singh I was secretly preparing for a showdown with his Mughal allies.

NAHARGARH FORT

If Jaigarh was one of the hill forts guarding the approach to Amber, the other was Nahargarh, the "tiger Fort". Originally this site was thickly forested and inhabited by deadly accurate Mina archers. It also happened to be the site of the cenotape of a Rathor prince, Nahar Singh. However, in 1734, Raja Sawai Jai Singh II decided that this was the precise spot on which he wanted to build a new fort. According to legend, the ghost of Nahar Singh would not let the fort to be built: whatever walls were erected by day came crumbling down by night. Finally, tantric rites were performed to appease the agitated ghost, and the fort, once completed, was named after the prince. The fort's thick crenelated ramparts and arches make it a superb example of Rajput military architecture. Over by the edge of the precipice is Hazari Burj, an artillery emplacement ideally positioned for the Kachhawaha guns to decimate any would-be attackers on the killing fields far below.

MADHAVENDRA BHAWAN. By the 19th century, Nahargarh Fort was converted to more peaceful purposes, and a palace was built here, with delicately cusped arches and ornately frescoed walls (above). As you enter, you can see the suites of the maharaja and his nine queens. All of them are notable for the beautiful florally painted *arayish* on their walls, which is still amazingly well-preserved. The palace complex is laid out with courtyards and terraces, and a Hawa Ghar ("breeze chamber"), from where the ranis could get a view of the city.

"MARBLE" FINISH
At Nahargarh (as at other old Rajput palaces), you can see a unique plasterwork technique called *arayish,* which had a finish as smooth as marble. *Arayish* is made from highly refined limestones, mixed with various exotic substances, including egg, *jaggery* (hardened palm syrup), gum and marble powder. Preparing it was an extremely painstaking process. The final stage was hand-polishing with a piece of agate. The finish was so smooth it was sometimes almost indistinguishable from marble.

Nahargarh Fort (left).
Fresco in palace
(above).

155

Sisodia Rani ka Bagh

Located 6 miles east of Jaipur is Sisodia Rani ka Bagh, a little palace laid out in formal terraced gardens with fountains (right). This was built for a Sisodia princess from Udaipur who was married to Raja Sawai Jai Singh II. It was merely a political marriage between the two antagonistic states, one of the terms of which was that the son born of this union would succeed to the Jaipur throne. But tired of the constant intriguing against her at Jaipur's City Palace and fearful for the life of her son, the unhappy princess came away here to live under its domed and canopied roof. The upper storey of the palace has some charming murals of hunting scenes, polo matches, mythical beasts and episodes from the life of Lord Krishna and Radha.

HOLY CLEANSING
Galta is a pilgrimage center for Hindus, and the waters of its seven tanks are considered to be as holy as those of the River Ganges. A dip in the tanks is said to cleanse believers of their worldly sins.

Galta

Just beyond Sisodia Rani ka Bagh, in a picturesque gorge, is the temple of Galta. This is the spot where the great sage Galav is supposed to have lived and performed his penance. On the ridge there is an 18th-century temple of Surya, the sun god, built by one of Raja Sawai Jai Singh II's courtiers. The view of the city from here is splendid. It is said that the temple's sacred tanks never run dry because of a spring that flows out of a rock carved with the shape of a cow's face.

View of Galta (above). Cenotaphs of Gaitor.

GAITOR

The graceful white marble cenotaphs of the Kachhawaha rulers lie in a valley beneath Nahargarh Fort, 4 miles north of Jaipur. The most impressive of them is that of Raja Sawai Jai Singh II, the great mathematician and astronomer-king ● 35, 131. Here, on his death, as Colonel Tod records, "his wives and several concubines ascended on his funeral pyre, on which science expired with him." The cenotaph or *chhatri* (the word literally means "umbrella") has a marble dome and surrounding cupolas, all supported by twenty pillars, lavishly carved with mythological figures. Raja Madho Singh II's *chhatri,* with its beautiful frieze of carved peacock, is also worth seeing. By the time you come to the *chhatri* of the last ruling maharaja, who died in the early 1970's, however. you will see how the standards of craftsmanship have sadly waned in recent times. What is particularly touching at Gaitor are the miniature *chhatris* in the complex: these are the shrines of the two sons born to Madho Singh II by his concubines. The ranis' *chhatris,* according to tradition, lie in a separate complex, not far away.

JAL MAHAL

In the middle of the lake of Man Sagar, en route to Amber, lies Jal Mahal ("Water Palace") with its graceful cupolas and *bangaldar* eaves reflecting prettily in the waters. Built by Madho Singh I (reigned 1750-68) ▲ *137,* it was obviously inspired by Udaipur's Jag Mandir ▲ *251,* where the raja spent his childhood. In the 19th century, it was turned into a hunting lodge.

Jal Mahal.

A TASTE OF RAJASTHAN
Choki Dhani, en route to Sanganer, is a novel "food village" (one can't call it a mere restaurant) serving authentic Rajasthan food in a charming rustic setting, complete with puppeteers, ballad singers, bangle-makers and potters. Its sprawling campus is lit entirely by flickering hurricane lamps. The food is served on leafplatters while you are seated on the floor in the traditional manner.

ORIGIN OF CENOTAPHS
The idea of erecting beautiful marble *chhatris* or cenotaphs (like the ones at Gaitor) probably originated from the impressive tombs that the Rajput kings saw their Muslim counterparts leave behind. Since they themselves were cremated (and had their ashes dispersed in the holy River Ganges), they developed the concept of memorials like these to mark the spot where they were cremated. Every Rajput kingdom had a hauntingly beautiful complex of cenotaphs for its rulers.

157

SANGANER

The old walled town of Sanganer, 10 miles south of Jaipur, is known for its traditional textile printing. It was named after a Kachhawaha prince, Sangaji. You enter the town through the ornate tripolia (triple arched) gateways in the ruined walls. Here you can see fabric being printed with hand-blocks, as has been done for centuries ● 56. The printers here were under the patronage of Jaipur's royal family and therefore developed a highly sophisticated sense of style. The printed calicoes of Sanganer are said to have been so popular in Britain in the 18th century that they began to affect the sales of woolen flax, and were therefore actually banned by statute in 1721. They are still exported to various fashion centres all over the world and are known for their delicate motifs of flowers, foliage, peacocks, and other animals. It is fascinating to wander through the sandy, winding alleyways of Sanganer and watch the hand-block printers at work. The entire town is one large, bustling, colorful workshop that often spills out into its narrow lanes. The printing, done with intricate, hand-carved wooden blocks, is an enormously laborious process: each yard of printed fabric may call for up to thirty separate blocks and up to 350 separate impressions. Sanganer is also a well-known center for blue pottery and handmade paper. There are some old temples here as well (above), the most beautiful being a 15th-century Jain temple with stone carvings so intricate that they are reminiscent of the great Dilwara temples at Mount Abu ● 94, ▲ 270.

HANDMADE PAPER
If you've ever used handmade paper from India, chances are it was made in Sanganer. The craftsmen are the descendants of those who, for generations, made paper for the Rajput princes, and the technique hasn't changed: the raw material is ordinary scrap paper, which is ripped up, stamped into pulp by foot, and washed. Then it is bleached, dyed, and very dexterously lifted out, layer by layer... each layer, of course, being a fresh sheet. The sheets are then dried, either by hanging them from clothes-lines, or by sticking them up on the walls of the town's houses. (The latter gives a more interesting texture.) Finally, they are smoothed out with heavy stones and speckled, if necessary with gold.

BAGRU

Beyond Sanganer, 20 miles southwest of Jaipur, is another old textile-printing town, Bagru. The hand-block printing technique here is similar to that of Sanganer ● 56, but what makes Bagru unique is that it is one of the last bastions of printers still predominantly using traditional vegetable dyes. For example, blues are often derived from indigo, greens from indigo mixed with pomegranate rinds, reds from the madder root and yellows from the turmeric root. For black, an iron horse-shoe is placed with molasses or vinegar in a clay pot and made to stand in the sun for several days. The printers of Bagru are said to have been brought here in the late 17th century by the local raja from various different

Hand-block printer at Bagru.

Decorative details in the palace complex at Tonk.

parts of northern and northeastern Rajasthan. Over the centuries they became known for the earthy, rustic printed fabrics they created for the villages of this region. In recent years, however, their unique use of vegetable dyes and their dramatic designs have put this sleepy little town on the international fashion map. As always, in Rajasthan, there is a legend behind this craft of printing. It is said that Surasen, the son of Arjuna, the hero of the epic *Mahabharata,* had to renounce his warrior caste for a small misdeed. In order to give him an alternative trade (and caste), a goddess appeared in his dreams and revealed the heavenly secret of making dyes from the vegetables and minerals of the earth. The craftsmen of Bagru thus considered theirs to be a divinely ordained craft. There is also a small deserted 17th-century fort here in Bagru, one of the girdle of garrison forts that provided Jaipur's first line of defence.

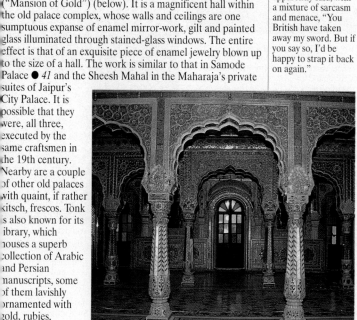

A magnificent armored coat belonging to the nawab of Tonk.

TONK

The small town of Tonk, 58 miles southeast of Jaipur, was the capital of what was once the only Muslim state of Rajasthan. The first nawab of Tonk, Amir Khan, was a fierce Pathan warlord who had once served the powerful Maratha ruler of Indore, in central India. When he became a threat to British interests, they attempted to subdue him by creating this new state for him in 1817, prudently ensuring that it was divided into three separate pieces, rather than one contiguous chunk. The town of Tonk is rather unattractive, but one thing that makes a visit here worthwhile in itself is the Sunehri Kothi ("Mansion of Gold") (below). It is a magnificent hall within the old palace complex, whose walls and ceilings are one sumptuous expanse of enamel mirror-work, gilt and painted glass illuminated through stained-glass windows. The entire effect is that of an exquisite piece of enamel jewelry blown up to the size of a hall. The work is similar to that in Samode Palace ● *41* and the Sheesh Mahal in the Maharaja's private suites of Jaipur's City Palace. It is possible that they were, all three, executed by the same craftsmen in the 19th century. Nearby are a couple of other old palaces with quaint, if rather kitsch, frescos. Tonk is also known for its library, which houses a superb collection of Arabic and Persian manuscripts, some of them lavishly ornamented with gold, rubies, emeralds, and pearls.

WORD OF HONOR
Once, a sword was as essential a part of an Indian nobleman's costume as his turban. According to legend, Amir Khan, the first nawab of Tonk, once appeared at the British Resident's *durbar* without his sword. When eyebrows were raised at this impropriety, he apparently said, with a mixture of sarcasm and menace, "You British have taken away my sword. But if you say so, I'd be happy to strap it back on again."

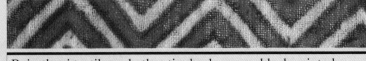

Rajasthani textiles, whether tie-dyed, woven, block-printed, appliquéd, embroidered, or hand-painted, use certain motifs not generally seen elsewhere. The motifs are mostly derived from the flora and fauna found in the region. Some flowers, like the marigold, jasmine, rose, *champa*, or *raibel*, have sacred associations, and some animals such as the elephant, lion and monkey are considered more important than others. Caparisoned elephants and camels, peacocks, or a girl holding a flower or in a dance pose, add more Rajasthani character than other motifs. However, motifs based on geometrical forms, trellises (*jalis*), symbolic patterns used in age-old paintings, or decorations in daily rituals by the village women (for example the *mandana* motifs used to decorate mud houses during Diwali in certain parts of Rajasthan), and flowers and flowering plants are also common.

FLORAL MOTIFS
The Rajasthani block printers cater to the needs of an ever-expanding market and use numerous floral motifs, specially for the field design. In these fifty-year-old specimens (top), where the printers still used vegetable colors and printed with hand-blocks, four popular floral motifs are shown, clockwise from top left, *kela* (banana), *nimsher* (neem flower), *bade phool* (large flower), and *nargis*.

CHAMPA (FRANGIPANI)
Besides large flower heads of lotus, marigold, hibiscus, chrysanthemum, and various bulbiferous flowers such as *nargis*, lily tuberose, and local flowers such as rose, *champa* (*Michelia champeca*), and *raibel* are also popular. This motif is from a woven silk material used for the royal wardrobe.

ELEPHANT, LION, BIRD, AND DANCING GIRL
Elephants are very much an integral part of the Rajasthani festive scene. Be it a royal procession or a religious festival, or the wedding of a prince or a nobleman, rows of well-decorated elephants would steal the show. The skillful dyers of Rajasthan have combined elephants, lions, birds, and a dancing girl in this 19th-century piece of tie-and-dye work. Such intricate designs are not common now, though not impossible to find.

DOTS AND FLOWERS.
The tie-dyed veil, or *chunari*, used by the traditional Rajasthani women, has designs of dots and petals of two or three colors arranged like rows of bright flower heads. This exquisite piece was used for a Diwali outfit, as revealed by its deep blue ground color. The design is known *kamal phool* or lotus flower.

HAJARA (CHRYSANTHEMUM)
This 18th-century work (right) shows the *hajara* motif at its finest and best with the outlines overprinted with gold leaf.

WOMAN WITH FLOWER
Women appear in Rajasthani textiles in various forms, standing, holding a flower, or a parrot, or a garland, dancing or worshipping in a shrine. Some of the motifs are derived from Mughal figured silks and brocades. This is an early piece from the border of a *kanat* (tent wall) segment or a curtain.

Arabesqued
façade of Arhai
Din ka Jhonpra
(right).

Pilgrims at the
dargah (below).

The small town of Ajmer, 78 miles west of
Jaipur, played a surprisingly important
role in India's history. Set at the point
where the rocky Aravalli hills end and the
Thar Desert begins, this was originally the
stronghold of the powerful Chauhan
dynasty of Rajputs ● *35*, who built India's
first ever hill fort here in the 7th century,
Taragarh ("Star Fort"), whose ruins you
can still see today. Ajmer was ruled by the
great Raja Prithviraj Chauhan ● *35, 55*,
the last Hindu king of Delhi, until his

**EMPTYING THE
CAULDRON**
There are two
enormous *degs* or
cauldrons at Ajmer's
dargah, one of them
nearly 10 feet in
diameter. During the
saint's annual festival,
food is cooked in
them. During the
ritual of "looting the
degs", attendants
empty the entire
cauldron at lightning
speed, leaping into
the steaming hot
interiors to scrape
out the dregs. The
whole process takes
just three to four
minutes! The food is
then distributed to
the devotees.

defeat in 1192. After having changed hands several times, in
1556 Ajmer finally came under the Mughal Emperor, Akbar,
who used it as the headquarters for his vitally important
operations in Rajasthan. It was here, a generation later, that
the first British Ambassador, Sir Thomas Roe, had an historic
meeting with Emperor Jahangir in 1615. And it was here, half
a century later, that the critical battle between the Mughal
crown prince, Dara Shukoh, and the usurper, later Emperor,
Aurangzeb, took place. (If the former had in fact won, along
with his Rajput allies, as seemed very likely at one point,
historians say India's entire history would have turned out
very differently indeed.) In the 19th century, Ajmer became a
little British enclave, from where the British Chief
Commissioner for Rajputana kept an eagle eye on all the
Rajput kingdoms. Today Ajmer is, frankly, not the most

charming of towns, unlike its heyday in
the 17th century when it was Emperor
Shah Jahan's pleasure resort. You can still
see the white marble pleasure pavilions
the Emperor built by the Ana Sagar Lake.
There are also various buildings of
historical interest to visit here.

Fortress and town of
Ajmer (right).

DARGAH SHARIF

Dargah Sharif is the shrine of the 12th-century Muslim saint,
Khwaja Mu'in-ud-din Chisti (1142–1236), perhaps the most
important Muslim shrine in the entire Indian
subcontinent ● *51*. The saint was greatly
venerated by the Mughal emperors, and
Emperor Akbar is said to have made
two pilgrimages here on foot all the
way from Agra: once when an
heir was finally born to him, to
fulfill a vow that he had made
● *99*, and again when he won
against Chittor. The shrine is
believed by people of different
faiths to have the power to
make their prayers come true.
During the saint's *urs* (death
anniversary celebrations),
celebrated between the first
and sixth of Rajab, the
seventh month of the lunar
calendar, tens of thousands of
pilgrims come here from all

ETON OF THE EAST
Mayo College in
Ajmer is a fabled
institution, once
described as "the
Eton of the East".
Modeled on a British
public school, it was
set up in the 19th
century to prepare
young Rajput princes
for their royal duties.
Today it is a well-
known public school,
run on rather more
egalitarian lines. Its
white marble main
building was designed
by Sir Swinton Jacob
▲ *134*.

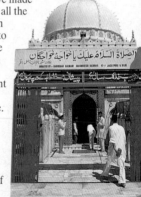

"AJMER IS THE FRANKFURT OF RAJASTHAN AND ITS NUMEROUS ROTHSCHILDS HAVE RIVALLED EACH OTHER IN ENRICHING IT WITH SUPERB MONUMENTS."

LOUIS ROUSSELET, *INDIA AND ITS NATIVE PRINCES*, 1878

over the sub-continent. Female pilgrims often sweep the shrine's courtyard with their long hair – as the Mughal princess, Jehanara, is said to have once done when a prayer she made here was fulfilled.

ARHAI DIN KA JHONPRA

This was originally a Sanskrit college, which was destroyed and converted into a mosque by Sultan Qutbuddin Aibak of Delhi in 1198. According to Cunningham, an eminent 19th-century archeologist, "For gorgeous prodigality of ornament, richness of tracery, delicate sharpness of finish… this may be one of the noblest buildings the world has produced." Its ornately carved sandstone façade is a masterpiece, and it is interesting to see how the original Hindu columns were re-erected in triple layers during its reconstruction in 1198. The name Arhai Din ka Jhonpra literally means "The Hut of the Two-and-a-Half Days", referring to the two-and-a-half days in which it was hurriedly demolished and built, or perhaps to the two-and-a-half days that *fakirs* (mendicants) would gather here during an *urs* in the 18th century.

SCENT OF ROSES
It is not commonly known that the famous perfume, "Ittar of Roses", was invented here in Ajmer, during the reign of Emperor Jahangir. Today the roses of this area are exported to perfumiers all over the world.

Arhai Din ka Jhonpra (above).

AKBAR'S PALACE

This sandstone palace lies in the heart of the old walled city. It has a beautiful gateway, through which you can see the window where the Mughal emperors used to sit and listen to public petitions. Today it houses the Government Museum, which has an interesting collection of 6th and 7th-century sculptures, including a fine black marble image of Kali and a 13th-century Jain *tirthankara* carving.

NASIYAN

Nasiyan Temple (right) is an ornate 19th-century Jain temple. It has a splendid double-storied hall, with a rich display of gilded figures from Jain mythology. Visiting it is a fascinating experience. You can see how Jain temple architecture has evolved over the centuries from the medieval temples of Dilwara and Ranakpur

● 94 ▲ 262, 270.

Holy lake and town of Pushkar.

The picturesque little temple town of Pushkar, 7 miles northeast of Ajmer, is one of the holiest centers of Hinduism. Each year, it is the site of an astonishingly colorful camel fair, one of the largest fairs of its kind in Asia. There is an interesting legend behind the creation of Pushkar. It is said that Lord Brahma, the Creator of the Universe, once did battle with the demon, Vajra Nabh, and slew him with a lotus blossom. The petals of the lotus floated down to earth and landed at three places in and around Pushkar, where three beautiful lakes immediately gushed forth. Brahma thereupon performed a *yagna*, an elaborate sacred rite, which was attended by all of the gods and goddesses. A temple was developed around this site, which is one of the five essential pilgrimage centers that a Hindu must visit in his lifetime, along with Badrinath, Puri, Rameshwaram and Dwarka. The town of Pushkar has been written about over the centuries by writers as diverse as the immortal Sanskrit poet Kalidasa (in his great classic *Abhigyan Shakuntalam*), the 6th-century Chinese traveler, Fa-hsein, and the 11th-century Arab traveler, Alberuni ● *33*. Later in the 17th century, Emperor Jahangir wrote in his memoirs, "While in Ajmer I visited nine times the mausoleum of the revered Khwaja, and fifteen times went to look at Pushkar Lake." Pushkar is said to have nearly five hundred temples, large and small, dedicated to various deities, and fifty-two palaces (as several rajas and maharajas from all over India maintained palaces here for their pilgrimages).

BRAHMA TEMPLE

A WIFE'S WRATH
Brahma Temple is, surprisingly, virtually the only temple dedicated to Brahma, the Creator of the Universe ● *45*. According to one legend, when Brahma was performing a great *yagna* (sacred ritual) ceremony at Pushkar, his wife Savitri was absent. Since the presence of a wife was essential for the ritual, Brahma hastily married a local maiden, Gayatri. Savitri flew into a rage about this and cursed Brahma, saying that henceforth he would not be worshiped anywhere except at Pushkar.

Brahma Temple (left) is probably the most important of all the temples at Pushkar – and one of the very few Brahma temples in existence in India. This is curious as Brahma (the Creator) is one of the Hindu Trinity; along with Vishnu (the Preserver), and Shiva (the Destroyer), and there are numerous temples dedicated to the latter two all over India. There are several interesting legends and intellectual theories to explain this fact. Inside the temple's sanctum is a fine, four-armed life-sized statue of Brahma. Another interesting feature are the coins studded in the floor of the temple, placed by devotees from all over India to commemorate the births and deaths of their loved ones.

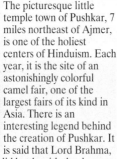

Temples of Pushkar.

VARAH TEMPLE

Originally built in the 12th century, Varah Temple was, like many others, destroyed by the bigoted Emperor Aurangzeb (who, it is said, was particularly upset by the huge idol here of Varah, the god with the body of a man and the head of a boar). Reconstructed by Raja Sawai Jai Singh II of Jaipur in 1727, the temple has an interesting and richly ornamented image house.

CAMEL EXTRAVAGANZA
During the exuberant camel fair every year, ● *82* numerous contests, such as camel races and the traditional "loading of the camels" contest, are held. The aim of the latter is to see how many riders can pile onto a single camel. Camel polo, is of course, *de rigueur*.

MAHADEVA TEMPLE

A beautiful temple built in the 19th century, it was described by a British traveler of the time as "by far the most remarkable, for the elegance of its structure and the nature of its ornaments, of all the temples Pushkar boasts of." It is also noteworthy for its white marble Mahadeva image, with its five faces (and its traditional tufts of hair).

RAMAVAIKUNTH TEMPLE

One of Pushkar's largest and most intricate temples is Ramavaikunth Temple (left), built in the 1920's. It has a beautifully sculpted stone *gopuram*, or pagoda, sculpted with the images of no less than 361 different deities. The ornate outer *gopuram* over the entrance is said to have been built by a team of masons specially brought here from south India.

BAZAAR

Pushkar's fascinating old bazaar is a maze of narrow lanes interspersed with little temples, *ashrams* and picturesque old homes with archways and ornate balconies. Every few yards there are broad, formal stepped *ghats* that lead off the side, down to the pretty Pushkar Lake ● *47*.

SHOPPERS' DELIGHT
Pushkar's bazaars are one of the best places in Rajasthan to buy vivid embroidery and painted textiles. It is also a great place to shop for old silver jewelry.

▲ KISHANGARH AND MAKRANA

Darwaan (royal retainer) outside Kishangarh Fort.

INDIAN MONA LISA
In the 18th century a Kishangarh court artist immortalized the love of Raja Samant Singh for the beautiful court singer, Bani Thani, and the two are depicted as Radha and Krishna. Bani Thani, with her enormous, languorous eyes, curved eyebrows and tiny waist, appears frequently in Kishangarh miniature paintings, and the people here are particularly fond of referring to her as "the Mona Lisa of Rajasthan"!

Miniature of the Maharaja of Kishangarh (above).

KISHANGARH

Kishangarh, 18 miles north of Ajmer, was the capital of one of the smaller Rajput kingdoms, but one whose unique cultural heritage belied its small size. Founded in 1597 by a Rathor prince from Jodhpur, the kingdom of Kishangarh remained on friendly terms with the Mughal emperors, and the peaceful conditions that resulted from this relationship made for a great flowering of culture and the arts here – and the emergence of one of India's most celebrated schools of miniature painting. One of the great patrons of the arts was Raja Samant Singh (reigned 1699–1764), a remarkable combination of warrior, poet and mystic.
KISHANGARH SCHOOL. The Kishangarh school of miniature paintings ● *64* is known for its elegant and graceful depictions of the divine lovers, Radha and Krishna. These splendid paintings are imbued with a rare tenderness and lyricism. They are rich with layer upon layer of meaning, the love of Radha and Krishna being a metaphor for the soul in its quest for the Divine.
PHOOLGARH FORT. The fort is reflected in the waters of a pretty little lake. Entering through its lofty, arched gateway, flanked on both sides by elephant murals, you come upon its courtyards, now in splendid decay, surrounded by delicate pavilions and latticed windows. The royal family of Kishangarh have recently restored Rupangarh Palace, an earlier seat of power and refinement for over a century. This is now a hotel with rooms the size of tennis courts.

MAKRANA

MARBLE SUPPLIER
Makrana has become synonymous with the beautiful marble yielded up by its quarries ■ *18*. It was this marble that was used for monuments all over India – from the Taj Mahal in Agra to the Victoria Memorial in Calcutta.

Makrana, which lies 36 miles from Kishangarh, is famous for its beautiful white marble, which has been mined here for centuries. As Colonel Tod noted in the 1820's, "to the marble quarries of Makrana…all the splendid edifices of the imperial cities owe their grandeur. The materials used in the palaces of Delhi and Agra, their mosques and tombs have been conveyed from (here)." The marble quarries of Makrana, where quarrying methods have changed little in the last thousand years, are interesting to visit. There are also numerous little marble workshops here, where traditional craftsmen carve delicately shaped marble artefacts, many of which are later sent to Agra for its famed marble inlay work. The vast salt lake of Sambhar is close by, creating a very eerie white landscape.

The temple tank at the Banai Vilas Palace.

COAT-OF-ARMS
The Alwar coat-of-arms shows a shield bearing a traditional Rajput *katar*, or dagger. It is flanked by a tiger and a bull, the symbols of Rajput bravery and piety respectively (the maharajas of Alwar took their role as descendants of the Hindu god, Lord Rama, very seriously). The coat-of-arms is topped by the curiously shaped Alwar crown.

"[Maharaja Jai Singh] is the centre of innumerable stories... of hideous cruelty, and sometimes darker inferences that remind one of tales of black magic and evil possession. You may think of him as Poet and Hero – until you catch the gleam of that wild animal smile or hear the goat wail once too often."
Yvonne Fitzroy, *Courts and Camps of India*, 1926

Plan of the fort and city.

Street scene, Alwar.

HISTORY

Alwar, paradoxically, was both the oldest and newest of all the Rajput kingdoms. On the one hand, it traced its traditions back to the kingdom of Viratnagar that flourished here around 1500 BC. On the other, it was officially created – carved out of the Maratha territories – by the British as late as the 1770's. The rulers of Alwar were distantly related to the Kachhawaha dynasty of Jaipur and, until the mid-18th century, were merely the chieftains of two villages in Jaipur state. But, by skillfully aligning themselves with the right party at the right time – the Jats of Bharatpur, the Kachhawahas, the Mughals and, finally, the East India Company – they rapidly jockeyed themselves into a position of political consequence.

THE MAHARAJAS OF ALWAR. As a result of their relatively junior status, perhaps, the maharajas of Alwar conducted themselves with great ostentation: their palaces were the most ornate, their pageantry the most spectacular, and their tiger *shikars* the most elaborately organized. They even affected the title of Sawai, "The One-and-a-Quarter", following their grander cousins from Jaipur. It was this innate desire on their part to outshine their fellow princes that made Alwar the picturesque place it is today, with its splendid palaces. But since Alwar was a poorer state than many others, the maharajas also made themselves fairly unpopular with their subjects in the process. Alwar and its surrounding areas are one of the most interesting and undiscovered parts of Rajasthan. And one of the things that contributes toward making it so are the tales of Maharaja Jai Singh (reigned 1892–1937), its brilliant but weird ruler in the early part of this century.

> "THE CONICAL-SHAPED MOUNTAINS OF ULWUR, CROWNED WITH
> BATTLEMENTS…, LEAVING ONLY A NARROW STRIP OF LAND
> CROWDED WITH FAIRY-LIKE PALACES AND TEMPLES."
> LOUIS ROUSSELET, *INDIA AND ITS NATIVE PRINCES*, 1878

ALWAR TODAY

The town of Alwar lies at the point where the Aravalli hills of
Rajasthan flare up one final time before subsiding into the
plains of northern India. A significant part of the town was
built between these craggy hills by Raja Banai Singh (reigned
1815–57), an esthete and builder of renown. In medieval
times, Alwar was a town of great strategic importance because
of its commanding position on the southern approach to
Delhi. Today, however, it is a modest little trading center for
the gram, barley and wheat grown in this region. It
has a few industries, including textiles and glass-
bangle making, but what is quite amazing here
is the craft of double-sided dyeing, practiced
by a handful of Alwar artisans: they are
able to dye one side of a sari in one color
and the other side in a totally different
color.

OLD MONUMENTS. The layout of the town
clearly reflects its turbulent history. One
side of the town was protected by the
steep, rocky hills, topped by the fort, Bala
Qila; the other three sides were guarded
by strongly fortified walls and, in addition,
a deep moat, the latter being a rare feature
in Rajasthan. Alwar has some fine old
monuments, chief among them being the
sumptuous Banai Vilas palace complex and the
rugged Bala Qila Fort, with its eagle's eye view of the
surrounding plains. But in addition to these, there are various
other sights, including the splendid cenotaph of Raja
Bakhtawar Singh; the imposing, domed, 17th-century
mausoleum of Fateh Jung; the graceful, old, pink sandstone
railway station; and various palaces built by the maharajas of
Alwar.

PRINCE "CHARMING"
Maharaja Jai Singh of
Alwar was one of the
most fascinating
princes of his time.
He was brilliant,
urbane, erudite,
always gorgeously
dressed, and was
gifted with a magnetic
personality. However,
there was a dark side
to him, and he was
described by
someone who
knew him
well as
"sinister
beyond
belief".
He was
known to
be an
eccentric
and a
sadist,
and was
rumored to
practice
black magic.
He was finally
deposed by the
British when,
unhappy with one of
his polo ponies after a
match, he doused it
with petrol and set
fire to it.

169

Seal of Alwar State.

CITY PALACE ★

The City Palace ("Vinay Vilas", as it is officially called) (left) was built in 1793 by Raja Bakhtawar Singh at the foot of a rugged, towering hill and was added to over the centuries by his successors. The palace is a marriage of Rajput and Mughal styles – an almost baroque profusion of arches, balconies, pavilions and porticos, with an accent on *bangaldar* eaves, which seem characteristic of northeastern Rajasthan. Once, this palace was part of the maharajas' ornate lifestyle and housed, among other things, a drinking cup cut out of a single emerald in its treasury and a mammoth, double-storied, four-elephant carriage in its stables. Today, however, the palace has been converted into the district's collectorate, and its halls and chambers have been turned into government offices.

CENTRAL COURTYARD. The central courtyard of the palace (below) is impressive, with its graceful marble pavilions set on lotus-flower bases, its inner walls lined with canopied balconies and its dramatic marble checkerboard floor. Once dancing girls performed here by moonlight, but today it is often the venue for rowdy teenagers' cricket matches.

DURBAR HALL. Beyond the marble pavilions lies the splendid, old *durbar* hall, its walls and ceilings richly covered with gilded arabesques still remarkably fresh. In an antechamber beyond is an exquisite frieze of miniature paintings, sealed under glass and set in gilt, running along the wall. Permission to see this section, however, has to be obtained from the maharaja, who now lives in Delhi.

RANI MOOSI CHHATRI. Behind the palace lies the old temple tank and the cenotaph of Raja Bakhtawar Singh and Rani Moosi, who performed *sati*. It is a superb example of early 19th-century Rajput architecture, with its graceful brown Karauli sandstone structure and its nine white marble canopies. Its style is

SHAKESPEARE WALLAH
One of the more unusual moments in the history of the City Palace occurred when it was used for the shooting of Merchant and Ivory's *Shakespeare Wallah*. The "Anthony and Cleopatra" scene was shot in a courtyard of Zenana Mahal, with the actors appearing out of its cupolaed pavilions and trellised balconies.

CAR FANATIC
Maharaja Jai Singh was apparently very fond of blue Bugattis, which he bought in threes. When he tired of the cars, it is said that, in his own eccentric fashion, he had them buried in the hillsides around Alwar, where, presumably, their remains still lie.

A view of the
City Palace.

Miniature paintings
from the Alwar
school (below).

completely different from those of other
cenotaphs in the rest of Rajasthan.
Beneath the dome you can see interesting
frescos of scenes from the epics *Ramayana*
and *Mahabharata*.

THE MUSEUM. The palace museum has a
wonderful collection of exhibits, reflecting
the eclectic tastes – and the personal
wealth – of the maharajas of Alwar. There
are some excellent manuscripts here,
including an illustrated *Mahabharata*, on a
200-foot-long scroll, made from a single length of
paper, with writing so tiny it must be read with a
magnifying glass. Other prize pieces here are
illustrated manuscripts of *Gulistan*, *Shah Nama*, and on
Emperor Babur's life. There are also some fine *Ragamala*
paintings and miniatures from the Alwar, Bundi, and
Mughal schools. (Don't miss the miniature of the
incarnations of Vishnu.) In the armory section you will
find several historic swords, including those belonging to
Sultan Mohammad Ghori, as well as the Mughal
emperors Akbar and Aurangzeb. You will also find a
fascinating collection of armor (including a suit of
crocodile leather armor) and the usual strange Rajput
weapons, such as a *nagphas*, a carpet-beater shaped
weapon ingeniously designed for strangling the
enemy. There are various other heirlooms from
the maharajas' collection, from perfumed
sandalwood fly-whisks to a solid silver dining table
(with *trompe-l'œil* waves shimmering across it for good
measure). One thing that is *not* here, however, is
Maharaja Jai Singh's favorite car: a gold
Lanchester, shaped in the form of
the King of England's
coronation carriage, but
without the horses!

Jewelry (above) and a
jade vase (below)
from Alwar's royal
collection.

This miniature
painting shows the
presentation of
Gulistan to Maharaja
Vinay Singh of Alwar.
Gulistan is the most
valued manuscript in
the Alwar Museum.

171

Remains of Moti
Doongri Palace.

Bala Qila ramparts.

Interior of Nikumbh
Mahal Palace
(center).

MILITARY BACKING
Bala Qila and
Rajgarh Fort were
held by the great
founder of Alwar,
Raja Pratap Singh
(above). Originally a
nobleman of the
Jaipur court, he
achieved great fame
after an astrologer,
seeing the rings in his
eyes, predicted, "Take
your armies wherever
you will, victory will
always be yours."

MOTI DOONGRI

Visiting Moti Doongri ("Pearl Hill") is a bizarre experience.
All that now exists is a massive fortified wall, with a flat,
empty space at the crest of the hill. The elegant hundred-
roomed palace that stood here was dynamited out of
existence by Maharaja Jai Singh. The reason remains a
mystery. Was he looking for buried treasure here, as some
people say? Was it in grief at the suicide of his favorite wife?
Was it to destroy the tomb of a *fakir* nearby? Or was it merely
his eccentricity? Nobody knows. The fact is that the
demolition took two years and cost more than the building of
the palace itself. Jai Singh possibly wanted
to build another palace here.

BALA QILA ★

Towering on a craggy hill that
dominates the town is Bala
Qila ("Young Fort"). Built
on the foundations of an
ancient mud fort
constructed in AD 928 by
the Nikumbh Rajputs, it has
had a turbulent history and
was successively occupied by
the warring Mughals,
Pathans and Jats before
finally being captured by Raja
Pratap Singh in 1775. Bala Qila
is accessible only by jeep (with
special permission from the
Superintendent of Police, for there is a
police wireless station located in its citadel today). As you
drive up the steep slope you can see the amazing fortifications
that run all the way along the hill, often at crazy, seemingly
impossible, angles. Passing through a series of massive gates,
you finally enter Nikumbh Mahal Palace at the top. Built in
the early 19th century, it has graceful *bangaldar* eaves, carved
marble columns and delicate latticed balconies opening onto
a central courtyard (where the police wireless station is now
incongruously sited). Inside the *baradari* (pavilion), there are
some beautiful gilded frescos on the walls and ceilings
(above). And outside, beneath the canopies surrounding the
courtyard, are traces of other delicately painted panels. From
here there is a stunning view of the
surrounding
countryside, and
you can also see
the miles of
ramparts that
enclose the fort: a
feat of military
engineering,
sometimes running
vertically up the
hill, and provided
with literally
thousands of steps

Frescos in Bala Qila.

built for the sentries who patrolled its top. You can also see, on a nearby ridge, the palace of the Mughal prince Salim, later Emperor Jahangir, who was exiled here for three years for trying to assassinate Abu'l Fazal, one of the celebrated "Nine Gems" of his father Akbar's court.

VIJAY MANDIR

Vijay Mandir, a sprawling, cupolaed palace with 105 rooms and a beautifully laid out garden, lies 6 miles outside Alwar. Reflected picturesquely in the waters of Vijay Sagar Lake, it is said to have been designed along the lines of a ship. Like all the ventures of its builder, the sinister and dazzling Maharaja Jai Singh, it has a curious history. The Maharaja had earlier commissioned another lovely Italianate palace, Yeshwant Niwas. When it was completed, he promptly decided he didn't like it. He never lived in it and immediately began work on Vijay Mandir instead. You need permission from the present Maharaja of Alwar to see this palace, but it is worth viewing from the outside anyway.

Painting of Akbar and Abu'l Fazal in court.

PAPER-THIN POTS
Alwar is known for its delicate *kagazi*, or literally "paper-thin", pots. Crafted from roots, these unique pots have beautiful patterns carved into their delicate double walls.

RAJGARH

Located 22 miles south of Alwar, among the prettily wooded valleys that are characteristic of this part of Rajasthan, is the old hilltop fort of Rajgarh. It was built by Raja Pratap Singh, the founder of the State of Alwar and often referred to as the "Bismarck of Alwar", in 1771. The fort was the site of the old capital before the new capital was set up at Alwar. It was later turned into a summer palace. A 19th-century British traveler described this valley as "a perfect earthly paradise. There the walls of the well-kept fort of Rajgarh are picturesquely perched on a hill which rises out of a green and fertile tree embowered valley." Today the fort is somewhat dilapidated, but still worth visiting, with its curious fading frescos, its old Sheesh Mahal and its tales of secret passages. (Peep into the old toilets with their quaint disposal system!) At the bottom of the hill is a town with narrow alleyways and old *havelis* set amid the citrus groves. The entire surrounding region is dotted with the ruins of old hill forts, standing like silent sentinels.

Vijay Mandir.

Siliserh Palace.

SILISERH

En route to Sariska, 8 miles southwest of Alwar, is the water palace of Siliserh and a pretty lake ringed by low, wooded hills. There is a romantic legend about this palace. Once, a young raja of Alwar was out riding when he heard a beautiful village maiden singing. He immediately fell in love with her. She seemed to reciprocate his feelings, but her brothers suddenly arrived on the scene and, infuriated at what they saw to be an insult to their sister's honor, were about to kill the raja. The raja then revealed his identity and promised to marry the girl. He built this palace for her so that she could look out at her old village across the lake's waters. The palace is now a rather shabby hotel, but it's worth stopping here briefly, sitting on the lovely terrace, and watching the cormorants diving for fish in the waters of the lake.

SARISKA ★

HUNTING STRATEGY
The eccentric Maharaja Jai Singh's tiger hunts in the Sariska forest were perhaps the most elaborate in India. He would combine these hunts with the military exercises of the Alwar army, using whole battalions of his infantry to drive the tigers toward the *shikaris*. He had superb hunting elephants, whom he spent years training, and he also took pride in his prowess in the highly dangerous sport of hunting wild boar on foot with a knife.

SARISKA TIGER RESERVE. This game sanctuary, 20 miles southwest of Alwar, was once the personal hunting ground of the maharajas of Alwar. It became a sanctuary in 1955 and was taken up under Project Tiger in 1979. It covers an area of 320 square miles (with a core area of 192 square miles). The forested hills of Sariska are among the best places to view tigers in India. There is a tiger population of approximately thirty here. Unlike other sanctuaries, the tigers here can sometimes be sighted by day. These daytime sightings are on the increase, with the tigers gradually becoming more confident with human beings around. The best time of the year to see the tigers is during the summer months, when they come out to the water-holes to drink and when there is less jungle foliage to provide them with cover. Other animals here are panthers (which tend not to overlap in the same areas with tigers), jungle cats, and caracals. In addition, there are the *nilgai, chital, sambar*, wild boar, and porcupine. The reserve is also rich in birds, including gray partridge, quail, sandgrouse, and white-breasted kingfisher. The best way to see the animals is to drive through the reserve either in the early morning or in the late

Kankwari Fort.

evening. While there are paved roads within the reserve, and you can drive through it by car, it might be preferable to hire a jeep so that you can go off the regular track into the interiors of the forest. In the core areas, especially, you can see from the lovely forests what much of the Indian countryside must have looked like, right up to the first half of this century. Also, it is a unique experience to visit the remote little villages in the outer areas of the reserve to see how the way of life, totally untouched by outside influences, remains virtually the same as it has been for centuries. The villagers still live, for instance, with the daily threat of their cattle being carried away by leopards!

SARISKA PALACE. Set inside the Sariska Tiger Reserve, this was actually Maharaja Jai Singh's hunting lodge, where he would bring the guests whom he particularly wanted to impress. It has beautiful, sprawling lawns and contains some of the original antique furniture, but mercifully the Maharaja's tiger-skin patterned wall paper has been taken down. There are also some very interesting old photographs of the royal *shikar* parties of the 1920's here. (Incidentally, one of the Maharaja's eccentricities was that, being an ultra-orthodox Hindu, he always wore silk gloves to avoid touching either cow-hide or "untouchable" foreigners. It is interesting to note from these photographs that these gloves were not taken off, even when he was out hunting!)

KANKWARI FORT. Within Sariska Tiger Reserve, 12 miles from the gate, lies Kankwari Fort. It is a superb example of a *vanadurg*, or jungle-fort, as described in the ancient Indian texts. Even today it is so inaccessible, deep in the tiger-infested forests (and approachable only by jeep), that one can only wonder at how it was built, back in the 17th century, and how it was supplied. It was here, apparently, that the heir to the Mughal throne, Prince Dara Shukoh, was held captive by his usurper brother, Aurangzeb, after the fateful Battle of Deorai, near Ajmer, in 1659. The fort is still impressive, though the interiors are overgrown with weeds. In the citadel is a fine old painted *baradari*, now in ruins.

NEELKANTH

Beyond the Kankwari Fort, 20 miles from the Sariska Reserve's gate, and approachable only by jeep, lies the ruined ancient temple town of Neelkanth. Once there were over eighty beautifully carved temples here, which, some say, date back as early as the 6th to 9th centuries. However, the town was abandoned, and the temples are now covered by forest. It was only in the 1950's that the town was rediscovered (local villagers were using the old sculpted pillars and statues to build their huts) and excavations began. Today perhaps just a quarter of the temples have been excavated. Neelkantheshwar Temple is still in use, but what is really interesting is the superb pink sandstone monolith of the Jain *tirthankara*, Parshvanath, in Naugaza Temple. There are several other little ruined temples dotting the landscape.

ACCESS TO WATER
Kankwari Fort has an unusual feature: a fortified double wall projects out of its ramparts and runs down to the bottom of the hill to provide the garrison with access to the water supply even in times of siege. The double wall is narrow and runs zig-zag, so that it was easy to defend.

Sariska Palace.

SACRED ANTELOPE
The *nilgai*, the largest of all Asian antelopes, is a singularly fortunate animal. It has somehow acquired the name *"gai"*, which means "cow", and by virtue of its name, is sacred to Hindus. In addition, it has the prefix *"nil"*, which means "blue", and is therefore associated by some with the blue-complexioned deity, Lord Krishna. This makes it doubly sacred: it cannot be killed, despite the damage it often causes to crops.

The private and privileged nature of the royal hunts of the past resulted paradoxically in the careful nurturing of forests to ensure the supply of regular sport, and many of today's national parks, such as Ranthambhor, were exclusive royal shooting preserves ■ *24*. Devastation for the tiger in India came post-Independence, when it was caught in the cross-fire between the *shikar* (hunt), trade in ingredients for traditional medicine, and widespread habitat destruction.

SHIKAR GUESTS
The British were the royal *shikar* guests of the maharajas, alongside fellow princes. Hunting was an exclusive privilege conferred by the maharajas.

TIGER TRADE
The destruction of the tiger's habitat, its prey species, and the species itself for skins, trophies, and bones threatens the tiger population. Whereas tiger skins were much in demand earlier, the trade has been overtaken by the demand for bones and other parts, including fat and whiskers, in oriental medicine, for ailments such as arthritis and as potency charms.

PROJECT TIGER
SHOOTING, TRAPPING, KILLING OF WILD ANIMALS ARE PROHIBITED.

PROJECT TIGER
Project Tiger was launched in 1973 to save the species. Ranthambhor and Sariska, the past hunting reserves of the maharajas of Jaipur and Alwar respectively, are among the twenty tiger reserves in India listed under Project Tiger ▲ *304*.

ENDANGERED SPECIES
A widely accepted estimation of the tiger population in India at the turn of the century is 40,000. By 1972 this figure had dropped to an all-time low of 2000. The tiger count in India today is officially in the region of 4000, with experts placing it far below official estimates.

Gate of Sariska Tiger Reserve.

SHIKARS
Rajasthan was
once the home of
the tigers. The
maharajas preserved
the species and its habitats
as royal reserves for *shikar* parties.
The more elaborate hunting methods
involved many men, mounts, and *machans*
(platforms), as well as beaters and baits.

HUNTING STRATEGY
A standard hunting practice
was to surround a forest
with hundreds of beaters
and a line of elephants in
order to bring the tiger to a
point where the hunter waited
for a sure shot.

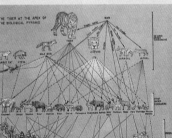

FIGHT FOR SURVIVAL
The tiger is not a
doomed species in
the evolutionary
process. It is highly
adaptive to climate,
terrain, and even
food. In procuring its
prey, the tiger
adheres to the law
that the intake of
energy should exceed
the output of labor.

HUNTING PORTRAITS
The Maharaja of
Kota hunting from a
boat in the Chambal
Valley (right). Royal
hunts were a popular
subject for court
artists ● *65*.

177

Ancient ruins at Bhangarh.

NEEMRANA – A LABOUR OF LOVE
The story of Neemrana Palace, situated 40 miles northwest of Alwar and Rajasthan's closest palace to New Delhi, is a fascinating one ◆ *340*. Built in 1464, it was abandoned by its raja in 1947 and slowly fell into ruins. A few years ago, it was discovered by two explorers of Rajasthan from Delhi, Aman Nath and Francis Wacziarg, and they have since restored it, using mainly the local village craftsmen. Neemrana Palace has been turned into an elegant hotel, possibly one of the oldest in the world. It has become a favorite retreat of the smart set from Delhi and the international jet set, who come for its beauty and calm as well as its French and Rajasthani cuisine.

BHANGARH

On the outskirts of Sariska Tiger Reserve, 33 miles from its gate, lies the splendid, old, ruined town of Bhangarh – its crumbling pavilions, walls and temples silent in the wilderness, against the backdrop of the forested hills. Built in the early 17th century by Raja Madho Singh, the brother of Amber's celebrated Raja Man Singh I, this was once a city of ten thousand homes. The medieval bazaar, recently restored, is fascinating and evocative of the town's ancient prosperity. Beyond it, at the foot of the hills, lie the ruins of the old palace and Someshwar Temple, with its fine carvings and its tank (where the villagers still come to bathe). Nearby is the temple of Gopinath (left), with its carved pillars and corbeled dome. Not far away is another ruined monument, now indelicately labeled "Randiyon ka Mahal" ("Palace of the Prostitute"). Overlooking all of this is a cupola on the hill, from where, if you are adventurous, you can get a great view of the superb landscape. According to legend, the town was cursed by an evil magician and had to be abandoned. The curse is still believed to operate and the local villagers tread warily.

BAIRAT

The village of Bairat, 40 miles southwest of Alwar, has a remarkably rich history, boasting monuments and legends from at least three different epochs. Here, on a low hill, are the ruins of a 3rd-century BC Buddhist *chaitya*, or chapel, the oldest freestanding structure anywhere in India. You can see the foundations of the circular building and the niches for the twenty-six octagonal wooden pillars that once supported it. Among the huge rock overhead are the remains of a monastery. Not far away is a rock edict of Emperor Ashoka, also from the 3rd century, indicating that this was an important town in that era. However, the history of Bairat goes back even further, to the time of the epic *Mahabharata*, around 1100 BC, and this is said to have been the site of the great city of Viratnagar, where the Pandava heroes, with their wife, Draupadi, spent the thirteenth year of their exile. Nothing remains of the ancient city, although archeological finds do indicate the area's great antiquity. Nearby is a little-known, neglected, but charming 16th-century *chhatri* where Emperor Akbar is said to have hunted and stayed overnight en route on his pilgrimage to Ajmer. (It is worth seeing for the elegant murals that adorn its chambers.)

EARLIEST KNOWN MURALS
The frescos at Bairat's Mughal hunting lodge are especially interesting: dating back to the early 17th century, they are probably the very earliest of their kind in Rajasthan and, directly or indirectly, a model for all the other later frescos in the region.

SHEKHAVATI

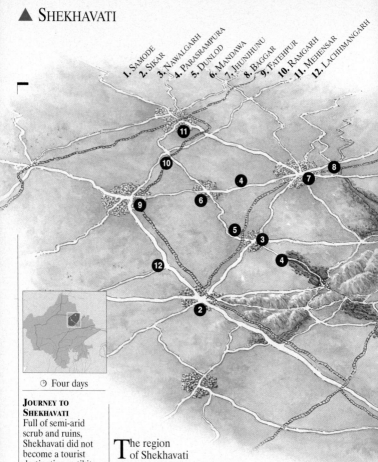

1. SAMODE 2. SIKAR 3. NAWALGARH 4. PARASRAMPURA 5. DUNLOD 6. MANDAWA 7. JHUNJHUNU 8. BAGGAR 9. FATEHPUR 10. RAMGARH 11. MEHENSAR 12. LACHHMANGARH

🕚 Four days

JOURNEY TO SHEKHAVATI

Full of semi-arid scrub and ruins, Shekhavati did not become a tourist destination until its attractions were publicized in *Rajasthan – The Painted Walls of Shekhavati*. The authors, Francis Wacziarg and Aman Nath, traveled extensively throughout the region before publishing their book in 1982. It sparked off new interest in the cultural heritage of the local people and the wealthy Marwari community, who still own the painted *havelis*.

The region of Shekhavati (literally, "Garden of Shekha") was originally a part of the Amber-Jaipur kingdom. Its founder was Rao Shekha (reigned 1433–88) who made it independent till 1738 when it reverted back to Jaipur. His descendants ruled their small kingdoms as vassals of the maharajas of Jaipur till after India's independence in 1947 ● *39*.

HAVELIS OF THE MARWARIS

These mansions were built mainly between 1860 and 1900 by the Marwari merchants of Shekhavati who had ventured out to Calcutta and the other new emerging commercial centers of India. With their business success came a spirit of architectural one-upmanship, and each sought to outdo the other with the lavishness of his *haveli*. Gradually, later generations of Marwari merchants and their families began to leave their *havelis* behind. Today the little towns of Shekhavati are strange ghost towns, packed with their splendid *havelis*, all of them empty, but for a lonely caretaker or two. The busy owners themselves return for perhaps only a couple of days in the year for some family ceremony and then return to Calcutta or Bombay, or wherever it is they are now settled.

SAMODE ★

En route to the region of Shekhavati, 24 miles from Jaipur, lies Samode, with its fairy-tale palace ● *41* ◆ *341*. Samode

"AT PRESENT THE TRADITION IS RAPIDLY
DEGENERATING....HOUSES ARE DECORATED WITH COPIES OF
PSEUDO-GOTHIC SCROLLWORK...."

HERMAN GOETZ, END OF THE 19TH CENTURY

Palace was built in the late 19th century by a kinsman (and Prime Minister) of the Maharaja of Jaipur. Its Rang Mahal ("Palace of Colors") is a little gem of ornamentation, with its gilded and painted walls and mirror-worked ceilings. Beyond this lies Sheesh Mahal, with its dazzling inlays of mirror-work and glass, and painted friezes of hunts and *durbar* scenes. The palace, now a romantic hotel, was used as a location for a film based on *The Far Pavilions*.

AGE-OLD MERCHANTS
The Marwari business community, which hails from Shekhavati, is an amazing sociological phenomenon. According to an American sociologist "it is estimated that more than half the assets in the modern sector of the Indian economy are controlled by the trading castes originating in the northern half of Rajasthan." And of these, a majority originate in just a dozen little towns of Shekhavati (including four out of India's eight largest business houses). They trace their ancestry back to the merchants who did business at this ancient meeting point of the camel caravans from the Middle East, China and India. As the old trading routes dwindled away in the late 18th century, the Marwari merchants moved to the new emerging commercial centers of British India, where their trading genius, honed over generations, made them enormously successful.

SIKAR

Sikar's unusual Biyani Haveli, with its blue painted frescos (below), adds a different palette to the Shekhavati frescos. It represented a new level of one-upmanship because blue was a color that was traditionally difficult to achieve on wet lime plaster – and was only made possible by the expensive, new synthetic dyes imported from Germany in the 1870's. The temples of Gopinath, Raghunath and Madan Mohan, too, have some interesting frescos. Sikar Fort, now in decay, is also worth a visit.

Sikar Fort.

181

NAWALGARH

Nawalgarh has one of the biggest groups of *havelis* in Shekhavati. There are literally dozens of them to wander into. Aath Haveli ("Eight Havelis") is interesting, with amusing European influences reflected in its frescos. Chhawchhariya and Poddar *havelis* are perhaps the most splendid. The latter has been converted into what must surely be the world's most picturesque school. Uttarian Haveli is notorious for its resident ghost. Here, even the telephone exchange has frescos that are worth seeing. But the *pièce de résistance* is Bala Qila Fort, whose frescoed kiosk is perhaps one of the finest examples of the art in all of Shekhavati.

Poddar Haveli (above); cenotaph of Shardul Singh (below).

PARASRAMPURA

It is worth driving out to Parasrampura from Nawalgarh, just to see the cenotaph of Shardul Singh, the eighth descendant of Rao Shekha, the founder of Shekhavati. On the ceiling of its cupola are some of the oldest frescos in the region, dating back to the mid-18th century, depicting scenes from the epics *Ramayana* and *Mahabharata*.

DUNLOD

Dunlod, off the road from Nawalgarh to Mandawa, is noted for its two impressive Goenka *havelis* and its painted Goenka *chhatri,* or cenotaphs. There is also a quaint fort here, almost Scottish in its design. Inside is an interesting Mughal-style *diwan khana,* or hall, with copies of Louis XIV furniture and old family portraits of the local *thakur*'s (chieftain's) family. The fort has now been converted into a hotel.

MYSTERIOUS FORT
The mysterious little desert fort at Mandawa was originally built in the 1750's. It was (in the manner of all Rajput forts) added to, generation by generation, and is a maze of dark interconnecting galleries and secret passageways. In fact, the owners, who have converted it into a hotel, recently discovered dungeons and chambers that they never knew existed.

Mandawa Castle.

MANDAWA

One of the very earliest frescos in all of Shekhavati, dating back to the 1760's, is within Mandawa Castle. The castle is now a hotel of great charm and character ◆ *340*. It was guarded in the past by a cannon and a wickedly spiked gate that served as a defense against elephant attacks. Here, in the old desert tradition, time is still kept by the striking of a gong every hour (right). Chokhani, Saraf and Goenka *havelis* in Mandawa are also worth seeing. By the way, do not miss the way the artist of Goenka Haveli has skillfully integrated the mansion's windows into the design. There are also some frescos influenced by the British East India Company style of art at the Madanlal and Newatia *havelis*. In the former, an Englishman rides a bicycle, but the artist, obviously never having seen one of these contraptions, has got its details delightfully wrong. In the latter, you can see the Wright Brothers in a strange-looking

Murals from a *haveli* in Mandawa.

flying machine with only one wing, and one of the poor brothers left suspended in mid-air.

JHUNJHUNU

Jhunjhunu is known for its Chhe Haveli ("Six Havelis") complex. Tibdiwala and Modi *havelis* are particularly interesting, while Khatri Haveli is unusually elegant in its artistic approach. Rani Sati Temple is also worth seeing for its riotously colorful frescos and kitschy cement sculptures.

FATEHPUR

Fatehpur has one of the largest groups of *havelis* in this region. Devra, Singhania (bottom picture), and Goenka *havelis* are especially worth visiting. Devra Haveli has a superbly painted ceiling, with a series of medallioned portraits: everybody from a Mughal emperor to an English gentleman with a dog! Goenka Haveli has an intricately painted chamber. Don't miss the curious painting here of Lord Krishna riding an elephant which is actually composed of eight maidens. Two other quirky *havelis* were built later, perhaps in the 1920's, by the Jalan and the Bhartia families. The latter has some amusingly kitsch mirror-work and Japanese tiles.

BAGGAR

Known for a large white gate built to honor the Maharaja of Jaipur's visit in 1928, Baggar is the only painted town of Shekhavati where you can stay in a traditional Marwari home. Piramal Haveli (above) serves excellent vegetarian cuisine and is a charming eight-roomed hotel, built in the colonial Rajasthani style. When driving from Delhi, Baggar is the gateway to Shekhavati.

Portraits of the maharajas of Jaipur, Sawai Ram Singh II (reigned 1835–80) and Sawai Madho Singh II (reigned 1880–1927) ● *137*, on the walls at Dunlod Fort. Except between 1471 and 1738, the Shekhavati chieftains served under Jaipur.

Stylistically the frescos of Shekhavati, which date between 1750 and 1930, follow a folk-Mughal or sub-imperial beginning, through a provincial Jaipur school development into the Company School eclecticism with British influences. The style decays into a kitsch, calendar art form made popular with the arrival of the printing press in India. The technique of painting began with the more tedious fresco *buono* painted on wet plaster, ending with the simpler fresco *secco* where paint is applied on dry lime-faced walls.

SWANKY DUDES
Two Englishmen in hats and shoes pose with their walking sticks on a mid-19th century *haveli* façade.

RAMA AND HANUMAN
An early fresco in natural pigments shows Rama and his brother helped by the monkey god Hanuman and his army, en route to Sri Lanka to battle the demon-king Ravana.

HINDU MYTHOLOGY
Mythological scenes of the popular god Krishna show him with his beloved Radha (above), on a swing with the cowherd girls who were eternally and metaphorically charmed by his flute (opposite, top), and with royal devotees (right, above).

184

Since the migrant merchants of Shekhavati amassed fortunes which were largely disproportionate with the times, besides building their elaborate *havelis* and cenotaphs, each erected at least five things to be well remembered by posterity: a temple, a well or reservoir, a school, a cow shed, and a garden, which was indeed a luxury in the desert. Yet they remained socially modest, seldom commissioning a portrait of themselves. The Rajputs who were the warrior rulers of this region, however, followed the example of the imperial rulers of Delhi. They commissioned grand portraits of themselves with royal attributes such as horses and arms, as well as peacetime versions with flowers.

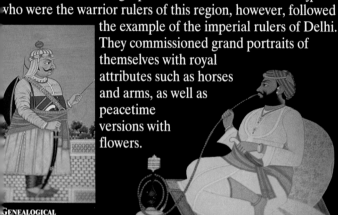

GENEALOGICAL PORTRAITS
These old family portraits of the local *Thakur's* (chieftain's) family decorate the walls of the fort in Dunlod.

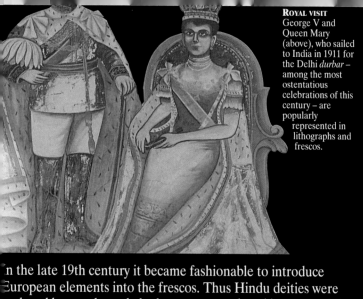

In the late 19th century it became fashionable to introduce
European elements into the frescos. Thus Hindu deities were
replaced by angels, and elephants were replaced by automobiles
and airplanes. Gentlemen on bicycles and ladies with low
necklines began to make an appearance. The inspiration for
these was all second-hand,
from European
lithographs and
photographs, which is
why so many of the
details, particularly of
mechanical objects, are
amusingly incorrect.

WEDDING
The bridesmaid seems to fall off her chair in this fresco which is obviously copied from a wedding photograph.

MERCENARIES
Foreign mercenaries with European headgear often helped decide the fate of battles in the early 19th century. An Irishman George Thomas was one such mercenary famous in Shekhavati.

FLYING KRISHNA
Lord Krishna, the divine charioteer in the epic battle of the *Mahabharata*, depicted in a flying car ▲ *45*.

FAMED FRESCOS
The pigments used in Shekhavati were natural ores: saffron for the oranges, a kind of terracotta for the reds, antimony for the black and indigo for the blues. The brilliant yellows were derived from the urine of cows that had been fed solely on a diet of mango leaves! The frescos in Soné Chandi ki Haveli are lavishly embellished with gilt.

RAMGARH

Two *havelis*, belonging to the Poddar and Ruia families respectively, are worth seeing. There are more delightful paintings here of new-fangled mechanical devices that the artists had obviously never actually seen, like a car whose wheels are shaped like flowers. Also, do take a look at the local *chhatris* or cenotaphs, particularly the frescos around their entrance. The scenes from the *Ramayana* in Poddar Haveli are worth noticing. There is also an interesting old mud fort here, supposed to have once been a stronghold of local dacoits.

MAHENSAR

Mahensar is one of the less visited towns of Shekhavati, perhaps, but definitely one of the most rewarding. Soné Chandi ki Haveli ("Mansion of Gold and Silver") (left), which belonged to the Poddar family of jewelers, has the finest frescos in Shekhavati, bar none. The artists are said to have been the descendants of those who painted the spectacular Anup Mahal in Bikaner, and the similarity is evident. Don't miss the frieze of the battle scene, as delicate as a miniature painting.

LACHHMANGARH

The sprawling Char Chowki Haveli ("Haveli of the Four Courtyards"), belonging to the Ganeriwala family, is arguably the grandest in Shekhavati. Rathi Haveli is also interesting. Take a look, for instance, at the fresco of the *memsahib* playing a gramophone (left). The walk from Murlimanohar Temple to Chokhani Haveli is interesting. Don't miss the quaint painting in one of the *havelis* of a European incongruously holding up an umbrella at a ceremonial function and labeled, perhaps unnecessarily, "Foreigner". There is also an interesting fort in Lachhmangarh, perched on a hill, with a good view of the town and an unusual aerial view of the great Char Chowki Haveli.

ANTIQUES
Ramgarh is one of the best places in Shekhavati to buy antiques and replicas, especially ornate Rajasthani woodwork, although the prices aren't necessarily cheap.

Lachhmangarh Fort.

THE NORTHWEST

▲ Marwar
Bikaner

1. Bikaner 2. Deshnoke 3. Gajner 4. Kolayat 5. Nagaur 6. Khimsar 7. Jodhpur 8. Mandore 9. Osiyan 10. Pokharan 11. Jaisalmer 12. Samm 13. Khurri 14. Lodurva 15. Akal Fossils 16. Barmer

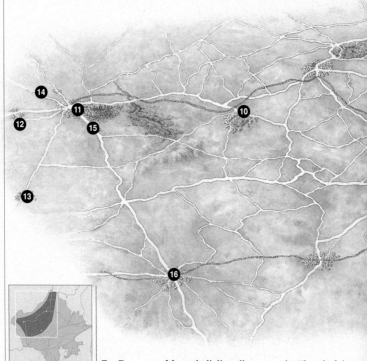

⏱ Twelve days

WRITING ABOUT THE DESERT
Colonel Tod wrote in 1829 that if the North African desert could be likened to a leopard's hide, spotted with oases, the Marusthali Desert was more like "that of the tiger, of which the long dark stripes would indicate the expansive belts of sand, elevated upon a plain only slightly less sandy."

The desert in Bikaner.

Marwar, or Marusthali, literally means the "Land of the Dead." It broadly comprises the harsh desert region of western Rajasthan, stretching from Bikaner in the north, down to the hills of Mewar in the south. It is an especially interesting part of Rajasthan; its relative remoteness tends to attract the genuine traveler keen to explore areas a little off the beaten track. There are three main destinations around Marwar – Bikaner, Jaisalmer and Jodhpur. From Bikaner you can drive out to Gajner, Deshnoke, or the archeological ruins of Kalibangan. From Jaisalmer, you can go on a camel safari, visit the Desert National Park or make side trips to Samm, Khurri, and Barmer. From Jodhpur you can take an excursion to the temples of Osiyan or to Khimsar and Nagaur.

History

Bikaner was founded in the 15th century by Rao Bika, the son of the Rathor Raja of Marwar (or Jodhpur) ● 34. Taking offence at a stray comment that his father made, he left with a small band of horsemen to set up his own kingdom in the deserts of the north. Spurred on by the blessing of a great female mystic, Karni Mata, whom he had met along the way and who had predicted that his fame and glory would some day exceed that of his father, Rao Bika fought the local desert clans for thirty years, and ultimately carved

192

"OUT OF THE SILKEN DARKNESS OF A DESERT DAWN EMERGED THE DREAM OF BIKANER."

TRADITIONAL BALLAD

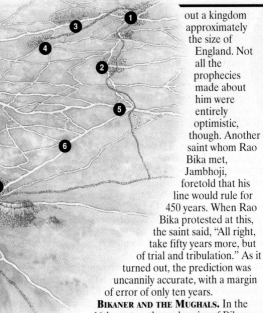

out a kingdom approximately the size of England. Not all the prophecies made about him were entirely optimistic, though. Another saint whom Rao Bika met, Jambhoji, foretold that his line would rule for 450 years. When Rao Bika protested at this, the saint said, "All right, take fifty years more, but of trial and tribulation." As it turned out, the prediction was uncannily accurate, with a margin of error of only ten years.

BIKANER AND THE MUGHALS. In the 16th century the maharajas of Bikaner came into conflict with the Mughal emperors in Delhi, who were in the process of setting up their new empire in Hindustan. Being located closer to Delhi, Bikaner spent much more time fighting the Mughals than other desert kingdoms, such as Jaisalmer or Jodhpur. With the harsh desert terrain on their side, the Bikaner armies soundly defeated the Mughals in their early encounters. By the late 16th century, however, they had been won over by the diplomacy of Emperor Akbar. As a result, several of Bikaner's rulers commanded the Mughal armies, fighting with distinction from Gujarat in the west to the Deccan in the south. One great ruler, Raja Prithviraj Singh, a poet and warrior, in fact, became one of the celebrated "Nine Gems" of Akbar's court. Bikaner, meanwhile, had become a flourishing town and an important trading post along the centuries-old caravan trails that connected India with the Middle East and China. As the town prospered, it became known for the handiwork of its gold and silversmiths, weavers, perfumiers and leather craftsmen. It also became known as an important center for the arts and music. It was especially well known for its school of miniature paintings, which were a delicate fusion of the Rajput and Mughal styles ● 65.

BIKANER AND THE BRITISH. However, with the eclipse of the Mughals in the 18th century, Bikaner, along with the rest of Rajasthan, fell into a slow decline, although its desert barriers at least spared it the depredations that the Marathas were wreaking on its other Rajput neighbors. This situation continued until the treaty with the British in 1818, in which "perpetual friendship, alliance and a unity of interests" were pledged.

COAT-OF-ARMS
Bikaner's coat-of-arms depicts two tigers, which symbolize the bravery of the Rajputs, and a shield containing three sacred kites, associated with Karni Mata, the dynasty's patron goddess ● 55 ▲ 206. The motto, which translates as "Hail, King of the Wastelands!", recalls an episode when the Raja of Bikaner agreed to spearhead a Rajput revolt against the Mughal Emperor Aurangzeb, provided the other rajas first accepted him as the overlord of the desert.

ENEMY ALERT
Rao Bika's bed, displayed in Phul Mahal within Junagarh Fort, has a strangely austere shape. The reason is that Rao Bika never forgot how his grandfather had been tied to his bed with his own turban and murdered. Hence his own bed was short, light and designed so that his feet projected well beyond its edge while he slept. The idea was that even if his enemies should ever tie him to the bed, he could still stand up and fight with it on his back!

VISIONARY RULER
Maharaja Ganga
Singh was a man of
extraordinary vision
and character. At the
end of World War
One he was one of
the signatories to the
Treaty of Versailles.
He presciently
objected to the
terms, noting that
any treaty that
"imposed such a
burden upon the
vanquished foe could
not be the harbinger
of a lasting peace".

TURN OF FORTUNE. By the mid-19th century the years of
internal strife and the financial and military pressures
being put on Bikaner by its new allies, the British, had
put the kingdom into debt. It became a shabby and
backward province. But, curiously, it was Bikaner's
famous camels that triggered off a process of economic
and political recovery. The British were involved in
fighting the Afghan War at the time and it was realized
that the only "vehicles" that could deliver their supplies in
that terrain were camels. The Maharaja of Bikaner cannily
cashed in on this opportunity by supplying the British army
with a steady stream of Bikaner's camels, long known for their
hardiness and load-carrying capacity. This resulted in a
turnaround in Bikaner's fortunes. A modern administrative
system was soon installed, the first hospitals established, and a
police force set up to handle the lawlessness and banditry that
were becoming rampant. In 1886, this remote desert kingdom
became the first Indian Princely State to introduce electricity.
MAHARAJA GANGA SINGH. It was Maharaja Ganga Singh
(reigned 1898–1944), one of the most remarkable rulers India
produced in the early 20th century, who was responsible for
putting Bikaner in a position of prominence on the map of
India ● *39*. Maharaja Ganga Singh, who was educated at the
celebrated Mayo College in Ajmer ▲ *162* (like most of the
other later Rajput maharajas), gave Bikaner a prominence far
beyond its size. First, he created the famous Bikaner Camel
Corps, or Ganga Risala, a flamboyant fighting force that he
personally led, on behalf of the British, first to China to help
put down the Boxer Rebellion in 1900, then to Somaliland to
quell the Somali Uprising in 1903, and finally to Egypt during
World War I ▲ *204*. (At the Suez Canal in 1915 the Ganga
Risala routed the Turks in a daredevil camel cavalry charge.)
Maharaja Ganga Singh also built up Bikaner's economy,
promoting, among other things, the Ganga Canal, an
ambitious irrigation project that was years ahead of its time,
and which turned the deserts of Bikaner into rich farmland
■ *22* ● *115*. But most of all, perhaps, Maharaja Ganga Singh
came to be known for his spectacular grouse shoots, to which
everybody from the Viceroy downward, including fellow
maharajas, vied to be invited. Maharaja Ganga Singh very

Officers of the
Bikaner Camel Corps
circa 1902.

> "IT APPEARED LIKE AN IMMENSE WALLED TOWN WITH BASTIONS, NOR COULD WE GIVE CREDIT TO OUR GUIDES WHEN THEY TALKED OF THE *SIYA KOT* ('CASTLE IN THE SKY')…"
>
> COLONEL TOD, *ANNALS AND ANTIQUITIES OF RAJASTHAN*, 1829

shrewdly treated these hunts as a diplomatic tool, using the opportunity to charm selected guests and win their support.

His guests at the great shoots included the Prince of Wales, later King George V, and French President, George Clemenceau. Maharaja Ganga Singh later became something of an international political figure, going on to lead the Indian delegation to the League of Nations. In 1949 the kingdom became part of the new state of Rajasthan in independent India ▲ 39.

BIKANER TODAY

Bikaner is still, at heart, a medieval, walled desert town. The thick crenelated walls encircling it are still there, studded with five huge gates that were once locked at night. Like Jaipur, it is also a "Pink City", in fact, perhaps even more so, as its impressive fort, palaces, mansions and public buildings are all carved from the rich pink-purple sandstone that is characteristic of this region. It has always been a surprisingly wealthy town because of its trade. An old saying talked of its "five famous treasures": its camels, wealthy merchants, rich candies, gold jewelry, and beautiful women. Bikaner was also, until the turn of the century, India's "Wild West" – plagued by bandit chieftains and robber barons. All that changed with the rule of Maharaja Ganga Singh, who created a modern administration and developed the kingdom's agricultural system and mineral industries. But the lingering flavor of the old, wild desert town is still there. Wander around the bazaars of Bikaner (near the walled town's old Kot Gate). Shops sell everything from camel-hair blankets to flamboyantly colored tie-and-dye fabrics ● 58. As you wander, you're constantly jostled by supremely arrogant-looking Bikaneri camels and camel carts. The latter have now gone high-tech: they now have truck tires instead of the old creaking wooden wheels. Bikaner is known particularly for its excellent *durries* and carpets, its ornately decorated lacquer-work and its camel-skin handicrafts ranging from delicate, translucent hand-painted lampshades to quaintly upturned *mojri* slippers, which, with wear, mold around the shape of your foot like a second skin (above). Bikaner is now an important military base. The surrounding region is no longer a desert wasteland, but thanks to the Ganga Canal and, later, Indira Gandhi Canal, one of the world's largest projects of its kind, it is now fertile farmland.

WATER POTS
With the scarcity of water in this desert area, water containers naturally assume a major importance. Bikaner is known for its graceful clay *kunjas*, traditionally shaped with narrow necks to prevent loss of water through evaporation.

A LEGACY OF THE PAST
The ancient sandalwood throne of the kings of Kannauj (the old dynasty from which Rao Bika was descended), dating back to the fifth century AD, is the oldest piece of furniture in India today. Along with a state umbrella, a diamond studded shield, war drums and an image of the family goddess, it was one of the dynasty's heirlooms, brought by Rao Bika from Jodhpur in 1486 ● 34.

JUNAGARH FORT

Junagarh Fort is one of the most interesting forts in Rajasthan. Its sumptuously decorated interiors are much better preserved than in almost any other in the region. Wandering through the halls of its palace complex, you can easily imagine what life must have been like in those medieval times. Built in 1588 by Raja Rai Singh (reigned 1571–1611), it is unusual in the sense that it was one of the few major forts of Rajasthan that was not built on a hilltop. Instead, it was built on the desert plains, perhaps using the very inconspicuousness of its location as a defense. Its rugged sandstone bastions and graceful pavilions and balconies are silhouetted against the sky. As you enter through the main gateway, Suraj Pol, you can see the twin statues of the fort's guardians, Jaimal and Patta, the warrior-heroes of Chittorgarh's defense. Beyond this lies a complex of splendid palaces, each one built by a different ruler over the centuries. The last portions were added on as recently as 1943.

MIRACULOUS FEATS
In Junagarh Fort, you can see curious platforms made of swords on which the *sadhus* of Bikaner would dance. Lady Reading, the Viceroy's wife, wrote in 1922 of "a wizard who walked with bare feet on swords I could not touch, so sharp were their points...it was hopelessly uncanny, but wonderful and gorgeous."

Suraj Pol.

KARAN MAHAL. This lies in the second of the palace complex's courtyards. It is remarkable for its walls, which look like marble *pietra dura* inlaid with semi-precious stones as in Agra's Taj Mahal but which actually turn out, on closer inspection, to be a superb example of gilded *arayish* plaster-work.

DURGA NIWAS. Beyond Karan Mahal is Durga Niwas, a beautiful enclosure with superbly painted walls and a white marble pool. The pool was built to cool this part of the palace in summer. During the spring festival of Holi it would be filled with colored water, with which the maharajas and their ranis would riotously splash each other in the customary manner.

LAL NIWAS. Nearby is Lal Niwas, the oldest part of the palace complex, dating back to 1595. It is notable for the richly painted stylized floral motifs in red and gold that cover its walls. Another notable feature is the revolutionary absence of columns to support the ceiling, which accounts for the narrowness of the hall. As you go upstairs, you come to Gaj Mandir and, right at the summit, the breezy Chhattar Niwas. Built in the 1880's, it has walls idiosyncrati-

Lal Niwas (top) and its red-and-gold frescos (bottom).

Chandra Mahal.

Anup Mahal.

cally decorated with English plates bearing old prints of "Oriental Field Sports".

ANUP MAHAL. One of the truly exceptional parts of Junagarh's palace complex is Anup Mahal. Built in 1669, it has a magnificent coronation room with ornately lacquered walls in red and gold and panels of dazzling colored glass inlay set over a throne. The marble columns are covered with delicate paint work, and the entire effect is simply breathtaking. Do not miss the small side chamber with its aquamarine blue walls, richly inlaid with gold leaf.

CHANDRA MAHAL AND PHUL MAHAL. Almost as impressive are Chandra Mahal ("Moon Palace") and the nearby Phul Mahal ("Flower Palace") built in the mid-18th century, with their superbly painted walls and elaborate mirror inlay work (below). A member of the Viceroy's party which visited Junagarh Fort in the 1920's wrote of the Maharaja's jewelry collection once housed here, "those of the Maharajah of Benares are splinters in comparison. Such pearls and emeralds, the latter in strings of about six chains and then knobs of uncut emeralds and diamonds…I tried everything on and blazed like a chandelier." Another, rather different, observation was that of the famous film director, James Ivory (who shot part of his film, *The Guru*, here at Junagarh), who

WATER FANTASY
In a desert kingdom like Bikaner, where rain is a rare phenomenon, this fresco of rain clouds in Badal Mahal represents a fantasy.

noted, "So much has happened in these palaces. Nearly every story has violent death as a theme; there are terrible tales of revenge, poisonings, patricides, mass widow burnings. Finally, it is all – well, just weird and unnerving."

It is said that the artist was specially commissioned to paint it, so that when the rains finally *did* come the children of the royal household would not be frightened by it. A touching folk saying of the region goes, "Through snake bite, accident, lightning or the sword death may strike us; but let it not strike us by denying us rain."

Ganga Niwas.

FORT MUSEUM. Ganga Niwas, a great pink sandstone hall, its walls entirely carved with delicate tracery and scroll-work, was Maharaja Ganga Singh's contribution to Junagarh Palace in the early 20th century.

Once used as the Diwan-i-Am ("Hall of Public Audience"), it now houses part of the fort museum. Here you can see an exotic array of antique Rajput weaponry, from jade-handled daggers to ivory inlaid muskets. Also, unexpectedly, you'll discover a World War One biplane in here! Other interesting items in the museum collection are an eclectic collection of royal costumes, *hookahs*, bric-à-brac, carpets, jewelry and the drums of Jambhoji (below), the saint who predicted that Rao Bika's dynasty would rule for only 450 years. There is a collection of personal memorabilia of the redoubtable Maharaja Ganga Singh, from old photographs of him with various great international statesmen with whom he rubbed shoulders, to an amusing soup spoon specially designed to accommodate his enormous upturned mustache.

The museum also contains some beautiful examples of miniatures from the Bikaner school, as well as illuminated Sanskrit and Persian manuscripts.

THE GENERAL'S ARMOR
The armor of Raja Anup Singh (reigned 1674–98) is in the fort museum. A great renaissance man, he was, in addition to being a superb general, a mathematician, astronomer, scholar, and patron of the arts and music.

Lallgarh Palace (top) and old prints of its dining room (bottom left) and smoking room (bottom right).

LALLGARH PALACE

Around the turn of the 20th century, Maharaja Ganga Singh decided that it was time to move out of Junagarh Fort and build a modern palace that more clearly reflected the progressive new character of his kingdom. The result was the impressive Lallgarh Palace (in purple-pink sandstone again, like most of Bikaner's buildings). It took twenty-four years to complete, from 1902 to 1926. Designed by Sir Swinton Jacob ▲ *134*, and considered by many to be his greatest masterpiece, the opulent Lallgarh Palace draws its inspiration largely from the Rajput tradition, with virtually no trace of a Mughal influence. Its façade, like a Rajput fort, has almost no decorative features, except its topping of arrayed cupolas. The inside of the palace is

Bikaner miniatures reflect an exquisite marriage between the traditions of 16th-century Jain art and Mughal art.

centered around two courtyards and has a wealth of carved pillars, ornamental friezes, delicate stonework lattices and arcaded balconies. The cloistered courtyard of Laxmi Vilas, for instance, is considered to be a little architectural gem. In the grand expanses of Maharaja Ganga Singh's Durbar Hall, one can imagine how matters of great international import must have once been discussed here in remote little Bikaner. While the details of Lallgarh Palace are entirely Rajput, there is a strong touch of the Renaissance in the way it has been laid out, with its colonnades and corridors. As you wander through it, you can see its old halls, suites, billiard room and smoking room, all largely unchanged from the days of Maharaja Ganga Singh, with their Bohemian chandeliers and hunting trophies on the walls (some of them souvenirs from a hunting trip to Bavaria). There is a banquet hall that can seat up to four hundred people, and in one corner, a huge indoor swimming pool (now dry). The palace also has a significant collection of rare Sanskrit manuscripts, which in fact is one of the finest collections of ancient Sanskrit manuscripts in the world. It is open to research scholars. Many of these manuscripts were brought back from the Deccan by Raja Anup Singh, who led the Mughal armies against Golconda and Bijapur in the 17th century. A great patron of the arts and music, it is said that he came back from his south Indian campaign laden with, instead of booty, an enormous collection of sacred manuscripts and idols that he had saved, all of which are now here in Bikaner. The royal family still lives in a wing of Lallgarh Palace, but the rest of it has now been converted into a charming hotel ◆ *338*.

BIKANER MUSEUM. In Lallgarh Palace is a fascinating little museum, filled with the sundry possessions of the later maharajas (which give you a vivid glimpse of their lifestyle): everything from a 1921 model Simplex movie projector to the British tin soldiers that some little Bikaner prince used to play with once.

SWINGING MAIDENS
This exotic lacquered wooden swing in the Junagarh collection is ornamented with carvings of maidens on its supporting columns. These were ingeniously connected with the swing's mechanism, so that as you gently swung on it, the maidens would automatically "dance" for you.

Antique Rajput weaponry from the Fort Museum.

Rhinoceros-hide shield (right), and sword belonging to Raja Man Singh I of Jaipur (left).

Weapons, not surprisingly, played an important part in the lives of the martial Rajputs. Of Maharao Umed Singh of Bundi (reigned 1771–1819), for instance, it is said that he habitually carried "a matchlock, a lance, a sword, a dagger and their appurtenances of knives, pouches and priming horn; he had a battle-axe, a javelin, a tomahawk, a discus, bow and quiver of arrows". Colonel Tod noted that the keeper of the armory was regarded as one of a prince's most confidential officers.

DEVOTED TO ARMS
Colonel Tod, in *Annals and Antiquities of Rajasthan*, describes how the Rajputs worshiped their arms: "The devotion of the Rajput is still paid to his arms...He swears by the steel and prostrates himself before his defensive buckler, his sword, or his dagger."

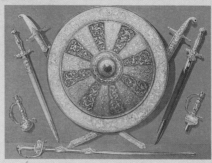

WAGH NAKH
Wagh nakh was an apt name for this strange and gruesome weapon. Literally meaning "tiger's claws", it was slipped unobtrusively over one's fingers and used to maul one's opponent in close combat.

VARIETY OF SHIELDS
Rajput shields were made from a variety of materials: wood, steel, bamboo, crocodile hide or rhino hide. The latter was by far the favorite, as it was believed to offer a warrior the greatest protection.

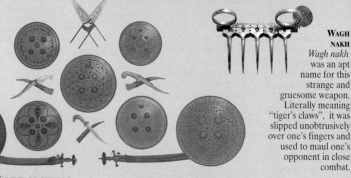

ANCIENT WEAPON
Rajput warriors often used a heavy mace in battle. This weapon has an ancient tradition that goes back to Lord Bhima, the great warrior in the Hindu epic, the *Mahabharata*.

CURVED FAVORITE
The Rajputs used a wide variety of different types of sabres. But their favorite was the *sirohi*, with its light, narrow, slightly curved blade, formed like that of a Damascus sword.

"NO PRINCE OR CHIEF IS WITHOUT HIS SILEH KHANA, OR ARMOURY, WHERE HE PASSES HOURS IN VIEWING AND ARRANGING HIS ARMS..."
COLONEL TOD, *ANNALS AND ANTIQUITIES OF RAJASTHAN*, 1829

EXQUISITE SWORDS
Rajput swords were superbly tempered and often exquisitely ornamented. They covered a wide variety of types, from the long sword for cut-and-thrust to the heavy double-edged *khanda*.

WEIGHTY ARMOR
Rajput warriors wore suits of armor so heavy that you wonder at the strength of the man who could fight from underneath it all. For instance, Maharana Pratap of Udaipur's armor, along with his weapons, weighed a total of 165 pounds.

RAJA ANUP SINGH'S ARMOR
Raja Anup Singh's 17th-century armor must have seen action on numerous battlefields, from Kabul in the north to Golconda in the south. It was worn with an unusually shaped rhino-hide helmet.

DAGGERED FIST
A *katar* was the traditional broad-bladed dagger worn over the fist. Sometimes it was designed with little pistols projecting from the sides of its handle, which could be fired by squeezing the handle.

▲ BIKANER
HAVELIS, TEMPLES, AND CAMEL FARM

HAVELIS

During medieval times, Bikaner became a haven for rich traders and bankers who felt safe here, in the desert, from the turmoil that frequently swept across north India. Several of them left their families – and their wealth – in Bikaner, as they plied their business elsewhere (paying handsomely, by the way, for the protection). That is the origin of the town's beautiful old *havelis* or mansions, which date back to the 17th century. These handsome sandstone buildings, often multi-storied, have ornately carved lattice screens, balconies and balustrades. The windows, made from solid wood, bound with iron bands, contrast graphically with the delicacy of the carved purple sandstone. Inside, hidden away from the outside world, the descendants of those wealthy traders'

families continue to live, as they have for centuries. The *havelis* of Bikaner are clustered together in the narrow lanes of the old walled city. Rampuria Haveli and Kothari Haveli are among the most impressive.

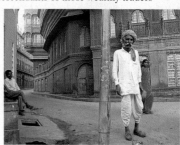

SANDESHWAR TEMPLE

There are two very interesting Jain temples here, the Sandeshwar and Bhandeshwar temples, said to have been built by two wealthy merchant brothers in the 14th century. Sandeshwar Temple is a minor masterpiece. Dedicated to the Jain *tirthankara* (saint), Neminath, its interiors are ablaze with enamel and gold-leaf frescos and leafwork scrollery. The ceiling is vaulted, arched and ornately decorated. At one end is a statue of Neminath meditating on a lotus pedestal, beneath which are rows of wonderful marble statues of other Jain saints.

LEGEND OF A DESERT TREE
The *khejri* (*Prosopis cineraria*) is one of the few trees that flourishes in the hostile conditions of the desert ■ 30. According to legend, Raja Gaj Singh of Bikaner, on a campaign in the Deccan with Emperor Aurangzeb's armies, came upon a *khejri* tree and began to weep, as it reminded him of his own distant kingdom. The Emperor gave him leave to go home for six months, but asked that his cousin, Raja Zorawar Singh of Khimsar, another Rajput general, stand guarantee for his return. When Raja Gaj Singh did not return in time, Raja Zorawar Singh promptly gave up three-quarters of his own kingdom of Khimsar to honor his promise to the Emperor.

After war or famine, if a girl cannot be married for want of a groom, the betrothal ceremony can be performed with a *khejri* tree. This subject appears in paintings (left).

BHANDESHWAR TEMPLE

Dedicated to the Jain saint, Parashvanath, this temple has interestingly carved wooden columns decorated with motifs of dancing maidens. In the center lies the sanctum, which is covered with mirrorwork and gilt and houses a fine marble statue of the saint. In the temple's circular *mandapa,* or hall, you will find some superb frescos depicting processions, court scenes and battles. The red sandstone galleries and porches were later additions in the 17th century. There are several other fascinating temples in Bikaner, but if you don't have time for all of them, at least take a look at the impressive Rattan Bihari Temple opposite Junagarh Fort.

CAMEL FARM

The camels of Bikaner played a major role in the history of the kingdom, contributing greatly to its economy, as well as its defense, over the centuries. The camel breeding farm (below), set amid rolling sand dunes, was formed in 1960 to produce superior strains of camels. One of the efforts at the farm, interestingly, is to breed camels with longer, thicker eyelashes, which offer greater protection in sandstorms! Bikaner's camels have traditionally been renowned for their heavy load-carrying capacity (while Jaisalmer's camels are known for their speed). The camel farm breeds camels both for domestic haulage as well as, even today, for military use. The Indian army still boasts a crack Camel Corps, indispensable for desert warfare ▲ 194, 204. It traces its origins back to the Ganga Risala regiment, raised by Maharaja Ganga Singh in the late 19th century. The regiment's temperamental beasts were so superbly trained that a member of a visiting Viceroy's party to Bikaner in the 1920s, on seeing a guard of honor, noted that the camels were "immoveable, as if carved out of gray granite." Incidentally, Maharaja Ganga Singh, shrewd showman that he was, used to arrange dramatic military tattoos featuring legions of camel warriors dressed in black chain-mail armor in order to impress his important guests.

THIRST QUENCHER
Traveling through the desert, you frequently see people selling melons by the roadside as thirst quenchers. Colonel Tod, writing in the 1820s, remarked on "the superior magnitude of the water melons of the desert", adding that "one is sufficient to allay the thirst both of a horse and his rider." Emperor Babur, the first Mughal, had called India an uncivilized country because, among other things, it had no melons. He is reputed to have introduced these, along with the Mughal gardens ▲ 314.

SNAKE DEITY
All around Bikaner, as well as other parts of Rajasthan, you see the sacred slabs of Gogaji, a popular folk deity, often represented by a coiling snake with a hood. He is supposed to offer immunity against snake bites – important in this snake-infested desert region. His main shrine is in the nearby village of Gogamedi, where he is believed to reveal himself to his devotees each year, astride his blue horse, on three nights in the monsoon month of Bhadon.

Camel breeding farm (left).

203

▲ BIKANER CAMEL CORPS

The Camel Corps is even advertised on cigarette packs.

The Bikaner Camel Corps had its early beginnings in 1465 when Rao Bika, the founder, led a corps of three hundred *sowars*, or camel riders, to conquer the adjoining territories. Subsequently, in the 19th century, during the reign of Ganga Singh, the Bikaner *durbar* offered to raise a camel corps of five hundred Rathor Rajputs as Imperial Service troops for the British Army ▲ 194. The unit, known as the Ganga Risala after the name of the ruler, served in the Boxer Rebellion in 1900, the Somaliland Campaign from 1902 to 1904, and the two World Wars. After India gained independence, the regiment was effective in the desert areas during India's border disputes with Pakistan between 1965 and 1971.

THE OFFICER AND HIS CAMEL
The tall, proud Rajput soldier is dressed resplendently in his white uniform and red and gold turban, while his camel is caparisoned in bright colors. According to a popular story, there was an attempt to introduce shoes for the camels as part of their uniform to protect their soft, padded feet from being damaged by the tarred roads which they had to traverse. The camels sat down en masse on the road, obstinately refusing to move till the shoes were discarded – a clear case of mutiny.

"SHIPS OF THE DESERT"
When Rao Bikaji in the 15th century started to deploy camels for his army, the best specimens of the *sowari*, or riding camels, were from the districts of Jaisalmer and Bikaner. Even today they are used by the Indian post for delivering mail in the remote desert regions.

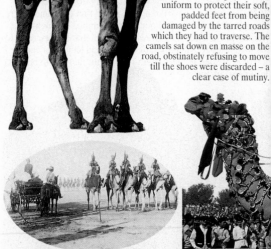

Military review of the Bikaner Camel Corps, the pride of Bikaner State Forces.

GANGA RISALA

Situated in the desert and near the international border, Bikaner had to maintain a well-trained and sizeable army. The Ganga Risala consisted of six units which looked after specific functions. When it was first set up, British officers were appointed to supervise the training and equipping of the units.

GANGA-JAISALMER RISALA

In 1951, the Ganga Risala amalgamated with the Jaisalmer Camel Corps to become the Ganga-Jaisalmer Risala. It was redesignated as the 13th Battalion of the Grenadiers in the Indian Army on March 4, 1955. The corps is stationed at Bikaner as part of the Border Security Force (left), a paramilitary force which patrols India's borders from the icy Himalayan passes to the desert in the west.

CEREMONIAL PARADE

The Camel Corps officiates on special occasions during peacetime. It forms part of the ceremonial parade in New Delhi on Republic Day. Its officers also excel in mounted sports such as camel polo.

RAT LEGEND
According to legend, Karni Mata once attempted to bring a dead child back to life. However, she failed because Yama, the god of death, explained to her that the child had already been reincarnated on earth. Angrily, Karni Mata proclaimed that nobody from her tribe would ever fall into the hands of Yama. Instead, when they died they would temporarily inhabit the body of a rat before being reborn into the tribe.

Karni Mata Temple.

KARNI MATA'S VICTORY
The heavy chased silver doors of the Karni Mata Temple depict the patron goddess, calm and composed after her victory over Mahishasura, the great buffalo-demon (whose head is seen at the end of her trident) while her rodent followers leap about her in glee.

DEVIKUND

The royal cenotaphs of Bikaner (above), beautifully carved in sandstone and marble and grouped around a large pool, are located 5 miles outside Bikaner. The cenotaphs are carved with the symbol of the sun, for the dynasty is *suryavanshi* ("of the family of the sun"). The cenotaphs of the ranis are signified by lotus flowers, or footmarks to mark those who had performed *sati*. The cenotaphs of the children, touchingly, bear hollowed cups, supposedly to hold milk for the child. It was once prophesied, apparently, that all the maharajas of Bikaner would be cremated within this complex at Devikund. Uncannily, with the cremation of the last ruling maharaja, Sadul Singh, in 1950, the complex was full.

GAJNER

The old royal hunting lodge of Gajner, 20 miles west of Bikaner, was the venue of Maharaja Ganga Singh's legendary *shikar* parties. The lodge itself, a sprawling deep-pink affair, ornamented with delicate lattice screens and cupolas, is set in lush gardens by the side of a picturesque lake (above). A member of a viceregal party that was once entertained here later reminisced, "You can't imagine the beauty, it was like 'Arabian Nights' in the desert." Incidentally, for all his huntsmanship, Maharaja Ganga Singh was also a dedicated wildlife conservationist. He enforced strict laws to prevent hunting out of season and made sure that the animals were well looked after. He even had slabs of rock salt tied to the trees on one occasion, when it was learned that a certain species of deer was suffering from a salt deficiency. Today Gajner is a good place to see blackbuck, *chinkara*, *chital*, *sambar*, wild boar, and bustard. The maharaja still uses the lodge for weekends, but most of it, like Lallgarh Palace, has been converted into a hotel.

KOLAYAT

Beyond Gajner, in the middle of the desert, is a large lake and the temple complex of Kolayat, associated with a famous ancient sage, Kapil Muni. There are several marble temples, pavilions and bathing ghats here, where pilgrims and holy men take a dip in the waters.

"THE LAKE [AT GAJNER] HAS CLOSED OVER THAT
WONDERFUL PINK PALACE, COMPELLED BY
SOME LIGHT-HEARTED… MAGICIAN."

YVONNE FITZROY, *COURTS AND CAMPS OF INDIA*, 1926

DESHNOKE

KARNI MATA TEMPLE.
Located 19 miles south of
Bikaner, Karni Mata
Temple is one of the
strangest in India ● 46.
Karni Mata is the patron
goddess of the maharajas
of Bikaner ▲ 193. The
temple is populated by
hundreds of sacred
rats – quite harmless,
incidentally – who
are fed on the
offerings of the
devotees.
The temple
itself is
superbly
carved in
white marble,
with lavishly
decorated
gateways,
pavilions,
columns, and
balconies. Its
heavy chased
silver gates are
particularly
admirable.

Shiva temple in
Kolayat.

KALIBANGAN

The pre-historic ruined town of Kalibangan lies 175 miles
north of Bikaner, but the journey is worth making.
Kalibangan was a city of the Harappan civilization that
flourished between 3500 and 4500 years ago ● 32. In fact, it
was a sister city to the great Indus Valley cities of
Mohenjodaro and Harappa, designed on basically the same
plan, and almost as large. Kalibangan literally means "Black
Bangles", from the numerous fragments of weather-stained
terracotta bangles that were found strewn all over the
excavation site. The excavations here reveal the portrait of an
amazingly sophisticated urban lifestyle. The town was built
around a central acropolis, with a fine system of streets that
intersected at right angles, and an advanced drainage system.
The houses were made of kiln-fired bricks and had bathrooms
with terracotta water pipes and even faucets. Other finds
range from a sophisticated system of weights and
measures to a charming array of children's toys,
including a delightful whistle shaped in the form
of a bird. Subsequent excavations
nearby have unearthed relics of an
even more ancient culture,
simply dubbed "pre-
Harappan", which goes back
five thousand years in time.

**ROYAL HUNTING
PARTY**
The itineraries of
visiting English
dignitaries and
monarchs in India
were often arranged
to fit in a hunt with
Maharaja Ganga
Singh at Gajner,
usually over
Christmas. They
would hunt blackbuck
at 50 miles per hour
from open-roof Rolls
Royces in the desert.
Or, more frequently,
they would hunt
imperial sandgrouse
at Gajner Lake. The
birds swept down to
the lake, as an
English guest once
wrote, "not in the
hundreds, but in the
thousands. Not for
half an hour, but for
three hours on and …
in perfect military
formation." An
invitation to a grouse
hunt was much
coveted and
Maharaja Ganga
Singh was
sometimes
referred to
as "The
Maharaja
by the
Grouse of
God".

The flag of Jaisalmer flies over the fort citadel.

COAT-OF-ARMS
Jaisalmer's coat-of-arms is emblazoned with a desert fort and a naked arm holding a broken spear because, as Rudyard Kipling noted, "The legend goes that Jeysulmir was once galled by a horse with a magic spear." The hawk is a symbol of Durga, the dynasty's patron goddess. The desert antelopes below are spangled with gold coins – a tribute to Jaisalmer's wealthy Jain bankers.

DESERT MINSTRELS
The Manganiyars are wandering desert minstrels ● 79. Historically, they had a close relationship with the Rajputs of Jaisalmer. It was the duty of the Muslim Manganiyars to entertain the Rajput before battle, as well as to stay beside him when he died, maintaining a vigil over the corpse until the ceremonies for the departed soul were over.

HISTORY

The medieval fortress town of Jaisalmer rises out of the remote deserts of Rajasthan, like a city at the very end of the world. According to mythology, after the epic battle of the *Mahabharata*, Lord Krishna and the Pandav hero, Bhima, came here for a ceremony. Lord Krishna then prophesied that a descendant of his Yadava clan would one day establish a glorious kingdom here in the desert. Then, with his discus, he smote a rock and a sweet water spring sprang forth. In the 12th century, a Bhatti Rajput prince, Rao Jaisal, came upon the great triangular rock (where Jaisalmer now stands). Here he met a hermit, Eesul, who blessed him and learning that Rao Jaisal was descended from the Yadavas, showed him Lord Krishna's prophecy engraved on a rock. Rao Jaisal, inspired by this, decided to shift his capital here from nearby Lodurva, despite the fact that the hermit also prophesied that this new capital would be sacked two and a half times. The great fort was built in 1156, supposedly the second oldest of Rajasthan's major forts after Chittorgarh. Jaisalmer was located right on the route of the caravans from Egypt, Arabia, Persia and Central Asia carrying their spices, silks and dried fruits to the emporia of Delhi in the east, and Gujarat in the south. Thus it became an extremely prosperous town. The Bhatti rulers of Jaisalmer were romantic marauders, known as the "wolf-packs of the desert".

THE THREE SACKINGS. In 1294, the first of the "two-and-a-half sackings" of Jaisalmer prophesied by the sage Eesul took place. When the princes of Jaisalmer ambushed and captured a treasure caravan of three thousand horses and mules belonging to Sultan Alauddin Khilji of Delhi, the Sultan launched a punitive raid on Jaisalmer and the siege is said to have lasted for eight years. Eventually, Jaisalmer fell, but not before 24,000 of its women performed *jauhar* by leaping into the flames to prevent themselves from falling into the enemy's hands. The second of the prophesied sackings took place not long after, when one of Jaisalmer's princes caringly carried away the prize steed of Sultan Feroz Shah of Delhi. Once again the womenfolk of the fort performed *jauhar*. The third – the "half sacking" of the ancient prophecy – was the most curious of them all. In the 16th century, a neighboring Patina chieftain played a Trojan horse trick on Jaisalmer, by bringing into its fort a retinue of palanquins supposedly carrying the ladies

of his court, but filled, instead, with armed warriors. A fierce hand-to-hand battle broke out and when it seemed that the defenders were surely going to lose, the Rawal of Jaisalmer killed all his womenfolk with his own sword – since there was no time for a *jauhar*. Tragically, it turned out to have been in vain because, shortly after, reinforcements arrived and the attackers were wiped out.

Portrait of Rao Jaisal.

END OF HOSTILITIES. In the 16th century the maharawals of Jaisalmer were attacked several times by the Mughals, but resisted defiantly. Finally, however, in the 1650's Rawal Sabal Sigh (reigned 1651–61) recognized the sovereignty of Delhi, and with the end of hostilities a new era of prosperity began for Jaisalmer. It was also an era of brilliant architectural activity during which the wealthy merchants of town, as well as the maharawals themselves, used their vast riches for building exquisite *havelis* and palaces.

BRITISH RULE. By the 19th century Jaisalmer had come under the influence of the British – one of the last of the Rajput kingdoms to sign a treaty with them. Colonel James Tod, the celebrated scholar of the Rajput civilization and author of the magnum opus, *Annals and Antiquities of Rajasthan*, was himself sent here as the British Political Agent. It is amusing to note that during this period, remote little Jaisalmer briefly figured in the arena of international geopolitics. With the then Russian Empire looking for its long sought-after access to the warm water ports of the Indian Ocean, and the threat of its invasion, the possession of Jaisalmer became, for the British, "of vital importance, by giving us the command of...the most practicable point of advance into India."

GODDESS OF WAR
Bhawani, whose temple is by Bhointia Pol, is the goddess of war. The Bhatti warriors sought her blessings before riding into battle and came back to thank her for her protection on their safe return. The warriors' terrifying battle cry was "Jai Bhawani" ("Victory to Bhawani").

Painting of a battle scene on the wall of Jaisalmer Fort.

▲ JAISALMER
THE CITY

COURTESAN'S GATE
Telia, the beautiful courtesan of a Bhatti prince, built the ghats and ornate gateway that lead to Jaisalmer's Gadsisar Lake. The royal family was furious at her effrontery and threatened to destroy the gate. The shrewd Telia quickly installed a temple to Lord Krishna above the gate so nobody would be able to pull it down. The royal family, however, has never used the gate.

WEB OF INTRIGUE. The early century saw an era of bitter intrigue in the court of Jaisalmer between the maharawals and their powerful hereditary prime ministers, the Mehtas. Swarup Singh Mehta was beheaded by a prince of Jaisalmer when he insulted the prince over a debt owed to him. He was succeeded by his young son, Salim Singh, who had secretly sworn revenge on the Rawal's family. Salim Singh grew up to become a Borgia-like tyrant who very neatly ruined both the Rawal and the kingdom of Jaisalmer itself, and was finally stabbed to death. He was so hated by everybody that it is recorded that "since there was some fear that the (stab) wound might heal, his wife gave him poison".

JAISALMER TODAY

Jaisalmer, even today, has an exotically medieval flavor to it. Most of the town lies within the thick stone walls of the fort, 1485 feet long and 890 feet wide, and wandering through it is almost like stepping into the pages of the Arabian Nights. For a thousand years the town flourished because of its position on the main caravan trail up through Afghanistan. According to a persistent legend, Marco Polo stopped here during his travels to China. By the 19th century, however, with the coming of the British and their new system of octroi and the opening up of ports such as Bombay, the caravan trade and,

DEPARTMENT OF NARCOTICS
Ornately crafted wood and silver boxes were used for carrying opium. The smoking of opium was historically a part of the way of life in the harsh deserts of Marwar. Warriors took a double dose before going into battle. Opium was crushed in a bowl embellished, significantly, with a cobra's hood. It was considered an insult for guests to refuse opium offered. A milder version is *bhang*, often crushed with rose petals, aniseed, and black pepper, and served in buttermilk, candies, or fried snacks. You can get *bhang* in shops licensed by a government body, interestingly named "The Department of Narcotics".

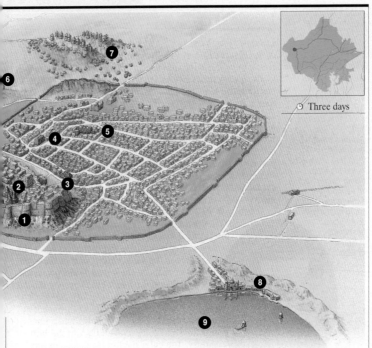

Three days

consequently, the importance of this town dwindled. In the wake of the 1965 war between India and Pakistan, the entire area became a major military base. Today Jaisalmer's economy depends largely on the earnings of camels, sheep and cattle. But with the opening of the new Indira Gandhi Canal, the desert landscape will probably soon be transformed by agricultural use. In addition, there are prospects of major sources of natural gas beneath the desert sands. Still, this region is an astonishingly arid place. Sometimes it does not rain here for five years at a time. It is said that the children, who have sometimes never seen rain, are terrified at the prospect of their first shower! But the surrounding desert region has a harsh, terrible beauty about it, and going out on a camel safari is an experience not to be missed. Jaisalmer, till the very end, remained one of the kingdoms of Rajasthan that was most insulated from the outside world: there was no proper road to Jaisalmer till 1958, and it was only in 1968 that a railway line was installed. It is still surprisingly untouched by progress, part of the reason perhaps being the absence of an airport, and its relative inaccessibility to the outside world. Best is to come around the time of the spectacular annual Desert Festival in February, when dancers, musicians, puppeteers and other performers (including fire-walkers and sword swallowers) congregate here from all over Rajasthan. An ironic footnote: a splendid new desert fort was built at Mohangarh near Jaisalmer, as late as 1940. Barely thirty-five years later, just 50 miles away, outside Pokharan, the Indian Government tested a nuclear device.

EMPORIUM OF THE EAST
Jaisalmer's bazaars are evocative of the days of the medieval camel caravans when the region was a trading emporium for splendid carpets from Herat, scimitars from Damascus, stallions from Arabia and wines from Shiraz."

Old cannon at Jaisalmer Fort.

HURLING STONES
Colonel Tod, who was the British Political Agent in Jaisalmer, wrote that the fort had "very few cannons mounted". Its defenses were therefore reinforced by having huge, round stones placed all around its battlements, which could be hurled down upon the enemy in times of siege.

Hawa Pol.

JAISALMER FORT

Jaisalmer Fort looks like a giant child's sandcastle, or the set of the desert castle in a Hollywood epic production of *Beau Geste*. In fact, it is the ultimate in desert forts, dominating the landscape for miles around from the top of Trikuta Hill, as it has for more than eight hundred years. One of the fascinating things about the fort is its color: its massive sandstone walls are a tawny lion color during the day, turning to a magical honey-gold as the sun sets. When Satyajit Ray, the celebrated Indian film director, saw it, he was inspired to make a film called *Sonar Kila* (The Golden Fort) ▲ *346*, a charming fantasy about a treasure guarded by a peacock. The fort stands on a triangular hill 250 feet high, enclosed by a thick, crenelated wall of over 30 feet high and reinforced with ninety-nine bastions, most of which were built in the mid-17th century ● *90*. Remarkably, these walls used no mortar at all. They were made entirely from huge, intricately interlocking blocks of stone. At one time the town of Jaisalmer lay entirely within the fort walls but sometime in the 17th century, part of the town moved outside, on the leeward side, protected by the hill and the fort itself. However, much of the town still lives within the fort, making it a kind of living museum. Walking through it at night, especially, is like stepping into a time machine and going straight back to the 14th century. You enter the fort up a steep incline paved with enormous flagstones, through a series of four huge gates, passing along the way a second fort wall running parallel to the outer one, and rising to half its height. Reaching the innermost gate, Hawa Pol ("Gate of the Winds"), so named because of the beautiful breezes it catches, you enter the spacious Chauhata Square. This is the heart of the fort complex. In front are the palaces of the maharawals. Toward the left

WEATHER FORECAST
This curious device atop the fort was used to forecast the weather in Jaisalmer. Each year on a day in April, a flag would be planted in its center, and the direction in which it blew was believed to determine the weather for the year. If it blew to the west, for instance, it meant a good monsoon, but if it blew to the north it indicated famine.

Jaisalmer Fort.

A hive of activity within Jaisalmer Fort (below).

is a flight of marble steps topped by a white marble throne, where the maharawal used to sit, listening to petitions or reviewing his troops. This was also the place, by the way, where the womenfolk performed *jauhar*; it was here that they leapt into the flames en masse. By the side of the square is Rao Jaisal's well where the sage Eesul is supposed to have shown Rao Jaisal the prophecy of Lord Krishna carved on a rock ▲ 208.

JAISALMER PALACE

As you enter the palace, you find it is actually a maze of interconnecting palaces, the oldest of which is Juna Mahal dating back to the early 16th century. Rang Mahal, built in the 18th century, is especially interesting, with its richly frescoed walls (look for the scenes of old Jaisalmer, as well as of Jaipur and Udaipur) and the superbly carved stone screen that you assume is a dark wooden lattice turns out to be cut from solid stone! Equally interesting is the slightly older Sarvottam Vilas, with its blue tiles and glass mosaics. You will also come across amusing little touches here in the palace, such as the ornate 19th-century American street lamp you suddenly discover up on the citadel, made, according to the signature, by the Pan American Light Company of Warren Street, New York. It is incongruously positioned right beside a medieval weather forecasting device and the fluttering royal Jaisalmer banner.

JAIN TEMPLES. Also within the fort are some old Jain temples, dating back to the 12th century. The most interesting are the temples of Rishabhdevji and Sambhavnath. Rishabhdevji Temple ● 48 has a splendidly carved *torana* archway over its entrance, and a striking group of *tirthankara* images, with jeweled eyes that sparkle in the dark. Next door is Sambhavnath Temple. It has a fabulous library in the basement, reputed to contain some of India's oldest and rarest palm-leaf manuscripts, dating back to the 11th century.

OLD MANUSCRIPTS
Old and rare manuscripts are kept in Sambhavnath Temple's library, including what is thought to be the oldest surviving manuscript in India – an 11th-century manuscript of one of the great *rishi* (sage), Dronacharya.

HAUNTING HANDPRINTS
Sati stones mark all the queens of a fort who have performed *sati*, immolating themselves on their husband's funeral pyres. Before leaving her dead husband's home for the last time the widow would traditionally leave a scarlet handprint on the gatepost as a reminder of her loyalty.

One of the remarkable things about Jaisalmer is the *havelis* or mansions built by its wealthy merchants and nobles in the 19th century. They are famed for their exquisitely carved sandstone façades – a feat of stone-carving unmatched anywhere else in India, not even by the intricate marble screens at Agra's Taj Mahal.

PATWON KI HAVELI

The largest and most elaborate of these *havelis* is Patwon ki Haveli ("Mansion of the Brocade Merchants") (left), built in 1805 by Guman Chand Patwa, a merchant and banker, who is said to have had three hundred trading centers between Afghanistan and China. Built for his five sons, this ornate five-storied complex took fifty years to complete. It stands in the privacy of a little cul-de-sac, behind a lofty arched gateway. Its entire frontage is beautifully carved, with its sixty latticed balconies looking as if they have been created from sandalwood rather than from stone. Inside are the remnants of some fine old murals.

NATHMALJI KI HAVELI

Even more beautifully carved is Nathmalji ki Haveli (below), built by a Prime Minister of Jaisalmer as late as 1885. Its façade is a riot of ornamentation: flowers, birds, elephants, soldiers, as well as a bicycle and a steam engine! It was apparently carved by two brothers, Hathu and Lallu, each of whom completed one side of the *haveli*. You can see how the whole looks perfectly harmonious but that the right and left side differ in their details. Also, extraordinarily, the building was carved out of boulders – not dressed stone – and you can see the raw boulder faces in the fascinating rooms inside.

TORANAS
Traditionally, every home in Jaisalmer has an auspicious *torana* over the archway of the main door. They are put up over a bride's home, and never taken down. The bridegroom, when he first enters the house on horseback, touches the *torana* with his sword to indicate that he will, if necessary, take his bride by force.

Façade of Patwon ki Haveli.

SALIM SINGH KI HAVELI

The third of the great *havelis* is the one built by the cruel scheming Prime Minister, Salim Singh, in 1815 (left). What makes it unique is the way it is narrow at the base, but suddenly flares out its cantilevered upper story. The *haveli* has a beautiful arched roof, capped with blue cupolas and superbly carved details. Do not miss its elegant peacock brackets. It is said that the Machiavellian Salim Singh slowly became more powerful than the maharawals themselves, and was once planning to build a passage from the upper story of this *haveli* to connect directly to the maharawal's palace, but the maharawal finally managed to scotch the idea.

BAZAARS

Wandering through the narrow alleys and bazaars of Jaisalmer, you are transported back to the time when this was the place where the products of India and China were exchanged for those of Persia, Arabia, Africa, and Europe, when "chintz, dried fruit, opium, silks, arms and salts" were traded for "elephant's teeth, dates, sandalwood, spices and coffee." A good place to start is Manak Chowk ("The Ruby Square"), the main market square, with its ancient water trough, where the town's animals are still watered. Across the road are stalls selling everything from traditional candies (the bright yellow little balls of *ghotua* are a specialty of Jaisalmer) to hardware, blankets, water containers, and desert supplies. As you walk through the narrow winding lanes, you pass by camels, desert gypsies, wandering cattle and children playing with primitive little handmade wooden toys. Jaisalmer is also a great place to shop for chunky rustic silver jewelry. There

are dozens of different types of jewelry designed for different parts of the female body: forehead, nose, ears, fingers, waist, ankles, toes, even an ornament called a *chupara* for the teeth! Other things to look for are colorful embroidery and mirrorwork, brightly colored tie-and-dye fabrics, rugged looking camel-skin *mojri* slippers, traditional shawls, rugs, and woodcarving.

SADDLED FOR COMFORT
To soften an uncomfortable camel ride, a typical Jaisalmer camel saddle is specially designed with several layers. The first is a layer of wool followed by four layers of cotton and a layer of cloth, often elaborately embroidered. Over this is placed a wooden seat, embellished with engraved copper and brass and attached to a leather cushion. A well-crafted saddle can cost up to one sixth of the price of a camel.

DELICATE CARVINGS
The *silavats* (stone carvers) of Jaisalmer are known for their incredibly delicate carving. The celebrated film director Satyajit Ray wrote of a sandstone tea cup he was once shown by the Maharawal on a visit to the palace, which was carved so finely that it actually floated when placed in water! He added, "It was like magic, and we all but applauded."

Handicrafts being sold in an alley off Patwon ki Haveli (left).

Vyas Chhatri.

Shrine to the Bhatti princess at Bhattiani Sati Rani.

BHATTIANI SATI RANI

South of Jaisalmer Fort is a shrine to a 19th-century Bhatti princess who performed *sati*. The story goes that her husband and his younger brother had gone out into battle. A messenger appeared at the end of the battle bearing her husband's turban, thus indicating his death. The princess immediately performed all the necessary rites and was about to perform *sati* when the dead body was brought back, and it was discovered that it was not her husband, after all, but his young brother who had died in battle. The princess decided to go ahead with the self-immolation, saying she would become a *mahasati* – one who performs *sati* not for her husband but for her son, for the young prince was like a son to her. The keepers of this Hindu shrine are, interestingly, Muslim Manganiyars, who sing romantic ballads in praise of the dead princess and light the lamp before her memorial tablet.

BARA BAGH

DUNG BEETLE
The dung beetle of the desert is a remarkable insect known to roll balls of dung much larger than itself. It is designed like a high-tech flying machine with wings that swing out for take-off from under an armored shield!

Situated 4 miles away in the desert is Bara Bagh ("The Great Garden") with its clusters of hauntingly beautiful cupolaed marble cenotaphs of the maharawals of Jaisalmer, set on an incline by the water of the Jait Bund. Do not miss the fine carving on the ceilings. Closer to town lies another complex of graceful marble cenotaphs, almost as impressive, belonging to the Brahmins of Jaisalmer, called Vyas Chhatri.

AMARSAGAR

DESERT GYPSIES
The Kalbeliyas are gypsies from the deserts near Jaisalmer who are known for their music, dances
● 79 and snake charmers' skills. One branch of the Kalbeliyas is believed to have wandered westward over the centuries and mingled with the gypsies of Europe. There is a startling resemblance, significantly between the dances and music of Spain and those of the Kalbeliyas.

Lying 4 miles west of Jaisalmer is a small lake with a 17th-century sandstone pleasure palace built by Rawal Amar Singh, its courtyard once laid with large, formal gardens. Beside the palace are pavilions and broad ghats or steps that lead down to the water of the lake. Take a look at the animal heads carved into the stone by the lake: there are also three

fine Jain temples, with beautifully screened walls and carved balconies, and some good examples of old step-wells.

LODURVA

The ancient Bhatti capital of Lodurva lies 5 miles beyond Amarsagar. You can still see traces of the ruins of the city in the desert, but the one monument that is intact is the Jain Temple of Parshvanatha. Rebuilt in the 17th century, its ornate *torana* archway (right) is perhaps the finest example of its kind in Rajasthan. Inside the temple is a Kalpavriksha, a representation of the Celestial Tree, with its carved copper leaves, believed to have the power to bestow any favor asked of it by a devotee. This temple, it is said, is connected by a secret underground passage to Sambhavnath Temple in Jaisalmer Fort 9 miles away. Nearby is the bed of the River Kak that has now run dry. Legend associates it with the star-crossed lovers, Prince Mahendru of Amarkot and the beautiful Princess Moomal who lived on the banks of the River Kak. Separated by a tragic misunderstanding they were reunited too late; weakened by their travails they died in each other's arms. That day the River Kak, they say, dried up in sadness and has not flowed since. Nearby are the ruins of a building that is said to have been Moomal's palace.

Jain temples at Lodurva (above). Cenotaphs of Bara Bagh (bottom).

AKAL AND KANDIALA

The Fossil Park of Akal lies 10 miles southeast of Jaisalmer. The petrified fossils of a forest of great trees that grew here 180 million years ago lie in the red, rocky terrain that now glitters with mica. At Kandiala not far away are fossils of a different kind – fossilized rocks from a probably older but undated past, when this desert was actually part of the ocean bed (as you can tell from the tiny sea shells embedded in the rocks).

SHRINE OF BHAIRONJI
Bhairon, a folk manifestation of Lord Shiva, is believed to have lived in Jaisalmer. His main shrine is at Bara Bagh, but his wayside images depicting him with his legendary dog are popularly worshiped all over Rajasthan, particularly by childless women who make offerings to him of their *kanchlis* (corsets) in the hope of becoming fertile.

217

The great
Indian bustard.

**FLOOR AND WALL
MOTIFS**
The desert huts of
Jaisalmer and Barmer
are known for the
fascinating, elaborate
mandana,
decorations on their
floor and walls. These
are considered
auspicious, and as the
saying goes, "It does
not matter if your son
remains unmarried
but your courtyard
floor should never be
left unadorned."
Drawn by the women
with white lime paste,
or red earth, the floor
patterns are usually
geometric while the
wall patterns are
usually animated
▲ 236. Of the
numerous traditional
motifs, each has its
own name and
special significance.
Different motifs are
associated with
different festivals
and rituals. Thus
the *feenia* (candy)
motif is associated
with the Makar
Sankranti festival,
the *paglia*
(footprint) motif
denotes a birth in
the family, and so
on.

Pokharan Fort
museum.

SAMM

The sand dunes at Samm, 26 miles west of Jaisalmer, have an
awesome beauty about them (below). The silken smooth
sands are sculpted into huge, rippled hummocks by the wind.
The best time to view them is at dawn: sunrise over the dunes
is spectacular. These active sand dunes can be as treacherous
as they are scenic. In summer, lifted by the desert winds, they
eerily disappear and reappear several
yards away within a matter of a
few minutes. A particularly
interesting way to get to
Samm is to go on a camel
safari. A popular safari
covering Samm and various
desert villages, ruins and
temples takes three nights.
Sleeping overnight under a
desert starscape is an
unforgettable experience.

DESERT NATIONAL PARK

Located 27 miles west of Jaisalmer, Desert National Park
■ *24* contains a number of species of fauna and flora, quite
remarkable for a desert region. In fact
much of this 1280-square-mile park
consists not of rolling sand dunes but
scrubland with its own characteristic trees
and flowers. In its arid grasslands you can
see the *chinkara*, blackbuck, *nilgai*, wolf,
and desert cat. There is also a wide range
of birdlife, including the spotted eagle,
tawny eagle, kestrel and lanner falcon,
sandgrouse, desert courser and of course the rare desert bird
known as the great Indian bustard.

POKHARAN

This interesting little garrison town at the very gates of
Jaisalmer was the outpost of the rival kingdom of Jodhpur. It
has a little fort and some beautiful
sandstone *chhatris* or cenotaphs.

218

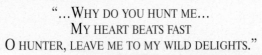
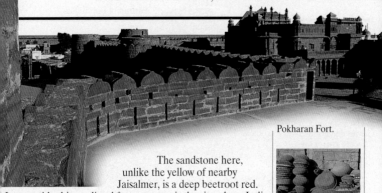

Pokharan Fort.

The sandstone here, unlike the yellow of nearby Jaisalmer, is a deep beetroot red. Just outside this medieval fortress town is the site where India tested its nuclear device in 1974. This links back curiously to a legend from the *Ramayana*, according to which Lord Rama once fitted a terrifying arrow that generated great heat – a kind of atomic missile – into his bow in order to dry up the seas near Sri Lanka. Persuaded by the gods not to do so, he fired this missile instead into the ancient Saraswati River that flowed here. The great, flaming explosion of its impact, it is said, dried up the river and turned the region into a desert.

CLEVER CLAY PITCHERS
The clay water pitchers of Rajasthan are ingeniously conceived. The water continually seeps through the porous clay and evaporates, thus automatically cooling the water within. Each different part of Rajasthan has its own distinctive type of water pitcher, the ones from the desert regions having narrower mouths, so as to help reduce the loss of water through evaporation.

KHURRI

This fascinating desert village, located near sand dunes, lies 30 miles southwest of Jaisalmer. Its huts, typical of the desert regions of Rajasthan, are brilliant examples of folk design: at once highly functional (they are designed to withstand 122°F temperatures and 84 miles per hour desert winds) as well as being highly esthetic. Made of clay mixed with cow dung, each hut is actually a complex of different functional spaces around a central courtyard, the whole of which – walls, floor and rooms – seems to be molded out of one single piece of clay ● *84*. Their strikingly decorative folk art, ornate papier-mâché storage systems and *mandana* floor patterns are not to be missed.

BARMER

Going further off the beaten track, you come to the little town of Barmer, 95 miles from Jaisalmer. Some of the most picturesque desert huts of Rajasthan are found in this harsh, remote wasteland – their *mandana* patterns are sometimes so ornate that they look almost like beautiful Persians carpets that have been thrown over the floors and walls. In the absence of agriculture, the people of this area have developed a rare skill with handicrafts. Barmer is known for its outstanding woodcarvings, unique, laboriously hand-printed *ajrakh* fabrics with characteristically bold indigo and red patterns ● *59*, and embroidered textiles (right).

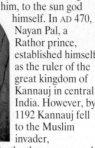

Portrait of Rao Jodha.

HISTORY

The kingdom of Jodhpur was ruled by the powerful Rathor clan. The Rathors trace their ancestry back to Lord Rama, the hero of the epic *Ramayana,* and, through him, to the sun god himself. In AD 470, Nayan Pal, a Rathor prince, established himself as the ruler of the great kingdom of Kannauj in central India. However, by 1192 Kannauj fell to the Muslim invader, Mohammed Ghori. Rao Siyaji, an heir to the throne, escaped with the traditional *panchranga* ("five-colored") flag of the Rathors and marched into the deserts of Rajasthan with his followers to set up a new kingdom there. By the 15th century the Rathors ruled all of Marwar, with their capital at Mandore. Shortly after, they went to war with the maharanas of Mewar over the accession to the throne of Chittorgarh. The conflict was successfully resolved in 1459. Rao Jodha, the ruler of Marwar, abandoned his old capital and built a new fort on the rocky cliffs of what is now Jodhpur. Unfortunately, the legend goes, in the process he had to displace a hermit who was meditating at the site, and the hermit placed a curse on his descendants, saying henceforth they would be plagued by famine every year. Rao Jodha later placated the holy man, but the curse could not be withdrawn completely – which, they say, is the reason why, even today, there is a drought in Jodhpur every three or four years.

MEWAR AND THE MUGHALS. Rao Ganga Singh of Jodhpur (reigned 1516–32) fought alongside the army of the great warrior king of Mewar, Rana Sanga, against the first Mughal emperor, Babur ● *36.* But over the next half century or so, the rulers of Jodhpur allied themselves with Babur's grandson, Akbar. Several rulers of Jodhpur became trusted lieutenants of the Mughals, such as Raja Sur, who conquered Gujarat and much of the Deccan for Akbar, and Raja Gaj Singh, who put down the rebellion of the Mughal prince, Khurram, against his father, Jahangir. With the support of the Mughals, the court of Jodhpur flourished and the kingdom became a great center of the arts and culture. In the 17th century Jodhpur became a flourishing center of trade for the camel caravans moving from Central Asia to the ports of Gujarat and vice versa. In 1657, however, Maharaja Jaswant Singh (reigned 1638–78) backed the wrong prince in the great war of succession to the Mughal throne. He was in power for almost twenty-five years with Aurangzeb before he was sent out to the frontier as viceroy in Afghanistan ● *37.* Aurangzeb then tried to seize his infant son, but loyal retainers smuggled the

COAT-OF-ARMS
The Jodhpur coat-of-arms depicts the sacred kite of the goddess Durga and the Rathor clan's battle cry, "*Ran banka Rathor*", which means "Rathor, invincible in battle". What is interesting is the grains of millet depicted on the shield. They represent the words of Sher Shah, Sultan of Delhi, who having very narrowly defeated the Jodhpur armies, ruefully commented, "For just a handful of millet, I nearly lost all of Hindustan."

JODHPUR LANCERS
The Jodhpur Lancers were a crack regiment raised in the late 19th century. They sailed to China in 1899 to help the British put down the Boxer Rebellion. The first time they went on a cavalry charge, they gallantly (and foolhardily) went in with their lances reversed, until their commander, Sir Pratap Singh, had the honor of drawing first blood. They fought alongside the Cossacks and are said to have been slightly disdainful of the latter's inferior standards of horsemanship.

Seal of Jodhpur.

little prince out of his clutches, hidden, they say, in a basket of sweets.

POLITICAL STRIFE. The kingdom of Jodhpur then formed a triple alliance with Udaipur and Jaipur, which together threw off the Mughal yoke. As a result, the maharajas of Jodhpur finally regained the privilege of marrying Udaipur princesses – something they had forfeited when they had allied themselves with the Mughals. A condition of these marriages, however, was that the sons born of the Udaipur princesses would be first in line to the Jodhpur throne. This soon led to considerable jealousy. Nearly a century of turmoil followed, culminating in Jodhpur falling under the influence of, first, the Marathas, and then, in 1818, the British. The state of affairs was such that a young Rathor prince, when asked where Jodhpur was, simply pointed to the sheath of his dagger and said, "Inside here".

SIR PRATAP SINGH. In the 1870's, a remarkable man came to the fore in Jodhpur: Sir Pratap Singh (left) ● *114*. A son of the Maharaja of Jodhpur, he himself ruled a small neighboring kingdom called Idar, but abdicated to become Regent of Jodhpur, which he ruled, in effect, for nearly fifty years. Sir Pratap Singh was a great warrior and the epitome of Rajput chivalry. He became an intimate friend of three British sovereigns. At Queen Victoria's *durbar* he is said to have presented her not with mere jewels, like everyone else, but with his own sword, his most valuable possession as a Rajput warrior. Sir Pratap Singh laid the foundation of a modern state in Jodhpur, which Maharaja Umaid Singh (reigned 1918–47) built upon ▲ *223*.

The kingdom of Jodhpur was not merely the largest of the Rajput states, but also one of the most progressive. In 1949, after the independence of India, it was merged into the newly created state of Rajasthan ● *39*.

AND THEN CAME JODHPURS...
Sir Pratap Singh was the inventor of "jodhpurs", or riding breeches, as we know them today. Since he virtually lived on horseback, he gradually evolved this item of clothing with the help of his tailor to meet his own riding needs. It all began, apparently, when he got tired of the way his traditional Rajput riding pyjamas would get frayed on the inside of the knees, as he rode. He later went on to invent ankle-length jodhpur boots and the close-collared Jodhpuri coat – which came to be adopted as the semi-formal dress of the Jodhpur court.

FISH-SHAPED IMPERIAL STANDARD
The *Mahi Maratib* was the fish-shaped imperial standard that the Mughal emperors granted only to their most trusted allies. It was granted to Raja Ajit Singh of Jodhpur.

City of Jodhpur c. 1900.

221

▲ JODHPUR
THE CITY

🕐 Three days

PIONEER AIR ROUTE
Jodhpur's airport, surprisingly, was one of the first international airports to be set up, in the early 1930's, on the original air route from Europe to the Far East. It served KLM and Imperial Airways, the two pioneer airlines on this route (between whom there was considerable rivalry). Later came Air France, en route to French Indochina.

THE BLUE CITY
If Jaipur is the "Pink City", Jodhpur may be called the "Blue City" from the characteristic pale indigo color of its traditional homes. Originally, the color signified the home of a Jodhpuri Brahmin. The story goes that centuries ago, the Brahmins of the town painted their homes thus, because they had discovered that the color wards off mosquitoes.

The blue houses of Jodhpur.

JODHPUR TODAY

Jodhpur is today the second largest city of Rajasthan, with a population of 650,000. It is a major military base and an important center of research in arid-zone agriculture. Yet, in many ways, it has not changed all that much from the old fortified town that was built under the protective cover of the brooding Mehrangarh Fort. The 15th-century town walls are still there, punctuated by massive gates; and the old quarter of Jodhpur is a fascinating place, with its narrow jumble of lanes, its *havelis* and its fine medieval water tanks. Take a walk through its lanes, starting from the old Fateh Pol ("Victory Gate"), past the 15th-century Jetha Bera tank, through the colorful little lane of Jaisalmeriyon ki Gali, past the beautiful Talati ka Mahal, a palace-turned-hospital, and ending, finally, at the Juni

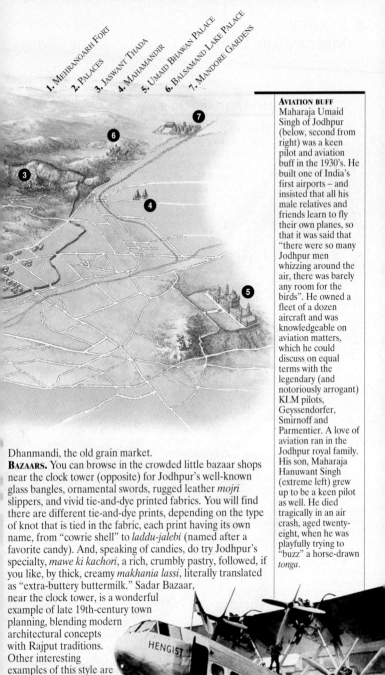

AVIATION BUFF
Maharaja Umaid Singh of Jodhpur (below, second from right) was a keen pilot and aviation buff in the 1930's. He built one of India's first airports – and insisted that all his male relatives and friends learn to fly their own planes, so that it was said that "there were so many Jodhpur men whizzing around the air, there was barely any room for the birds". He owned a fleet of a dozen aircraft and was knowledgeable on aviation matters, which he could discuss on equal terms with the legendary (and notoriously arrogant) KLM pilots, Geyssendorfer, Smirnoff and Parmentier. A love of aviation ran in the Jodhpur royal family. His son, Maharaja Hanuwant Singh (extreme left) grew up to be a keen pilot as well. He died tragically in an air crash, aged twenty-eight, when he was playfully trying to "buzz" a horse-drawn *tonga*.

Dhanmandi, the old grain market.

BAZAARS. You can browse in the crowded little bazaar shops near the clock tower (opposite) for Jodhpur's well-known glass bangles, ornamental swords, rugged leather *mojri* slippers, and vivid tie-and-dye printed fabrics. You will find there are different tie-and-dye prints, depending on the type of knot that is tied in the fabric, each print having its own name, from "cowrie shell" to *laddu-jalebi* (named after a favorite candy). And, speaking of candies, do try Jodhpur's specialty, *mawe ki kachori*, a rich, crumbly pastry, followed, if you like, by thick, creamy *makhania lassi*, literally translated as "extra-buttery buttermilk." Sadar Bazaar, near the clock tower, is a wonderful example of late 19th-century town planning, blending modern architectural concepts with Rajput traditions. Other interesting examples of this style are Jodhpur's fine old public buildings, such as the old railway station, the High Court, the old hospital and the Air Force Mess, which used to be a hotel, built by Maharaja Umaid Singh for the early air travelers who used to touch down here in the 1930's, en route to Batavia (Jakarta), Australia and French Indochina.

▲ JODHPUR
MEHRANGARH FORT

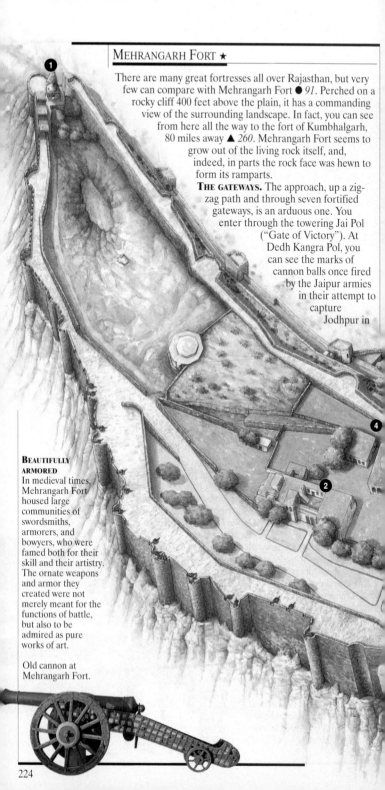

MEHRANGARH FORT ★

There are many great fortresses all over Rajasthan, but very few can compare with Mehrangarh Fort ● *91*. Perched on a rocky cliff 400 feet above the plain, it has a commanding view of the surrounding landscape. In fact, you can see from here all the way to the fort of Kumbhalgarh, 80 miles away ▲ *260*. Mehrangarh Fort seems to grow out of the living rock itself, and, indeed, in parts the rock face was hewn to form its ramparts.

THE GATEWAYS. The approach, up a zig-zag path and through seven fortified gateways, is an arduous one. You enter through the towering Jai Pol ("Gate of Victory"). At Dedh Kangra Pol, you can see the marks of cannon balls once fired by the Jaipur armies in their attempt to capture Jodhpur in

BEAUTIFULLY ARMORED
In medieval times, Mehrangarh Fort housed large communities of swordsmiths, armorers, and bowyers, who were famed both for their skill and their artistry. The ornate weapons and armor they created were not merely meant for the functions of battle, but also to be admired as pure works of art.

Old cannon at Mehrangarh Fort.

> "…HE WHO WALKS THROUGH IT LOSES SENSE OF BEING AMONG BUILDINGS. IT IS AS THOUGH HE WALKED THROUGH MOUNTAIN-GORGES…"
>
> RUDYARD KIPLING, *LETTERS OF MARQUE*, 1899

1807. After Dedh Kangra Pol, there is a sharp U-turn to thwart would-be attackers, and finally you come to Loha Pol, the 15th-century "Iron Gate", beside which you can see the handprints of fifteen royal *satis*, Jodhpur ranis who immolated themselves on the funeral pyres of their dead husbands. On the fort ramparts, which are 130 feet high in places, you can see a battery of fine medieval cannons. Some of these cannons were spoils of war, won in battles against the rival kingdoms of Gujarat and Jalore.

Fort ramparts.

THE FORT. The fort itself is divided broadly into three areas: the outer court, with its old stables and kitchens; the *durbar* hall, reception rooms and maharajas' palaces; and, finally, the *zenana*, or queens' palaces. This palace complex, constructed around a series of interconnecting courtyards and adorned with breathtakingly carved sandstone filigree work, was first built in 1459 and added to, over the centuries, by successive generations of maharajas. It is one of the most impressive palace complexes in Rajasthan. On your right, as you enter, is the white marble coronation throne, where every ruler of Jodhpur has been crowned since the 15th century.

1. CHAMUNDA TEMPLE
2. SALIM KOT
3. NAGNECHIAJI TEMPLE
4. MURLI MANOHARJI TEMPLE
5. SINGHAR CHOWK (DURBAR COURT)
6. DAULAT KHANA CHOWK
7. ZENANA CHOWK
8. JANKI MAHAL
9. FATEH MAHAL
10. JAI POL
11. CHOKELAO PALACE AND GARDEN

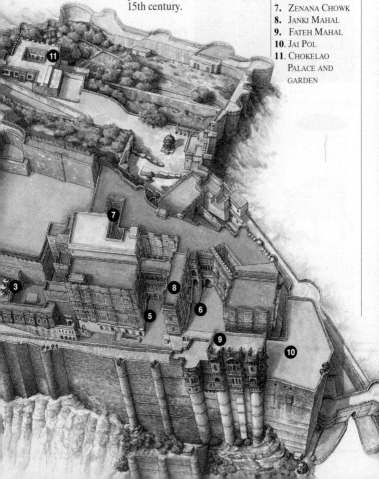

Façade of the palace apartments.

Mirrored walls in the fort-palace.

Palanquin in Fort Museum.

Golden wooden throne from Jodhpur.

HANGING LACE
A unique feature of the Mehrangarh Palace is the profusion of delicately latticed, overhanging *jharokhas* (balconies), which give what the celebrated architectural historian G.H.R. Tillotson has described as "the appearance of a piece of hanging lace".

FORT MUSEUM.
This is one of the finest museums in Rajasthan and certainly the best laid out. In the palanquin section of the fort museum, you can see an interesting collection of old royal palanquins, including the elaborate domed gilt Mahadol palanquin, which was won in battle from the Governor of Gujarat in 1730. Next comes the *howdah* section, with perhaps one of the finest collections of ornate elephant *howdahs* in the world.

MAAN VILAS. Maan Vilas, the armory section, has one of the finest collections of weapons in India: everything from medieval mortars shaped like crocodiles to shields decorated with semi-precious stones. The swords here are particularly noteworthy (right). They range from exquisite damascened Mughal swords (including

the sword of Emperor Akbar himself) to Rao Jodha's enormous *khanda*, weighing over 7 pounds. There is also a very interesting collection of over a hundred different types of turbans from the different parts of Rajasthan, including a strange hunting turban with a visor and back-flap.

UMAID VILAS. As you pass into Umaid Vilas,

you will see an excellent collection of miniature paintings from all the major schools of Rajasthan, but mainly, obviously, from Jodhpur itself. The early Jodhpur miniatures were strongly influenced by Jain art, but by the 18th century, because of Jodhpur's close links with the Delhi court, a marked Mughal influence began to manifest itself. Two particularly interesting paintings here, incidentally, are one portraying a maharaja playing *holi* with his queens, splashing each other with ceremonial colors, and one depicting a maharaja and his queens playing polo together.

Lithograph of Mehrangarh Fort.

ROYAL CRADLE
The present Maharaja of Jodhpur once slept in a quixotic cradle, which ran on electricity and was automatically rocked by the arms of the figurines on either side, while ornately carved fairies – and the infant's father – looked down on him protectively. It was a gift to the little prince from Jodhpur's Public Works Department, and was inscribed "with profound loyalty".

TAKHAT MAHAL. Takhat Mahal is a huge royal bedchamber, with exquisitely lacquered walls depicting scenes of dancing girls and legendary lovers. (You might wonder about the glittering colored globes hanging from the fine beamed ceilings, but then you'll realize that they're just Christmas decorations that someone, curiously, decided to add to the decor in the 1930's!) In Ajit Vilas nearby you can see the extravagant, old brocade and silk costumes of the generations of maharajas.

PHOOL MAHAL. Going up the stairs you come to Phool Mahal ("Flower Palace"), which is perhaps even more impressive than Moti Mahal. Built in the 18th century as a Hall of Private Audience, it has magnificently painted walls depicting the various musical *ragas* (classical Indian patterns of melody and rhythm) and their changing moods. If you look closely, you might detect a faint European influence in these 19th-century murals.

Stained-glass windows of the royal bedroom in a palace.

NOT KING-SIZED
A feature of many Rajput palaces is the fact that the maharajas' apartments always occupied a much smaller area than the ranis' apartments. The reason is that, in medieval times, the maharaja spent most of the year out on his military campaigns, so the permanent residents of the palace were mainly the womenfolk.

227

Singhar Chowk, the courtyard of the palace complex.

SHOEING THE MISTRESS
The pearl shoes of Angoori Bai, a favorite mistress of Raja Gaj Singh (reigned 1620–38), played an interesting little role in altering the course of Jodhpur's history in the 17th century. Raja Gaj Singh's ambitious younger son, Jaswant Singh, presented these shoes to Angoori Bai, kneeling humbly to shoe her feet himself. In return, Angoori Bai persuaded his father to name Jaswant Singh as his successor in place of the rightful successor, the valiant and chivalrous Amar Singh.

SARDAR VILAS. In Sardar Vilas there are some classic examples of Jodhpur's celebrated traditional woodwork, including an array of doors in a variety of styles, superbly carved, lacquered, ornamented with gilt and inlaid with ivory.
KHAB KA MAHAL AND JHANKI MAHAL. Through Khab ka Mahal, which used to house the office of the Prime Minister, and an old conference room for Rathor's nobles, you come to Jhanki Mahal ("Palace of the Glimpses"). This palace got its name from the exquisitely carved sandstone lattice windows, through which the ladies used to view the world outside, without themselves being seen by prying eyes. The stone latticework here is so fine, it actually resembles lace. There are nearly 250 different latticework patterns used all over the palace complex, each of which has its own name, such as *chaubla*, or checkerboard, and *chaufulia*, an elaborate, four-petalled flower pattern. On the walls of Jhanki Mahal, you can see old mirrors, in which generation after generation of beautiful Jodhpur ranis must have admired themselves. Here there is also a fascinating display of royal infants' cradles, which range from the exotic (do not miss the splendidly mirrored cradle with the peacock motifs) to the idiosyncratic.
MOTI MAHAL. Moti Mahal ("Pearl Palace") is a throne room built in the late 16th century. Judging from its magnificence and size, it was originally conceived as a Hall of Public Audience. Its ceiling is gorgeously embellished with mirror-work and gilt. (It is said that nearly 80 pounds of gold was used here!) Its walls are lustrously polished, and decorated with a triple band of ornate niches in which lamps once flickered, reflecting off the polished walls. At the far end is an octagonal silver throne, a rare and priceless heirloom dating back to the 17th century.
JASWANT THADA. On the way down from the fort, on your left, is Jaswant Thada, the graceful marble cenotaph of Maharaja Jaswant Singh II (reigned 1873–95) and those of the other maharajas of Jodhpur who died in this century. Wives and concubines committed *sati* on Jaswanti funeral pyre. The cenotaphs of earlier maharajas and maharanis are at Mandore ▲ *232*.

Jaswant Thada.

UMAID BHAWAN PALACE

PUPPET SHOW
The finest puppeteers of Rajasthan are the Barlai Bhatts, originally from the Jodhpur area. A favorite theme of their puppet shows is the bravery of the Rathor prince, Amar Singh, who was killed after single-handedly slaying five Mughal noblemen. Another popular theme of the puppeteers is the comic drama of the washerman and his shrew of a wife in their ongoing marital battle.

MELTING INTO CORNERS
When Umaid Bhawan Palace's gigantic dome was being built, a young Jodhpur engineer thought up an ingenious way to install the cornerstones without damaging them. He first positioned huge blocks of ice in the corners and then placed the cornerstones on top of them. As the ice slowly melted, the cornerstones settled perfectly – and flawlessly – into place.

The gigantic Umaid Bhawan Palace has the distinction of having been one of the largest private residences in the world ● 88. It has 347 rooms and used over 2.5 million cubic feet of sandstone and marble! But what is probably even more remarkable is the reason it was built in the first place: there was a major famine in Jodhpur in the early 1920's, and the construction of this enormous palace was one of the public works projects devised to offer employment to the people of the kingdom. It took fifteen years to complete. The palace was designed by a British architect, H.V. Lanchester, who was an admirer of Lutyens, the designer of New Delhi, and in both the style and the scale of the Umaid Bhawan you can see a reflection of Delhi's Viceregal Lodge (now Rashtrapati Bhawan). The interior of the palace was decorated in the Beaux Arts and Art Deco styles. And it incorporated everything from two theaters and an indoor swimming pool to its own central air-cooling plant. Unfortunately, however, not everything went according to plan. The furniture for the palace, ordered from Maples of London, was lost twice – the first time when the ship carrying it to India got torpedoed during World War II, and the second time when the company's warehouses in London were bombed by the Luftwaffe. If you think the palace's entrance hall with its sweeping marble staircases and wildlife trophies is impressive, just wait till you come to the Central Hall, under the

Umaid Bhawan Palace.

dome, 198 feet high. (Old-timers in the palace will tell you of a banquet held here in the 1940's – a sit-down affair for a thousand people.) The reception room is worth seeing, with its murals by a refugee Polish artist, which can only be termed "Ashokan Art Deco"! Wander around the spacious old billiard room, the maharaja's personal office, now a lounge, and try to take a look at some of the suites – the Maharaja suite, for instance, where the black marble Art Deco bathroom speaks volumes of the old princely lifestyle. There is also an excellent little museum here of some of the royal family's possessions: everything from ornate mirrored French furniture to fine china. The present Maharaja now lives on the first floor of the palace, while the rest of the palace has been turned into a luxury hotel.

MAHAMANDIR

The great Shiva temple of Mahamandir was the first structure in Jodhpur to be built outside the city walls. It had to be surrounded by its own fortified ramparts, an indication of how insecure life was in Rajasthan in the early 19th century. It is notable for its profusion of finely carved pillars, one hundred of them in all. One of the manifestations of Lord Shiva is the Maha Yogi or "Great Yogi", and the murals on the temple walls, depicting various *yogic* postures, are especially interesting. Mahamandir is an excellent example of the architectural and artistic impulses of Jodhpur during the reign of Raja Man Singh (reigned 1803–43), himself an esthete, scholar and patron of the arts.

ROYAL RAILWAY SALOON
A luxury train called the "Palace on Wheels", which takes you through Rajasthan, has been ranked by travel writers as one of "The World's Ten Best Railway Journeys" ◆ 348. However, the old saloons of the Maharaja of Jodhpur (above) are now "parked" at the Umaid Bhawan Palace. Carefully maintaining their original 1930's charm, they are being converted into suites, a dining car and lounge, and guests can stay on board!

TREND-SETTING TURBAN
Each region of Rajasthan takes great pride in its own distinctive way of tying a turban. The people of Jodhpur, however, claim that the Jodhpuri turban is superior to all the rest, pointing to the fact that it has been adopted by trend-setters all over Rajasthan, from Bikaner to Jaipur.

Cenotaphs of
Jodhpur's rulers.

Hall dedicated to
heroes and gods,
Mandore (right).

VILLAGE DURRIES
The villages around
Jodhpur are famed
for some of the finest
Indian *durries* ● 68.
Woven on quaint,
primitive looms by
family members, the
durries eventually end
up in fashionable
boutiques all over the
world.

MANDORE

Mandore, located about 5 miles north of
Jodhpur, was the former capital of the
maharajas of Marwar, but was later
abandoned for the security of
Mehrangarh Fort. Here you will find the *dewals,* or cenotaphs,
of Jodhpur's former rulers. Unlike the usual *chhatri*-shaped
cenotaphs typical of Rajasthan, they are built along the lines
of a Hindu temple, four stories high, with fine columns and
an elegant spire, all in red sandstone. The most impressive
is the *dewal* of Maharaja Ajit Singh (reigned
1678–1724). These cenotaphs are set
in beautiful landscaped gardens.
Nearby is the Hall of Heroes,
dedicated to various deities
and fabled Rajput folk heroes, whose
statues (each one astride his steed) are
carved out of rock and painted in bright
colors. Next door is a larger hall called
"The Shrine of the Three Hundred Million
Gods", filled with brightly colored images of
various Hindu gods (above). And as you climb up the hill, you
come to the ruined city of Mandore, with its old palace. Don't
miss the extraordinarily beautiful maharani's cenotaphs set
apart on a rocky outcrop – a ten-minute walk over the hill.

BALSAMAND

This pretty lakeside pleasure palace of the maharajas, 4 miles
from Jodhpur, is a small oasis in the desert. Set by the side of
an artificial lake created in the 12th century, measuring nearly
half a mile long, the palace itself was built in the late 19th
century, during the time when the lake was being enlarged.
The red sandstone façade is richly carved with traditional
Hindu motifs, but the interiors are clearly
European, with a strong Italian influence.
Around the palace is a pleasant
garden and a small bird sanctuary.

BISHNOI VILLAGES

All around Jodhpur lie the
picturesque villages of the Bishnoi
community. They are worth seeing,

"It was more quiet and empty and lonely than any other place I know on earth…I thought the cenotaphs themselves resembled vultures."

Ruth Prawer Jhabvala, *Autobiography of a Princess*, 1975

not just for their folk architecture – an ingenious marriage of the functional and the esthetic – but also for a close look at the Bishnoi's fascinating, rustic way of life. Probably the best way to do it is to take one of the well-known jeep safaris of Maharaj Swaroop Singh and let the Maharaj (himself a very colorful personality) take you into the villages and explain the significance of the everyday rituals you see. The visit will provide a unique insight into the ways of rural India. (Check with Ajit Bhawan Palace for details of the safaris.)

Osiyan ★

The temple complex of Osiyan lies 40 miles northwest of Jodhpur. Once a great religious center, its ruins today present one of the finest depictions anywhere of how Indian temple architecture evolved between the 8th and 12th centuries. There are altogether sixteen Jain and Hindu temples here. Start with the oldest, the small Sun Temple III (early 8th century), remarkable for its carved doorway, and considered one of the most impressive in India. Its vestibule is also worth seeing, with its fine carved ceiling and its frieze of Lord Krishna. The temples especially worth visiting are (in order) the Harihara Temple I, the Harihara Temple III, the Sun Temple II, and the Sachiya Mata Temple.

Harihara temples. The Harihara Temple I (mid 8th century) is noteworthy for its delicate cornice frieze depicting the Krishna-lila legends. But the most beautiful of all the temples at Osiyan is the Harihara Temple III (early 9th century). In

Sachiya Mata Temple (top); Mahavira Temple (above); stairway in Sachiya Mata Temple (below).

fact, it is one of the finest examples of how the ancient Indian builders married architectural grace with sculptural exuberance. Don't miss the exquisite doorway and columns of the sanctum, and the highly ornamented dome-like ceiling. The richly carved outer walls of the sanctuary are also worth seeing.

Sun Temple and Sachiya Mata Temple. The Sun Temple II (8th century) is interesting mainly for its curiously Grecian-looking porch columns. The Sachiya Mata Temple (11th to 12th centuries), still in use as a temple, is notable mainly for its imposing multi-turreted spire.

Although now a nondescript little town in the middle of an arid expanse, Osiyan was from the 8th to the 11th centuries an important commercial, cultural, and religious center. During that time, a group of Hindu and Jain temples were built at this site. Of great stylistic significance, this group includes handsome examples of the earliest structural temples built in western India. The Mahavira Temple of the Jains is the best preserved at Osiyan because the Jains carefully conserved their temples through repairs and renovations. For the Jains, Osiyan has special significance because it is associated with the origin of the Oswal Jain community of merchants.

FIGURE IN A NICHE
Many temples of western India feature the eight *dik-palas* (guardians of the cardinal directions) on their exterior wall facing their particular direction. These figures are usually accompanied by their animal vehicles. In this temple, the *dik-palas* are placed in niches framed by pilasters and surmounted by a trellis roof which echoes the style of the spire and the domical roof of the temple.

PILLARS
The pillars in the temple are decorated with auspicious vase and foliage motifs popular in Indian religious architecture. The delicate and elaborate treatment of the motifs contrasts superbly with the plain surface of the pillars.

Mahavira Temple.

TEMPLE SPIRE

Built of sandstone, the temple complex stands on a vast terrace. As was the prevalent practice, all the various components of the temple are united in one structure along its longitudinal axis. The spire was rebuilt in the 11th century to replace the original one that had collapsed.

CHAPELS

In the enclosure of the temple are seven *devakulikas* (chapels), each with its shrine chamber and portico (above). Each of the chapels with its decorative moldings and carvings is an architectural masterpiece. Unlike the later Jain temples of the region, the number of chapels here does not correspond to any established convention because the style is still in its emergent stages. Chapels along the enclosure walls became an essential characteristic of Jain temple-complexes in the centuries that followed. Generally they assumed the form of simple cells joined together with a common colonnaded corridor.

Strut figures on ceiling.

CEILING

Elaborately conceived and decorated, the ceiling (above) consists of a succession of receding concentric courses with delicately embellished lace-like scalloped motifs and a hanging pendant. The most striking feature of this arrangement is the radial struts portraying standing female dancers and musicians in an aureole, often formed by the foliage of trees.

235

Folk motifs.

Decorative art has been used in Rajasthan to offset the starkness of the desert. Everything in daily use is painted or decorated, from the walls of houses to pots, pitchers, musical instruments, animal carts, and even the animals themselves, thus making Rajasthan a treasure trove of traditional art. As the anthropologist, Verrier Elwin, says, "God put the tool in the wood-carver's hand. He gave the brush to the village woman."

MANDANA
Wall paintings are usually executed with a small piece of cloth wrapped around the fingers. The designs can be symbolic, geometrical, or floral. Before each festival, the walls are "painted" with a mixture of cow dung and mud, and then adorned with new designs.

A GRAND BEAUTY
Any animal which provides a livelihood is treated with great respect. The *mahout's* (elephant keeper's) family will bathe the elephant and then decorate it, either by themselves or by engaging a painter.

MEHENDI
Mehendi, the art of henna decoration, is commonly practiced in Rajasthan. Traditionally, the art involved forming hand patterns by rolling henna paste between thumb and index finger and forming the strands into *jali*

designs on the palms. The less adept used matchsticks or polythene cones as brushes. The henna pattern is allowed to dry for some hours, then the henna scraped off. The pattern remains on the hand for two to three days.

RANGOLI
Rangoli designs are made out of rice paste or lime. Laid outside the entrance, they were supposed to keep evil forces out of the house.

CLAY FIGURES
Clay is molded into toys in the shape of human or animal figures. The link between ritual and play is intimate. The same figures serve a dual purpose, as toys

and as votive offerings. A clay doll could be dressed up in red and worshiped as Gangaur or Parvati. Animal figures are sometimes found at tribal shrines as votive offerings.

ART FOR CAMELS
Camels are painted and decorated with the *gorbandh*, colorful strings plaited together with cowrie shells and bells, made by the women of the family. A famous folk song describes the preparation of the material and the making of the *gorbandh*.

WALL PAINTINGS OF DEITIES
Since most forms of traditional art have religious themes as their subject, it is not unusual to see images of deities (above) painted on the walls of houses.

PAINTINGS AROUND DOORWAYS
The white walls around the doorways are often decorated with figures of elephants and horses, symbols of strength and longevity.

DECORATED HOUSES
Following a 5000-year-old tradition, Rajasthani women decorate the walls of their houses ● 85. The role of decoration for its own sake results in many geometric and abstract patterns. Specific areas are decorated, especially the entrance. The intricacy and beauty of the decorative detail denotes the wealth and status of the owner. A decorated house is considered auspicious, whereas absence of decoration indicates misfortune. Houses are not painted for a year when a death occurs.

237

▲ AROUND JODHPUR

CURE FOR SNAKE BITES
Tejaji is a folk deity, originally from Nagaur, who is believed to offer a miraculous snakebite cure. The legend goes that a snake was about to bite Tejaji, but he pleaded that he had some urgent work to finish first. Having completed the work, true to his word, Tejaji returned and offered himself to the snake. The snake duly bit and killed him, but it proclaimed that henceforth anyone chanting Tejaji's name would be cured of snakebite. Today there are Tejaji shrines all over Rajasthan which, indeed, report some miraculous cases of recovery from snakebites.

Medieval cooling system.

Fresco of Krishna and the *gopis* on palace wall within Nagaur Fort.

KHIMSAR

The 15th-century fortress of Khimsar, with its long-forgotten but dramatic history, lies 37 miles northeast of Jodhpur ▲ *202*. Over the centuries it was besieged five times – the last being a siege by an army of Jodhpur as recently as April 4, 1944! Ironically, the tank commander who led this attack was himself a Khimsar prince. He is supposed to have said, in the typical Rajput tradition, "Yes, I shall smash open the fort and enter – but I shall then immediately resign my commission and join my kinsmen to defend the fort." The fort, where Emperor Aurangzeb once came and stayed as a guest, has been converted to a hotel. It serves as a wonderful base for visits to the surrounding Bishnoi villages and for wildlife safaris.

NAGAUR

The historic, fortified town of Nagaur lies 84 miles north of Jodhpur. The mighty Nagaur Fort (right) was originally built in the 4th century, but most of what you see today dates from the 12th

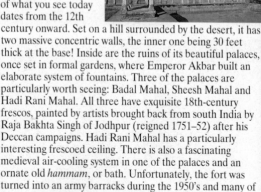

century onward. Set on a hill surrounded by the desert, it has two massive concentric walls, the inner one being 30 feet thick at the base! Inside are the ruins of its beautiful palaces, once set in formal gardens, where Emperor Akbar built an elaborate system of fountains. Three of the palaces are particularly worth seeing: Badal Mahal, Sheesh Mahal and Hadi Rani Mahal. All three have exquisite 18th-century frescos, painted by artists brought back from south India by Raja Bakhta Singh of Jodhpur (reigned 1751–52) after his Deccan campaigns. Hadi Rani Mahal has a particularly interesting frescoed ceiling. There is also a fascinating medieval air-cooling system in one of the palaces and an ornate old *hammam*, or bath. Unfortunately, the fort was turned into an army barracks during the 1950's and many of the frescos were vandalized. Nagaur is also known for its puppeteers and colorful annual cattle fair ● *82*.

THE SOUTH

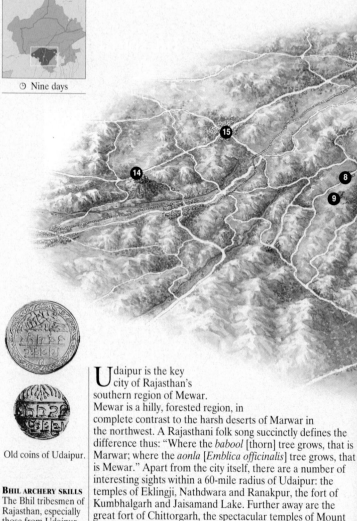

⊙ Nine days

Old coins of Udaipur.

BHIL ARCHERY SKILLS
The Bhil tribesmen of
Rajasthan, especially
those from Udaipur,
are famed for their
deadly archery skills.
The epic
Mahabharata speaks
of a Bhil called
Eklavya who was the
only man alive who
could beat the
legendary warrior,
Arjuna, at archery.
Ultimately, Eklavya,
in sacrifice for his
guru, destroyed his
own archery skills in
deference to Arjuna
by chopping off his
right thumb.

Udaipur is the key
city of Rajasthan's
southern region of Mewar.
Mewar is a hilly, forested region, in
complete contrast to the harsh deserts of Marwar in
the northwest. A Rajasthani folk song succinctly defines the
difference thus: "Where the *babool* [thorn] tree grows, that is
Marwar; where the *aonla* [*Emblica officinalis*] tree grows, that
is Mewar." Apart from the city itself, there are a number of
interesting sights within a 60-mile radius of Udaipur: the
temples of Eklingji, Nathdwara and Ranakpur, the fort of
Kumbhalgarh and Jaisamand Lake. Further away are the
great fort of Chittorgarh, the spectacular temples of Mount
Abu and the splendid palaces of Dungarpur.

HISTORY

Of all the kingdoms of Rajasthan, the kingdom of Mewar (or
Udaipur) was considered of prime importance, and its ruler
acknowledged as being the most senior of all the Rajput
princes ● *34*. This is because the Sisodia dynasty of Mewar
was probably the oldest dynasty in the world, tracing its
origins directly back through seventy-six generations to its
founder, Guhil, who came to power in AD 566. However, it is
not the antiquity of their lineage alone for which the Sisodias
were respected, but also for the fierce zeal with which they
upheld their independence and their Rajput values through
the centuries. Of all the Rajput kingdoms, Mewar was the

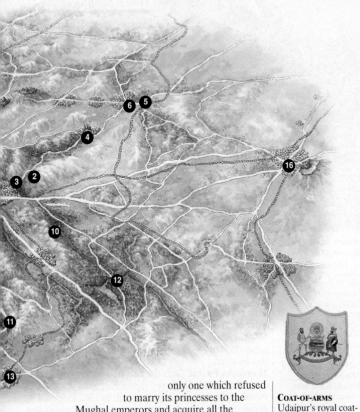

only one which refused to marry its princesses to the Mughal emperors and acquire all the political advantages that accrued. The Sisodias were also staunch defenders of the Hindu faith. In fact, the dynasty's name comes from the word *sisa*, or lead, for the legend goes that a certain prince of the line was unwittingly made to eat a piece of beef. When he later discovered this, he chose to atone for his sin by swallowing molten lead. In AD 734, Bappa Rawal, the first of the great Sisodia kings, came to the throne. It was Bappa Rawal who moved his capital to the strategic hilltop fortress of Chittorgarh, which was to remain the capital of Mewar for the next eight hundred years.

COAT-OF-ARMS
Udaipur's royal coat-of-arms depicts a blazing sun, from which its maharanas claimed direct descent. The central shield is flanked by a Rajput warrior and a Bhil archer, indicating the important role that the Bhil tribesmen played in the history of Mewar. From time immemorial, at the coronation of each maharana, a Bhil chieftain would cut his own thumb, apply a *tika* (auspicious mark) of his blood on the maharana's forehead and then lead him by the arm to his new throne.

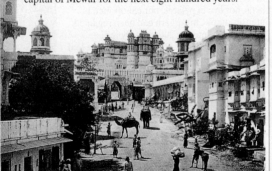

Street scene, Udaipur.

241

THREE SISODIA KINGS

The most glorious and eventful years of Mewar's history were probably in the 15th and 16th centuries, or more particularly, during the reign of three great Sisodia kings, Rana Kumbha, Rana Sanga and Maharana Pratap.

RANA KUMBHA. Rana Kumbha (reigned 1433–68) was a remarkably versatile man: a brilliant general, poet and musician. He built Mewar up to a position of unassailable military strength by building a chain of thirty-two forts that girdled the kingdom. But, perhaps more important, he was a patron of the arts to rival Lorenzo de Medici, and he made Chittorgarh a dazzling cultural center whose fame spread right across Hindustan.

RANA SANGA. Rana Sanga (reigned 1509–27) was a fearless warrior and a man of great chivalry and honor ● *34*. But his reign was marked by a series of continual battles, in the course of which he is said to have lost one arm and one eye, been crippled in one leg and received eighty-four different wounds on his body. The last of his battles was against the Mughal invader, Babur, in 1527. Deserted by one of his own generals, Rana Sanga was wounded in the battle and died shortly after.

MAHARANA PRATAP. Over the next half-century, most of the other Rajput rulers allowed themselves to be wooed over by the Mughals; Mewar alone held out. In 1567 Emperor Akbar decided to teach it a lesson: he attacked Chittorgarh and razed it to the ground. Five years later Maharana Pratap (reigned 1572–97) came to rule Mewar – a king without a capital. He continued to defy Akbar, and in 1576, confronted the imperial armies at Haldighati ● *36*. The battle ended in a stalemate and Maharana Pratap and his followers withdrew to the craggy hills of Mewar, from where they continued to harry the Mughals through guerilla warfare for the next twenty years. Maharana Pratap made his descendants vow that they would not sleep on beds, nor live in palaces, nor eat off metal utensils, until Chittorgarh had been regained. In fact, right into the 20th century the maharanas of Mewar continued to place a leaf platter under their regular utensils and a reed mat under their beds in symbolic continuance of this vow. When news of Maharana Pratap's death reached Emperor Akbar in 1597, it is said that the Emperor's eyes filled with tears, and he ordered his court poet to compose a poem in honor of his gallant foe.

BATTLE OF HALDIGHATI
The Battle of Haldighati in 1576, one of the most famous in Indian history, pitted the forces of Mewar against those of the Mughals ● *36*. It is interesting to note that the armies of Mewar were led by a Muslim general, Hakim Khan Suri, while the Mughal armies were led by a Rajput general, Raja Man Singh I of Jaipur.

VALIANT HERO
Maharana Pratap of Mewar is one of the greatest heroes in Rajput history. Single-handedly, for a quarter of a century, he defied the Mughal Emperor, Akbar, living in the wilderness and fighting a series of guerilla battles.

> "THERE IS NOT A PASS IN THE ALPINE ARAVALLI THAT IS NOT SANCTIFIED BY SOME DEED OF [MAHARANA] PRATAP – SOME BRILLIANT VICTORY, OR OFTENER, MORE GLORIOUS DEFEAT."
>
> COLONEL TOD, *ANNALS AND ANTIQUITIES OF RAJASTHAN*, 1829

FOUNDING OF UDAIPUR

One day in 1559 Rana Udai Singh II (reigned 1537–72) was out hunting on the banks of a lake when he came across a hermit meditating. The hermit blessed the young prince and advised him that this very spot would be an auspicious site for him to build a new city. After the fall of Chittorgarh to the Mughal army of Emperor Akbar, Rana Udai Singh II, needing a new capital, followed the advice he had received years before. Thus the city of Udaipur was born, watered by the beautiful Pichola Lake and guarded by hills on all four sides. It could not have been more fortunately sited.

CULTURAL RENAISSANCE. In the early 17th century, after decades of continuous battling with the Mughals, Rana Amar Singh (reigned 1597–1620) finally negotiated a treaty of peace with Emperor Jahangir under one condition: that his descendants would never appear personally at the Mughal court. This new era of peace saw a great renaissance of the arts in Udaipur, with the building of a series of beautiful palaces along the lake front and the blossoming of the Mewar school of painting. In the early 18th century, with the disintegration of the Mughal Empire, the maharanas, with their new independence, began to set up a splendid court. The unemployed artists of Delhi found a welcome haven under its patronage.

BRITISH RULE. Shortly after, a period of strife began, with internal dissensions, followed by incursions of the Maratha armies. In 1818 the Rana of Udaipur finally signed a treaty accepting the paramountcy of the British.

Courtly procession (below top). Maharana Bhim Singh receiving Colonel Tod at the Mewar court (below bottom).

MEWAR SCHOOL OF MINIATURES
The Mewar school of miniatures is the oldest in Rajasthan, dating back to the 15th century. The paintings are unique in their liveliness, both through the way they depict human figures and in their brilliant primary colors: scarlets, golden yellows and lapis lazuli. Of all the miniature schools of Rajasthan, the Mewar school remained, for reasons political as well as artistic, the one that was least influenced by the Mughals. The paintings are incredibly intricate in their details, often having being painted with just a single hair plucked from the throat of a squirrel.

Durbar of the Maharana of Udaipur, late 19th century.

A PIECE OF VENICE
Udaipur today is one of the most picturesque cities in India, set as it is on three beautiful lakes and surrounded by an amphitheater of hills. In fact, Lord Northbrook, the 19th-century British viceroy, described it thus: "Take a lake about the size of Orta, with lower hills and of a lighter colour; put the walls of Verona on the lower hills with a fort or two, add islands smaller than those on Lake Maggiore, covered with marble pleasure palaces and domes… Pile up half a dozen French châteaux on the side and end with a piece of Venice."

UDAIPUR TODAY

Udaipur is a city with a population of 300,000. It is a road and rail junction, and an agricultural market town with a sprinkling of industries, ranging from handicrafts to chemicals. But more than this, it is perhaps one of the most romantic and picturesque cities in Rajasthan, with its lakes, hills and splendid palaces. The old city, once surrounded by fortified walls, like any medieval Rajput town, has five great gates: Hathi Pol ("Elephant Gate"), Suraj Pol ("Sun Gate"), Chand Pol ("Moon Gate"), Kishan Pol ("Gate of Kishan") and Delhi Gate. At one time the gates were shut each night. Today they serve as popular landmarks. Udaipur's streets are narrow and twisting, and the traditional old, whitewashed houses are painted over with brightly colored folk murals of elephants, horsemen or peacocks – auspicious motifs, usually painted on the occasion of festivals or weddings ▲ 236.

BAZAARS. Udaipur has some fascinating bazaars. Start at Jagdish Temple and wander through Bara Bazaar, turning left at Suraj Pol into Bapu Bazaar. You will discover a vivid sprawl of little shops selling the tie-and-dye fabrics for which the city is famed, particularly the *laharia* (or wave-patterned) ones ● 58, which are, perhaps naturally, associated with this city of lakes. Other good buys are Udaipur's brightly colored folk toys, *pichhvais* ● 67 and enamel jewelry ● 62 from nearby Nathdwara, copies of the celebrated miniature paintings of the Mewar School, terracottas from Molela ● 72, chunky silver jewelry, lacquer-work curios, embroidered textiles, antiques and ornamental swords (a 19th-century European traveler once remarked that Udaipur's main industry seemed to be sword-making, and everybody above the age of twelve carried a sword). Until not so long ago, you

could also buy
what must surely have been one
of the world's most strangely named products: a soft drink
named Pee Cola, now, alas, withdrawn from the market.
AYURVEDA CENTER. One of Udaipur's lesser-known claims to
fame is that it is an important center of *ayurveda* – the three-
thousand-year-old Hindu system of medicine which is
founded on a belief in the holistic relationship between man
and the cosmos, and which is thought to have inspired the
ancient Greek system of medicine. There is an ayurvedic
hospital, an ayurvedic research center, and an ayurvedic
college here.

Old city gate.

245

The City Palace (above) is a blend of stern Rajput military architecture on the outside and lavish Mughal-inspired decorative art on the inside ● 89. Set on a hill overlooking Pichola Lake, it is a sprawling edifice made up of at least four separate, interconnecting palaces, built over a period of nearly three centuries. The entire palace is oriented to face the east, aptly, perhaps, for a dynasty which claimed descent from the sun. The earliest parts of the palace are reminiscent of the architectural style of Chittorgarh, but subsequent additions show an interesting evolution of style, although this is sometimes disguised by later remodeling. You enter the palace through two great gates, Bari Pol and Tripolia Pol, and carved *torana* archways. The maharanas used to be weighed here, the equivalent in gold then being distributed in charity. Through Ganesh Deori, dedicated to the god of fortune, with its kitschy Japanese tiles, you come to Raj Angan, built in 1559, the oldest part of the palace. Legend says this was the very spot where Rana Udai Singh II met the sage who suggested this location for his new capital ▲ *243*, and that the first thing he built was the Dhuni Mata Temple you see here.

UNUSED CHAIR
The special chair of Maharana Fateh Singh (reigned 1884–1930), from the great *durbar* held for King George V in Delhi in 1913, is on display at the City Palace Museum. Just as his ancestors refused to attend the *durbars* of the Mughal emperors, Maharana Fateh Singh also refused to attend the *durbar* of the King of England, although he went to Delhi. He was probably the only one of India's 562 rajas and maharajas who didn't sit on the chair.

Elephant fight in Udaipur, early 20th century.

Lithograph of City Palace.

BARI MAHAL. Climbing a flight of steep steps you come to Bari Mahal, a delightful garden, nearly 90 feet above the ground. Around the garden is a marble courtyard with a square, central pool and fluted, balustered columns, reminiscent of the Mughal style. This was a royal playground once. Old miniature paintings portray the maharanas at play with the ladies of their court, sprinkling them with colored water during Holi. Looking down from here you can see the courtyard below, where Udaipur's great elephant fights were once staged, the last one being as recently as the 1950's.

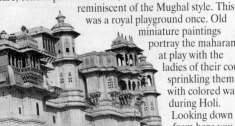

A miniature of Bari Mahal. The garden is actually the summit of a small hill completely enclosed within the palace's high walls.

DILKHUSH MAHAL. Beyond this lies Dilkhush Mahal ("Palace of Joy"), originally built in the 1620's, with two splendid chambers, Kanch ki Burj ("Turret of Glass") and Chitran ki Burj ("Painted Turret"). Kanch ki Burj is a 19th-century Sheesh Mahal, with elaborate gray and red mirror-work walls and ceilings, set off by a carved ivory door. Chitran ki Burj is a little 18th-century masterpiece, its walls covered with frescos of hunting scenes, festivals and court life in princely Udaipur. There is a tragic story connected with this chamber: it was once the bedchamber of a beautiful sixteen-year-old Mewar princess who was being ardently sought by the rival rajas of Jaipur and Jodhpur. Since agreeing to marriage with either one would mean provoking a bloody war with the other, she chose to commit suicide here, by drinking a cup of poppy extract. Take a look also at the curious little glass portrait of Rana Karan Singh (reigned 1620–28) on one of the walls: his costume suddenly turns color from blue to gold, depending on the angle from which you look at it.

TURRET OF GLASS
Kanch ki Burj ("Turret of Glass") was perhaps a 19th-century development of the traditional Sheesh Mahal concept. What makes it unusual is the fact that not only did it have mirror-worked walls and ceilings, but it also had a decorative glass floor, upon which, until only recently, visitors were allowed to walk with their shoes on.

European-influenced Dutch tile inlays at Chini Chitrashala.

CHINI CHITRASHALA. Next you see the 18th-century Chini Chitrashala ("Porcelain Painted Gallery") (above), with its striking blue Dutch inlaid tile work, an amusing European influence that suddenly appears to compete with the Rajput and Mughal styles of the rest of the palace. Don't miss the detail of Joseph and Mary with the infant Jesus on their flight into Egypt.

Moti Mahal.

Relief of peacock at Mor Chowk.

OCTOPUSSY
One of the more unusual moments in Shiv Niwas's colorful history was when it was used as a location for the shooting of the James Bond film, *Octopussy*.

PALACE BUILDINGS. Moti Mahal ("Pearl Palace"), built in 1620, is another Sheesh Mahal in the City Palace. Its walls are decorated with plates of mirror-work and colored glass, creating a magical interplay of reflections. Beside it is Bhim Vilas, a small prayer room, with fine murals depicting episodes from the legends of Lord Krishna and Radha. Across the courtyard is Priyatam Niwas, the simple little apartment where Maharana Bhopal Singh (reigned 1930–55) (below) used to live, right up to 1955. You can see some of his memorabilia here, including, touchingly, his wheelchair. He was paralysed from the waist down, but nevertheless was an expert hunter, going out on *shikar* strapped onto his horse

● *39*. Below these apartments is the grand Mor Chowk ("Peacock Courtyard"), its wall covered with a dramatic mosaic relief of dancing peacocks. It is one of the more celebrated features of the City Palace, though severely criticized by the famous scholar of Rajput architecture, G.H.R. Tillotson, as having "execrable glass mosaics…added in the late 19th century." Nearby is another well-known feature of the palace, Surya Gokhra ("Sun Window"),

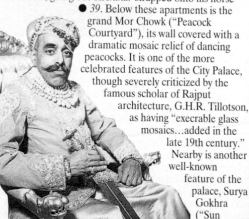

from where, apparently, the maharanas – descendants of the sun god himself – would show themselves to the people in times of misfortune, to reassure them that the sun was still shining on Mewar. Manak Mahal ("Ruby Palace") was built in 1620 as a dining room. It has walls inlaid with ornate mirror-work and colored glass. (Try striking a match and see how the myriad tiny convex mirrors pick up dozens of pinpoints of light.) Inside it are the amusing mosaics of 18th-century Englishmen being served wine by Rajput maidens.

An old photograph of the City Palace, with Shiv Niwas on the right.

Courtyard of City Palace (left).

PALACE MUSEUM. The palace museum contains a wonderful collection of old Rajput weaponry. One of the weapons looks

like an ordinary sword, but is actually a traditional two-swords-in-one scabbard (which you would draw simultaneously, so that you have one sword in each hand). Somewhat more wicked-looking are the old maces. But what is positively gruesome is an arrow with a large crescent-shaped arrowhead – the idea being to aim for the victim's throat and thus neatly slice off his head. Other historic pieces include Maharana Pratap's suit of armor and the war bugle and drums of Rana Sanga.

FAKE TRUNK
In the palace museum, you will see the battle armor worn by Maharana Pratap's famous horse, Chetak. It has an unusual feature: a fake elephant trunk. This was specially designed so that in battle the enemy horses would mistake it for an elephant and get intimidated by it, while the enemy elephants, thinking it was a baby elephant, would hesitate to attack.

SHIV NIWAS AND FATEH PRAKASH PALACES. Later additions that have been built just south of the main City Palace complex are Shiv Niwas and Fateh Prakash. Both were originally intended to be guest houses for the personal guests of the maharanas, but have now been turned into hotels. Shiv Niwas is built around a large, impressive semi-circular courtyard. Its interiors are decorated with mosaics, mirror-work and enamel, as would befit Rajasthan's premier dynasty. One of its suites, until recently, was furnished with a set of solid crystal furniture. The palace has played host, over the years, to celebrities ranging from Jackie Onassis to Queen Elizabeth II. It is said that when Maharana Bhagwat Singh was escorting the latter, he naturally gave her precedence, but she apparently demurred, saying "Please lead the way. You come from a much older family than I do." The smaller Fateh Prakash has some of the most exquisite Mewar miniature paintings from the Maharana's private collection.

Belgian glass crystal furniture at Fateh Prakash.

CURSE OF THE TIGHTROPE WALKER
Natani ka Chabutra ("Platform of the Lady Acrobat") in Pichola Lake commemorates a 19th-century acrobat to whom the maharana, half in jest, promised half his kingdom if she could cross Pichola Lake on a tightrope. She accepted the challenge, and had almost completed the feat when a shrewd courtier cut the rope, and the poor girl drowned in the lake. She apparently cursed the maharana, saying that his line would never again have any direct heirs. Strangely, after that, six out of the next seven maharanas were adopted heirs.

The banquet hall's ceiling in Jag Niwas.

PICHOLA LAKE

Perhaps the best way to see Udaipur is by boat on Pichola Lake, preferably at sunset, sailing past its picturesque ghats and palaces. Pichola Lake was originally created in the 15th century by a Banjara grain merchant, who built a small dam here in order to allow his grain carts to cross over during the monsoon. As you sail up toward the north of the city, you pass slowly by its various sights: first, the old hillside hunting box of the maharanas and the remnants of the old fortified walls; the City Palace, with its high towers and turrets; the lakeside *havelis* of the old city, with their cupolaed balconies reflected in the waters of the lake, and the high, triple-arched Gangaur Ghat (above right), where women bathe and wash their clothes and where the colorful Gangaur festival is celebrated each year in spring. Finally, past the lakeside temples, you come to the island palaces of Jag Niwas and Jag Mandir.

JAG NIWAS ★

Jag Niwas, better known as the Lake Palace (below), seems to float, as if by magic, on the waters of Pichola Lake. Built in 1746, this pleasure palace has a romantic history. The story goes that the young prince, Jagat Singh, asked his father for permission to go with the ladies of his court to the nearby Jag Mandir. His father, the Rana, refused, saying that if the prince wanted to spend his time so frivolously he should build his own pleasure palace. In a fit of pique the prince did precisely that. The palace he created covers an area of nearly four acres. It is a dreamlike confection of white marble that has been called "one of the most romantic creations of man" and was designed to catch

Jag Niwas, or the
Lake Palace.

Sajjan Niwas, a guest
room in Jag Niwas.

the soft
lakeside breezes
that waft through the
elegant courtyards, cupolaed
pavilions and fountained gardens. Its apartments are
elaborately decorated with cusped arches, beautiful wall
paintings, mirror-work, inlaid stones and stained glass.
Colonel Tod, writing about life in the palace in the 19th
century, says, "Here they listened to the tale of the bard and
slept off their noonday opiate amidst the cool breezes of the
lake, wafting delicious odors from myriads of lotus flowers
which covered the surface of the waters." Today the Lake
Palace is a hotel, perhaps one of the most romantic in the
world. It has hosted a whole who's who of international
celebrities.

JAG MANDIR

This older water palace, built in 1620, played an important
role in Udaipur's history. The Mughal prince, Khurram,
exiled by his father, Emperor Jahangir, chose to seek refuge
here with the Mughals' most implacable enemy, the Rana of
Mewar ● *37*. Prince Khurram was here at Jag Mandir when
news of his father's death came in 1627, and he was
announced as the new Emperor Shah Jahan. The close
relationship between the two rulers led to an important new
era of peace, prosperity and architectural renaissance in
Udaipur. The apartment where Shah Jahan lived is a small
curiosity, its lower floor designed in the Hindu tradition and
its upper floor in the Mughal tradition. Jag Mandir saw
another dramatic episode enacted during the great
Uprising of 1857, when it sheltered the British families
who had fled from nearby Neemuch. The Rana of
Mewar chivalrously lodged them here, after taking the
precaution of destroying all the town's boats so that the
angry rebels would not be able to get to the island.

Jag Mandir as
portrayed in a
miniature (above)
and a lithograph
(below).

The early British settlers in India, often referred to as Nabobs, married local women and emulated local customs and lifestyles. But after the Uprising of 1857, the British sought to establish their own identity as rulers and formed their own enclaves. Although Princely Rajasthan and British India were two different worlds, they were bound together by treaties and *sanads* (grants) between *gaddi* (Rajput throne) and Crown. Political Agents, Residents, Governor-Generals and British royalty were lavishly entertained with banquets and sports such as fishing, polo and *shikars* (hunting parties). The maharajas were wonderful hosts and these visits were attended with pomp and pageantry.

GUN SALUTES
The British instituted complicated systems of precedence and protocol, rewarding princes who toed the line with impressive titles and gun salutes. Maharaja Ganga Singh of Bikaner (above, extreme right), for instance, was entitled to a seventeen-gun salute. Known for the sandgrouse shoots he held in Bikaner ▲ 194, he kept close personal ties with British royalty. He is shown here with King George V.

ROYAL RECEPTION
The Maharaja of Jaipur sends off his British guest at a railway station, c. 1902. Some rajas went to great lengths to satisfy the predilections of their more important British guests. Even the most fleeting visits could cause a total disruption to the smooth running of the state, prompting a flurry of road-building and spring-cleaning.

FINAL GATHERING
Lord and Lady Mountbatten stand in the center of this group photograph (right) taken during the last gathering of Indian princes at the Silver Jubilee celebrations of the Maharaja of Jaipur in 1948. Many princes felt let down by Mountbatten when he partitioned the country and cajoled them into acceding to India or Pakistan ● 39.

POLITICAL AGENTS

British Political Agents, responsible for relations between the Indian Princely States and the British rulers, were appointed to the states of Udaipur, Jaipur, Jodhpur, Bharatpur, and Kota. The photograph above shows British officers and their guests waiting for the Viceroy outside the railway station at Bikaner.

RAJ LIFESTYLE

The British lived like mini-potentates in spacious bungalows, served by a battery of servants including cooks, bearers, ayahs, maids, sweepers, and gardeners. They were members of exclusive clubs and moved to the hills during the heat of summer. Their lifestyle reflected the might of Empire and reaffirmed the belief that Britannia ruled the waves.

Saheliyon ki Bari.

RURAL LIVING
Just outside Udaipur is Shilpagram, an interesting "living ethnographic museum". You can get a glimpse into the lifestyle of the rural folk of Rajasthan (and other parts of western India) by visiting the village huts, which are furnished with traditional household articles. Also see the craftsmen and folk musicians perform their everyday tasks.

SAHELIYON KI BARI

These beautiful gardens (literally, "Gardens of the Maids of Honor") were laid out in the mid-18th century for a retinue of forty-eight young ladies-in-waiting who were sent to Udaipur as part of a princess's dowry. The gardens have beautiful lawns, lotus pools, marble pavilions, and marble elephant-shaped fountains. Once the site for royal picnics, the gardens are now a somewhat neglected public park.

JAGDISH MANDIR

Dedicated to Lord Vishnu, Jagdish Mandir was built in the classical Hindu style in the mid-17th century. The temple's bold *shikhara*, or pagoda, 79 feet high, is covered with carved friezes of dancers, musicians, elephants, and horsemen. Its archway is also impressive. Be sure not to miss the small shrine opposite the temple entrance, which houses an excellent bronze statue of Garuda, the mythical bird which is the vehicle of Lord Vishnu.

Jagdish Mandir.

BHARATIYA LOK KALA MANDAL

Bharatiya Lok Kala Mandal has been doing admirable work over the past forty years, recording Rajasthani folklore and music and supporting the traditional folk arts. A collection of Rajasthani folk art – costumes,

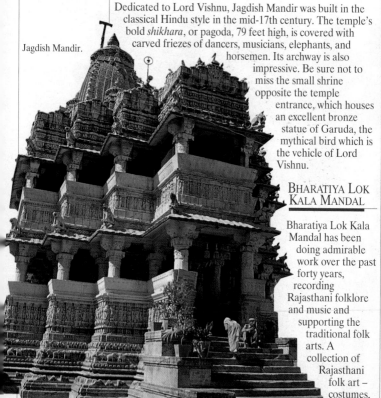

Garuda statue at Jagdish Mandir

musical instruments, paintings, folk deities, masks, dolls, and weapons – can be seen here. The puppet collection is particularly interesting.

SAJJANGARH

High on a hilltop just outside Udaipur lies this dramatic 18th-century palace (below), with a breathtaking view of the Mewar countryside. On a clear day, it is said, you can see the fortress of Chittorgarh from here, so it naturally held a very special place in the hearts of the maharanas. Originally intended to be a towering five-story astronomical center, it was later abandoned and used as a monsoon palace and hunting lodge. Today entry into the building itself is restricted because it has been taken over for governmental use, but the view alone makes a visit worthwhile. At night it is gaudily lit up in pink and green, causing it to be described as "tutti-frutti" by Udaipur's inhabitants.

AHAR

This ancient capital of the Sisodias, en route from the airport, lies 2 miles east of Udaipur. It used to be the capital of the clan until Bappa Rawal founded Chittorgarh in the 8th century. There is a fine complex of royal cenotaphs here, built around the sacred tank of Gangabhar Kund (below). In all, nineteen maharanas of Mewar were cremated here, along with their ranis. Their cenotaphs were built of white marble and resemble small, graceful, colonnaded temples, each one bearing an image of Eklingji and of the maharana and his wives. The most impressive of them is the cenotaph of Rana Amar Singh (reigned 1597–1620), with its four-faced image in the center and a beautiful carved frieze depicting the *sati* of his ranis. Another beautiful cenotaph is that of Rana Sangram Singh (reigned 1710–34), with its fifty-six pillared portico and its octagonal dome. Nearby are two carved 10th-century temples dedicated to the saints Mirabai and Adinatha. There is also an archeological museum here, containing excavated specimens of an ancient civilization discovered in the vicinity, dating back three thousand years: shards of pottery ■ 20, terracotta toys and a large earthenware grain storage pot. There are also a number of stone sculptures here from later periods, including an impressive 10th-century Surya, or sun-god image. The excavations around Ahar are of great archeological and historical interest.

OF MAHARANA JAI SINGHJI

**HANDMADE
TERRACOTTAS**
Molela, near
Nathdwara, is known
for its unique
terracotta folk art
● 72. These
terracottas, depicting
various local deities
and legendary heroes,
have a charming
rustic beauty about
them. They are
dexterously made by
hand, using only the
most primitive of
tools – no molds –
and painted in bright
colors. With
traditions going back
two thousand years,
this is, unfortunately,
a dying art, practiced
today only by about
twenty families in
Molela.

Sas Temple.

EKLINGJI TEMPLE

This temple, actually a
complex of 108 small
temples (right), lies in a
remote, hilly gorge 14
miles north of Udaipur.
Eklingji, an incarnation
of Lord Shiva, was the
tutelary deity of the
maharanas of Mewar. This
temple is said to have been built
in the 8th century by Bappa Rawal, the
first of the great Sisodia kings, and rebuilt in the 15th century.
The main temple is of an unusual design: built of marble, it
has a clustered, curved tower and a *mandapa* (pillared hall)
roofed with a pyramid of miniature architectural motifs.
Inside is the main four-faced Eklingji image, carved in black
marble. Outside the main sanctuary is a large statue of Bappa
Rawal standing beside Nandi, Lord Shiva's bull. According to
legend, Allaudin Khilji, Sultan of Delhi, attacked the temple
in the late 13th century and struck this Nandi idol with his
mace. Out of its hollow interior a swarm of angry bees
emerged and attacked the Sultan, forcing him to call off his
attack.

NAGDA

SAS AND BAHU TEMPLES. The 10th-century Sas and Bahu
temples (literally, "Temples of the Mother-in-law and
Daughter-in-law"), dedicated to Lord Vishnu, and known for
their beautiful carvings, are situated by the side of a lake,
two-and-a-half
miles from
Eklingji.

Details of carvings in
Sas Temple (right
and below).

Sas Temple (the larger of the two) has a richly carved porch. On its walls are elaborate friezes with scenes from the *Ramayana* and depictions of trysting lovers, as well as images of the Hindu trinity of Brahma, Shiva and Vishnu. The dome, too, has some wonderful carvings, although they are not in a very good condition today. The sanctuary itself, in contrast to the porch and *mandapa*, is simple and unadorned. Bahu Temple has a beautifully carved *torana* archway in front of it (right). Apparently the image of the presiding (Vishnu) deity was swung from the archway, to the singing of hymns, on ceremonial occasions. The basic scheme of the temple is similar to that of Sas Temple next door, although on a smaller scale. The portico, however, is open. The columns are richly carved and the octagonal ceiling is decorated with eight female figurines.

NATHDWARA

The important pilgrim center of Nathdwara, with its temple of Shrinathji or Lord Krishna, lies 30 miles north of Udaipur. According to legend, the temple's image of Shrinathji was originally located in Mathura. However, in 1691, fearing an attack on the temple by the fanatical Mughal Emperor, Aurangzeb, it was decided that the image should be smuggled away to a safer, more remote place. When the carriage carrying the image arrived at Nathdwara, its wheels got stuck in the sands and could not be moved. Taking this as a message from Lord Krishna, the guardians of the image decided to build a new temple on the spot. The temple itself is architecturally very simple. The Shrinathji image, carved in black marble, has the quality of a mysterious and powerful monolith, with wide hypnotic eyes and one hand held up, as if

to support a mountain. It is treated with great ritual and ceremony: its clothes and jewelry are changed six times a day between *puja* (prayer) services, when it is presented before the devotees in the various different aspects of Lord Krishna. The temple is open only to Hindus. Outside the temple are colorful bazaars, where you can find Nathdwara's famed *pichvai* paintings ● 67 and *minakari* jewelry, and artists who will engrave your name on a single grain of rice.

RELIGIOUS PICHHVAIS
The *pichhvai* paintings of Nathdwara are a unique art form that evolved at Shrinathji Temple in Nathdwara ● 67. They were originally created as a cloth backdrop to be hung behind the temple's idol (the word *pichhvai* literally means "at the back"). The paintings depict different episodes from Lord Krishna's life, and are changed regularly to create different moods, depending on the occasion or ritual. The *pichhvai* paintings of the 19th century were exquisite works of art, created with great passion and reflecting a symbolic imagery of their own. Swirling ink-blue clouds, for example, represent Lord Krishna, with his dark complexion; dancing peacocks again symbolize Lord Krishna, while cows symbolize devotees yearning for the god.

257

Carved façade of Dayal
Shah Mandir (below).

BRAINWAVE FOR IRRIGATION
The "Persian wheels" that you see all over Mewar were an ingenious medieval invention ■ *23*. A large loop of water-containers is placed above a well and connected to a yoked bull (or camel) with a simple mechanical device. As the bull is driven around in a circle, the water containers are dipped into the well, brought up and emptied into a water channel, which then provides a steady stream of water for irrigating the farmer's fields.

RAJSAMAND AND KANKROLI

The royal lake of Rajsamand, with the village of Kankroli on its shores, lies about 40 miles north of Udaipur. This large, artificial lake was constructed in the 1660's. By the lake stands Nauchowki ("Nine Pavilions"). An elegant stepped embankment goes right down to the water's edge, punctuated by gracefully carved *torana* archways and marble pavilions. The entire complex was built by Rana Raj Singh I (reigned 1652–80) to commemorate an act of defiance against Emperor Aurangzeb. When Aurangzeb proposed marriage to Princess Charumati, a Rajput princess of Kishangarh, she could not refuse, so she turned to Raj Singh I to save her. The Rana gallantly married her himself.

TEMPLES. Nearby are two interesting temples, the 16th-century temple of Dwarakadhish or Lord Krishna, and a large Jain temple built by Dayal Shah. The latter has some exquisite marble carvings, almost as intricate and delicate as the ones at the Dilwara temples at Mount Abu ● *94* ▲ *270*. The other interesting feature of Rajsamand is Raj Prashasti, a history of Mewar in verse, whose 1017 stanzas were carved on twenty-seven slabs of stone in the 17th century. It is believed to be the longest literary work ever carved in stone.

SUMMER HUNTING PARTIES
The forests around Jaisamand were once the scene of the maharanas' hunting parties in summer. These were elaborate, highly organized expeditions. Signalers, positioned on the hilltops, would first signal the locations of the panther or wild boar. The strategy would then be worked out: whether to go in with beaters, elephants or lancers. The maharana decided which of his guests would have the honor of shooting which animal. Now, of course, there is a game sanctuary in these forests.

JAGAT

AMBIKA MATA TEMPLE. Located 35 miles southeast of Udaipur is the village of Jagat and the 10th-century temple of Ambika Mata. The temple is small, but elaborately carved. The porch outside has friezes and a carved panel of a dancing Ganesha. A decorated gateway leads into the towered sanctuary. Inside are images of Durga, the goddess of destruction, attended by sensuous maidens in seductive postures. On the walls are more carvings: musicians, sages and amorous couples, reminiscent of the erotic carvings of Khajuraho.

RISHABDEO

The 15th-century temple of Lord Rishabdeo, 25 miles south of Udaipur, is an

Carvings in Ambika Mata Temple.

important center of pilgrimage for both Jains and Hindus ● 48. The Jains consider the deity to be one of the twenty-four *tirthankaras* of Jainism, while the Hindus consider him to be one of the ten incarnations of Lord Vishnu. This is a fascinating temple, with a black marble image of Rishabdeo, smeared with saffron by the devotees. Each pilgrim can wash off the saffron paste applied by the previous pilgrim and anoint it afresh. On ceremonial occasions the image is dressed in an extravagant diamond-studded garment which was presented to the temple by the maharanas of Mewar.

JAISAMAND

Jaisamand, a vast artificial lake 32 miles southeast of Udaipur, was created by Raja Jai Singh in 1691. With an area of 13½ square miles, it was the largest artificial lake in the world, until superseded by the lake that was formed by the Aswan Dam in Egypt. This is an exceptionally picturesque place, surrounded by wooded hills. On the banks of the lake are vast marble steps descending to the water, embellished with pretty domed pavilions and sculpted elephants. On either end is a small water palace, and in the center a temple dedicated to Lord Shiva. The forests around Jaisamand were once hunting grounds of the maharanas of Mewar, where they came to shoot panthers and wild boars in summer. Now the entire area has, of course, been turned into a game sanctuary. Here you can see *chitals*, *chinkaras*, wild boars, panthers and crocodiles, as well as a wide variety of birds, including several migratory species drawn to this huge lake.

THE CHITAL AND THE LANGUR MONKEY
The *chital*, or spotted deer, which can be seen at Jaisamand, is considered one of the most beautiful species of deer in the world ■ 25. It has a curious, symbiotic relationship with the black-faced langur monkey. *Chitals* have often been seen with a langur monkey astride their backs, in the manner of a rider.

Terraced embankment of the lake at Jaisamand.

Lithograph of
Kumbhalgarh
Fort (opposite).

KUMBHALGARH FORT

Of the thirty-two forts that the great warrior king, Rana Kumbha (reigned 1433–68), built all over Mewar, the most spectacular was Kumbhalgarh. In many ways, in fact, it is even more impressive than the Mewar citadel of Chittorgarh itself. Built high in the hills west of Chittorgarh in the mid-15th century, Kumbhalgarh was called the "eye of Mewar" because of its strategic position in relation to the kingdom's aggressive neighbors in Gujarat and Marwar. It was impregnable, having withstood several attacks from the armies of Gujarat, Malwa and the Mughals. Even Emperor Akbar, after the conquest of Chittorgarh, could not get beyond Kumbhalgarh's mighty second gate. Actually, an ancient fortress had existed on this site ever since the 3rd century, but Rana Kumbha won it over from the local Mer ruler, constructing its fortifications anew, with massive walls, rounded bastions, tall watchtowers and secret passages, designed in accordance with the ancient Hindu treatise, *Vastu Shastra*. The outer wall encloses an area of 32 square miles, and the fort is said to have once contained 252 palaces.

THE GREAT WALL
The massive ramparts of Kumbhalgarh run for 2¹⁄₂ miles along the rugged Aravalli hillsides, and are wide enough for eight horsemen to ride abreast on top of them. They have been compared in their conception, by some, to the Great Wall of China.

FORT GATES. You approach the fort through thick forests and ravines and enter through the first of seven strongly fortified gates, Arait Pol, from whose watchtower mirrored signals could be flashed up to the citadel. The other gates continue to throw up barriers to would-be invaders, one after the other, all the way up the hill. The second gate, Hulla Pol ("Gate of Disturbance") was named such because the invading Mughal forces had reached up to here after the fall of Chittorgarh. You can still see the marks of their old cannon balls on this gate. Bhairon Pol bears a stone tablet inscribed with an order for the exile of a treacherous 19th-century prime minister. Paghra Pol ("Stirrup Gate") (right) was where the Mewar cavalry would amass before riding out into battle. Topkhana Pol ("Cannon Gate") housed an artillery emplacement, as well as, it is said, a secret passage out of the fort. As you

"[It] RISES, LIKE THE CROWN OF THE HINDU CYBELE, TIER ABOVE TIER OF BATTLEMENTS TO THE SUMMIT, WHICH IS CROWNED WITH THE BADAL MAHAL, OR 'CLOUD-PALACE' OF THE RANAS."

COLONEL TOD, *ANNALS AND ANTIQUITIES OF RAJASTHAN*, 1829

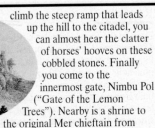

climb the steep ramp that leads up the hill to the citadel, you can almost hear the clatter of horses' hooves on these cobbled stones. Finally you come to the innermost gate, Nimbu Pol ("Gate of the Lemon Trees"). Nearby is a shrine to the original Mer chieftain from whom Raja Kumbha won over this fort. According to a gory and fanciful legend, the Mer offered to sacrifice himself for the building of the fort: he had his head cut off at the bottom of the hill, and yet his body continued to walk up to this point, where it finally fell. There are small shrines that supposedly mark both these points.

BADAL MAHAL. At the citadel lies Badal Mahal ("Cloud Palace"), with its beautiful apartments painted with delicate pastel-colored murals in the 19th century. In these chambers you can see an ingenious "air-conditioning" system, with a series of ducts that draw cool air into the rooms and ventilate them from the bottom, rather than from the top, as convention might dictate. Two other curiosities to see are the quaint toilets and the royal bedchamber with its (presumably erotic) echo effects! The view from Badal Mahal of the surrounding countryside is stunning. There is a romantic story about how Rana Kumbha once carried away a beautiful Jalore princess from her betrothed, a prince of Marwar, and brought her here to Kumbhalgarh. It is said the dejected Marwar prince would sit at night in his palace at Mandore, over 72 miles away, and watch the lights in the towers of Kumbhalgarh, knowing that there was no way he could storm the mighty fortress and win his princess back.

OTHER BUILDINGS. Apart from the palace, there are various other buildings that are worth seeing. Near Ram Pol, for instance, is the beautiful three-storied Vedi building, with its massive columns and sculpted parapet, where the consecration of the fort was celebrated in 1458. There are also some fine old temples here: the Kumbhaswami, Mahadev and Neelkant temples are just some of the 365 temples that the fort is said to have once contained. And, of course, there is the cenotaph of Rana Kumbha, who was murdered here by his own son, known to history only as Hathiaro ("The Murderer")

GARRISON FORTS
Around each of the major forts of Rajputana were several little garrison forts, which were commanded by the chieftains of the ruler, and which acted as the first line of defense in case of invasion. One of the garrison forts around Kumbhalgarh was the one at Ghanerao, with a late 16th-century palace beside it. The palace is now a charming little hotel ◆ *338*.

Wall painting at Badal Mahal.

Neelkanth Temple.

Vedi building.

LORD PARSHVA
According to a Jain legend, Prince Parshva once saved a snake from being killed by the evil Kamatha. Years later, Kamatha, reborn as a heavenly being through his penances, saw Parshva deep in meditation, and whipped up a terrible storm to kill him. Despite the rising storm waters that threatened to drown him, Parshva continued to meditate

serenely. The snake whom he had saved years earlier, now reborn as the Lord of the Snakes, came to his rescue, coiling his body below Parshva, thereby raising him above the water's level. Spreading his thousand hoods over Parshva's head, the snake shielded him from the cyclonic winds ▲ 265.

RANAKPUR

Deep in the forest, 56 miles north of Udaipur, is the huge 15th-century Adinatha Temple at Ranakpur ● 94. It is the largest and most complex Jain temple in India, with twenty-nine halls covering 4,320 square yards. Holding up its domes and spires are 420 ornately carved pillars. The temple was built by a wealthy Jain merchant, Dharna Sah. According to legend, one night he dreamed of a celestial vehicle. Enchanted by this vision, he vowed to make it a reality and invited architects from all over India to present designs. Finally, a sculptor named Depa produced a design that perfectly captured Dharna Sah's vision. The construction of the main shrine took fifty years.

DESIGN. The temple is one of the five great holy places of the Jain sect. It is so complex in form and overwhelming in scale that at first it leaves you quite bewildered. But, as you walk through its chambers, the pattern gradually emerges. It takes an unusual form, as Indian temples go, for it rejects the traditional longitudinal plan in favor of a cruciform plan, with four separate entrances, one on each side. Each of these leads, through a series of columned halls, to the central court and cruciform sanctum chamber with its four-faced Adinatha image. The temple is enclosed on all four sides by rows of chapels (eighty-six in all), and is topped by twenty domes and five spires. Perhaps the best view of the temple is from the upper level, from where you can see it as a whole and admire its halls and pillars.

STONE CARVINGS. What makes the Adinatha Temple truly remarkable, of course, is the fact that all these grand architectural elements are completely covered with carvings, so profuse and so intricate that they resemble lace-work, rather than stone-carving ▲ 264. The ceiling panels are decorated with geometric patterns and scrollery; the domes are embellished with ornate concentric friezes

Adinatha Temple (right) and Jain pilgrims entering the temple (above).

and descending pendants; the brackets supporting the domes are designed with dancing goddesses. And when you study the richly carved pillars, you will realize that each one of them is carved with a different pattern from the rest. Look out also for one of the columns facing the sanctum, on which there is a small panel depicting a man with his hands joined. This is supposed to be Dharna Sah, the man who built this temple, while the figure next to him is Depa, his sculptor and architect. The temple is also remarkable for its spatial complexity. The pillared *mandapas* (halls) around the sanctum and the surrounding colonnades regularly open up to create large, octagonal areas which are double or even triple-storied and which are ornamented with corbeled domes and delicate balconies. Architectural scholars have been uniformly eloquent in their praise of the temple. Fischer wrote of the "unending vistas of the columns, interrupted at intervals by open courts, each compartment covered with carving of a most intricate character, and the whole illuminated by light that is thrown from pavement to pillar, and from pillar to screen to penetrate into all parts." In the temple courtyard is a tree that is believed to be over four hundred years old, having been planted at the time the temple was built.

OTHER TEMPLES. There are two other temples nearby, a 15th-century Jain Parshvanatha temple, remarkable especially for its ornately pierced stone windows, and another 15th-century Hindu Surya temple. Ranakpur is named after Rana Kumbha ▲ *242*, whom Dharna Sah approached when he had the vision of his great temple, to ask for the land for its construction. Rana Kumbha apparently agreed on condition that the temple be named after him.

Interior of Adinatha Temple.

LIGHT AND SHADOW
The temple of Ranakpur is held up by a forest of 1444 carved pillars. One of the remarkable things about the temple is the wonderful play of shadow and light, as the sun's rays shift through the day, changing the pillars' color from gold to pale blue.

NEMI'S RENUNCIATION
Nemi, one of the great Jain *tirthankaras*, was riding to his marriage ceremony when he heard the piteous cries of the animals being slaughtered for his wedding feast. Deeply saddened, Nemi immediately renounced the world and its pleasures, and, leaving his young bride-to-be, embarked on the life of an ascetic.

263

▲ HYMN IN MARBLE
DHARNA VIHARA, RANAKPUR

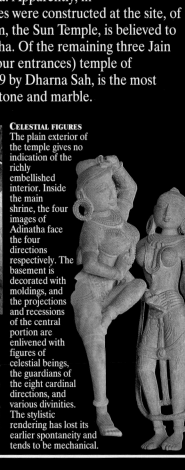

On the curve of a boulder-strewn river, in a tiny enclave within the forested Aravalli hills, lies the sacred site of Ranakpur. There, Dharna Sah, a minister of the Rana of Mewar, sought permission to construct a Jain temple. The Rana desired that with the temple, a small township should also be built. Accordingly, a settlement was created on the western slopes of the hills and was named Ranakpur, in honor of the Rana. Apparently, in the 15th century, several temples were constructed at the site, of which four survive. One of them, the Sun Temple, is believed to have been built by Rana Kumbha. Of the remaining three Jain temples, the *chaumukh* (with four entrances) temple of Adinatha, completed in AD 1439 by Dharna Sah, is the most imposing, a veritable hymn in stone and marble.

CELESTIAL FIGURES
The plain exterior of the temple gives no indication of the richly embellished interior. Inside the main shrine, the four images of Adinatha face the four directions respectively. The basement is decorated with moldings, and the projections and recessions of the central portion are enlivened with figures of celestial beings, the guardians of the eight cardinal directions, and various divinities. The stylistic rendering has lost its earlier spontaneity and tends to be mechanical.

PILLARED HALL
Though conforming to the prevailing architectural tenets, the temple is exceptional because of its compact plan, pillared vistas, soaring domes, and open courts. The pillars are not conceived in one single piece, but as a series of drums of varying heights and receding diameter. They are placed one upon another to form an elegant tapering shaft. The temple has more than 1400 pillars, each of which, interestingly, displays a different decorative design.

CEILING
It is not clear exactly when the town of Ranakpur was abandoned after the Muslims desecrated the temples. The ruined Adinatha Temple became a hiding place for dacoits and wild animals. At the end of the 19th century, the site was cleared and fortified. The renovation of the Adinatha Temple was entrusted to the descendants of Depa, the original architect of the temple. Depa's family had been practicing the art of temple architecture as a living tradition for centuries, and only the discerning eye can easily differentiate between the original and renovated elements in the reconstructed ceilings and pillars.

PLAQUE OF PARSHVA
This plaque, approximately 3 feet in diameter, is a later addition to the temple. Placed against the wall of the southern side shrine in the row of chapels, it depicts Parshva, the twenty-third *tirthankara*, a historical figure who lived in the 8th century BC. On either side of Parshva is a Jina, and an attendant. A cobra protects the three Jinas with his thousand hoods. This common motif of Jain iconography has been treated very innovatively.

PILLARS
The carved patterns on the pillars reveal a preference for floral, vegetal, and scroll motifs over depictions of human figures, probably a consequence of Muslim influence.

Spine of the Temple of Adinatha.

Udai Villas.

TROPHY ROOM
Most of the
maharajas of
Rajasthan were
expert *shikaris* or
huntsmen and had
splendid collections
of hunting trophies.
But the trophy room
in Dungarpur Palace
is said to house one
of the finest
collections of such
trophies in all of Asia.

Durbar hall in Juna
Mahal.

HIS WEIGHT IN GOLD
A carved stone arch
in Dungarpur's Udai
Vilas was supposedly
part of an elaborate
weighing device. The
reigning maharawal
was balanced on it,
and his weight would
determine the
amount of silver or
gold that was to be
distributed to the
populace as charity.

DUNGARPUR

Situated 69 miles south of Udaipur, the town of Dungarpur
was the capital of a kingdom of the same name. The rulers of
Dungarpur were Sisodias, who branched away from the main
line of Mewar in the 12th century. There are various stories
behind this, but the most colorful one tells of a
misunderstanding between the eldest prince of Mewar and
his father, the Rana. The prince was getting married,
and the bride's family sent him the customary
ceremonial coconut. By mistake the coconut was
accepted by the prince's father. The prince
thereupon got angry and said, "Since you accepted
the coconut, you marry the girl. I will leave
Chittorgarh forever." He rode south with his
followers to found the kingdom of Dungarpur,
while his younger brother succeeded to the throne
of Mewar (thus making Dungarpur the senior
branch of the Sisodias). The region surrounding
Dungarpur was an inhospitable place known,
apparently, for five things: water, rocks, thorns,
thieves, and foul language. Here, on an enormous
rock, the town of Dungarpur was founded. Juna
Mahal and Udai Vilas palaces in Dungarpur
represent some of the finest examples of art and
architecture in existence in Rajasthan today.
JUNA MAHAL. Juna Mahal rises above the town in a fierce,
medieval jumble of white battlements, turrets, and
watchtowers. In complete contrast to this warlike exterior, the
apartments within the palace are sumptuously covered with
paintings, inlay work and ornamentation. Its walls and
ceilings are alive with scenes from Dungarpur's history and
portraits of bygone princes, all
dating from the 16th to the 18th
centuries. What's more, since the
palace is so remote – and has
been unused since the 18th
century – Juna Mahal's art work
is far better preserved than any
other palace in Rajasthan.
UDAI VILAS. Another nearby
palace, Udai Vilas, was built in
the late 18th century. This,
too, is equally interesting,
for in the middle of its
courtyard rises an
extraordinarily ornate carved

pleasure pavilion. Its lower level is a mass of intricate friezes, columns and arches, but the second story is even more ornate, with decorative brackets, unusually sculpted figurines and extravagantly carved pillars. Above this is a terrace with a profusion of kiosks, canopies, and balustrades. Inside, the apartment walls are created in inlaid marble, as at the Taj Mahal. The palace is one of the most exuberant and fantastical examples of Rajput architecture.

DEOLIA

The town of Deolia, about 100 miles southeast of Udaipur, is off the usual beaten tourist track. But if you are adventurous it is worth visiting for the brilliant wall paintings in its ruined palace. The palace was built in the 16th century, and one can imagine that it must have had a glorious past, but it now lies neglected and crumbling. Inside, especially in the royal bedchamber and the large *durbar* hall, are some truly exquisite wall paintings, which appear to have been painted in the early 19th century. Do not miss the rich crimson glass paintings embellished with gilt on the vaulted ceiling of one of the chambers, nor the frieze of wall paintings appearing like an endless row of framed miniatures. A predominant theme here is Lord Krishna as the great lover. Several of the paintings are charmingly erotic, like the ones in the bedchamber. These paintings are similar in style to the highly intricate style of the Mewar school ▲ *243*. This is not surprising, as the royal family of Deolia was an offshoot of the Sisodias of Mewar, with whom, over the centuries, it had a love-hate relationship. Deolia is also famed for its splendid Partabgarh *thewa* enamel-work on glass.

Five examples of frescos in Juna Mahal are shown above. The erotic painting below is also from Juna Mahal.

FAMILY SECRET
An exquisite and unusual (but unfortunately dying) art of Rajasthan is the *thewa* work of Deolia. A silver wire frame is covered with delicately patterned gold leaf and then sunk into a softened layer of green or crimson enamel or glass. This is then used as a plaque or an ornamental box top. Common design themes are religious and court scenes. There is only one family left in Deolia who knows the secret of this craft, and they guard it jealously. Not even the daughters, it is said, are taught the secret, as they will one day marry and leave the family.

267

Lake at Mount Abu.

THOU SHALT NOT KILL
The Jain religion teaches that all living beings possess a soul, and must therefore be treated on a par with human beings ● 48. Not only will a Jain never consciously kill any animal or insect, but devout Jains actually wear a cloth to cover their mouths in order to avoid accidentally killing insects by inhaling them.

HISTORY

Mount Abu was the site of a little colonial hill station, set, surprisingly, in the middle of this desert state. "A sort of Simla of Rajputana," as somebody once called it. It has a fascinating history that goes back, layer by layer, into deepest antiquity and has long been considered a holy spot by both Hindus and Jains. Once the tranquil hilltop retreat of meditating *rishis,* or holy men, it is supposed to have been home to no less than 330 million different gods and goddesses. To the Rajputs, however, this was a Mount Olympus, the scene of the great *agni-kunda* (sacred fire pit) of ancient times, out of which thirty-six Rajput warrior clans were born ● 32. The legend goes that snake-like demons were ravaging this region, so the Brahmins perform an elaborate fire rite. In response to their prayers, Rajput warriors emerged from the fire, vanquished the demons and saved the land. Historians say the story is an allegory: the "demons" were actually the Indo-Scythian invaders of the 6th century; the ritual was an elaborate purification ceremony by which various lesser castes were given the exalted status of warriors and thereby inducted into the defending armies.

PILGRIMAGE CENTER. By the 11th century, Mount Abu had become an important Jain center of pilgrimage. Over the next two centuries, some of India's most spectacular marble temples were built here. In the 15th century these hills were conquered by Rana Kumbha of Mewar (who built a fortress here ▲ 274).

HILL STATION. In the early 19th century, Mount Abu was developed into its present form as a hill station, where the British from the hot, dusty

plains of Rajasthan could seek refuge during the summer
months, amid the eucalyptus trees and oleanders. Charming
English countryside cottages were built around Nakki Lake.
As time passed it became a British enclave, the official
summer capital to which the Chief Commissioner for
Rajputana would shift his office from Ajmer for two months
each year. With the emergence of an administrative center,
most of the major Rajput maharajas, too, built palaces here
(some of which have now been converted into hotels). There
was cricket and golf at the Rajputana Club and considerable
intrigue at the British Residency. The maharajas used the
opportunities Mount Abu offered for casual encounters with
the Chief Commissioner for political ends, since approaching
him here was much more discreet than public visits to Ajmer.

MOUNT ABU TODAY

While the surrounding hills, with
their waterfalls and bamboo and
eucalyptus groves, are still
extremely charming, Mount Abu
has become an overcrowded and
somewhat gaudy little town. If
you can imagine an Indian
version of Las Vegas and Disney World rolled into one, this
would probably be it. Still, its bazaars are fascinating as a
living museum of contemporary Indian kitsch. The temples of
Dilwara, of course, simply have to be seen ● 94 ▲ 270. Some
of the old palaces make interesting viewing, such as Bikaner
Palace, where Maharaja Ganga Singh used to come every year
with a retinue of four hundred people, and the gothic towered
palace of the bizarre Maharaja Jai Singh of Alwar ▲ 173.

The gothic-style
palace built by
Maharaja Jai Singh of
Alwar. The palace has
some interesting
anecdotes associated
with it. On one
occasion, the story
goes, when a fellow
maharaja was hosting
a dinner to which he
had pointedly not
been invited,
Maharaja Jai Singh
bought up all the food
supplies for miles
around, forcing the
dinner to be canceled.
He then added insult
to injury by inviting
everybody to his place
instead.

Interior of
Jain temple.

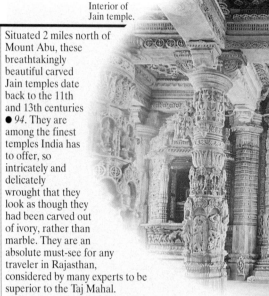

Temples at Dilwara.

POETIC BEAUTIES
The marble *nayikas*
(maidens) that adorn
the Dilwara temples
are not just ethereally
beautiful in form, but
they are often
presented in a highly
poetic context. One
of them, for instance,
is depicted as having
just emerged wet
from her bath. The
droplets of water
falling from her long
hair are being drunk
by a swan sitting by
her feet!

Situated 2 miles north of
Mount Abu, these
breathtakingly
beautiful carved
Jain temples date
back to the 11th
and 13th centuries
● *94*. They are
among the finest
temples India has
to offer, so
intricately and
delicately
wrought that they
look as though they
had been carved out
of ivory, rather than
marble. They are an
absolute must-see for any
traveler in Rajasthan,
considered by many experts to be
superior to the Taj Mahal.

VIMALA-VASAHI TEMPLE ★

Built in AD 1030 by Vimala Shah, a minister of Gujarat, to
atone for his earthly sins, the temple is said to have involved a
work force of 2700 men, and taken a total of fourteen years to
complete. The cost at that time is supposed to have been over
US$6 million! From the outside the temple is deceptively
austere, but as you enter through the ornate doorway, the
beauty of the marble carvings is simply overwhelming. The
temple is a classic example of Jain architecture, with a central
shrine, a colonnaded hall and an ambulatory passage around
it, with fifty-two small shrines against the surrounding wall,
each one containing the image of a Jain *tirthankara*. The

Interior of Vimala
Vasahi Temple at
Dilwara.

inner sanctum houses the image of
Adinatha, the great Jain saint. The real
beauty of the temple, of course, lies in its
profuse and intricate decorations. The
columns are carved with figures and
friezes of scrollwork. The domes and
vaults of the ceilings are corbeled and
embellished with row upon row of
musicians, dancers, warriors and
elephants, set around beautiful
medallions decorated with lotus-blossom
motifs. Each of the canopies of the roof
is said to have been carved by two
workers, one on either side, and yet they
match perfectly in the center. The large
dome of the open *ranga mandapa* (main
hall) is an especially impressive feature
of the temple, with roof brackets carved
in the form of seductive maidens, and a
clustered lotus pendant. Take a look also
at the splendid carved panels in the
aisles, depicting figures from Jain, as
well as Hindu, mythology. In the porch

TWO MONK SECTS
Jain monks are divided into two sects: Svetambaras, the "white-robed", and Digambaras, the "sky-clad" (naked) ascetics ● 48. One can recognize which of the two groups a *tirthankara* statue represents by looking at its eyes. Wide open, enameled eyes mark a *Svetambara*, while closed eyes indicate a *Digambara*.

there is a marble figure seated on a horse, believed to be the builder, Vimala Shah.

LUNA-VASAHI TEMPLE ★

Built in AD 1232 by two wealthy brothers, Luna-Vasahi Temple is similar in form to Vimala-Vasahi Temple, but smaller. Its carved ornamentation is even richer, denser and more delicate – resembling paper cut-outs more than marble. In some places, in fact, the marble is carved so finely that it is actually translucent! The doorways of the temple are framed by ornate pediments and pilasters; the columns are magnificently carved; and the ceiling is ablaze with mythological figures, processions of horsemen, elephants and dancers. The carvings on the corners of the ceilings in the fourth, fifth and sixth cells are exceptional. Other features worth taking a closer look at are the caparisoned elephants in the elephant chamber and the magnificent image of Lord Adinatha seated in a triple-storied marble tower with Jain devotees on its four sides. However, the greatest masterpiece in the entire Dilwara complex is the *ranga mandapa* of the Luna-Vasahi, and, more specifically, its ceiling. From its center hangs a clustered marble pendant of unsurpassed richness and delicacy (someone described it as a "cluster of crystal drops", which sounds overly poetic, but under the circumstances, entirely appropriate). On a nearby frieze are sixty-eight maidens caught in different dance poses on the petals of a lotus, and on a raised platform above is an arrangement of nine canopies with more examples of superbly intricate carving. The two *gokhadas*, or filigreed marble niches, containing Jain idols and images of the goddess Lakshmi, are also worth taking a closer look at. There are two other temples in the complex, dedicated to Parshvanatha and Adinatha. The former is notable for its columned *mandapa* (hall), and the latter for its carved pillars and its massive brass idol.

PAINSTAKING REWARD
The marble pendant that descends from the ceiling of Luna-Vasahi Temple's main hall is so delicately carved that it simply takes one's breath away. It is said that this astonishing delicacy of carving was achieved by offering the artisans the weight of their marble shavings in gold: the more finely they carved, the more they earned.

On the summit of the lofty mountain of Mount Abu are two magnificent Jain temples built in marble. The earlier of the two, completed in AD 1030, the Vimala-Vasahi, dedicated to Lord Adinatha, was commissioned by Vimala, the Commander-in-Chief of Bhimadeva I, the ruler of Gujarat. The other, enshrining the image of Lord Neminatha, was constructed two hundred years later in AD 1232 by the Minister, Tejpala, the brother of Vastupala. Both Tejpala and Vastupala were famous for having constructed more than fifty Jain shrines. Tejpala built the Luna-Vasahi temple for the spiritual welfare of his wife and his son, Lavanyasimha, after whom the temple was named.

INTERIOR OF VIMALA-VASAHI TEMPLE
Scenes from Jain myths, gods and goddesses, portrayals of *Tirthankaras*, and monks with devotees are carved in relief on every possible surface – door frames, pillars, niches, ceilings, and arches. The exquisite workmanship heightens the translucency and shell-like delicacy of the carvings, which owe their fragile beauty not to the process of chiseling but to the painstaking technique of thinning the marble into the incredible shapes by gently scraping it.

KALPAVALLI MEDALLION
The architectural vocabulary of the region included ornamental renderings of flowers and creepers. The motif of the *kalpavalli*, a filigreed scroll in varied and replicated forms was prevalent. In the 15th century, it is encountered again on a ceiling in the Jain temple of Adinatha at Ranakpur.

DIVINITIES
The portrayal of Yakshini Chakreshwari, the attendant deity of Adinatha, is an integral part of the scheme of figural sculptures of the temple. The figures have broad faces, sharp facial features, and narrow waists, in keeping with prevailing esthetic norms. The plastic grace of the earlier expression at Osiyan gradually yielded to greater stylization and stiffness at Mount Abu.

ARCHES
In the interior of the temples at Mount Abu, a dramatic accent is added by the intricately sculpted arches connecting the pillars. They are of two varieties – the wave, with its regular undulations, and the caterpillar, with its exaggerated curves. The latter variety, preferred in the temples of Gujarat, occurs in the Vimala-Vasahi Temple, adding to the richness of its interior.

CEILING PENDANT
Of incomparable beauty are the ornamental pendants hanging from the decorated domical ceiling of the temples at Mount Abu. The patterns of the ceilings in the corridor and vestibules are variations on certain geometrical and floral motifs that have been integral to the architectural tradition of the region. Often, however, the inventive genius of the sculptor creates a different pattern of light and shade by carving the motif at varying depths and in different arrangements.

DAMASCENED SWORDS
The kingdom of Sirohi, near Mount Abu, has traditionally been famous for its damascened swords. These slender, slightly curved swords were the favorites of the Rajputs. They were called *sirohis*, after the town itself. The sword-makers would first chase the motif on the steel with a sharp chisel. Then fine gold or silver wire would be painstakingly hammered into the groove. The hammering was so skillfully done that the wire actually became welded to the steel surface. After the hammering process, the slight spreading of the inlaid wire would be carefully scraped away by the sword-maker, just as a jeweler would do. The mark of a good *sirohi* sword is that if you run your finger along its flat surface, the wire and steel would form a single, perfectly smooth surface.

Sketch of Gomukh Temple (right); a deity in the temple (below).

NAKKI LAKE

The name of this lake (right) has a curious origin. The word *nakki* means fingernails, reflecting the belief that the lake was clawed out of the earth by the fingernails of the gods. It is a pretty lake, surrounded by wooded hills, which, as in many Indian hill stations, was the focal point of the entire town. Boating is a popular pastime here, and a walk along the banks is quite pleasant. From here you can see the strange rock formation called "Toad's Rock", one of many fascinating rock formations sculpted by the forces of nature in the area. Southwest of the lake is Sunset Point, with its lovely view of the surrounding hills. From here you can see the sun set spectacularly between two rocky peaks.

GOMUKH TEMPLE

Located about 2 miles from Mount Abu, this is the site of the ancient *agnikunda*, where the great fire rite is said to have been carried out by the Brahmins. Gomukh Temple contains images of Lord Rama and Lord Krishna, both of whom are considered to have been incarnations of Vishnu, "The Preserver" of the Hindu trinity. The name "Gomukh" literally means "cow's face", referring to a spring here which flows through a rock carved in the shape of a cow's mouth. The spring water, said to have sacred, purifying properties, is taken home by pilgrims.

ACHALGARH FORT

The ruins of this 15th-century fort, built by the warrior king, Rana Kumbha, who conquered Mount Abu from its Chauhan rulers ▲ 268, lie 5 miles from Mount Abu. This was one of a girdle of thirty-two forts that he constructed all over Mewar in order to secure the kingdom against invaders. From its crumbling battlements there is a superb view of the surrounding plains. Nearby are the remains of several ancient temples. Of these, the most interesting is the 15th-century temple of Lord Shiva, where you are shown what is said to be Lord Shiva's toenail. It is unusual for a Shiva temple, as it does not have a characteristic *Shivalinga*; instead there is a deep pit that is believed to lead straight down into the underworld. The peak of Guru Shikhar, the highest point in Rajasthan, at an altitude of 5,676 feet, lies 2 ½ miles beyond Achalgarh. There are more dramatic views of the surrounding countryside from here, of wooded hills, waterfalls and the plains.

Plains near Achalgarh Fort.

SIROHI

The little town of Sirohi, once the capital of the Deora Chauhan clan of Rajputs, is situated down on the plains, 36 miles from Mount Abu. Founded in 1347, after the clan had been driven south by the Muslim invaders, Sirohi, protected by the surrounding Aravalli hills, was able to retain its independence in the face of attacks by the Mughals, the Marathas and the Rathors of Marwar. An indication of the volatility of those times is the fact that the 16th- century ruler, Rao Sultan Singh, fought fifty-two battles in the fifty-one years of his reign! Sirohi, a fascinating little town, rather off the usual beaten tourist track, is known for its fine ornamental swords and daggers. Kesar Vilas Palace has some fine gesso ornamentation in gold and white, reminiscent of Junagarh Fort in Bikaner and the City Palace in Jaipur. It is the private property of the Maharao, but if you are lucky, you may be able to obtain permission to see it. There are also some 17th-century frescos in Sirohi Fort and the 1621 *chhatri* of Rao Raj Singh in the nearby fortified hill temple of Sarneshwar Mahadev. One of Sirohi's claims to fame, incidentally, was that it was the very last Rajput kingdom to sign a treaty of "perpetual friendship" with the British: while all the other kingdoms signed treaties between 1817 and 1818, Sirohi held out until 1823.

Achalgarh Fort.

SON OF THE HIMALAYAS
According to legend, Mount Abu is the "Son of the Himalayans". The nearby peak of Guru Shikhar is, in fact, the highest peak between the Himalayas in the north and the Nilgiri Hills in southern India. It takes its name from Arbuda, the great serpent who rescued Lord Shiva's bull, Nandi, from a chasm into which it had fallen.

Throne in Sirohi Palace (above).

The town of Sirohi has twenty-eight temples on one street, which they consider a world record (left).

275

Chittorgarh Fort.

Chittorgarh, the awe-inspiring hill fort built on a massive rock 3 miles long and 495 feet high, lies 72 miles northeast of Udaipur. It was said that this fort was the key to all of Rajputana, and any conqueror who had ambitions on Rajputana had to first wrest control of it. It is considered by many to be the finest medieval Hindu fort in existence. But more than that, it is cloaked in legends of valor, chivalry and glorious death and occupies a preeminent position in the Rajput psyche. Chittorgarh was built in the 8th century by Bappa Rawal (reigned AD 734–53), the first of the great Sisodia rulers (although legend traces it all the way back to Bhima, the mighty warrior of the epic *Mahabharata*). Between then and 1567 it fell victim to three bloody sieges, each one ending in glorious defeat and *jauhar*, the mass self-sacrifice of its womenfolk in a sacred fire.

THE SIEGES OF CHITTORGARH. The first great siege was in 1303, at the hands of Alauddin Khilji, Sultan of Delhi. It is said that the Sultan had heard of the legendary beauty of Rani Padmini, the wife of the then Rana, and requested that he be allowed to gaze at her face, just once. It was finally agreed that although this would not be permitted directly, he would be allowed to see her reflection in the waters of a pool, which in turn would be reflected in a mirror. Having seen her beauty, and being completely smitten by it, the Sultan ambushed and captured the Rana and demanded the hand of

A PRINCESS'S HYMNS
Mirabai, the celebrated 16th-century poet, singer and saint, was a Rajput princess who lived at Chittorgarh. The daughter-in-law of the great warrior king, Rana Sangha, she was an ardent devotee of Lord Krishna, in praise of whom she composed and sang her hymns. It was scandalous in those distant times for a rani to profess her love for anyone but her husband, even if it was a god. There was much intrigue in the court against her, but she stood firm in her devotion, ultimately leaving her family to follow the trail of Lord Krishna to Brindavan and Dwarka. Her hymns are widely sung all over India today.

Mughal miniature portraying the siege of Chittorgarh by Akbar's forces in 1567.

"I GAZED UNTIL THE SUN'S LAST BEAM FELL ON THE 'RINGLET OF CHITTOR', ILLUMINATING ITS GREY AND GRIEF-WORN ASPECT, LIKE A LAMBENT GLEAM LIGHTING UP THE FACE OF SORROW."

COLONEL TOD, *ANNALS AND ANTIQUITIES OF RAJASTHAN*, 1829

Rani Padmini in ransom. The Rajputs agreed and sent a procession of palanquins to Alauddin's camp, ostensibly carrying the Rani and her ladies, but in fact filled with armed warriors. The Rana was rescued, but a massive battle ensued, in which 50,000 Rajput warriors were slain, and Rani Padmini, along with the rest of the womenfolk, threw herself into the flames rather than fall into the hands of the enemy. The *jauhar* was repeated a second time in 1535 when Sultan Bahadur Shah of Gujarat captured Chittorgarh. On this occasion, it is recorded that 32,000 warriors fell on the battlefield and 13,000 womenfolk died in the *jauhar*. The third and final sack of Chittorgarh took place in 1567, at the hands of no other than the Mughal Emperor Akbar. Two young Rajput chieftains, Jaimal and Patta, both in their teens, led the fortress's defense. Both died fighting valiantly, the former with his mother and wife fighting beside him. And, once again, a great *jauhar* was called, and the womenfolk hurled themselves into the flames. It is said that Akbar, on returning to his capital after the fall of Chittorgarh, had statues erected to commemorate the valiant young chieftains, Jaimal and Patta. The ascent to the fort is by a tortuous, winding road, defended by seven fortified gateways. Bhairon Pol was where Jaimal fell, while the innermost, Ram Pol, was where Patta fell. Both these sites are marked by cenotaphs.

RANA KUMBHA'S PALACE. Past the crenelated, loopholed fort wall, you come to the oldest palace of Chittorgarh, Rana Kumbha's palace, with its beautiful series of cantilevered, canopied balconies and a stepped outer wall. Beneath its courtyard is an underground passage leading to the chamber where Rani Padmini is said to have performed *jauhar*. Opposite this palace lies Kunwar Pade ka Mahal ("Crown Prince's Palace"), a wonderful example of early Rajput architecture. Just beyond lies the imposing temple of Vraj-ji, built by Rana Kumbha, and, nearby, the temple of Mirabai, the celebrated 16th-century poet-saint.

TOWER OF VICTORY Vijaystambha, ("Tower of Victory") is an extraordinary structure, visible from the plains below for miles around. Built by Rana Kumbha to celebrate a great victory over the Sultan of Malwa in 1440, the nine-storied structure is profusely carved with images of gods and goddesses. Lithograph of Vijaystambha (below left).

VIJAYSTAMBHA. The real architectural masterpiece at Chittorgarh, however, is Rana Kumbha's great Vijaystambha ("Tower of Victory"), built in a Jain revivalist style. It has been restored subsequently, but if you look at the upper stories, you can see the splendidly carved original panels, depicting a variety of Hindu gods and goddesses. As you walk south from the Vijaystambha, you come to the Mahasati, the terrace where the maharanas were cremated. This was also the site of Chittorgarh's second great *jauhar* in 1535. Just beyond this lies Gomukh, a large tank, fed by a perennial spring through a rock carved with the face of a cow.

Spring water flows from a "cow's mouth" in Gomukh tank.

Kalika Mata Temple (left);
Patta's palace (right).

NOMADIC BLACKSMITHS
The Gadholia Lohars, whom you see all over Rajasthan today, are a tribe of nomadic blacksmiths who trace their origins back to Chittorgarh. The legend goes that after the fall of Chittorgarh in 1567, they vowed that they would not cease to wander until the fortress was reconquered. They have never given up their nomadic ways.

PALACES OF PATTA AND JAIMAL. South of the Gomukh tank are the ruins of a row of great mansions, including those of the heroes who defended Chittorgarh, Patta and Jaimal. These two palaces were among the last of the monuments to be built in the fort before it was destroyed in 1567. Patta's palace echoes the style of the palace of Rana Kumbha and Kunwar Pade ka Mahal, with a stepped wall in the case of the former, and rich decorations in the case of the latter. If you look closely, you can see the ornamented blue tiles that once adorned many of the buildings here. Jaimal's palace, on the other hand, is solid and austere, but displays the perfect symmetry of plan that can be traced back to even the oldest Rajput palaces. Nearby is the Bundi Chief's palace, with its beautiful old pool, lined with bathing terraces, and beyond it lie the ruins of Chittorgarh's old Pearl Market.

KALIKA MATA TEMPLE. Toward the south end of the fort is Kalika Mata Temple, originally dedicated to Surya, the sun god. It dates back to the 8th century, making it the oldest structure in the fort.

PADMINI'S PALACE. Still further south, beyond Chonda's Palace, lies the palace of Rani Padmini ▲ *118*. According to legend, she is said to have been a Sri Lankan princess, so fair and delicate that when she drank water, you could see it pass through her throat! The original palace was a beautiful water palace, a forerunner of the later Jag Mandir and Jag Niwas in Udaipur ▲ *250*. What you see today, however, is a 19th-century recreation that bears little resemblance to the original. However, you are shown a mirror on the wall of an adjacent building and invited to simulate for yourself how Alauddin Khilji must have gazed on the reflection of Rani Padmini in the waters behind him. As you turn north again, and continue along the eastern ramparts, you come to Suraj Pol. Look down on the plains below from here: this is where Akbar's forces are said to have camped during their final campaign for Chittorgarh.

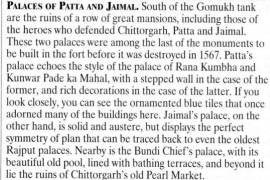

Palace of Padmini.

DIFFERENT ROLES
While Emperor Akbar was responsible for the destruction of Chittorgarh, his father, Humayun, ironically, played a defensive role in its history. In 1535 Rani Karnavati of Chittorgarh, under siege from the Sultan of Gujarat, sent Humayun a *rakhi*, the traditional ornamented wristlet that a sister presents to her brother, and asked for his assistance. Humayun rushed here from Bengal. He defeated the Sultan of Gujarat and expelled him from Chittorgarh.

TOWER OF FAME. Further north lies another fine tower, the seven-story Kirtistambha ("Tower of Fame") (left), dating back to the 12th century and dedicated to the great Jain saint, Adinatha. Still further north, on the great rock of Chittorgarh, lie the ruins of Rana Ratan Singh's beautiful palace. Set by a small lake, it is similar in style to Rana Kumbha's palace, except that it is perfectly rectangular in shape, a fact that is somewhat obscured now by the ruins and subsequent alterations.

THE SOUTHEAST

▲ Kota

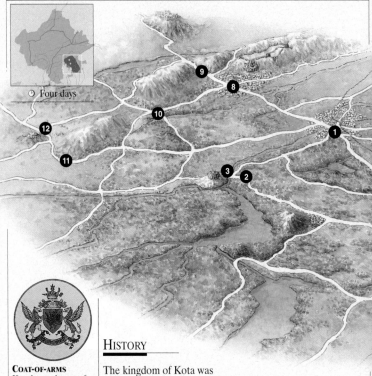

◷ Four days

COAT-OF-ARMS
Kota's royal coat-of-arms shows the great mythological bird, Garuda, the mount of Lord Vishnu, set within a central shield. This is topped by a warrior emerging from the flames, symbolizing the emergence of the ruling family from the great sacred fire at Mount Abu, out of which it is said to have been born ▲ 269. The winged gryphons flanking the shield seem to have a curiously European touch, thought up by the British heraldry experts who were commissioned to devise coats-of-arms for all the Rajput states.

History

The kingdom of Kota was carved out of Bundi in 1579 by a ruler of Bundi as a gift for a favorite younger prince, Rao Madho Singh, who is said to have proven himself as a successful and courageous general at the tender age of fourteen. This great martial tradition continued down the family: fighting on behalf of the ageing Mughal emperor, Shah Jahan, against the usurper prince, Aurangzeb, five of Rao Madho Singh's sons died on the battlefield. The sixth, who narrowly survived, lived on to count no less than fifty wounds on his body, acquired during the course of a long and eventful military career. Kota has a complex history, with great swings of fortune, unlike its sister kingdom of Bundi, hidden away behind its rampart of hills. Menaced over the centuries by various Mughal rulers, the maharajas of Jaipur and Mewar, the Maratha warlords,

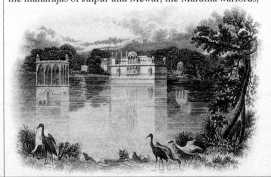

Country seat of the Kota princes (right).

An artist's impression of the city of Kota.

and even sometimes their own cousins in Bundi, the rulers of Kota developed a keenly honed instinct for diplomacy. One result was a treaty with the Marathas in the 18th century to keep the Kachhawaha rulers of Jaipur at bay.

ZALIM SINGH'S LEADERSHIP. It was around this time that Kota produced one of the most fascinating characters of modern Rajput history: Zalim Singh, a statesman and diplomat who has been referred to as the "Talleyrand of North India" and the "Machiavelli of Rajwarra." Starting out as a general of the Kota armies, he became Regent of the kingdom when the ruler died, leaving an infant son on the throne. He then set about manipulating the kingdom's belligerent neighbors, parleying with them and shrewdly setting one against the other. Meanwhile, he also reorganized the kingdom completely, setting up a modern administration, adopting European weapons and tactics for its armies and creating a comprehensive revenue system that taxed everything from widows to brooms. In doing all this, he certainly was not without personal ambition – the result of which was that there were numerous attempts on his life, including a memorable one when he was set up by a rani and attacked by a band of armed ladies in the *purdah* palace.

KOTA AND THE BRITISH. In 1817, under Zalim Singh's leadership, Kota became one of the first of the Rajput states to sign a treaty with the British, in return for which Zalim Singh extracted an agreement that the kingdom would be divided, and a separate kingdom carved out of it for his own descendants. The result was the new kingdom of Jhalawar, formed in 1838. The rulers of Kota had their little revenge on the British: during the great Uprising of 1857, Kota was one of the few states of Rajputana where the Indian troops rebelled, discreetly aided, it is said, by the ruler.

Zalim Singh is famed for the legendary gardens he laid out at Kota. Almost defying the laws of nature, he grew a variety of exotic fruits here, "where even grass could not grow": coconuts and palmyras from Malabar, apples and quinces from Kabul, oranges from Bengal and the famed "golden plantains" from the Deccan. He also, incidentally, invited weavers from Kashmir to settle here in Kota, weaving shawls to rival the finest that Kashmir could produce.

KOTA MINIATURES
The celebrated miniature paintings of the Kota school frequently depict the kingdom's jungle-covered hills and flowing rivers, combining these with scenes of hunting (which was a passion of its maharajas). The Kota school was an offshoot of the Bundi school; it is often difficult to distinguish between the two.

281

SOLAR CLOCK
The sun clock in the Kota Palace Museum incorporated a miniature cannon, which was automatically fired by the sun's rays precisely at noon each day. This signaled the firing of a regular cannon that would indicate the time to the townspeople. Made by the old British firm of Lawrence and Mayo in Bombay, the sun clock was carefully calibrated, so that you could adjust it according to your latitude for perfect accuracy.

City Palace.

KOTA TODAY

Kota today is a complete contrast to its neighboring town, Bundi, only 14 miles away, which seems to be still caught in a medieval time warp. Kota is one of Rajasthan's premier industrial and commercial centers, with a major hydro-electric plant, an atomic power station, as well as various manufacturing industries, ranging from precision instruments to synthetic fibers. Unfortunately, the city has paid a price for this – losing a great deal of its olden-day character. However, it has some interesting palaces and old Indo-Victorian public buildings, such as the Herbert College, Curzon Wylie Memorial, and Crossthwaite Institute. But even more interesting, perhaps, is the fact that it is the key to a fascinating and largely undiscovered region of Rajasthan, studded with forts, temples, pleasure palaces and opportunities for wildlife safaris.

CITY PALACE

Built from 1625 onward, Kota's City Palace reflects the city's stormy history – its exterior marrying rugged bastions and ramparts with delicate cupolas and balustrades. Basically Rajput in form, it also reflects the close connections the kingdom had with the Mughals in its graceful Mughal-style design elements. The palace is a rambling complex of suites and apartments built by different rulers at different times. You enter through the 17th-century Hathi Pol ("Elephant Gate"), typical of the Hadauti region of southwest Rajasthan in design, with its bracketed elephants forming an archway with their raised trunks. Inside lies the grand Raj Mahal, with ornate medieval glass and mirror inlay-work covering its walls and ceilings. There are also some fine 18th-century frescos here, mainly depicting scenes from the legends of Lord Krishna. Adjoining this is a gallery with a fine collection of period Rajput weaponry, including Prithviraj Chauhan's historic scimitar and a fascinating array of old firearms, many of them superbly inlaid with gold and ivory. Beyond this lies another gallery with old family photographs from the Maharaja's personal albums, depicting the princely lifestyle of the 19th century. Still further beyond lies an art gallery with some interesting examples of *Kotah Kalaam* miniature paintings. (Look, for instance, for the amusing scene of the holy man being entertained by

"The appearance of Kotah is very imposing, and impresses the mind with a more lively notion of wealth and activity than most cities in India."

Colonel Tod, *Annals and Antiquities of Rajasthan*, 1829

devoted ladies of the court.) Across the courtyard outside is Akhade ka Mahal ("The Palace of the Wrestling Arena"), where there is a collection of treasures and memorabilia of the maharajas, from an elephant *howdah* and ivory palanquin to a mysterious-looking 17th-century astronomical device. Bhim Mahal, on the first floor, has some superb friezes of Rajput miniature paintings covering its walls, set off by beautiful ebony and ivory inlaid doors. Climbing up the stairs you come to Bada Mahal and Chhatar Mahal, with more exquisite paintings, ornate glass inlay and frescos. However, these lie in the personal palace of the maharaja and require special permission to visit. In the ornate Hawa Mahal ("Palace of the Winds") is the Government Museum, with some excellent stone carvings and antiquities.

LETHAL WEAPON
Yet another of the strange and bloodthirsty weapons of the Rajputs, these *bhujtrans* in the Kota Palace Museum are shaped rather like knuckle-dusters, but with three lethal daggers in place of mere studs.

BRIJRAJ BHAWAN

Another interesting palace, now converted into a hotel and therefore accessible to travelers, is Brijraj Bhawan. Built in 1840, high above the banks of the River Chambal, this white-pillared colonial building was once the British Residency and is said to be haunted by the ghost (apparently benign) of the Resident, Major Charles Burton, who was killed here during the Uprising of 1857.

UMED BHAWAN

Umed Bhawan Palace, designed by Sir Swinton Jacob ▲ *134* and built in 1904, is a charming creation in beige stone that seems more Edwardian than Rajput, with features such as a billiard room, tennis courts and a beautiful English-style garden, well known for its beautiful herbaceous borders. It is now the personal residence of the maharaja.

Interior of Umed Bhawan Palace.

JAGMANDIR

Jagmandir is a graceful 18th-century pleasure palace built on the waters of Kishor Sagar Lake, along the lines of Udaipur's Jag Niwas Palace. Colonel Tod described it as "a little fairy islet with its light Saracenic summer abode". A trifle neglected today, it makes a picturesque sight reflected in the lake's waters. Nearby, on the shore, are the splendid old royal cenotaphs, also, alas, in a state of neglect.

Ivory palanquin.

Jagmandir.

Kansuan Temple.

Kota is known for its gossamer-fine Kota Doria fabrics, woven with a cotton warp and silk weft, and often embellished with delicate floral motifs. The fabrics have an interesting history behind them. The weavers were brought here from faraway Mysore in the 17th century by the then Rao of Kota, who discovered them during his military campaigns in south India. Incidentally,

the handicraft still flourishes here, while it has died out in its original home in Mysore. The fabric is also called Kota-Masuria, recalling its ancestry.

Weaving the fine Kota Doria fabric.

Temple ruins at Baroli (above). Ghateshwara Temple (center).

KANSUAN TEMPLE

This ancient Shiva temple, with an inscription dating back to AD 738, lies 6 miles from Kota. Within a walled enclosure is the main temple and various smaller shrines, pavilions and *Shivalingas*. It must have been an extremely beautiful temple once, but is now in a somewhat weathered condition.

BAROLI TEMPLES

The ruins of this superb 9th–12th century temple complex (left), one of the finest of its kind in Rajasthan, picturesquely sited in a forest, are located 34 miles southwest of Kota. Colonel Tod, visiting the Baroli Temples in 1820, was so impressed that he proceeded to devote entire eleven pages of his book, *Annals and Antiquities of Rajasthan,* to the wonders he saw there. The principal temple of the complex is Ghateshwara Temple (center), with its richly ornamented porch, ceilings and pillars, the latter exquisitely carved with images of celestial nymphs. The *shikhara,* or pagoda, is profusely and delicately embellished, and there are some elegant sculptures set around the walls: a dancing Shiva; Shiva slaying the demon, Andhaka; and Chamunda. By the sanctum doorway is another dancing Shiva, this one surrounded by Brahma, Vishnu and various other mythological figures. Do not miss the temple's wonderfully carved *torana* archway. Two other temples within the complex that are especially interesting are the 10th-century Trimurti and Mahishasuramardini temples. Near the former are the carved columns of an old gateway, decorated with gracefully proportioned maidens, devotees and floral garlands.

In Mahishasuramardini Temple, do take a close look at the curved pagoda, with its intricately etched motifs, almost like a fine screen. There is also a picturesque little Shiva temple nearby, set inside a pool of water.

> "To describe its [the Baroli Temples'] stupendous and diversified architecture is impossible…The carving on the capital of each column would require pages of explanation."
>
> Colonel Tod, *Annals and Antiquities of Rajasthan*, 1829

Bhensrorgarh Fort

Colonel Tod wrote in the 1820's, "The Castle of Bhainsror is most romantically situated upon the extreme point of a ridge." The ridge itself is composed of solid rock, 230 feet high, just a few miles beyond Baroli. Protected by the River Chambal on two sides, this 14th-century fort was once one of the most powerful in Rajasthan – it was never captured. It is worth seeing on your way back from Baroli to Kota.

Bhensrorgarh Fort.

Darrah Wildlife Sanctuary

Darrah, once the private hunting grounds of the maharajas of Kota – and the place where many of the splendid hunt scenes in the Kota miniature paintings were set – is situated 35 miles south of Kota. Spread over an area of 106 square miles, these forests were once thick with everything from tigers to rhinoceros. Today neither the wildlife nor the forests themselves are as rich as they used to be, but Darrah is still worth visiting. You can view animals such as the leopard, sloth bear, *chinkara* and wolf, from the old hunting boxes of the maharajas.

The word *darrah* literally means a "pass", and these forests were once a place of great strategic importance, opening up the hills of Hadauti to the plains of Malwa in the east. They were also the scene of several battles between the Rajputs, the Marathas and, later, the British. Another very pretty, and almost totally undiscovered, little sanctuary 30 miles southeast of Kota is Sorsan. It is a naturalist's paradise, with its rich species of birdlife, and reputedly the best place in India to view the endangered great Indian bustard ■ 27.

Within the Shiva Temple at Ramgarh are some very interesting erotic sculptures (above), reminiscent of those at Khajuraho.

Ramgarh

Located 40 miles north of Kota, Ramgarh is known for its fine 10th-century temple ruins, accessible only by jeep and therefore somewhat off the beaten track. Here, in the middle of the wilderness, is a Shiva temple, carved in rich mauve-brown stone, with superbly ornamented columns. Nearby are several other ruins, notably Kishnai Mata Temple, sited on a hilltop. There's also a ruined medieval palace by the side of the hill.

Temple at Ramgarh.

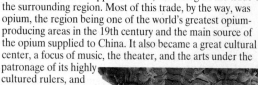

Garh Palace, Jhalawar.

COAT-OF-ARMS
The Jhalawar coat-of-arms depicts Hanuman, the great monkey-god of the epic *Ramayana*, on the central shield. The shield is flanked by a horse and a lion. A trident is positioned over the shield to represent the Goddess Durga.

JHALAWAR

Jhalawar, 54 miles south of Kota, is a fascinating little Rajput town, all the more interesting because it is relatively undiscovered, and therefore quite unspoiled. It also lies in one of the most scenic parts of Rajasthan, and the drive from Kota, through the Darrah forest, is in itself a part of the experience. Jhalawar (literally "Place of the Jhala Clan") was the principality specially set up for that remarkable 19th-century statesman, Zalim Singh, in 1838, on the understanding that it would be ruled by his descendants ▲ *281*. Zalim Singh encouraged the wealthiest people of the region to settle here and set up an amazingly modern, well-planned town. It was, in fact, the first town anywhere in India to have its own municipality. Progressive a man as he was, he also had, back in those feudal days, a charter of rights of the city inscribed on a stone pillar, which made Colonel Tod observe that it had elements of "that commercial greatness which made the free cities of Europe the instruments of general liberty." As a result the town soon became "the grand commercial mart of Upper Malwa", absorbing all the trade of the surrounding region. Most of this trade, by the way, was opium, the region being one of the world's greatest opium-producing areas in the 19th century and the main source of the opium supplied to China. It also became a great cultural center, a focus of music, the theater, and the arts under the patronage of its highly cultured rulers, and actually boasted one of the finest Western-style opera houses in India.

RAVI AND UDAY SHANKAR
The family of the celebrated *sitar* maestro, Ravi Shankar, is from Jhalawar. Originally from the distant state of Bengal, they moved to Jhalawar, where Ravi Shankar's father was the Prime Minister. His old family bungalow is still here.
The legendary oriental dancer, Uday Shankar (Ravi Shankar's elder brother), who grew up in Jhalawar, danced at the Natyashala long before he was discovered by Anna Pavlova in Europe, with whom he later danced.

Interior of Surya Temple, Jhalrapatan (center).

JHALAWAR TODAY. Jhalawar is a sleepy little town which belies the highly progressive spirit of its 19th-century beginnings. Visiting the old Garh Palace of the maharajas is a slightly bizarre experience, for its marvelously frescoed 1840's halls and chambers have now been converted into government offices, and you

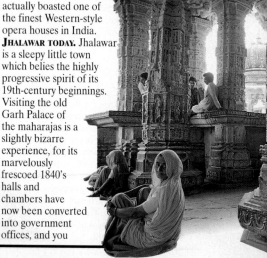

wander from office to office, peeping past conferring officials at the gloriously decorated walls and ceilings. The Deputy Superintendent's office with its glass paintings and mirrored ceilings is perhaps the only one of its kind in Rajasthan. Valiant efforts are being made by conservationists to preserve the frescos. Within the palace walls is Bhawani Natya Shala, the old theater, built along the lines of the opera houses that Maharaja Bhawani Singh (reigned 1899–1929) had seen in Europe, fitted with a remarkable acoustic system. Nearby is the Government Museum with some very good old sculptures from the 8th-century ruined township of Chandravati nearby. The oldest exhibit here is a stone inscription, dating back to the 5th century.

Opera theater in palace, Jhalawar.

JHALRAPATAN

Adjoining Jhalawar is the ancient walled town of Jhalrapatan (or, picturesquely, "The Town of the Temple Bells"). It was once a temple town with no less than 108 temples. The finest of them is the 11th-century Surya Temple, with its ornately carved 10-foot high curved dome, surrounded by miniature tower-like motifs of different sizes. The temple is reminiscent of the famous Surya Temple at Konarak. It used to house a spectacular gold image of the sun god, said to have been the finest in India, but this was carried away by dacoits who plundered the temple in 1857. There are some fine carvings on the *torana* archway and the columns, which are worth taking a close look at. What is also interesting is the quaint, lithographed European-style tiles of Lord Vishnu and Lord Krishna on either side of the sanctum. Nearby are three other ancient Hindu temples and a fascinating 11th-century Jain temple. At the Jain temple, take a look at the curious painted frieze of murals on a wall in one of the corners, graphically specifying the punishments in the hereafter for various lapses in behavior. The bazaars of Jhalrapatan are especially interesting to wander through, with their colorful hodge-podge of little shops, temples and old houses.

Surya Temple, Jhalrapatan (left), and detail of sculpture from the temple (above).

PRITHVI VILAS
Originally built as a garden-house in the mid-19th century, the Prithvi Vilas was expanded at the turn of the century to accommodate the personal library of Maharaja Bhawani Singh. Its collection of European books is today considered one of the finest in Rajasthan and contains many hand-painted manuscripts and first editions.

Chandravati Temples: doorway (right) and a view of the temple grounds (below).

PROTECTED BY WATER AND JUNGLE

According to the ancient Sanskrit texts, there were basically six types of forts: *dhanva durg* (protected by desert), *giri durg* (protected by mountains), *mahi durg* (protected by mud walls), *nara durg* (protected by men), *jala durg* (protected by water) and *vana durg* (protected by jungle). Obviously, in the largely desert area of Rajasthan, the last two types of forts are the most uncommon. However, Gagron Fort is an example of both a *jala durg* and a *vana durg*, having been protected both by the river that forms its natural moat and the thick forest that once grew here.

CHANDRAVATI TEMPLES

Gagron Fort.

Just outside Jhalawar are the ruins of the ancient temple town of Chandravati ("The Gardens of the Moon"), one of India's most ancient towns. Here you can see, by the banks of a stream, a group of temples dating back to the 6th century. Chandramauleshwar Temple, in particular, is an outstanding example of ancient temple art, with its ornately carved pillars and gateways. It was described by Cunningham, the well-known 19th-century archeologist, as one of the finest of its kind in India. Chandravati was once one of India's most important centers of dance and music. The temples here, with their traditional temple dancers, contributed greatly to the evolution of classical Indian dance forms.

Life-sized Ganesha in old temple at Kakuni.

GAGRON FORT

The splendid Gagron Fort, a rare example of a *jala durg* (a fort protected by water) in Rajasthan, lies 6 miles from Jhalawar. Spectacularly located at the confluence of two rivers and set against a backdrop of hills, this fort has had a long and turbulent 1200-year history, having gone through fourteen major battles and three acts of *jauhar*, when the womenfolk immolated themselves in the sacred fire rather than fall into the hands of the enemy. Sultan Alauddin Khilji of Delhi is said to have besieged it – unsuccessfully – for eleven years. Captured ultimately by the Mughal emperor Akbar in 1561, it was ceded to the Maharaja of Kota in 1715 by the Mughals. The interiors of the fort are now in ruins, overgrown with weeds, but you can still see the remains of the township that was located inside here, with its barracks, stables, gunpowder magazine, and beautiful palace complex. Wandering through the palace, you can see the remains of its ornately carved walls, canopied balconies and even the hooks in the ceilings for the traditional swings that the rulers must have reclined upon.

PARROT'S TONGUE
Gagron is famed for its "Ram Tota" parrots. Much sought after, as they are reputed to be the finest talking parrots in India.

Temple ruins.

KAKUNI

The ancient ruins of Kakuni, a majestic group of temples dating back to the 8th century, are scattered in the wilderness 40 miles east of Jhalawar. Here, you can see an enormous, life-sized idol of Lord Ganesha, the elephant-headed god of fortune, and the impressive 8th-century *Shivalinga*, the phallic symbol of Lord Shiva. Evidence shows that this was once an important town, a major center of trade and religion. Nearby, across the river, lie the ruins of Bhimgarh Fort, also worth visiting.

SHERGARH FORT

This splendid medieval fort, 33 miles east of Jhalawar, is another fine example of a *jala durg* or water fort. Built on the banks of the river Parwan, it was renamed after Sher Shah, the 16th-century Afghan ruler of Delhi. However, evidence shows that its history goes back much earlier, to the 10th century, when there was a major center of Shiva worship here. Subsequently Jain religious influences played an important role. Take a look at the fort walls, which have interesting statues and icons from different periods of history embedded in them. Later Shergarh became an important frontier fort of the Kota kingdom, the first line of defence against its belligerent neighbors in Malwa.

MANGO ORCHARDS
According to a local legend, during Sultan Alauddin Khilji's eleven-year siege of Gagron Fort, his soldiers ate a ration of mangos. It is said that the mango seeds they threw away gave birth to the noted mango orchards of this area.

An old painting of Bundi town, dominated by the imposing Taragarh Fort.

COAT-OF-ARMS
Bundi's royal coat-of-arms depicts a Hara Chauhan warrior emerging from the flames of the sacred *agni-kunda* fire pit. On either side of the shield are bulls, representing *dharma*, or piety. It is topped by a diagonal *katar* or dagger, which, according to Rudyard Kipling, was "in commemoration of the defeat of an Imperial Prince who rebelled against the Delhi Throne in the days of Jehangir".

The town of Bundi.

FATAL ENCOUNTER
An ancient prophecy made by a dying *sati* foretold that if a maharao of Bundi and a maharana of Mewar should ever meet at the annual Aheria (Bundi's ritual spring hunt), one of the two would surely die. Over the next three centuries, it is said, such a meeting took place four times, and on each of the four occasions, one of the two princes ended up being slain by the other.

HISTORY

The rulers of the kingdom of Bundi were Hara Chauhans, a clan of warriors said to have been born from the ancient fire ceremony conducted by the Brahmins on top of Mount Abu to save the land from a plague of demons ▲ *269*. They were considered superior to all of the other Rajput clans, having been born not of woman, but of the sacred fire. Originally, the Hara Chauhans ruled Ajmer, but after being defeated by Muhammad Ghori, in 1192, they drifted down to Mewar. One of the great Hara chieftains in the 14th century was Rao Dewa, of whom it is said that he possessed a magnificent horse, so swift that it could cross a stream "without wetting its hooves". The Sultan of Delhi coveted the horse and tried to imprison Rao Dewa, but the latter escaped, shouting out the admonishment, "There are three things you must never ask of a Rajput: his horse, his mistress and his sword." It was this spirit of pride perhaps that led Rao Dewa out of Mewar into the rocky hills of the Chambal Valley, where in 1342, he founded the kingdom of Haravati ("The Garden of the Haras"), with its capital at Bundi. Here the Haras ruled, largely protected from the influences of the outside world by the hill country around them.

BUNDI AND THE MUGHALS. When the Mughal emperor Akbar began his policy of winning over the allegiance of the Rajputs in the mid-16th century, he guaranteed Rao Suran of Bundi religious freedom and regal privileges for his descendants. Subsequently, the rulers of Bundi became one of the Mughals' closest allies in Hindustan. In fact, it is said that in two battles on behalf of the Mughal emperors in the 17th century, the Bundi armies lost twelve royal princes and the head of every single Hara clan. One of the great rulers of Bundi in the 17th century was Rao Chhatar Sal, who served the Mughals with such distinction that Emperor Shah Jahan

A step-well inside Taragarh Fort.

made him the Governor of the imperial city of Delhi, a rare privilege for a Rajput. He was a loyal ally, and when the usurper prince, Aurangzeb, tried to woo him over in his battle for the throne, Rao Chhatar Sal refused, even in the face of the greatest of temptations. He was killed fighting Aurangzeb at the head of a *gole*, a terrifying battle formation invented by the Bundi armies, whereby they formed a tight circle, bristling with spears and swords, and rushed at the enemy "like an angry porcupine". It was a highly effective tactic in its time, but became a suicidal exercise with the introduction of artillery. And yet the Bundi armies defiantly persisted with it. Apart from fighting on behalf of their Mughal allies, the rulers of Bundi were continually at war with their powerful and somewhat overbearing Rajput neighbors: the maharanas of Mewar could never forget that Bundi had originally been carved out of Mewar's territories and therefore constantly attempted to subjugate it. Later the maharajas of the increasingly powerful kingdom of Amber tried repeatedly to annex Bundi's territories, leading Rao Umed Singh to lament that the kingdom he inherited was nothing more than "a heap of cotton".

BUNDI AND THE BRITISH. In 1818 Bundi succumbed to the British and signed a treaty with them, like all the other Rajput kingdoms. However, despite this fact, the maharaos of Bundi steadfastly refused to admit any British influence in their state.

BUNDI TODAY

Remote as it is in its hilly terrain, Bundi continues to be a place where life is largely untouched by the outside world. In fact, even today, Bundi is one place in Rajasthan that has a delightfully medieval flavor – visiting it is like stepping into some kind of time warp. The town nestles at the foot of a large rocky hill, dominated by Taragarh Fort and Garh Palace. It is a town of numerous ornate step-wells dating back to the 17th century. The tiny, winding lanes of its bazaars are among the most fascinating you will find anywhere in Rajasthan.

CITY OF WELLS
Bundi has been known as a "city of wells", with over fifty beautifully designed old step-wells and tanks. One of the finest examples is Sabirna-dha-ka-Kund, a deep 17th-century step-well, whose marvelous geometry gave the maximum number of people access to the water, regardless of erratic annual fluctuations in the water level.

Portrait of Maharao Raja Sir Raghubir Singh Bahadur of Bundi, a colorful man who paid special attention to traditional regalia and ceremony.

Cityscape as seen from the Fort.

▲ GARH PALACE

GARH PALACE

THUNDEROUS!
The Bhim Burj bastion was built to house Bundi's famous 16th-century cannon, Garbh Gunjam, one of the largest, most feared artillery pieces of medieval Rajputana. Its sound was so terrifying that, legend says, it used to cause pregnant women to lose their unborn children.

Garh Palace.

Garh Palace is not a single palace but actually a whole complex of different palaces, built by different rulers at different times. Hugging the steep hillside, the complex looks, if viewed from above, like a checkerboard. The most impressive of all the palaces, however, is Chhattar Mahal, built by Rao Chhattar Sal in 1660. Rao Chhattar Sal was a veteran of fifty-two battles and a man of unbending pride. It is perhaps characteristic of the man, therefore, that despite his closeness to the Mughal emperors, he allowed no Mughal influence to dilute the proud Rajput style of his palace. The material he used was not the sandstone that was favored by the Mughals (and by other Rajput princes), but the green serpentine from Bundi's own quarries. Nor did Rao Chhattar Sal use the arches and columns typical of the Mughal style of architecture; instead he retained the traditional Rajput style, with its characteristic lotus-flower spandrels, recurrent elephant motifs, richly ornamented brackets and a profusion of drooping, arcuated roofs, kiosks, and pavilions. A steep ramp takes you up through two towering gates, Hazari Pol ("The Gate of the One Thousand") and Hathi Pol ("Elephant Gate"). Hathi Pol is topped with two enormous elephants with raised trunks, once apparently cast from brass, but later replaced by plaster elephants painted in bright yellows, reds, and blues. Through Hathi Pol you come to a small, rough courtyard faced by an arched arcade and stables. (It is very clear that this palace was a warrior's retreat, and not some luxurious Mughal-style court.) Here you will find the Diwan-i-Am ("Hall of Public Audience"), with a white marble throne set

> "THE PALACE OF BOONDI, EVEN IN BROAD DAYLIGHT, IS SUCH A PALACE THAT MEN BUILD FOR THEMSELVES IN UNEASY DREAMS – THE WORK OF GOBLINS RATHER THAN OF MEN."
>
> RUDYARD KIPLING, *LETTERS OF MARQUE*, 1899

in a canopied balcony, from where the maharaos would give audience to their subjects in the courtyard below. To the right lies the celebrated Chitra Mahal ("Palace of the Paintings"). In front of Chitra Mahal is a splendid courtyard, now overgrown, where fountains once played and goldfish swam in lily-pools. It was probably this courtyard that prompted Colonel Tod to write in the 1820's that "whoever has seen the Palace of Boondi can easily picture to himself the Hanging Gardens of Semiramis". Around this courtyard lies a gallery lavishly decorated with murals, some of the finest ever in the history of Rajput art. Painted in the style of the Bundi school of miniatures, these murals are executed in the characteristic shades of blue, green, and maroon (above). They cover a wide range of subjects: on the maroon dados are depicted a series of elephant fights; higher up are scenes from the legends of Lord Krishna, battle scenes, lovers' trysts, and scenes of Garh Palace as it was during the 19th century, including an interesting panel on Chitra Mahal itself. (Be sure you look inside the inner chamber of the gallery, with its murals in glowing colors, untouched by the effects of sunlight and rain over the centuries.) Garh Palace had had a dark and tangled history, and there are numerous chilling legends associated with it, like that of Hada Rani, who beheaded herself and had her head sent to her husband on the eve of battle, so that he would not be distracted by thoughts of her while fighting the enemy.

A BEEHIVE OF ACTIVITY
When Rudyard Kipling visited Bundi's Garh Palace, he saw some of the later frescos being painted. He noted that there was a great deal of activity and noise there, like "a broken beescomb, with the whole hive busily at work".

The results are fine examples of wall paintings in the distinctive Bundi style, with subjects ranging from palace life to scenes of Lord Krishna and the *gopis*.

"The *coup d'œil* of the castellated Palace of Boondi, from whichever side you approach it, is perhaps the most striking in India." Colonel Tod, *Annals and Antiquities of Rajasthan*, 1829

Walls of fort.

MISSING TREASURE
According to an old
legend, there is a
secret treasure
hidden inside
Taragarh Fort that
each ruler was
allowed to visit just
once in his lifetime.
The treasure was
guarded over the
centuries by a family
of loyal Pathan
retainers.
Unfortunately, the
last of the old
Pathans died during
World War Two,
taking the secret of
the treasure with him.
When the young
Maharao Bahadur
Singh returned from
Burma, where he was
serving during the
War, he launched a
major treasure hunt
within the fort,
but nothing
was found.
The
treasure
must still
be there
somewhere.

The steep ramps of
Taragarh Fort down
which the water
gushes during the
annual flooding
▲ 297.

TARAGARH FORT

Taragarh ("Star Fort") dominates the top of a steep, craggy hill, with a magnificent view of the Aravalli hills on one side and the dusty plains on the other. Like many other Rajput forts, it was conceived in such a way that it provided a final point of retreat from the palace in times of siege. The two, in fact, form a single complex, with an outwork of the fort wall encircling the palace wall and providing it with a formidable double fortification. The fort's outer walls are, in many places, over 10 feet thick and run for miles along the hillsides. Yet, as Rao Umed Singh once said, these walls "are not required against an equal foe, and are no defence against a superior foe…Bundi's best defence is always its hills." You enter the fort through a strongly fortified main gate to find that it is roughly square in shape, with large bastions at each corner (below). The fort is dominated by a huge masonry tower called Bhim Burj, built in the 16th century to house Bundi's legendary cannon, the Garbh Gunjam (which roughly translates as "The Thunder that Echoes in the Womb") ▲ 292. It was one of the most powerful – and dreaded – artillery pieces in all of Rajputana. Its sound was so loud that a deep pit was provided alongside the emplacement, into which its gun crew had to jump after lighting its fuse, in order to protect their eardrums! Today there is not much else left standing within the fort, apart from the old water tank that provided the garrison's water supply and Rani Mahal, with its fading murals and stained-glass windows. But most interesting of all are the tales of the secret underground passages that are said to have once honeycombed the entire hillside, leading to the palace, the town below and the neighboring hills, to provide a variety of escape routes for the fort's defenders. These secrets, alas, are now lost forever.

It has been estimated that there are approximately one thousand different styles and types of turban in Rajasthan.

WHAT THE TURBAN REVEALS

A *safa* (turban) is much more than a just an item of headgear to protect the wearer from the sun's heat. By its shape, color, and size it tells you a great deal about the man, such as where he comes from, what he does for a living, and his position in society. A *safa* is about 30 feet long and about 4 feet wide. It was traditionally considered an essential part of a man's clothing, and to appear in public without one was a sign of grossly bad behavior. The color, pattern, and style of tying a turban vary according to community, region, and even district. Thus it is said that the dialect of men's turbans changes every 12 miles in Rajasthan. *Safa*-tying is considered a fine art. Men who have mastered it take great pride in the fact. Some colors and patterns are seasonal, such as the white and red *falguniya* turban that is worn in spring. Others signify family circumstances; for instance, the dotted *chunri* pattern or bright colors signify a marriage or the birth of a child. On the other hand, colors like dark blue, maroon, or khaki signify a death in the family. Wearing the wrong type of turban under the wrong circumstances can make you an object of ridicule.

RANIJI KI BAORI

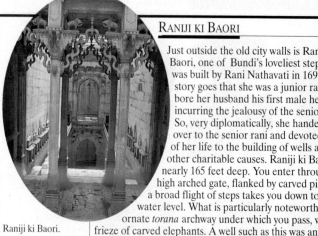

Just outside the old city walls is Raniji ki Baori, one of Bundi's loveliest step-wells. It was built by Rani Nathavati in 1699. The story goes that she was a junior rani who bore her husband his first male heir, incurring the jealousy of the senior rani. So, very diplomatically, she handed her son over to the senior rani and devoted the rest of her life to the building of wells and to other charitable causes. Raniji ki Baori is nearly 165 feet deep. You enter through a high arched gate, flanked by carved pillars, and a broad flight of steps takes you down to the water level. What is particularly noteworthy is the ornate *torana* archway under which you pass, with its frieze of carved elephants. A well such as this was an important center of the town's social and religious life in the olden days.

Raniji ki Baori.

BUNDI MINIATURES
Bundi miniature paintings are considered to be among the finest in Rajasthan ● *65*. Reaching their zenith in the 18th century, they are known for their brilliant colors, their elegant sense of design and their masterful technique. Favorite subjects were court and hunting scenes and episodes from the Radha and Krishna mythology. But what is most fascinating is the depictions of sensuous Bundi maidens, bathing, pining for absent lovers, flirting, or sometimes indulging in more wine than is good for them.

CHAURASI KHAMBON KI CHHATRI

Chaurasi Khambon ki Chhatri ("Cenotaph with the eighty-four Pillars") (right) was raised in memory of Deva, the son of the wet nurse of Rao Raja Anirudh Singh, in 1683. Built on a high platform, this unique double *chhatri* has a large *Shivalinga* in the center – which makes it both a temple as well as a cenotaph. The sides of the plinth are covered with delicate sculptures of various beasts, and beautiful etchings decorate the columns. The ceiling is covered with paintings depicting various subjects, from battle scenes to traditional fish symbols.

SUKH MAHAL

Sukh Mahal is a delicate pleasure palace, built in 1773, on Sukh Sagar Lake, which was supposed to have been the scene of a great deal of revelry between the princes of Bundi and the ladies of their court. Around the lake you can see the low forested hills which once teemed with wildlife, and which were the scene of Bundi's great Aheria ▲ *290*, the celebrated annual boar hunt that heralded the coming of spring. Further down the lakeside is Shikar Burj, an old hunting lodge of Bundi's maharaos.

KESAR BAGH

On the other side of the lake from Sukh Mahal lie the old cenotaphs – sixty-six of them – commemorating Bundi's

Kesar Bagh (left);
Sukh Niwas (right).

kings, queens and princes. The garden is now overgrown with weeds, but the cenotaphs are beautiful, many of them with elegantly carved marble ceilings, decorative friezes and elephants, and topped with a characteristic *Shivalinga*. They span, between them, a period of two-and-a-half centuries, from 1581 to 1821.

BAZAARS

In the tiny, twisting lanes of Sadar Bazaar and Chaumukh Bazaar (left) at the base of Taragarh Hill, you will discover one of the quaintest bazaars in Rajasthan today, virtually untouched by the outside influences that creep into the larger towns. Some of the shops – as you can tell from looking at their architecture and crumbling masonry – date back to the 17th century. You can browse in them for items such as silver jewelry or brightly colored turbans.

BIJOLIYAN TEMPLES

On the road to Chittorgarh are the ruins of three temples rising out of a field, just outside the fortified walls of Bijoliyan. This, sadly, is all that remains of a complex of over one hundred temples built here from the 11th century onward. The finest of these is the 13th-century Undeshwar Temple, with its curving pagoda covered with bands of beautifully carved stone motifs. It represents a tradition of ancient Hindu architecture, according to which surface decoration was just as important as structural form. The unusual feature of this temple is that the inner sanctum is submerged in water, out of which you can see a *Shivalinga* emerge. Nearby is the Mandakini Kund temple tank and two other temples, including a lovely, old Ganesha temple, which has the unusual feature of four elevated *chhatris* surrounding its main pagoda. There is also a fine image of Ganesha guarding the entrance. In the surrounding fields you can see the ruins of other old temples. This was the site of a great cultural center of the Chauhan kingdom, and inscriptions found in the temples, dating back to 1170, give us the first ever historical mention of the city of Delhi.

Temples of Menal.

GOLD ARROWHEAD
Mandalgarh is an ancient Solanki fort lying 20 miles south of Menal. Rebuilt by Rana Kumbha of Mewar, it became one of the most important of his chain of thirty-two forts, because of its strategic location at the gates of Mewar. Captured by Emperor Akbar during his campaign against Chittorgarh, it was later recaptured by the maharanas of Mewar in 1706. The fort has an interesting legend behind it. According to Colonel Tod, a local Bhil named Mandu, while sharpening his arrow on a stone, suddenly found that his arrowhead had turned to gold. He immediately took the *paras patthar* (philosopher's stone) to his chieftain, who used the resultant wealth to build this fine fort, which he named Mandalgarh after the fortunate Bhil.

MENAL

In the middle of beautifully wooded ravines, 10 miles from Bijoliyan, is a gorge of the Menal River, and the ruins of what used to be a 12th-century mountain retreat of the great raja, Prithviraj Chauhan ● *35, 55*. On the banks of the river are the ruins of an ancient palace, and nearby, a complex of beautiful temples. You enter the complex through a handsome double-story gateway carved with images of Bhairava and Ganesha. In the courtyard is an imposing Shiva temple, a wonderful example of the western Indian temple style, but also incorporating central Indian elements, such as the meshed bands in the middle of its pagoda and tiers of miniature tower-like motifs on either side. On the walls are graceful carvings of Shiva and Parvati in various aspects, as well as of dancers, attendants, musicians and animals, including, halfway up the tower, a curious mythical lion. Opposite the Shiva temple lie the ruins of several other smaller temples, one of which has a beautifully carved double *torana* archway.

HINDOLI FORT

The long-forgotten 15th-century hill fort of Hindoli (left) lies 9 miles northwest of Bundi. Described by Professor Herman Goetz as "a gem of early Rajput architecture", it is visited by only very few people today. Set among low hills surrounding a picturesque lake, it has all the strength and austerity of design of classical Rajput architecture prior to the ornamental influences of the Muslims. Yet, its walls and apartments are notable for their perfect harmony of proportion. With its strategic location on the frontier guarding Bundi from powerful Mewar, Hindoli had a dramatic history, changing hands several times over the centuries. For a while it was occupied by Maharana Pratap of Mewar (who added to its fortifications) but finally, in 1659, it was won back by Rao Bhao Singh of Bundi. As Professor Goetz wrote, "in the dust of these ruins there still lives the breath of the Golden Age of early Rajput civilization".

Bharatpur to Karauli

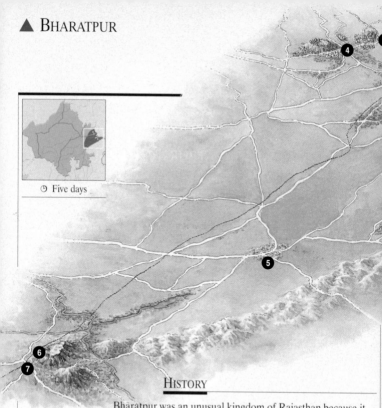

⏲ Five days

COAT-OF-ARMS
The Bharatpur coat-of-arms depicts a shield flanked by a lion and an elephant, the symbol of royalty. The shield itself bears a bull, symbolizing piety, and a pair of crossed *katars* or daggers. All this is topped by the representation of a fort flying the banner of Hanuman, the great monkey god of the epic *Ramayana*. The motto beneath says "Shri Gokulendurjati". Jats being of peasant stock, the maharajas of Bharatpur were never completely accepted by the other Rajput princes of Rajasthan despite all their efforts to assert their royal status.

HISTORY

Bharatpur was an unusual kingdom of Rajasthan because it was the only one that was ruled by a dynasty of Jats – peasant sons of the soil – rather than Rajputs ● 35. Under its aggressive rulers, the kingdom of Bharatpur became a major military and political force in the 18th and 19th centuries, its armies sweeping the plains of northern India, virtually lords and masters of all they surveyed. However, the history of Bharatpur goes back far, far earlier, to the great ancient kingdom of Matsyadesh that flourished here around the 5th century BC. There are several fine archeological remains of this civilization which you can see in the Bharatpur Museum.
17TH AND 18TH CENTURIES. The region came to the fore in the late 17th century when a powerful Jat village headman named Churaman rose up against the Mughals. His armies ranged the countryside, raiding and pillaging, until finally in 1721, the Mughals came down with a heavy hand, killed Churaman and smashed the Jat strongholds. The Jats, however, were not to be put down. Under Badan Singh, they rose up again, and by 1750 their marauding armies controlled a wide expanse of territory, almost from Delhi to Agra, until their ruler was finally, fearfully, recognized by the Mughal emperor and given the hereditary title of Raja. Raja Badan Singh's son, Raja Surajmal, consolidated all this power and used the enormous wealth that his armies had acquired for him to good effect: he built numerous forts and palaces across his kingdom, including the exquisite pleasure palace complex in Deeg ▲ *310* and the great fort of Bharatpur, said to have been one of the mightiest ever built in Indian history ▲ *302*. By the 1760s, with the Mughal Empire in tatters, Raja Surajmal began to get even more ambitious, regularly raiding the imperial cities of Delhi and Agra and carrying away a vast amount of booty. He actually dismantled entire Mughal palaces and brought them back with him to Bharatpur, and, on one particularly brazen occasion, even plundered the very

1. BHARATPUR
2. KEOLADEO GHANA SANCTUARY
3. GOVARDHAN
4. DEEG
5. KARAULI
6. RANTHAMBHOR
7. SAWAI MADHOPUR
8. DHOLPUR

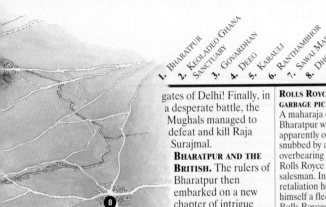

gates of Delhi! Finally, in a desperate battle, the Mughals managed to defeat and kill Raja Surajmal.

BHARATPUR AND THE BRITISH. The rulers of Bharatpur then embarked on a new chapter of intrigue and diplomacy with the new emerging powers in India, the Marathas and the East India Company. This culminated in British attacks on Bharatpur Fort in the early 19th century. The attackers, to their great surprise, were repulsed and defeated. Finally, in 1818, Bharatpur entered into a treaty with the British, one of the very first states in Rajasthan to do so. Bharatpur's most important role in the pages of Indian history, however, was an episode that was written – by default – in the 1820's. For it was here that the British, involved in a succession struggle to the Bharatpur throne, first developed the Doctrine of Paramountcy over the princes, which ultimately led to their becoming the supreme political power in India ● 35.

BIRD-LANDS. In the years that followed, the maharajas of Bharatpur became known mainly for one thing: the bird-lands they carefully developed in the marshes just outside Bharatpur and the spectacular duck shoots – perhaps among the most famous in the world – that they hosted for visiting British dignitaries (and fellow maharajas) ▲ 306, 308. These splendid bird-lands have now been converted into a remarkable little national park, considered to be one of the wonders of the natural world. Bharatpur as a town is not overly attractive, but it is a useful jumping-off point for a region that is rich and quite undiscovered, a region dotted with the old forts and palaces of the Jat kings. Deeg, with its pleasure palaces, is, of course, almost as much of a "must-see" as Agra's Taj Mahal, but there are also other interesting places such as Dholpur, Karauli, Govardhan and Bayana, for which Bharatpur is a convenient springboard.

ROLLS ROYCE GARBAGE PICK-UP
A maharaja of Bharatpur was apparently once snubbed by an overbearing young Rolls Royce salesman. In retaliation he bought himself a fleet of Rolls Royces and had them shipped back to Bharatpur, where they were put to use as municipal garbage collection vehicles!

Residence of the British Political Agent in Bharatpur, circa 1900.

General view of Bharatpur.

▲ BHARATPUR

Ashtadhati Gateway,
Lohagarh Fort.

LOHAGARH FORT

"Lohagarh" literally means "Iron Fort", and it was an apt name, for it was virtually impregnable. Built by Raja Surajmal in the mid-18th century, its defense systems are said to have been inspired by a description given in the epic, *Ramayana*. It had two formidable concentric ramparts, made of beaten earth and rubble, each surrounded by a moat 149 feet wide and 60 feet deep. The outer wall, about 7 miles long, took eight years to construct. What's more, being a *mahi durg*, or "mud fort", as described in the ancient Sanskrit scriptures, Lohagarh's thick walls were able to absorb even the most furious of artillery barrages. The cannon balls would simply sink into the mud walls, to be collected later and used against the enemy. As a result, the fort had stood up to several attacks by the Mughal armies, and no less than four attacks by the British, before it finally fell. The fort's outer ramparts were demolished by the British after the Treaty of 1818, but the inner battlements remain, punctuated by two massive towers commemorating two great victories of the Bharatpur armies: the first tower, Jawahar Burj, marking Raja Surajmal's storming of Delhi in 1764, and the second, Fateh Burj, commemorating the rout of Lord Lake's British armies, when the attackers were repulsed, leaving three thousand men dead in the battlefield. At Jawahar Burj, do not miss the iron "Victory Column", bearing the inscriptions of the genealogy of the Jat kings. There are two imposing gates to the fort: in the north is the historic Ashtadhati Gate, with its huge, rounded bastions and war elephants

Lohagarh Fort was protected by deep moats, and according to legend, would fall "only when a crocodile swallowed up all the water of the moat".

THE UNDOING OF A GENERAL
Bharatpur's Lohagarh Fort proved to be the undoing of Lord Lake (above), until then, one of the most successful British generals. His armies decimated in the bloody siege of Bharatpur, Lord Lake disappeared into obscurity, paving the way for an up-and-coming young officer named Arthur Wellesley, later to become famous as Duke of Wellington. Wellesley ultimately managed to capture Bharatpur, but not before it had given him some anxious moments.

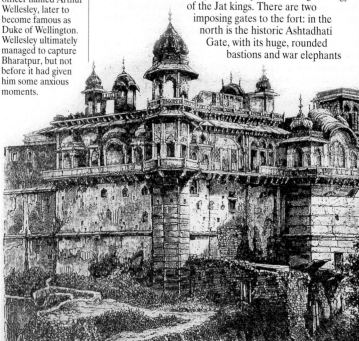

painted on either side, and in the south, Loha Gate. Both of these were torn down from the walls of the imperial capital of Delhi and brought back by the victorious Jat armies in an act of supreme military arrogance.

PALACES AND MUSEUM. Within Lohagarh Fort is a complex of three palaces: Mahal Khas, Kamra Palace and Raja Badan Singh's Palace, built by successive generations of Bharatpur's rulers – and set around a small, but elegant, old Mughal garden (above). Mahal Khas, built by Raja Balwant Singh (reigned 1826–53), houses the royal apartments, which reflect the simple lifestyle of the Jat rulers. Its chambers are small, with ornate pierced stone windows and patterned marble tiled floors. In the corners are octagonal chambers with domed ceilings and delicately painted walls. On the lower floor is an

interesting *hammam*, or sunken bath house. Raja Badan Singh's Palace, adjacent to Mahal Khas, has an imposing sandstone *durbar* hall, with finely carved walls, pillars and archways, and a beautiful alcove set into the far wall, from where the Raja himself would hold court. Today this palace houses part of Bharatpur's Archeological Museum, with Kamra Palace next door housing the other half. The museum has some carvings dating back to the second century and terracotta toys from the first century, excavated at the village of Noh, just a few miles east of here. Some of the carvings worth taking a closer look at are the 7th-century image of Shiva and Parvati, the 11th-century image of the Jain saint, Parshvanatha, and the 10th-century Ganesha. However, the prized piece here is the unique 2nd-century red sandstone *Shivalinga* (above).

GOLBAGH PALACE

Built in the early 1900's, this fascinating palace drew its inspiration freely from a variety of sources, ranging from the pleasure palaces of Deeg to the Art Nouveau salons of Europe. Set in Mughal gardens, it is a riot of lotus arches, ornate balconies, canopies, and delicate latticework screens. Take a close look at some of the latticed windows and you will see the curious influence of the Art Nouveau style that was so fashionable at the time. Once the home of Maharaja Kishan Singh, the palace has now been converted into a hotel, after the royal family moved in to Moti Mahal Palace next door.

HAVE GATE WILL TRAVEL
Ashtadhati ("Eight-Metal") Gate of Lohagarh Fort has a history behind it. It is said to have originally been the gate of Chittorgarh Fort, but was carried away by Sultan Alauddin Khilji of Delhi. In 1764 it was torn down from the walls of the Mughal capital of Delhi and brought back in triumph to Bharatpur.

Raja Badan Singh's palace.

FAMILY HISTORY ON COLUMN
The Vijay Stambha, ("Victory Column"), erected inside the Fort by the maharajas of Bharatpur, has engravings tracing their family history back, generation by generation, to the Hindu god, Lord Krishna himself.

303

▲ RANTHAMBHOR

CATCHING PREY
The tiger has developed a high degree of cunning to overcome the highly evolved self-preservation systems of all its prey species. When attacking its prey it creeps up as if in slow-motion, often taking up to fifteen minutes to cover about 165 feet. Then, pausing cautiously for a long while – perhaps two to three minutes – it leaps upon the unsuspecting beast with lightning speed. However, it gives man, the craftiest of predators, a very wide berth indeed.

PROJECT TIGER
In the late 1960's it was realized that the tiger was on its way to extinction – with only two thousand of these magnificent beasts still surviving. As a result, Project Tiger ▲ *176* was launched in 1972 – an ambitious project based on the premise that the species could be saved only by the total conservation of its habitat, based on an ecosystem approach. It is considered to be one of Asia's most important conservation efforts.

Gray partridge, Ranthambhor National Park.

RANTHAMBHOR FORT

Of all the forts in Rajasthan, one of the most dramatic is the mysterious jungle-fort of Ranthambhor (below). Set high on a rock cliff, its ruined battlements loom over the dense surrounding foliage. It is one of the finest examples of the ancient Hindu concept of a *vana-durg*, or a fort protected by a jungle. Built in AD 944, this fort has had a bloody and complex history. In 1192 it was taken over by the Chauhans, who had been forced out of their own strongholds in Ajmer and Delhi. In the late 13th century it went through a glorious epoch, during the reign of Raja Hamir Dev, but was sacked by Sultan Alauddin Khilji in 1303. Regained by the Rajputs, it was once again lost in 1569, this time to the Mughal emperor Akbar, who, after a 37-day artillery barrage, finally took it through an audacious bluff. Disguising himself as an ordinary mace-bearer, he entered the fort with one of his Rajput generals, and in a bewilderingly rapid sequence of events, was placed upon its throne. You enter the fort through a narrow, fortified defile in the jungle, via a steep, serpentine ramp. Here you can see the four massive gateways that any attacking army would have to break through, defended by elephant spikes, massive chains and tricky zig-zag configurations. By the way, do not miss the enigmatic ancient Ranthambhor monolith by the side of the third gate. The fourth gate is at the head of a steep flight of stairs: a thick bastion, reinforced by a turret. From here a long vaulted tunnel takes you into the fort itself. The interiors of the fort now lie in splendid ruin. You can see two small, old temples here and the remains of a fine tank. From the battlements there is a great view of the surrounding forests, and a sheer drop of over 200 feet.

Lawns of Sawai Madhopur Lodge, the royal hunting lodge of the Maharaja of Jaipur in the 1930's.

RANTHAMBHOR NATIONAL PARK

This must certainly be one of the most picturesque game reserves in the world, the entire forest being dominated by the silent, ruined battlements of Ranthambhor Fort. Seeing a tiger roaming over these ruins, as one often does here, is a moment of eerie beauty. The park has a core area of 158 square miles, and is one of the parks covered by Project Tiger ▲ *176,* a conservation project. Ranthambhor is noted for its tigers, who are not merely nocturnal, but frequently seen during the day, often stalking their prey in full view of visitors. As a result of such sightings, Ranthambhor has become a favorite place for wildlife buffs and professional wildlife photographers. Its tiger population, which had dropped to just fourteen in 1973, has now grown to about forty. The park also has a large population of panthers. Their habitat does not overlap with that of the tigers: they keep to the outer areas. Other predators here are the caracal, hyena, jackal and jungle cat. Marsh crocodiles can also be seen basking by the banks of the lakes. There are various species of deer, such as the *sambar, chital, chinkara,* and *nilgai.* Ranthambhor is also known for its rich birdlife, drawn here by the wide variety of flora and the lakes. Some of its many species of birds are the great Indian horned owl, various species of eagle, painted and white-necked stork, spoonbill, partridge and quail. Another interesting feature of the park, incidentally, is a huge banyan tree – supposedly one of the world's largest – near the graceful Jogi Mahal water palace.

PRIVATE GAME RESERVE
Ranthambhor was once the private game reserve of the maharajas of Jaipur, who used to bring their personal guests here for tiger shoots ▲ *176.* Royal hunts have a tradition that goes back to at least the 12th century. Historical records show that Prithviraj Chauhan, the last Hindu raja of Delhi, was an enthusiastic hunter, so much so that his hunting activities in other rajas' territories frequently led to war!

Animals grazing at Ranthambhor National Park (left). *Sambar* (above) can be seen at the park.

305

▲ BHARATPUR
KEOLADEO GHANA SANCTUARY

DUCK-SHOOT RITUAL
The maharajas of Bharatpur developed the marshlands of Ghana into a hunting reserve ▲ *301*. Their great duck shoots were a major event on the sporting calendar of old Imperial India, and the British pro-consuls and generals used to vie for invitations. Each duck shoot took months to arrange and allotting the shooting butts was said to be "as tricky an exercise as making the seating arrangements at a formal banquet". The firing would begin at the sound of a bugle call and ended strictly at the sound of a second bugle call hours later.

Just outside Bharatpur lies this small, but amazingly rich, bird sanctuary, considered to be one of the world's outstanding heronries ▲ *308*. Covering an area of just 12 square miles, it is an interlocking ecosystem of woodlands, swamps, wet prairies and dry savannah, home to over 370 varieties of birds, of which more than 115 are migrants flying in from Central Asia, Siberia and western China during the winter months. Perhaps no other bird sanctuary in the world offers so many different species within so small a compass, creating a uniquely rewarding bird-watching experience. The park, originally called Ghana, which means "dense", takes its name from the ancient temple of Keoladeo, or Lord Shiva, that you will find inside it. It was painstakingly created in the 19th century out of the arid surrounding scrubland by diverting the waters of a nearby canal and creating a series of dykes and dams. The new ecosystem that emerged became an ideal habitat for birds of all kinds. It is perhaps surprising that so many birds continue to flock here, given the park's rather bloody history: from 1902 to 1947, this was the site of some of the most extravagant duck shoots the world has known. The most notorious one was in November 1938, when the British Viceroy, Lord Linlithgow (right), and his party massacred 4273 ducks and geese.

It was recorded that the Viceroy himself had two loaders to help him reload, and his guns got so hot that they had to be cooled down by sloshing them regularly with water. The Maharaja of Bharatpur used Rolls Royces, which he converted into shooting brakes, to transport his guests within Ghana. Today motor vehicles are forbidden. One has to travel either by boat, bicycle or cycle-rickshaw.

STORKS AND CRANES. The highlight of the park is perhaps its storks and cranes. Most famous of all is the nearly extinct Siberian crane that flies in each winter from Siberia ■ *27*. It stands up to 4½ feet tall and has a wing span of over 6 feet. It has been called the "lily of birds", for as an ornithologist once noted, "It is the most elegant of birds and, stand in what position it may, its head, neck and body presents a series of the most graceful and harmonious curves." Being the wintering ground of this rare species, Keoladeo has been included among the World Heritage sites. About thirty Siberian cranes visit Keoladeo each year, although for unknown reasons not a single bird arrived in the winter of 1994. The birds in Keoladeo are often enormous in size: the

Clockwise from top left: Large cormorants, spoonbills, red-crested pochard and white ibis.

Graylag geese (left) and nesting
painted stork (right).

White-breasted
kingfisher.

tallest bird in North America, for instance, the great blue
heron, approximately 4½ feet tall, would be completely
dwarfed by birds here such as the greater adjutant stork and
the black-necked stork, which are up to 6 feet tall, about the
height of a man. Keoladeo is also
Asia's largest breeding ground of the
painted stork.

OTHER SPECIES. Other notable
species of birds found here are
the openbill stork (below),
spoonbill, white ibis, heron,
egret, cormorant and
several species of splendid, brilliantly
colored kingfisher. Among the migrant
species are the steppe eagle (one of the
largest species of eagle), peregrine
falcon, marsh harrier, graylag geese,
plover, sandpiper and rosy pelican. In
addition, there are larger numbers of
gadwal, shoveler, wigeon, whistling and
common teal. Keoladeo is also famed for
its ducks: in winter they sometimes
completely cover the sky, and when they
suddenly rise from the lake, as a wildlife
writer once noted, "they make a noise
like thunder." The park also has some
interesting species of animals such as
the *sambar*, *chital*, blackbuck, wild
boar, and various species of
wild cat and large rock
python, found especially
near Python Point.

**TILL DEATH DO US
PART**
The sarus crane is
celebrated in Indian
mythology for its
fidelity: it mates with
the same partner for
a lifetime ■ 28. Its
mating dance – a
magnificent aerial
ballet – is an
unforgettable sight.

WINTER'S FLIGHT
The Siberian crane,
one of the world's
rarest birds ■ 27,
migrates here in
winter from the
frozen tundras of
south Siberia – a
journey of two
months. Incredibly, it
flies 3900 miles to this
tiny patch of
marshlands, just 12
square miles in size.

**WORLD'S TALLEST
STORK**
The black-necked
stork, seen in
Keoladeo in large
numbers, is the
world's tallest stork,
standing up to 6 feet
tall. Its dramatic
black and white wings
span up to 8 feet.

307

"A LIVING SOUP"
Bharatpur's wetland habitat
has been graphically described as "a
living soup", and it is the birds' specialized
and differentiated feeding habits that allow the
"soup" to go around.

Keoladeo Ghana in
Bharatpur, where thousands of
migratory waterfowl arrive every winter,
is part of the Indo-gangetic plains of
India where waterbirds nest in thousands
during the monsoon ▲ 306.
Created in the late 19th century by the
maharaja of Bharatpur to bring the
pleasures of wildfowl hunting to his
doorstep, the reserve came into being
by the simple act of diverting
water from a nearby irrigation
canal. The lowlands holding the
monsoon flood water have
been an ageless avian
paradise, and were where the
maharaja of Bharatpur hosted
duck shoots for British luminaries
(above).

SNAKE BIRD
The snake bird, or darter, hunts for fish
with its spring-like neck, which acts as
a "javelin" at short distance. As its
feathers lack waterproofing,
the bird is commonly seen
drying itself with
wings spread.

**LISTING THE BIG
SHOTS**
At the entrance of the
sanctuary, a veritable
who's who lists the
big shots of the 1930's
with details of the
shoot.

DATE	ON THE OCCASION OF THE VISIT OF	BAC
1902 1ST DEC.	1ST SHOOT H.E. VICEROY LORD CURZON H.E. C-IN-C LORD KITCHENER	540
1905 9TH FEB	2ND SHOOT H.R.H. THE DUKE OF CONNAUGHT	780
1905 26 MARCH	1ST SHOOT H.E. VICEROY LORD CURZON	
1907 15TH NOV	1ST SHOOT HON'BLE MR E. COLVIN A.G.G.	173
1908 20TH NOV	1ST SHOOT HON'BLE COL. PINHEY A.G.G.	214
1908 12TH NOV	2ND SHOOT	108

These waters, rich in microbes, insects, fish, frogs, and reptiles, provide food for the nesting waterbirds. Nests are built with strong and elastic material from acacia trees ■ *30* and the soft lining is from algae and water plants.

BAR-HEADED GOOSE
Once India's most common goose – the 19th-century naturalist, A. O. Hume, counted over ten thousand in 1877 along a single 10-mile stretch – this snow-white bird with black markings has dwindled to under one thousand in recent winters.

A WINTER'S TALE
Aristotle speculated about where the swallows went in winter. Today, scientific studies on the accuracy, regularity, velocity, and altitude of the birds' migratory flight are carried out.

BIRDS' HABITAT
Keoladeo Ghana Sanctuary is home to over 370 varieties of birds from over fifty families, of which some 120 species nest here.

PAINTED STORKS
The painted stork is symbolic of Keoladeo Ghana, where it nests in colonies of thousands on tree tops. It visits the sanctuary between July and October during the monsoon to breed.

DEEG

Deeg, with its exquisite complex of pleasure palaces (above), lies 22 miles north of Bharatpur. Created in pale yellow sandstone and set around large, formal Mughal gardens, these palaces are architectural gems, considered by some to be second only to Agra's Taj Mahal in their beauty and symmetry. The palaces were laid out in the mid-1700's by Raja Badan Singh and, later, Raja Surajmal, as an idyllic place of refuge from the battles in which they were constantly engaged. In creating them, the Bharatpur rulers freely sought inspiration from the architectural traditions of the Mughals. Ironically, they succeeded brilliantly in this endeavor, at a time when Mughal architecture was becoming a sad parody of itself. The main pavilion of the complex is Gopal Bhawan, built by the banks of a large tank in 1763. It is an elegant piece of architecture, and fascinatingly designed: what appears to be a two-storied structure actually has four stories that descend gracefully down to the waters of the tank. This is where the Bharatpur royal family lived until 1951. Inside you can still see their furniture and some of their objets d'art. Gopal Bhawan is flanked by two beautiful little pavilions named Sawan and Bhadon, named after the two months of the monsoon. With their drooping *bangaldar* eaves perfectly mirrored in the still waters of the tank, they were designed to look like house boats, rather than buildings. To the east lie the beautiful Mughal gardens, interspersed with pools, water channels and five hundred fountains, which are still turned on once a year – although without the rainbow colors that used to play in them during the days of the maharajas ▲ *312*. South of the gardens lies Kishan Bhawan, another beautiful, yellow sandstone pavilion with splendidly carved archways, covered with rich arabesque motifs. Inside, it is embellished with carved motifs of flowers and peacocks, with an alcoved balcony set into its wall, where the maharaja used to sit. The dining room with a low horseshoe-shaped marble table was used for Indian meals partaken in silver *thalis* while sitting on the floor. The open end of the table was used for service.

SITE PLAN

TEMPLE

RAM BHAWAN

SINGH POL

NAND BHAWAN

TEMPLE

RANI GARDEN

GOPAL SAGAR

RUP SAGAR

GOPAL BHAWAN

KESAV BHAWAN

SURAJ BHAWAN

KISHAN BHAWAN

SHEESH MAHAL

SURAJ GATE

TANK

PURANA MAHAL

HARDEV BHAWAN

Badal Mahal.

> "THE APARTMENTS WE OCCUPIED WERE UNIQUE…PAVED WITH FINE MARBLE, IN WHICH BOUQUETS OF FLOWERS ARE REPRESENTED BY ONYX, LAPIS LAZULI AND AGATE…"
>
> LOUIS ROUSSELET, *INDIA AND ITS NATIVE PRINCES*, 1878

There are two other very interesting pavilions set around the gardens, Keshav Bhawan and Nand Bhawan. Keshav Bhawan, an open, columned summer pavilion, is particularly charming. To the far south of the complex is the beautiful, white marbled, verandahed Suraj Mahal pavilion, with its delicate mosaic inlay work in semi-precious stones. It bears a particularly close resemblance to the Mughal architecture of Shah Jahan's times – which is not surprising, for it is actually made from several pillaged Mughal buildings brought back by the Jats from Delhi and reassembled here. As a result, when you look closely, you will notice how its marble slabs are not perfectly matched. An interesting architectural feature of the palace complex is the projecting double cornices which give the buildings a striking appearance, and creating a subtle balance of shadow and light. The complex, incidentally, is only half-finished. Raja Surajmal was planning to build a mirror image of it on the other side when he was killed in battle. Near the palace complex is Deeg Fort, which is also worth a visit.

A royal carriage at Deeg, circa 1902.

Frescos at a cenotaph in Govardhan.

GOVARDHAN

The small sacred town of Govardhan is located 9 miles east of Deeg. Associated with legends of the Hindu deity, Lord Krishna, who is said to have lived in these parts, it is an important place of pilgrimage. In its narrow winding lanes you can feel the pulse of the real India. Harideva Temple, built in the 16th century, is particularly worth a visit. The impressive cenotaph of Raja Surajmal, 2 miles north of here, has some fascinating frescos of scenes from the Raja's life under its dome. Near Harideva Temple is another interesting complex of cenotaphs of the Bharatpur maharajas, which are also notable for their frescoed ceilings. Their curved cornices and multiple domes and pavilions are typical architectural features of northeastern Rajasthan.

SHIELDED FROM CYCLONE

According to legend, Lord Krishna once protected the people of Braj from a cosmic cyclone hurled at them by Lord Indra, the god of the rain. To shield them from the rain and floods, Krishna lifted Mount Giriraj, near Govardhan, on the tip of his little finger and held it aloft for seven days and nights, like an umbrella, until the cyclone finally died out, and Indra apologized at the feet of Krishna – a subject much represented in Indian art.

DHOLPUR

Situated 66 miles southeast of Bharatpur is the town of Dholpur, once the capital of a little kingdom of the same name. Dholpur was founded in the 11th century by Raja Dholan Deo, and its rulers were vassals of the Hindu rajas of Delhi. One of them, Palun Singh, died leading the troops of the last great Hindu raja of Delhi, Prithviraj Chauhan ● *35, 55*, into battle in AD 1175. This region saw several historic battles, including a decisive one in 1658 between the Mughal heir, Dara Shukoh, and his younger brother,

BABUR'S GARDEN
Just outside Dholpur lie the remains of a splendid Mughal garden laid out in 1529 by the first Mughal emperor, Babur. Lost for centuries, it was rediscovered in 1978 by Elizabeth Moynihan, the wife of the then United States Ambassador to India. Using Babur's autobiography as a guide, she followed a trail of clues from Uzbekistan to Dholpur. The gardens have long since vanished, but there are still traces of the beautiful old lotus pools hewn from the living rock, around which the gardens were laid.

Aurangzeb, the usurper who became emperor ● *36*. Dholpur is an interesting town to visit, particularly because it is far from the usual tourist track and is quite undiscovered. It is famed for its pink sandstone quarries, whose stone was specially selected by Lutyens for the building of the new city of Delhi in the early part of this century. Dholpur Palace, a splendid early 19th-century sandstone edifice, is worth seeing, particularly for its extensive use of Art Deco English tiles that cover the walls of each room from floor to ceiling. See also the 16th-century mausoleum of Sadiq Khan (now converted into a school).

BARI

Bari, 18 miles southwest of Dholpur, has an elegant 17th-century lakeside pleasure palace built by Emperor Shah Jahan. Nearby, there is also an interesting 13th-century fortress and two wildlife sanctuaries, Vana Vihar and Ram Sagar.

KARAULI

The picturesque old fortified town of Karauli, about 76 miles southwest of Bharatpur, was founded in 1348. Its richly ornamented 18th-century City Palace is worth visiting for its orange sandstone cupolas, its elaborate stucco-work details and its impressive *durbar* hall. There are also some interesting frescos inside, which you should not miss. The Maharaja of Karauli has converted his country palace into a heritage hotel which can be used as a base to discover some fascinating old temples, as well as a game sanctuary with wonderful opportunities for jeep safaris.

Karauli's coat-of-arms (right).

PRACTICAL
INFORMATION

The best time to visit Rajasthan is from October to March. The climate becomes cooler, and as the dust settles, the sky turns beautifully blue. Important festive spectacles such as the Pushkar Fair, Diwali, Desert Festival, Elephant Festival, and Holi take place during this time. Expect some chilly days and cold nights, and some winter showers, in December and January. If you visit in summer, be prepared for the scorching heat, hot winds, and dust storms.

VISA FORMALITIES

Visitors should obtain an Indian visa before arrival. Visas are readily available from your nearest Indian Consulate. In countries where there is no Indian Diplomatic Mission, normally the British Consulate would issue the visa. Usually, a multiple entry visa valid for a period of 120 days is granted to tourists, simplifying the procedure for visiting neighboring countries such as Nepal and Sri Lanka.

VACCINATIONS

No vaccinations are required apart from yellow fever vaccinations for people arriving within six days after leaving or in transit from infected or endemic areas. However, it is advisable to vaccinate against typhoid, tetanus, and polio. A gamma globulin injection may also be useful to protect against hepatitis infection.

EMBASSIES AND CONSULATES

UNITED KINGDOM:
Indian High Commission,
India House,
Aldwych, London
WC2B 4NA
Tel. (0171) 836 8484
Fax. (0171) 836 4331

UNITED STATES:
Embassy of India
2107, Massachusetts
Ave, N.W.,
Washington, D.C.
20008
Tel. (202) 939-7070/
7069/7000
Fax. (202) 939-7027

Consulate General of India
3 East 64th Street,
New York, NY 10021
Tel. (212) 879-7800
Fax. (212) 988-6423

FRANCE:
Embassy of India
15, rue Alfred
Dehodencq,
75016, Paris
Tel. 45 20 39 30
Fax 40 50 09 96

OPENING HOURS

Banks are open till 2pm (Mon.–Fri.), and till noon on Saturday. Markets, offices, and banks are closed on Sunday. Central government offices are closed on Saturdays. State government offices close on the second Saturday of the month.

TOURIST INFORMATION

It is useful to visit the overseas branches of the Government of India Tourist Office for the latest information. They can supply maps, brochures, a festival calendar, information on domestic air services, trains, and package tours.

UNITED KINGDOM:
7, Cork Street,
London WIX 2AB
Tel. (0171) 437 3677
24-hour brochure line:
01233 211 999
Fax. (0171) 494 1048

UNITED STATES:
30, Rockefeller
Plaza, Suite 15,
North Mezzanine,
New York, NY 10020
Tel. (212) 586-4901
Fax. (212) 582-3270

3550, Wilshire
Boulevard (Res)
Room No. 204
Los Angeles,
California 90010
Tel. (213) 477-3824
Fax. (213) 380-6111

FRANCE:
8, Blvd. de la
Madeleine,
Paris 75009
Tel. 42 65 83 86/77 06

TRAVEL TIPS

To avoid heat stroke, drink lots of water. A green mango juice, locally called *panna* or *kairi ki chanch*, and butter milk is recommended. Include raw onion in meals.

MAJOR AIRLINES FLYING TO INDIA

AIR INDIA

UNITED KINGDOM:
17/19, New Bond
Street,
London W1Y OBD
Tel. (0171) 493 4050
Fax. (0171) 493 0693

UNITED STATES:
Regional Office
345, Park Avenue,
New York, NY10154
Tel. (212) 407-1379
Fax. (212) 753-8964

BRITISH AIRWAYS

UNITED KINGDOM:
156, Regent Street,
London WIR 6LB
101/2, Cheapside,
London EC2V 6DT
Victoria Railway
Station, London SW1
Tel. (0345) 222111

UNITED STATES:
530, Fifth Avenue,
1 World Trade Tower,
North Tower,
New York, NY
Tel. (718) 397 4000

LUFTHANSA

UNITED KINGDOM:
10, Old Bond Street,
London W1X 4EN,
Tel. (0345) 737747

UNITED STATES:
680, Fifth Avenue,
New York 10017
Tel. (212) 745-0700

K.L.M.

UNITED KINGDOM:
Heathrow Airport
Terminal Four, London
Tel. (0181) 750 9000

UNITED STATES:
437, Madison Avenue,
New York, NY 10022
Tel. (212) 702-3000

AIR FRANCE

UNITED KINGDOM:
Colet Court, 100,
Hammersmith Road,
London W6 7JP
Tel. (0181) 742 6600

UNITED STATES:
125 West 55th Street,
New York NY 10019
Tel. (212) 247-0100

SINGAPORE AIRLINES

UNITED KINGDOM:
143-7, Regent Street,
London W1R 7LB
Tel. (0171) 439 8111

UNITED STATES:
55 East 59th Street,
Suite 20B, New York,
NY 10022
Tel. (212) 644-8805

PUBLIC HOLIDAYS

Jan 26   Republic Day
Aug 15   Independence Day
Oct 2   Gandhi Jayanti
Many public holidays such as the national festivals follow the lunar calendar, so it is not possible to give exact dates.

January to March

High tourist season.

Date	Festival		Average rainfall	Temperature
11–13 February (fixed)	**HADOTI FESTIVAL,** Kota	**JAIPUR**	9MM	50°-79° ☁
13–16 February	**NAGAUR FAIR,** Nagaur			
17– 22 February	**BANESHWAR FAIR,** Baneshwar, Dungarpur			
20–22 February	**DESERT FESTIVAL,** Jaisalmer	**JODHPUR**	4.6MM	54°-83° ☁
19–21 MARCH	**BRIJ FESTIVALS,** Bharatpur			
23 March	**ELEPHANT FESTIVAL,** Jaipur			
31 MARCH	**SHITALA ASHTAMI,** Chaksu (Jaipur)	**UDAIPUR**	4MM	52°-81° ☁
4 APRIL	**KELADAVI FAIR,** Karauli, Sawai Madhopur			

★ Desert Festival, Elephant Festival

April to June

The heat in April is still bearable, but avoid the scorching heat from May to June. If you are traveling in summer, go out in the early hours and late evenings rather than midday.

Date	Festival		Average rainfall	Temperature
10–11 APRIL	**MEWAR FESTIVAL,** Udaipur	**JAIPUR**	25MM	79°-102° ☀
10–11 APRIL	**GANGAUR FAIR,** Jaipur			
16 – 22 APRIL	**MAHAVEERJI FAIR,** Mahaveerji	**JODHPUR**	13MM	79°-105° ☀
1–3 JUNE	**SUMMAR FESTIVAL,** Mount Abu			
		UDAIPUR	32MM	76°-102° ☀

★ Gangaur Fair

July to September

The heat abates from August to September, cooled by rains, but humidity increases. Torrential rains may be experienced during the short monsoon period (July to August), turning roads into water pools and leaving people stranded.

Date	Festival		Average rainfall	Temperature
6–7 AUGUST	**TEEJ FAIR,** Jaipur	**JAIPUR**	162MM	76°-93° 🌧☀
18 AUGUST	**GOGAMEDI FAIR,** Gogamedi (Ganganagar)			
20–21 AUGUST	**KAJLI TEEJ,** Bundi	**JODHPUR**	104MM	77°-95° 🌧☀
18 AUGUST AND 16 SEPTEMBER	**GOGAMEDI FAIR,** Gogamedi (Ganganagar)			
11–12 SEPTEMBER	**RAMDEORA FAIR,** Pokharan (Jaisalmer)	**UDAIPUR**	164MM	73°-87° 🌧☀

★ Teej Fair

October to December

High tourist season.

Date	Festival		Average rainfall	Temperature
9–11 OCTOBER	**DUSSEHRA FAIR,** Kota	**JAIPUR**	8MM	55°-83° ☁
15–16 OCTOBER	**MARWAR FESTIVAL,** Jodhpur			
11–14 NOVEMBER	**PUSHKAR FAIR,** Pushkar (Ajmer)			
11–19 NOVEMBER	**KOLAYAT FAIR,** Kolayat (Bikaner)	**JODHPUR**	3.7MM	59°-88° ☁
13–15 NOVEMBER	**CHANDRABHAGA FAIR,** Jhalawar			
14–15 NOVEMBER	**BIKANER FESTIVAL,** Bikaner			
		UDAIPUR	6.5MM	55°-86° ☁

★ Pushkar Fair

☀ sunny and warm   ☁ cool   🌧 rainy

The average minimum and maximum temperatures are given in degrees Fahrenheit.
Festival dates given above are for 1997.

BUDGET FOR A TRAVELING COUPLE

BIKANER, JAISALMER, JODHPUR
(Five nights, six days)

Airfare	US$3000/£2000
Hotel:	
Medium range	US$190.50/£127
Deluxe range	US$354/£236
Transportation	US$300/£200

BIKANER, JAISALMER, JODHPUR, MOUNT ABU, UDAIPUR (Nine nights, ten days)

Airfare	US$1350/£900
Hotel:	
Medium range	US$430.50/£287
Deluxe range	US$1272/£848
Transportation	US$675/£450

LUNAR CALENDAR DATES

Dates of festivals follow the lunar calendar and vary every year. Check with the Tourism Office for dates in other years.

EVENT	1998	1999
Nagaur fair	3–6 Feb.	24–27 Jan.
Desert Festival	9–11 Feb.	29–31 Jan.
Elephant Festival	12 Mar.	1 Mar.
Brij Festival	8–10 Mar.	26–28 Feb.
Shitala Ashtami	20 Mar.	10 Mar.
Gangaur Fair	30 Apr.–1 May	20–21 Mar.
Mewar Festival	30 Apr.–1 May	20–21 Mar.
Teej Festival	26–27 Jul.	14–15 Aug.
Ramdeora Fair	31 Aug–1 Sept	19– 20 Sept
Marwar Festival	4–5 Oct.	23–24 Oct.
Pushkar Fair	1–4 Nov.	20–23 Nov.
Bikaner Festival	4–5 Nov.	23–24 Nov.
Kolayat Fair	31 Oct–8 Nov.	19–27 Nov.

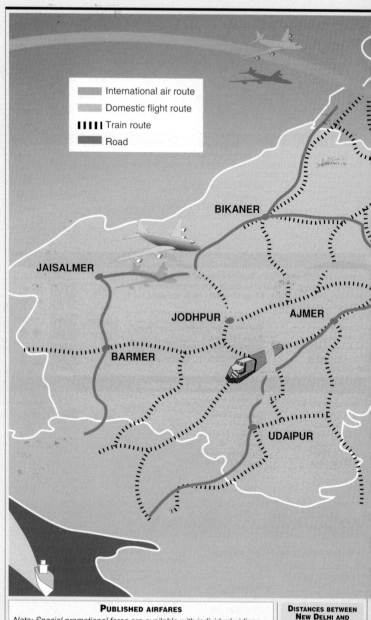

International air route
Domestic flight route
Train route
Road

BIKANER

JAISALMER

JODHPUR

AJMER

BARMER

UDAIPUR

PUBLISHED AIRFARES		
Note: Special promotional fares are available with individual airlines.		
From Europe	**Time**	**Average cost**
Executive flight from London	9 hours	£2074
Economy flight from London	9 hours	£1466
From the United States		
Executive flight from New York	16 hours	US$5202
Economy flight from New York	16 hours	US$2263
Executive flight from Los Angeles	16 hours	US$4432
Economy flight from Los Angeles	16 hours	US$3766

DISTANCES BETWEEN NEW DELHI AND MAJOR CITIES	
CITY	MILES
PARIS	4402
LONDON	4598
ROME	3934
FRANKFURT	4174
MOSCOW	3132
HONG KONG	2965
NEW YORK	8136
TOKYO	4398

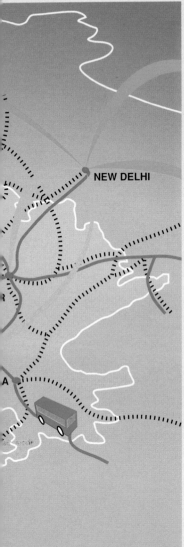

NEW DELHI

BY CAR
National Highway No. 8 connects Delhi and Jaipur. The drive takes five and half hours (including a break of 20 minutes). Chauffeur-driven cars can be hired from leading travel agencies as well as hotel counters and taxi stands. You have to pay return taxi fare if you travel to Jaipur. Per kilometer charge varies for a petrol and a diesel vehicle. A petrol-driven Ambassador car charges Rs.3.25 to Rs.3.50 per kilometer. Passengers have to pay Rs.250 on the border with the state of Haryana.

BY BUS
The Rajasthan Roadways operates a fleet of deluxe and air-conditioned buses between 5.30am to 1pm. Bikaner House, near India Gate, is the most convenient boarding point. Fare: Rs.125 for the deluxe bus and Rs.225 for the air-conditioned Pink Line.

BY TRAIN
The newest, most comfortable train is the Shatabdi Express between Jaipur and New Delhi. Covering the distance in four and a half hours, the fare on the air-conditioned train includes breakfast. Advanced booking is a must. The Garib Nawaz Express leaves Delhi at 6.15am daily and returns from Jaipur at 4.45pm. A five-hour run, it provides a convenient link in chair-seating compartments. An overnight train to Jaipur with air-conditioned coaches can also be taken. It is better to reserve seats in advance on

payment in dollars. Indrail passes valid for a day, a week, fifteen days, three weeks, and one or two months can be bought. These are sold by the general sales agents in New York, London, Paris, Frankfurt, and Amsterdam, among other major cities, and within India. The passes can also be bought from the main railway stations in major cities. In Rajasthan they are available only in Jaipur.

TOURIST OFFICES
DELHI
Tourist Reception Center, Government of Rajasthan, Bikaner House, Near India Gate, New Delhi
Tel: 383837, 389525, 3381884
Government of India, Tourist Office, 88, Janpath, New Delhi
Tel: 3320005, 3320008, 3320109

BOMBAY
Tourist Information Bureau, Government of Rajasthan, Dr. D.N. Road, Bombay
Tel: 2835603

CALCUTTA
Tourist Information Bureau, Government of Rajasthan, 2, Ganesh Chandra Avenue, Calcutta
Tel: 279051

MADRAS
Tourist Information Bureau, Government of Rajasthan, 28, Commander-in-Chief Road, Madras
Tel: 8772093

BY AIR
The nearest international airport to Rajasthan is the Indira Gandhi International Airport (IGI), New Delhi. Jaipur is the closest point to fly to and from Delhi. Indian Airlines flies twice a day from Palam Airport, 5½ miles from the IGI airport. A shuttle service connects the two airports. Other private operators connecting to Jaipur are Skyline Nepc., three times a week; Sahara and ModiLuft daily. It takes 35 minutes to fly to Jaipur ◆ 321.

317

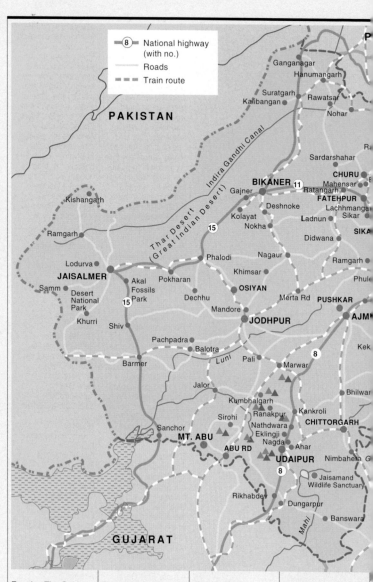

Forming The Golden Triangle with New Delhi and Agra, Jaipur is the main entry point for foreign tourists.

BY AIR
Daily air service connects Jaipur with New Delhi and Bombay, and with the major tourist destinations within Rajasthan such as Jodhpur and Udaipur.

During the peak season more flights are provided. For latest schedules and fares contact a travel agent or Indian Airlines in Jaipur at Nehru Place, Tonk Road, Tel. 514500, 514407; Airport Tel: 550222/ 0519/0718. Many flights are also operated by private carriers.

Skyline Nepc., Near Chanakya, Ganesh Complex, Tel. 362278. U.P. Airways, Anukampa Travel, Anukampa Building, Phase II, M.I. Road, opp. Raymond Showroom, Tel. 378206, 370266. ModiLuft, Techno Travels, Nav Jeevan Chambers, Vinobha Bhave Marg,

C-Scheme. Tel. 363373, 379693. Sahara, 309 Vijaypath, Tilak Nagar, Tel. 620781. Tickets can be bought directly from the airline office or through a travel agent. No handling charges. Porters charge per piece of baggage. Trolleys are free.

Railway Station, Jaipur.

PACKAGE TOURS
During the tourist season the Rajasthan Tourism Development Corporation, Delhi, operates package tours. For details contact the Manager, Tours, RTDC Bikaner House, Tel. 3383837, 3389525

BY TRAIN
There are slow and fast trains referred to as *passenger* and *mail* or *super fast* trains respectively. Two types of coaches, air-conditioned first class and non-air-conditioned second class, are available, but some of the fast trains have air-conditioning in both first and second-class coaches. Train tickets can be booked at the main railway stations. Advanced booking must be made to reserve a berth or a seat by paying a reservation charge. Do not take chances in the unreserved compartments, which can be too crowded and uncomfortable. Waitlist tickets need to be confirmed. Cancellation charges are levied on the confirmed tickets but not the waitlist tickets.

PALACE ON WHEELS
During the tourist season (September to April) a luxury train operates from Delhi Cantonment station every Wednesday ◆ 348. The train was recently modernised and no longer has the character of the original.

BY BUS/COACH
The Rajasthan Roadways operates buses throughout the state linking all the major tourist destinations. Super-deluxe and air-conditioned buses run between New Delhi and Jaipur, and semi-deluxe buses run to other cities using the deluxe coaches at a lower tariff. Advance reservation should be made. Book your tickets at the Rajasthan Roadways, Deluxe Counter, Sindhi Camp, Station Road, Tel. 375834.
Ordinary buses are generally too crowded for even standing space. Super-deluxe buses stop en route at wayside facilities provided by RTDC.

BY CAR
You can hire a car with a driver from the local travel and excursion agents or from the taxi stands. A taxi is provided on a per kilometer basis charge, and the minimum run is 150 miles, with an additional night charge. Per kilometer charges vary between Rs.2.50/US$0.08/ £0.05 and Rs.10/ US$0.33/£0.20, depending on the type of car. The rate for petrol vehicles is higher than for diesel vehicles.
CAR WITH DRIVER
Most of the better hotels arrange for cars to take you sightseeing.
EURO CAR
Tholia Circle, M.I. Road, Jaipur, Tel. 378377, 367735
SITA TRAVELS
D'Villa, Station Road, Tel. 374722, 368266
TRAVEL HOUSE
Welcomgroup Rajputana Palace Sheraton, Tel. 368431, 363211
RAJASTHAN TOURISM DEVELOPMENT CORPORATION
Transport Unit, Tourist Hotel, opposite General Post Office, M.I. Road, Tel. 375466
SELF-DRIVE CARS
These are provided by Wheels-rent-a-car in slots of 4 hours/50 km or 8 hours/80 km and beyond. Tel. 383867, 383870
Hertz, NGS-42 Nehru Place, Tonk Road, Tel. 514672

INDIAN AIRLINES' OFFICES

Udaipur
L.I.C. Building, Delhi Gate, Tel. 28995
City Office Tel. 28999
Airport Tel. 28011

Jodhpur
Circuit House Road, Near Bhati Cross Roads, Tel. 28600
City Office Tel. 36757
Airport Tel. 30617

AIRFARES	Rs	US$	£
Jaipur to Jodhpur	1197	37.40	24.00
Jaipur to Udaipur	1197	37.40	24.00
Jaipur to Delhi	1013	31.65	20.25
Jaipur to Bombay	2727	85.20	54.54

319

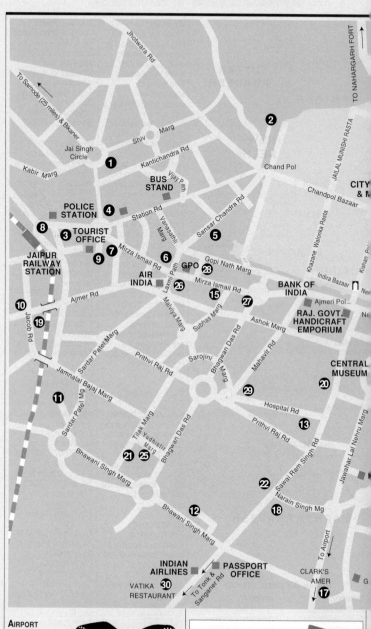

To Samode (25 miles) & Bikaner

Jhotwara Rd

Shiv Marg

Jai Singh Circle

Kabir Marg

Kantichandra Rd

Vijay Path

BUS STAND

Chand Pol

Chandpol Bazaar

CITY & M

JAILAL MUNISH RASTA

TO NAHARGARH FORT

POLICE STATION

Station Rd

Vanasathli Marg

Sansar Chandra Rd

Khazane Walonka Rasta

Kishan Po

Indira Bazaar

TOURIST OFFICE

Mirza Ismail Rd

Gopi Nath Marg

JAIPUR RAILWAY STATION

AIR INDIA

GPO

Laxmi Path

Mirza Ismail Rd

BANK OF INDIA

Ajmeri Pol

Ne

Ajmer Rd

Jacob Rd

Malviya Marg

Subhas Marg

RAJ. GOVT. HANDICRAFT EMPORIUM

Sardar Patel Marg

Prithvi Raj Rd

Sarojini

Bhagwan Das Marg

Ashok Marg

Mahavir Rd

CENTRAL MUSEUM

Jamnalal Bajaj Marg

Sardar Patel Mg

Tilak Marg

Bhawani Singh Marg

Yudhistir Marg

Bhagwan Das Rd

Hospital Rd

Prithvi Raj Rd

Sawai Ram Singh Rd

Jawahar Lal Nehru Rd

Bhawani Singh Marg

Sawai Ram Singh Rd

Narain Singh Mg

To Airport

INDIAN AIRLINES

PASSPORT OFFICE

CLARK'S AMER

G

VATIKA RESTAURANT

To Tonk & Sanganer Rd

AIRPORT TRANSFER
Jaipur's Sanganer Airport lies 6¹/2 miles south of the city center, about half an hour's journey. Unmetered taxis charge around

Rs.125/US$4.07/ £2.55, while auto-rickshaws can be hired at half the price after bargaining.

JAIPUR VISION
For the latest tourist information and tips, refer to *Jaipur Vision*, the city's only monthly tourist magazine, available in the hotels and book shops. Costs Rs.20/US$0.65/£0.40.

Cycle-rickshaws and auto-rickshaws are two local means of transport.

ALKATORA TANK

GOVIND DEVJI

VIDHAN SABHA

ANTAR ANTAR

Gangapol

N

TO GAITRO & AMBER

Moti Katla Bazaar

Hawa Mahal Bazaar

HAWA MAHAL

CHAR DARWAJA

JAMA ASJID

a Bazaar

Ram Ganj Bazaar

Johari Bazaar

Surajpol Bazaar

Suraj Pol

To Galta
To The Oberoi

pu Bazaar   Sanganer Pol

AGRA MARG

M NIWAS DEN & ZOO

OF GY

rial Rd

ry

a

HOTELS:

1 JAIPUR ASHOK
2 BISSAU PALACE
3 RTDC SWAGATAM
4 RTDC TEEJ
5 ARYA NIWAS
6 MANSINGH
7 RTDC GANGAUR
8 RAJPUTANA PALACE
9 KHASA KOTHI
10 JAI MAHAL PALACE
11 RAJMAHAL PALACE
12 RAMBAGH PALACE
13 DIGGI PALACE
14 LMB HOTEL & RESTAURANT
15 TOURIST HOTEL
16 HOTEL JAIPUR PALACE

17 HOTEL CLARK'S AMER
18 NARAIN NIWAS PALACE
19 ACHROL HOUSE
20 MERU PALACE
21 HOTEL SAKET
22 LAKSHMI VILLAS
23 HOTEL HOLIDAY INN
24 SAMODE HAVELI
25 SHIKHA

RESTAURANTS:

26 COPPER CHIMNEY
27 NIRO'S
28 CHANAKYA
29 GARDEN CAFE
30 VATIKA RESTAURANT

MOVING AROUND JAIPUR

Since there are no standard road signs, the best way is to ask the locals who are usually very helpful, or ask the traffic policeman. In the old town it is difficult to get lost as the main roads cut the side lanes at a right angle like the streets of Manhattan.

LOCAL TRANSPORT

Cycle- and auto-rickshaws are the most common means of transport. Fix the price before boarding. Cycle rickshaws charge Rs.5/US$0.16/£0.11 per km and can be booked for half a day for Rs.50–Rs.75/ US$1.63–$2.44/ £1.02–£1.53 and Rs.75–Rs.100/ US$1.63–$3.25/ £2.04 for a full day. Auto-rickshaws are supposed to run the meter but they do not. Charges for one hour or eight km are Rs.35–Rs.40/ US$1.14–$1.30/ £0.71–£0.82. Metered taxis or cars from the local agents are usually unavailable and taxis cannot be hired for a half day or a full day. The package rate is Rs.340/US$11.06/ £6.93 for four hours, and Rs.520/ US$16.92 /£10.60 for eight hours. Almost all deluxe hotels have a travel desk to help with car hire. Conducted tours to important tourist sites are operated by the RTDC. Price: Rs.60/ US$1.93/£1.27 for half a day and Rs.90/US$2.90/£1.91 for a full day, excluding entrance fees. For bookings, contact the Tourist Information Bureau at the Railway Station. Tipping is optional.

TOURIST OFFICES AND INFORMATION CENTERS

GOVERNMENT OF INDIA
Hotel Khas Kothi
Tel. 372200
9am to 6pm

GOVERNMENT OF RAJASTHAN
Railway Station
Tel. 315714
6am to 8pm

FOREIGNERS REGIONAL REGISTRATION OFFICE
Behind Hawa Mahal
Rajasthan Police
Head Office
Tel. 49391

TOURIST INFORMATION BUREAU
Central Bus Stand, Sindhi Camp
10am to 5pm

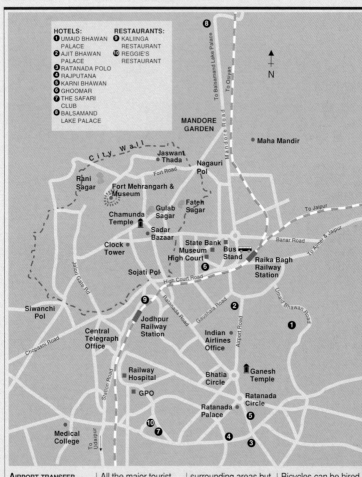

HOTELS:
- ❶ UMAID BHAWAN PALACE
- ❷ AJIT BHAWAN PALACE
- ❸ RATANADA POLO
- ❹ RAJPUTANA
- ❺ KARNI BHAWAN
- ❻ GHOOMAR
- ❼ THE SAFARI CLUB
- ❽ BALSAMAND LAKE PALACE

RESTAURANTS:
- ❾ KALINGA RESTAURANT
- ❿ REGGIE'S RESTAURANT

AIRPORT TRANSFER
The airport is 3 miles from the city center. Airport transfers cost Rs.115–Rs.135/ US$3.75–$4.40/ £2.35–£2.75. Jodhpur is connected by Indian Airlines with Jaipur, Udaipur, Bombay, New Delhi, and Aurangabad. Jagson Airways connects it with Delhi and Jaisalmer, Tel. 43813. Modiluft, Tel. 48333 U.P. Airways, Tel. 49826 Airport Tel. 37516

LOCAL TRANSPORT
Use Ghoomar Tourist Hotel as the central reference point.

All the major tourist attractions, the old city, bus stand, railway station, and airport are within 6 miles of it. Unmetered auto-rickshaws are easily available, while taxis can be booked through the hotel reception counter or the Tourist Reception Center. Prices keep fluctuating. Check with the Tourist Office. You have to bargain in any case. Auto-rickshaw costs Rs.30–50/ US$0.98–$1.63/ £0.61–£1.02. Taxi fares: Rs.65–70/ US$2.12–2.28/ £1.33–£1.43. City buses travel to

surrounding areas but not the fort and Umaid Bhawan Palace. The old city can only be covered on foot.

Tourist Reception Center, Ghoomar Tourist Hotel, High Court Road, Jodhpur Tel. 45083 9am–1pm/ 2–6pm

Bicycles can be hired from the lodge opposite the main Railway Station.

CONDUCTED TOURS
Ticket: Rs.50/ US$1.63/£1.02. Itinerary includes Umaid Bhawan Palace, Mehrangarh Fort, Jaswant Thada, and Mandore.

TAXI HIRE/TOUR AGENTS

TOURIST GUIDE SERVICE
Airport Road
Tel. 33054

TRAVEL AID
Umaid Bhawan Palace
Tel. 33316

RAJASTHAN TOURS
AIRPORT ROAD
Tel. 32694

CAR/BUS OPERATORS:
MEGHMALA TRAVELS
Opp. Railway Station
Tel. 26338

SOLANKI TRAVELS
Station Road
Tel. 39572

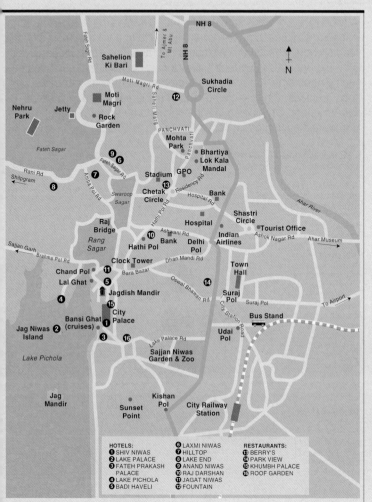

HOTELS:
1. SHIV NIWAS
2. LAKE PALACE
3. FATEH PRAKASH PALACE
4. LAKE PICHOLA
5. BADI HAVELI
6. LAXMI NIWAS
7. HILLTOP
8. LAKE END
9. ANAND NIWAS
10. RAJ DARSHAN
11. JAGAT NIWAS
12. FOUNTAIN

RESTAURANTS:
13. BERRY'S
14. PARK VIEW
15. KHUMBH PALACE
16. ROOF GARDEN

AIRPORT TRANSFER

The city center is 15 miles away from the airport. No airport bus is available. Taxis can be hired for Rs.125–130/ US$4.06–$4.23/ £2.55–£.2.65. If you book through a travel agent, it costs Rs.190–225/US$6.18 –$7.32/£4.58–£5.48. The local bus is cheap but you have to walk about ten minutes to get a bus along the main road.

LOCAL TRANSPORT

The old city is located on the eastern side of Lake Pichola. Kajari Tourist Hotel is just outside of the city wall, and only half a mile to the northeast of the bus stand. Unmetered auto–rickshaws cost Rs.10–15/US$0.33– $0.49/£0.20–£0.30 within the city area, regardless of distance. The city bus service is also available.

Bicycles can be hired at a reasonable price.

CONDUCTED TOURS

RAJASTHAN TOURISM DEVELOPMENT CORPORATION Kajari Tourist Hotel 8am–1pm
City Tour
Price: Rs.30/US$1/ £0.60. Daily tours to Haldighati, Eklingji, and Nathdwara. 2pm–7pm.

Price: Rs.70/ US$2/£1.40
Package tours to the surrounding areas are also available. For more information, contact Tourist Information Bureau at Kajari Tourist Hotel. Tel. 29535.

CAR HIRE

JAI MEWAR
Tel. 25287
KAJARI HOTEL (RTDC)
Tel. 29509
TAXI STAND
Chetak Circle
Tel. 29112

LAKE PALACE TRADE AND TRAVELS
Tel. 29158
T.G.S. TOURS AND TRAVELS
Tel. 29626, 29661

A wide range of experience can be had, from living in a palace to camping amid sand dunes, or enjoying life in a village. India's two leading hotel chains, the Welcomgroup and Taj Group, operate five-star luxury hotels in various cities. A new concept that has become highly popular is that of the heritage hotels, converted from the forts, palaces, *havelis* (old houses of noblemen), and retreats of former rulers. Or you can live in a local home under a recently introduced paying guest scheme.

MONEY MATTERS

Credit cards, traveler's checks, and Indian currency are the usual modes of payment. Apart from the tickets for bus and train travel, hotels and flight tickets can be paid with credit cards. Traveler's checks are the safest way to carry money around in India. No restriction is placed on the amount of cash being brought in, but if it is more than US$10,000/£6667, a Customs Declaration Form has to be filled in at the airport on arrival.

DENOMINATIONS

The Indian currency is available in notes in 500, 100, 50, 20, 10, 5, 2, and 1 rupees. In coins, there are 5, 2, and 1 rupees, and 50, 25, 20, 10, 5, and 1 paise.

EXCHANGE RATE

The exchange rate for the Indian rupee is 31 Indian rupees to US$1 and 49 Indian rupees to £1. Keep exchange receipts to change back remainder rupees.

TIPPING

This is not a must as in some parts of the world. However service personnel such as waiters do expect a tip, which can be up to 10 percent of the bill. Ten rupees is a reasonable tip for porters. Don't misunderstand tip as *bakshish*, a word often used by beggars.

BANKS

Banks are normally open between 10am and 2pm (Mon.–Fri.), and 10am–noon (Sat.). Some banks have evening branches. This includes the State Bank of India and Rajasthan Bank. The evening counters are open from 3pm to 6pm. Some branches in leading hotels are open till 8.30pm.

LOCAL TAXES

Food and beverages in hotels and restaurants are levied with a 12 percent sales tax. For hotel rooms with tariffs above Rs.1200/ US$39.04/£24.50, an expenditure tax of 20 percent is charged.

LAUNDRY

The *dhobi* or washermen charge nominal rates. Good only for cotton and fast colours. Drycleaners are available in the big cities and are not too expensive. They can take urgent orders and return the clothes by the evening or in twenty-four hours.

TRY THE BEST SPAGHETTI OF RAJASTHAN

FOOD

An average meal in a good restaurant costs US$5–7/£3.33–£4.67 and US$0.50–1.50/ £0.33–£1 in a local wayside joint known as *dhaba*. Some restaurants serve Chinese and Italian dishes to attract foreign tourists. *Halwai* sell snacks and Indian sweets. *Samosa, kachori* and

WHAT TO AVOID
◆ Hot spicy food, unless your stomach can accept it.
◆ Fresh salads.
◆ Drinking water from the tap.

mirchi vada are the popular local spicy snacks. Try freshly made sweets such as *jalebi*. These are sold by many shops. *Ras malai* and *mawa kachori* are quite delicious.

Indian sweets.

HOTEL BOOKINGS

FIVE-STAR HOTELS
It is advisable to book a room well in advance through your travel agent before leaving your country.

TAJ GROUP OF HOTELS
London:
Tel. 0171/963 8300
Fax. 0171/834 8629
United States:
Tel. 1-800-1-LUV-TAJ
(Toll-free line)

WELCOMGROUP OF HOTELS
United Kingdom:
Tel. 1-800-325-3535
(Toll-free lines)
United States:
Tel. 1-800-325-3535
(Toll-free lines)

◆ MID-RANGE
RTDC HOTELS
You may take the chance of booking a room on the spot. During the peak season, however, it is better to book in advance through the Central Reservation at RTDC Hotel Swagatam, Railway Station Road, Jaipur
Tel. (0141) 60586, 79252, 74203
Fax. (0141) 76245

BOOKING ADVICE
◆ Contact the local office of the Government of India Tourist Office for assistance.
◆ For last-minute bookings, contact the Government of Rajasthan's tourism offices all over the state.
◆ For paying guest accommodation, ask for the local directory of the listed guest houses at the Rajasthan Tourism Office. Speak personally to the host on the phone. If possible visit the place first before deciding. The drivers of scooter rickshaws and other public vehicles may not help you in this sort of booking as no commissions are involved. You can also refer to the latest directory at the Indian Embassy or consult the overseas offices of the Government of India.

ACCOMMODATION

The Welcomgroup and Taj Group are the two leading chains in India operating five-star luxury hotels with rooms from US$125/ £83 upward. While the Welcomgroup has its hotels in Jaipur, Jodhpur, Bikaner and Kota, the Taj Group operates in Jaipur, Udaipur, and Sawai Madhopur. The Oberoi chain will soon open hotels in Jaipur, Jodhpur, Jaisalmer and Bundi. Other chains are in the pipeline. You should experience staying in one of the heritage hotels and imagine what it is like living in the residences of erstwhile rulers and noblemen. You might meet a maharaja.

LEVEL OF COMFORT
◆ FIVE STAR DELUXE
HOTELS
These hotels offer high-quality accommodation and service often comparable with hotels around the world. Extras such as

swimming pool, tennis courts, and other standard facilites are available.
◆ HERITAGE HOTELS
These hotels offer a varied level of service. Some are professionally managed and the owners personally see to it that the guests are provided with the best service.
◆ MIDDLE RANGE
HOTELS
Some of these hotels can be good while others provide only essential services.
◆ RTDC HOTELS
The Rajasthan Tourism Development Corporation (RTDC) has been upgrading their hotels but sometimes you may just get a dingy room.
◆ PAYING GUEST
SERVICE
The local hosts try to provide all basic comforts. See below.
◆ CHEAP HOTELS
Very often, these hotels may provide a dingy room without a window or bedding.

PAYING GUEST SCHEME

A great alternative is to live in a home listed under the recently launched paying guest scheme of Rajasthan Tourism. You get a room with an attached bathroom with hot water and home-cooked meals in a good location for around US$12–15/ £8–£10.

FOOD GLOSSARY

aanda: egg
bhat/chaval: rice
chapatti/roti: unleavened bread
dahi: plain yogurt
dal: lentils
gosht: meat
halwa: sweet made from semolina, carrots or lentils
jalebi: deep fried circles of batter soaked in syrup
kachori: puff-pastry filled with lentils or spices
kadhi: a curry made of yogurt and chickpea flour

laddu: round sweet snack
lassi: iced yogurt drink
macchi: fish
makhan: butter
mirchi: spicy/chillied
murgi: chicken
namkeen: savory snack
nan: leavened bread baked in a tandoor
pani: water
papad: crispy Indian cracker
puri: deep fried, puffed bread
sabzi/sag: green vegetable

The best way to experience Rajasthan is to spend some time in the market area, which enables you to enjoy the most colorful images of local life. There are big shops as well as small wayside vendors. Some people make a living by selling fruits and vegetables or utility items at a spot on the pavement. The traffic scene in the city centers, doubtless chaotic, can be fascinating: you can see a camel cart, a scooter rickshaw, and a Maruti car maneuvering their way alongside an elephant. There may be a good chance to catch a festive procession.

Rajasthan Art Emporium.

HANDICRAFTS

Be careful when shopping at handicraft shops to save yourself from being cheated. Take a proper receipt/bill from all shops. Handicraft shops around the monuments are open from 8.30am to 8.30pm.
◆ For Rajasthani handicrafts, the only government shop is Rajasthali.
◆ Handloom House, Khadi Ghar, and the State Emporia are the only government-owned outlets selling hand-crafted textiles.
◆ A so-called government-approved shop is only approved for money-changing.
◆ Take a proper bill and receipt when paying with a credit card.
◆ Take your time and go on your own so you do not have to pay the commissions, which can be as much as 100 percent.

TEMPLES

All temples and mosques have definite timings for visitors. The times differ from shrine to shrine, so check beforehand. In Hindu and Jain temples, both men and women can join in prayer; in a mosque only men can participate. Visitors are advised to take off their shoes while visiting any holy place in Rajasthan and to cover the head when entering a mosque. No leather objects are allowed in Hindu temples.

Brahma Temple, Pushkar.

NEWSPAPERS

National dailies published in New Delhi are available at bookshops, newspaper stalls, and vendors throughout Rajasthan. Most important towns have a radio station known as Akashvani Kendra. The regional television station on Doordarshan Kendra is located in Jaipur. Foreign newspapers are not available. Magazines such as *Time, Newsweek* and the *Economic Times* can be picked up from leading bookshops.

TRAVELERS' TIPS

For those Westerners who do not wish to feel like a tourist, there is not much chance as even in the tourist centers such as Jaipur, they cannot skip the attention of the local people. Here are some tips.
◆ Wear dresses that are not revealing. For women, wear a knee-length dress, even if it is a bit too warm. For men, shorts are acceptable.
◆ Enjoy the company of the friendly local people but don't let the young man hovering around lead you to a dingy den for the cheapest price as you could end up being robbed or fleeced.
◆ When crossing at a zebra crossing, do look left and right, as Rajasthanis do, for your own safety.
◆ Learn a few words of Hindi and see the magical effect it has.
◆ Adopt a flexible attitude toward time-keeping – the person you're waiting for will eventually turn up or contact you.
◆ Just be friendly and offer a cup of tea or a little souvenir to get your work done. Give up the colonial attitude of giving *bakshish* or tipping unnecessarily.

Mail boxes.

POST OFFICE

There is a main post office in every town known as the General Post Office, or GPO, and each area has its own post office. A special postal service provided in the main Railway Station is popularly referred to as the RMS.

OPENING HOURS
All post offices are open 10am–5pm (Mon.–Fri.) and 10am–noon (Sat). The GPO closes at 7pm, and the RMS at 8pm. Registered mail and money orders are available till 3pm on weekdays and till 1pm on Saturdays. A superfast service delivering letters within twenty-four to forty-eight hours is known as the SPEEDPOST, for which extra charges have to be paid. GPO and RMS are open on Sundays. Some hotels have counters selling stamps and postal stationery and also have a mail box.

TELEPHONE

HOTELS
You may use the direct line or go through the operator. The latter comes with a service charge of up to 20 percent in five-star hotels.
PUBLIC CALL BOXES
These are not common. Local calls can be made by inserting a one-rupee coin.
STD-ISD SHOPS
It is most convenient to make calls from these shops located in the main markets. From 9pm to 6am, the rate is a quarter of the normal, and from 7am to 8am and 7pm to 9pm, it is half the normal rate.

NORMAL RATES
Jaipur-Delhi rate: Rs.18.75/US$0.60/ £0.38 per minute. Rajasthan-UK & USA:Rs.75/US$2.44/ £1.53 per minute.
OVERSEAS CALLS
International Direct Dialing Numbers
United Kingdom: 0044
United States: 001
International call booking: 186
TIME DIFFERENCES
UK: IST less 05.30 hours
USA (West Coast): IST less 10.30 hours.

Mail delivery with camel.

BARGAINING

Bargaining is a way of life in Rajasthan. Prices vary, so compare and haggle before buying. Sometimes it is possible to reduce the quoted price by 50 percent. All handicraft shops, big or small, pay heavy commissions to the guides as well as travel agents in India and abroad. Shops included in your itinerary or package tours pay an advance commission to the program makers and the driver who takes you to the shop. However, general utility items have a stated price. Look out for banners advertising clearance and seasonal festival sales for textiles and leather goods.

AREA CODES WITHIN RAJASTHAN	
Alwar	0144
Ajmer	0145
Bharatpur	05644
Bikaner	0151
Bundi	0747
Jaipur	0141
Jaisalmer	02992
Jodhpur	0291
Kota	0744
Mandawa	01592
Mount Abu	029742
Nawalgarh	015952
Pushkar	145
Sawai Madhopur	07462
Sikar	015752
Udaipur	0294

SOME SAMPLE PRICES

A CUP OF COFFEE
Rs.3/Rs.6/Rs.30
SOFT DRINKS
Rs.6/Rs.30
BEER
Rs.25 upward

BREAKFAST
(CONTINENTAL)
Rs.70–165
(INDIAN)
Rs.70–165
MAIN MEAL
Rs.25–325

ENTRY TO MUSEUMS
Rs.1–30

MOVIE THEATER
TICKETS
Rs.6–16

1˚ ROLL OF FILM
(FUJI)
Rs.80–250
(KONIKA)
Rs.90
(KODAK GOLD II)
Rs.100

Girls at the Desert Festival, Jaisalmer.

Villagers at the Nagaur Fair.

There are few places on earth where history comes alive the way it does in Rajasthan. This is partly because of the numerous splendid forts and palaces, many dating back to the 16th century, that dot this region. But more than that, the old legends of the great Rajput warriors, whose glorious tradition of valor and chivalry bring to mind the shining knights of medieval Europe, are still retold, as if it was just yesterday.

The Great Indian Bustard.

GEOGRAPHY

Rajasthan is India's westernmost state, forming a large part of its border with Pakistan, from the marshes of Kachchha in the south, through the great Thar Desert, to the plains of the Punjab in the

north. The state covers an area of over 130,000 square miles, and falls, very broadly, into three parts ■ 16. In the west lie the deserts of Marusthali or Marwar ("The Land of Death"), covering an area of 80,000 square miles. It is a unique desert ecosystem, with a sandy, rocky terrain, where thorny bushes and hardy trees, such as the Acacia nilotica and Prosopsis cineraria grow. In the center, running like a vast diagonal slash across the state, lie the sharp, craggy conical hills of the Aravalli range. And to the east lie forests, river valleys and plains that merge southward into the Vindhya hills of Central India.

HISTORY

In Rajasthan you can find traces of a civilization that flourished here as far back as 4500 years ago. However, it was in the 6th to 7th centuries that this region really began to come to the fore, with the formation of various Rajput warrior clans. By the 12th century these clans had consolidated themselves into powerful royal houses, which came into conflict with the Muslim invaders from the northwest. In the mid-16th century, the Mughal Emperor Akbar, recognizing their power, formed a series of alliances with almost all of the Rajput rulers and coopted them into his army as its main sword-arm ● 36. It

was a synergetic relationship, and as a result, the Rajputs moved from being a regional power to a subcontinental power, ranging across the length and breadth of India at the head of the Mughal armies. In the 18th century, the Rajputs went slowly into decline, partly because of internal confusion, and partly as a result of external attacks from forces like the Marathas. Finally, between 1817 and 1823, the Rajput states signed treaties of friendship with the British ● 39. After India's independence in 1947, the Princely States of the region were merged, and ultimately formed into a single administrative unit that was named Rajasthan.

POPULATION

The population of Rajasthan, according to the 1991 census, is 43.9 million. However, what is significant is the low density of population within the state, which is, in fact, one of the lowest in India. Because of the

Wall painting in Bindeswara Temple, Bikaner.

Bikaneri miniature.

Kumbhalgarh Fort.

Ghats at Lake Pichola, Udaipur.

harsh geographic conditions, the average density of population is 128 persons per square kilometer, and the figure goes down to just nine persons per square kilometer in Jaisalmer district! The population of Rajasthan is made up of a number of communities, but the single most influential community has historically been the Rajputs, who have deeply influenced the rest of society with their own cultural values of martial spirit and chivalry. Another interesting feature of Rajasthan's population is the relatively large proportion of tribals, who account for over 12 percent, and who have their own distinctive ethnographic ways ● *52*. The two largest tribes are the Bhils of southern Rajasthan, and the Minas of north-central Rajasthan.

ECONOMY
Traditionally, the economy of Rajasthan depended mainly on its livestock, agriculture,

and handicrafts. In medieval times, interestingly, military conquest gave a major economic boost to the region, when the Rajput warrior-kings came back from their military campaigns all over India, bearing the prizes of war. In the modern period a major economic landmark was the building of the far-sighted Ganga Canal irrigation project in the 1920's and 1930's, which turned the arid desert of the northeast into prime farmland ▲ *194*. Since 1947, several other major irrigation projects have followed suit. Also, since 1947, a substantial industrial base has been built up in the state, spanning everything from synthetic yarn to zinc, from automotive products to electronic equipment. Another important – and growing – contributor to the state's economy, of course, is tourism. It is also now believed that a major source of natural gas lies below Rajasthan's

desert sands, waiting to be tapped.

CULTURE
Rajasthan is famed for its rich variety of folk dance and folk music forms ● *78*. Each area has its own very special dialect of dance, ranging from the hypnotic, sinuous dances of the Kalbeliya nomads of Jaisalmer to the vigorous, energetic drum dance of Jalore, from the graceful, rhythmic *ghoomar* dance performed by the ladies of Udaipur to the daredevil fire dance of Bikaner, performed live on burning coals. Also you'll discover a fascinating variety of folk music here, ranging from the simple, haunting music of the wandering desert minstrels of the Langa and Manganiyar communities to the somewhat more sophisticated *mand*, traditionally sung at the courts of the Rajput rulers. Rajasthan is also known for its puppet shows ● *73*, based on popular legends, and for the *pabuji ki phad*, a unique bardic narration of the Pabuji legend, illustrated by a 30-foot illuminated scroll, like some medieval forerunner of the modern animated movie ● *54*. The best

showcase of Rajasthani culture is the famed Desert Festival that is held in Jaisalmer each year, where the finest performers from all over the state gather to vie with each other for honors ● *81*.

Idol of Karni Mata, Karni Mata Temple, Deshnoke ▲ 207.

RELIGION
The predominant religion of Rajasthan is, of course, Hinduism ● *44*. However it is perhaps Hinduism with a slightly different flavor, for the dominant force within Hindu society was the warrior caste of the Rajput Kshatriyas rather than the priestly Brahmins, as was the case in most of the rest of India. Another interesting religious feature of Rajasthan is the various folk cults that have developed and flourished here, based on local deities and folk heroes, such as Pabuji, Ramdeoji, Gogaji, Mehaji, Harbhuji, and Tejaji ● *52*. Other significant religious groups in the state are the Jains ● *48* and the Muslims ● *50*.

Main entrance, Samode.

Poddar Haveli.

This itinerary covers a number of cities – Jaipur, Shekhavati, Udaipur, Jaisalmer, Jodhpur, and the surrounding areas. If you prefer a more leisurely pace, reserve some cities for another trip. Rajasthan is, after all, a big state!

DAY 1
Start in Jaipur (**A**). Visit the 18th-century City Palace and its Museum ▲ *136*. Just outside is Jantar Mantar, the fantastic 18th-century observatory ▲ *140*. In the afternoon explore Jaipur's amazing scientifically planned 18th-century "Pink City" quarter and see the Albert Hall Museum ▲ *144*. In the evening visit the splendid Rambagh Palace (now converted into a hotel) ▲ *144*. Visit the Panghat Complex ◆ *342* with its countryside ambience. You can enjoy delicious food and also see a colorful performance at the theater.

DAY 2
Drive to the Amber Fort (**B**) ▲ *146* (taking a packed lunch). Visit the royal cenotaphs at Gaitor and the Jal Mahal water palace en route ▲ *157*. The 16th-century Amber Fort is a complex of mighty defense systems and exquisite palaces. In the afternoon, drive up to Amber's sister forts of Jaigarh and Nahargarh ▲ *154*. Later, visit the charming 18th-century garden palace of Sisodia Rani ka Bagh and the Hindu pilgrimage centre of Galta ▲ *156*.

DAY 3
Visit the old *haveli* mansions of Jaipur. Shop in the bazaars for Jaipur's well-known hand-printed textiles and enamel jewelry ▲ *142*. In the afternoon drive to the quaint little textile printing towns of Sanganer and Bagru ▲ *158*. Both are on different roads, in different directions. Sanganer has a very special handmade paper industry where recycled, hand-printed paper is made. On the way back stop for dinner at the rustic "food village" of Choki Dhani ▲ *157*.

DAY 4
Drive out to Shekhavati early morning. Stop at Samode and see its exquisite frescoed palace ▲ *180*. At Sikar (**C**) see the Biyani Haveli ▲ *181*. At Lachhmangarh (**D**) see the Char Chowki Haveli (one of Shekhavati's grandest). At Fatehpur (**E**) see the Devra, Singhania, and Bhartia *havelis* ▲ *183*. Finally you arrive at Mandawa (**F**) with its Chokhani, Goenka, and Saraf *havelis* and its medieval fort (now a very charming hotel, where you can spend the night) ▲ *182*.

DAY 5
Drive to Ramgarh (**G**), with its cenotaphs and *havelis* of the Poddar family ▲ *190*. It's also a great place to shop for antiques. At

Haveli, Jaisalmer.

Bazaar, Udaipur.

Mahensar **(H)** see the Sone Chandi ki Haveli (with the finest frescos in all Shekhavati) ▲ *190.* At Bissau **(I)** see the cenotaphs of the local *thakurs* (chieftains). Turning back, stop at Jhunjhunu **(J)** and see the Tibdiwalal *haveli* ▲ *183.* At Nawalgarh **(K)** there are some superb frescos inside the fort, and also the Poddar and Chhawchhariya *havelis* ▲ *182.* At Dunlod **(L)** there's a very interesting little fort, and the Goenka Haveli and cenotaphs ▲ *182.* Return to Jaipur.

DAY 6
Take the early morning flight to Udaipur **(M).** Visit Udaipur's City Palace, with its ornately decorated suites and its museum ▲ *246.* Nearby are the more recent palaces of Fateh Prakash and Shiv Nivas ▲ *249.* Take a boat to the fabulous marble Lake Palace (now a hotel) ▲ *250.* After lunch, visit the Jagdish Mandir and shop in Udaipur's bazaars. At sunset take a cruise past the sights of this lovely lake city.

DAY 7
Drive to Chittorgarh **(N),** 69 miles away ▲ *276.* The fort is truly awe-inspiring. On the way back, visit the Sas and Bahu temples at Nagda **(O)**

and the Eklingji Temple **(P)** ▲ *256.*

DAY 8
See the beautiful old gardens of Saheliyon ki Bari ▲ *254.* Drive on to the royal cenotaphs at Ahar **(Q)** ▲ *255.* By noon set out for the great fortress of Kumbhalgarh **(R),** 43 miles away ▲ *260.* Spend the night at the 18th-century Ghanerao Royal Castle (now a charming hotel) ◆ *339.*

DAY 9
Visit the Kumbhalgarh Game Sanctuary. Then set out for the great 15th-century Jain temple at Ranakpur **(S)** ▲ *262,* which is open to tourists from noon to 5pm. Drive back to Udaipur, and visit Shilpagram, an interesting "living ethnographic museum" ▲ *254* ◆*342.* Catch the evening flight to Jodhpur **(T)** (7pm).

DAY 10
Visit Jodhpur's impregnable hilltop Mehrangarh Fort ▲ *224,* with its beautiful palace complex. See the nearby Jaswant Thada cenotaph ▲ *228.* In the afternoon take a walk through the town's old medieval quarter and shop for Jodhpur's handicrafts along the way. In the evening see the colossal domed

1930's Umaid Bhawan Palace (now a hotel) ▲ *230.* Take a late-night train to Jaisalmer **(U)** (10.30pm).

DAY 11
Go to the Gadsisar Tank, with its historic (and controversial) archway ▲ *210.* Spend the day exploring the mighty 12th-century yellow sandstone fort ▲ *212.* Inside are some wonderful Jain temples, and astonishingly carved *havelis.* Shop in the bazaar for Jaisalmer's famed desert handicrafts. Later, see the Jaisalmer Palace (from the outside only, unfortunately), the Jawahar Nivas royal guest house, and the Vyas Chhatri cenotaphs ▲ *216.* In the evening drive out to the desert village of Samm 27 miles away **(V),** or to Khurri **(W)** 24 miles away ▲ *218,* and spend the night there ▲ *219.*

DAY 12
Take a desert camel safari from Khurri. Starting at 8am, it takes you through the vast, empty sand-

duned country. At midday you stop at a desert village for lunch. At 4pm drive back to Jaisalmer.

DAY 13
Drive out to the beautiful royal cenotaphs at Bara Bagh, the Amarsagar tank ▲ *216* and palace, the ancient capital of Lodurva **(K),** and Akal and Kandiala ▲ *217,* with their interesting fossils. In the evening visit the romantic Bhattiani Sati Rani temple.Take the night train back to Jodhpur (9.15pm).

DAY 14
Drive out from Jodhpur to the great ruined temple town of Osiyan **(Y)** ▲ *233,* dating back to the 8th century, located 40 miles away. On your way back, stop at Mandore **(Z),** with its unique royal cenotaphs and its curious "Hall of Heroes" ▲ *232.* Back in Jodhpur, visit the impressive many-pillared Mahamandir Temple ▲ *231.* Catch the night flight to Delhi.

City Palace Museum.

Sheesh Mahal, Amber Fort.

DAY 1

MORNING
Begin at the City Palace (**A**), a sprawling 18th-century complex of palaces and courtyards designed in a formal Rajput-Mughal style ▲ 136. The museum here has a fine collection of heirlooms of the maharajas of Jaipur. Adjoining the palace is the Jantar Mantar (**B**) an amazing 18th-century observatory ▲ 140. There is a gigantic 89-foot high sundial here, for instance, that keeps time accurate to three seconds! Also part of the palace complex is

AMBER: THE PALACES

the picturesque Hawa Mahal (**C**), the five-storied "Palace of the Winds," created for the pleasure of the ladies of the court ● 93 ▲ 139.

AFTERNOON
Have lunch at Lakshmi Mishtan Bhandar (**D**) nearby (the *dahi wadas,*

savory donuts in yogurt; *kachoris,* deep-fried spiced puffs; and *kulfi,* a traditional saffron-flavoured ice cream, are recommended) ▲ 142. After lunch take a slow rickshaw ride through Jaipur's old Pink City quarter (**E**), laid out in the 18th century in a

remarkably scientific grid system of town planning ● 92 ▲ 132. This is where Jaipur's colorful, bustling bazaar lies ▲ 142. Just beyond is the Albert Hall Museum ▲ 144, worth a visit if only to see its magnificent 17th-century Persian garden carpet.

EVENING
Go to the Rambagh Palace (**F**) for dinner ▲ 144. In the 1930's this was the palace of the jet-setting Maharaja Sawai Man Singh II. Today it is a hotel and in its charming Polo Bar you can have a drink

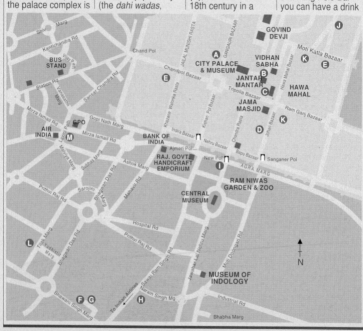

Polo Bar, Rambagh Hotel.

Chand Pol bazaar.

among the trophies of the Maharaja's legendary polo team. Make sure you get to the Rambagh before sundown, so you can see its beautiful grounds, and the graceful cupolated building, designed by the famed architect, Sir Swinton Jacob ▲ *134*. For dinner visit the Panghat Complex (**G**), the latest addition to the city, offering a country-like ambience and a colorful show at the theater ◆ *342*.

DAY 2

MORNING
Take a packed lunch and drive to Gaitor, the beautiful marble cenotaphs of the maharajas of Jaipur ▲ *157*. Nearby is Jal Mahal, the water palace built in the center of a lake ▲ *157*. This lake was the site of Sawai Jai Singh II's great Horse Sacrifice, to mark his pre-eminence as the greatest Hindu king of his time. From here, it's a short drive to the splendid 16th-century Amber Fort ▲ *146*. It was built by Raja Man Singh I with an eye to both war and pleasure: mighty battlements and watchtowers enclose exquisite pleasure palaces. Don't miss the Sheesh Mahal, with its magnificently mirrored walls and ceiling, and Sukh

Niwas, with its ingenious medieval "air-conditioning" system.

AFTERNOON
After lunch, drive up the hills behind Amber to Jaigarh ▲ *154*, the mysterious, brooding hill fort that was part of Amber's complex defense system. Here you can see the mammoth Jaivana, probably the largest cannon in the world, and the palace complex, a replica of the one at Amber. Don't miss the royal baths at Lakshmi Vilas, with their intriguing medieval system for hot and cold water. Drive on to Nahargarh ▲ *155*, another old hill fort nearby, with its romantic pleasure palace complex built by Madho Singh II for his nine maharanis. Until recently, cannons were fired daily at midday to mark the time. Drive on to Sisodia Rani ka Bagh, a double-storied 18th-century pleasure palace, built for a Sisodia princess ▲ *156*. It is surrounded by a beautiful multi-leveled landscaped garden, with fountains and cascades. From here, carry on to Galta, with its Sun Temple perched high on a hill overlooking a gorge, and its sacred water tanks, where pilgrims gather on auspicious

occasions to wash away their earthly sins ▲ *156*.

DAY 3

MORNING
Visit the *havelis* of Jaipur, the mansions of the kingdom's erstwhile nobility ▲ *145*. Many of them have now been converted into charming hotels. Narain Niwas (**H**) and Samode Haveli (**J**) are some of the more interesting ones. Nearby are the bazaars (**K**) ▲ *142*, where you can shop for Jaipur's famed hand-printed fabrics and *minakari* enamel jewelry. For exclusive fashion garments straight out of the pages of *Elle*, try Anokhi on Tilak Road (**L**) ▲ *143* ◆ *340* and Soma Blocks on Jacob Road, and for silver jewelry try Amrapali International, Miss India and Tholia's Kuber, all on M.I. Road, and Silver Mountain, Chameliwala Market (**M**), opposite the General Post Office.

AFTERNOON
For lunch, try one of Rajasthan's favorite delicacies, *dal bati churma* (you'll get it at Lakshmi Bhojanalaya on M.I. Road). Then drive out to Sanganer, 6 miles away, famed since the 17th century for its handprinted textiles, and its handmade paper ▲ *158*. Both of these industries spill out into Sanganer's maze of sandy lanes and it is fascinating to watch the craftsmen at work. There's also a fine 15th-century Jain temple here. Drive on from here to Bagru ▲ *158*, further south, another interesting old textile printing town, where craftsmen from all over Rajasthan were invited by the local raja three hundred years ago to practice their crafts. Today their bold, earthy prints have put this sleepy little town on the international fashion map.

EVENING
You can visit one of Jaipur's many village resorts.

Mehrangarh Fort overlooking the city.

Umaid Bhawan Palace.

DAY 1

MORNING

Explore the awe-inspiring Mehrangarh Fort (**A**) ▲ *224*, which seems to somehow grow organically out of the craggy, towering hill overlooking the town. You enter its mighty walls through a series of cunningly planned fortified gates, and at the summit is a complex of splendid palaces (noted, particularly, for their exquisitely carved sandstone latticework). There is also an interesting museum here, with a collection of royal heirlooms – from superb antique weaponry to elephant *howdahs* of different types, and even a strange assortment of ornate cradles in which the royal babies were rocked. Another especially fascinating exhibit here depicts the various different styles of turbans worn in Rajasthan – about a hundred of them. There is a spectacular view from the ramparts, and on a clear day you can see all the way to the rival fort of Kumbhalgarh, 77 miles away ▲ *260*. On your way down stop off at Jaswant Thada (**B**), the white marble cenotaph of

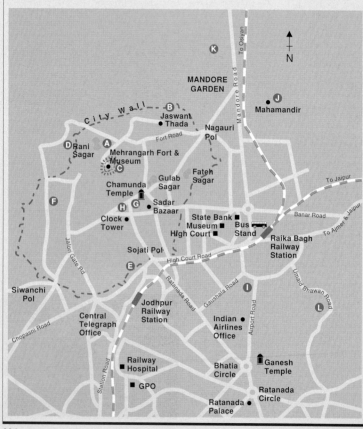

Interior of Ajit Bhawan Palace.

Village house.

Maharaja Jaswant Singh II ▲ 228.

AFTERNOON
Try a typical Rajasthani meal. Two restaurants that are recommended are Pokhar Sweet House (**C**) and Pankaj, at Jalori Gate, near the base of the fort. After lunch there is an interesting walking tour you can take through the town's maze of little medieval lanes. Start at the fort's Fateh Pol Gate, turn right toward the old 16th-century water tanks of Rani Sar and Padam Sar (**D**). Then double back to the beautiful old mansion of Mohnoton ki Haveli, past Jaisalmeriyon ki Gali (**E**), with its picturesque old houses, and the splendid carved 16th-century Talati ka Mahal palace (**F**). You will then come to the Old Grain Market (**G**), which is surrounded by some fine old temples and buildings. In the bazaar nearby you can shop for Jodhpur's brightly colored handprinted fabric, glass bangles, and leather *mojri* slippers. At the end of the afternoon, cool off at the Shri Misrilal Hotel, near the clock tower (**H**), with a *makhaniya lassi*, buttermilk so thick you can stand a spoon in it.

EVENING
A very good place to shop is the emporium at the Ajit Bhawan Palace (**I**) ◆ 339. It has an excellent selection of everything from handicrafts and "neo antiques" to authentic Jodhpur riding breeches. Stay on for a drink and dinner at the Ajit Bhawan. Dinner is in the traditional Rajasthani style, served in the palace's carved sandstone courtyard under the stars, and while you eat you are entertained by *bhopa* folk bards ▲ 54, singing folk songs of bravery and chivalry. By the way, make bookings here for tomorrow morning's village safari, organized by the Ajit Bhawan Palace.

DAY 2
MORNING
Go out on a jeep safari to the Bishnoi villages surrounding Jodhpur ▲ 232. You get a rare and wonderful insight into the life and customs of an Indian village – with Maharaj Swaroop Singh providing a vivid commentary. The experience may cover such things as having tea and a puff of the *hookah* with the villagers, learning about their rituals, folklore, and superstitions, watching weavers

and potters at work, learning how a *dhoti* is tied, or even receiving a small ritual draft of opium as a mark of hospitality from your village host. The safari also gives you the opportunity to see the local wildlife along the way, specifically the blackbuck and the rare Great Indian Bustard.

AFTERNOON
Have lunch at Ajit Bhawan – a simple earthy Rajasthani meal served in the hotel's "village complex" – and set out for Mahamandir (**J**). This is a great Shiva temple with a veritable forest of wonderfully carved pillars and some fascinating murals of yogic postures ▲ 231. Drive on from here to the old royal lakeside pleasure resort of Balsamand, and to Mandore (**K**) ▲ 232. The latter was the ancient capital of the Jodhpur kingdom, and you can see the graceful spired cenotaphs of the maharajas. Rao Ajit Singh's is the most impressive. There's also a fascinating "Hall of Heroes" here, with row upon row of equestrian statues of Rajput folk heroes. Do not miss the tombs of the Maharanis, a ten-minute walk over the hill.

EVENING
Visit the colossal Umaid Bhawan Palace (**L**) ▲ 230, once one of the world's largest private residences, with 347 rooms. It looks like something designed by Albert Speer from the outside, and its interiors are a mixture of Art Deco and Beaux Arts. Now, of course, it is a luxury hotel, but it gives you a pretty good idea of what the lifestyle of the maharajas was like. There is a very interesting royal museum here. If you can, do try and see some of the lavish suites. The palace's verandah is a great place for a sundowner. Have dinner in the palace's grand dining hall, under the towering vaulted ceilings. Also, there is usually a program of Rajasthani folk dances held at the Umaid Bhawan in the evenings.

Lake Palace.

Jag Mandir.

DAY 1

MORNING

Visit the 16th-century City Palace (**A**) ▲ 246, with its high walls surmounted by towers, cupolas, and balconies in the traditional, formidable Rajput manner. Inside is a succession of palaces which became more decorative and sumptuous as the centuries passed, with fine mosaics, frescos and intricate mirrorwork. There is also a hanging garden where, surprisingly, full-grown trees flourish 90 feet above the ground, and a museum with a terrifying array of old Rajput weaponry.

AFTERNOON

Take a packed lunch and set out early for the magnificient Ranakpur Temple (**B**), 60 miles away ▲ 262. It closes at 5pm, so tell your driver to step on it. Built in 1439, the temple is overwhelming in its scale and complexity, as well as its intricacy of carving. It is held up by 1414 carved pillars, and if you look closely you'll discover that no two pillars are the same.

EVENING

From Ranakpur, drive on to Ghanerao, where you can spend the night at the Ghanerao Royal Castle, a Rajput palace dating back to the 17th century, and now converted into a charming hotel ◆ 339.

DAY 2

MORNING

Set out early for the great fort of Kumbhalgarh ▲ 260. Built in the 15th century, this enormous fort is, in many ways, even more awe-inspiring than the Chittorgarh Fort. Its miles of outlying walls, running across the hillsides, are wide enough for eight horsemen to ride abreast, and have been likened in their conception to the Great Wall of China. At the citadel, within the fort's seven concentric defensive rings, is the Badal Mahal ("Cloud Palace"), with its delicately frescoed halls and chambers.

AFTERNOON

Returning to Udaipur, head for the Lake Palace (**C**) for lunch. This 18th-century marble palace ▲ 250 floating in the middle of Lake Pichola is like something out of an oriental fantasy, with cupoled pavilions, courtyards, fountains and frescos. Today it has been converted into a hotel, described by the well-known travel writer René Lecler as "the most beautiful hotel in the world". Then visit the 17th-century Jagdish Mandir (**D**) ▲ 254 near the City Palace gates. Make sure you don't miss the superb bronze statue of Garuda in the shrine near the temple entrance. Browse in the bazaar just outside the temple for copies of Udaipur's famed miniature and *pichhvai* paintings, and other handicrafts.

EVENING

Take a lake cruise at sunset, sailing leisurely past the sights of this lakeside town: the old fortified walls, the *haveli* mansions, the picturesque bathing ghats, and the Jag Mandir (**E**) island palace. Then back to the Lake Palace for a sundowner, a colorful Rajasthani folk puppet show and dinner.

THEMATIC
ITINERARIES

A not-to-be-missed experience in Rajasthan is the opportunity to stay in the many old palaces-turned-hotels that pepper the state. Most of them are run by former princes or chieftains, and visitors are treated almost like personal guests of the family. Here we spotlight ten of the classified heritage hotels.

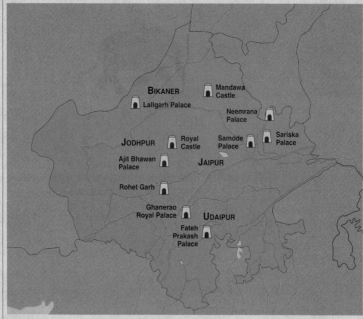

◆ **MANDAWA CASTLE, MANDAWA (SHEKHAVATI)**
Mandawa Castle is a mysterious medieval fortress. Staying here is like stepping back through a time-warp ▲ *182*.

◆ **SAMODE PALACE, SAMODE (NEAR JAIPUR)**
The exquisite, frescoed 19th-century Samode Palace was the location for the TV serial based on M.M. Kaye's best-seller, *The Far Pavillions* ▲ *180*.

◆ **ROHET GARH, ROHET (NEAR JODHPUR)**
At the Rohet Garh Palace, you are hosted by the family of the local raja, who will also take you on interesting safaris.

◆ **GHANERAO ROYAL CASTLE, GHANERAO (NEAR UDAIPUR)**
Ghanerao Royal Castle is characterized by a rambling 17th-century mélange of cupolas and balconies.

◆ **AJIT BHAWAN PALACE, JODHPUR**
Ajit Bhawan Palace is a charming 19th-century sandstone palace filled with family heirlooms and old hunting trophies. The village safaris they organize from here are a must.

◆ **NEEMRANA PALACE, NEEMRANA (NEAR ALWAR)**
Built in 1464 and painstakingly restored over the past few years, Neemrana Palace is one of the most romantic hotels in Rajasthan ▲ *178*.

◆ **ROYAL CASTLE, KHIMSAR (NEAR JODHPUR)**
Built in the late 15th century, Khimsar's Royal Castle was already over two hundred years old when it played host to the Mughal emperor Aurangzeb in the 1680's.

◆ **FATEH PRAKASH PALACE, UDAIPUR**
Fateh Prakash Palace, a small but elegantly restored old palace, has rooms decorated with priceless miniature paintings from the Maharana of Udaipur's personal collection ▲ *249*.

◆ **LALLGARH PALACE, BIKANER**
A sprawling sandstone fantasy designed by Sir Swinton Jacob, Lallgarh Palace is one of the grandest palaces in Rajasthan ▲ *198*.

◆ **SARISKA PALACE, SARISKA (NEAR ALWAR)**
A magnificent hunting lodge, Sariska Palace was built by the eccentric and sinister Maharaja Jai Singh of Alwar in honor of the Prince of Wales' visit in 1905 ▲ *175*.

Lallgarh Palace

Ghanerao Royal Castle

Rohet Garh

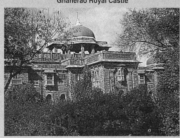

Ajit Bhawan Palace

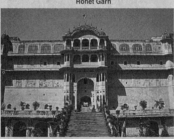

Samode Palace

Sariska Palace

Fateh Prakash Palace

Mandawa Castle

Royal Castle

Neemrana Palaces

Block-printed textiles.

Tie-and-dye textiles.

Leather embroidery work.

A centuries-old crafts tradition has turned Rajasthan into a shopper's paradise. The rulers of the former Princely States can be credited for giving Rajasthan a rich heritage of handicrafts as they had extended patronage to talented craftsmen from other states. Today a number of official organizations, such as the All India Handicraft Board, the Rajasthan Small Scale Industries Corporation, and the Ministry of Textiles provide financial and other support to meet the demand for local crafts.

RAJASTHANI TEXTILES

Rajasthan is extremely rich in vibrant textiles. Two ancient techniques of tie-and-dye and block printing ● 56, 58 are still widely practiced. In tie-and-dye art, there are two distinct patterns: the dot motif, or *bandhej*, and the stripes, or *laharia*. There is a wide selection of block prints from Sanganer and Bagru near Jaipur, and Barmer. You can see block-printing in process as well as buy the material in these areas. Anokhi at Tilak Marg is the main outlet for hand-embroidered and mirrorwork textiles in Jaipur. Tel. 381619, 381558. Check out the stores on M.I. Road, such as:

GOVERNMENT EMPORIA
Handloom House
Rituraj Bldg.
M.I. Road, Jaipur

RAJASTHALI
Ajmeri Gate,
M.I. Road, Jaipur
Tel. 367176

ITEM	PRICE RANGE
Cotton fabric (per meter)	Rs.15–20/ US$0.49–$0.65/ £0.30–0.41
Silk fabric (per meter)	Rs.75–100/ US$2.44–$3.25/ £1.53–£2.03
Bed cover, Single	Rs. 70–90/ US$2.28–$2.93/ £1.43–£1.84
Bed cover, Double	Rs.100–200/ US$3.25–6.50/ £2.03–£4.08
Sari, cotton	Rs.90–100/ US$2.93–$3.25/ £1.84–£2.03

CARPETS AND DURRIES

Rajasthan is an important center for the manufacture and export of high-quality carpets ● 68. Around Jaipur there are several villages actively producing carpets that compare well with Persian ones and are available at very competitive prices. Cotton, silk, and woolen floor coverings with oriental and contemporary motifs are made in and around the cities of Jaipur and Jodhpur. Shyam Ahuja, a world-famous designer and manufacturer of rugs, durries, fabrics and other home accessories, will be opening a new outlet in Jaipur. You can see their showrooms in Bombay and Delhi.

HANDMADE PAPER

This cottage industry is located at Sanganer ● 158. Non-forest material such as tailor cutting, jute and agro waste, hoisery cuttings, and waste paper are used. After recycling the waste material, skilled hands turn it into beautiful paper which is converted into letter paper, cards, carrier bags, and gift boxes.

Blue pottery.

Jootis.

Miniature painter.

"JOOTIS"

Worn by locals, these leather slip-on shoes are becoming increasingly fashionable.
Price range: Rs.90–250/US$3–$8/£1.80–£5.

MINIATURE PAINTINGS

Miniature paintings of distinctive schools ● *64* are reproduced on silk, ivory, cotton, and paper. As you wander in the cities of Rajasthan, you can see the painters at work. Some have their works exhibited in museums abroad and their works command a high price. One such artist is Ved Pal Sharma Banno, Chankya Marg, near Jorawar Singh Gate, Jaipur Tel. 43450.
Price range: Rs. 250–5000/US$8–163/£5–102 and upward.

BLUE POTTERY

The blue pottery of Jaipur is world famous ● *72*. One of the veterans who revived this art is Kripal Singh Shekhawat in whose studio at Kripal Kumbha, Shiv Marg, Bani Park, Tel. 311229, you can pick up some collectible pieces. Jaipur's blue pottery center at Sanganer is worth visiting, to see the craftsmen at work and to pick up some pieces at a bargain price. Prices of pots vary with size and the quality of the workmanship.
Price range: Small pieces at Rs.30–100/US$1–$3.30/£0.60–£2. Big pieces at Rs.60–400/US$2–$13/£1.30–£8.20. Earrings at Rs.15–40/US$0.50–$1.30/£0.30–£0.80; necklaces at Rs.40–300/US$1.30–$9.80/£0.80–£6.15.

PRACTICAL SHOPPING TIPS

◆ Prices are quoted high and can be brought down considerably by bargaining.
◆ Craft shops around the monuments are often not the best places to get a fair deal.
◆ Browse first to develop a sense of appreciation when buying miniature paintings, embroidered pieces, and so on.
◆ When paying by credit card, ask for a bill and receipt.

JEWELRY

MINAKARI JEWELRY
The art of embellishing gold jewelry with enamel work, or *minakari*, originated from Lahore at the end of the 16th century ● *62*. The technique of enameling is the same as that of *champlevé* work in Europe but the designs and the motifs reflect the strong influence of Mughal art. There are two variations of enameled jewelry. One is designed using only the enamels while the other is a combination of enamelwork and the inlay art known as *kundan* work. For enameled gold jewelry, 23½ carat gold and a touch of copper is used to achieve the perfect finish. This art is also practiced for some of the most exquisite objets d'art. It is important to know the gold weight to figure out the right price. See master

craftsmen, such as Sardar Kudrat Singh at Jadiyon Ka Rasta and Jaswant Kumar at Gopalji ka Rasta, at work.

PRECIOUS STONES
Jaipur is a world-famous center for the cutting and polishing of imported raw stones. In the walled city's Johri Bazaar, Haldiyon Ka Rasta, and Gopalji Ka Rasta are the shops, or *gaddies*, that produce these gems. In the back alleys around the market, artisans cut and polish the stones. You need to bargain wisely as there are no fixed prices for these gemstones.

SILVER JEWELRY
The jewelry worn by villagers for centuries are now high fashion items. Browse in the shops in the old city markets. Silver is sold at a per-gram rate or on the percentage of silver. Price range: Rs.6–15/ US$0.20–$0.49/ £0.13–£0.30 per gram.

RAJASTHALI

Rajasthali, the state government's outlet found in the major towns, is recommended for its range of crafts and fixed prices. Even if you shop outside the towns, visit Rajasthali to get an idea of the price range and workmanship.

◆ CULTURAL PERFORMANCES

Panghat Theater.

Musicians.

Folk traditions and classical forms found royal patronage in Rajasthan. In the state of Jaipur, distinctive styles of classical arts, such as the Jaipur School of Kathak and the world-famous Dhrupad singing, flourished. The Bhatti rulers of Jaisalmer extended patronage to the Manganiyar community ● *79* and the Rathors of Jodhpur; the rich Sindhi Muslims patronized both the Langas and the Manganiyars. The Manganiyars and Langas have an extremely rich repertoire of songs. A characteristic style of singing, *Maand*, marked ceremonial occasions and musical feasts, or *mehfils*.

PANGHAT THEATER

The recently opened Panghat Theater at the Rambagh Palace, Jaipur, is highly recommended during the tourist season (October to April). The Bird's repertory of performers from all over the state performs, directed by Himmat Singh, who also designed this picturesque theater under the trees. For reservations, contact The Rambagh Palace Tel. 381919 Cost: Rs. 600/ US$10/£6.50 inclusive of dinner.

REGULAR SHOWS

◆ Panghat Theater Rambagh Palace, Jaipur
7.15pm to 8pm. The show includes folk dances such as Chari, Terah Tali, Kalbeliya, and Chakari ● *78*. Langas and Manganiyars play instruments such as *satara, morchang*, and *kamaycha*.

◆ Bharatiya Lok Kala Mandal, Chetak Circle, Udaipur Puppet theater from 6pm to 6.30pm. Folk dances from 6.30pm to 7pm. Rs.20/US$0.65/£0.40
◆ Meera Kala Mandir, 7pm to 8pm. Choreographed folk dances available throughout the year. Rs.30/US$0.98/£0.62

OTHER THEATERS

All major towns have theaters or town halls available for performances brought in by cultural organizations in the form of plays, classical and folk shows, as well as entertainment shows with film personalities or other maestros. The best way to keep in touch is through the local Tourist Office because some of these shows may be open to members of certain clubs and cultural organizations only.

JAWAHAR KALA KENDRA

Located along the Jawahar Lal Nehru Marg in Jaipur, this cultural complex comprises two theaters and a village arena. Performances representing the arts of Rajasthan and sometimes those of other states in India and even foreign countries are organized all year round. One normally has to keep in touch with the center for information since wide publicity is given only to the bigger events.

SHILPAGRAM, UDAIPUR

This village complex on Rani Road near Fateh Sagar Lake has recently gained popularity as a performance venue since local craftsmen and artisans gather here to demonstrate their skills ● *254*. Open from 2pm to 7.30pm.

Gair dance.

Puppet theater.

SHOWS IN HOTELS

Hotels all over the state of Rajasthan vie with each other in putting on a variety of cultural shows every evening with the available local talent. Since not much else happens here as far as evening entertainment goes, these shows are often the only exposure to the folk dance, music, and puppetry of the region. Some, admittedly, may not be as authentic as others. In the hotels of Jaisalmer and Jodhpur, where the traditional musical communities, the Manganiyars and Langas, live, the performances are definitely more authentic. The presence of puppeteers and snake charmers are, however, abundant in hotels all over Rajasthan. Some places even have paid shows, while others arrange a dinner cum free cultural show, where the performers earn handsome tips from the guests. Artistes are also available for personalized performances should any tourist so desire. Earnings from tourism in the state have helped to keep these traditional art forms alive.

Snake charmer.

PUPPETRY

The traditional puppeteers known as the Bhatts ● 73 live all over Rajasthan, but they prefer to sell puppets rather than perform. The best place to see the traditional puppet theater is the Bharatiya Lok Kala Mandal at Udaipur ▲ 254. Set up in 1952, the center is renowned for its outstanding puppet productions and experimental folk dances. Its puppet theater and dance group has performed all over the world, in London, Paris, Berlin, Munich, Hamburg, Rome, Geneva, and elsewhere. The institution also houses a folklore museum.

FAIRS AND FESTIVALS

Tourists can catch authentic cultural performances in the many fairs and festivals held in Rajasthan throughout the year ● 80–2 ◆ 315.

MUSIC AND VIDEO TAPES

Music Today and HMV have released the music of the Langas, Manganiyars, and Mand singers, and that of the late Alla Jillai Bai and Gauri Devi on tape. The tapes are available in major music shops.

Music Today: Rs.65/US$2/£1.50
HMV: Rs.26/US$0.85/£0.53
The Bird has undertaken the production work for a video recording. For details, contact: C-267, Bhabha Marg, Tilak Nagar, Jaipur 302004 Tel. 622185

Jaisalmer Fort.

Jain temple, Mount Abu.

SUNSET OVER JAISALMER FORT

Watch the Jaisalmer Fort ▲ 212 at sunset and you'll see the curious phenomenon of its battlements changing color.

Each evening, as twilight falls, they turn from a dull buff-yellow to a glowing pink-gold.

TRANSLUCENT MARBLE

The marble temples at Mount Abu ▲ 270 are carved with such breathtaking intricacy that the effect is not of marble at all, but of

frilly paper-cuttings. In some places, indeed, the marble is so finely shaved that it is actually translucent.

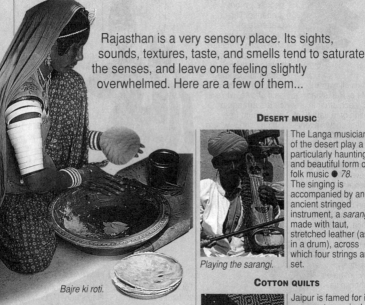

Rajasthan is a very sensory place. Its sights, sounds, textures, taste, and smells tend to saturate the senses, and leave one feeling slightly overwhelmed. Here are a few of them...

DESERT MUSIC

Playing the sarangi.

The Langa musicians of the desert play a particularly haunting and beautiful form of folk music ● 78. The singing is accompanied by an ancient stringed instrument, a *sarangi*, made with taut, stretched leather (as in a drum), across which four strings are set.

Bajre ki roti.

RAJASTHANI FLAVORS

Bajre ki roti, the simple rustic bread of Rajasthan, is thick, coarse, and deliciously grainy. Made from stone ground millet, it is traditionally eaten with garlic chutney. Celebrated in folk songs, this bread is a favorite of everyone from peasant to princeling. Another favorite is *gajak*, a

delicious north Rajasthani candy, made from *jaggery* and *til* (sesame seed). It is dried into wafer-thin flaky, crumbly sheets that literally melt in one's mouth. *Daal-baati-churma* is a traditional Rajasthani delicacy – roasted wheat flour balls crushed with lashings of hot *ghee*, lentils, and *jaggery*.

COTTON QUILTS

Quilt.

Jaipur is famed for its snug, yet amazingly light cotton quilts – just the thing for a freezing desert winter's night. Sometimes musk or ambergris *attar* is sprinkled on the whipped cotton filling, as it is believed that such *attars* have a subtle "heating" quality.

Rural house.

Pushkar fair.

RUSTIC FENCES

The villagers of Rajasthan use fences made of thorny *babool* branches (above, the overhanging branches of a *babool* tree) to keep their domestic animals from straying. This was perhaps a natural predecessor of the modern barbed wire. Another type of fence is made from *khus*, a dry reed that is woven into screens which form an ingenious, if primitive, "air-conditioning" system. The screens are regularly drenched with water so that the hot desert air that blows through them is automatically cooled and perfumed. In summer, you can get the delightful cooling fragrance of *khus* wherever you go.

CRYING CAMELS

At the end of the great annual camel fair at Pushkar ● *82*, you hear a strange wailing sound in the air. It is, you learn, the sound of the departing mother camels crying at being parted from their young ones, which have been auctioned off.

HOT SANDS

A contingent discomfort of traveling in the desert regions of Rajasthan is the naggingly gritty feel of sand in one's eyes. The Camel Breeding Farm in Bikaner ▲ *203* has specially bred a strain of camels with thicker eyelashes to give them greater protection in dust storms.

"LILY OF BIRDS"

The Siberian Crane.

The rare Siberian crane ● *27* is perhaps one of the most graceful birds in existence. Described by an ornithologist as "the lily of birds", it presents the eye with a series of harmonious, flowing curves. It has been seen every winter in the Keoladeo Ghana Sanctuary ● *307*.

"BIDIS"

Smoking a bidi.

Bidis, the rustic "mini-cigarettes" that are smoked in Rajasthan, have a pungent, acrid fragrance all their own. Made of crude rolled tobacco leaves, they are traditionally smoked in a curious fashion: the *bidi* is held between the little finger and ring finger of a clenched fist and the smoke is inhaled through the gap between the thumb and the index finger.

Devotees at Karni Mata Temple.

SCURRYING RATS

A truly bizarre experience is feeling the sacred rats of the Karni Mata temple ● *46* ▲ *207*, near Bikaner, scurrying over your bare feet. However, if one of the rats does climb onto you it is said to be a sign of good fortune.

Rajasthan seems as if it was created specifically to be a movie set, with its 70 mm desert landscapes, spectacular palaces and forts, picturesque bazaars, and colorfully veiled women. Added to all these are the romantic legends of Rajasthan that fire the movie-maker's imagination. Satyajit Ray, for instance, once confessed that although he filmed in Rajasthan six times, "proximity has done nothing to dispel the aura....If anything, by making me aware of its richness and diversity, it has entrenched itself even more deeply in my imagination."

Scene from "Shakespeare Wallah" filmed at City Palace, Alwar.

SHAKESPEARE WALLAH

When filming *Shakespeare Wallah*, Ismail Merchant and James Ivory needed a palace to shoot the scene where the itinerant Shakespearean company performs *Antony and Cleopatra* for a maharaja. The place they had set their hearts on was the grand, many-pillared Diwan-i-Khas at the Deeg Monsoon Palace ▲ *310*, but the duo were unable to obtain permission to shoot there. They finally used the interior courtyard of the City Palace, Alwar ▲ *170*, having the Shakespearean actors appear from its trellised windows and domed balconies, while the maharaja sat in the courtyard below.

THE FAR PAVILIONS

Based on M.M. Kaye's famous novel, the movie was shot in Rajasthan and involved a cast of many local people as extras. The Hollywood cast included Omar Sharif, Christopher Lee, and Ben Cross in the lead.

AUTOBIOGRAPHY OF A PRINCESS

This is one of the most interesting movies set in Rajasthan. The idea for the movie was born when, in the 1970's, Merchant and Ivory discovered some priceless old 16 mm documentary footage lying in the Maharaja of Jodhpur's store-rooms. It depicted the royal lifestyle of Jodhpur in the 1920's and 1930's: everything from polo matches to wedding pageants. Merchant and Ivory ingeniously interwove this footage with a contemporary story of a dispossessed Indian princess (Madhur Jaffrey) recollecting fond memories over tea with her father's retired secretary (James Mason).

SONAR KELLAR

Satyajit Ray once wrote that, thanks to the tales he had read as a child, the name Rajasthan "seemed magically to evoke a faraway fairytale land... Indeed the lure of the enchanted land grew over the years, and as soon as I found an opportunity, I decided to go filming in Rajasthan." The movie was

Sonar Kellar (*The Golden Fortress*), inspired by the Jaisalmer Fort. It was a delightful tale about a treasure guarded by a magic peacock.

Shiv Niwas Palace.

Mehrangarh Fort.

OCTOPUSSY

The James Bond movie *Octopussy* was shot in the lake city of Udaipur. (The other option considered was apparently Hawaii.) The exotic arches and cupolas of the Shiv Niwas Palace ▲ 249 provided a suitably sybaritic setting for 007's capers. One of the highlights of the movie is an auto-rickshaw chase through the crowded bazaars of Udaipur. Even today you find little stores in the bazaar displaying autographed photographs of Roger Moore, the actor who played James Bond in the movie.

THE JUNGLE BOOK

Mehrangarh Fort ▲ 224 was one of the locations for the shooting of Walt Disney Productions' movie *The Jungle*

Book, based on Rudyard Kipling's classic novel. However, the fort that actually provided Kipling with part of his inspiration was Chittorgarh, which is said to be the basis for the threatening python and monkey infested "Cold Lairs" in Mowgli's jungle.

JEWEL IN THE CROWN

Udaipur was one of the main locations for the TV serial based on Paul Scott's widely acclaimed *Raj Quartet*. It is the setting for the fictional princely state of "Mirat", and the Lake Palace served as the "Nawab's Palace" in the story. The royal cenotaphs nearby were the "Bibighar"

Gardens", where Daphne Manners was assaulted.

Actor from "The Deceivers".

THE DECEIVERS

This movie, based on a John Masters' novel and produced by Ismail Merchant, was shot in Rajasthan. Set in the 1830's, it is a romanticization of the true story of Sir William Sleeman, the man who stamped out the cult of the Thugs, who ritually strangled unwary travelers as a sacrifice to Kali, the goddess of death. The movie ran into a controversy when demonstrators picketed the shooting, claiming that it glorified the practice of *sati*, the ritual self-immolation of a woman on her husband's funeral pyre.

SIDDHARTA

Although Merchant and Ivory couldn't get permission to shoot at the Deeg Palace complex, Conrad Rookes managed to do so when he was filming Hermann Hesse's *Siddhartha*. The movie caused a scandal in strait-laced India, because the Indian actress, Simi Grewal, appeared semi-nude in one of the scenes. The Indian public reacted to this with a mixture of outrage and titillated interest. Publicity posters with the actress in the offending semi-nude pose had to be withdrawn and replaced with something more modest.

◆ RAJASTHAN BY TRAIN

Traveling by train allows you to see the surrounding landscape and the vivid scenes of life in Rajasthan. You meet a variety of people, some of whom will love to talk about their land to the foreign visitor and ask about your country – a delightful form of cultural exchange.

PALACE ON WHEELS

The train takes you through Rajasthan the "maharaja" way. The coaches of the Princely States were initially used before they were declared unserviceable and substituted with new coaches. A six-day trip covers Jaipur, Chittorgarh, Udaipur, Jaisalmer, Jodhpur, Bharatpur, Fatehpur Sikri, and Agra. The coupés are well provided with amenities, with each coach attended by its own staff. Breakfast is served on board. All arrangements for local sightseeing and meals at leading hotels are inclusive in the package. You can also buy a single destination ticket.

Contact Central Reservation, Palace on Wheels, Rajasthan Tourist Development Corporation (RTDC), Swagat Hotel, Near Railway Station, Jaipur 302006
Tel: 310586, 317052
Fax: 316045
OSD/POW/Sr. Manager, Accommodation and Package Tours, Tourist Reception Centre, Bikaner House, Pandara Road,
New Delhi 110001
Tel: 3383837, 3381884, 3389525
Fax: 3382823
A package costs US$425/ person/ night (single); US$300 (double); US$240 (triple).

ITINERARY OF THE PALACE ON WHEELS

Facilities on board include a library, a bar, money exchange, conference facilities and restaurants serving Indian, Continental, and Chinese cuisine.

DAY 1
Dinner is served on board at Delhi Cantt (**A**) before the train leaves for Jaipur at 10.45pm.

DAY 2
After arriving at Jaipur (**B**), you leave for Hawa Mahal and Amber Palace , taking an elephant ride. Shop later at the State Emporium. Lunch is arranged at Rambagh Palace Hotel, after which you visit the City Palace and Jantar Mantar. Dinner comes with a cultural show at Nahargarh. You head for Chittorgarh (**C**) at 10.10pm.

DAY 3
In the morning, you visit Chittorgarh Fort. Then take a coach to Udaipur (**D**), stopping en route at Nagda. After lunch at the Lake Palace Hotel, you visit the City Palace and Crystal Gallery. Head toward Sahelion ki Bari and have tea at Pratap Memorial, Moti Magri. On returning to Chittor, you board the train for Sawai Madhopur (**E**) at 10pm.

DAY 4
After breakfast at Castle Jhoomar Baori, visit the Ranthambor Sanctuary. Board the train by noon and leave for Jaisalmer (**F**). Lunch and dinner is served on board.

DAY 5
On arriving in Jaisalmer, you visit the *havelis* and fort. After lunch at Gorbund Palace, head toward Samm to see the sand dunes and take a camel safari, followed by tea. Dine at Moomal Tourist Bunglow. You leave for Jodhpur (**G**) at 10.40pm.

DAY 6
In the morning, visit Mehrangarh Fort and Jaswant Thada. Lunch is at the Umaid Bhawan Palace Hotel, while tea and dinner are served on board.

DAY 7
After arriving at Bharatpur (**H**), you leave for the Keoladeo Ghana Bird Sanctuary. You then journey by coach to Fatehpur Sikri. See the Taj Mahal and Agra Fort (**I**). You board the train for Delhi Cantt. at 8 pm after some last-minute shopping.

DAY 8
Breakfast is served on board on arriving at Delhi Cantt, the last day of your tour.

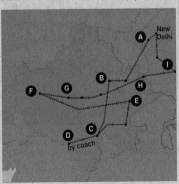

Itinerary route of Palace on Wheels.

MAHARAJA'S SALOONS

The old saloons of the Maharaja of Jodhpur used to operate between Jodhpur and Jaisalmer, but stopped after the change in the railway gauge-line. They are now "parked" at the Umaid Bhawan

Palace and guests can stay on board. The ten coupés have attached baths. The original coupé of His Highness is being converted into a suite. In addition, there will be a dining car and lounge. The price is not yet fixed.

Palace on Wheels.

The Royal Orient Express.

ORDINARY TRAINS

Traveling by train is an experience in itself. You meet a variety of people and could strike up a conversation with fellow passengers. Be careful when accepting edible items. Recently a tourist was drugged with a biscuit and was robbed of all his belongings.

You can see a marked difference between the sahib-type passengers in the first and second upper-class sections and the economy section. Make a reservation if you want to be sure of a seat. The toilets in the first-class section are clean but you have to learn to bear with the ones in the second class section. It is useful to carry paper rolls, soap, tissue paper, and even paper toilet covers. The ordinary train journey to Jaisalmer is rather dusty, and the only measure is to close the windows. Dust is unavoidable as it is part of life in the desert. If you are traveling first class, you can order a bed roll while reserving your ticket or before boarding the train, but you cannot be assured of one on certain routes despite booking in advance; for example, the Jodhpur-Jaisalmer route. Most Indians bring along their own beddings and it is ideal to bring a sleeping bag or sheets. A light quilt is advised for the winter season as the trains can be freezingly cold. Bring along books or a pack of cards to help you while away the journey. The railway platforms are a kaleidoscope of activity. As the train chugs into the station, there is total chaos, with hoards of people trying to get into the unreserved classes and *chaiwalas* trying to sell as many drinks as possible to transit passengers.

TRAIN SCHEDULES TO/FROM JAIPUR

FROM DELHI
Pink City Express: Departs at 6am. Arrives at noon.
Delhi Express: Departs at 9.20am. Arrives at 5.10pm.
Super Fast: Departs at 6.10pm. Arrives at 11.45pm.

TO DELHI
Pink City Express: Departs at 4.45pm. Arrives at 10.30pm.
Delhi Express: Departs at 10.45am. Arrives at 10.40pm.
Chetak: Departs at 6.50am. Arrives at 3.05pm.

FROM BOMBAY
Gangaur Express: Departs at 7pm. Arrives at 12.45pm.

TO BOMBAY
Gangaur Express: Departs at 1.35 pm. Arrives at 7.55 am.

FROM CALCUTTA
Sealdah Express: Departs at 8.15 pm. Arrives at.7.40 am. (Day Three).

TO CALCUTTA
Sealdah Express: Departs 7.15 pm. Arrives at 7.15 am.

THE ROYAL ORIENT EXPRESS

Jointly operated by Indian Railways and Gujarat Tourism, the Royal Orient Express offers yet another journey back in time. Operating between September and April, it has thirteen exotic saloon cars that are embossed in gold. The week-long trip takes you to some of the "royal" cities of Rajasthan and Gujarat. These include Udaipur, Chittorgarh, Jaipur, Palitana, Sasangir, Ahmedabad, and Junagadh. Accommodation is provided in the coupés, and each carriage is equipped with a lounge, a mini-bar, and a kitchenette. The train departs from Delhi Cantonment railway station at 2.30pm every Wednesday and returns at 6am the following Wednesday. The package prices are US$525/£350 per person per night (single); US$300/£200 per person per night (twin-sharing); US$262.50/£175 per person per night (triple-sharing). Bookings are confirmed after placing a 10 percent deposit.
For reservations, contact:
Central Reservation Office,
A-6, State Emporia Building
Baba Karak Singh Marg
New Delhi - 110001
Tel. 3734015   Fax 3732482

Jodhpur's railway station.

Camel safari.

Horse safari.

Safaris are the best way to discover villages that are away from the beaten track. Camel safaris are the most popular, although horse and jeep safaris are also available. An innovative idea is the recently introduced elephant safari.

CAMEL SAFARIS

In Jaisalmer, you can go on a day-long safari to see the sand dunes as well as an eleven-day safari to Bikaner. A camel covers 12 to 18 miles a day. Camel safaris are also organized in Bikaner, Jodhpur, and the Shekhavati region. For an overnight journey, two camels are provided, one for the tourist and the other for luggage. The rates vary according to the degree of comfort and facilities provided. A well-organized camel safari should include a cook, tents for overnight stay, bedding, a night watchman, and a radio in case of emergency. Do not be lured by cheap rates as the camels may not be well-trained and the facilities far from satisfactory. If locally organized, the prices range from Rs.600/US$19.50/£12.30 to Rs.1500/US$48.80/£30.60 for a first-class overnight safari, although a camel can be hired for Rs.150–200/US$4.90–$6.50/£3–£4 a day. Useful items to bring along are a hat or scarf, a sunscreen, a first-aid box and ointment for muscle and joint pains. Wear cotton during the day and woolens during the early morning and late evening. Before going on a safari, it is important to know the area(s) you are going to visit and the facilities provided.

HORSE SAFARIS

Horse safaris are available around Udaipur and Chittorgarh. Organizing a horse safari requires expertise and is best done by the horse breeder. For a well-organized safari, expect prices of Rs. 1200–3500/US$39–$114/£24.50–£71.40 per person.

Organizers:
Narendra Singh
Pratap Country Inn
Jaisamand Road
Udaipur 313001
Tel. 583138

JEEP SAFARIS

Jeep safaris are for visitors who prefer to be less adventurous. They are quite commonly organized around Jaipur and Jaisalmer, and cost around Rs400–600/US$13–$19.50/£8.20–£12.30 per jeep. Hotels organize these safaris as well.

Sajjan Singh,
Ghanerao,
Jhalamand House,
Ratanada,
Jodhpur
Tel. 33054

The Safari Club
High Court Colony
Jodhpur 342001
Tel. 37023, 32695
Fax 0291-37023

Shekhavati Brigade
Horse Safari
Roop Niwas Palace
Navalgarh
Shekhavati
Tel. 01594-22008

ELEPHANT SAFARIS

Elephant safaris are relatively new. Jaipur Vision organizes these special safari programs for groups who book in advance.
Tel. 0141-622185
Fax 0141-561492

ORGANIZERS OF CAMEL SAFARIS

JAISALMER
Jaisal Castle
Narain Niwas

SHEKHAVATI
Devendra Singh
Roop Niwas
Nawalgarh
Tel. 01594-2008

The Rajasthan Tourism Development Corporation (RTDC)
The Executive Director, RTDC
Swagatam Tourist Hotel, Jaipur
Tel. 0141-317052

USEFUL ADDRESSES

- 🖅 CREDIT CARDS
- 🇨 CENTRAL
- ☀ VIEW
- ⌂ QUIET
- 🖅• SECLUDED
- ⌇ SWIMMING POOL
- ♫ MUSIC
- ▢ TELEVISION
- ☎ PHONE
- 🎺 LIVE BANDS

◆ CHOOSING A HOTEL

◆ < US$15 / £10
◆◆ US$15 to $110 / £10 to £75
◆◆◆ > US$110 / £75

	PAGE	PRICE	EXCEPTIONAL VIEW/GARDENS	LIVE ENTERTAINMENT	AC/CEILING FAN	HOT WATER	EXCEPTIONAL ARCHITECTURE	RESTAURANT AND/OR BAR	ROOMS
EAST RAJASTHAN (JAIPUR, SAMODE)									
ACHROL HOUSE	365	◆◆			●	●			7
ADITYA	364	◆◆		●	●	●		●	24
BISSAU PALACE	364	◆◆		●	●	●	●		30
CLARK'S AMER	364	◆◆	●	●	●	●		●	202
DIGGI PALACE	364	◆◆	●	●	●	●	●		45
FORT UNIARA	365	◆◆		●	●	●		●	12
GANGAUR	359	◆◆			●	●			63
HOLIDAY INN	364	◆◆		●	●	●			99
JAI MAHAL PALACE	363	◆◆◆	●	●	●	●		●	102
JAIPUR ASHOK	364	◆◆			●	●			99
JAIPUR PALACE	363	◆◆	●	●	●	●		●	59
KHASA KOTHI	363	◆◆◆	●	●	●	●			36
MANDAWA HOUSE	364	◆◆			●				19
MANSINGH HOTEL	364	◆◆		●	●	●		●	91
MERU PALACE	364	◆◆			●	●			48
NARAIN NIWAS PALACE	364	◆◆	●		●	●		●	36
RAMBAGH PALACE*****	363	◆◆◆	●	●	●	●	●	●	106
RAMGARH LODGE	363	◆◆	●		●	●		●	11
RAJMAHAL PALACE*****	363	◆◆◆	●		●	●		●	12
RAJPUTANA PALACE*****	364	◆◆◆	●	●	●	●		●	218
TEEJ	359	◆◆			●	●			46
SAMODE PALACE	365	◆◆	●	●	●	●	●	●	22
EAST RAJASTHAN (AJMER, PUSHKAR)									
AMBASSADOR	366	◆			●	●		●	44
FORT BAGHERA, BAGHERA	366	◆◆			●	●	●		4
MAN SINGH PALACE	365	◆◆			●	●		●	112
PRITHVI RAJ	366	◆			●	●		●	50
ROOPANGARH FORT	366	◆◆	●		●	●	●		15
THE SAFARI CLUB, PUSHKAR	366	◆◆	●		●	●		●	30
EAST RAJASTHAN (ALWAR)									
ARAVALI HOTEL	366	◆◆			●	●		●	28
LAKE PALACE, SILISERH	367	◆◆	●	●	●	●			10
MEENAL	359	◆			●	●			6
NEEMRANA	366	◆◆◆	●	●	●	●	●	●	27
SARISKA PALACE	366	◆◆	●	●	●	●			40
DUNGARPUR									
UDAI BILAS PALACE	376	◆◆	●	●	●	●	●	●	10
SHEKHAVATI									
MANDAWA CASTLE	368	◆◆	●	●	●	●	●	●	51
DERA DUNDLOD KILA	369	◆◆		●	●	●	●	●	25
DESERT RESORT, MANDAWA	368	◆◆	●	●	●	●			51
DUNDLOD CASTLE	369	◆◆	●	●	●	●			22
MUKUNDGARH FORT	369	◆◆	●	●	●		●		42
RAMESH JANGID'S TOURIST PENSION	369	◆◆		●	●	●			5
ROOP NIVAS PALACE, NAWALGARH	369	◆◆	●	●	●	●			30
SHIV SHEKHAVATI, JHUNJHUNU	327	◆◆		●	●	●			20
EAST RAJASTHAN (BHARATPUR, SAWAI MADHOPUR, RANTHAMBHOR)									
C.J.B., SAWAI MADHOPUR	359	◆◆	●		●	●			12
EAGLE'S NEST, BHARATPUR	367	◆◆		●	●	●			12
FOREST LODGE, BHARATPUR	367	◆◆	●		●	●			17
GOVIND NIWAS, BHARATPUR	367	◆◆	●		●	●		●	6
PARK PALACE, BHARATPUR	367	◆			●	●			24
SARAS, BHARATPUR	359	◆◆			●	●		●	24
SAWAI MADHOPUR LODGE	368	◆◆			●	●			28
KAMDHENU, SAWAI MADHOPUR	359	◆◆		●	●	●		●	22
TOURIST GUEST HOUSE, BHARATPUR	367	◆◆◆	●	●		●			6
THE SAFARI CLUB, RANTHAMBHOR	368	◆◆		●	●	●		●	6

	PAGE	PRICE	EXCEPTIONAL VIEW/GARDENS	LIVE ENTERTAINMENT	AC/CEILING FAN	HOT WATER	EXCEPTIONAL ARCHITECTURE	RESTAURANT AND/OR BAR	ROOMS
NORTHWEST RAJASTHAN (JODHPUR)									
AJIT BHAWAN PALACE	370	♦♦♦	●	●	●	●	●	●	50
BALSAMAND LAKE PALACE	371	♦♦	●	●	●	●	●		36
FLETCHER HOUSE KUDI OASIS	371	♦♦	●		●	●	●		4
FORT CHANWA, LUNI	371	♦♦♦	●		●	●	●	●	12
KARNI BHAWAN	370	♦♦	●		●	●		●	25
RAJPUTANA PALACE	370	♦♦			●	●		●	24
RATANADA POLO PALACE	370	♦♦♦			●	●		●	62
THE SAFARI CLUB	370	♦♦	●		●	●	●	●	13
UMAID BHAWAN PALACE*****	370	♦♦♦	●	●	●	●	●	●	100
NORTHWEST RAJASTHAN (PALI)									
JAGRAM DURG	328	♦♦	●		●	●	●	●	5
ROHET GARH	328	♦♦	●		●	●	●		25
SARDAR SAMAND PALACE	371	♦♦	●		●	●	●		19
NORTHWEST RAJASTHAN (BIKANER)									
BHANWAR NIWAS	372	♦♦			●	●	●	●	14
GAJNER PALACE	372	♦♦	●		●	●	●		25
KARNI BHAWAN PALACE	372	♦♦			●	●	●	●	15
LALLGARH PALACE	372	♦♦	●		●	●	●	●	40
NORTHWEST RAJASTHAN (JAISALMER)									
FORT POKHARAN	373	♦♦	●		●	●	●	●	10
GORBANDH PALACE	373	♦♦			●	●		●	67
HERITAGE INN	373	♦♦	●		●	●	●	●	36
HIMMATGARH PALACE	373	♦♦♦	●		●	●	●	●	35
JAISAL CASTLE	373	♦♦	●		●	●	●	●	10
JAWAHAR NIWAS PALACE	373	♦♦	●		●	●	●		26
NARAYAN NIWAS PALACE	373	♦♦			●	●	●	●	38
NORTHWEST RAJASTHAN (KHIMSAR)									
ROYAL CASTLE, KHIMSAR	371	♦♦♦	●		●	●	●	●	24
KHIMSAR FORT, KHIMSAR	370	♦♦	●		●	●	●	●	40
SOUTH RAJASTHAN (UDAIPUR)									
ANAND BHAWAN	375	♦♦	●		●	●		●	22
FATEH PRAKASH PALACE	375	♦♦♦	●	●	●	●	●	●	9
GOKUL VILAS, DEOGARH	376	♦♦	●	●	●	●	●	●	8
HILLTOP	375	♦♦			●	●		●	55
KOTRI RAOLA	372	♦♦	●		●	●	●	●	10
LAKE END	375	♦♦	●		●	●		●	78
LAKE PALACE HOTEL*****	375	♦♦♦	●		●	●	●	●	81
LAKE PICHOLA HOTEL	376	♦♦	●		●	●	●	●	25
LAKSHMI VILAS PALACE*****	375	♦♦♦	●		●	●		●	54
ORIENTAL PALACE	375	♦♦	●		●	●	●	●	35
RAJ DARSHAN	375	♦♦			●	●		●	52
SHIKARABADI	375	♦♦♦	●	●	●	●		●	25
SHIV NIWAS*****	375	♦♦♦	●	●	●	●	●	●	31
SOUTH RAJASTHAN (MOUNT ABU)									
CONNAUGHT HOUSE	378	♦♦			●	●		●	14
DARBARGADH POSHINA	378	♦♦	●	●	●	●	●	●	8
HOTEL MADHUBAN	377	♦♦	●		●	●		●	14
KESAR BHAWAN PALACE	377	♦♦	●		●	●		●	10
PALACE HOTEL	377	♦♦♦	●		●	●	●	●	35
SAVERA PALACE	377	♦♦			●	●		●	24
SUNRISE PALACE	377	♦♦	●		●	●	●		16
SUNSET INN	377	♦♦	●		●	●		●	40
SOUTHEAST RAJASTHAN (KOTA)									
BRIJRAJ BHAWAN PALACE	378	♦♦	●		●	●	●	●	6
SOUTHEAST RAJASTHAN (BUNDI)									
ISHWARI NIWAS PALACE	378	♦♦			●	●			17
HAVELI BRAJ BHUSHANJEE	378	♦♦	●			●	●		14

◆ CHOOSING A RESTAURANT

Exchange rate US$1=Rs.31
£1=Rs.49
- ◆ < Rs.150/US$5
- ◆◆ Rs.150–300/US$5–10
- ◆◆◆ Rs.30/US$100

	PAGE	PRICE	VEGETARIAN	NON-VEGETARIAN	RAJASTHANI CUISINE	INDIAN CUISINE	WESTERN CUISINE	LIVE ENTERTAINMENT	EXCEPTIONAL AMBIENCE
EAST RAJASTHAN (JAIPUR)									
AANGAN	363	◆◆◆	●	●	●	●			
BHUWANESHWARI	362	◆◆	●	●	●	●	●	●	●
CHANAKYA	362	◆◆	●			●			
CHANDRAVANSHI PAVILION	363	◆◆	●	●	●	●		●	●
COPPER CHIMNEY	363	◆	●	●		●			
GARDEN CAFE	363	◆	●	●		●	●		
GULAB MAHAL	362	◆◆	●	●	●	●		●	●
JAL MAHAL	363	◆◆	●	●	●	●			
LAKSHMI MISHTAN BHANDAR (LMB)	362	◆◆	●		●	●			
NIRO'S	362	◆		●		●	●		
PALMS	363	◆◆◆	●	●		●	●		
SHEESH MAHAL	363	◆◆◆	●	●	●	●		●	●
SHIVIR	362	◆◆◆	●	●	●	●			
ZAIKA	363	◆◆	●	●		●	●	●	
EAST RAJASTHAN (AJMER/PUSHKAR)									
HONEY DEW	365	◆◆	●			●	●		
JAI HIND, AJMER	365	◆	●			●	●		
PRINCE'S, PUSHKAR	366	◆	●		●	●	●	●	●
SHEESH MAHAL	365	◆◆◆	●	●	●	●	●	●	●
EAST RAJASTHAN (ALWAR)									
CIRCUIT HOUSE RESTAURANT	366	◆◆	●	●	●	●			
LAKE PALACE, SILISERAH	367	◆◆	●	●	●	●			●
NEEMRANA FORT	366	◆◆◆	●	●	●	●	●	●	●
SARISKA PALACE	366	◆◆	●	●	●	●			●
THE HILL FORT, KESROLI	366	◆◆	●	●	●	●	●	●	●
EAST RAJASTHAN (DUNGARPUR)									
UDAI BILAS PALACE	376	◆◆	●	●	●	●	●	●	●
EAST RAJASTHAN (SHEKHAVATI)									
MANDAWA CASTLE	368	◆◆	●	●	●	●	●	●	●
DUNLOD CASTLE	368	◆◆	●	●	●	●	●	●	●
LAKSHMI VILAS PALACE HOTEL	367	◆◆	●	●	●	●	●	●	●
ROOP NIWAS PALACE, NAWALGARH	368	◆◆	●	●	●	●		●	
SHIV SHEKHAVATI	368	◆◆	●	●	●	●			●
THE DESERT RESORT, MANDAWA	368	◆◆	●	●	●	●		●	●
AST RAJASTHAN (BHARATPUR, SAWAI MADHOPUR)									
KAMDHENU	359	◆◆	●	●	●	●			
KOHINOOR, BHARATPUR	367	◆◆	●		●	●			
ON THE ROCKS	370	◆◆		●	●	●	●		●
SPOON BILL, BHARATPUR	367	◆◆	●	●	●	●	●		
SAWAI MADHOPUR LODGE	368	◆◆	●	●	●	●			●
NORTHWEST RAJASTHAN (JODHPUR)									
BALSAMAND LAKE PALACE	370	◆◆	●	●	●	●	●	●	●
COURTYARD RESTAURANT	369	◆◆◆	●	●	●	●	●	●	●
KHAMAGHANI	370	◆◆◆	●	●	●	●	●		
MARWAR HALL	368	◆◆◆	●	●	●	●	●		
ON THE ROCKS	370	◆◆◆	●	●	●	●	●		
REGGIE'S RESTAURANT	369	◆◆	●	●	●	●	●	●	●
RISALA	369	◆◆◆	●	●	●	●	●		

	PAGE	PRICE	VEGETARIAN	NON-VEGETARIAN	RAJASTHANI CUISINE	INDIAN CUISINE	WESTERN CUISINE	LIVE ENTERTAINMENT	EXCEPTIONAL AMBIENCE
THE PILLARS	369	◆◆◆	●	●	●	●	●	●	●
TORAN	370	◆	●	●	●	●	●	●	●
NORTHWEST RAJASTHAN (BIKANER)									
AMBER	372	◆	●		●	●	●		
ANNAPURNA	372	◆	●	●	●	●			
CHOTU-MUTU	372	◆◆	●		●	●			
DHOLA MARU	372	◆◆	●	●	●	●	●		
DINING ROOM	372	◆◆◆	●	●	●	●			●
LAKSHMI NIWAS	372	◆	●		●	●			
NORTHWEST RAJASTHAN (JAISALMER)									
8TH JULY	373	◆◆	●	●	●	●	●		●
FORT VIEW	373	◆	●		●	●	●	●	
GAY TIME	373	◆	●		●	●			
KALPANA	373	◆◆	●		●	●	●		
KOTRI RAOLA, PALI	372	◆◆	●	●	●	●	●	●	●
MOTI MAHAL	373	◆	●		●	●	●		
NATRAJ	373	◆	●		●	●	●		
THE TRIO	373	◆◆	●	●	●	●	●	●	●
TOP DECK	373	◆◆	●		●	●	●		●
WEST RAJASTHAN (KHIMSAR)									
ROYAL CASTLE	370	◆◆	●	●	●	●	●	●	●
SOUTH RAJASTHAN (UDAIPUR)									
BAITHAK	375	◆◆	●	●	●	●	●	●	●
BERRY'S	374	◆◆	●	●	●	●	●		
CHEETAL	375	◆◆	●	●	●	●	●		●
JHAROKHA	374	◆◆◆	●	●	●	●	●	●	●
KHUMBHA PALACE	375	◆◆	●	●	●	●	●		
LAKE END HOTEL	331	◆◆	●	●	●	●			
ORIENTAL PALACE	375	◆◆◆	●	●	●	●	●	●	
PADMANI	374	◆◆◆	●	●	●	●	●		●
PARK VIEW	374	◆◆	●	●	●	●	●		
RAJ DARSHAN	375	◆◆◆	●	●	●	●	●	●	●
ROOF GARDEN CAFE	375	◆◆	●	●	●	●	●		
SAI NIWAS	331	◆◆	●	●	●	●	●		
SHIV NIWAS PALACE	375	◆◆	●	●	●	●	●	●	●
SOUTH RAJASTHAN (MOUNT ABU)									
AANGAN	377	◆◆	●		●	●			
HAVELI	377	◆◆◆	●	●	●	●			
INDIAN COFFEE HOUSE	377	◆	●			●			
JUNGLE CORNER	377	◆	●			●			
MK	377	◆	●			●			
PALACE HOTEL	377	◆◆◆	●	●	●	●	●		
SOUTHEAST RAJASTHAN (KOTA)									
BRIJ RAJ BHAWAN PALACE	378	◆◆	●	●	●	●			
HOTEL SURYA	378	◆◆	●	●					
SOUTHEAST RAJASTHAN (BUNDI)									
BUNDI CAFE & CRAFTS	378	◆◆	●	●	●	●		●	●
DIAMOND	378	◆◆	●	●	●	●			
ISHWARI KOTHI	331	◆◆	●	●	●	●			

RAJASTHAN

USEFUL INFORMATION

IMMIGRATION
PASSPORT OFFICE
Opposite Muncipal
Corporation Office
Tonk Road
Tel. 510884, 513511

Renew your visa at
least one week prior to
expiry at:
FOREIGNER'S
REGISTRATION OFFICE
Behind Hawa Mahal,
Jaipur

POLICE STATIONS
JAIPUR
Tel. 100
Flying Squad
Tel. 565555
City Kotwali
Tel. 321444

JODHPUR
Tel. 100, 47180

JAISALMER
Tel. 52100, 52495

UDAIPUR
Tel. 100, 414600

AJMER
Tel. 100, 21000

BHARATPUR
Tel. 100, 22670

BIKANER
Tel. 100, 61100

MOUNT ABU
Tel. 3333

KOTA
Tel.100, 450229

BUNDI
Tel. 3356

ALWAR
Tel. 21100, 22333

SAWAI MADHOPUR
Tel. 35310

CHITTORGARH
Tel. 40088

HOSPITALS
JAIPUR
S.M.S. Hospital
Sawai Ram Singh Road
Tel. 560291, 564222

SONI HOSPITAL
J.L. Nehru Marg
Tel. 562028

SANTOKBA DURLABHJI
HOSPITAL
Bhawani Singh Road
Tel. 566251

GETWELL POLY CLINIC
J.L. Nehru Road
Tel. 563743

JAISALMER
SRI JAWAHAR HOSPITAL
Hanuman Circle
Tel. 52343

JODHPUR
MAHATMA GANDHI
Near Jalori Gate
Tel. 36437, 36390

UMAID FOR WOMEN &
CHILDREN
Siwanchi Gate
Tel. 35720
Ambulance
Tel. 102

AJMER
JAWAHAR LAL NEHRU
Tel. 50231
LADIES HOSPITAL
Tel. 32305

KOTA
GENERAL HOSPITAL
Tel. 23578
Ambulance
Tel. 23578, 25335

ALWAR
GENERAL HOSPITAL
Tel. 22333/32
Ladies Hospital
Tel. 22323

MOUNT ABU
GOVERNMENT HOSPITAL
Tel. 3535

BUNDI
GOVERNMENT HOSPITAL
Tel. 32833

BHARATPUR
GOVERNMENT HOSPITAL
Hospital Road
Tel. 528811
NAYA HOSPITAL
Circular Road, Co. Bagh
Tel. 22451
Ambulance
Tel. 528811

PHARMACY
opposite S.M.S.Hospital
and on M.I. Road, Jaipur

BANKS AND BUREAUX DE CHANGE

BANKS
Banking hours are
10.30am–2.30pm
(Mon.–Fri.),10.30am–
12 noon (Sat.) except
evening banks ◆ 324.

STATE BANK OF INDIA
*This is one of the most
important banks, with
branches dealing in
foreign exchange all
over the state.*
10am–2pm (Mon. to Fri.)
Sat. till 2pm

JAIPUR
Sanganeri Gate
Tel. 565114, 565001,
561163
Fax 564597

JODHPUR
High Court Compound
Tel. 45090
Fax 45178

JAISALMER
Nachna House
Tel. 2398

BIKANER
Ganga Shahar Road
Tel. 28052
Dauji Road
Tel. 61496

MOUNT ABU
RAYKIYA HOSPITAL
Nakki Lake
Tel. 3535

ALWAR
Mahal Chowk
Tel. 21488
Opposite Muwa
Boarding, Arya Nagar
Tel. 21889

KOTA
L.I.C. Building,
Chawni Chauraha
Tel. 25412

UDAIPUR
Hospital Road
Tel. 528811

SAWAI MADHOPUR
Man Town
Tel. 20248

BHARATPUR
Kumhare Gate
Tel. 22409

BIKANER
P.B.M Hospital,
Ambedkar Circle
Tel. 27851

CHITTORGARH
Meera Nagari
Near Collectorate,
Chaurana
Tel. 2902

SANGANER
(NEAR JAIPUR)
Main Market
Tel. 550684

BUREAUX DE CHANGE
Most hotels have a
counter for exchange of
foreign currency, as do
the leading banks. We
list some currency
exchange outlets here.
BANK OF RAJASTHAN
Rambagh Palace,
Jaipur
Tel. 381416
7.30am–8.30pm

CENTRAL BANK OF INDIA
Sansar Chandra Road,
Jaipur
Tel. 364141

STATE BANK OF INDIA
Tilak Marg, C-Scheme
Jaipur
Tel. 380421

BUREAUX THOMAS COOK
Jaipur Towers,
Opposite All India Radio,
Jaipur
Tel. 360940/974/801
9am–6pm

TRANSCORP
INTERNATIONAL BUREAU
Shanti Sadan,
Church Road,

Jaipur
Tel. 368406, 360839
10am–6pm

CROWN TOURS
Near York Hotel,
M.I. Road, Jaipur
Tel. 378057, 372124
10am–6pm

CREDIT CARDS
Accepted cards are
Visa, American Express,
and MasterCard. In case
of need, these
representatives can be
contacted in Jaipur:

VISA
ANDHRA BANK
M.I. Road
Tel. 364094, 369606

CANARA BANK
Jayanti Market
Tel. 360467, 372749

BANK OF BARODA
Tripolia Gate
Tel. 314079, 312451

MASTERCARD
CENTRAL BANK OF INDIA
Sansar Chandra Road
Tel. 364141/44

POSTAL SERVICES

JAIPUR
GENERAL POST OFFICE
M.I. Road
Tel. 374000

CENTRAL TELEGRAPH
OFFICE
M.I. Road
Tel. 367001

JODHPUR
GENERAL POST OFFICE
Near Railway Station
Tel. 27864

CENTRAL TELEGRAPH
OFFICE
Sardarpura
Tel. 31303

JAISALMER
GENERAL POST OFFICE
Near Police Station
Tel. 52407

UDAIPUR
GENERAL POST OFFICE
Chetak Circle
Tel. 26003, 526003

KOTA
GENERAL POST OFFICE
Opposite M.B.S.
Hospital Civil Lines
Tel. 27592

AJMER
GENERAL POST OFFICE

Madar Gate Circle
Tel. 23203

MOUNT ABU
GENERAL POST OFFICE
Telecom Centre
Tel. 3107
CITY POST OFFICE
Raj Bhavan Road
Tel. 3170

BHARATPUR
GENERAL POST OFFICE
Delhi Gate
opp. Gandhi Park
Tel. 23586

BIKANER
GENERAL POST OFFICE
Behind Junagarh Fort
CITY POST OFFICE
Inside Kote Gate

BUNDI
GENERAL POST OFFICE
Nainwa Road
Tel. 26230

ALWAR
GENERAL POST OFFICE
Raghu Marg
Tel. 22631

CONSULATES

All diplomatic missions
are based in New Delhi.
Most have consulate
offices in the other cities
such as Bombay,
Calcutta, and Madras.
There are no
representatives in
Rajasthan.

AMERICAN EMBASSY
Shanti Path,
Chanakyapuri,
New Delhi 110021
Tel. 91-11-600651
Fax 91-11-6872028

BRITISH HIGH
COMMISSION
Chanakyapuri
New Delhi 110021
Tel. 91-11-6872161
Fax 91-11-6872882

AUSTRALIAN HIGH
COMMISSION
Australian Compound
1/50-G, Shanti Path,
Chanakyapuri

New Delhi 110021
Tel. 91-11-6888223
Fax 91-11-6885199

EMBASSY OF FRANCE
2/50-E, Shanti Path,
Chanakyapuri,
New Delhi 110021
Tel. 91-11-6118790
Fax 91-11-6872305

TOURIST INFORMATION

**RAJASTHAN TOURIST
INFORMATION OFFICES**
JAIPUR
Railway Station
Platform No. 1
6am–8pm
Tel. 0141-315714
Tourist Reception Center
Tourist Hotel
M.I. Road
Tel. 370180 - ext. 203

AJMER
Hotel Khadim
Railway station
Tel. 0145-52426

CHITTORGARH
Janta Awas Grah
Tel. 01472-41089

UDAIPUR
Tourist Reception Center
Fateh Memorial
Suraj Pol.
Tel. 0294-29535
Dabok Airport
Tel. 0294-23011

MOUNT ABU
Opposite bus stand
Tel. 0297742-3151

JODHPUR
Hotel Ghoomar
near High Court
Tel. 0291-45083

JAISALMER
Station Road
Tel. 02992-52406

KOTA
Hotel Chambal
Nayapura
Tel. 0744-27695
BUNDI
Circuit House
Tel. 0747-22697

SAWAI MADHOPUR
Tiger Project Office
Tel. 07462-20808

ALWAR
Information Center
opposite Purjan Bihar
Garden
Tel. 0144-21868

BHARATPUR
Hotel Saras Tourist
Guest House
Tel. 05644-22542

AMBER
Elephant Stand
Tel. 530264

BIKANER
Junagarh Fort
Tel. 0151-27445

BANSWARA
Information Center
Banswara
Tel. 02962-41081

JHUNJHUNU
Hotel Shiv
Shekhavati
Tel. 1592-32909

Outside the state:
NEW DELHI
Bikaner House
Pandara Road
Tel. 3383837, 3889525
Fax 3382823

DOMESTIC AIRPORT
INFORMATION COUNTER
Tel. 91-11-3265296

INTERNATIONAL AIRPORT
INFORMATION COUNTER
Tel. 91-11-3291171

CALCUTTA
"Embassy"
4, Shakespeare Sarani
Calcutta 700071
Tel. 033-242140,
2421475, 2425813
Fax 033-2423521

BOMBAY
123, Maharishi Karve
Marg, opposite
Churchgate
Bombay 400020
Tel. 022-203293,
203314/5, 2036054
Fax 022-2014496

MADRAS
154, Anna Salai
Madras 600002
Tel. 044-8269685,
8269695
Fax 044-8266893

TRANSPORT

AIRPORT
JAIPUR
SANGANER AIRPORT
6½ miles from city.
Connected by Indian
Airlines, Modiluft,
Sahara, and Damania.

JODHPUR
3½ miles from city.
Connected by Indian
Airlines, and Jagson.

UDAIPUR
DABOK AIRPORT
15 miles from city.
Connected by Indian
Airlines. Modiluft also
operates but not in the
summer. Connected
with New Delhi, Jaipur,
Bombay, Aurangabad,
and Ahmedabad.

BIKANER
The nearest airport is
Nal, 9 miles from city.
No air service is
available at present. An
air taxi service may
operate soon.

TOUR AND
EXCURSION AGENTS

*Here are a few of the
reputable licensed
travel and excursion
agents in Jaipur.*

TOUR OPERATORS
JET AIR
TRANSPORTATION
M.I. Road
Tel. 377051, 370509
SITA WORLD TRAVELS (I)
D'villa, Station Road,
near Polo Victory
Tel. 364104, 374722,
368226

TRAVEL CORPORATION OF
INDIA
Jamnalal Bajaj Marg
Tel. 380050, 381071

TRAVEL HOUSE
Welcomgroup
Rajputana Palace
Sheraton, Palace Road,
Jaipur 302 006
Tel. 368431, 363211

EXCURSION AGENTS
RAJASTHAN TOURS
Rambagh Palace Hotel
Jaipur 302006
Tel. 381041

TOURIST GUIDE SERVICES
Panch Batti, M.I. Road
Tel. 378377, 376251

ELEPHANT SAFARIS
A safari becomes a
special experience in the
hands of good
organizers ◆ 350. The
local publisher of *Jaipur
Vision*, a monthly tourist
guide booklet,
organizes elephant
safaris for groups who
book in advance. For
details, fax
0141-561492.

CAMEL AND JEEP
SAFARIS
These two types of
safaris operate around
Jaisalmer, Bikaner,
Jodhpur, and the
Shekhavati region. The
duration of the trip
ranges from one day to
a week to ten days.
Contact:
The Executive Director
RAJASTHAN TOURISM
DEVELOPMENT
CORPORATION (RTDC)
Swagatam Tourist Hotel
Jaipur 302006
Tel. 0141-317052

HORSE SAFARI
OPERATORS
THE SAFARI CLUB
High Court Colony,
Jodhpur 342001
Tel. 0291-37023, 32695
Fax 0291-37023
*Safaris are conducted in
and around Jodhpur,
Ranthambhor, and
Pushkar. Upmarket.*

SHEKHAVATI BRIGADE
HORSE SAFARI
Roop Niwas Palace
Complex, Nawalgarh,
Shekhavati
Tel. 01594-22008
*Upmarket safaris
operating in the
Shekhavati region.*

PRATAP COUNTRY INN
c/o Maharaja Narendra
Singh
Jaisamand Road
Udaipur 313001
Tel. 0294-83138
Fax 0294-83058
*Pioneers in horse
safaris. Operating in the
Udaipur region, this
upmarket organizer also
has overseas
representatives.*

SIDDARTH SINGH ROHET
Rohetgarh Village Pos,
Rohet, District Pali
Tel. 02932-82431
*Operates safaris in and
around Jodhpur. Mid-
range prices.*

CAMPING
Youth Hostel, near
Stadium, Jaipur
Tel. 0141-373311

ACCOMMODATION

PAYING GUEST SCHEME
Jaipur was one of the
first cities to introduce
the Paying Guest
Scheme. Started in
1991, the scheme
has become quite
popular and there are
about 150 homes
offering decent
accommodation at
reasonable rates. Most
serve home-cooked
meals. A comprehensive

*Directory of Paying
Guest Accommodation*
is available at all offices
of RTDC and GOI tourist
offices. Paying Guest
services are now
available in many of the
other tourist centers
of Rajasthan.
The following are a
sample of these paying
guest houses in Jaipur.

MRS. B. PANDEY
"Indragan"
C-267, Bhabha Marg,
Tilak Nagar,
Jaipur 302004
Tel. 622185
*One double room with
attached bath, Rs.250.
One double room
without attached bath,
Rs.200.
Vegetarian meals
available. Facilities:
TV/Cable Language
spoken: English, Hindi.
Accepts foreigners only
(couples and women).
Located close to
Ganesh Temple and
Moti Doongri Castle.*

MR. R.A. RANA
7-KA-4, Jawahar Nagar
Rs. 75-150

COL. O.P. DRALL
61, Hatroi Fort
Tel. 376525
Rs. 350

MRS. KAMLA SINGH
GAUR
24-B, Ganesh Colony
Imliwala Pathak
Jyoti Nagar
Tel. 513803
Rs. 100-150

MR. HEMANT GOYAL
B-119, Kabir Marg
Bani Park
Tel. 317823
Rs. 200-300

MR. S.D. KULSHRESHTHA
B-33, Sethi Colony
Tel. 604570
Rs. 300-600

MR. BHUVANESHWARI
KUMARI
Rashouse, 9-Barwara
Colony Civil Lines
Tel. 381796
Rs. 300-350

RAJASTHAN TOURISM
DEVELOPMENT
CORPORATION (RTDC)
HOTELS
Every RTDC hotel is
located near the railway
station, bus station, and

airport. Most of these are priced below US$10/£6 per night and are good value for money for budget travelers. Most offer bathroom facilities on a sharing basis. Most hotels/motels offer different rates for high and low seasons. For more information, contact the Senior Manager, Accommodation, at this address: RAJASTHAN TOURISM DEVELOPMENT CORPORATION (RTDC) Central Reservation Office, Hotel Swagatam Campus, near Railway Station, Jaipur Tel. 319351, 310586 Fax 316045

RTDC HOTELS
The following is a list of RTDC hotels.
Price range:
Rs.350–600/US$10–$20 /£7–12 (super deluxe), Rs.200–350/US$6.50–$11/£4–7 (deluxe), Rs.80–200/US$3–6/ £2–4 (ordinary). Extra beds available. Dormitory beds cost an average of Rs.40/US$1.25/ £0.80 per person. Some offer rooms for day use for six-hour slots.

EAST RAJASTHAN

HOTEL GANGAUR
M.I. Road,
Jaipur 302006
Tel. 371641, 371642–7
*Sixty-three rooms,
Rs.500-1200.
Driver's dormitory,
Rs.30/head.*

HOTEL SWAGATAM
Station Road,
Jaipur 302006
Tel. 310595
*Thirty-nine rooms.
Rs.100–300*

HOTEL TEEJ
Sawai Singh Hwy,
Jaipur 302006
Tel. 374206
*Forty-six rooms/dormitory.
Rs.250–450*

DURG NAHARGARH
Jaipur 302002
Tel. 383202
Rs.250

TOURIST HOTEL
Opposite General Post Office, M.I. Road,
Jaipur 302002
Tel. 383163, 360238
*Forty rooms/dormitory.
Rs.100–250*

HOTEL KHADIM
Near R.P.S.Office,
Civil Lines,
Ajmer 305001
Tel. 20490
*Fifty rooms, eleven AC,
and dormitory.
Rs.150–600*

TOURIST VILLAGE
Pushkar Nagaur Road
Pushkar (Ajmer)
Tel. 014581-2074
*Twenty-eight rooms.
Rs.100–200*

HOTEL SAROVAR
Near Pushkar Lake
Tel. 014581-2074/2040
*Forty rooms.
Rs.40–300*

HOTEL MEENAL
Alwar 301001
Tel. 22852
*Six rooms.
Rs.250–450*

HOTEL LAKE PALACE
Siliserh, Alwar
Tel. 0144-22991
*Ten rooms.
Rs.200–600*

HOTEL TIGER DEN
Jaipur Road, Sariska,
Alwar
Tel. 014441-342
*Twenty-seven rooms/
dormitory.
Rs.200–700*

HOTEL HAVELI
On NH 11, Bikaner-
Fatehpur,
Fatehpur 332301
Tel. 01571-20293
*Nine rooms.
Rs.100–400*

JHEEL RAMGARH
Ramgarh (Jaipur)
303109
Tel. 014262-370
*Ten huts.
Rs.150–200*

**CASTLE JHOOMAR
BAORI**
Ranthambor Road
Sawai Madhopur
Tel. 07462-20495
*Twelve rooms.
Rs.375–750*

HOTEL VINAYAK
Ranthambor Road
Sawai Madhopur
Tel. 07462-21333
Rs.100-450

HOTEL SARAS
Fatehpur Sikri Road
Bharatpur 321001
Tel. 05644-23700
*Twenty-five rooms/
dormitory.
Rs.200–550*

NORTHWEST RAJASTHAN

HOTEL DHOLA MARU
Puran Singh Circle,
near Gandhi Path,
Bikaner 334001
Tel. 0151-28621
*Twenty-seven rooms/
dormitory.
Rs.100–400.*

HOTEL MOOMAL
Amar Sagar Road,
near Central Bus Stand,
Jaisalmer 345001
Tel. 02992-52392
*Sixty rooms.
Rs.150–550*

HOTEL GHOOMAR
High Court Road,
opposite Rani Ka Bagh
Railway Station,
Jodhpur 342006
Tel. 0291-44010
*Seventy-four rooms/
dormitory.
Rs.200–500*

SOUTH RAJASTHAN

HOTEL KAJRI
Shastri Circle,
Udaipur 313001
Tel. 0294-29509
*Fifty-three rooms/
dormitory.
Rs.150–500*

HOTEL HALDIGHATI
Haldighati,
near Udaipur
Rs.75–100

HOTEL SAM DHANI
Sam Village,
Jaisalmer
*Eight huts/dormitory.
Rs.100–150*

HOTEL GOKUL
Near Lal Bagh,
Nathdwara 313301
Tel. 02953-2685
*Seven rooms/dormitory.
Rs.200-250*

HOTEL GAVRI
Rishabdeo 313802
Tel. 029072-245
*Eight rooms/dormitory.
Rs.200–250*

HOTEL SHILPI
Jain Temple Road,
Ranakpur
Tel. 02934-3674

Thirteen rooms.
Rs.125–250

HOTEL SHIKHAR
near Central Bus Stand,
Mount Abu
Tel. 02974-3129
Eighty rooms/cottage.
Rs.125–600

HOTEL PANNA
CHITTOR
Near Railway Station
Chittorgarh 312001
Tel. 01472-41238
Thirty-one rooms/
dormitory.
Rs.350–450

HOTEL JANTA AVAS
GRAH
Chittorgarh
Tel. 0747-3238
Two rooms.
Rs.30–60

SOUTHEAST
RAJASTHAN

HOTEL CHAMBAL
Near Chambal Garden,
Kota 324001
Tel.0744 -26527
Fifteen rooms/dormitory.
Rs100–400

HOTEL CHANDRAVATI
Patan Road, Jhalawar
Tel. 07432-3015
Six rooms/dormitory.
Rs.100–250

HOTEL VRINDAWATI
near Jait Sagar Lake
Bundi 323001
Tel. 0747-3473
Two rooms/tents.
Rs.200–300

RTDC MOTELS
MOTEL BEHROR
On NH 8, Jaipur-Delhi
Midway
Tel. 01494-20049
Thirteen rooms.
Rs.250–450

MOTEL MAHUWA
Jaipur-Agra Highway
Tel. 07461-4260
Four rooms/dormitory.
Rs.150–250

MOTEL BARR
On NH 8 between Jaipur
and Jodhpur
Tel. 02937-4221
Two rooms.
Rs.100–200

MOTEL RATANGARH
NH 11, Agra-Bikaner
Tel. 01567-2286

MOTEL DEOGARH
Udaipur-Rajsamand

Road. Tel. 02904-52011
Two rooms.
Rs.100–150

MOTEL POKRAN
Jodhpur-Jaisalmer
Highway
Tel.029942-2275
Two rooms.
Rs.300–200

MOTEL RATANPUR
NH Udaipur-Ahmedabad
Four rooms.
Rs.200–300.

MOTEL SHAHPURA
Jaipur Devi Road,
Tel: 01422-2264
Two rooms.
Rs.300–350.

USEFUL
INFORMATION

JAIPUR
STD Code 0141

TELEPHONE SERVICE
Local enquiry
Tel. 197
Morning alarm
Tel. 173
Trunk booking
Tel. 180
Trunk assistance
Tel. 181

Overseas booking
Tel. 186
Trunk information
Tel. 183

EMERGENCIES
POLICE
Tel. 100
FIRE
Tel. 101
AMBULANCE
Tel. 102

TOURIST SERVICES
AND INFORMATION
CENTERS
FOREIGNERS REGIONAL
REGISTRATION OFFICE
Behind Hawa Mahal,
RAJASTHAN POLICE HEAD
OFFICE
Tel. 49391
GOVERNMENT OF INDIA
TOURIST OFFICE

Hotel Khasa Kothi
Tel. 372200
9am–6pm
RTDC OFFICE
Railway Station
Tel. 315714
6am–8pm
INFORMATION CENTER,
RAJASTHAN
GOVERNMENT
Ram Singh Road
Tel. 372345
TOURIST INFORMATION
BUREAU
Central Bus Stand,
Sindhi Camp
10am–5pm

COMMUNICATIONS
Phone, facsimile, STD,
and ISD (IDD) facilities
are available at
numerous shops all over
the city. The more
reliable places have
metered readings for the
time clocked per call and
the service charges
incurred.

TRANSPORT
AIRLINES
AIR INDIA
Ratan Mansion
M.I. Road
Tel. 368569

INDIAN AIRLINES
City Office
Nehru Place,
Tonk Road
Tel. 514500, 514407,
515324
AIRPORT
Tel. 550222, 550519
Flight enquiry
Tel. 141142

ARCHANA AIRWAYS
Anukampa Phase II
M.I. Road
Tel. 370266

MODILUFT
Techno Travel
Nav Jeevan Chambers,
opposite Maharashtra
Mandal,
Vinobha Bhave Marg,
C-Scheme,
Tel. 363373

SKYLINE NEPC.
Near Chanakya
Restaurant,
Ganeshan Complex.
Tel. 362278

SAHARA
Viajy Path
Tilak Nagar
Tel. 620781

U.P. AIRWAYS
Anukampa Travel
Anukampa Building

Phase II - M.I. Road
Tel. 378206, 370266

RAILWAY
Railway enquiry
Tel. 131
Railway reservation
Tel. 135

RAJASTHAN ROADWAYS
Central bus stand
Sindhi Camp
Tel. 375834

CAR RENTAL
Most hotels arrange for
car hire. Wheels rent-a-
car has cars for city and
inter-city use. They are
available in packages of
4 hours/30 miles or
8 hours/48 miles and
beyond.
Tel. 383867, 383870
Hotel Clark's Amer
Tel. 550616
HERTZ
NGS-42 Nehru Place
Tonk Road
Tel. 514672

PHOTO STORES
TAK STUDIO
SMS Highway,
New Gate
Tel. 373546

PICTORIALS
Panch Bathi,
M.I. Road
Tel. 373834

K.K. COLOUR LAB.
Ajmeri Gate
Tel. 376784

GOYAL COLOUR LAB
Ajmeri Gate
Tel. 368333

KLIK
Nehru Bazaar
Tel. 317363

PHOTO EYE
11, Kishan Pol Bazaar
Tel. 620950

SPOTLITE
Nehru Bazaar
Tel. 373495

CULTURE

MUSEUMS/GALLERIES
CITY PALACE
Tel. 48146
9.30am–4.45pm
Admission: Rs.20,
Rs.6 (students)
Closed on national
holidays.
A collection of textiles,
paintings, armory,
carpets, among other
things ▲ 136. Some of

its textiles, carpets, and silver pots are listed in the Guinness Book of Records.

ALBERT HALL MUSEUM
Ramniwas Garden
Tel. 560796
10am–5pm
Admission Rs.3,
Rs. 2 (students)
Free on Monday.
Closed on Friday.

AMBER FORT-PALACE,
TEMPLES, GOVERNMENT
MUSEUM
Jaipur-Amer Road,
6½ miles to the north of
Jaipur
Tel. 530293
9am–4.30pm
Shila Devi Temple is
open
5am–12 noon, 4–8pm.
Free admission.
Admission fee to fort:
Rs.2
Closed on national
holidays.
*Don't miss Diwan-i-am,
Sheesh Mahal, and
Shila Devi Temple ▲ 146.*

OBSERVATORY
JANTAR MANTAR
Located in the City
Palace complex.
9am–4.30pm
Admission fee: Rs.2
Free on Mondays.
*Maharaja Jai Singh's
open-air observatory of
outsized astronomical
instruments, built in
1728–34, is the largest
and best preserved of
the five he built in North
India ▲ 140.*

PALACES/FORTS
JAIPUR
HAWA MAHAL
10am–5pm
Free admission.
*The five-story pink
sandstone structure of
the "Palace of Winds",
built in 1799, is one of
Jaipur's most famous
landmarks. From behind
its 953 niches, windows,
and balconies, the royal
ladies would watch the
scenes in the streets
below ▲ 139.*

JAIGARH FORT
Jaipur Amer Road
Tel. 45594
9.30am–4.45pm.
Admission fee: Rs.10,
Rs.5 (students)
Closed on national
holidays.
SISODIA RANI KI BAGH

Jaipur Amer Road
Tel. 45594
8am–6pm
Admission fee: Rs.1

SAMODE
SAMODE PALACE
30 miles north via
Chomu.
Tel. 01423-4123
Admission fee: Rs.50
*See the exquisite mirror
inlay work and the
paintings in the Diwan-i-
Khas ▲ 180.*

DANCE/THEATER
PANGHAT THEATER
Rambagh Palace
Tel. 381919
7pm–8pm
October to April.
*Authentic performances
◆ 342. An absolute
must.*

CRAFTS

If you want to see
artisans at work, go into
the narrow side lanes
and experience Jaipur's
cottage industry first-
hand. Visit Ramganj
Bazaar for *mojris*
(shoes); Kishanpol
Bazaar for tie-and-dye
textiles; Maniharon Ka
Rasta (Tripoli Bazaar)
for lac work; Achrol
House, Subhash Chowk
for carpets;
Khajanewalon Ka Rasta
for marble carving;
Sanganer village for
block-printed textiles,
handmade paper, and
blue pottery.

SHOPPING ◆ 340
Stores generally open
from 10am to 7pm.

GOLD AND SILVER
JEWELRY
SILVER MOUNTAINS
S-2, Chameliwala
Market, M.I. Road,
Jaipur
Tel. 377399
*Manufacturers and
exporters of gems and
jewelry, particularly the
famed silver ornaments
of Rajasthan.*

GEM PALACE
M.I. Road, Jaipur
Tel. 374175
*Precious stones and
jewelry.*

BHURAMAL RAJMAL
SURANA,
Johari Bazar, Jaipur
Tel. 560628

*Kundan (gold inlay) and
enamel jewelry.*

AMRAPALI
Tholia Building, Panch
Batti, M.I. Road, Jaipur
Tel. 377940
*Gold, silver and tribal
jewelry.*

DWARKA'S
H-20, Bhagat Singh
Marg,
near Govt. Press,
C-Scheme, Jaipur
Tel. 360301, 368341
Fax 372932
*Gold and silver jewelry
studded with diamonds
and precious stones.*

THOLIA'S KUBER
Tholia Building,
M.I. Road, Jaipur
Tel. 367334
*Silver and tribal jewelry
and objets d'art.*

MANEEKA
H-10, Chameliwali
Market, opposite
General Post Office,
Jaipur
Tel. 375913
*Old tribal silver
ornaments.*

TEXTILES
For authentic
Sanganeri or
Bagru hand-
printed fabrics,
one must visit the
Chaupar stalls or the
upmarket handicraft
stores on M.I. Road.
Silks and the famed
Rajasthani quilts are
also available here.

GOVERNMENT
EMPORIA
HANDLOOM HOUSE
Rituraj Building,
M.I. Road, Jaipur

KHADI GHAR
M.I. Road, Jaipur
Tel. 373745

RAJASTHALI
Ajmeri Gate,
M.I. Road, Jaipur
Tel. 367176

CARPETS AND
DURRIES
ANKUR EXPORTS
opposite Rambagh
Palace, Jaipur
Tel. 515121, 515553

AMBIKA EXPORTS
Naila House, Moti
Doongri Road
Jaipur 302004
Tel. & fax 609821
*Sells durries,
environment-friendly
natural fibre rugs.*

ART AGE
2, Bhawani Singh Road,
Jaipur
Tel. 381720, 381726

SIDDHARTH CARPET
MANUFACTURING CO.
B-84 Ganesh Marg
Bapu Nagar, Jaipur
Tel. 5197954
Fax 565905

RUNGEEN BAZAAR
Mayur Apartments,
Raj Bhawan Road,
Civil Lines, Jaipur

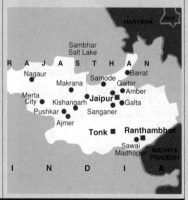

Tel. 383079
*Clothing and fabrics for
the home in classical
styles using vegetable
dyes.*

SHYAM AHUJA
Rambagh Palace Hotel
3, Bhawani Singh Road
Jaipur
Tel. 381448
*World-famous designer
and manufacturer of
rugs, durries, fabrics,
and home accessories.*

BOUTIQUES
ANOKHI
Tilak Marg, Behind
Secretariat, Jaipur
Tel. 381619, 381558
*Ready-made garments,
furnishings, fabrics, and
accessories in exclusive
prints.*

NEERJA
S-19, Bhawani Singh
Road, Jaipur
Tel. 380395
*Blue pottery and
costume jewelry.*

NAYIKA
Tholia Building,
M.I. Road, Jaipur
Tel. 367334

SOMA
5, Jacob Road,
Civil Lines,
Jaipur
Tel. 382986-87
Fax 380076
Furnishings, ready-

*made garments and
accessories.*

SALIM'S PAPER
Handmade paper and
board industries,
Gramodyog Road,
Sanganer, Jaipur
Tel. 550552, 552772
Fax 552552
*Eco-friendly paper
handmade from agro,
jute, cloth, and recycled
paper ▲ 158.*

**PAINTING AND OBJETS
D'ART**
ART FAIR
U-2, Chameliwala
Market, opp. GPO,
M.I. Road, Jaipur
Tel. 362915, 373042

EXPO PLUS
C-86, Prithviraj Road,
C-Scheme, near Bagria
Bhawan, Jaipur
Tel. 383044
Fax 361879
*Handmade metal, wood,
papier maché, ceramic
items, jewelry, and
textiles.*

**EMBROIDERED
TEXTILES**
SAURASHTRA ORIENTAL
ARTS
5–6 Jorawar Singh
Gate, opposite
Ayurvedic College, Amer
Road, Jaipur
Tel. 42609, 552026
*It has a fascinating
collection of
embroidered pieces.*

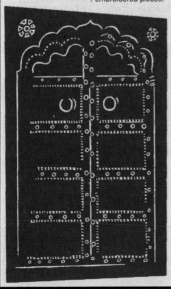

RESTAURANTS

*Tipping: Usually 10
percent of the bill.
Deluxe restaurants
apply a 12-percent sales
tax and moderately
priced ones charge 8
percent. Inexpensive
restaurants usually do
not levy any taxes or
service charge. But
tipping is expected.*

BHUWANESHWARI
Bissau Palace Hotel
outside Chandpol,
Jaipur
Tel. 320191, 310371
Fax 317628
6am–11pm
*Royal dining room with
intimate atmosphere.
Serves Rajasthani
special dishes.*
▭ ◖ ⌂ ⊡⋯

NIROS RESTAURANT
M.I. Road, Jaipur
Tel. 374493, 371874
9.30am–11pm
*Government-approved,
air-conditioned
restaurant. Serves
Tandoori, Mughlai,
continental, and
Chinese cuisine;
vegetarian dishes
included. Moderately
priced.*
▭ ◖

**LAKSHMI MISHTAN
BHANDAR**
Johari Bazaar, Jaipur
Tel. 565844, 560845,
565846, 565847
Fax 562176
8am–10.30pm
*Specializes in North
Indian cuisine. Serves
authentic Rajasthani
food and Indian chaat,
or snacks, such as dahi
bada, potato chop, papri
chaat. It is the largest
confectioner of Indian
sweets. Most popular
items include Rasmalai,
Paneer Gharver, Mishi
Mawa. Pure vegetarian
dishes also available.*

COPPER CHIMNEY
opposite General Post
Office, M.I. Road, Jaipur
Tel. 372275
12.30–3.30pm,
6.30–11pm
*An air-conditioned
restaurant serving
Indian (Mughlai) food
and vegetarian dishes.*

CHANAKYA
2AB, M.I. Road, Jaipur

Tel. 376161/378461
12 noon–11pm
*North Indian and
Rajasthani vegetarian
food, with emphasis on
"home-made" cuisine.
Paneer butter masala
and malai kofta are
favorites.*
▭

GULAB MAHAL
Jai Mahal Palace Hotel,
Jacob Road, Civil Lines,
Jaipur
Tel. 371616
Lunch and dinner.
*The main dining hall of
the palace-hotel
preserves its royal
heritage through its
elegance and service.
Managed by the Taj
Group, the cuisine
ranges from continental
to Indian. It has the best
Rajasthani thali in town.
The typical local fare
includes lahsuni murg
tikka, aloo mangodi, and
safed naans.*
▭ ◖ ⋇ ⌂ ♫ ⊨

SHIVIR
Hotel Mansingh,
Sansar Chander Road,
Jaipur
Tel: 378771
Fax: 377582
12.30pm–3pm,
7.30pm–11.30pm
*A rooftop restaurant in a
contemporary luxury
hotel, Shivir affords a
pretty view of the city.
Their range of thali
meals is noteworthy.
There is Panna
(vegetarian), Ameri
(traditional), and Mumal
(a royal repast). An array
of succulent meats and
poultry dishes.*
▭ ⌂ ⊨

PALMS
Holiday Inn Jaipur
Amer Road, Jaipur
Tel. 609090
*Serves continental and
Indian cuisine.*
▭

AANGAN
Holiday Inn Jaipur
Amer Road, Jaipur
Tel. 609000
12 noon–3.30pm,
7.30pm–11.30pm
*The restaurant overlooks
the traditional haveli
courtyard. Typical
Rajasthani ambience
with jarokhas. Serves
authentic Mughlai
cuisine.*

ANGITHI MAHRANI PALACE
Station Road
Tel. 374104
Barbeque in the poolside terrace garden.

GARDEN CAFE
A-6, Mahaveer Marg,
C-Scheme, Jaipur
Tel. 620811
11am–11pm (summer), 10am–10pm (winter). An open-air fast food outlet, serving South Indian food, burgers, pizzas, drinks, ice-cream. Casual decor, friendly atmosphere.
📷••

GAURI
Gangaur Tourist Hotel
Gopal Bari,
Hathroi Fort Road,
off M.I. Road,
Jaipur
Tel. 371641, 371647
*7am–1pm
An air-conditioned restaurant where South Indian and Chinese food are available.*

CHANDRAVANSH PAVILION
Welcomgroup
Rajputana Palace
Sheraton,
Palace Road,
Jaipur
Tel. 360011
*Open 24 hours.
Serves Indian (all regional cuisines), Western (French, English, Italian), and Indian and Chinese vegetarian food.*
📷 🅲 ✂ 🏠 🎵

JAL MAHAL
Welcomgroup
Rajputana Palace
Sheraton, Palace Road,
Jaipur
Tel. 360011
*6.30–10am, 12 noon–3pm, 7–11pm
Serves Indian (all regional cuisines), Western (French, English, Italian), and Indian and Chinese vegetarian food.*
📷 🅲 🏠 🎵

ANNAPURNA
C-20, Radha Marg,
C-Scheme, near
Rajmandir cinema,
Jaipur
Tel. 368759, 371305
Vegetarian Indian, Rajasthani and Gujarati specialties.

ARAVALLI
Jaipur Ashok, Jaipur
Tel. 320091, 320098
Vegetarian Indian and continental cuisine.

CHANDRALOK
M.I. Road (above Laxmi
Commercial Bank),
Jaipur
Traditional Rajasthani thalis.

ZAIKA
Uniara Garden Haveli
Hotel, Trimurti, JN Road,
Jaipur
Tel. 620668, 620386
Located in the haveli, it serves multi-cuisine in a quiet, pleasing atmosphere.

SURYA MAHAL
M.I. Road,
Jaipur
Tel. 369840, 371862
Fax 366323
Multi-cuisine, including South Indian, Indian, Chinese, continental food. Also serves pizzas, snacks, and shakes.

KHASA RASODA
Maharani Farms,
Durgapura, Jaipur
An open-air restaurant with guests seated on the terrace. Dinner is served by candlelight.
✂

SHEESH MAHAL
Samode Palace,
District Jaipur
The stunning "Palace of Mirrors" in the palace is worth a visit just for the ambience. Food is good too.

ACCOMMODATION

The Heritage Hotels
Association
9 Sardar Patel Marg,
C-Scheme,
Jaipur 302001
Tel./Fax 382214, 381804
The association can supply a list of classified hotels which ensure a certain level of services and comfort apart from other member hotels.

JAIPUR KHASA KOTHI
M.I. Road,
Jaipur 302001
Tel. 375151–55
Fax 374040
*Located in the heart of the city, close to the railway station and bus stand, this is a regal, white mansion set among old, tall trees. It was the summer palace of the former Maharaja of Jaipur. Audio and video music system installed. Dance performance can be arranged on demand and ghazals are also arranged occasionally. Thirty-six rooms.
Rs.570–1800/
US$19–59/£12–37*
📷 🅲 ✂ 🏠 📡•• ⌷
🎵 ⌷ ☎

HOTEL JAIPUR PALACE
Tonk Road,
Jaipur 302015
Tel. 512961
Fax 512966
*A modern hotel with a palace look. Located 3 miles from the city. Fifty-nine rooms. Serves Indian, continental, and Chinese food.
Rs. 1195–Rs.2350/
US$40–80/£24–48*
📷 🅲 ⌷ ⌷ ☎ 🍴

JAI MAHAL PALACE
Jacob Road, Civil Lines,
Jaipur 302006
Tel. 371616
Fax 365237
*Built in the typical palace fashion with high domed chhatris and cupolas, and intricate latticework, the hotel is a fine blend of Mughal and Rajput styles. Most rooms have a panoramic view of the beautifully landscaped Mughal gardens.
102 rooms.
US$172.50–637.50/
£115–425*
🅲 ✂ 🏠 ⌷ 🎵 ⌷
☎ 🍴

MAHRANI PALACE
Station Road,
Jaipur 302001
Tel. 374104
Fax 372816, 367431
*Located close to the Railway Station, this is a modern hotel with well furnished rooms, roof-top swimming pool, barbecue served in the terrace garden and multi-cuisine restaurant. Bed and breakfast.
Rs.1150-2500/
US$40-83/£24–53*
⌷ ✂ ⌷ 🎵 ⌷

THE RAMBAGH PALACE
Bhawani Singh Road,
Jaipur 302005
Tel. 381919
Fax 381098
Spread over 47 acres of fine gardens, it was a hunting lodge for Maharaja Madho Singh (1880–1922) and was later renovated when Sawai Man Singh II
▲ 133 *moved in, raising its status to that of a maharaja's palace. Magnificently painted ceiling of Suvarna Mahal and the mirror-work bamboos of the Oriental Room. Splendid swimming pool in garden pavilion.
106 rooms
Rs.4650–19,500/
US$155–$650/
£93–390*
⌷ ⌷ 🎵 ⌷

THE RAJMAHAL PALACE HOTEL
Sardar Patel Marg
Jaipur 302001
Tel. 381757, 381625
Fax 381887
*Set amid 15 acres of lush green lawns, it was built in 1729 by Sawai Jai Singh of Jaipur for his favorite queen. From 1821, the palace functioned as the residency of the British Resident of Jaipur, and in 1956 Maharaja Sawai Man Singh II renovated and renamed this palace, which served as his residence till his death. Throughout that period, it provided lodging for aristocracy of the old order as well as the new, from Queen Elizabeth II to Mrs Jacqueline Kennedy. Twelve rooms.
Rs.1350–4000/
US$45–135/£27–80*
📷 🅲 ✂ 🏠 ⌷ ⌷
☎

MANSINGH
Sansar Chander Road,
Jaipur 302001
Tel. 378771
Fax 377582
A contemporary luxury hotel which caters to foreign tourists and local business groups. 8 miles from airport, 2 miles from railway station. Ninety-one rooms. Rs.2390/US$80/£48

WELCOMGROUP RAJPUTANA PALACE SHERATON
Palace Road,
Jaipur 302006
Tel. 360011
Fax 367848
Modern, constructed along the lines of traditional haveli architecture. 218 rooms, one presidential suite. Folk/nomadic dance performances everyday. Rs.3875–21,700/ US$125–700/£77–434

HOLIDAY INN JAIPUR
Amer Road,
Jaipur 302002
Tel. 609000
Fax 609090
A new hotel with traditional haveli structure – a central open-to-sky courtyard and open corridors. Seventy-two rooms and suites. Rs.1800–3008/ US$58–97/£36–60

HOTEL JAIPUR ASHOK
Jai Singh Circle, Bani Park,
Jaipur 302016
Tel. 320091-98
Fax 322999
In the heart of town. Ninety-nine rooms. Rajasthani folk dance performance every evening. Rs.1195–2200/ US$38–75/£57–112

HOTEL ADITYA
2 Bhawani Singh Road,
Jaipur 302005
Tel. 381750/20/26/27
Fax 381730
Twenty-four rooms. Rajasthani folk dance and ghazal on request. Rs.930–1800/ US$30–60/ £19–36

CLARK'S AMER
Jawahar Lal Nehru Marg, Jaipur 302017
Tel. 550616, 550701
Fax 550013
Close to the city and only five minutes away from the airport, the hotel is situated amid lush green surroundings. 202 rooms. Rs.2480–2790/ US$80–90/£120–135

MERU PALACE
Sawai Ram Singh Road,
Jaipur 302001
Tel. 371111–16
Fax 378882
Forty-eight rooms. Rs. 1195–1400/ US$38–$45/£24–£28

BISSAU PALACE HOTEL
Outside Chandpol, Near Saroj cinema,
Jaipur 302016
Tel. 320191, 310371
Fax 317628
Situated on the foothills of Tiger Fort, this is the traditional summer residence of the Rawal of Bissau. It has a special museum displaying portraits, armory, and jewelry. Restaurant serves Indian, continental, and Rajasthani specialties. Folk dances and sitar recitals are staged. Rs.495–1320/ US$16–43/£10–27

NARAIN NIWAS PALACE
Kanota Bagh, Narain Singh Road,
Jaipur 302004
Tel. 561291
Fax 563448
Thirty-six rooms. A house built by a Rajput chieftain, it is surrounded by gardens. Interesting architecture, original frescos. Heritage hotel. Rs.1000–1800/ US$32– 58/£21–38

SAKET
Opposite Udyog Bhawan,
C-Scheme,
Jaipur 302001
Tel. 381791/381769
Twenty-nine rooms. Restaurant serves Indian, continental, and Chinese cuisine.

Rs.350–850/ US$11–28/£7–17

MANDAWA HOUSE
Sansar Chandra Road,
Jaipur 302001
Tel. 365398
Fax 371795
Nineteen rooms. Built in 1896 by the Mandawa family, this haveli is now a heritage property. Rs.600–800/ US$20–25/£12–16

DIGGI PALACE
Sawai Ram Singh Road,
Shivaji Marg,
Jaipur 302004
Tel. 373091, 370359
A family-run hotel set in a 250-year-old haveli, with a 30,000 square foot lawn. Forty-five rooms, fifteen air-conditioned and the rest provided with fans and air coolers, all with running hot and cold water. Horse-riding available. Five minutes walk from the walls of the city. Rs.150–600/ US$5–19./£3–12

THE OBEROI
Gajner Road,
off Agra Road,
Jaipur 302001
Tel. 5563232
Fax 5563001
Old palace. Fifty-two rooms, including deluxe cottages with three rooms each.

Air-conditioned tents. There is an old Shankar Temple within the complex which is being restored to its former glory. Rs.18,000/US$600/ £360; tents Rs.6000/ US$200/£120

KARAN'S GUEST HOUSE
D-70 Shiv Heera Path,
Chomu House,
C-Scheme,
Jaipur 302001
Tel. 380081
Fax 382810
An eight-roomed guest house offering deluxe comforts at budget price. Rs.675–725/ US$22–24/£13–14

LAKSHMI VILAS
Sawai Ram Singh Road,
Jaipur 302001
Tel. 381567, 381569
Twenty-two rooms. Rs.300–500/ US$10–16/£6–10

ACHROL HOUSE
Jacob Road,
Civil Lines, Jaipur 302006
Tel. 382154
Fax 382810
This hotel is of 1930 Rajasthani vintage and comes with a large garden. Seven rooms. Rs.300–850/ US$10–27/£6–17

L.M.B. Hotel
Johari Bazaar,
Jaipur 302003
Tel. 565844
Fax 562176
*Thirty-three rooms.
Rs.725–Rs.1275/
US$23–41/£14–£25*
☐ 🄲 🛏

Arya Niwas
Sansar Chandra Road,
Behind Amber Tower,
Jaipur 302001
Tel. 372456, 368524,
370612
Fax 364376
*Old palace renovated
haveli style, with typical
Jaipur style of façade,
verandah, and
courtyards.
Seventy rooms.
Rs.200–500/
US$6–16/£4–10*

The Ramgarh Lodge
Jamuva Ramgarh
Jaipur 303104
Tel. 262217
Fax 381098
*Situated on the shores
of the famous Ramgarh
Lake, 24 miles from
Jaipur, it was the
hunting lodge of the
former rulers of Jaipur.
An idyllic retreat, it also
gives an idea of how
royalty "roughed it".
Beautiful prints of
hunting scenes
decorate the walls of
the rooms and corridors.
Recreation facilities
include tennis, squash,
and billiards.
Breakfast and either
lunch or dinner
included.
Rs.1550–2480/
US$50–80/ £31–50*
☐

Royal Castle
Agra Road, 8½ miles
from Jaipur, Kanota
Tel. 561291
Fax 563448
*This 18th-century fort
offers a unique chance
to enjoy the village life.
Special attraction here is
the library with a
collection of 10,000 rare
books, manuscripts,
miniature paintings, old
arms, buggies and
saddlery.
Rs. 950-1300/
US$31-41/ £20-28*
☐••

The Fort Uniara
Near Trimurti,
J.N. Road,

Jaipur 302001
Tel. 620668, 620386
*A twelve-roomed haveli
hotel located on the
road to the airport.
Rs.800–1000/
US$26–32/£16–20*
☐ ⇟ 🏠 ☎ ⌇

Fort Hotel
Kuchaman,
District Nagaur
Tel. 01856-20880/2,
20035
*Perched on the top of a
hillock, like an eagle's
nest, the fort overlooks
the Salt Lake, city and
plains. High ramparts,
thirty-two bastions, ten
gates and various
defenses make this
formidable fort an
architectural marvel.
Rs1150–2170/
US$37–70/£23–43*
⇟ 🏠 ♫

Samode Palace
Samode 303806
Office: Gangapole,
Jaipur 302002
Tel. 01423-602407,
47068
Fax 01423-602370
*Approved heritage hotel.
25 miles outside Jaipur
on the Jaipur-Sikar
route. Live Rajasthani
folk music every
evening, folk dances on
request.
Thirty-five rooms.
Rs.1195–2500/
US$40–80/£24–50*
☐ ⇟ 🏠 ♫

Samode Bagh
Samode 303806
Tel. 01423-4113
*Near the palace, this
Mughal-style garden has
forty tents with attached
bathroom.
Rs.1195–2500/
US$40–80/£24–50*
☐ ⇟ 🏠 ♫

Samode Haveli
Gangapole,
Jaipur 302002
Tel. 47068, 602407
Fax 602370
*Approved heritage hotel
just outside Jaipur.*

*Old palatial building with
huge garden and lawns.
Twenty-two rooms.
Rs.1195–2100/
US$40–78/£24–42*
☐ ⇟ 🏠 ♫

Choki Dhani
Tonk Road
Jaipur 302015
Tel. 550118
Fax 381888
*Newly built ethnic resort
with multi-cuisine
restaurant, bar,
swimming pool, riding
and in-house boating
facilities.*
☐ ⌇ ♫ ☐

Castle Awan
Garh Awan
Tel. 01434–8508
Bookings: 3, Naru Path
Govind Marg,
Jaipur 302004
Tel. 560731, 381543
*An old fort which was
the hunting lodge of the
Uniara family. It is
famed for its 'bawaris'
(wells). Situated 93
miles from Jaipur, 7 1/2
miles off Jaipur/Kotah
Highway.
Rs 660–1200/
US$22–36/£13–22*
♫ ☐

Hotel Bhadrawati Palace
Bhandarej,
District Dausa
Tel. 01427-8351
Fax 0141-382810
*Outside the city, on the
Agra-Jaipur road. The
town is of historical
importance. The palace-
hotel comprises a
restaurant, Sheesh
Mahal (seemingly a
common name in the
region!), and serves
multi-cuisine.
Twenty-five rooms.
Rs.1000–1600/
US$33–53/£20–31*
☐••

Ajmer and its

Environs

Useful Information

Ajmer
STD Code 0145

Culture

Mosque
Ajmer
Khwaja Mu'-in-ud-din
Chisti's Dargah
*Holy place of Muslims.
Also commands the
respect of other
believers. A superb
example of Indo-Islamic
architecture ▲162.*

Temple
Pushkar
Pushkar lake, temples
and ghats.
6½ miles from Ajmer.
See the Brahma
Temple, Rangji Temple,
and ghats around the
lake ▲164.

Restaurants

Bhola
Agra Gate, Sabzi Mandi
Tel. 23844
*Excellent thalis. Pure
vegetarian Indian and
Rajasthani food.*
○

Honey Dew
Opposite the railway
station.
Tel. 32498
*Vegetarian food.
Pleasant, shady garden.*
○

JAI HIND
Opposite the railway station, Madar Gate, behind the clock tower.
Tel. 22546, 22757
Serving very tasty vegetarian dishes for almost three decades now. Good value for money. Clean surroundings.
○

SHEESH MAHAL
Man Singh Palace Hotel
Tel. 425855/57, 425702
Excellent tandoori and Indian cuisine.

ACCOMMODATION

As Ajmer is the nearest base to Pushkar, prices rise sharply – as much as ten times – during the week of the Pushkar Fair. The camel and cattle fair is held in October/November during the Kartik Purnima (full moon). Most hotels are booked well in advance.

HOTEL MAN SINGH PALACE
Ana Sagar Road, Vaishali Nagar
Tel. 425855/57, 425702
Fax 0145-62635
112 rooms, including fifty air-conditioned double rooms. Bar and conference hall.
Rs.1200–2000/
US$40–66/£24–40
☐ ☎

HOTEL REGENCY
Delhi Gate, Ajmer
Tel. 30296/31750/24439
Fifty-six rooms, including seven air-conditioned double rooms, eight ordinary double rooms, three suites. Conference hall.
Rs.425–495/
US$14–/6/£8–10

HOTEL PRITHVI RAJ
Jaipur Road, Ajmer
Tel. 23297
Fifty rooms, including eighteen air-cooled double rooms and two air-conditioned rooms.
Rs.160–600/
US$5–20/ £3–12

AMBASSADOR
Ashok Marg, Ajmer 305001
Tel. 425095
Twenty-one rooms.

Centrally located near the hospital.
Rs.300–1100/
US$10–31/£2–22
⌂ ☐ ☐ ☐ ☎

ROOPANGARH FORT
Roopangarh 305814, District Ajmer
Tel. 01463-7217
Fifteen double rooms and one suite. In the center of the village.
Rs.1100–1350/
US$36–43/£22–27
☐ ☐ ☐ ☎

PUSHKAR
STD code 145

RESTAURANTS

PRINCE'S RESTAURANT
Hotel Pushkar Palace
Tel. 72001,72041/2/3
Fax 72226
6.30am–1pm
Offers a view of the lake. There is a terrace garden as well. Can accommodate up to fifty persons at a time. Serves a large variety of vegetarian cuisine.

ACCOMMODATION

THE SAFARI CLUB
Pushkar
Office: The Safari Club, High Court Colony, Jodhpur 342001
Tel. 0291-37023, 32695
Fax 0291-37023
Enjoy the experience of living in a tent in the midst of the desert. Particularly memorable during the Pushkar Fair. The camp in Pushkar operates only during the fair. Book in advance.
30 tents with attached baths.
Rs.4100/US$68/£43
(double occupancy)
☐ ⌂ ☐·· ☐ ⊨

PUSHKAR PALACE
Pushkar
Tel.145-72001, 72401/2/3
Fax 72226
Overlooking a lake, this heritage property was built around four

hundred years ago by the Maharaja of Kishangarh. The royal family would come here to take a holy dip in the lake.
Thirty six rooms.
Rs.950–1050/
US$32–35/£19–21
⌂ ⚬⃠ ⌂ ♫

ALWAR AND ITS ENVIRONS

USEFUL INFORMATION

STD Code 0144

NATURE RESERVE

SARISKA TIGER RESERVE
Admission fee: Rs.25
Bus hire: Rs.100
Car hire: Rs.75
Two-wheeler hire: Rs.10
Take a drive in the forest to see wildlife species ▲ 174. The tiger is rarely spotted.

CULTURE

CITY PALACE
10am–5pm
Admission fee: Rs.2, Rs.1 (students)
Closed on Friday and national holidays.
The Government Museum is on the ground floor.
Unique architecture with symmetrical ghats ▲170. Contains a collection of 18th- and 19th-century Rajput and Mughal paintings, manuscripts in Arabic, Sanskrit, and Urdu.

RESTAURANTS

THE HILL FORT
Kesroli, Tehsil Ramgarh, District Alwar

Tel. 4616145, 4625214, 4618962 (Delhi)
1pm–3pm, 8pm–10pm
Specializes in Indian and continental cuisine.
Rs.150–300/
US$5-10/£3–6

ACCOMMODATION

ARAVALLI HOTEL
Near the railway station. Educational packages, visits to tiger sanctuary, trekking.
Tel. 70316/70011/70883
Twenty-eight rooms.
Rs.300–1400/US$10–47/£6–28
⌂ ☐ ☐ ⌂ ⌣ ♫ ☐ ☎ ⊨

HOTEL SARISKA PALACE
Sariska, District Alwar
Tel. 014441-322
Booking: A-15/27, Vasant Vihar, New Delhi 110057
Tel. 6883544
Built in 1892–1900 by Maharaja Jai Singh of Alwar as a royal hunting lodge, it is now a modern hotel etched against the backdrop of the Sariska nature reserve. The nearest town, Alwar, is 21 miles away. The palace uses original Louis XIV and art-deco furniture. Offers numerous excursions in the region.
Forty rooms.
Rs.1147–2170/
US$37–70/£23–43
⚬⃠ ⌂ ☐··

NEEMRANA FORT-PALACE
Neemrana, District Alwar 301705
Tel. 01494-6005/6/8
Office: A-58 Nizamuddin East, New Delhi 110013
Tel. 011-4616145/4618962 /5214
Bookings: 4634208
Fax 011-4621112
Built in 1464, Neemrana Fort-Palace is Rajasthan's closest palace to New Delhi, two hours' drive away on the Delhi-Jaipur highway. The rooms in this reconstructed fort-palace are furnished with an eclectic mix of traditional Indian and colonial furniture, antiques, and objets d'art.
Rs.1000–5000
US$35-166/£20–100
⚬⃠ ⌂ ☐··

HARYANA
I N D I A
UTTAR PRADESH
Alwar
Deeg
Sariska Sanctuary
Agra
Rajgarh
Bharatpur
■ Jaipur
Dholpur
R A J A S T H A N
MADHYA PRADESH

THE HILL FORT
Kesroli, Tehsil Ramgarh,
District Alwar
Tel. 011-4616145,
4625214, 4618962
(Delhi)
Fax 011-4621112,
4634208
*A martial fort located on
top of a hill, with a
commanding view of
the countryside.
Medieval Rajasthani
architecture.
Ten rooms.
Rs.1200–1500/
US$40–49/£25–31*
⌂ ▭ ⚲ ⌂ ▭•• ♫

LAKE PALACE HOTEL
Siliserh, District Alwar
Tel. 0144-22991
*An erstwhile royal
residence with
traditional Rajput and
Islamic architecture.
A lakeside castle that is
now a hotel.
Ten rooms/dormitory.
Rs.250–500/
US$8–16/£5–10*
⌂ ⌂ ▭••

USEFUL
INFORMATION

STD Code 05644
*The nearest airport is at
Agra, 33 miles from
where one can take a
bus or taxi. The railway
station is at
Bharatpur town.*

NATURE

KEOLADEO GHANA BIRD
SANCTUARY
4pm–6pm
Admission: Rs.25
Bicycle: Rs.3
Car hire: Rs.75
Bus: Rs.100
Boat hire: Rs.60
*An absolute must. Some
374 migratory birds
camp here. During
winter nesting birds
include rosy and
dalmation pelicans,
flamingos, bareheaded
geese, and many others
▲ 306.*

CULTURE

DEEG PALACE
20¹/₂ miles north of
Bharatpur
8am–12 noon, 1–6pm
*Romantically beautiful
palace-complex ▲ 310.*

RESTAURANTS

KOHINOOR
Near Power House,
Bharatpur
Tel. 23733
8am–10pm
*Specializes in Indian
(tandoori) food,
including vegetarian
dishes.*

SPOON BILL
Near Saras Hotel,
Bharatpur
Tel. 23571
8am–10pm
*Serves Indian,
continental, and Chinese
vegetarian and non-
vegetarian dishes.*

DEEPALI
Hotel Park Palace,
Kumher Gate
Tel: 23222, 23783
Vegetarian and non-

*vegetarian Rajasthani
and Indian cuisine.*
○

ACCOMMODATION

FOREST LODGE
Keoladeo National Park,
Bharatpur
Tel. 22722, 22760
Fax 22864
*Seventeen rooms.
High season,
October–April,
Rs.1195–1450
Low season, May to
September,
Rs.900–1050/
US$30–33/£18–21*
▭••

SPOON BILL ROOMS
Near Saras Hotel,
Bharatpur 321001
Tel. 23571
*A kind of paying-guest
scheme for visitors.
Bikes, bird books and
binoculars are available
on hire for the bird lover.
One can spend winter
evenings around a
sparkling camp fire.*
▭

TOURIST GUEST
HOUSE
Near Saras Circle,
Bharatpur 321001
Tel. 25402
*Four rooms and two
tents. Offers bird-
watching facilities.
Rs.75–300/
US$2.50–10/£1.50–6*
▭ ⌂

LAKSHMI VILAS
PALACE HOTEL
Kakaji ki Kothi
Bharatpur 321001
Tel. 25259, 23523
Fax 25259
*Another heritage hotel.
The century-old palace
was built for the
younger son of the then
Maharaja of Bharatpur.
Set amid 40 acres of
picturesquely
landscaped environs, it
was designated as the
'zenana' – the
residence of the
beautiful, veiled
princesses. Located a
stone's throw from the
bird sanctuary, it is an
hour's drive from the Taj
Mahal at Agra.
Twenty-two rooms.
Rs. 750–2200/
US$24–71/£15–44*
▭ ⎘ ⚲ ⌂ ▭•• ▭
⌂

GOVIND NIWAS
Gol Bagh Road,
Bharatpur 321001
Tel. 23247
*An old colonial house
run by the owner
offering personalized
service. Six rooms.
Rs.800–1400/
US$ 26–47/£16–28*
⌂ ⚲ ⌂ ▭••

HOTEL PARK PALACE
Kumher Gate,
Bharatpur 321001
Tel. 23222, 23783
Fax 23170
*An elegant Dholpur
stone-clad building,
located in open
grounds; the rooms are
well-ventilated and
bright.
Rs 250-550/
US$8–18/£5–11*
⌂ ⎘ ▭ ☎

HOTEL EAGLE'S NEST
Tel. 25144
*Camp-fire parties on
request. Twelve rooms.
Oct–April. Rs.450–600/
$15–20/£9–12,
May–Sept. Rs.300–450
$10–12/£6–9*
⌂ ⌂

USEFUL
INFORMATION

STD Code 07462

NATURE

RANTHAMBHOR
RANTHAMBHOR NATIONAL
PARK
6 miles from Sawai
Madhopur.
7am–7pm
Closed from July 1 to
September 30.
Admission: Rs.25/visitor
plus Rs.75 for vehicle.
Rs.500/gypsy. A jeep
accommodates five
tourists and one guide.
Rs.50/person Open
safari bus with twenty-
two seats.

Covering some 160 square miles, the scenic national park is traditionally well-known for tigers. Summer: 6am to 9.30am, 3pm to 6pm. Winter: 6.30am to 10am, 2pm to 5pm (may close half an hour earlier or later depending on daylight).

CULTURE

RANTHAMBHOR
RANTHAMBHOR FORT. Tenth-century ruins with a series of well-established artificial lakes ▲ 304.

ACCOMMODATION

SAWAI MADHOPUR LODGE
Ranthambhor National Park Road, Sawai Madhopur 322001 Tel. 07462-20541/20247 Fax. 07462-20718 A heritage hotel. Twenty-two rooms, including six tents. The highlight of your stay is a visit to the Ranthambhor National Park, which has remarkably rich and diverse flora and fauna ▲305. Rs. 3410–3720/ US$110–120/£68–74

THE SAFARI CLUB
Office: The Safari Club, High Court Colony, Jodhpur 342001 Tel. 37023,32695 Fax 37023 Permanent safari camp. Price is inclusive of safari, meals, evening entertainment, boat across River Chambal, guides, and wildlife movies/documentaries. Two nights, Rs. 5425–7130/

US$175–$230/ £108–143 Three nights Rs.6510–8680/ US$210–$280 / £130–174

BHANWAR VILAS PALACE
Karauli 322241, District Sawai Madhopur Tel: 07464-20024 Bookings: Karauli House, New Sanganer Road, Sodala, Jaipur 302019 Tel. 0141-367532, 370512 Fax 0141-382810 A delightful location if you want to participate in camel, horse, and jeep safaris. Local fairs and festivals provide a great deal of color and flavor. Twenty rooms. Tents available on request. Rs 750–1000/ US$25–33/£15–20

SHEKHAVATI

USEFUL INFORMATION

STD code 015965

TRANSPORT
RAIL
The railway stations in the region are at Sikar, Nawalgarh, Fatehpur, Jhunjhunu, and Mukundgarh. Tel. 2395, 2396
AIR
There is a proposal to connect Jhunjhunu by air taxi.
BUS
Regular bus services connect all the important centers. Deluxe buses ply from Jaipur to Sikar, Jhunjhunu, and Fatehpur.

CULTURE

The havelis of Marwari businessmen are a legacy. The towns here are known for their profusely painted walls ▲184, step wells, and temples.

SIKAR
Located 70 miles from Jaipur.
Chotilal Sagarmal Sodhani Haveli, Raghunath Temple, and stepwell.

MANDAWA
Located 15 miles from Jhunjhunu.
Havelis of Ramnath Goenka, Bansidhar Newatia, and Gulab Rai Ladia. Fort. Majisa ka Kuan well.

NAWALGARH
Located 24 miles from Jhunjhunu.
Anand Lal, Poddar Haveli.

FATEHPUR
Located 30 miles from Jhunjhunu.
Havelis of Goenka, Devra, and Singhania. Remains of a 17th-century step-well.

RAMGARH
Located 13 miles from Fatehpur.
Poddar Haveli and cenotaphs.

JHUNJHUNU
110½ miles from Jaipur via Sikar.
Havelis of Modi and Tibrewala.

DUNDLOD
19 miles from Jhunjhunu.
Goenka haveli.

MAHENSAR
27 miles from Jhunjhunu.
Soné Chandi ki Haveli.

MUKUNGARH
5 miles from Dundlod
Kanoria and Ganeriwala havelis.

RESTAURANTS

ROOP NIWAS PALACE
Nawalgarh 333042 Tel. 01594-22008 Serves fixed meals and à la carte. Both vegetarian and non-vegetarian Indian and Rajasthani cuisine.

ACCOMMODATION

JHUNJHUNU
HOTEL SHIV SHEKHAVATI
Near Muni Ashram, Jhunjhunu 333001 Tel. 01592-32651 Twenty rooms and restaurant. Folk music and dance can be arranged on request. Rs.150–800/ US$5–25/£3–16

HOTEL SANGAM
opposite Central Bus Stand, Jhunjhunu 333001 Tel. 1592-32544 Fax 33432, 33086 Thirty rooms. Rs.150–700/ US$5–22/£3–12

JAMUNA RESORT
Near Nathji Ka Teela, Jhunjhunu 333001 Tel. 01592-32871 Three traditional cottages, air-conditioned. Rs.400–500 US$13–16/ £8–10

MANDAWA
CASTLE MANDAWA
Tel. 0159289-23124
Fax 23171
Heritage hotel. Chariot, camel, and horse rides are available. Jeep rides can be arranged on request. Folk dances and puppet show. Fifty-one rooms.
Rs.800–1100/
US$27–37/£16– 22
□••

THE DESERT RESORT
District Jhunjhunu
333704
Tel. 01592-23151
(c/o Castle Mandawa)
Office: 9, Sardar Patel
Marg, Jaipur 302001
Tel. 0141-381906
Fax 0141-382214
for reservations.
Fifty-one cottages built as a mud-walled tourist hamlet on a sand dune overlooking the desert. Traditional frescos and local crafts make for a unique ambience.
Rs.675–850/
US$21–28/£13–17
⚘ ⌂ □• ♫

NAWALGARH
ROOP NIWAS PALACE
Nawalgarh 333042
Tel. 01594-22008
Situated in the heart of Shekhavati, the hotel is a blend of European and Rajput styles of architecture. Thirty rooms with ceiling fans and air coolers. Serves Indian/Rajasthani cuisine. Camel and horse rides, puppet shows, folk dances and jeep drives on request.
Rs.700–900/
US$23–29/£14–18
⚘ ⌂ ⌖ ♫

APANI DHANI
Jhunjhunu Road,
Nawalgarh 333042,
Shekhavati
Tel. 01594-22239
Fax 01592-33432
Traditional "mud/straw architecture" of Rajasthan in the middle of an ecological farm. All huts have attached organic toilets. Ten rooms with ceiling fans and coolers. Hot water available; heated by solar panels. Serves Indian/Rajasthani vegetarian food. About half a mile east of Apani Dhani.

Rs.500/US$16/£11
□••

RAMESH JANGID'S TOURIST PENSION
Behind Maur Hospital,
Nawalgarh 333042
Shekhavati
Tel. 01594-22129,
22829
Fax 01592-33432
Five double rooms with ceiling fans and coolers. The family kitchen serves Indian and Rajasthani vegetarian food.
Rs.150–250/
US$5–8/£3–5

DUNDLOD
DUNDLOD CASTLE
Dundlod 333702,
District Jhunjhunu
Tel. 01594-52180
Fax 0141-373318
(Jaipur reservation office, Tel. 361611)
The castle, built in 1750, has beautiful medieval architecture, a mixture of Mughal and Rajput styles. Twenty-two rooms. A large restaurant caters to more than fifty guests. Well-equipped big conference room with a capacity for seventy people. Full of atmosphere, interesting murals. Rides/safaris, entertainment.
Rs.850–2500/
US$28–80/£17–43
♫

DERA DUNDLOD KILA
Dundlod Fort,
Dundlod 333702,
Jhunjhunu
Tel. 0141-366276
Fax 0141-366276,
0141-15945-2519
Within the Dundlod Castle. Twenty-five rooms with ceiling fans and coolers.
Rs.700–2340/
US$22–75/£14–47
⌖ ♫

MUKUNDGAH FORT HERITAGE HOTEL
c/o PTC Travels
Nawalgarh District,
Shekhavati
Tel. 015945-2395-96
Forty-two rooms.
Rs.1100-2200/
US$35–71/£22–44
□••

USEFUL INFORMATION

STD Code 0291

EMERGENCIES
Tourist Reception
Center
Tel. 45083, 44010
Police Assistance
S.P. Police Line
Tel. 33700 (office)
30700 (res.)

TRANSPORT
Air enquiry
Tel. 36757, 30617
Rail enquiry
Tel. 131, 132
Reservations
Tel. 20842
Bus enquiry
Tel. 44686, 44989

COMMUNICATIONS
POST AND TELEGRAPH
OFFICE
General Post Office
Near Railway Station
Tel. 27864

PHOTO STORES
TAK STUDIO
Sojati Gate
Tel. 20728

FAMOUS STUDIOS
High Court Road
Tel. 24689

URGENT STUDIO
Hospital Road
Tel. 26192

CULTURE

MEHRANGARH FORT
9am–5pm
Admission: Rs. 35 with a guide, Rs.10 without a guide.
Closed on national holidays.
The museum contains the royal collection, including elephant howdahs, cradles, and cannons.

JASWANT THADA
9am–5pm
Free admission.

A white Makrana marble chhatri (cenotaph) built by the Maharaja at the end of the 19th century.

UMAID BHAWAN PALACE
9am–5pm
Part of it is a museum which is open to visitors.

MANDORE GARDENS
5½ miles from Jodhpur.
The glory of this lush, shady, landscaped gardens are its six dewals, the domed chhatris of the Rathors, built on the spot where each ruler was cremated ▲ 232.

JODHPUR
RESTAURANTS

MARWAR HALL
Welcomgroup Umaid
Bhawan Palace Hotel
Jodhpur 342006
Tel. 33316
The grand dining hall of the palace hotel has a buffet for all three meals. In addition it serves Chinese, Indian, continental, and Rajasthani cuisine.
□ ⌂ ♫

RISALA
Welcomgroup Umaid
Bhawan Palace Hotel
Jodhpur 342006
Tel. 33316
Open for lunch and dinner. An à la carte restaurant serving Indian, Chinese, and continental cuisine. Sitar performance.
□ ⌂ ♫

THE PILLARS
Welcomgroup Umaid
Bhawan Palace Hotel
Jodhpur 342006
Tel. 33316
6am–11pm
The open-air restaurant overlooking the lush green lawns of the palace offers a view of the fort.
□ ⚘ ⌂ ♫

COURTYARD RESTAURANT
Ajit Bhawan Palace Hotel, opposite Circuit House, Jodhpur 342006
Tel. 37410
Fax 37774
7.30pm–10.30pm
Exquisitely intricate latticework stone screens and turbaned men in service recreate the charismatic atmosphere of the legendary past with daily folk music and dance performances. Serves Indian/Rajasthani cuisine, including vegetarian food.
🖂 ⤼ 🏠 ♫

ON THE ROCKS
Ajit Bhawan Palace Hotel, opposite Circuit House, Jodhpur
Tel. 37410
Fax 37774
7.30pm –10.30pm
A garden restaurant with rocky surroundings and fountains. Serving barbecue and Indian food.
🖂 ⤼ 🏠 ♫

REGGIE'S RESTAURANT
Near The Safari Club High Court Colony Jodhpur
Tel./Fax 37023
7pm–12pm (in summer, dinner only), 6.30pm–11.30pm
A rooftop restaurant with a Texas ranch-like look. Catering to foreign tourists, with lots of black-and-white photographs of Frank Sinatra, Dean Martin, Bing Crosby, and so on. Excellent tandoori or

barbecue and Western cuisine from grilled chicken to baked fish.
C ⤼ 🏠 ⤶ ☎ ⬳

KHAMAGHANI
Hotel Ratanada Polo Palace, Presidency Road, Jodhpur
Tel. 31910 (5 lines)
Serves Indian, tandoori, Chinese, and continental cuisine.

TORAN
Hotel Rajputana Palace Panch Batti Circle, Airport Road, Jodhpur
Tel. 31672, 38059
Fax 38672
7am–10.30pm
Serves Rajasthani, Indian, Chinese, and continental meals. Live folk music and dances on request at extra cost.
🖂 ⤼ 🏠 ▢

KALINGA
Station Road, Jodhpur
Tel. 24066, 26939
7am–10pm
Serves Rajasthani, South Indian, Gujarati, continental, and Chinese food. Children's menu available.
⤼

BALSAMAND LAKE PALACE
Mandore Road, Jodhpur
Tel. 33316
Fax 35373
Dine on Indian and Western vegetarian and non-vegetarian cuisine in an exceptional setting. The restaurant is in the beautiful old Lake Palace.
🖂

KHIMSAR FORT
Village Khimsar, District Nagaur
Tel. 01585-2345, 0141- 382314
Fax: 01585-228, 0141-381150
Three restaurants: on rooftop, within the 16th-century ruins and near the pool. Serves Rajasthani and continental cuisine.
⤼ 🏠 ☕ ♫ ☎

ACCOMMODATION

WELCOMGROUP UMAID BHAWAN PALACE
Jodhpur 342006
Tel. 33316
Fax 35373
*One hundred palatial rooms, overlooking lush, green lawns. One-hour folk dances in the evening at the pillars.
Rs.3900–4800/US$156–160/£78–£98 (single room), Rs.4200–5300/US$137–$173/£86–£100 (double room) Rs.6100–28,000/US$199–$911/£124–£570 (Suites)*
🖂 ⤼ 🏠 ♫

HOTEL RATANADA POLO PALACE
Residency Road, Jodhpur 342001
Tel. 31910 (5 lines), 33359, 33360
Fax 33118
*Sixty-two rooms. Poolside parties arranged with Rajasthani folk music and dance on request.
Rs.2000–5500/US$70–$185/£40–£100*
🖂 ☕ ♫

HOTEL RAJPUTANA PALACE
Panch Batti Circle, Airport Road, Jodhpur 342011
Tel. 31672, 38059
Fax 38072
*Twenty-four rooms, ten air-conditioned and fourteen air-cooled. Live folk music and dance on request (extra cost). 2 miles from town, near to airport.
Rs.550–900/US$18–29/£11–18*
🖂 C 🏠 ▢ ☎

HOTEL KARNI BHAWAN
Palace Road, Jodhpur 342006
Tel. 32220, 39380

Fax 33495
*Twenty-five rooms, eleven luxury and fourteen deluxe rooms. Restaurant serves thali Indian meals. Folk music and dance on request (extra cost).
Rs.880–1595/US$30–53/£18–33*
🏠 ⤼ 🖂 ☕ ♫ ▢ ☎ ⬳

HOTEL AJIT BHAWAN PALACE
Opposite Circuit House, Jodhpur 342006
Tel. 37410
Fax 37132
*A legendary resort with traditional palace architecture and a garden laid out in traditional Rajasthani style. Personalized hospitality provided by the late Maharaja's family, who still live here. Fifty rooms, thirty-eight cottages, four suites, and five tents. The open-air restaurant serves Indian and continental meals. Rajasthani folk music and dance every evening during dinner. Village safari by jeep is very popular
Deluxe room, Rs.1199/US$39/£25 (single room), Rs.2195/US$72/£45 (double room), extra bed, Rs.300/US$9.80/ £6.20, Cottage Rs.1075/US$35/£22 (single room), Rs.1175/US$38/£24 (double room), extra bed, Rs.250/US$8/£5*
🖂 ⤼ 🏠 ☕ ♫ ☎

THE SAFARI CLUB
High Court Colony, Jodhpur 342001
Tel. 37023, 32695
Fax 37023
A modern bungalow, with an old family house beside it, it is located

slightly more than a mile from the railway station. The guest house is run by Reggie Singh, the grandson of Maharaj Ratan Singh, known for his polo and shikar exploits. Guests are treated to personalized hospitality. Thirteen spacious double bedrooms with attached bath, with running hot and cold water. Three of the rooms are air-conditioned and the rest are air-cooled. There is an excellent rooftop restaurant. Breakfast is served on a big lawn. Village safari, horse safari, or jungle drive available. Boat across River Chambal can be arranged. The only place in town playing recorded jazz, blues, reggae, and rock-and-roll music, with a small dance floor. Occasionally cultural performances are held. Rs.500–1800/US$16–59/£10–37

BALSAMAND LAKE PALACE
Mandore Road, Jodhpur 342001
Tel. 33316
Fax 35373
This beautiful old Lake Palace, set within lush green gardens, has for centuries been a venue for royal parties and picnics. Thirty rooms and six suites.
Rs.2000–2500/suite
Rs.5000–7000/US$70–80/US$167–233/£40–50/£100–140

GHOOMAR TOURIST BUNGALOW
High Court Road, Jodhpur 342001
Tel. 44010
RTDC hotel. Eighty rooms and dormitory,

with air-conditioning and TV in ten rooms. Serves Indian and continental meals.
Rs.200–600/US$7–20/£4–12

FLETCHER HOUSE KURI OASIS
Pali Road, P.O. Jhaomand, District Jodhpur (34 miles)
Bookings: Dhamli House, 11-A Old Public Park, Rai-ka-Bagh, Jodhpur 342001
Tel. 22114, 41614
Three rooms, one dormitory. Live music and dance. Jeep safaris available.
Rs.430–530/US$14–18/£9–11

HOTEL FORT CHANWA
Village Luni, District Jodhpur
Tel./Fax 32460
On the Luni River which is dry much of the year; owned and restored by uncle of present Maharaja. The fort is carved out of the famous red sandstone of Jodhpur, with ornately carved latticework friezes and intricate jarokhas (balcony windows). Twelve luxurious suites each with its own charm. Serves Rajasthani cuisine. Camel, horse, and jeep safaris to the nearby villages.
Rs.950–1050/US$31–$34/£19–21

KHIMSAR FORT
Village Khimsar, District Nagaur
Tel. 01585-2345
Fax 01585-2228
A 16th-century fort situated about half a mile from the village center. Forty air-conditioned rooms.
Rs.1150–2480/US$38–80/£25–£53

PALI
STD Code 0291

RESTAURANTS

SARDAR SAMAND PALACE LAKE RESORT
P. O. Sardar Samand,

via Sojat City, District Pali
Tel. 33316
A multi-cuisine restaurant in a palace ambience overlooking the lake.
6.30am–11.30pm

MAHARANI BAGH ORCHARD
Near Ranakpur, Sadri, District Pali
Tel. 33316
Fax 35373
Vegetarian and non-vegetarian restaurant in an orchard setting. Live singing. Good base for exploring Ranakpur and Kumbhalgarh.

ACCOMMODATION

ROHET GARH
Village/P.O. Rohet
District Pali
c/o Rohet House, P.W.D. Road, Jodhpur 342001
Tel. 02932-66231 (Rohet), 0291-31161 (Jodhpur)
Heritage hotel with traditional décor, run with traditional hospitality. Situated on the bank of a big lake which provides drinking water to about fifty surrounding villages, the place is like an oasis in the desert with lawns and lush green plants. Jeep safaris to Bishnoi shepherd and weaver/potter villages are the highlight. Horse or camel safaris can be arranged. 24 miles from Jodhpur on the Jodhpur-Udaipur route. Twenty-five rooms.
Rs.990–1250/US$33–41/£21–26

JAGRAM DURG (FORT)
P.O. Nimaj, District Pali
Tel. 02939-6522
Rs. 450 –600/US$15–20/ £.9–12

RAWALA NARLAI
Village Narlai, via Desuri
District Pali
Tel. 02934-7725/7743
Bookings: Ajit Bhawan, Jodhpur
Tel. 37410
Fax 37774
A centrally located 17th-century fortress

renovated in the 20th century.
Twelve rooms.
Rs. 1190–1495/US$38–48/£24–30

SARDAR SAMAND PALACE LAKE RESORT
P. O. Sardar Samand, via Sojat City, District Pali 306403
Tel. 0291-33316
Fax 0291-35373
This Art Deco hunting lodge built by Maharaja Singh Singh in 1933 is still used by the present family. Full of atmosphere; wonderful views of the lake and flamingos.
Nineteen rooms.
Rs 1190–2390/$40-80/£24–48

KOTRI KAOLA
Village/Post. Kotri, District Pali (via Nandol)
Tel. 6324
Bookings: Ghanerao Hotels Pvt. Ltd., 2-A, New Fatehpura, Udaipur 313001
Tel. 560822
An ideal getaway for those wanting a quiet holiday. Horse, jeep, and buggy rides and safaris can be arranged.
Rs.850–950/US$28–31/ £17–19

CULTURE

CAMEL FARM
3pm–5pm
Free admission.
Closed on Sunday.
A great sight at sunset. Hundreds of camels breed here ▲ 203.

Junagarh Fort-Palaces
Tel. 24876
10am–4.30pm
Admission fee: Rs.25
See Chandra Mahal, Anup Mahal, Phul Mahal. Exquisite paintings and mirrorwork ▲ 196.

Lallgarh Palace
10am–5pm
Admission fee: Rs.5
Closed on Sunday.
Part of the palace is the Shri Sadul Museum, which contains the personal collection of the former maharaja ▲ 198.

Karni Mata Temple
18 miles from Bikaner.
Closed 12 noon to 4pm.
Karni Mata is believed to be an incarnation of Goddess Durga. The temple is famed for the rats that roam about here. Also known as the Temple of Rats ▲ 207.

Restaurants

Dining Room
Lallgarh Palace, Bikaner 334001
Tel. 522105, 523963
7–10am (breakfast), 1–3pm (lunch), 7.30–10pm (dinner)
Serves Indian, continental, and Rajasthani specialties.

Amber
Station Road, Bikaner
Tel. 61861, 23288, 26321
Fax 523104
Moderately priced. Serves vegetarian Rajasthani and Indian cuisine. Their cheese cutlets, cheese 'naan' (Indian bread) and shahi vegetables are highly recommended.

Chotu-Motu
Station Road, Bikaner
Tel. 44666
Local fare and Indian vegetarian dishes.

Dhola Maru
Near Puran Singh Circle, Bikaner
Tel. 28621
Non-vegetarian and vegetarian Indian and Rajasthani food.

Lakshmi Niwas
Near Lallgarh Palace, Bikaner
Tel. 25020
Indian, Rajasthani food.

Annapurna
Mahatma Gandhi Road, Bikaner
Tel. 27674
South Indian and continental dishes. Keep to the South Indian as they are very good.

Accommodation

Lallgarh Palace
Bikaner 334001
Tel. 522105, 523963, 26103
Fax 522253
A heritage hotel. Indo-Saracenic-style palace set amid sprawling lawns. Forty rooms.
Rs.1440–2720/ US$45 –$85/£30–60 (breakfast included)

Karni Bhawan Palace Hotel
Bikaner 334001
Tel. 522408
This modern residence was built by His Late Highness Dr Karni Singhji of Bikaner in the art-deco style. Fifteen rooms.
Rs.1000 –1100/ US$33–35/£20–22

Gajner Palace
Gajner, 20 miles from Bikaner 334001
Bookings: Karni Bhawan Palace Hotel, Bikaner 334001
Tel. 5039, 5001-5
The hotel, built of red sandstone, is situated besides a lake. Twenty-five well appointed rooms.
Rs.1000–1100/ US$33–35/£20–22

Dhola Maru
Near Puran Singh Circle, Bikaner 334001
Tel. 28621
Twenty-six rooms/ dormitory.
Rs.300–600/ US$10–20/£6–12

Bhanwar Niwas
Rampuria Mohalla, Bikaner 334005
Tel. 61880, 71043
Fax 61880
A luxurious heritage hotel, its architecture and décor are a fascinating potpourri of Indian and European styles. This haveli has beautiful public areas and fourteen stunningly appointed rooms.
Rs.1175-2350/ US$39–78/£23–47

Thar Hotel
Hospital Road
Ambedkar Circle, Bikaner 334001
Tel. 27180
Special sight-seeing trips, safaris and desert trekkings can be arranged from the hotel. Thirty rooms.
Rs.300–420/ US$10–12/£6–7

Delight Rest House
Opposite Gole Katra, Station Road, Bikaner 334001
Tel. 24966
Twenty rooms.
Rs.45–125/ US$1.50–4/£1–2.50

Inder Lodge
Opposite Tata Co., G.S. Road, Bikaner 334001
Tel. 524813
Twenty rooms. TV on request.
Rs.55–110/US$2–4/£1–2

Hotel Shri Shanti Niwas
Ganag-Shahar Road, Bikaner 334001
Tel. 25025
Fifty-seven rooms.
Rs.60–250/ US$2–8/£1.30–5

JAISALMER

Useful Information

STD Code 02992

Culture

Patwon Ki Haveli, Nathmal Ji Ki Haveli, Salim Singh Ji Ki Haveli
10.30am–5pm
See the intricate stone carvings and architectural details ▲ 214.

Jain Temples
8am–12 noon
Within the fort complex these 12th–15th century temples were built with funds donated by the wealthy Marwaris (business community).

Fort/City Palace
8am–1pm
Admission fee: Rs.5
Built with the famous Jurassic sandstone, the fort and its environs take on a golden tinge. It is known as "Sonar Kellar" (Golden Fort) ▲ 212. *The palace stands on the highest point within double ramparts.*

Gadsisar Lake
3pm–5pm
An artificial lake which had been the main source of water supply to Jaisalmer ▲ 210. *Watch the sunrise here.*

Samm Desert
Located 24 miles north of Jaisalmer. *View the sand dunes at sunset* ▲ 218.

Restaurants

A number of restaurants such as Sky Room, Top Deck, The Trio, The Golden Fort, and Mid Town are located within the fort.

Fort Pokharan
P. O. Pokaran 345021
District Jaisalmer
Tel. 02994-22274
The old Durbar Hall has been converted into a restaurant. Indian and Rajasthani cuisine is served in an exceptional ambience within the sandstone fort.

8th July
Fort, Jaisalmer
Tel. 53164
Located in the fort, it overlooks the main square. Offers an extensive and imaginative menu.

Fort View
Fort View Hotel, Gola Chowk, Jaisalmer

Tel. 52214
*A rooftop hotel
restaurant offering a
view of the fort from
every table. Serves
good, reasonably priced
cuisine.*
🅒 ⤵ ⌂

TOP DECK
Gandhi Chowk,
Jaisalmer
Tel. 53244
*Rooftop restaurant
offering a good view.
Serves a variety of food.
Reasonably priced.*
◯ ⤵

GAY TIME
Gandhi Chowk,
Jaisalmer
*Vegetarian Indian and
Rajasthani food.*

KALPANA
Gandhi Chowk,
Jaisalmer
Tel. 52469
*Punjabi cuisine and
tandoori dishes.
Open-air seating.*

MOTI MAHAL
Opposite Salim Singh's
Haveli, Jaisalmer
Tel. 52677, 53077,
52049
*Non-vegetarian,
vegetarian meals.
Excellent and
inexpensive.*
♫ ▢ ⇴

NATRAJ
Facing Salim Singh's
Haveli, Jaisalmer
Tel. 52667, 52194
*Has a government-
approved beer bar.
High-quality vegetarian
and non-vegetarian
Indian food is served in
this rooftop restaurant.*
⤵ ⇴

THE TRIO
Mandir Palace,
Gandhi Chowk,
Jaisalmer
Tel. 52733
Fax 52778
*Indian, Chinese, and
Western cuisine.
Delicious food, good
service, and a very
pleasant ambience.
Offers a panoramic view
of the fort. Assistance
provided for camel and
jeep safaris into the
heart of the Thar Desert.
Live folk music. Open
from 6am to midnight.*
▢

ACCOMMODATION

GORBANDH PALACE
1, Tourist Complex,
Samm Road,
Jaisalmer
Tel. 53111
*Inspired by the fort, this
hotel is built of yellow
sandstone. Lying a
couple of miles outside
the city, it makes a
tranquil hideaway. It is
the only hotel in
Jaisalmer that has a
swimming pool.
Sixty-seven air-
conditioned rooms.
Rs.1195–2395/
US$40–80/£24–48*
🏛 ⌂ 🖿⋯ ⤳

FORT POKHARAN
P.O. Pokaran 345021
District Jaisalmer
Tel. 22274
Bookings: Pokaran
House, Jodhpur 342001
Tel. 20614
*Part of the 14th-century
fort is converted into a
hotel, making it a unique
place to stay in. It was
the site of India's
nuclear test explosion in
1974. Ten rooms.
The restaurant serves
mouth-watering desert
cuisine.
Rs 350–1710/
US$25–57/£7–34*
🅒 ⤵ ⌂ ♫ ▢
⇴

HOTEL HERITAGE INN
Samm Road
P.O. Box No. 43
Jaisalmer 345001
Tel. 52769, 40200,
40400
Fax 53038
*Thirty-six rooms and six
family suites with
modern amenities.
Rs.1100–2500/
US$36–83/£22–50*
▢ ⤵ ⌂ ♫ ▢
⇴

**HOTEL HIMMATGARH
PALACE**
1, Ramgarh Road,
Jaisalmer 345001
Tel. 52002/3/4,
Fax 52005
*Built of the same yellow
sandstone as the fort
and situated opposite
the Vyas Chhatris, it
provides a spectacular
view of the entire fort.
Thirty-five rooms.
Rs.1195–3750/
US$40–125/£24–75*
▢ ⤵ ⌂ ⤳ ♫ ▢

**NARAYAN NIWAS
PALACE**
Malka Prol, Near
Ramesh Takies,
Jaisalmer 345001
Tel. 52408, 52601
Fax 52101
*Thirty-eight rooms, five
air-conditioned, and
thirty-three air-cooled.
Rs.1075–1475/
US$35–47/ £21–30*
🏛

**JAWAHAR NIWAS
PALACE**
Amarsagar Road,
Jaisalmer 345001
Tel. 52208
*Twenty-six rooms.
Rs.700–800/
US$22–26/£14–16*

HOTEL SONA
Majdoor Para,
Jaisalmer 345001
Tel. 52468
*Forty-five beds, two with
air-conditioning.
Rs.550–750/
US$18–24 /£11–15*

HOTEL JAISAL CASTLE
Fort, Jaisalmer
Tel. 52362
*Ten rooms. A highly
interesting place to stay
within the fort.
Picturesque sunrise and
sunsets from the roof.
Rs.500–650/
US$16–21/£10–13*

HOTEL SURAJ
Behind Jain Temple,
On Fort, Jaisalmer
Tel. 53023
*Located inside the fort,
the over-five-hundred-
year-old havelis
retained its original
paintings and carvings.
It is the second highest
point in the fort. Ten
beds.
Rs.300–650/
US$10–21/£6–11*
▢ ⤵ ⌂

LAUGHING CAMEL INN
Near Hanuman Circle
Tel. 53164
*Air-cooled rooms.
Rs. 150-350/
US$5-11/£3-8*

HOTEL PLEASURE
Near Bank of Baroda,
Gandhi Chowk,
Jaisalmer 345001
Tel. 52323
*Fifteen rooms, air-
cooled and with ceiling
fans.
Rs.60–80/US$2–3/£1–2*
▢ ⇴

UDAIPUR AND ITS ENVIRONS

USEFUL INFORMATION

STD code 0294

TRANSPORT
AIRPORT DABOK
15 miles from the city
Tel. 28011
RAILWAY STATION
Tel. 131
BUS STAND
Tel. 27191
POLICE
Surajpol Thana
Tel. 29107
Hathipol Thana
Tel. 27866
BOATING FACILITIES
Pichola Lake
Tel. 28239/41

TOURIST INFORMATION
TOURIST RECEPTION
CENTRE
Fateh Memorial,
Suraj Pol
Tel. 411535

CULTURE

**UDAIPUR
CITY PALACE**
9.30am–4.30pm
Admission fee: Rs.10
*Largest palace complex
in Rajasthan* ▲ 246.

The main part of the palace is now a museum. See Mor Chowk for its beautiful mosaic work, Manak Mahal for glass and porcelain figures, and Krishna Vilas for miniature painting.

LAKE PICHOLA

17th-century Indo-Aryan temples edge this lake along with havelis, gardens, and hillocks. It is one of Udaipur's most scenic lakes. On two of the islands are the Jag Mandir ▲ 251, known for its domed pavilion, Gul Mahal. On Jag Niwas island is the famed Lake Palace ▲ 250. A pleasant boat cruise around the lake can be taken without stopovers.

JAGDISH TEMPLE

6am–2pm, 6pm–10pm

WEST ZONE CULTURAL CENTER

9.30am–6pm
Admission fee: Rs. 20
The office is located in

Bagore ki Haveli at Fateh Sagar, Lake Pichola. The village, Shilpagram, is situated 2 miles away. This is created with replicas of huts from Rajasthan, Gujarat, Maharashtra, and Goa. It also houses a collection of colorful art ▲ 254 ◆ 342.

BHARATIYA LOK KALA MANDAL

Tel. 24296
9am–6pm
Admission fee: Rs.5
Puppet show, 6–7pm
Fee: Rs. 20
This is a museum of folk arts ▲ 254 ◆ 343.

SAHELIYON KI BARI

9am–6pm
Admission fee: Rs.2
Early 18th-century gardens for the Maids of Honor ▲ 254.

RANAKPUR JAIN TEMPLES

54 miles from Udaipur.
12 noon–7pm

Admission fee: Rs.5
Chaumukh four-faced temples dedicated to Lord Adinatha supported by 1444 pillars ▲ 262.

RESTAURANTS

JHAROKHA

The Lake Palace Hotel P.B.5, Lake Pichola, Udaipur
Tel. 527961
Fax. 527974
Open round-the-clock, the spectacular setting and panoramic view of the City Palace and Lake Pichola make it an ideal choice.

PADMANI

Lakshmi Vilas Palace Hotel, Fateh Sagar Road, Udaipur
Tel. 529711/2/3/4/5
Fax. 525536
Serves Indian and continental cuisine.

ARSI VILAS

Lake Pichola, Udaipur
Tel. 529387
An exclusive island built by Maharana Arsi Singh so he could watch the sunset from the middle of the lake. An attached lower platform serves as a helipad, making its location unique.

GALLERY RESTAURANT

Fateh Prakash Palace, Palace Road, Udaipur
Tel. 528410-14
An ideal spot to have a cup of afternoon tea and scones while you gaze across Lake Pichola.

RISALA

Shikarabadi Hotel Goverdhan Vilas, Udaipur
Tel. 583200–4
Fax 584841
An open-air restaurant on the grounds of the lodge, where one can enjoy a camp fire and a barbecue.

BERRY'S

Chetak Circle, Udaipur
Tel. 525132
9am–11pm
An air-conditioned restaurant serving Indian, continental, and Chinese food. Specialties: seekh kabab, shami kabab, tomato fish, tandoori/butter chicken. Vegetarian dishes and children's menu available.

PARK VIEW

Opposite Town Hall, Udaipur
Tel. 528098
Serves Indian (including South Indian), continental, and Chinese cuisine. Specialties: butter chicken, paneer butter masala, chillied chicken. Open 8.30am to 11pm.

SAI NIWAS

75, Navghat Road, near City Palace, Udaipur
Tel. 524909
Highly recommended for its fresh food and excellent service. Local Indian cuisine.

GARDEN RESTAURANT

Opposite Gulab Bagh (Rose Gardens), Udaipur

R A J A S T H A N

Ranakpur
Bhilwara
Chittorgarh
Bijolia
Haldi Ghati
Nathdwara
Barolli
Kailashpuri (Eklingji)
Udaipur
Jaisamand
Rikhabdev
Dungarpur
Banswara
Galiakot
GUJARAT
MADHYA PRADESH
I N D I A

Tel. 528410
A colonial-style building with high ceilings and white columns, it was the place where the palace cars were garaged. An old petrol pump in the forecourt bears testimony to this. Serves typical Gujarati vegetarian thalis.

KUMBHA PALACE
Bhatina Chotta, next to Mona Lisa Hotel, Udaipur
Run by an English woman. Recommended for its Western dishes and pizzas. Try the home-made chocolate cake.

SHILPI VILLAGE RESTAURANT
Near Shilpagram, Rani Road, Udaipur
Tel. 522475
11am–11pm
An open-air restaurant serving Indian (including South Indian) and Chinese food, as well as special vegetarian dishes.
○

ROOF GARDEN CAFE
Delwara House, opposite Lake Palace's main gate, Udaipur
Tel. 29748
8am–10pm
An open-air rooftop restaurant offering a magnificent view of the palace. Serves Indian, Western, and Chinese food. Specialties: Tandoori items, chicken Hong Kong, chillied chicken.

CHEETAL
Shikarabadi Hotel, Goverdhan Vilas, Udaipur
Tel.583200/4
Decorated with antique paintings and baskets of flowers hanging from the ceiling, it provides a pleasing ambience. A variety of cuisines, both Indian and Western, is served.

BAITHAK
Shikarabadi Hotel, Goverdhan Vilas, Udaipur
Tel. 583200-4
An open-air restaurant

with a special camp-style atmosphere. It is highly popular during winter when meals can be had around the bonfire.

ORIENTAL PALACE RESORTS
Subash Nagar, Udaipur
Tel. 411238
Open round-the-clock, the restaurant serves Indian, Chinese, and continental cuisine.

ACCOMMODATION

THE LAKE PALACE HOTEL
P.B.5, Lake Pichola, Udaipur 313001
Tel. 527961
Fax 527974
Located in the middle of Lake Pichola. Belonging to the Historic Resort Hotels, this palace is straight out of a fairytale. It allows you a glimpse into the princely life of the Rajputs, with all its many splendors. Eighty-one rooms including suites.
Rs.4960–18,600/
US$160–600/£100–372

LAKSHMI VILAS PALACE HOTEL
Fateh Sagar Road, Udaipur 313001
Tel. 529711/15
Fax 525536
Fifty-four rooms. Puppet show every evening, and dancing on request.
Rs.2700–6000/
US$90–199/£54–120

SHIV NIWAS PALACE HOTEL
City Palace, Udaipur 313001
Tel. 528019
Fax 523823
The most charming hotel in Udaipur, part of the royal palace with wonderful views of the lake.
Thirty-one rooms.
Rs.1705–10,850/
US$55–350/£34–217

FATEH PRAKASH PALACE HOTEL
Palace Road, Udaipur 313001

Tel. 528016
Part of the City Palace complex, built in the early 20th century, the hotel is situated on the shores of Lake Pichola. A royal ambience with well-decorated rooms. Offers an exceptional view. A visit to the Crystal Gallery and Durbar Hall is a must. Six suites and three deluxe rooms.

SHIKARABADI HOTEL
Goverdhan Vilas, Udaipur 313001
Tel. 583200/4
Fax 584841
A forest hunting lodge with traditional architecture. The original shikarbadi (hunting lodge), which is almost a hundred years old, lies to the left of the present structure, its architecture reminiscent of a pol (gate). Twenty-five rooms including three suites. Serves Indian, continental, and Mewari food. Horse-riding, polo and shooting available. The hotel, which faces a small lake, is near a Deer Park. On national highway No. 8, 5 miles away from city.
Rs 1200–3000/
US$40–100/£24–60

HOTEL HILLTOP
5, Ambavgarh, Fateh Sagar, Udaipur 313001
Tel. 28708, 28709, 28764
Fifty-five rooms. A modern hotel located high above Fateh Sagar. Daily puppet show, and folk dance on request.
Rs.1150–1400/
US$40–45/£24–£30

RAJ DARSHAN
18, Panna Dhai Marg, Udaipur 313001
Tel. 526601-5

Fifty-two rooms. Puppet show and dance on request.
Rs.1100–1500/
US$35–50/£22–30

ORIENTAL PALACE RESORTS
Subash Nagar, Udaipur 313001
Tel. 411238
Thirty-five rooms. Folk music and dance and puppet show every evening.
Rs.800–2350/
US$24–80/£16–48

HOTEL ANAND BHAWAN
Fateh Sagar Road, Udaipur 313001
Tel. 523256–523018
Fax 523247
Twenty-two rooms. Good value, excellent view. Serves Indian, continental, and Rajasthani food.
Rs.500–Rs.950/
US$17–31/£10-19

LAKE END HOTEL
Alkapuri Fateh Sagar Lake, Udaipur 313001
Tel. 523841, 528008, 529032, 528009
Fax 523898
Modern with lakeside gardens and a panoramic view of the Aravalli range. Seventy-eight rooms.
Rs.1100–3000/
US$36–100/£2260

LAKE PICHOLA HOTEL
Outside Chandra Pol, Udaipur 313001
Tel. 29197/29387
Twenty-five rooms. Live music and puppet show on request.
Rs.575–900/
US$19–30/£11–18

PRATAP INN
Raj Samand Road, Udaipur 313001
Tel. 583138

Rs 100–400/
US$4–12/£2–9
🖵 🛏 🎵

HOTEL PADMINI
27 Gulab Bagh Road
Udaipur 313001
Tel. 27860
*Situated in the heart of
the city in peaceful
surroundings. Near the
famous Gulab Bagh
garden.*
*Rs.350–790/
US$11–25/£8–19*
🛗 🖵 ⛾ 🏠 🛏 🎵
🖵 ☎

SAI NIWAS HOTEL
75, Navghat Road, near
City Palace,
Udaipur 313001
Tel. 524909
*A haveli-style hotel
reputed for its excellent
cuisine.*
🖵⋯

**JAGAT NIWAS PALACE
HOTEL**
25, Lal Ghat,
Udaipur 313001
Tel. 529728
Fax 520028
*A traditional haveli
converted into a hotel.
Located in the heart of
town, the hotel offers a
panoramic view,
overlooking the Lake
Palace Hotel and the
historical Pichola Lake.
Twenty-two rooms,
fifteen with attached
bathroom.*
*Rs.175–750/
US$6–24/£4–15*
🅲 ⛾ 🏠 🎵

RANG NIWAS HOTEL
Rang Niwas, Lake
Palace Road,
Udaipur 313001
Tel. 523890/1
Fax 520294
*Twenty-two rooms.
Rs.125-650/
US$4–21/£3–13*
⛾ 🛏 🎵

**LALGHAT GUEST
HOUSE**
Behind Jagdish Temple,
Udaipur 313001
Tel. 525301
*Twenty-five rooms and
ten beds in a dormitory.
Situated on the bank of
the lake, some rooms
offer a view of the lake
and palace. There is a
large open courtyard to
sit out in.*
*Rs.50–400/
US$1.5–12/£1–8*
⛾

HERITAGE RESORTS
Lake Bagela, Sas Bahu
Temple, Nagda, District
Udaipur 313202
Tel. 414076, 528628
Fax 527549
Bookings:Tushar, 774,
O.T.C. Scheme, Rani
Road, Udaipur.
*Located amid the
Aravalli Hills on the
fringe of Lake Bagela, it
overlooks the Nagda
Temples. Twenty-six
rooms.*
*Rs.2062–2433/
US$69–81/£41–48*
🖵 ⛾ 🏠 🛏 🎵 🖵
☎

GOKUL VILAS
Deogarh, District
Rajsamand 313331
Tel. 52904-52017
*A 150-year-old guest
house with just four
rooms. Once a royal
retreat of the Deogarh
nobility, it is now a home
to the present
Rawatsahib and
Ranisahiba. A paradise
for bird-watchers.
Superb food.*
*Rs 1200–1500/
US$40–50/£20-30*
⛾ 🏠 🖵⋯ 🎵 ☎

CHITTORGARH

USEFUL INFORMATION

STD code 01472

CULTURE

FORT
Closed on Friday.
Fee: Rs.0.50
Allow four hours for a
tour of the fort. See the
"Tower of Victory"
▲ 277, Rana Kumbha's
Palace, Vijay Stambh,
Padmini's Palace,
Gomukh reservoir, and
Meera Mandir.

NAGRI
8½ miles north of
Chittorgarh. One of the
oldest towns with Hindu
and Buddhist remains
dating from 3 BC.

RESTAURANTS

MORCHA
Hotel Pratap Palace,
near Head Post Office,
Chittorgarh
Tel. 40099
Fax 41042
*Traditionally decorated,
the restaurant serves
delicious vegetarian and
non-vegetarian
Rajasthani and Mewari
cuisine.*

SHAKTI
Castle Bijaipur,
Village/Post, Bijaipur,
Chittorgarh
Tel. 40099
Fax 41042
*Located in a 16th-
century castle, it is a
perfect setting for
traditional Mewari
cuisine.*

ACCOMMODATION

CASTLE BIJAIPUR
Village/Post Bijaipur,
Chittorgarh 312001
Tel. 40099
Fax 41042
*Set amid the serene
Vindhyachal ranges, this
16th-century castle is a
symbol of Rajput*

*pageantry and
hospitality. Attractions in
the vicinity are camel
safaris, boating in Lotus
Lake, village excursions
and a visit to the 12th-
century Pangarh Fort.
Sixteen rooms.*
*Rs.500–1100/
US$16–35 /£10–21*
⛾ 🏠 🖵⋯

PRATAP PALACE
Near Head Post Office,
Chittorgarh 312001
Tel. 40099
Fax 41042
*The twelve-roomed
hotel is located
centrally and is run by
the same family that
manages Castle
Bijaipur.*
*Rs.330–480/
US$11–15 /£6–10*
🛏 🎵 🖵 ☎ 🍴

DUNGARPUR

USEFUL INFORMATION

STD Code 02964

ACCOMMODATION

UDAI BILAS PALACE
Dungarpur 314001
Tel. 30808
Fax 31008
Bookings: Curvett India
Pvt. Ltd., New Delhi
Fax 011–6822856,
6919116
North West Safaris,
Gujarat
Tel. 02712-23729
Fax 31008
*Located on the banks of
Lake Gaibsagar, this
19th-century palace built
by the Maharawals of
Dungarpur is still
occupied by his
descendants. Art-deco
furniture combines with
exquisite carvings to
form an architectural
marvel. Ten rooms
which include three
suites. Sight-seeing
tours are arranged.*
*Rs 950–2200/
US$ 30–75/£19–44*

MOUNT ABU AND ITS ENVIRONS

USEFUL INFORMATION

STD code 029742

CULTURE

MOUNT ABU DILWARA TEMPLES
12 noon to 4pm daily.
Jain temples built in the
11th to 13th centuries.
Vimal Vasahi, built in
AD 1031, is the oldest,
constructed with white
marble. The profusely
carved pillars and
latticework on the ceiling
are exquisite ▲ 270.

NAKKI LAKE
*An artificial lake sacred
to the Hindus. Nowhere
else in the country does
a lake exist at 3960 feet
above sea level. In
legend it is believed to
have been scooped out
by the fingernails (nakki)
of the gods while trying
to escape the wrath of a
demon ▲ 274. Boats
can be hired.*

TOAD ROCK
*Named because of its
resemblance to a toad,
it overhangs Nakki Lake
which is ringed by hills
▲ 274.*

ADHAR DEVI TEMPLE
*15th-century Durga
temple carved out of
rock. A flight of 220
steep steps leads up to
it. Offers a panoramic
view.*

RESTAURANTS

Almost all the
restaurants listed below
are located along Nakki
Lake.

AANGAN
near the Tourist
Information Office,
Mount Abu
Tel. 38305
Serves Gujarati thalis.

CLOUD 9
Sunrise Palace,
Old Bharatpur Kothi,
Mount Abu
Tel. 3573
Fax 3775
*Located on top of a
hillock it has glass walls
on three sides offering a
spectacular view of the
surroundings. A multi-
cuisine restaurant.*
🍽

HAVELI
Nakki Lake.
*Expensive, but worth the
price. Very tasty Punjabi
food.*

JUNGLE CORNER
Hotel Kesar Bhawan
Palace Sunset Road,
Mount Abu
Tel. 3647
*Serves excellent
Gujarati (vegetarian)
meals.*

MADHUBAN
Hotel Madhuban
Near Bus Stand,
Mount Abu
Tel. 3122, 3111
*Serves Indian,
Rajasthani, and Gujarati
cuisine (both vegetarian
and non-vegetarian).*

MADRAS CAFE
Near Chacha Museum
Tel. 38168
*Range of ice creams,
fruit juices, and milk
shakes.*

MK
Nakki Lake.
Tel. 3531
Chinese cuisine. Good.

VEENA
Near Taxi Stand.
Tel. 38033
*Open-air restaurant
serving vegetarian
South Indian and
Gujarati meals.*

SHER-E-PUNJAB
Main Bazaar
Tel. 3344
*Serves vegetarian, non-
vegetarian and tandoori
meals.*

ACCOMMODATION

*Most of the following
hotels offer 50 percent
discount during the off-
peak season. All rooms
have attached hot and
cold water bath.*

SUNRISE PALACE
Old Bharatpur Kothi,
Mount Abu 30750
Tel. 3573, 3775
Fax 3775
*Sixteen rooms, with two
air-conditioned suites;
all rooms with attached
bath. On the crest of a
hill, with a panoramic
view.
Rs.600–1150/
US$20–38/£12–23*
🍽 🏠 📺 🎵 📺
🛏

PALACE HOTEL
Bikaner House
Dilwara Road,
Mount Abu 307501
Tel. 3121, 3673
Fax 3674
*Thirty-five rooms.
A former summer
palace with its own
lake. A peaceful haven
with a number of
facilities, including
tennis court.
Rs.1025–1300/
US$33–42/£20–26*
🍽 🏠 📺

SAVERA PALACE
P.B. 23, Sunset Road,
Mount Abu 307501
Tel. 3354, 3254
Fax 3354
*Twenty-four rooms.
Rs.700–800/*

US$23–26/£14–16
📺 🍽 📺

SUNSET INN
P.B. 24, Sunset Road,
Mount Abu 307501
Tel. 3194
Fax 3515
*Forty rooms of which
fourteen are air-
conditioned.
Rs.500-900/
US$16–30/£10–18*
📺 🍽 🏠 📺 🎵
📺 ☎

HOTEL MADHUBAN
Near Bus Stand,
P.B. 33
Mount Abu 307501
Tel. 3111, 3122
Fax 3576 ("Attention:
Madhuban")
*Centrally located.
Fourteen rooms, air-
cooled and equipped
with ceiling fans. Offers
off-peak discount of up
to 50 percent.
Rs.500–750/
US$16–24/£10–15*
🍽 🏠 📺 📺 ☎

KESAR BHAWAN PALACE
Sunset Road,
Mount Abu 307501
Tel. 3647
*Ten rooms.
Rs.850/US$28/£17*
🍽 🏠 📺

HOTEL HILLTONE
Near Bus Stand
Mount Abu 30750
Tel. 3112, 3114
*Modern hotel with
swimming pool. The
restaurant serves Indian,
Gujarati, continental and
Chinese food.
Rs 500–1000/
US$16–32/£10–21*
📺 🍽 🎵 📺 ☎

HOTEL HILLOCK
Near Tourist Bungalow
Mount Abu 30750
Tel. 3277
*Hotel with panoramic
views and swimming
pool. The restaurant
serves Indian, Chinese
and continental food.
Rs 990–1300/
US$31–41/£21–27*
📺 🍽 🍽 🎵 📺
☎

CONNAUGHT HOUSE
Rajendra Marg,
Mount Abu 30750
Tel. 3360, 3439
Fax 0291-35373
*A charming country
cottage set in shady*

gardens within easy walking distance of the town of Mount Abu and the famous Nakki Lake. This property of the Maharaja was formerly the official summer residence of the Chief Minister of the Princely State of Marwar-Jodhpur.
Fourteen air-cooled rooms.
Rs.850–1150/
US$28–37/£17–23.50

DARBARGADH POSHINA

Village Poshina, via Khedbrahma, Sabarkanta.
Tel. 02775-83325
Fax 02712-23729
("Attn. North West Safaris")
Six rooms, two deluxe suites.
Part of a 15th-century fortress with havelis dating from the 17th to 19th century. Period furnishings, carvings, and pleasant surroundings. Antiques and handicraft shop. Can arrange safaris to neighboring hamlets and scenic spots.
Rs.600–1200/
US$20–40/£12–24

KOTA AND ITS ENVIRONS

USEFUL INFORMATION

STD code 0744

CULTURE

KOTA CITY PALACE

11am–4pm

Admission fee: Rs.25
Closed on Friday.
The City Palace and the Rao Madho Singh Museum has the best preserved murals in the state. Beautiful architecture ▲ 282.

BAROLI

33½ miles from Kota. On the way to Rana Pratap Sagar. One of the oldest temples of the state ▲ 284. Has the finest examples of 10th-century Pratihara temples in the country.

JHALARAPATAN

48 miles south of Kota, 4 miles from Jhalawar. 10th-century temples and beautiful sculptures ▲ 287.

RESTAURANT

BRIJ RAJ BHAWAN PALACE

Civil Lines, Kota
Tel. 25203
The hotel's dining room offers a wide range of vegetarian and non-vegetarian cuisine. It is the only recommended place to eat in this city.

ACCOMMODATION

UMED BHAWAN PALACE

Civil Lines, Kota 324001
Tel. 25262-65
Fax 24701
Has been taken over by the Welcomgroup and is currently undergoing renovations ▲ 283. Starting with seventeen rooms, this hotel will finally have thirty-five rooms. Billiard room and badminton court.
Rs. 1150-1800/
US$37-58/£24-38

BRIJ RAJ BHAWAN PALACE

Near PWD Office, Civil Lines,
Kota 324001
Tel. 450529
Fax 450057

A small palace by the river. Relaxing ambience. Three air-conditioned rooms, two double rooms and one single room.
Rs.360–950/
US$12–32/£7–19

BUNDI

USEFUL INFORMATION

STD code 0747

CULTURE

BUNDI GARH PALACE

Only the Chitra Mahal and Umed Mahal are open to the public ▲ 292. The Chitra Mahal is famous for the Bundi school of painting ● 65.

RANIJI KI BAORI

Outside the old city wall is a fine example of a step-well ▲ 296. The Raniji ki Baori has a high arched gate and ornate carvings on the pillars. It was built by a queen of the royal house.

RESTAURANTS

BUNDI CAFE & CRAFTS

Opposite Ayurvedic Hospital, Bundi
Tel. 32322
Fax 32142
Located in the hotel. The restaurant,

Darikhana, is in a large hall with an adjoining terrace. You can also try eating meals, Indian-style, on the floor. Good meals. An interesting handicrafts shop.

DIAMOND

Tel. 22656
Vegetarian North Indian and tandoori cuisine.

ACCOMMODATION

ISHWARI NIWAS PALACE

Opposite Circuit House, Bundi
Tel. 22541, 32414
Old heritage mansion belonging to the Raja's family. Friendly ambience. Good restaurant with home-cooked meals. Seventeen rooms.
Rs.200–600/
US$6–20/£4–12

HAVELI BRAJ BHUSHANJEE

Opposite Ayurvedic Hospital, Bundi 323001
Tel. 32322, 32127, 32509
Fax 32142
Situated below the palace, the 150-year-old building, with an architecture typical of its period, has some exquisite examples of wall paintings of the Bundi miniature school.
Rs.300 –900/
US$10–30/£6–18

DIAMOND

Tel. 22656
A ten-bed hotel. The rooms have en-suite baths.

APPENDICES

◆ Bibliography

◆ ESSENTIAL READING ◆

◆ DAVIDSON (ROBYN): *Desert Places*, Viking, London, 1996.
◆ PALLING (BRUCE): *India: a Literary Companion*, John Murray, London, 1992.
◆ DEVI, MAHARANI (GAYATRI) AND RAMA RAU (SANTHA), *A Princess Remembers, The Memoirs of the Maharani of Jaipur*, Wiedenfield & Nicholson, London, 1976.
◆ PATNAIK (NAVEEN): *A Second Paradise: Indian Courtly Life, 1590-1947*, Sidgwick & Jackson, London, 1985.
◆ TOD (JAMES COLONEL): *Annals and Antiquities of Rajasthan*, Low Price Publications, Delhi, 1990.

◆ ARCHITECTURE ◆

◆ DAVIES (PHILIP): *The Penguin Guide to the Monuments of India, Vol. II, (Islamic, Rajput, European)*, Penguin Group, London, 1989.
◆ EDWARDES (MICHAEL): *Indian Temples and Palaces*, Hamlyn, London, 1969.
◆ GHURYE (G.S.):*Rajput Architecture*, Popular Prakashan, Bombay, 1968.
◆ GOETZ (HERMANN): *Rajput Art and Architecture*, Franz, Steiner, Verlag, Wiesbaden, 1978.
◆ GOETZ (HERMANN) AND CASSIRER (BRUNO): *The Art and Architecture of Bikaner*, Oxford, 1950.
◆ MITCHELL (GEORGE): *The Penguin Guide to the Monuments of India, Vol.1, (Buddhist, Jain,* *Hindu)*, Penguin Group, London, 1989.
◆ TILLOTSON (G.H.R.): *The Rajput Palaces*, Oxford University Press, Bombay, Calcutta, Madras, 1987.

◆ THE ARTS ◆

◆ AGARWALA (R.A.): *Marwar Murals*, Agam Prakashan, New Delhi, 1977.
◆ ARCHER (MILDRED) AND FALK (TOBY): *Indian Miniatures in the India Office Library*, Sotheby, Parke, Bernet, London, 1981.
◆ ARCHER (WILLIAM G.): *Indian Painting in Bundi and Kota*, Victoria and Albert Museum, London, 1959.
◆ CHANDRA (MOTI): *Mewar Painting*, Lalit Kala Akademi, New Delhi, 1955.
◆ COOMARASWAMY (ANANDA): *Rajput Painting*, Hacker Books, New York, 1975.
◆ COOPER (ILAY),*The Painted Towns of Shekhavati*, Mapin Publishing, Ahmedabad, 1994.
◆ NEERAJ (JAI SINGH): *Splendour of Rajasthani Painting*, Abhinav Publications, New Delhi, 1992.
◆ RANDHAWA (MOHINDER SINGH) AND SCHREIER (DORIS): *Kishangarh Painting*, Randhawa, Vakils, Feffer & Simon, Bombay, 1980.
◆ TOPSFIELD (ANDREW): *Paintings from Rajasthan*, National Gallery of Victoria, Melbourne, 1980.
◆ WACZIARG (FRANCIS) AND NATH (AMAN): *The Painted Walls of Shekhavati*, Croom, Helm, London, 1982.

◆ THE CRAFTS ◆

◆ WACZIARG (FRANCIS) AND NATH (AMAN): *Arts and Crafts of Rajasthan*, Mapin International, New York, 1987.
◆ BHISHAM (PAL H.): *Handicrafts of Rajasthan*, Asia Book Corporation, Delhi, 1984.

◆ FICTION ◆

◆ ACKERLEY (J.R.): *Hindoo Holiday*, Penguin 20th century Classics, London, 1994.
◆ FORSTER (E.M.): *The Hill of Devi*, Edward Arnold, London, 1953.
◆ KIPLING (RUDYARD): *Collected Stories*, Everyman's Library, London/Alfred A Knopf, New York, 1995.
◆ MEHTA (GITA): *Raj*, Jonathan Cape, London, 1989.
◆ MEHTA (RAMA): *Inside the Haveli*, Arnold Heinemann, Delhi, 1981.
◆ RICHARDSON (JANE): *Virgin Princess*, India Book Distributors, Bombay, 1992.

◆ GENERAL ◆

◆ ANAND (MULK RAJ): *Private Life of an Indian Prince*, Hutchinson, London, 1985.
◆ ANAND (UMA) AND ANAND (VIVEK): *Mansions of the Sun*, Al Falak Scorpion, London, 1982.
◆ AHUJA (D.R.): *Folklore of Rajasthan*, National Book Trust, New Delhi, 1980.
◆ DUBE (DINA N.): *Folk Tales of Rajasthan*, Asia Book Corporation, Delhi, 1983.
◆ ERDMAN (JOAN L.): *Patrons and Performers in Rajasthan, The* *Subtle Tradition*, Chanakya Publications, New Delhi, 1985.
◆ FASS (VIRGINIA): *The Forts of India*, Collins, London, 1986.
◆ FASS (VIRGINIA) AND MAHARAJA OF BARODA: *The Palaces of India*, Collins, London, 1980.
◆ FITZROY (YVONNE): *Courts and Camps of India*, Methuen, London, 1987.
◆ FRATER (ALEXANDER): *Beyond the Blue Horizon*, Penguin, London, 1987.
◆ HOLKAR (SHIVAJI RAO) AND HOLKAR (SHALINI DEVI): *Cooking of the Maharajas, The Royal Recipes of India*, Viking Press, New York, 1975.
◆ HUXLEY (ALDOUS): *Jesting Pilate, An Intellectual Holiday*, Doran, New York, 1926.
◆ IWATA (HIROKO): *Desert Villages, Life and Crafts of Gujarat and Rajasthan*, Yobisha, Tokyo, 1984.
◆ JAIN (KAILASH CHAND): *Ancient Cities and Towns of Rajasthan*, Motilal Banarsidas, Delhi, 1972.
◆ KHANGAROT (R.S.) AND NATHAWAT (P.S.): *Jaigarh, The Invincible Fort of Amber*, RBSA Publishers, Jaipur, 1990.
◆ KIPLING (RUDYARD): *Letters of Marque*, P.F. Collier & Son, New York, 1891.
◆ LOTHIAN, SIR (ARTHUR): *Kingdoms of Yesterday*, John Murray, London, 1951.
◆ MERCHANT (ISMAIL): *Hullabaloo in Old Jeypore, The Making of "The Deceivers"*, Viking, London, 1988.
◆ RUDOLPH

(SUZANNA AND LLOYD): *Essays on Rajputana*, Concept Publishing, New Delhi, 1984.

◆ SCHOMER (KARINE), ERDMAN (JOAN L.), LODRICK (DERYCK O.), RUDOLPH (LLOYD I.) (EDS.): *The Idea of Rajasthan*, Manohar Publications, New Delhi, 1994.

◆ SHARMA (DASHARATH): *Lectures on Rajput History and Culture*, Motilal Banarasidass, Delhi, 1970.

◆ SHARMA (G.N): *Social Life in Medieval Rajasthan*, Laxmi Narain Agarwal, Agra, 1968.

◆ SHERRING (M.A): *Tribes and Castes of Rajasthan*, Cosmo Publications, New Delhi, 1975.

◆ SMITH (JOHN D.): *The Epic of Papuji*, Cambridge University Press, Cambridge, 1991.

◆ SUGICH (M): *Palaces of India*, Pavilion Books, London, 1992.

◆ GEOGRAPHY ◆

◆ MISRA, DR (V.C.): *Geography of Rajasthan*, National Book Trust, New Delhi, 1967.

◆ HISTORY ◆

◆ DAVENPORT (HUGH): *Trials and Triumphs of the Mewar Kingdom*, Maharana of Mewar Charitable Foundation, Udaipur, 1975.

◆ GASCOIGNE (BAMBER): *The Great Mughals*, Cape Publications, London, 1971.

◆ HALLISEY (ROBERT C.): *The Rajput Rebellion Against Aurangzeb*, University of Missouri Press, Columbia & London, 1977.

◆ MENON (V.P.): *The Story of The Integration of the Indian States*, Longman, London, 1956.

◆ QANUNGO (K.R.): *Studies in Rajput History*, S. Chand & Co., Delhi, 1969.

◆ SARKAR (JADUMATI): *A History of Jaipur*, Longman, Hyderabad, 1984.

◆ SHARMA (DASHARATH): *Rajasthan through the Ages*, Rajasthan State Archives, Bikaner, 1966.

◆ SHARMA (G.N): *Mewar and the Mughal Emperors*, Shiv Lal & Sons, Agra, 1962.

◆ SINGH (BRIJRAJ M.K.): *The Kingdom that was Kotah*, Lalit Kala Akademi, New Delhi, 1985.

◆ SINGH (R.B.): *Origin of the Rajputs*, Sahitya Sansar Prakashan, Buxipur, 1975.

◆ SPEAR (PERCIVAL): *A History of India*, Penguin, Harmondsworth, 1965.

◆ ROYALTY ◆

◆ ALLEN (CHARLES) AND DWIVEDI (SHARADA): *Lives of the Indian Princes*, Century, London, 1984.

◆ BARTON, SIR (WILLIAM): *The Princes of India*, Nisbet & Co., London, 1934.

◆ CORFIELD, SIR (CONRAD): *The Princely India I knew*, George Thomas for the Indo-British Historical Society, Madras, 1975.

◆ CREWE (QUENTIN): *The Last Maharajah*, Michael Joseph, London, 1985.

◆ DASS (DIWAN JARMANI): *Maharajah*, Allied Publishers, Bombay, 1969.

◆ FITZE, SIR (KENNETH): *Twilight of the Maharajahs*, J. Murray, London, 1956.

◆ GRIFFITH (M): *India's Princes, Short Life Sketches of the Native Rulers of India*, W.H. Allen, London, 1894.

◆ HENDLEY (THOMAS HOLBEIN): *Rulers of India and Chiefs of Rajputana, 1550–1897*, W. Griggs, London, 1897.

◆ IVORY (JAMES): *Autobiography of a Princess*, Harper & Row, New York, 1975.

◆ LORD (JOHN): *The Maharajahs*, BI Publications, New Delhi, 1982.

◆ MASTERS (BRIAN): *Maharana*, Mapin Publishing, Ahmedabad, 1990.

◆ PATNAIK (NAVEEN): *Desert Kingdom*, Wiedenfield & Nicholson, London, 1990.

◆ ROUSSELET (LOUIS): *India and its Native Princes*, Bickers, London, 1882.

◆ SINGH (DHANANJAYA): *The House of Marwar*, Roli Books, Delhi, 1994.

◆ VAN WART (R.B.): *The Life of Lt. General H.H. Sir Pratap Singh*, Oxford University Press, London, 1926.

◆ PHOTOGRAPHY ◆

◆ BENY (ROLOFF): *Rajasthan, Land of Kings*, Frederick Muller, London, 1984.

◆ GUTMAN (JUDITH MARA): *Through Indian Eyes, 19th & Early 20th Century Photography from India*, Oxford University Press & International Centre for Photography, New York, 1982.

◆ MITCHELL (GEORGE) AND MARTINELLI (ANTONIO): *The Royal Palaces of India*, Thames & Hudson, London, 1994.

◆ MORAES (DOM) AND GAJWANI (GOPI): *Rajasthan, Splendour in the Wilderness*, Himalayan Books, New Delhi, 1988.

◆ PATANKAR (ADITYA) AND NINAN (SEVANTI): *Rajasthan*, Lustre Press, New Delhi, 1988.

◆ NATH (AMAN) AND JODHA (SAMAR): *Jaipur, the Last Destination*, India Book House, 1992.

◆ SINGH (RAGHUBIR): *Rajasthan, India's Enchanted Land*, Perennial Press, Hong Kong, 1981.

◆ TOUTAINE (PIERRE) AND BUSQUET (GERARD): *Rajasthan*, Harrap Columbus Ltd., London, 1988.

◆ UCHIYAMA (SUMIO) AND ROBINSON (ANDREW): *Maharaja, The Spectacular Heritage of Princely India*, The Vendome Press, New York, 1988.

◆ WILDLIFE ◆

◆ ISRAEL (SAMUEL) AND SINCLAIR (TONY) (ED.): *Indian Wildlife*, APA Productions, Hong Kong, 1987.

◆ GEE (E.P.): *The Wildlife of India*, Dutton, New York, 1964.

◆ SINGH, LT. COL. (KESRI): *The Tiger of Rajasthan*, Jaico Publishing House, 1967.

◆ THAPAR (VALMIK) AND RATHORE (FATEH SINGH): *Tigers, The Secret Life*, Elm Tree Books, London, 1989.

◆ GLOSSARY

◆ A ◆

◆ AANGAN: Courtyard.

◆ AARTI: The ritual of passing an oil lamp or flame in a circular movement in an act of devotion or homage.

◆ ACHAKAN: Traditional Indian long, formal coat.

◆ AGARBATTI: Incense.

◆ AGNIKULA: Literally "Fire-born". A set of thirty-six Rajput clans who trace their ancestry not to the Sun or Moon (like the others), but to a great ancient fire rite.

◆ AHIMSA: Non-violence.

◆ AJRAKH: Handprinted fabric, typical of Barmer.

◆ ANGRAKHI: A loose, double-breasted jacket worn by men.

◆ AONLA: A yellow-blossomed tree typical of southern Rajasthan, which bears sour berries.

◆ ARAYISH: A traditional lime plaster technique with a finish as smooth as marble.

◆ ATMASUKH: A quilted jacket. Literally "the happiness of the soul".

◆ ATTAR: Traditional Indian perfume. Also spelled *ittar*.

◆ AYURVEDA: Traditional Hindu medicine.

◆ B ◆

◆ BABOOL: Thorny tree, characteristic of the desert region of Rajasthan.

◆ BAGH: Garden.

◆ BAJRA: Millet.

◆ BANDHANI: Tie-and-dye fabric, typical of Rajasthan. The origin of the English word "bandanna".

◆ BANGALDHAR: A style of drooping eaves found in Rajput architecture, inspired by Bengali village huts.

◆ BANIYA: Trader or moneylender caste.

◆ BARAAT: Wedding procession.

◆ BARADARI: Pavilion.

◆ BATTI: Light or lamp.

◆ BAZAAR: Market.

◆ BHAGWAN: God.

◆ BHAJAN: Hindu devotional song.

◆ BHAKTI: Devotion.

◆ BHALA: Spear.

◆ BHANG: Dried hemp leaves. A narcotic often mixed with drinks or food.

◆ BHATT: A community of bards.

◆ BHIL: Aboriginal tribals of southern Rajasthan, known for their archery skills.

◆ BIDI: Traditional Indian "mini-cigarette" made from rolled tobacco leaves.

◆ BRAHMA: One of the Hindu Trinity, considered the god of creation.

◆ BRAHMIN: Hindu priestly caste.

◆ C ◆

◆ CHANDRAVANSHI: Rajput clan, believed to be descended from the moon.

◆ CHAPPATI: Flat, circular Indian bread.

◆ CHARAN: A community of bards and poets, believed to have special spiritual powers.

◆ CHHATRI: Literally "umbrella", used to signify the royal cenotaphs of the Rajputs.

◆ CHIK: Reed screen to provide shade from the hot summer sun.

◆ CHITAL: A species of small, graceful deer.

◆ CHITRASHALA: Frescoed hall. Literally, "Hall of Paintings".

◆ CHOLI: Woman's blouse.

◆ CHOWK: Public square.

◆ CHURIDAR: A kind of skin-tight pyjamas, with horizontal folds around the ankles. Literally, "the pyjamas with bangles."

◆ D ◆

◆ DAAL: Lentils.

◆ DAHI-WADA: Savory snack soaked in yogurt and spices.

◆ DARGAH: Mausoleum or memorial of Muslim saint.

◆ DARSHAN: An audience or viewing, usually of a Hindu deity, royalty or important personage.

◆ DARWAZA: Door or gateway.

◆ DESERT-COOLER: A kind of primitive "air-conditioner" that blows air through a moistened reed screen at high velocity.

◆ DEV: God. Also *devata*.

◆ DHABA: Little roadside eatery.

◆ DHOBI: Washerman.

◆ DHOL: Drum.

◆ DHOTI: Hindu man's garment comprising a long white cloth that is folded intricately around one's waist and legs.

◆ DURRIE: A flat, woven floor covering.

◆ DIWAN: Prime Minister.

◆ DIWAN-I-AM: Hall of Public Audience in a medieval palace.

◆ DIWAN-I-KHAS: Hall of Private Audience in a medieval palace.

◆ DURBAR: Gathering of a king's court.

◆ DURG: Sanskrit word for fort.

◆ DURGA: Hindu goddess of destruction. An incarnation of Parvati, wife of Lord Shiva. Another incarnation is Kali, goddess of death.

◆ DWARPALA: Sentry or symbolic carvings flanking a doorway. Literally "door-keeper".

◆ F ◆

◆ FAKIR: Muslim mendicant.

◆ G ◆

◆ GADDI: Throne.

◆ GAJAK: A flaky candy made from jaggery and sesame seeds.

◆ GALLI: Alley or narrow lane.

◆ GANESHA: Elephant-headed Hindu god of fortune.

◆ GAON: Village.

◆ GAZAL: Urdu poetry, usually of romantic mood.

◆ GARH: Fort. Also *kila*.

◆ GHAGRA: Loose, pleated Indian skirt.

◆ GHAT: Steps going down to lake.

◆ GHEE: Clarified butter.

◆ GHEVAR: A crunchy, honey-comb shaped candy made from cottage cheese.

◆ GHODA: Horse.

◆ GHOTUA: Yellow, ball-shaped candy typical of Jaisalmer.

◆ GURU: Teacher, spiritual guide.

◆ H ◆

◆ HALDI: Turmeric, a root considered to have beneficial properties.

◆ HAMMAM: Medieval bath.

◆ HATHI: Elephant.

◆ HAVELI: Mansion.

◆ HAWA MAHAL: Literally "Palace of the Winds", where royal ladies could enjoy the breeze without being seen. Also called "Hawa Ghar" (house).

◆ HOLI: Hindu festival of spring, celebrated by sprinkling colors on people.

◆ HOOKAH: Hubble-bubble.

◆ HOWDAH: Elephant seat.

◆ I ◆

◆ ISHWAR: God.

◆ IZZAT: Honor, prestige.

◆ J ◆

◆ JAI: Victory.

◆ JALI: Lattice.

◆ JAUHAR: Ritual mass immolation of women at the time of defeat, to save themselves from falling into the hands of the enemy.

◆ JHAROKHA: Window of a balcony.

◆ JI: A suffix that is added to a person's name as a mark of respect.

◆ JOHRI: Jeweler.

◆ JUAR: Coarse millet grain.

◆ K ◆

◆ KACHORI: Fried savory snack. Like a puff-pastry with a filling.

◆ KALA: Art.

◆ KARMA: Action. Also used to signify "Fate".

◆ KATAR: Traditional Indian dagger.

◆ KATHPUTLI: Puppet.

◆ KAVAD: A small portable temple with brightly painted wooden panels depicting various deities.

◆ KER-SANGRI: A favorite vegetable dish in the desert areas of Rajasthan.

◆ KESAR: Saffron.

◆ KHAMBA: Pillar.

◆ KHANDA: Heavy sabre.

◆ KHAZANA: Treasure.

◆ KHEJRI: A tree that blooms in the deserts of Rajasthan (*Prosopis cineraria*).

◆ KHUS: Scented shrub, believed to have cooling powers. Often used for making screens and awnings.

◆ KILA (or *qila*): Fort.

◆ KOTHI: Mansion.

◆ KRISHNA: Hindu god. Known for his amorous exploits in his youth; later the mentor of the Pandavas in the epic *Mahabharata*.

◆ KSHATRIYA: Hindu military caste.

◆ KUAN: Well.

◆ KUM-KUM: Red powder used by Hindus in rituals. Also worn as a dot on the forehead or in the parting of the hair by married women.

◆ KUNDAN: Jewelry setting of uncut gems in gold.

◆ KUNJA: A narrow-necked earthen pitcher.

◆ KUNWAR: Prince.

◆ KURTA OR KAMEEZ:

Traditional loose Indian shirt.

◆ L ◆

◆ LAKH: 100,000.
◆ LASSI: Thick buttermilk.
◆ LAHARIA: Wave-patterned fabric or turban.
◆ LOO: Dust storm.

◆ M ◆

◆ MAHABHARATA: Hindu epic telling of the war between the clan of the virtuous Pandavas and their cousins, the wicked Kauravas.
◆ MAHAL: Palace.
◆ MAHARAJA: Literally "Great King". The rulers of most major Rajput kingdoms were called thus. There were variants on this: the ruler of Mewar was a *maharana*; the rulers of Jaisalmer and Dungarpur were *maharawals*; the ruler of Bundi was a *maharao*.
◆ MAHARANI: Literally "Great Queen". Wife of a maharaja.
◆ MAHARAJKUMAR: Literally "Great Prince". Son of a maharaja.
◆ MANDAPA: Pillared hall of temple.
◆ MANDIR: Temple.
◆ MANDANA: Traditional auspicious floor or wall patterns in Rajasthani village.
◆ MARDANA: Men's quarters in a palace.
◆ MARG: Main road or street.
◆ MATKA: Large, round-shaped earthen pitcher.
◆ MEHENDI: Henna decorations on the palm of a woman's hand.
◆ MELA: Village fair.
◆ MEMSAHIB: Lady. A term of respect.
◆ MINAKARI: Enamel-work ornamentation rendered on jewelry.
◆ MOJRI: Traditional Rajput slippers with pointed, upturned "toes". Also called *jootis*.
◆ MOOCHH: Mustache.
◆ MOR: Peacock. Also called *mayoor*.

◆ N ◆

◆ NAGADA: Ceremonial drum.
◆ NAWAB: Muslim ruler.
◆ NILGAI: A species of deer often considered sacred by Hindus.
◆ NIWAS: Abode.
◆ NAMASTE: Traditional Hindu greeting. Said with folded hands. Also *namaskar*.

◆ O ◆

◆ ODHNI: A long scarf worn by women over the head, shoulders, and bosom. Also called *dupatta*.
◆ OONT: Camel.

◆ P ◆

◆ PAGARI: A small turban, smaller and less flamboyant than a *safa*.
◆ PAISA: Money.
◆ PALKI: Palanquin.
◆ PANCHAYAT: Village council.
◆ PANDIT: Hindu priest or scholar.
◆ PANKHA: Fan, including the hand-held variety.
◆ PARVATI: Consort of Lord Shiva.
◆ PATWARI: Leader of a village.
◆ PHAD: Traditional painting depicting the legends of the Rajasthani folk hero, Pabuji.
◆ PICHHVAI: Paintings based on the life of Lord Krishna. Typical of the area north of Udaipur. Literally, "That which hangs behind."
◆ POL: Gate. A variant in some places is *prole*.
◆ PUJA: Hindu religious ritual.
◆ PUKKA: Proper. Colloquially it means "definite", a promise or commitment.
◆ PURDAH: Veil or curtain. Also the practice of keeping the women secluded from the men.
◆ PUROHIT: Hindu priest.
◆ PYJAMAS: Literally, "leg covering". Traditional Indian trousers, usually worn loose.

◆ Q ◆

◆ QILA (or *kila*): Fort.

◆ R ◆

◆ RAGA: Traditional Indian melody.
◆ RAJ: Reign, sovereignty, or government.
◆ RAJA: King.
◆ RAJKUMAR: Prince.
◆ RAJKUMARI: Princess.
◆ RAJPUT: A member of the Kshatriya community of Rajasthan. Literally, "son of a king."
◆ RAJPUTANA: The old name for the present state of Rajasthan. Literally, "The land of the Rajputs."
◆ RAMA: Hindu god. Hero of the epic *Ramayana*. An incarnation of Vishnu.
◆ RAMAYANA: Hindu epic, whose hero is Lord Rama.
◆ RANG MAHAL: Literally, "Palace of Colours". A frescoed palace.
◆ RANGOLI: Traditional, auspicious floor patterns drawn in brightly colored powders.
◆ RANI: Queen.
◆ RAVANHATTA: A stringed folk music instrument.
◆ REGISTAN: Desert.
◆ RETI: Sand.
◆ RAZAI: Quilt.
◆ RISHI: Hindu sage.
◆ ROTI: Indian bread.

◆ S ◆

◆ SADHU: Hindu mendicant.
◆ SALAAM: A greeting. Literally "peace".
◆ SAFA: Turban.
◆ SAGAR: Lake or pond.
◆ SAHIB: Gentleman. A term of respect for a man.
◆ SALWAR: Loose trousers worn by women.
◆ SAMBAR: A species of deer.
◆ SANSAYI: Hindu hermit.
◆ SARANGI: A stringed musical instrument.
◆ SARASWATI: Hindu Goddess of Learning.
◆ SARDAR: Chieftain.
◆ SATI: The immolation of a wife on her husband's funeral pyre.
◆ SHAMIANA: A large, open-sided tent.
◆ SHASTRA: A Hindu scripture or text.
◆ SHEESH MAHAL: Hall of mirrors.
◆ SHEHNAI: Traditional Indian wind instrument, played on ceremonial occasions.
◆ SHERWANI: Knee-length coat worn by men, usually over *churidars*.
◆ SHIKAR: Hunt.
◆ SHILPA SHASTRA: Ancient Hindu treatise on architecture.
◆ SHIVA: One of the Hindu Trinity, considered the god of destruction.
◆ SHIVALINGA: The symbol of Lord Shiva's phallus, symbolizing fertility.
◆ SILEH KHANA: Armory.
◆ SINGH: Literally "lion". Also used as a family name by Rajputs.
◆ SIROHI: A light, curved sword favored by the Rajputs.
◆ SOWAR: Horsemen.
◆ SURAHI: Narrow-necked earthen pitcher.

◆ SURYA: Sun or sun god.
◆ SURYAVANSHI: Rajput clan, believed to be descended from the sun.

◆ T ◆

◆ TABLA: Small Indian drum.
◆ TEEJ: Festival welcoming the monsoons.
◆ THAKUR: Chieftain or nobleman.
◆ THALI: Large, circular stainless steel eating utensil, with small bowls known as *katoris* for curries, yogurt and sweet dishes; also refers to a set meal.
◆ THEWA: Enamel-worked glass ornaments typical of Deolia, near Udaipur.
◆ TIKKA: Ritual anointing of the forehead with *kum-kum* or sandalwood paste.
◆ TIRTHANKARA: Jain saint.
◆ TORANA: Ornate archway.
◆ TOSHAKHANA: Treasury or wardrobe.
◆ TRIPOLIA: Triple arched gateway.
◆ TRIMURTI: Represents the Hindu Trinity of Shiva, Vishnu, and Brahma.
◆ TRISHUL: A trident, symbolic of Lord Shiva.

◆ V ◆

◆ VIJAY: Victory.
◆ VIMANA: Temple tower or pagoda.
◆ VISHNU: Hindu god. One of the Hindu Trinity, considered the god of preservation.

◆ W ◆

◆ WAGH: Tiger.
◆ WAGHNAKH: A curious weapon shaped like a set of tiger claws and used in close combat.
◆ WALLAH: Person. A suffix used as an occupational name such as *"phool-wallah"* (flower-seller), *"akhbar-wallah"* (newspaper vendor), etc.

◆ Y ◆

◆ YAGNA: An elaborate Hindu ritual.

◆ Z ◆

◆ ZAMINDAR: Landlord.
◆ ZENANA: Women's quarters in a palace.

PRONUNCIATION NOTE:

a = a, as in arm
ch = ch, as in chair
e = e, as in mermaid
u = oo, long or short,
as in book or pool, tool
g = hard g, as in get
The nasal sound is
denoted by a " ` "
symbol on top of the
vowel which is to be
pronounced nasally:
for example, "Maì" is
pronounced with a
nasal sound of "ì", and
"Hà" is pronounced
with a nasal sound of
"à". All words with the
final "n" consonant
take on the nasal
sound at the end.

ESSENTIALS

I/me: *main*
we: *hum*
you: *aap/tum*
he/she/they: *woh*
what?: *kya*
who?: *kaun*
when?: *kab*
where?: *kahà(n)*
how?: *kaise*
why?: *kyun*
this: *yeh*
that: *woh*
here: *yahan*
there: *wahan*
from: *yahan se*
to (a place): *wahà tak*

USEFUL WORDS

help: *madat karo/
bachao*
to meet: *milnà*
to come: *aanà*
to go: *janà*
to enter: *andar chalo*
to sit: *baitho*
to stand: *khare ho*
to rest: *aaram karo*
to read: *padho*
to see: *dekha*
to bathe: *nahanà*
to wait: *thairo*
to leave: *bahar jao*
to sleep: *sonà*
arrive at: *pahunchnà*
early/quick: *jaldi*
late: *der se*
far: *dur*
near: *najdik*
good: *achha*
bad: *bura*
hot: *garam*
cold: *thanda*
sick: *bimar/bukhar*
headache: *seer darad*
pain/ache: *darad*
house: *ghar/kothi*
room: *kamra*
book: *kitab*
newspaper: *akhbar*

GREETINGS

Hello: *namaste.*
How are you?: *aap
kaise hai?*
I am fine, thank you:
maì(n)thik hoo(n).
Thank you:
dhanyavad.
See you again: *phir*
milenge.
Good morning,
afternoon or evening:
namaste.
Good night: *shubh
ratri.*
Goodbye/Bon voyage:
namaste, bye-bye.
Okay: *achha.*

GENERAL

What is your name?:
aap ka naam kya hai?
My name is…: *mera
naam…hai.*
Where do you live?:
aap kahà(n) rahte ho?
I live in…: *mai(n)…
mei(n) rahta hoo(n).*
That's alright: *thik hai.*
Yes: *ha(n)*
No: *nahi(n)*
I don't speak Hindi:
mujhe Hindi nahi aati.
Do you understand
me?: *aap mujhe
samjhate ho?*
I don't understand:
main samajta nahin.
May I use the phone?:
mujhe phone karnah?
Where are the toilets?:
sandas or *bathroom
kaha(n)?*
I want to go to the
doctor: *mujhe
doctor(vaidya) ke
paas janà hai.*
I want to speak to…:
*main ....se baat
karna chaata hoon.*
How much for one
night's stay?: *ek raat
rahne ke kitne paise?*
I am sorry: *mujhe
maaf kardo.*
I am hungry: *Mujhe
bhukh lagi hai.*

DINING

hungry: *bhuuk*
thirsty: *pyaas*
food: *khanà*
drink: *paani*
Indian bread: *roti/
paratha/naan/puri*
rice: *chawal*
vegetables: *sabji*
fish: *machhi*
chicken: *murgi*
mutton: *gosht/maas*
beef: *gaye ka maas*
egg: *aanda*
fruits: *phal*
mango: *aam*
banana: *kela*
apple: *seb*
orange: *santra*
vegetarian: *maas
nahin khaata*
restaurant: *hotel*
table: *maiz*
chair: *kursi*
I do not want spicy
food: *mujhe tikha
khana (mirch wala)
nahi chahiye.*
sweet: *mitha*
hot: *tikha/mirchwala*
sour: *khatta*
bitter: *kadva*
sugar: *chini*

SHOPPING

I want to buy…: *maì(n)
…kharidna chahata
hoon.*
price: *daam*
to buy: *kharidnà*
to sell: *bechnà*
shirt: *khamij*
shoes: *jooti*
tie and dye cloth:
bandhani ka kapda
handicraft: *hasta-kala*
expensive: *mehenga*
cheap: *susta*
big/large: *bada*
small: *chhota*
embroidery: *haat-ka-
kaam*
color: *rang*
different: *alag*
to change: *badalna*
good: *achha*
defective/bad:
khaarab
to look: *dekho*
How much?: *kitna?*
Is there something
cheaper?: *is say
sasta hain?*
I'll come back later:
baad main aaonga.

GETTING AROUND

I want to go now:
mujhe abhi jana hai.
Where is the… : *...
kaha(n) hai?*
How can I go to the
…?: *mai(n)…kaise ja
sakta hoo(n)?*
How far is the…?: *...
kitna dur hai?*
How long will it take to
go to …? *jane ke liye
kitna samay lagega?*
How much will it cost?
kitne paise lagenge?
temple: *mandir*
garden: *baag*
palace: *mahal*
fort: *kila*
lake: *talab*
bus stop: *bus thamba*
shop: *dukan*
market: *bazar*
hospital: *aspatal*
doctor: *doctor*
medicine: *davaie*
pharmacy: *davaie-ki-
dukan*
police station: *pulis
thana*
post office: *daak ghar*
vehicle/car: *gaadi*
office: *daftar*
road: *raasta*
city: *shahar*
country: *desh*
airport: *hawai adda*
I want to go to…:
main ....jana chata
How far is the…?: *...*

salt: *namak*
milk: *dudh*
coffee: *coffee*
tea: *chai*
boiled water: *ubla hua
paani*
mineral water: *botal
ka paani* (bottled
water)

SHOPPING

kitna dur hai?
Where do I get off?:
main kahan utruga?
Please take me to…:
mujhe …le jao.
Where to?: *kahan?*
Right: *daine*
Left: *bayen*
Straight: *seedha jao*
Stop here: *roko*
North: *uttar*
South: *dakshin*
East: *purab*
West: *paschim*

NUMBERS

0 : *shunya*
1 : *ek*
2 : *do*
3 : *teen*
4 : *char*
5 : *paanch*
6 : *chhe*
7 : *saat*
8 : *aath*
9 : *nau*
10 : *dus*
11 : *gyarah*
12 : *baarah*
13 : *terah*
14 : *chaudah*
15 : *pandrah*
16 : *solah*
17 : *satrah*
18 : *atharah*
19 : *unnis*
20 : *bees*
30 : *tees*
40 : *chalis*
50 : *pachas*
60 : *saath*
70 : *sattar*
80 : *assi*
90 : *nabbe*
100 : *sau*
1,000 : *ek hajaar*
100,000 : *ek laakh*

TIME

day: *din*
time: *samay*
hour: *ghanta*
minute: *minit*
What is the time?: *ab
hi kitne baje hai?*
8 o'clock: *aath bajai*

CALENDAR

Monday: *somwar*
Tuesday: *mangalwar*
Wednesday: *budhwar*
Thursday: *guruwar*
Friday: *shukrawar*
Saturday: *shaniwar*
Sunday: *raviwar*
year: *warsh/sal*
month: *mahina*
week: *saptah/hapta*
today: *aaj*
yesterday/tomorrow:
kal
day after tomorrow:
parsoon

FAMILY

family: *parivar*
female: *aurat*
male: *aadmi*
mother: *ma/mata*
father: *baap/pita*
child: *bachcha*

LIST OF ILLUSTRATIONS

We have not been able to trace the heirs or publishers of certain documents. An account is being held open for them at our offices.

INDEX

◆ Index